The Classics of Western Philosophy

A Reader's Guide

Edited by

Jorge J. E. Gracia, Gregory M. Reichberg, and Bernard N. Schumacher

Blackwell
Publishing

© 2003 by Blackwell Publishing Ltd

350 Main Street, Malden, MA 02148-5018, USA
108 Cowley Road, Oxford OX4 1JF, UK
550 Swanston Street, Carlton South, Melbourne, Victoria 3053, Australia
Kurfürstendamm 57, 10707 Berlin, Germany

The right of Jorge J. E. Gracia, Gregory M. Reichberg, and Bernard N. Schumacher to be identified as the Authors of the Editorial Material in this Work has been asserted in accordance with the UK Copyright, Designs and Patents Act 1988.

First published 2003 by Blackwell Publishing Ltd

Library of Congress Cataloguing-in-Publication Data

The classics of Western philosophy : a reader's guide / edited by Jorge J.E. Gracia, Gregory M. Reichberg, Bernard N. Schumacher.
    p. cm.
    Includes bibliographical references and index.
    ISBN 0-631-21906-4 (alk. paper) – ISBN 0-631-23611-2 (pbk. : alk. paper)
    1. Philosophy – History.   I. Gracia, Jorge J. E. II. Reichberg, Gregory M. III. Schumacher, Bernard N.

B29 .C537 2002
190 – dc21

2002071050

A catalogue record for this title is available from the British Library

Set in 10 on 12.5 pt Galliard
by Ace Filmsetting Ltd, Frome, Somerset
Printed and bound in the United Kingdom
by T. J. International, Padstow, Cornwall

For further information on
Blackwell Publishing, visit our website:
http://www.blackwellpublishing.com

Contents

Notes on Contributors

Laird Addis is Professor of Philosophy at the University of Iowa. His books include *The Logic of Society: A Philosophical Study* (1975), *Natural Signs: A Theory of Intentionality* (1989), and *Of Mind and Music* (1999).

Thomas Baldwin is Professor of Philosophy at the University of York. His publications include *G. E. Moore* (1990) and *Contemporary Philosophy: Philosophy in English* (2001).

Endre Begby is Fulbright Fellow in the Department of Philosophy at the University of Pittsburgh and Research Associate at the International Peace Research Institute, Oslo (PRIO). He has published articles on hermeneutics, the philosophy of language, philosophy of science, ethics, and social theory.

David Bell is Professor of Philosophy at Sheffield University. He is the author of *Frege's Theory of Judgement* (1979) and *Husserl* (1990).

Deborah L. Black is Associate Professor of Medieval Studies and Philosophy at the University of Toronto. She is the author of *Logic and Aristotle's "Rhetoric" and "Poetics" in Medieval Arabic Philosophy* (1990), as well as articles on Islamic philosophy and its impact on the Christian West.

David W. Carrithers is Adolph Ochs Professor of Government at the University of Tennessee (Chattanooga). He is the editor of *Montesquieu's The Spirit of Laws: A Compendium of the First English Edition* (1977). He is also co-editor of *Montesquieu's Science of Politics: Essays on The Spirit of Laws* (2001) and of *Montesquieu and the Spirit of Modernity* (2002).

Peter Casarella is Associate Professor of Systematic Theology at the Catholic University of America. His publications include (co-edited with George Schner) *Christian Spirituality and the Culture of Modernity: The Thought of Louis Dupré* (1998) and *Word as Bread: Language and Theology in Nicholas of Cusa* (forthcoming).

Vere Chappell is Professor of Philosophy at the University of Massachusetts (Amherst). He is the editor of the *Cambridge Companion to Locke* (1994) and of *Locke* (1998) in the Oxford Readings in Philosophy Series. He has also edited volumes on Hume (1966, 1968), Descartes (1997), Hobbes and Bramhall (1999), and seventeenth-century philosophers in general (12 vols, 1992). He is the author of many articles on seventeenth-

and eighteenth-century philosophy, and co-author, with Willis Doney, of *Twenty-Five Years of Descartes Scholarship* (1984).

Vincent Colapietro is Professor of Philosophy at Pennsylvania State University. He is the author of *Peirce's Approach to the Self* (1989), and has published numerous articles on Peirce, pragmatism, and semiotics.

Daniel O. Dahlstrom is Professor of Philosophy at Boston University. He is co-editor and translator of Schiller's *Essays* (1993) and the author of *Heidegger's Concept of Truth* (2001).

Randall Dipert is C. S. Peirce Professor of American Philosophy at SUNY University Center at Buffalo. He is the author of *Artifacts, Art, and Agency* (1993) and "The Mathematical Structure of the World: The World as Graph," *Journal of Philosophy*, 94 (1997): 329–58, as well as articles on Peirce and logic.

Kenneth Dorter is Professor of Philosophy at the University of Guelph in Canada. He is the author of *Plato's Phaedo: An Interpretation* (1982) and *Form and Good in Plato's Eleatic Dialogues: The Parmenides, Theaetetus, Sophist, and Statesman* (1994).

Michael Dummett is Emeritus Professor at the University of Oxford having retired from his post as Wykeham Professor of Logic at the university in September 1992. He is a fellow of the British Academy, an Honorary Fellow of New College, Oxford, and an Emeritus Fellow of All Soul's College, Oxford. Among other books, he has published *Frege: Philosophy of Language* (1973, 1981), *Truth and Other Enigmas* (1978), *Origins of Analytical Philosophy* (1988, 1993), *The Logical Basis of Metaphysics* (1991), *Frege: Philosophy of Mathematics* (1993), and *On Immigration and Refugees* (2001).

Robert K. Faulkner is Professor of Political Science at Boston College. He is the author of *The Jurisprudence of John Marshall* (1968), *Richard Hooker and the Politics of a Christian England* (1981), and *Francis Bacon and the Project of Progress* (1993).

Thomas R. Flynn is Samuel Candler Dobbs Professor of Philosophy at Emory University. His books include *Sartre and Marxist Existentialism: The Test Case of Collective Responsibility* (1984), *Dialectic and Narrative* (edited with Dalia Judovitz, 1993), and a two-volume study, *Sartre, Foucault and Historical Reason*, vol. 1: *Toward an Existentialist Theory of History* (1997); vol. 2: *A Poststructuralist Mapping of History* (forthcoming).

Nicholas Fotion is Professor of Philosophy at Emory University. His latest major publication is *John Searle* (2001). He has also published books and articles on ethics, military ethics, medical ethics, and the philosophy of language.

Don Garrett is Kenan Distinguished Professor for Teaching Excellence at the University of North Carolina at Chapel Hill. He is the editor of *The Cambridge Companion to Spinoza* (1996) and the author of *Cognition and Commitment in Hume's Philosophy* (1997).

Newton Garver is SUNY Distinguished Service Professor and Professor Emeritus of Philosophy at the State University at Buffalo. His works include *This Complicated Form of Life* (1994), (with Seung-Chong Lee) *Derrida and Wittgenstein* (1994), and (with Eric Reitan) *Nonviolence and Community* (1995).

Hans-Johann Glock is Reader in Philosophy at the University of Reading. He has edited several volumes on Wittgenstein and on analytic philosophy, and he is the author of *A Wittgenstein Dictionary* (1996) and of *Quine and Davidson* (2002).

Jorge J. E. Gracia is Samuel P. Capen Chair and SUNY Distinguished Professor of Philosophy at the State University at Buffalo. His publications include *Introduction to the Problem of Individuation in the Early Middle Ages* (1986, 1988), *Individuality* (1988), *Philosophy and its History* (1992), *A Theory of Textuality* (1995), *Texts* (1996), *Metaphysics and its Task* (1999), and *How Can We Know what God Means?* (2001). He is editor of several books, including (with Timothy B. Noone) Blackwell's *A Companion to Philosophy in the Middle Ages* (2003).

Emily R. Grosholz is Professor of Philosophy and African American Studies at the Pennsylvania State University, and a Life Member of Clare Hall, University of Cambridge. She is the author of *Cartesian Method and the Problem of Reduction* (1991), co-author of *Leibniz's Science of the Rational* (1998), and co-editor of *On Race and Culture* by W. E. B. Du Bois (1996) and *The Growth of Mathematical Knowledge* (2000).

Jasper Hopkins is Professor of Philosophy at the University of Minnesota (Minneapolis). He is the translator of the *Complete Philosophical and Theological Treatises of Nicholas of Cusa*, 2 vols (2001) and co-translator of *Complete Philosophical and Theological Treatises of Anselm of Canterbury* (2000).

Stephen Houlgate is Professor of Philosophy at the University of Warwick. He is the author of *Hegel, Nietzsche and the Criticism of Metaphysics* (1986) and *Freedom, Truth and History: An Introduction to Hegel's Philosophy* (1991), and the editor of *The Hegel Reader* (1998). He is currently editor of the *Bulletin of the Hegel Society of Great Britain*.

T. H. Irwin is Susan Linn Sage Professor of Philosophy and Humane Letters at Cornell University. His publications include *Aristotle's First Principles* (1988), *Classical Thought* (1989), *Plato's Ethics* (1995), and *Aristotle's Nicomachean Ethics*, translation and notes (2nd edn, 1999).

Alfred L. Ivry is the Skirball Professor of Jewish Philosophy and Professor of Middle East Studies at New York University. Author and editor of many articles and books, he has recently edited and translated Averroës' *Middle Commentary* on Aristotle's *De anima*.

Michael J. Loux is George Schuster Professor of Philosophy at the University of Notre Dame. He is the author of *Substance and Attribute* (1978), *Primary Ousia* (1991), and *Metaphysics* (2001).

George R. Lucas, Jr is Professor of Philosophy and Associate Chair in the Department of Leadership, Ethics and Law at the United States Naval Academy (Annapolis, MD). He is Philosophy Editor for the State University of New York Press, author of *The Rehabilitation of Whitehead* (1989), and has published a number of essays analyzing Whitehead against the backdrop of the history of modern European philosophy.

William McBride is Arthur G. Hansen Distinguished Professor of Philosophy at Purdue University. His publications include *The Philosophy of Marx* (1977), *Philosophical Reflections on the Changes in Eastern Europe* (1999), and *Yugoslav Praxis to Global Pathos: Anti-Hegemonic Post-post-Marxist Essays* (2001).

John McDermott is Distinguished Professor of Philosophy and Humanities and Abell Professor of Liberal Arts at Texas A&M University. He has edited *The Philosophy of John Dewey* (2 vols, 1981), and is the General Editor of *The Correspondence of William James* (12 vols, 1992–).

Scott MacDonald is Professor of Philosophy and Norma K. Regan Professor in Christian Studies at Cornell University. He has published widely in medieval philosophy and edits the journal *Medieval Philosophy and Theology*.

John Marenbon is a Fellow of Trinity College, Cambridge, and Director of Studies in the History of Philosophy. Among his books are *Early Medieval Philosophy (480–1150): An Introduction* (1983), *Later Medieval Philosophy (1150–1350): An Introduction* (1987), *The Philosophy of Peter Abelard* (1997), *Aristotelian Logic, Platonism and the Context of Early Medieval Philosophy in the West* (2000), and *Boethius* (forthcoming). He has edited *Medieval Philosophy* (1998), and (with G. Orlandi) *Peter Abelard "Collationes"* (2001).

Gareth B. Matthews is Professor of Philosophy at the University of Massachusetts (Amherst). He is the author of *Thought's Ego in Augustine and Descartes* (1992) and *Socratic Perplexity and the Nature of Philosophy* (1999), and editor of *The Augustinian Tradition* (1999).

F. C. T. Moore is Emeritus Professor of Philosophy at the University of Hong Kong. He is the author of *Bergson: Thinking Backwards* (1996).

Timothy B. Noone is Associate Professor of Philosophy at the Catholic University of America and the Director of the Scotus Project. Among his publications are the critical editions of Duns Scotus's *Opera philosophica* (1997–) and (co-edited with Jorge J. E. Gracia) Blackwell's *A Companion to Philosophy in the Middle Ages* (2003).

Dominic J. O'Meara is Professor of Philosophy, Chair of Ancient Philosophy, University of Fribourg (Switzerland). His publications include *Michaelis Pselli Philosophica minora* II (1989), *Pythagoras Revived: Mathematics and Philosophy in Late Antiquity* (1989), *Plotinus: An Introduction to the Enneads* (1993), *The Structure of Being and the Search for the Good: Essays on Ancient and Early Medieval Platonism* (1998), and *Plotin Traité 51* (1999).

Claude Panaccio is Professor of Philosophy at the University of Quebec in Trois-Rivières. He is the author of *Les Mots, les concepts et les choses: la sémantique de Guillaume d'Ockham et le nominalisme contemporain* (1992) and *Le Discours intérieur: de Platon à Guillaume d'Ockham* (1999).

George Pappas is Professor of Philosophy at Ohio State University. He is the author of *Berkeley's Thought* (2000).

Stephen Priest is a Fellow and Tutor in Philosophy at Blackfriars Hall, Oxford and a member of Wolfson College, Oxford. He is the author of *The British Empiricists* (1990), *Theories of the Mind* (1991), *Merleau-Ponty* (1998), and *The Subject in Question* (2000). He is the editor of *Hegel's Critique of Kant* (1987) and *Jean-Paul Sartre: Basic Writings* (2001) and co-editor (with Antony Flew) of *A Dictionary of Philosophy* (2002).

Andrews Reath is Professor of Philosophy at the University of California-Riverside. He has written numerous articles on Kant's moral theory, and, with Barbara Herman and Christine Korsgaard, co-edited *Reclaiming the History of Ethics: Essays for John Rawls* (1997).

Jonathan Rée is a freelance philosopher and translator living in Oxford, England. His books include *Proletarian Philosophers* (1984), *Philosophical Tales* (1989), *Heidegger* (1999), and *I See a Voice* (2000).

C. D. C. Reeve is Professor of Philosophy at the University of North Carolina at Chapel Hill. He is the author of *Philosopher-kings: The Argument of Plato's Republic*

(1988), *Socrates in the Apology* (1990), *Practices of Reason: Aristotle's Nicomachean Ethics* (1992), *Substantial Knowledge: Aristotle's Metaphysics* (2000), and *Women in the Academy* (2001). He has translated Plato's *Republic* (1992), *Cratylus* (1998), *Euthyphro, Apology, Crito* (2002), and Aristotle's *Politics* (1998).

Gregory M. Reichberg is Senior Research Fellow at the International Peace Research Institute, Oslo (PRIO) and associate editor of the *Journal of Military Ethics*. He has published widely on the ethics of war and peace, and on topics in Thomistic philosophy. Recent articles include "Just war or perpetual peace?" *Journal of Military Ethics*, 1 (2002): 16–35; and "Beyond privation: moral evil in Aquinas's *De malo*," *The Review of Metaphysics*, 55 (2002): 732–64.

T. M. Robinson is Professor of Philosophy at the University of Toronto. Among his books are *Heraclitus: Fragments. A Text and Translation with a Commentary* (1987) and *Plato's Psychology* (2nd edn, 1995). He is co-editor of *The Phoenix Presocratics Series* (1978–).

Sandra B. Rosenthal is Provost Distinguished Professor of Philosophy at Loyola University New Orleans. Her works include *Speculative Pragmatism* (1986, 1990), *Charles Peirce's Pragmatic Pluralism* (1994), (with Rogene A. Buchholz) *Rethinking Business Ethics: A Pragmatic Perspective* (2000), and *Time, Continuity, and Indeterminacy* (2000).

James F. Ross is Professor of Philosophy and Law at the University of Pennsylvania. He has written on cognitive voluntarism opposing evidentialism, on semantic contagion as an account of diversity of meaning, and is presently completing a metaphysics book, *Hidden Necessities and the Master of Falsity*. Other works include *Philosophical Theology* (1968, 1979) and *Portraying Analogy* (1982).

Richard Schacht is Professor of Philosophy and Jubilee Professor of Liberal Arts and Sciences at the University of Illinois at Urbana-Champaign. His books include *Hegel and After* (1975), *Nietzsche* (1983), *Classical Modern Philosophers* (1984), *The Future of Alienation* (1994), and *Making Sense of Nietzsche* (1995).

Bernard N. Schumacher is Privatdocent of Philosophy at the University of Fribourg (Switzerland). He is the author of *Une philosophie de l'espérance* (2000) and *Auseinandersetzung mit dem Tode* (2003).

David Sedley is Laurence Professor of Ancient Philosophy at the University of Cambridge. His publications include *The Hellenistic Philosophers* (1987) (with A. A. Long) and *Lucretius and the Transformation of Greek Wisdom* (1998).

Stewart Shapiro is O'Donnell Professor of Philosophy at Ohio State University and Arché Professorial Fellow at the University of St Andrews. He is the author of *Foundations without Foundationalism* (1991), *Philosophy of Mathematics: Structure and Ontology* (1997), and *Thinking about Mathematics* (2000).

Robert Sleigh is Emeritus Professor of Philosophy at the University of Massachusetts (Amherst). Much of his scholarly work focuses on the philosophy of Leibniz. He and Daniel Garber are co-editors of the Yale *Leibniz*. He is the author of *Leibniz and Arnauld: A Commentary on their Correspondence* (1990).

David Woodruff Smith is Professor of Philosophy at the University of California, Irvine. He is the author of *Husserl and Intentionality* (1982) (with Ronald McIntyre) and *The Circle of Acquaintance* (1989), and the co-editor (with Barry Smith) of *The Cambridge Companion to Husserl* (1995).

G. W. Smith is Lecturer in Politics in the Department of Politics and International Relations at the University of Lancaster. He is the editor of *J. S. Mill's On Liberty in Focus* (1991) (with John Gray), *J. S. Mill's Social and Political Thought: Critical Assessments* (4 vols, 1998), and *Liberalism: Critical Assessments* (4 vols, 2002).

Henrik Syse is Senior Research Fellow at the International Peace Research Institute, Oslo (PRIO) and Associate Professor at the University of Oslo. He is the author of *Natural Law, Religion, and Rights* (forthcoming) and has published widely on normative aspects of war and other topics in international ethics.

Mariam Thalos is Associate Professor of Philosophy at the University of Utah. She is the author of numerous articles on the philosophy of science, metaphysics, and epistemology, including "Degrees of freedom: an essay on competitions between micro and macro in mechanics," *Philosophy and Phenomenological Research*, 59 (1999): 1–39; "Degrees of freedom in the social world: towards a systems analysis of decision," *Journal of Political Philosophy*, 7 (1999): 453–77; and "Explanation is a genus: on the varieties of scientific explanation," *Synthese*, 130 (2002): 317–54.

Bjørn Thommessen is Lecturer in Philosophy at the University of Oslo. His publications include essays on Augustine, Machiavelli, and Hobbes. He has also co-authored several textbooks on ethics and philosophical argumentation.

Richard Velkley is Associate Professor of Philosophy at the Catholic University of America. He is the author of *Freedom and the End of Reason: On the Moral Foundation of Kant's Critical Philosophy* (1989) and *Being after Rousseau: Philosophy and Culture in Question* (2002).

Donald Phillip Verene is Charles Howard Candler Professor of Metaphysics and Moral Philosophy and Director of the Institute for Vico Studies at Emory University. He is the author of, among other works, *Vico's Science of Imagination* (1981), *The New Art of Autobiography: An Essay on the "Life of Giambattista Vico, Written by Himself"* (1991), *Philosophy and the Return to Self-knowledge* (1997), and *The Art of Humane Education* (2002).

Merold Westphal is Distinguished Professor of Philosophy at Fordham University. Among his books are *Kierkegaard's Critique of Reason and Society* (1991), *Becoming a Self: A Reading of Kierkegaard's Concluding Unscientific Postscript* (1996), *History and Truth in Hegel's Phenomenology* (1998), *Suspicion and Faith: The Religious Uses of Modern Atheism* (1998), and *Overcoming Onto-theology: Toward a Postmodern Christian Faith* (2001).

Fred Wilson is Professor of Philosophy at the University of Toronto. Among his publications are *Hume's Defence of Causal Inference* (1997) and *The Logic and Methodology of Science in Early Modern Thought* (1999).

Allen W. Wood is Ward W. and Priscilla B. Woods Professor at Stanford University. His publications include *Kant's Moral Religion* (1970), *Karl Marx* (1981), *Hegel's Ethical Thought* (1990), and *Kant's Ethical Thought* (1999). He is also co-translator (with Paul Guyer) of Kant's *Critique of Pure Reason* (1998).

Preface

In a well-known essay, "Why Read the Classics?," Italo Calvino gives thirteen different definitions of what a classic is, and concludes that the "only reason that can be adduced in their favor is that reading the classics is always better that not reading them." Then, to prove his point, he cites Cioran, who writes: "While the hemlock was being prepared, Socrates was learning a melody on the flute. 'What use will that be to you?', he was asked. 'At least I will learn this melody before I die.'"

We cannot reproduce here all the thirteen definitions of a classic Calvino gives, nor do we assume he is right, but it is quite clear that the West has indeed agreed for the past two thousand years in thinking that it is better to read some philosophical texts than not to read them, and that it is better to read some texts rather than others. These texts, the ones that are read and re-read, we regard as classics in this book.

Which are these texts? Certainly many more than we have selected for discussion here. We have arbitrarily set a maximum number of sixty-one, mainly for reasons of economy. There are surely many more, although we hope that few of our colleagues, if any, will dispute that the sixty-one we have chosen are texts that are read and re-read by philosophers and that it is generally thought to be better to read them than not. Which books have been left out that should have been included? The readers are better judges of this than we are. But let us mention that, for the sake of balance, we have excluded many ancient texts which generally meet the criterion of classic that we have adopted. Which Dialogue of Plato or work by Aristotle does not qualify as a classic? But we had to leave some room for the moderns, so we have omitted most of the Platonic and Aristotelian corpus in order to make room for later authors. Indeed, we set a maximum limit of two works per author in order to help us achieve this goal.

The starting-point was not difficult to establish: Western philosophy begins with the pre-Socratics, and their texts are read and re-read mercilessly to this day. Is there any philosopher or student of philosophy who has not pondered what Thales meant by saying that everything is made out of water? The *terminus ad quem*, however, posed more difficulties. Where should we finish? Surely Wittgenstein's *Tractatus* and Heidegger's *Being and Time* had to be included. But what do we make of Gadamer's *Truth and Method*, Foucault's *The Order of Things*, or Rawls's *A Theory of Justice*?

These are texts that are read often these days, but will they be read in fifty years? History has yet to make this judgment. Still, some relatively recent texts seem to have survived their immediate time and continue to be the source of philosophical interest. We end the book with two of these: Kuhn's *The Structure of Scientific Revolutions* and Austin's *How to Do Things with Words*. It is possible that these will, like so many other books that enjoyed notoriety during their times or shortly thereafter, also be forgotten. But in our judgment it is unlikely.

For works composed before the printing press became available, we use the date at which they were completed, and in cases where they were left unfinished, we use the date at which their authors stopped working on them. For printed works, we use the date of first printing with the exception of Leibniz's *Monadology*, which was published more than a hundred years after it was written.

The length of each essay varies, reflecting the view of the editors of the relative importance the texts discussed occupy or have occupied in philosophical discourse. Some of these texts are read more than others, and some have been read much at particular times and little or none at others. But they have all been read repeatedly and tend to display a certain resilience; the philosophical community is reluctant to part with them permanently. By this we do not mean that the philosophical texts which do not meet the criterion of classic we use are completely ignored. Historians and anti-quarians abound who devote their efforts to studying them for the mere pleasure of knowing what went on in the past. What we mean is, rather, that they have ceased, permanently it seems, to be the subject of interest within the broader philosophical community.

Most of the authors of the essays included in this volume are senior, well-known, and established philosophers, but we also reserved some essays for younger, lesser-known individuals. Moreover, we especially tried to include philosophers who work in different philosophical traditions, so that this book would reflect the different approaches to the classics that are current. Finally, we did not request scholarly, encyclo-pedia-type articles. Rather, we encouraged the authors to speak their minds and treat this request as an opportunity to write essays that reflect their personal views of the value and importance of the texts in question. This, as readers will have occasion to see, has resulted in a volume which, we think, reflects the variety of philosophy at the beginning of the twenty-first century.

We are grateful to many colleagues and friends, too numerous to mention, for their advice and encouragement. But, most of all, we are grateful to the authors of the essays for their patience, good nature, and generosity. The value of the book is entirely a function of their efforts. Finally, we also appreciate Blackwell Publishers' willingness to give us a free hand in the composition of the volume and to take the financial risks which necessarily accompany a project such as this.

1

Pre-Socratics, *Fragments* (ca. 600–440 BC)

The Birth of Philosophical Investigation

T. M. Robinson

Our knowledge of Greek philosophers before Socrates comes to us in the form either of direct quotations from their now lost writings or of various *testimonia* concerning their views. These are to be found in a number of ancient authorities, ranging from someone as close to the time of the pre-Socratics as Plato (fourth century BC) to someone as far distant from them as Simplicius (sixth century AD). They were assembled about a century ago by Hermann Diels and Walter Kranz in their monumental *Die Fragmente der Vorsokratiker* and all references to "fragments" in what follows are references to the enumeration found in this volume. The earliest group of thinkers, the so-called "Milesians," lived in the sixth century BC, the rest in the fifth century.

The Milesians: Thales, Anaximander, Anaximenes, Xenophanes

It is generally acknowledged that the first major move in the West toward a more rational view of the universe took place in Miletus during the sixth century BC, spearheaded by Thales, Anaximander, and Anaximenes. Each seems to have sought to explain the world in terms of some feature of itself rather than some external agent or agents (such as the gods of Mount Olympus), and to explain it by preference in terms of a single "stuff" of which all things are constituted or of which they are in some way variants; and if the universe has a directive force (and all three of them are in agreement that it has), this stuff constitutes that directive force. For Thales the stuff in question is water; for Anaximenes, air; and for Anaximander, something he was unwilling to characterize in any particular way, preferring simply to call it the "indefinite" or "indeterminate" (*apeiron*), and leaving it unclear whether he meant indeterminate in quantity or indefinite in quality or both.

Another sense of *apeiron* – "boundless" or "unlimited" – leads us directly to an other question that intrigued early thinkers, and that is the *extent* of the universe. Anaximander may have wished to suggest, by his use of the multivalent term *apeiron*, that it is in fact without boundaries (or, as we would say, "open"), and in this he was very likely followed by Anaximenes, who also called it *apeiron*, though this time *characterized* in a very definite way as "air."

The fourth of the Milesian thinkers, Xenophanes, while sharing the physical and cosmological interests of his immediate forebears, is more famous for his attacks on the gods of organized religion, ridiculing them as being absurdly anthropomorphic and, given the immoral conduct so frequently attributed to them, wholly inappropriate as paradigms for human conduct. He has also, since ancient times, been credited with the view that there exists only one god, not many (as most Greeks assumed). This is very hard to excavate from the fragmentary evidence we have, however, which seems much rather to suggest that, whatever the nature of the other gods, there is one god that is undoubtedly supreme among them. Of this supreme god (the equivalent, presumably, of Zeus to other Greeks) he said, remarkably, "All of him sees, all of him ascertains, all of him hears" (fr. b24), setting in train a way of thinking of the divine that found its most eloquent expression in later thinkers such as Aristotle and Aquinas.

Xenophanes' second great claim to fame is his assertion that human knowledge is limited. Some have read this as being an assertion of universal skepticism, but it seems more probable that his skepticism was confined to what we might ever come to know with certainty about the divine and about the structure and operation of the macro-cosmic universe.

Heraclitus of Ephesus

The first to respond to Xenophanes' epistemological pessimism was Heraclitus of Ephesus, who made it clear that, not only is macro-cosmic knowledge possible, its specific and most significant object – the "plan" that directs the operations of the universe – in fact exhausts the plenitude of wisdom (fr. 41). As is clear at once, Heraclitus assumes, like his predecessors, that the universe is governed by a directive force, a force which seems to be co-extensive with the universe and is characterized by rationality. This rationality of the directive force is forever being exhibited in a continuing account (*logos*) that it is uttering about itself (fr. 1). The account is available to everyone (fr. 2), but most people are unaware of it, since it is couched in a language they have not taken the trouble, or are simply unable, to learn (fr. 107).

Were we to learn the language in which the universe-*qua*-rational is forever describing itself, we would learn, says Heraclitus, that the most important thing about the real is that it is a coherent unity, despite its appearance of being composed of sets of warring and apparently irreducibly "opposing" elements (like water and fire) or "opposing" states of affairs (like war and peace). As examples of this hidden unity that lies beneath surface discord, he points to the fact that a single thing has different effects on different people ("pigs like mud, [people don't]," fr. 13); that some things are only possible if we recognize their opposites (fr. 23); that different aspects of the same thing involve different descriptions (fr. 58); or that certain pairs of opposites are "the same" in the sense that they exist in invariable sequence to one another (fr. 88).

Claims like the above led Aristotle to believe that Heraclitus denied the law of non-contradiction, but this does not seem to have been the case. A careful reading of fragment 88, and especially the explanatory clause which concludes it, makes it clear that (as though he had been challenged to explain himself) Heraclitus is using the word "same" in the *softer* sense of the word only; he is not talking about arithmetical identity. The result is a world characterized by unity amidst diversity, by balance amidst tension, for which remarkable metaphors are (a) the abiding river and the ever-changing water which flows through, (b) the bow and the bowstring, and (c) the lyre and its strings. In another great metaphor he describes the unifying force of things as "warfare."

In view of this, it is hard to attribute to Heraclitus the famous "doctrine of flux" that he has been credited with since the writing of Plato's *Theaetetus*. The most that can be said is that, faced with a world of constant change and the push and pull of opposing elements and states of affairs, he was more drawn to the forces militating to make that world a great whole than those tending to fragment it.

A striking metaphor for this unity amidst change is that of fire. Like fire (and also, it seems, being at all times a variant *of* fire, like water for Thales or air for Anaximenes), the world, he maintains, is (synchronically) in an everlasting state of permanence amidst destruction. He may also (though this is still a matter of continuing dispute) have held the view, later espoused by the Stoics, that the world fluctuates (diachronically) be-tween totally opposite states, in which at one time all is fire and at another time fire has been broken down into its component elements, which will include what we call earth and water (whether he thought air too is physically real continues to be disputed).

Similarly disputed is a doctrine that has been frequently attributed to him, namely, that our rational self or soul (*psyche*) is made of fire. His meaning, however, is more probably that the life principle (*psyche*) that vivifies living things is on some sort of spectrum, one pole of which is fire. At the most basic level, life manifests itself in warm and damp situations. As life becomes more complex, and rationality starts to emerge as one of its manifestations, *psyche* becomes warmer and drier, and starts to take on some of the qualities of fire. One corollary of this is that we have it in our power to destroy our very selves. This is done by, for example, excessive drinking, which effectively both "puts out" that fire which is the soul-*qua*-rational principle and "drowns" that soul-*qua*-life principle (frs 117, 77).

Parmenides of Elea

It is commonly felt that Parmenides is the giant among Greek philosophers antecedent to Socrates. But interpretation of the detail of his doctrine continues to divide investi-gators. In a lengthy poem, large parts of the first section of which (often called "On Truth") have survived, Parmenides casts his views as a revelation from a goddess after he has completed a journey to the realm in which she dwells. Beginning with what seems to be a basic methodology for philosophical inquiry, the goddess says that there are only two routes available for our ascertainment (*noesai*), the first a route in terms of "is and cannot not-be," the second a route in terms of "is not and needs must not be" (fr. 2). This statement is, however, immediately followed by an affirmation that the second route in question is in fact *not* one that we can come to know, on the grounds that one could never come to know *what is not* or be able to point it out in words.

Whatever the meaning of these assertions (we shall need to return to them later), we can at least, by contrapositing the final statement, affirm with some certainty just what the poem is going to be about, and that is "what is" or "that which is." Parmenides very possibly expects us to do just that, since what is likely to be his very next statement (fr. 3), which purports to offer a reason for what has just been said, has "that which is" as part of it subject. Read literally, it says, "For to come to know and to be are one and the same." Failing to realize that the verb *noein* in early Greek is basically a verb of intellectual achievement, not just a vague verb of thinking, scholars have hitherto tended to see this as some sort of proto-Berkeleyan claim that "to think and to be are one and the same," or, alternatively, on a different reading of the sentence's syntactical structure, that "the same thing is there for being and for thinking." It is then a simple move to accuse Parmenides of a naïve modal fallacy of the form "If *A* thinks that *p*, then, necessarily *p*," and to write off his system as no doubt brilliant, but brilliantly vitiated.

But Parmenides seems much more likely to have meant something a good deal less obscure than this, and a good deal more plausible. If we accept that, like Heraclitus, he is using the word "same" in its softer sense, and thus saying that to come to know and to be are the same in the sense that they "go together" rather than that they "are identical," he is in fact propounding, for the first time in Western thought, an epistemological principle that has been basic to philosophy ever since, and that is, "If *A* knows that *p*, then *p*" (a principle Hintikka has rightly called "The Law of Parmenides").

It is also unsurprising, given the earlier realization by others such as Xenophanes and Heraclitus that no philosophical system can stand up to examination without a strong epistemological underpinning, to find him laying such stress at the outset on the elaboration of a basic epistemology. But what is to be understood by *p* is still to be examined. Is "that which is," seen as the subject of the poem, to be unpacked in terms of existence (i.e., "that which exists" or "that which is real"), predication ("that which is *p*", or "anything that is *p*") or veridication ("that which is the case" or "anything that is the case"), and, equally importantly, is it to be understood collectively or distributively (each is grammatically possible)? All three interpretations have been defended, but the strongest case still seems to be one in terms of "existence," not least because it firmly locates Parmenides in a context of investigation into "what is there," "what is real," which, as we have seen, characterizes the greater part of earlier and contemporary Greek philosophy. (The questions of predication and veridication will come into their own later on in the poem, when Parmenides turns to discussion of the *qualities* of the real and the nature of true propositions concerning it.)

On this interpretation, Parmenides is castigating those who claim that blank nothingness can ever come to be an object of knowledge. If there is knowledge, then, necessarily, there is knowledge of *something*, and that "something," which he now says clearly is "that which is" (fr. 8), turns out to have some remarkable features. *Qua* potential object of knowledge, that which is (or, as we might say, "the real") must first of all be seen simply *as* real, and also in its *totality*; knowledge of the particular is out of the question. Put slightly differently, we can indeed achieve knowledge of the universe, but only of the universe as seen from a universal optic and in terms of the most general thing that can be said about it; i.e., that of its simple *reality*. Once these conditions are fulfilled, we can then go on to say (fr. 8) that it is one, unchanging, homogeneous, complete, indivisible, without temporal beginning or end, and finite (its shape being ball-like).

Failing to understand how carefully Parmenides has circumscribed his argument, many have understood him as claiming that the shifting world of sense perception is a chimera, all that really exists being eternal, unchanging, homogeneous being. Others have understood him as saying there are two universes, the one (the object of "knowledge") being characterized as unchanging, homogeneous etc., the other (the object of "opinion") being the world open to sense perception. But both of these interpretations should be resisted. What Parmenides is saying, rather, is that there is only one universe, though it is only an object of knowledge if viewed in a very particular way. Viewed in terms of the ever-changing individual items that go to make it up, it will forever be the object of *opinions* of varying degrees of plausibility. The second part of his poem, of which we have only a few small fragments, is very likely just such a set of opinions of his own, on such items as the possible origin of the movements of the stars and planets (fr. 11), to add to those proffered by his predecessors and contemporaries.

The overall picture that emerges is remarkable. The real seen simply as real and as a totality is eternal, since nothing can come from nothing or be destroyed into nothing. It is also immobile, since, being by definition the totality of what is, there is no further, putative space into which it could conceivably move. It is furthermore indivisible into parts, since, by what we would now term the law of the identity of indiscernibles, each putative "part" would be simply (a) reality, and thereby indistinguishable from all others. And so on with all the other epithets set out in fragment 8: Parmenides has little difficulty showing that all make perfect sense if applied (though of course *only* if applied) to the real seen simply as real and as a totality. The only potential problem lies with his final statement, in which, influenced perhaps by the current view, ascribed to the Pythagoreans, that the sphere is the most "complete" of all geometrical figures, the real is described as being in mass like a perfectly rounded ball. To many it seems clear that Parmenides should in fact have concluded that his real is infinite in extent as well as in time, and a short time later his pupil Melissus attempts to help him out in this regard, it seems, when he argues that the real must necessarily be infinite in extension too.

As part of a discussion of the nature of the universe and in what way if any it can be "known" (i.e., in terms of what he called "totality" or "completeness"), Parmenides has in fact come close to formulating a second great epistemological tenet, eventually elaborated in detail by Aristotle; i.e., that knowledge claims involve universality. He is also possibly the first Greek to grapple with the question of the relationship between knowledge and true propositions, on one interpretation at any rate of a very difficult passage. At fr. 8, lines 34ff he says: "coming to know [something] and ascertainment that [that 'something'] *is* [real/the case] is one and the same [thing/process]. For you will not [ever] find [an instance of] coming to know without [also finding] that which *is* in [the proposition] in which [such ascertainment] has been affirmed" (translation mine).

At the level of philosophical psychology he may also have had a significant contribution to make, though once again evidence for this stems from one interpretation of a very obscure fragment (fr. 16). On this reading he says: "The *quality* of each person's understanding depends on the way his much-wandering body-components are co-ordinated. For *what* the body's nature knows is identical for all men and every man. For the *plenum* is ascertainment" (translation mine). The comment seems to be some sort of response to the question: how is it that perceptions of the real differ? In reply, Parmenides states that the genuine (if often unappreciated) object of knowledge is the real in its totality (now called the plenum; compare fr. 8, line 24, where the real was described as "all full of what is"). How we view it will be a function of who we are as physical individuals; but invariably our optic, however skewed (cf. fr. 6, line 6) or uncritically put forward, at least tangentially has the real as a totality as its object, since all objects in the universe of space–time are each in *some* sense real, however little else can be confidently affirmed about them.

If the above understanding of Parmenides is correct, he clearly deserves his reputation as the greatest of the pre-Socratic philosophers. However, the ambiguities in the use of the verb "to be" still largely eluded him, so much so that, like everyone else up to the time of Plato's *Sophist*, he tended to confuse negative existential and negative predicative propositions. Despite this, however, no Greek philosopher after him was prepared to propound any new system without first trying in one way or other to accommodate it to the challenges he had set down.

Zeno

Undoubtedly influenced by Parmenides' startling ideas, his friend and pupil Zeno of Elea has achieved fame for a series of arguments, perhaps the most famous of which involves Achilles never catching up with the tortoise, which set out to demonstrate the self-contradictory consequences of maintaining that motion and space are real. To do this he clearly operates on the assumption that his reader will make no distinction between physical and geometrical space, just as contemporary Pythagoreans apparently made no distinction between them as they set out, from the basis of a single point/unit/basic bit of material (the Greek word *hen* was used at this time to denote all three), to construct, as a single process, the physical universe of matter, the geometrical universe of points, and the arithmetical universe of units. To clarify and carefully distinguish the nature of the three universes has taken the time and energy of many thinkers, and it may well be a major claim to fame on Zeno's part that, being himself one of the first to be reasonably clear about the distinction, he could exploit the continuing confusion of other thinkers to show that, given their presuppositions, motion and place apparently had properties so manifestly contradictory that they could not in fact exist. Alternatively, he may have himself been still unclear about the distinction, and thus himself genuinely believed that motion and place had the properties he ascribed to them and hence could not be accounted for logically. And, finally, he could have been clear about the distinction, but believed that, even if we carefully confine ourselves to the universe of *physical* space, the notions of motion and place *still* cannot be accounted for logically.

In a further series of *reductio ad absurdum* arguments he sets out the contradictory consequences of believing in a plurality of things, and here too we are in the same state of unclarity about his intentions as we were about the arguments concerning space and motion: either he is aware that he is exploiting ambiguities that he knows his readership will very likely miss or he is himself still in a state of confusion about the matter.

Either way, it is uncertain how much of an ally Parmenides would have found him. If in beginning his arguments against plurality, for example, with the words "If there is a plurality" Zeno is to be understood as saying "If the real is a plurality" (the Greek would certainly allow for such an interpretation, and at one point in fr. 1 he does in fact use Parmenides' word "that which is" or "the real" [*to on*]), then Parmenides might well have seen him as a useful ally, since the epithets of the real that he goes on to defend in his arguments are precisely those affirmed by Parmenides of his own reality; i.e., unity and changelessness, though only of course if viewed *qua* real and as a totality.

But it is still a matter of broad dispute among scholars whether Zeno thought he was defending Parmenides by his arguments, and whether, if he did so think, he had in fact fully understood what his teacher was saying. One possibility is that Zeno felt that, in accepting the existence of space, motion, and plurality as part of the real *qua* object of opinion (though not, of course, of knowledge), Parmenides had failed to see that, even as supposed objects of opinion, they were still fundamentally unamenable to logical explanation, and his own (Zeno's) arguments had been set out to make this point very clear. This explanation, if correct, has the advantage of crediting Zeno with a *critical* knowledge of his teacher, as well as the logical skill to lay down a number of challenges to common-sense beliefs about space, motion, and plurality. But it is still only a guess, to add to the many that have been and continue to be put forward about what the enigmatic Zeno was up to.

Empedocles of Acragas

What Empedocles thought of the detail of Parmenides' views we do not know. But he clearly accepted the notion that the real in its totality is spheroid and a plenum, and that it is subject to neither coming into being nor destruction. His own interesting contribution to the discussion is his notion that what he calls the "roots" of things are four in number – earth, air, fire, and water. These four, which make up the totality of the real (there is no such thing as empty space), are in an unending state of combining and recombining to produce, in cosmic sequence across vast reaches of time, four stages of things, the two driving forces behind it all being what he calls Love and Strife and which we would likely call centripetal and centrifugal force. The four stages are those of (a) disunited limbs (an early stage in evolution in which nature has not yet made appropriate combinations: arms stray about unattached to shoulders, eyes are not embedded in foreheads, etc.); (b) monsters and deformities (creatures are by now fully formed, but oddities still abound: some creatures are both male and female, some humans have ox-heads, etc.); (c) "whole-natured forms" (a stage not unsimilar to what we see around us now, but without sexual differentiation); and (d) the world we now know.

The picture can be readily imagined as one in which, in stages (a) and (b), Love (centripetal force) is dominant, and in which, in stages (c) and (d), the forces of Strife (centrifugal force) have begun to take control. But the cycle is endless. As stage (d) draws to an end, Love begins to take control again in its turn, the process is reversed, and the cycle continues *ad infinitum*. On a macro-cosmic scale, the same forces are at work to produce the same effects. At a certain point in cosmic history, when Love is totally dominant, all four elements (earth, air, fire, and water) are massed together in so uniform a pattern as to be totally indistinguishable. By the time the polar opposite of this stage is reached, however, Strife has taken complete control, and the four world-masses have been totally separated, at which point the cycle starts again, *ad infinitum*. As for the way in which things are supposed to be *composed* from earth, air, fire, and water, he puts forward the view that it is a matter of the "ratio of the mixture" that makes things what they are (a ratio of 1/2/8/9, say, might be that of iron; one of 1/3/7/9 that of copper, etc.).

If in holding the above views Empedocles sounds remarkably modern in the contemporary scientific environment, where notions like evolution and oscillation theories of the universe have won a large measure of support, it is also the case that he held other beliefs which sound considerably less so. He held, for example, that the source of cognition is the blood around the heart – a view rejected later by Plato in favor of the brain, but unfortunately accepted by Aristotle, with long-lasting consequences. He was also, like the Pythagoreans, very much a psycho-physical dualist, believing, like them, in the transmigration of the human soul and its transformation into animal and plant forms, and claiming even to remember the time when he was "a boy and a girl, a bush and a bird and a mute sea fish" (fr. 117).

Anaxagoras of Clazomenae

Like all of his predecessors, Anaxagoras too felt that matter must always have existed, since he could not conceive of reality stemming from absolute nothingness. But his specific, and very startling, claim, in which we see further evidence that for some Greek thinkers physical and geometrical space were clearly not obviously distinguishable, was that matter is also infinitely divisible. As far as the world of sense perception is concerned, he believed that there have always existed what one might call basic things (or "seeds," to use his word); examples of these were blood, stone, water, and other natural bodies of this order (he also, less plausibly, seems to have included qualities like wetness, color, dryness, etc. in this list). All things in the world are made up of a combination of *all* of these, any individual thing getting its name from the dominant basic thing composing it (so blood is blood because of the preponderance of that basic thing "blood" within it). (The view has clear affinities with Empedocles' notion of the "ratio of the mixture"). As for the basic things themselves, they too will be infinitely divisible into smaller and smaller portions.

The significant motive force that accounts for the world we now have and its operations is not Love and Strife, but Mind. This Mind is exceptional in that, unlike everything else in the universe, it does not have a portion of all other basic things within it. It is thus "unmixed" and "pure," and can and does permeate the universe (fr. 12). It was the force which caused the initial spinning motion (fr. 13) that (a) brought our world into being from an initial state in which "all things were together, infinite in respect of their number and minuteness," and (b) across time brought it to that differentiated state which is the world we know.

The Atomists: Democritus and Leucippus

Now clearly distinguishing geometrical and physical space, Democritus and Leucippus took a diametrically opposite stance to that of Anaxagoras, arguing that, while matter is indeed uncreatable and indestructible, it has as its bedrock a multiplicity of "further unsplittable basic bits" (*a-toma*, "atoms"). These atoms are infinite in number; are of infinitely varied shapes; and are in eternal motion, clashing and combining (when their shapes fit) or rebounding (when they do not) in an infinity of space. With these four infinities at their disposal, Democritus and Leucippus go on to posit a universe of limitless variety, in which "worlds" (we would say "galaxies") are born and die, crash into one another, destroy and are destroyed. Some of these worlds, they say, will be like ours, some not; some will be large, some smaller, some will have suns and moons like ours, some not, and so on.

What has astonished very many people about this view is that it is wholly derived from reason, without benefit of telescope or microscope. It is simply a logical deduction from the positing of (a) four infinities, (b) chance, and (c) the operation of certain basic laws of physics. But it was a view that won few adherents at the time, since it left no room for the notion that the universe might manifest reason in some way. In particular it clashed with the ideas of a contemporary thinker, Diogenes of Apollonia, who was the first we know of to put forward the teleological claim that things in the universe are disposed in the best possible way. With this claim, and its immediate and unquestioning acceptance by Socrates, Plato, and others, the battle lines between teleological and non-teleological visions of the universe were drawn, and a new age of philosophizing began.

Bibliography

Editions and translations

Diels, H. and Kranz, W. (1952) *Die Fragmente der Vorsokratiker*, 6th edn. Dublin/Zurich: Weidmann.

Gallop, D. and Robinson, T. M. (1984–) *Phoenix Presocratics Series*. Toronto: Toronto University Press (commentaries by J. H. Lesher, T. M. Robinson, D. Gallop, B. Inwood, and C. C. W. Taylor).

Kirk, G. S., Raven, J. E., and Schofield, M. (eds) (1982) *The Presocratic Philosophers*, 2nd edn. Cambridge: Cambridge University Press.

Studies

Curd, P. (1998) *The Legacy of Parmenides*. Princeton, NJ: Princeton University Press.

Kahn, C. H. (1979) *The Art and Thought of Heraclitus*. Cambridge: Cambridge University Press.

McKirahan, R. D. (1994) *Philosophy before Socrates*. Indianapolis, IN: Hackett.

2

Plato, *Phaedo* (ca. 385 BC)

The Soul's Mediation between Corporeality and the Good

Kenneth Dorter

The *Phaedo* has always been one of Plato's (429–347 BC) most popular dialogues, both for philosophical and literary reasons. Philosophically it comprises more of Plato's best-known doctrines than any dialogue except for the much longer *Republic*: immortality, theory of forms, learning as recollection, method of hypothesis, virtue as purification. As literature it depicts the last hours of Socrates, culminating in a death scene that is the most moving episode in all of Plato. The popular appeal of the dialogue is echoed in the composition of Socrates' audience, which consists mostly of non-philosophers, and in the consequent use of religious metaphors to present the teachings.

The central philosophical discussion begins when Socrates tells his audience that not only should philosophers not regard death as an evil, but they should welcome it as a fulfillment. Philosophy is devoted to overcoming the petty and obsessive demands of bodily appetites and vanities, in order that our true self, reason, can achieve its goal of communion with intelligible reality. We strive, then, to separate the soul from the body as much as possible, and since that separation is the meaning of death, "philosophy is the practicing of death." Paradoxically, even if the fulfillment of the philosophical life lies in death, suicide is prohibited. Our life is in service to the gods and we must not deprive them of that service. The divine basis of reality both inspires philosophy to flee the body in a death-like pursuit of incorporeal divinity and at the same time forbids it from consummating that pursuit.

This tension between our inner impulse toward the incorporeal and divine (death) and our duty to serve the divine in the corporeal world (life) is the architectonic principle on which the *Phaedo* is based. Throughout the dialogue a three-level ontology is at work: the corporeal realm of becoming, the incorporeal intelligible realm of being, and the soul as intermediate between them. This first becomes evident when Cebes and Simmias challenge Socrates to defend his claim that the nature of philosophy implies the welcoming of death, and Socrates replies by considering in turn the nature of the body, the nature of the soul, and the nature of the intelligible realm: corporeal pleasure is not worthy of being a serious goal of life; the soul's pursuit of truth is most successful when it is most free from bodily disturbances; and because the forms or essences of things are intelligible rather than corporeal they can best be known when the soul is most detached from the body. When Cebes replies that death can only be regarded as a fulfillment of our being if the soul can be proved immortal, Socrates embarks on a series of three proofs, which once again proceed through the three levels of reality. The first examines the soul in relation to the nature of corporeal becoming; the second considers the nature of the soul's distinctive activity of acquiring knowledge; and the third shows the soul's affinity to the realm of intelligible form. Later, in response to an objection by Cebes, Socrates formulates a fourth argument in which all three levels of reality are explicitly combined: soul is what imparts the form of life to corporeality.

The *Phaedo* comprises roughly eleven sections: (1) a brief introductory scene; (2) the opening discussion of philosophy and its relation to virtue; (3–5) three arguments for immortality; (6) an interlude where Simmias and Cebes criticize the arguments; (7) Socrates' refutation of Simmias's criticism; (8) an autobiographical explanation of the method of hypothesis; (9) a fourth argument in reply to Cebes' criticism; (10) the myth of afterlife; and (11) the death scene.

Philosophy and Virtue (62b–69d)

Socrates describes his claim that suicide is prohibited because of our service to the gods as an (Orphic) mystery that is not easy to understand (62b). We can begin to understand it, however, when we notice that the characteristic of the gods that all three speakers insist on is their goodness (62d–63b), and that the principle of the good is the ultimate cause of all things (98c 99a). To say that we may not kill ourselves because our life is in service to goodness is to say that the world is somehow a better place for our presence, and that we must live up to that responsibility. Accordingly, this section culminates in a discussion of the nature of virtue.

Philosophy, as the practicing of death, is not a withdrawal from the world, for then we would be depriving the gods of our service as surely as if we killed ourselves. Rather, it is a way of life that recognizes the primacy of selfless (because universal) reason over the self-centeredness of bodily passions. Philosophers do not fear death because only in "Hades" will they find wisdom (68a) – "Hades," we later learn, refers not to Homer's unseen ("Hades" means "unseen") world of the dead but to the invisible realm of intelligible reality (80d, 81c). Those who fear death, then, are not lovers of wisdom (philosophers) but lovers of the body, and what they call virtue is really a kind of vice. Since they fear death they are courageous only because they fear something else (dishonor) even more, so their courage is cowardice; and since they love the body they limit their pleasure only when it interferes with other kinds of pleasure, so their moderation is indulgence. True virtue only belongs to those whose behavior is governed by selfless wisdom; that is, by those who purify themselves of selfish motives in order to serve divine goodness.

Reciprocity Argument (69e–72e)

We can find fulfillment in "Hades" only if the self or soul survives death, so Socrates must demonstrate immortality. As in the previous argument, he begins with a doctrine borrowed from religion: after the souls of the dead go to Hades they are reincarnated. If birth is actually reincarnation, then the soul must have existed posthumously. The demonstration can be summarized as follows:

1 Everything that has an opposite comes into being from it (bigger from smaller, waking from sleeping).
2 Being alive and being dead are opposites.
3 Consequently the living come from the dead.
4 Therefore our souls must exist in Hades after death so they can return to life.

A brief supplementary argument follows:

5 If the living died without returning to life, eventually everything would have been dead.
6 Therefore souls must be reincarnated.

Plato seems to recognize that, on the surface at least, there are difficulties with all the arguments in the dialogue because he portrays Socrates' audience as never completely convinced by them. One problem with the present argument is that the opposite (contradictory) of "alive" is not "dead" but "not-alive." We would agree that if something comes to be alive it must have been not-alive, but not that it must have been dead (previously alive). Socrates himself seems to be aware of the fallacy, for in the supplemental argument (steps 5 and 6) he says that even "if the living came from other things" than the dead, if nothing ever returned to life eventually everything would die out (72d–e). But to acknowledge that there are non-living things other than the dead is to admit that death is not the opposite of life, and that the first part of the argument is wrong. In fact this supplement seems meant to remedy that error by pointing out that the same conclusion follows nevertheless.

Why would Plato give us an invalid argument followed by a correction, instead of simply correcting the argument? Later Socrates warns that he is behaving as much like a polemicist as like a philosopher, and his audience should be careful lest they be taken in by bad arguments (91a–c). The reason becomes clear later: it is urgent that people believe in an afterlife as a deterrent to immorality (107c–d) – and Cebes had already pointed out that there is an irrational part of our nature which needs to be persuaded by emotional rather than logical means (77d–e, cf. *Timaeus* 71a–d). How we understand immortality depends on how we understand the self. For some the self is the individuality that distinguishes us from others, and immortality is personal; while for others the true self is what we share with everyone else, and immortality is impersonal. The *Phaedo* identifies the self with reason, and in the absence of appetites and competitiveness it is hard to see how one soul could be distinguished from another. In that case the *Phaedo*'s concept of immortality is an impersonal one, and would not satisfy the first type of person. Socrates' warning about his polemical arguments implies that the dialogue is written on two levels, one that appeals to abstract reason, and another that appeals to our emotions but does not stand up to rational analysis.

The first part of the argument, by insisting that the living come from the dead, suggests individual souls waiting to be reincarnated. The supplement, by quietly ac-knowledging that the non-living from which the living come need not be dead, no longer conveys an image of souls retaining their individuality after death: immortality seems more like conservation of energy than personal survival. In fact Socrates began by saying that the argument applied not only to humans but also to animals, plants, and everything that comes to be. But those who would not be satisfied with an immor-tality in which our soul is part of an eternal but undifferentiated life force could be won over by corresponding traditional images of Hades, the gods, and shades of the dead. Both this argument and the argument against suicide began as elaborations of reli-gious doctrines, where words like "gods" and "Hades" were used in a double sense. We can read the arguments of the *Phaedo* either as failed attempts to demonstrate what they claim, or as successful attempts to demonstrate something more subtle that they only imply. The second alternative is more plausible in view of Plato's portrait of Socrates' audience as reluctant to accept them at face value. Even after the final argu-ment Simmias says that, although he can find nothing wrong with it, he is uneasy because something may have escaped them, and Socrates replies "Not only that, Simmias, but you should more clearly examine both those things which you rightly mentioned and the first hypotheses, even if they are convincing to you" (107a–b).

Argument from Recollection (72e–77a)

After the reciprocity argument Cebes remarks that another proof for immortality is Socrates' claim that learning is recollection (see *Meno* 81d–86b), for "according to that view it is necessary for us to have learned at some earlier time what we now recollect. But that is impossible unless our soul existed somewhere before it was born in this human form" (72e–73a). Once again we are led to think of our souls pre-existing in Hades. The lengthy, complex argument can be paraphrased as follows.

1   Equal things sometimes seem equal and sometimes not.
2   We judge whether they are equal by an absolute standard of "equality itself."
3   Unlike equal things, which sometimes seem unequal, equality itself never seems unequal.
4   Therefore, our concept of equality itself cannot have been learned empirically from experience of equal things – they are only the occasion for recollecting it.
5   We must have acquired it before seeing equal things since we judge them by it.
6   We have perceived equal things since birth.
7   Therefore our souls acquired the concept of equality before we were born.
8   Therefore our souls existed before the body and are immortal.

The argument makes two general points: (1) since absolute concepts cannot be derived from sensory experience they are *a priori*; and (2) we must have acquired them before we were born. The first of these is plausible since the senses give us only relative qualities, but the second is problematic since we might suppose, with Kant and others, that the *a priori* is part of what it is to be human, and therefore does not exist before birth. In fact Simmias makes that very point: we may "acquire that knowledge at the time we are born' (76c). Socrates asks in reply, "But at what other time do we lose it?," and Simmias withdraws in confusion. But why must we lose it at another time? Why can we not acquire it as a potentiality that still needs to be activated? – which is what dormant memory is in any case. In fact both Simmias's and Socrates' words throughout this section imply that possibility. Six times in about half a page they repeat that "our souls existed before we were born as human beings" or simply ". . . before we were born" (76c–77a). This means that there is a difference between "our souls" and "we human beings." "We" can only acquire that knowledge at birth because "we" do not exist beforehand, only our souls do. Simmias is right after all, but he does not notice how the distinction between "us" and "our souls" supplies the answer to Socrates' challenge. The argument may still give us reason to believe that "our souls" are eternal, but it is no longer clear that "we" are eternal, in other words that our immortality is personal rather than impersonal.

Later Simmias recalls the conclusion of the argument rather differently: "Our soul exists even before it comes into the body just as its essence is the kind we designate as 'that which is'" (92d). In that case the soul has the same kind of being as forms like equality itself, and so it will know them from its own nature if it is not impeded by the body (see 79c–d). "We" acquire knowledge of the forms at birth, not before, because that is when the soul becomes a human being, and we lose it at the same time because that is when the soul's power to see the forms is obscured by the disruptions of the body. In that case there is another level to the argument than the mythological one conveyed by Cebes' suggestion that our soul "learned at some earlier time what we now recollect." Our soul does not literally have a prenatal learning experience that it forgets at birth; rather our soul (reason) *by nature* communes with eternal being, but "we" embodied souls who are caught up in the tumult of the body need to be made mindful of it, to "recollect" it.

The first argument demonstrated a naturalistic immortality as part of an eternal cyclical process of death and rebirth. This one gives us something more inward. We experience immortality not only externally as the stuff of eternal nature, but also internally through our knowledge of eternal forms. In the act of knowing we experience our soul's affinity with the forms that, like it, have the kind of essence we call "that which is," an essence not subject to becoming, and so eternal. At this level the argument leads naturally to the next, which assimilates the being of the soul to the being of the forms, and is introduced as a continuation of this one when, after a short interlude, Cebes asks to "return to the point from which we digressed" (78a–b).

The digression resulted from Simmias's complaint that the recollection argument proves only pre-existence, not immortality. Socrates suggests combining it with the first argument, which proved afterlife, so the two together demonstrate immortality past and future. But he also accuses Simmias and Cebes of being like children who fear that the soul disperses when it leaves the body. Cebes agrees that "perhaps there is a child in us who fears these things," and Socrates suggests that such fears need to be assuaged by "singing incantations" to that child – an image of how the mythological surface of the arguments complements the conceptual underpinnings by appealing to us at an emotional level (the concluding myth is explicitly called an incantation at 114d).

Affinity (78b–80b)

The affinity argument is the least rigorous and most hesitant of the arguments, weakening its assertions with qualifications such as "likely," and concluding anticlimactically that "the soul is completely indissoluble or close to it" (80b). It works from analogy and therefore claims only probability not certainty. An argument that shows two things to agree on certain points, and then concludes that they probably agree also on the point in question, can be dismissed by disputing either the initial comparisons or the extrapolation to the conclusion. But if it is logically the most modest, it is psychologically the most effective argument, for if the initial comparisons seem justified, the conclusion may seem to follow directly from our experience, and convince more effectively than one based on abstract, indirect inference. Among the proofs for the existence of God the argument from design, based on an analogy between human and divine creativity, is more persuasive than the abstract cosmological or ontological arguments because our experience of order in the world is more reason to believe in a creative force than all the conceptual insistence of the other arguments. Something of the kind is true of the affinity argument, the center of the dialogue's five arguments.

The argument contrasts the transient corporeal realm with the eternal intelligible realm, and shows that in at least three ways the body resembles the corporeal while the soul resembles the intelligible. It follows that, just as the body resembles the corporeal also in impermanence, the soul is likely to resemble the intelligible also in eternality. The three resemblances are drawn from the three realms of being – corporeality (the composite), soul (knowledge), and the forms (divinity).

1 Responding to the worry that the soul might scatter upon death, Socrates points out that only what is composite can scatter, and that things that change are more likely to be composite, while the changeless is more likely to be simple. Forms are unchanging and therefore simple, while things always change and are therefore composite. Our body, being visible, is more like the visible changing things; while our soul, being invisible, is more like what is invisible and unchanging.
2 In the soul's investigations, when it uses bodily senses it becomes confused because its subject is always changing, "whereas when it investigates through itself [reason] it goes to what is pure, eternal, immortal, and unchanging, and being akin to that it always stays with it whenever it [can]" (79d). So in respect of knowledge, too, soul is more like the forms while body is more like the realm of change.
3 In the soul–body composite one part rules while the other obeys, and it is natural for the divine to rule and the mortal to obey. In this respect as well the soul resembles the divine and the body the mortal.

On the basis of all these resemblances it is natural for the body to dissolve but not the soul. Although they are only analogies and can therefore be disputed, they point to the strongest experiential grounds for our belief in immortality. There is something in us which we feel remains unchanged through all the body's alterations, which in the experience of rational knowledge feels itself akin to the timelessness of its subject, and which seems to us to have something divine and sovereign about it. An experience of that kind is more persuasive than the most virtuosic exercise in deduction.

Misology and Method (80d–102a)

The affinity argument is followed by a depiction of our posthumous fate (such as reincarnation into creatures that reflect the life we led) and a return to the theme of philosophy as the practicing of death. At that point Simmias and Cebes express reservations about the arguments, and throw the audience into a perplexity that threatens to destroy their belief in rationality. Socrates combats the threat of misology by proposing a method of inquiry to protect us from random argumentation and its attendant confusion. This is the method of hypothesis, which he employs in his answers both to Simmias and to Cebes.

In a quasi-autobiographical account Socrates explains that he developed the method out of his frustration in trying to discover the ultimate causal principle, the good. We can satisfactorily understand the world only if we understand the reason why it is as it is – its goodness. Being unable to discover that principle, he resorted to a *deuteros plous*, a "secondary way" (literally, "second sailing"). The term refers to the use of oars in the absence of wind, so it is a slower, more laborious means to the same destination. The method of hypothesis is a gradual approach to the teleological principle of things, in three stages: (1) When we accept something as true we accept whatever agrees with it and reject whatever conflicts (100a). (2) But when the initial hypothesis itself comes into question we must examine its consequences to see whether they lead to disharmonious results (101d3–5). (3) And when we must give an account of it we do so in terms of the best of the higher hypotheses (101d5–e1). The first two stages are illustrated in Socrates' reply to Simmias, which preceded this account (Simmias anticipated stage one at 85c–d), and the third will be illustrated in his reply to Cebes.

Reply to Simmias: refutation of epiphenomenalism (85e–86d, 91c–95a)

Simmias's objection is that the soul may be invisible, incorporeal, beautiful, and divine – as the affinity argument claims – but so is the harmony of a tuned lyre, and since the harmony ceases to exist when the lyre is destroyed, the soul may perish when the body does. On that analogy the soul is a product of the body, an epiphenomenon. Socrates employs the first stage of the method of hypothesis by pointing out that since Simmias accepts the hypothesis (92d) of recollection he must reject epiphenomenalism because it conflicts with it by making the body prior to the soul. He employs the second stage by showing that the hypothesis (93c, 94b) of epiphenomenalism implies that the bodily elements are in perfect harmony, and that virtue itself is a kind of harmony, which leads to the absurd conclusion that all souls are equally virtuous. Moreover, since the soul rules the body, the epiphenomenalist hypothesis also entails the absurdity that a harmony can act against the elements that produce it.

Reply to Cebes: argument from essential attributes (86e–87b, 95b–107a)

Cebes' objection focuses on Socrates' weak claim that the soul is only "more like" the eternal than the body is, from which Socrates had argued that since the body does not fall apart upon death the soul would hardly do so either. Cebes points out that even if the soul is much longer lasting than any particular body, it passes through many incarnations and may die at the end of its final one, which may be ours. Socrates replies by considering the cause of generation and destruction, and at the same time illustrating the third stage of the method of hypothesis.

When his youthful attempt to explain everything by physical causation led to absurdities he looked for a "higher" explanation. Unable to discover the "true cause," the principle of the good, he settled for the best of the higher hypotheses, the hypothesis (100b) that the causes are forms. The third stage is then repeated at a higher level: although the theory of forms is "safe" from the previous absurdities, it too is dissonant: physicalism was at least sophisticated and informative (100c), but explanations like "things are beautiful because of beauty" are simplistic, artless, foolish, and ignorant (100d, 105c). Socrates accordingly replaces this second hypothesis with a higher one that unites the strengths of its two predecessors: "I see a safety beyond the first answer . . . not safe and ignorant . . . but [safe and] subtle" (105b). The new model introduces things that impart forms, and combines the forms with the natural causes spoken of earlier. This third hypothesis provides the basis for the fourth argument (105b–106e):

1   Some things impart certain forms to whatever they approach (snow imparts cold, fire heat).
2   These carriers can never have the opposite quality of the form they impart (snow can never be hot, or fire cold).
3   Soul imparts life to whatever it enters.
4   Therefore souls can never be qualified by death and are immortal, deathless.

But Socrates concludes on a note of caution: the argument proves only that a soul cannot be dead, not that it is imperishable – presumably because it might simply cease to exist rather than exist in a state of death. Therefore either they must agree that what cannot die is also imperishable, or else they will need an additional argument that the soul also cannot perish in some other way (105e–106d). Strangely, after introducing this difficulty, Plato has Cebes reply without explanation that no further argument is necessary – Cebes simply assumes in a subordinate clause what he needs to defend: "Hardly anything else would not admit destruction if the deathless, *which is eternal,* admitted destruction" (105d, emphasis added). Why does Plato end by allowing Cebes to beg the question he just raised through Socrates?

In earlier arguments where the overt conclusion was not supported, the implications of the premises pointed more cogently to a different conclusion that appealed to reason but not emotion. When Socrates says here that if deathless does not entail imperishability we need another argument, is there any indication of what that argument might be? Socrates responds to Cebes by saying, "The god, I believe, and the form of life itself, and anything else that may be deathless, everyone would agree that they never perish" (106d). Throughout the dialogue "god" has been taken to mean "good" by all three main speakers (62–63b, 80d), and previously Socrates told us that he fell back on the method of hypothesis only because of his inability to discern the true cause, the good. That method gave us the theory of forms, which is recalled here in Socrates' reference to "the form of life itself," but has not yet reached its goal of the good, which is implicit in Socrates' additional reference to "the god." (Socrates' advice immediately after this argument – to "more clearly examine the first hypotheses, even if they are convincing to you" [107a–b] – can be read as an invitation to take this next step on our own.) Its goal will be reached only if the additional argument is a teleological argument from the nature of the good: the universe is good, goodness requires life, therefore life exists necessarily and soul must be eternal. In other words the causality of the good requires the eternal presence of soul and life (our service to the gods).

It is not surprising that Plato would leave such an argument merely implicit. To defend it required almost the entire *Timaeus* (see *Timaeus* 29a–30b). Moreover, it does not imply that the soul is imperishable as an individual person. For the "child within us" who is led by emotion, it may be better to allow the argument to rest on an apparently rigorous though actually fallacious connection, while pointing toward a plausible but impersonal connection for those not satisfied as easily as Cebes. The efficacy of teleology is hinted at in the concluding myth's account of the rational formation of the world (Sedley, 1989).

Myth (107d–114d)

The last argument is followed by one of Plato's longest and greatest myths, according to which our fate after death depends on the rewards or punishments that our present behavior deserves. For those who believe in survival of the personality the myth provides a vivid image of our future experience. Some general claims like the sphericity of the earth are evidently to be taken literally, but details of rewards and punishments – some of which contradict the account at 80d–82b – seem to have more symbolic than factual value: "To rely upon these things as being just as I explained them would not be fitting for a reasonable man. But that they or some such things are true . . . seems to me to be fitting" (114d). The geography of the underworld sounds rather like biology: Tartarus pumps water through the river channels, and wind through the air, in much the way the heart and lungs operate in the living body (compare 112a–c with the *Timaeus*'s description of the heart and lungs at 70b–d). If the geography of the myth is an image of the living body, and the rewards and punishments are fitted to the nature of the virtues and vices that call them forth, the fate of the souls can be taken as images of what our way of life does to us while we are alive. Those who are slaves to their passions suffer appropriate torment, while those who purify their souls of lust experience the eternity of the divine.

Bibliography

Editions and translations

Plato (1911) *Phaedo*, ed. John Burnet (with intro. and notes). Oxford: Clarendon Press.

Plato (1977) *Phaedo*, trans. G. M. A. Grube. Indianapolis, IN: Hackett.

Plato (1993) *Phaedo / Plato*, ed. C. J. Rowe (with intro. and commentary). Cambridge: Cambridge University Press.

Studies

Dixsaut, M. (1991) *Phédon / Platon*, trans. and commentary. Paris: Flammarion.

Dorter, K. (1982) *Plato's Phaedo: An Interpretation*. Toronto: University of Toronto Press.

Dorter, K. (2001) "Deathless is indestructible, if not we need another argument": an implicit argument in the *Phaedo*. In A. Havlicek and F. Karfik (eds), *Plato's Phaedo: Proceedings of the Second Platonic Symposium in Prague*, pp. 406–23. Prague: Oikoumene.

Frede, D. (1999) *Platons "Phaidon": der Traum der Unsterblichkeit der Seele*. Darmstadt: Wissenschaftliche Buchgesellschaft.

Gallop, D. (1975) *Phaedo/Plato*, trans. and commentary. Oxford: Oxford University Press.

Sedley, D. (1989) Teleology and myth in the *Phaedo*. *Proceedings of the Boston Colloquium in Ancient Philosophy*, 5: 359–83.

Stern, P. (1993) *Socratic Rationalism and Political Philosophy: An Interpretation of Plato's Phaedo*. Albany, NY: State University of New York Press.

3

Plato, *Republic* (ca. 380 BC)

The Psycho-politics of Justice

C. D. C. Reeve

Plato was born in Athens in 429 BC and died there in 347–8. His father, Ariston, traced his descent to Codrus, the last king of Athens; his mother, Perictione, was related to Solon, architect of the Athenian constitution. While Plato was still a boy, his father died and his mother married Pyrilampes, a friend of the great Athenian statesman, Pericles. Plato was thus familiar with Athenian politics from childhood and was expected to enter it himself. Horrified by actual political events, however, especially the execution of Socrates in 399 BC, he turned instead to philosophy, thinking that only it could bring true justice to human beings and put an end to civil war and political upheaval (Plato, *Seventh Letter*, 324b–326b). In his greatest masterpiece, the *Republic*, written around 380 BC, he lays out the grounds for this at once pessimistic and optimistic assessment.

Behind these grounds, or underneath them, we can see Plato's entire philosophical heritage: (1) Socrates' compulsive search for definitions of the conventional moral virtues and his doctrine that virtue is knowledge and that weakness of will is impossible; (2) the sophists – represented in the *Republic* by Thrasymachus – whom Plato sees as Socrates' arch enemies; (3) Heraclitus of Ephesus, for whom all perceptible things and qualities are in constant flux; (4) Parmenides of Elea, for whom true being is permanent, unchanging, and accessible only to reason; and (5) Pythagoras of Samos, for whom mathematics holds the key to being and to our knowledge of it. It is in part the richness of this heritage, and the subtlety of Plato's response to it, that is responsible for the richness of the *Republic* itself. But one does not need to know anything of the work's heritage to feel its resonance. One measure of the *Republic*'s greatness, indeed, is that it so readily allows any reader to enter into creative engagement with the problems it discusses and explores.

The *Republic* is about justice, then, and begins with the characteristic Socratic search for a definition (*R* 331b–c). Polemarchus provides the first candidate: justice is giving to each what he is owed (*R* 331e). Socrates proceeds to examine this definition by testing its consistency with other beliefs Polemarchus holds and is unwilling to abandon. When it proves to be inconsistent with them, it is taken to have been refuted (*R* 335e). This sort of examination, which is Socrates' stock in trade, is called an *elenchus* (from the Greek verb *elegchein*, to examine or refute). In the ideal situation, it continues until a definition of justice is found that is not inconsistent with other beliefs.

Such a definition, Socrates claims, would capture the form (*eidos, idea*) of justice. This form is a first principle or starting-point (*archê*) of ethical knowledge (Aristotle, *Metaphysics* 1078b17–30), since it both causes just things to be just and is what some-one with knowledge (*epistêmê*) must use as a paradigm in judging which things are, or are not, just (Plato, *Euthyphro* 6d–e). It is because the form has this status that Socrates claims that he cannot know whether justice is a kind of virtue, or whether it makes its possessor happy, when he doesn't know what justice is (*R* 354b–c): if you don't know a first principle, you can't know anything posterior to it.

Socrates assumes that the *elenchus* can unmask inadequate definitions of justice. So he must presuppose, it seems, that some of Polemarchus' sincerely held ethical beliefs are true. After all, inconsistency with false beliefs is no guarantee of falsehood and consistency with them is no guarantee of truth. The problem is that there seems to be little reason to accept this presupposition.

Socrates' next interlocutor, Thrasymachus, explains why. He argues that those who are stronger in any society – the rulers – control education and socialization through legislation and enforcement. But the rulers, like everyone else, are self-interested. Hence they make laws and adopt conventions – including linguistic conventions – that are in their own best interests, not those of their weaker subjects. It is these conventions that largely determine a subject's conception of justice and the other virtues. By being trained to follow or obey them, therefore, a subject is unwittingly adopting an ideology – a code of values and behavior – that serves his ruler's, rather than his own, interests. Consequently, Thrasymachus defines justice, not as what socialized subjects, like Socrates, think it is (something genuinely noble and valuable that promotes their own happiness), but as what it really is in all cities: *the interest of the stronger*.

As in the case of Polemarchus, Socrates again uses the *elenchus* to try to refute Thrasymachus. But his attempts are not found wholly adequate, either by Thrasymachus himself or by the other interlocutors (*R* 350d–e, 357a–b, 358b–c). And we can see why: by arguing that ethical beliefs are an ideologically contaminated social product, Thrasymachus has undercut the *elenchus* altogether. *He* may get tied up in knots by Socrates, but his *theory* is invulnerable to elenctic refutation (as Thrasymachus points out at *R* 349a). That is why Plato has Socrates abandon the *elenchus* in subsequent books and attempt to answer Thrasymachus (whose views are taken over by Glaucon and Adeimantus) by developing a positive defense of justice of his own.

In the next section, I shall provide an outline of that defense. Then, in subsequent sections, I shall focus on particular topics: the theory of forms, which is the metaphysical and epistemological basis of Platonic ethics and politics; the principle of labor specialization, which is an integral part of the political system of the ideal city Plato describes; the problem of ideology, which is implicit in the fact that the rulers of the ideal city lie to the other citizens; the regulation of private life and property and the censorship of the arts embodied in the city's political system; and, finally, the severe limitations the system seems to impose on personal freedom.

The Argument in Outline

At the center of Socrates' defense of justice lie the philosopher-kings, who unite political power and authority with philosophical knowledge of the transcendent, unchanging form of the good (the good-itself). Because this knowledge is based in mathematics and science, it is unmediated by conventionally controlled concepts. Hence it is free from the distorting influence of power or ideology, and so is immune to the challenge Thrasymachus poses to the *elenchus*.

What the philosopher-kings do is construct a political system – including primarily a system of socialization and education – that will distribute the benefits of their specialized knowledge of the good among the citizens at large. The system they construct relies on Plato's theory of the soul or mind (*psyche*). According to it, there are three fundamentally different kinds of desires: *appetitive* ones for food, drink, sex, and the money with which to acquire them; *spirited* ones for honor, victory, and good reputation; and *rational* ones for knowledge and truth (*R* 437b ff, 580d ff). Each of these types of desire "rules" in the soul of a different type of person, determining his values. For people most value what they most desire, and so those ruled by different desires have very different conceptions of what is valuable or good or of what would make them happy. But just which type of desire "rules" an individual's soul depends on the relative strengths of his desires and on the kind of education and socialization he receives. The fundamental goal of ethical or political education isn't to provide knowledge, therefore, but to socialize desires, so as to turn people around (to the degree possible) from the pursuit of what they falsely believe to be happiness to the pursuit of true happiness (*R* 518b–519d).

The famous allegory of the cave illustrates the effects of such education (*R* 514a). Uneducated people, tethered by their unsocialized appetites, see only images of models of the good (shadows cast by puppets on the walls of the cave). They are not virtuous to any degree, since they act simply on their whims. When their appetites are shaped through physical training, and that mix of reading and writing, dance and song the Greeks call *mousikê* (musical training), they are released from these bonds and are ruled by their socialized appetites. They have at least that level of virtue required to act prudently and postpone gratification. Plato refers to them as *money-lovers* because they pursue money as the best means of reliably satisfying their appetitive desires in the long term (*R* 580d–581a). They see models of the good (the puppets that cast the shadows). For stable satisfaction of appetitive desires *is* a sort of good.

Further education, this time in mathematical science, leaves these people ruled by their spirited desires. They are *honor-lovers*, who seek success in difficult endeavors and the honor and approval it brings. They have the true beliefs about virtue required for such success, and hence that greater level of virtue Plato calls "civic" virtue (*R* 430c).

Finally, yet further education in dialectic (a sort of successor to the Socratic *elenchus*) and practical city management results in people who are bound only by their rational desires. They are free from illusion and see not mere images of the good, but the good-itself. They are *wisdom-lovers* or philosophers, who have knowledge rather than mere true belief about virtue, and so are fully virtuous.

Not everyone, however, is able to benefit from all these types of education: there are some at each stage whose desires are too strong for education to break. That is why there are producers, guardians, and philosopher-kings in the ideal city. That is why, too, these groups can cooperate with one another in a just system, where the money-loving producers trade their products for the protection provided by the honor-loving guardians and the knowledge provided by the wisdom-loving kings, rather than competing with one another for the very same goods (*R* 462e–463b). None the less, everyone in this ideal system is enabled to travel as far out of the cave of unsocialized desires as education can take him given the innate strength of those desires. Thus everyone comes as close to being fully virtuous, and so to pursuing and achieving genuine happiness, as he can. It is this that makes Plato's city both an ethical and a prudential ideal, both maximally just and maximally happy. And because it is both, it constitutes a response to the Thrasymachean challenge raised anew by Glaucon and Adeimantus in Book II. For if maximum justice and maximum happiness go together, then it pays in terms of happiness to be just rather than unjust.

The Theory of Forms

In a number of his dialogues, Plato connects the relativist doctrines he attributes to the sophists with the metaphysical theory of Heraclitus, according to which perceptible things or characteristics are in constant flux or change – always *becoming*, never *being*. In the *Theaetetus*, he argues that Protagoras' claim that "man is the measure of all things" presupposes that the world is in flux; in the *Cratylus*, he suggests that the theory of flux may itself be the result of projecting Protagorean relativism on to the world (*R* 411b–c). None the less, Plato seems to accept some version of this theory himself (see Aristotle, *Metaphysics* 987a32–4). In *Republic* V, for example, he characterizes perceptible things and characteristics as "rolling around as intermediates between what is not and what purely is" (*R* 478a–479d; see also *Timaeus* 52a).

The theory of flux clearly exacerbates the problem we noticed earlier with the Socratic *elenchus*. If perceptible things and characteristics are always in flux, how can justice and the other virtues be stable forms? How can there be stable definitions of them to serve as correct answers to Socrates' questions? And if there are no stable definitions, how can there be such a thing as ethical knowledge? More generally, if perceptible things and characteristics are always in flux, always *becoming*, how can anything *be* something definite or determinate? How can one know or say what anything *is*? Aristotle tells us that it was reflection on these fundamental questions that led Plato to "separate" the forms from perceptible things and characteristics (*Metaphysics* 987a29–b1). The allegories of the sun and line (*R* 507a–511e), which divide reality into the intelligible part and the visible (perceptible) part, seem to embody this separation.

Conceived in this way, forms seemed to Plato to offer solutions to the metaphysical and epistemological problems to which the *elenchus* and flux give rise. As intelligible objects, set apart from the perceptible world, they are above the sway of flux, and therefore available as stable objects of knowledge, stable meanings or referents for words. As real mind-independent entities, they provide the definitions of the virtues with the non-conventional subject matter Socratic ethics needs.

Like many proposed solutions to philosophical problems, however, Plato's raised new problems of its own. If forms really are separate from the world of flux our senses reveal to us, how can we know them? How can our words connect with them? If items in the perceptible world really are separate from forms, how can they owe whatever determinate being they have to forms? In the *Meno, Phaedo,* and *Phaedrus,* Plato answers the first of these questions by appeal to the doctrine of recollection (*anamnêsis*). We have knowledge of forms through prenatal direct contact with them; we forget this knowledge when our souls become embodied at birth; then we "recollect" it in this life when our memories are appropriately jogged (for example, when we undergo elenctic examination). He answers the second question by saying that items in the world of flux "participate" in forms by resembling them. Thus perceptible objects possess the characteristic of beauty because they resemble the form of beauty, which is itself something beautiful (see *Phaedo* 100c; *Symposium* 210b–211e).

The doctrine of recollection is a problematic doctrine, of course. Among other things, it presupposes the immortality of the soul – something Plato argues for in *Republic* X and elsewhere (*Phaedo* 69e ff; *Phaedrus* 245c ff). But perhaps because recollection is so problematic, he seems to have sought an alternative to it: recollection is not mentioned in the *Republic* or in the late dialogues. This supposed alternative is dialectic.

Dialectic is introduced in the *Republic* as having a special bearing on first principles – a feature it continues to possess in Aristotle (*Topics* 101a37–b4) – particularly on those of the mathematical sciences. The importance of these sciences in Plato's thought is twofold. First, they provided a compelling example of a rich body of precise knowledge organized into a deductive system of axioms, definitions, and theorems – a model of what philosophy itself might be. Second, the brilliant mathematical treatment of harmony (musical beauty), developed by Pythagoras of Samos and his followers (Aristotle, *Metaphysics* 987a29–988a17), suggested a role for mathematics within philosophy itself. For it opened up the possibility of giving precise definitions in wholly mathematical terms of all characteristics, including such apparently vague and evaluative ones as beauty and ugliness, justice and injustice, good and evil, and the other things of which Socrates sought definitions (*R* 530d–533e).

The problem Plato found with mathematical science lay in its first principles. Scientists treat these as "absolute starting-points" for which they provide no argument (*R* 510c–d). Yet if they are false, the entire system collapses. It is here that dialectic comes in. Dialectic defends these starting-points – it renders them "unhypothetical" – not by deriving them from something yet more primitive (which is impossible), but by defending them against all objections (*R* 534b–c, 437a). In the process, they undergo conceptual revamping, so that their consistency with one another – and hence their immunity to an *elenchus* – is revealed and assured. This enables the dialectician to knit them all together into a single unified theory of everything, and so to "see things as a whole" (*R* 557c). It is this unified, holistic theory, and not recollection, that is now supposed to provide the philosopher with genuine knowledge (*R* 533d–534a).

What one grasps by means of this theory, Plato claims, is the greatest object of knowledge (*R* 505a), the form of the good, which seems to be an ideal of rational order or unity expressed in mathematical terms. It is this, apparently mysterious, object that is supposed to provide the philosopher with the kind of knowledge he needs to design the kallipolis. On a larger scale, it also provides the maker of the cosmos – the

Demiurge – with the knowledge he needs to perform his cosmic task (*Timaeus* 29e ff). For even the gods are bound by the objective truths and values embodied in the forms (*Euthyphro* 10a ff).

Forms and the Good

In the discussion of music and poetry in *Republic* II, Socrates says: "You and I aren't poets at present, Adeimantus, but we *are* founding a city. And it's appropriate for the founders to know the patterns on which the poets must base their stories, and from which they mustn't deviate. But they shouldn't themselves make up any poems" (*R* 378e–379a). Adeimantus responds by asking what these patterns for stories about the gods actually are. Socrates' lengthy answer may be summed up without much loss as follows: No "bad images of what the gods and heroes are like" (*R* 377e); only stories that will make the guardians "least afraid of death" (*R* 386a); no "frightening and dreadful names for the underworld" (*R* 387b); no "lamentations of famous men" (*R* 387e); no representation of "worthwhile people as overcome by laughter" (*R* 388e–389a); no representation of gods or heroes as failing "to rule the pleasures of drink, sex, and food for themselves" (*R* 389d–e); no "headstrong words spoken in prose or poetry by private citizens against their rulers" (*R* 390a); no imitators except "the pure imitator of a good person" (*R* 397d); no musical harmonies except the Dorian and Phrygian (*R* 399a); no music played on flutes, triangular lutes, harps, or other "multistringed and polyharmonic instruments" (*R* 399c); no rhythms except those appropriate to "someone who leads an ordered and courageous life" (*R* 399d).

The way the philosopher reaches these patterns, moreover, is clear. He looks at the effects that various kinds of poetry have on a guardian's soul. He determines what kind of soul the guardians should have by looking to the role of guardians in the good city (*R* 500b–501c, 618b–e), and he determines what that role should be by looking to the good-itself, since it is only through knowing it that he knows any other kind of good at all (*R* 534b–c).

The patterns the philosopher reaches in this way are forms. But they are, as we have seen, quite unspecific: they are not detailed blueprints for actual poems. All they determine are the features that a *good* poem must have. The same, presumably, is true of the forms of other things. Thus the philosopher's pattern of an *F* simply specifies the features an *F* must have, or must lack, *if it is to be good*.

To see more clearly what such a form or pattern is, we turn to the allegory of the sun. This has both an epistemological side, dealing with knowledge and its objects, and a metaphysical or ontological side, dealing with being or reality. We shall begin with the former:

> [1] [a] What gives truth to the things known, and the power to know to the knower is the form of the good. And [b] though it is the cause of knowledge and truth, it is also an object of knowledge. [c] Both knowledge and truth are beautiful things but the good is other and more beautiful than they. In the visible realm, [d] light and sight are rightly considered sun-like, but it is wrong to think that they are the sun, so here it is right to think of knowledge and truth as good-like, but wrong to think that either of them is the good – for the good is yet more prized. (*R* VI 508e–509a)

The form of the good, then, is (1d) something like a self-illuminating object that can shed the intelligible analogue of light on other objects of knowledge – other paradigms – in such a way as to render them intelligible: it is an intelligible object that is somehow a condition of the intelligibility of other things. This suggests that the "light" the good itself gives off is something like rational or logical order, and that it itself is a paradigm of such order.

To make all this a little less metaphorical, suppose we have a correct definition of a form, *F*. Since the definition is correct, it must exhibit whatever level of rational or logical order is required for truth – at a minimum, it must be consistent. And because the definition is made true by *F*, that form itself must, at a minimum, possess the level of rational order that is an ontological correlate of consistency. Without rational order, then, there would be no truth, and so no knowledge. If the form of the good were indeed the form or paradigm of rational order, therefore, (1a) would be readily intelligible. But so, too, would (1b–c). For the good, as itself a form, would be an object of knowledge just like all the others. But as the cause of their intelligibility or knowability, it would be "other than they."

The metaphysical side of the allegory is described as follows:

> [2] You'll be willing to say, I think, that the sun not only provides visible things with the power to be seen but also with coming to be, growth, and nourishment [see 516b9–c2], although it is not itself coming to be . . . Therefore, you should also say that the objects of knowledge not only owe their being known to the good but their being is also due to it, although the good is not being, but superior to it in rank and power. (*R* 509b)

Visible things – including the sun – are components of the visible realm. But the sun has a very special role therein: without it there would be no such realm. The same holds of the form of the good considered as a paradigm of rational order: it is a component of the intelligible realm, without which there would be no such realm. Hence it is "not being, but superior to it in rank and power."

The relationship between the form of the good and the other forms is best revealed by the problematic case of "bad" forms, such as the form of the ugly or shameful, the form of injustice, and the form of the bad (*R* 402b–c, 475e–476a). For it is particularly hard to see how these can owe their being and knowability to the form of the *good*. Now "the bad," we are told, "is what in every case destroys and corrupts and the good is what preserves and benefits" (*R* 608e). But goodness and badness are not generic; rather, they are so indexed to kinds of things that only a kind's *natural* goodness or badness preserves or destroys it: rot not rust destroys wood, and rust not rot destroys iron (*R* 608e–609b). Relative to each kind of thing, then, we have a pair of opposed items, the (natural) good and the (natural) bad, each with a distinct function: the good preserves or benefits the kind; the bad destroys or corrupts it. On the (simplifying) assumption that preserving is low-level benefiting and destruction high-level corruption, we may refer to these three related items as *kinds*, *benefiters*, and *corrupters*.

If the good is a paradigm of rational order, all three of these items, as members of the intelligible realm, must be instances of rational order. Yet they differ significantly from one another. Perhaps the easiest way to capture these differences is as follows: a kind is an instance of rational order, which, *as such*, is neither good nor bad. To be good it needs to have its level of rational order enhanced by the appropriate benefiter; to be bad it needs to have its level of rational order reduced by the appropriate corrupter. For example, a body, as such, is neither bad nor good – it exhibits only a moderate level of rational order: "I believe that there are, as it were, three kinds – the good, the bad, and the neither good nor bad . . . Disease is a bad thing, and medicine is beneficial and good . . . But a body, of course, taken to be just a body, is neither good nor bad" (*Lysis* 216d5–217b3). Add health (the appropriate benefiter) to a body, then, and it has sufficient rational order to be a good body; add sickness (the corresponding corrupter) and it is sufficiently deficient in rational order to be a bad one. But despite the fact that a body as such is neither good nor bad, it yet owes a debt to the good. If there were no such thing as rational order, even the level of rational order exhibited by the form of a body as such – the level needed for it to be a truth maker for the definition of a body – would be impossible, and the form would not be an intelligible, knowable entity.

Now consider a corrupter, such as the form of injustice. It is a pattern of rational order – a knowable, intelligible thing, "a kind of civil war between the three parts [of the soul], a meddling and doing of another's work, a rebellion of some part against the whole soul in order to rule it inappropriately" (*R* 444b). Hence it owes its knowability or intelligibility – indeed its very being – to the existence of rational order, to the existence of the form of the good. But the fact that it is a pattern of rational order does not make it a good thing – it could be neither good nor bad (like a body as such) or it could be good (like health or virtue) or it could be bad (like rot or disease). What makes it in fact bad is that it is a pattern of rational order, opposed to the rational order of a kind, that will corrupt instances of the kind by causing their natural level of rational order to degrade to such an extent that they no longer fit the kind at all (*R* 609c). Contrariwise, what would make injustice a *benefiter*, if it were one, would be that it enhances the rational order of some kind.

The form of the good is a standard or paradigm, then, that enables the philosopher to determine what poetical, political, or any other kind of goodness is. That is why other types of expertise need philosophy. Consider shoemaking, for example. The shoemaker knows how to make a shoe – he has access to the form of a shoe (*R* 596b). But he does not, *qua* shoemaker, know how to make a good shoe – one that reliably contributes to human happiness. For that he must turn to the philosopher, since only he can judge the goodness of the cities of which shoemakers, and all other experts, must form a part if human happiness is to be reliably achieved. That, and the philosopher's rather differently based need of them, is what makes the good city possible in Plato's view (*R* 369b ff).

Specialization and the Structure of the Kallipolis

Due to divine inspiration, Socrates already knows the form of the good at the outset of the *Republic*, and so is in a position to act as a pretend philosopher-king (*R* 496a–e, 506d–e) – "pretend" because he isn't a king, only a philosopher. We might expect that his first step in this role will be to draft a set of laws for the kallipolis. Instead, he focuses almost exclusively on designing a social structure that will dispose all the citizens to virtue. The reason for this is ultimately psychological. Plato believes, first, that unless socialization (including education) makes our appetites and emotions as responsive as possible to reason, so that we acquire civic virtue, no system of laws will be effective; and, second, that once we acquire civic virtue, legislation is a routine matter (*R* 422e–427d). Put the other way around, he believes that the threat posed to political good order by "anarchic" appetites is the greatest political evil of all. It is this belief that explains so much that we are likely to find most abhorrent in the *Republic*, such as the lies of the rulers, the critique of the family and private property, and the censorship of art. Of more immediate relevance, it is also what explains the sort of labor specialization that Plato argues the kallipolis must exemplify.

In Books II–V Plato seems to accept the *unique aptitude doctrine* (UAD), according to which each person is born with a natural aptitude for a unique occupation or social role: "A physician has a different nature than a carpenter" (*R* 454d); "one woman is a physician by nature, another not, one is by nature musical, another non-musical" (*R* 455e). On the basis of this doctrine, moreover, he seems to accept as a normative *principle of specialization* (PS) that each member of the kallipolis *must* practice exclusively throughout life the unique craft or type of expertise for which he has a natural aptitude (*R* 370a–b, 374a–c, 394e, 423c–d, 433a, 443b–c, 453b). Yet despite all the apparent evidence to the contrary, it is a relief to discover that Plato ultimately accepts neither PS nor UAD: UAD is obviously false, after all, and PS horribly unattractive.

The first point to notice is that Plato's psychological theory absolutely excludes the possibility of one person having a natural aptitude for carpentry and another for pottery. For, according to it, all lovers of crafts have the same cognitive abilities – they have belief rather than knowledge (*R* 475d–480a) – and all of them are money-lovers, with the same ruling desires, the same conception of the good (*R* 580d ff). Something similar is true of rulers (wisdom-lovers) and guardians (honor-lovers). That is why, while we hear of the children of producers being taken off to be trained as guardians because of their natural aptitudes (*R* 415b–c), and of guardians being demoted to the ranks of producers for failing to live up to expectations (*R* 468a), we never hear of a carpenter's child being removed to a potter's house for upbringing because he has no aptitude for his father's craft. Indeed, Plato seems simply to assume that the normal thing is for a child to follow in the craft of his parents (*R* 456d, 467a).

Plato does not hold UAD, then, and so he cannot hold PS, which presupposes it. What he does accept is the very different *unique upper-bound doctrine* (UBD), according to which a person's ruling desires set a distinct upper limit to his cognitive development. Indeed, this doctrine, as we saw, is the very cornerstone of his psychological theory. Moreover, because he accepts UBD, he also accepts the *principle of quasi-specialization* (PQS), which states that each person in the kallipolis *must* practice exclusively throughout life whichever of producing, guardianship, or ruling demands of him the highest level of cognitive development of which he is capable: money-lovers must be producers of some kind; honor-lovers must be guardians; philosophers must be kings (*R* 434a–b).

That is why, in Book IV, PS is identified as a merely provisional first stab at PQS, and is explicitly replaced by it. If *all* the practitioners of the various ordinary crafts "exchange their tools and honors," so that PS is thoroughly violated, that does "no great harm to the city" (*R* 434a). Violations of PQS, on the other hand, are a political disaster, the "ruin of the city" (*R* 434a–b). For PS was never anything more than "a sort of image of justice" (*R* 443c), whereas PQS is its very essence (*R* 434c, 443c–d): a soul is just if its three constituent parts (reason, spirit, appetite) obey this new principle, as is a city when its parts (rulers, guardians, producers) do the same. Not only does PS have no place in Plato's psychological theory, therefore, it has no place in his politics or theory of justice either.

The Lies of the Rulers

On a number of occasions we are told that the philosopher-kings will often find it necessary or useful to lie to the guardians and producers. The specter of false ideology and exploitation is immediately raised. In this section, we shall try to determine how large an obstacle it poses to the ethical acceptability of Plato's politics.

At the end of Book II, Socrates distinguishes between two types of lies or falsehoods. A "genuine lie" or "what is really a lie" (*R* 382a, 382c) is a "lie about the governing things [told] to the governing parts of the soul" (*R* 382a–b). A "verbal lie" is a "sort of imitation" of a genuine lie (*R* 382b–c) that is useful "against enemies and those of one's so-called friends who, through madness or ignorance, are attempting to do some wrong, in order to turn them away from it" (*R* 382c–d).

To be a genuine lie, or the content of one, then, a proposition must be held or believed by reason, which is the governing part of the soul, concerned with the good of the soul as a whole (*R* 441e–442c). And it must so mislead reason as to prevent the soul from achieving that good. The account of verbal lies now becomes intelligible. *B* is attempting to do *x*, falsely believing – "through madness or ignorance" – that it is good to do it. *A* knows that it is not good for *B* to do *x*. Hence *A* tells *B* something he knows to be false in order to prevent *B* from doing *x*. *A* has lied to *B*. But *B* does not come to have a false belief about the good in the rational part of his soul as a result. Indeed, he is steered towards the good, not away from it. A genuine lie misleads reason about the good. A verbal lie may seem to do the same – especially to the person (*B* in our example) who discovers he has been lied to. For *B*, of course, believes that doing *x* *is* a good thing to do. That is why a verbal lie is "a sort of imitation" of a genuine lie. But it is not "an altogether pure" lie because it does not in fact mislead reason about the good. The verbal lie comes into being "after" the genuine lie (*R* 382b–c), because *A* cannot reliably lie in words until he knows the form of the good and is in a position to tell genuine lies that mislead reason about it. That is why everyone, except the philosopher-kings, who alone know the form of the good, must avoid lies altogether (*R* 389b–c).

That the lies of the rulers are all intended to be verbal rather than genuine is made clear by Plato's examples. One of these is the well-known myth of the metals (*R* 414b–415d). Since it is referred to as "one of those lies that are sometimes necessary, of which we were just now speaking, one noble lie" (*R* 414b–c), it is clearly intended to be verbal. Its function is to tie the members of the kallipolis to each other by bonds of love or friendship (*R* 415d). But their friendship is in fact well founded in mutual self-interest. So this lie fits our account. Those who believe it do not come to believe a genuine lie. For the belief benefits them, and leads them towards the good, not away from it.

We last hear about the lies of the rulers in Book V in connection with the lottery secretly rigged by the rulers to ensure that the best men "have sex with the best women as frequently as possible" (*R* 459c–460a). Here again the lie that luck not planning controls the sexual lottery is intended to be verbal, since it is supposed to benefit the city as a whole by preserving the quality of the guardian class. One cannot help feeling, however, that Plato's intentions are less than well realized here. For sex is something even honor-loving guardians enjoy: that is why getting to have it often is a reward for them (*R* 460b, 468b–c). Consequently, the loss of it, which inferior guardians suffer in the kallipolis, is a real loss – one, moreover, for which they are not compensated. If this is a defect in the kallipolis, however, it is surely a minor one. Plato has, for contingent historical reasons, simply chosen a less than optimum solution to the problem at hand. For he has no objection to sex *per se*: when guardians are beyond the age of reproduction they are allowed to have sex with anyone they want, provided they avoid incest (*R* 461b–c). Hence contraception would provide a better solution to the eugenics problem than rigged lotteries.

To grasp the philosophical significance of all this, we need to draw a few distinctions. If the citizens in a city falsely believe they are happier there than elsewhere, in part because the worldview they have been taught is false and known to be false by the rulers, they are the victims of *false ideology*. If, on the other hand, the citizens believe truly that they are happier, but do so because they have been taught to accept a worldview that is false and known to be false by their rulers, their ideology is *falsely sustained*. Finally, if the citizens in a city believe they are happier there and their belief is both true and sustained by a true worldview, they and their city are *ideology free*. Because the lies of the rulers are verbal lies it is clear that the producers and guardians who believe them are not the victims of false ideology. But because what they believe is false, and known by the philosopher-kings to be false, their ideology is falsely sustained.

However, the worldviews available to the producers and guardians in the kallipolis are intended to be as close to the truth as their natural abilities and ruling desires allow. For it is only when guided by the knowledge of the philosopher-kings that the producers' and guardians' (imperfect) access to the form of the good is as reliable as possible. So although the producers and guardians do not see their values or their place in the kallipolis with complete clarity, their vision is as undistorted as their natures, fully developed by education, allow.

It is obvious that everyone has a self-interested reason to avoid a city in which he is the victim of false ideology. But it is not so clear that everyone has a reason to avoid one in which his ideology is falsely sustained, especially if the degree of falsehood involved is minimal. Indeed, it may be rational for him to prefer such a city to one that is altogether ideology free. It all depends on what his natural abilities are, and on what he most wants in life. If, for example, he most enjoys a life devoted to the pleasure of knowing the truth, he will be maximally happy only in a city in which he is ideology free. But if what he most wants is the pleasure of making money or the pleasure of being honored, he has every reason to trade some truth in his worldview for more of his own favorite pleasure. Indeed, if he lacks the natural ability to escape ideology altogether, he may have no choice in the matter. So the fact that the ideologies of the guardians and producers are falsely sustained, while the philosopher-kings are ideology free, seems to be a strength in the kallipolis rather than a weakness. There, and only there, do honor-lovers and money-lovers get the benefits of the freedom from ideology of which they are themselves incapable. There and only there do philosophers get to see the world as it is.

Private Life and Private Property

Upon returning to the topic of the way of life appropriate to the guardians in Book V, Socrates raises the question of how female guardians should be trained and educated. Should they reduce the amount of work required of the males by sharing their duties, or "be kept indoors on the grounds that because they must bear and rear offspring they are unable to do so" (R 451d)? It is argued by Socrates' critic, as it has been throughout the ages, that a difference in reproductive roles does indeed entail a difference in social ones. Socrates sees through this, however, pointing out that it is not clear that one's role in reproduction has anything to do with one's aptitude for a type of work or occupation (R 454d–e). Individual women, he holds, are either money-lovers or honor-lovers or philosophers, just like individual men. Hence in the kallipolis women will not be confined to the home, but will be trained in the craft, whether it is producing or guarding or ruling (R 456a, 540c), for which their natural aptitude is highest.

While these provisions are certainly enlightened, even by our own standards, it may seem that they are intended to apply only to female *guardians*, not to female producers. Stray remarks which have clear application to female producers, however, suggest that this may not be the case. PS, for example, is said to apply to "children and women, slaves and freemen, producers, rulers, and ruled" (R 433d1–5). The implication is that female producers, being as subject to PS as any other member of the kallipolis, will be trained in the occupation for which they are naturally best suited. Since Socrates implies that there are women with a natural aptitude for carpentry (R 454d), explicitly mentions female physicians, and claims that natural aptitudes for each occupation are to be found in both sexes (R 455d–e), it is difficult to avoid the conclusion that female producers are intended to be apprenticed in an appropriate occupation in precisely the same way as the males.

It must be conceded, however, that Plato is not a feminist. He shows no interest in liberating women as such, and implies that they are generally inferior to men (R 455c–d). Moreover, his casual remarks reveal a streak of unregenerate sexism and misogyny (R 431b–c, 469d, 557c, 563b). But these are relatively small matters, and do not affect the general point that in the kallipolis men and women with the same natural assets receive the same education and have access to the same careers. Still, it must be admitted that Plato is regrettably vague about the producers, whether male or female, and has left us somewhat in the dark on the important question of who will do the housework, and rear the children, if both parents are employed full-time outside the household.

In the case of the guardians, though he is more forthcoming, what he describes may not appeal to us. If the guardians and producers were in competition for the same social goods, producers would fare very badly, since the guardians are armed and trained for warfare in a way that they are not (*R* 419a). But because the guardians are honor-lovers and the producers money-lovers, this problem can be solved. Education is, once again, a large part of the solution, though it needs to be reinforced by the structure of the kallipolis. Hence the guardians are segregated from the producers and denied both private property and private family life on the grounds that "if they acquire private lands, houses, and currency themselves, they'll be household managers and farmers instead of guardians – hostile masters of the other citizens instead of their allies" (*R* 417a–b). The result is sex by lottery as part of a state-sponsored eugenics program, state-run "rearing pens" for guardian offspring (*R* 451c–461e), and the totalitarian domination of the private sphere by the public. Scarcely anything in the *Republic* estranges our sympathies so thoroughly.

Rather than indulging in moral outrage, however, we do better to attempt diagnosis: what has led Plato in this unprepossessing direction? Part of the answer, no doubt, is his profound suspicion of the appetites, and the politically destructive potential of greed and self-interest. Removing the things that stimulate them therefore becomes appealing. But another part of the answer is more interesting. Men traditionally value honor and the competitive activities (including warfare) in which it is won, whereas women traditionally value domestic life, the having and rearing of children, and the emotional closeness and intimacy it makes possible. Consequently, if men and women were treated equally in the kallipolis, honor and emotional closeness have to be taken equally seriously as genuine human goods. But they aren't. Instead, Plato just assumes that honor is valuable, and that anyone, male or female, will want to win it if possible, while emotional closeness is implicitly treated as valueless (*R* 465b–c), and so is made wholly unavailable to the guardians. The result, it seems, is that Plato has not treated women justly at all, and has not promoted their welfare to the same extent as that of men. What he has done instead is, first, to make an entirely "masculinized" world and then given women the freedom to be "men" in it. The hegemony of males in the kallipolis is, therefore, more subtle and insidious than it first seems. And the awful result is the totalitarianism – the evisceration of the private sphere – that rightly disquiets the *Republic*'s contemporary readers.

Censorship

Even a cursory reading of the *Republic* leaves one in no doubt that Plato thinks that the most important political institutions in the kallipolis, or in any other society, are educational. The "one great thing," he says, is "education and upbringing." Hence the philosopher-kings must "guard *above all else* that there should be no change in musical and physical training . . . For musical training is not changed anywhere without change in the most important laws of the city" (*R* 423d–424c). It is no surprise, then, that, having completed the account of his own revolutionary educational proposals, and having justified them by showing that they promote both maximum justice and maximum happiness for those who receive them, Plato should turn in Book X to attack his competition – the poets and playwrights who were the purveyors of traditional Greek ethical education. The philosophers, not the poets, he argues, are the true teachers of virtue.

For, first of all, being able to imitate virtue or virtuous people in rhythms and rhymes that please and entertain most people does not qualify one to teach human beings how to live. The poet or dramatist writes for a non-specialist audience. Hence he must employ a conceptual framework similar to theirs. Character, motive, plot – all must be drawn from folk psychology not, say, from cognitive science or whatever the true theory of the soul turns out to be. This means that art represents people and their motives and actions not necessarily as they really are, but only as they seem to people without specialist training. The languages of art are not, then, the technical mathematics-like language of Platonic truth. The scientist, or philosopher-king, by contrast, is free of this constraint, since his is primarily an audience of fellow specialists (*R* 601a–b, 603b–605c).

Second, poetry and drama, like all art, aim to provide a certain characteristic pleasure or satisfaction (*R* 606b), which on Plato's view, as on Freud's, is related to repression. Art enables us to satisfy without reproach or shame the very desires we must repress in real life. These are characteristically appetitive desires, especially sexual ones. This might plausibly be taken to entail that representations of ethically good people do not provide the kind of satisfaction art typically provides and are not what a poet needs to know how to produce (*R* 604e–605a). If we suppose, as Plato does (*R* 485d), that even artistic indulgence of repressed desires strengthens them and weakens the repressive mechanisms, we will see reason here to mistrust art in general (*R* 605b, 606b).

Finally, we must look at the poet himself, and why he writes. Plato is confident that no one would be satisfied merely to represent life if he knew how to live it well, or could teach others how to do so (*R* 599b–601a). If we think again of the characteristic pleasure art provides, his view becomes intelligible, and again rather like a view of Freud's. A life devoted to making things that provide a fantasy satisfaction for unnecessary appetites could not rank very highly among lives.

These arguments may not command our assent, but there is surely much to admire in them. They make the philosophy of art continuous with ethics, politics, and the philosophy of mind, and that seems right. Moreover, the deep differences they identify between art and philosophy (at least as Plato conceives of it and its relations to science) are arguably there. Art is, and must be, bound up with ordinary life and thought in a way that philosophy need not be. Art is related to pleasure and to sex in a way that philosophy, perhaps, is not. Most important of all, even if they are inconclusive, Plato's arguments extend the right invitation to philosophers who think that art has something to teach us about how to live: develop a metaphysics, epistemology, psychology, and politics on the basis of which it will be clear that the knowledge a good poet or dramatist needs is relevant to ethics. It is precisely as an invitation, indeed, and not as what Berkeley calls "the killing blow," that Plato himself seems to understand those arguments (*R* 607d–e).

Freedom and Autonomy

A person's needs, wants, and interests are in part determined by the natural genetic lottery, in part by his education and upbringing, and in part by his actual circumstances. They also depend on his beliefs, which in turn depend to some extent on the same factors as his needs, wants, and interests themselves. His *real interests* are those he would form under optimal conditions – those in which his needs are satisfied, he is neither maltreated nor coerced nor the victim of false ideology, and is as aware as possible of his actual circumstances, and the real alternatives to them. Happiness is optimal satisfaction of real interests in the long term.

The relevance of this picture to the *Republic* should now be clear. For the kallipolis has emerged as a community intended by Plato to provide optimal conditions of the type in question. Each of its members has his needs satisfied and is neither maltreated nor coerced nor the victim of false ideology. Each is educated and trained so as to develop a conception of the world and his place in it that is as close to the truth as his nature, fully developed with an eye to his maximum happiness, permits. Each has his ruling desires satisfied throughout life. Thus each develops his real interests and is made really happy.

It sounds wonderful put like that. But that is not how the *Republic* feels to us when we read it. It feels authoritarian and repressive. But it feels that way as much because of controversial beliefs we bring to it as to what we find there. For example, because of where and when we live, we are inclined to presuppose that no amount of knowledge of the way the world is validates or underwrites a unique conception of the good (we cannot derive ought from is, value from fact). Different conceptions are determined by what different individuals happen to want or prefer. The state exists not to judge between these conceptions, but to allow each individual to realize his own conception as far as is compatible with others realizing theirs to the same extent. In this way, the state at once respects the individuality of its members and treats them equally. An activity, institution, or issue is paradigmatically political for us if it pertains to disputes between people who may have different conceptions of the good, yet must coexist and have dealings with one another in the same community or the same world. Individual freedom, on this broadly liberal conception, is freedom to do what one wants, freedom to live in accordance with a conception of the good that is rooted in one's own desires, preferences, or choices. And a state is free to the extent that it limits individual freedom only to guarantee equal freedom to all its members. It is not surprising, then, that when in imagination we project ourselves into the kallipolis *we* do feel repressed and unfree. For given our actual desires and interests, and presupposing the liberal conception of freedom, we would be repressed and unfree there.

This conception of political freedom is not the only one, however, and even if we leave aside worries about its metaphysical commitment to the distinction between facts and values, it is not clear that it is the best or most defensible conception. Freedom to do what we want – *instrumental* freedom – is certainly important. Its importance can be undermined, however, by the desires on which it depends. For if the desires we are free to satisfy are ones we would not have if we had engaged in a process of ideal, rational deliberation, being free to satisfy them is scarcely something worth caring about. If our desires themselves, like those of a drug addict, can make us unfree, instrumental freedom cannot be sufficient for real freedom or autonomy. Perhaps, then, we should move away from instrumental freedom towards *deliberative* freedom. Perhaps the freedom we should be concerned about is the freedom to have and to satisfy only the desires we would choose to have if we were aware of the relevant facts, were thinking clearly, and were free from distorting influences.

If we are persuaded to move in this direction, we can see at once that a state which guaranteed deliberative freedom might look and feel very repressive to someone solely concerned about instrumental freedom. It would very much depend on what his desires happened to be. Since the psychological and political cost of repression is high, however, we can well imagine that an enlightened state, committed to deliberative freedom, would want to devote much of its resources to education and training, so as to ensure that its members are as close to being deliberatively rational as possible. Such a state would already begin to look a little like the kallipolis, and to share some of its priorities.

Even a state whose citizens enjoy complete deliberative and instrumental freedom can seem to be defective from the point of view of what we might call *critical* freedom. For desires that are deliberatively rational may not be rational all things considered. Brought up in a capitalist democracy, which arguably does not provide optimal conditions for developing one's needs, wants, and interests, a person desires profit above everything else. And the more he deliberates under the aegis of that desire, the clearer it may become that his desire is perfectly rational. Yet, it may not be in his real interest to make profit his goal. But to discover this he would have to begin deliberating already possessed of desires other than those he actually has. If, for these sorts of reasons, deliberatively rational desires can fail to be the best ones for a person to have, then the same considerations that caused us to favor deliberatively free states over instrumentally free ones might cause us to favor critically free ones over those that are only deliberatively free. And this would certainly bring us closer still to the kallipolis. For like the kallipolis, any critically free state would have to devote much of its resources to ensuring that the actual interests of its citizens coincide as far as possible with their real interests. And that would require, not just extensive commitment to education and training, but extensive commitment to all branches of knowledge relevant to human beings and their interests. More than that, it would require political institutions that guarantee that knowledge thus gained would serve human good. If one cannot quite see producers, guardians, and philosopher-kings in all of that, one can, I think, see their outlines.

In any case, it seems clear that the kallipolis is intended to provide its members with as much critical freedom as their natures, fully developed in optimal conditions, permit:

> It is better for everyone to be ruled by divine reason, preferably within himself and his own, otherwise imposed from without, so that as far as possible all will be alike and friends, governed by the same thing . . . This is clearly the aim of the law, which is the ally of everyone. But it's also our aim in ruling our children, we don't allow them to be free until we establish a constitution in them, just as in a city, and – by fostering their best part with our own – equip them with a guardian and ruler similar to our own to take our place. Then, and only then, we set them free. (*R* 590d–591a; also 395b–c)

Thus even if we retain our liberal suspicion about the possibility of a science of values, we might still, by coming to see merit in the idea of critical freedom, also come to see the *Republic* not as predominantly a totalitarian hymn to the benefits of repression and unfreedom, but as an attempt to design a city whose members enjoy as much real happiness, and as much real freedom, as possible.

Conclusion

No one doubts that the *Republic* is one of the very greatest works of Western philosophy. Like nothing before it and very little since, it combines philosophical and literary resourcefulness of the highest order in an attempt to answer the most important question of all – how should we live? Moreover, the answer it develops is based on an unusually rich account of our nature and the nature of reality. Ethics, politics, aesthetics, philosophy of religion, philosophy of mind, philosophy of science, epistemology, and metaphysics are all woven together in it, and all have been decisively shaped by its contribution to them. Contemporary philosophers read the *Republic*, as their predecessors did, not out of piety, but because it continues to challenge, disquiet, and inspire. Western philosophy is not, to be sure, simply a series of footnotes to this amazing text, but many of its best stories begin there.

Bibliography

Editions and translations

Plato (1902) *Platonis Res Publica*, ed. J. Burnet (standard edition of the Greek text). Oxford: Oxford University Press.
Plato (1902) *The Republic*, ed. J. Adam (critical edition with notes and commentary). Cambridge: Cambridge University Press.
Plato (1992) *Plato: Republic*, ed. G. M. A. Grube and C. D. C. Reeve. Indianapolis, IN: Hackett (text citations are from this edition).

Studies

Annas, J. (1981) *An Introduction to Plato's Republic*. Oxford: Clarendon Press.
Burnyeat, M. (1987) Platonism and mathematics: a prelude to discussion. In A. Graeser (ed.), *Mathematics and Metaphysics in Aristotle*, pp. 213–40. Bern: Paul Haupt.
Cooper, J. M. (1977) The psychology of justice in Plato. *American Philosophical Quarterly*, 14: 151–7.
Cooper, J. M. (1984) Plato's theory of human motivation. *History of Philosophy Quarterly*, 1: 3–21.
Fine, G. (1984) Separation. *Oxford Studies in Ancient Philosophy*, 2: 31–87.
Fine, G. (1990) Knowledge and belief in *Republic* V–VII. In S. Levinson (ed.), *Companions to Ancient Thought*, vol. 1: *Epistemology*, pp. 85–115. Cambridge: Cambridge University Press.
Gosling, J. C. B. (1960) *Republic* Book V: *ta polla kala*. *Phronesis*, 5: 116–28.
Irwin, T. H. (1995) *Plato's Ethics*. New York: Oxford University Press.
Kraut, R. (ed.) (1997) *Plato's Republic: Critical Essays*. Lanham, MD: Rowman and Littlefield.
Murdoch, I. (1977) *The Fire and the Sun: Why Plato Banished the Artists*. Oxford: Oxford University Press.

Nehamas, A. (1982) Plato on imitation and poetry in *Republic* X. In J. Moravcsik and P. Temko (eds), *Plato on Beauty, Wisdom and the Arts*, pp. 47–78. Totowa, NJ: Rowman and Littlefield.

Popper, K. (1971) *The Open Society and its Enemies*, vol. 1. Princeton, NJ: Princeton University Press.

Reeve, C. D. C. (1988) *Philosopher-kings: The Argument of Plato's Republic*. Princeton, NJ: Princeton University Press.

Reeve, C. D. C. (1995) Platonic politics and the good. *Political Theory*, 23: 411–24.

Sachs, D. (1963) A fallacy in Plato's *Republic*. *Philosophical Review*, 72: 141–58.

Vlastos, G. (1977) The theory of social justice in the *polis* in Plato's *Republic*. In H. North (ed.), *Interpretations of Plato: A Swarthmore Symposium*, pp. 1–40. Leiden: Brill.

Vlastos, G. (1988) Elenchus and mathematics: a turning-point in Plato's philosophical development. *American Journal of Philology*, 109: 362–96.

Vlastos, G. (1989) Was Plato a feminist? *Times Literary Supplement*, 4, 288–9.

White, N. (1979) *A Companion to Plato's Republic*. Indianapolis, IN: Hackett.

4

Aristotle, *Metaphysics* (367–323 BC)

Substance, Form, and God

Michael J. Loux

What is supposed to tie the fourteen books of the *Metaphysics* together is the conception of a single discipline. We use the title of the text as the label for the discipline. That term, however, is not Aristotle's (384–322 BC), but the creation of later thinkers. He used a variety of labels to pick out the discipline: "wisdom," "theology," "the science of truth," "first philosophy," and just "philosophy." This discipline is supposed to be the most honorable or noble of disciplines, and the fourteen books are all supposed to be exercises in the discipline. None the less, they appear to be something of a hodgepodge. The first six books have an introductory cast: they seek to identify the subject matter for the discipline, to characterize its methodology, to identify the problems it must resolve, and to provide us with a vocabulary for research in the discipline; but these books do not proceed consecutively. They appear to have been composed independently; they make little reference to each other; and their positive contributions can seem flatly inconsistent. The remaining eight books are more substantive, but arguably even less unified than the first six. Books VII and VIII provide an account of the ontological structure of material substances; Book IX focuses on the notions of potentiality and actuality; Book X turns to the notion of unity; and Book XI is itself just a compilation and abbreviation of other texts from the *Metaphysics* and the *Physics*. Book XII takes the Prime Mover or God as its target; and the last two books deal with topics in the philosophy of mathematics.

Now, it may turn out that there is more unity to the *Metaphysics* than initial appearances suggest, but not even the most enthusiastic defenders of a unitarian approach to the text would want to claim that the *Metaphysics* presents us with a single line of argument with a clearly identifiable beginning, middle, and end. In discussing the overall shape of the text, we have little option but to approach the *Metaphysics* topically; and that is how I will proceed. I will deal with three sets of issues. In part I, I will address topics from the first six books focusing on the subject matter and methodology of what Aristotle calls "first philosophy." In parts II–IV, I will discuss the theory of material substance developed in what are often called the middle books, Books VII and VIII. Finally, in parts V–VII, I will examine Aristotle's views on immaterial or separated substance. Here, I will make a few comments on Aristotle's views about the subject matter of mathematics, but the focus will be Book XII's theology.

I

One aim of the first six books of the *Metaphysics* is the identification of the subject matter for the discipline the treatise is supposed to instantiate. Unfortunately, the books provide what look like two incompatible accounts of that subject matter. If we take "first philosophy" to be a neutral label for the discipline, then we can say that in Book I Aristotle introduces us to first philosophy under the title "wisdom." We are told that whereas the familiar sciences all seek to identify causes and principles, wisdom is the knowledge of first causes and first principles (981b29); and Aristotle goes on to tell us that wisdom is a "divine knowledge" since, first, God will most of all have it and, second, "God is thought to be among the causes of all things and to be a first principle" (983a8–10). In Book VI, the idea that first philosophy is a "divine knowledge" is reaffirmed. There, Aristotle calls first philosophy "theology"; and after telling us that the proper object for theological investigation is what exists separately and is unchangeable, he remarks that "if the divine is present anywhere, it is present in things of this sort" (1026a19–20).

Aristotle's wisdom or theology, then, seems to be what is called a special or departmental discipline. It seems to mark off a particular genus or kind – unchangeable substance – and to investigate that. The difficulty is that in other places Aristotle describes first philosophy in what appear to be quite different terms. Thus, at the beginning of *Metaphysics* IV, Aristotle tells us that first philosophy "investigates being qua being and the attributes which belong to it in virtue of its own nature" (1003a21), and he goes on to deny that it is any of the departmental disciplines (1003a23–25). On the contrary, it has universal scope; its subject matter spans the subjects of the various special sciences. It investigates everything that there is, and it does so from the most general perspective: it investigates the things that are precisely in so far as they are things that are. Now the concept of being can seem to be a rather thin notion; and that might suggest that there's not much for a discipline investigating being as being to tell us. Toward countering this suggestion, Aristotle reminds us of the distinctions marked by the categories (substance, quantity, quality, relation, etc.). Those distinctions, he tells us, represent a division of being itself. Accordingly, the categorial distinctions will fall under the purview of this universal discipline (1003b20–22 and 1026a35–36). The same is true of the contrast between actuality and potentiality (1026b1–2). But the focus on being does not exhaust the discipline. As Aristotle sees it, a discipline that seeks to understand being will deal as well with any concept necessarily co-extensive with being. Unity is such a concept, so it too provides material for this discipline; and, like being, it takes different categorial forms – unity in substance or sameness, unity in quality or similarity, unity in quantity or equality – so these notions too will fall under the science that studies being (1003b33–35). And since one and the same science studies opposites, this science will deal with notions like non-being, plurality, difference, dissimilarity, and inequality (1004a9ff). Finally, it will deal with any principles that hold true of things just in virtue of their being beings (1005a20–24). Since the most general principles underlying all demonstration (for example, the principle of non-contradiction – the principle that "the same attribute cannot at the same time belong and not belong to the same subject in the same respect" [1005b18–20]) are such principles, it is the role of this discipline to inquire into them.

So we have two different characterizations of first philosophy. Aristotle seems to be saying that it is both a departmental discipline concerned with first causes or unchangeable substance and a universal discipline concerned with everything that there is. It is difficult to see how the two characterizations can be anything but flatly incompatible. One and the same discipline cannot be both a departmental/special discipline and an inquiry into everything. A departmental discipline considers only a proper subset of the things that are, so it cannot be identified with a discipline that inquires into the nature of all the things that there are. The apparent inconsistency demands explanation. Providing that explanation is one of the most ancient problems in the interpretation of Aristotle. A popular strategy here is to explain the incompatibility in developmental terms: the two characterizations are supposed to represent two different stages in Aristotle's philosophical career. This strategy was especially popular in the twentieth century. Often, the proposed stages are characterized in terms of what are alleged to be Aristotle's changing reactions to Plato. The details here vary, but we are typically told that the conception of first philosophy as wisdom or theology represents an earlier conception of the most honorable discipline, a conception that ultimately gets displaced by the more mature idea of a universal discipline. Frequently, this story gets extended beyond the first six books to the rest of the *Metaphysics* in the form of a "patchwork" theory. The claim is that so far from being a unified treatise, the *Metaphysics* is a collection of independently composed and doctrinally inconsistent texts from different periods in Aristotle's career. Corresponding to the idea of wisdom or theology is Book XII's picture of a transcendent God in the person of the Prime Mover; whereas, corresponding to the idea of a universal science is the text encompassing Books VII and VIII, where we meet a straightforwardly naturalistic ontology including only material substances.

As I have said, virtually no one would want to claim that the *Metaphysics* is a text that runs smoothly and without interruption from Book I to Book XIV pursuing along the way a single train of argument. But conceding that the composition of the *Metaphysics* involved compilation hardly commits one to the view that the core texts making up the "book" embody flatly inconsistent metaphysical doctrines. Indeed, even a quick reading of the middle books and Book XII suggests a picture quite different from that developed by "patchwork" theorists. In Books VII and VIII, we find Aristotle repeatedly telling us that our discussion of sensible, material substance is meant to prepare us for the investigation of non-sensible, immaterial substance (see 1029a34–1029b13 and 1041a6–9), and the Aristotle of Book XII develops his account of the Prime Mover only after spending five chapters reviewing the main themes of Books VII and VIII, the implication being that the doctrine of the Prime Mover is intelligible only against the background of the theory of material substance developed in Books VII and VIII.

The fact that Aristotle himself seems to think that the metaphysical pictures expressed in the two contexts constitute a consistent whole suggests that we should look more closely at his accounts of the nature of first philosophy. When we do, we find that the apparent tension between the idea of a science of first causes and the idea of a science which investigates being as being disappears. When Aristotle first presents us with the idea of a body of knowledge that focuses on first causes and first principles, he tells us that the body of knowledge will have a universal dimension (982a21–23). In grasping what is primary, he suggests, we will have an implicit handle on all the items to which it is prior. Furthermore, it becomes clear as we move beyond Book I that the science that investigates the divine also deals with the propositions that constitute the first principles of the sciences (996b26–997a14); but these just are the propositions that hold true of beings in so far as they are beings. Hence, they fall under the purview of a universal discipline. And when Aristotle tells us that there is a science that "investigates being as being," he tells us that this discipline is the target of anyone concerned to identify first causes and first principles (1003a26–32). The idea is that our interest in first causes/principles is an interest in the causes/principles in virtue of which things are beings. What makes a cause primary, presumably, is that it is a cause responsible for that feature of things that is prior to every other feature they exhibit – their being or their existing. This idea gets repeated at the beginning of Book VI (1025b1ff); and, then, Aristotle concludes his discussion of the subject matter of first philosophy by telling us that theology, the science concerned with unchangeable, separable substance, is universal precisely because it is primary (1026a23–32). So the two characterizations look like characterizations of a single discipline. The universal science will study everything – God included; and the discipline that identifies and characterizes the Prime Mover cannot be a merely departmental discipline. It has to be a discipline that is concerned with being *qua* being; for what it does is identify the cause or principle on which the being of everything else depends.

II

When Aristotle introduces us to the science that studies being as being, he implicitly concedes that the idea of a universal discipline of this sort can appear problematic. The difficulty is that being is not a genus. There is no single kind encompassing all the things there are. The highest kinds are the categories, and the term "being" is equivocal over the categories. Substances, qualities, quantities, etc. are, in turn, each said to be in a unique and distinct sense of the term. But, then, the suggestion that all the things that are said to be beings constitute the subject matter for a single science seems bizarre. It is as though one were to insist that there is a single science whose subject matter is whatever is picked out by the word "bank" – a science whose inquiry spans the geology of river edges and the economics of financial institutions concerned with borrowing and lending money.

Aristotle's reaction to this problem is to argue that, while "being" is not univocal, it has a special kind of equivocity, one that is compatible with there being a single science of being (1003a32–1003b18). Although "being" is equivocal, its different senses are not like those of the word "bank" – totally unrelated to each other. "Being" exhibits what Aristotle calls *pros hen* equivocity or focal meaning. One of its senses is primary and its other senses are explained by reference to that primary sense. Aristotle's stock example of a *pros hen* term is "healthy." While "healthy" has a variety of different meanings, the sense of "healthy" in which it picks out the metabolically sound organism is the core or primary meaning of the term. It provides the focus for the other, secondary meanings. Thus, some things (e.g. a certain complexion or a certain red blood count) are said to be healthy because they are signs or symptoms of what is healthy in the core sense; other things (a certain diet or a certain kind of vitamin) are said to be healthy because they are productive of what is healthy in the core sense. In the same way, the term "being" has a primary sense – that in which it picks out substances. Everything else is called a being by reference to the being of substance. Thus, some things are said to be beings because they qualify what is a being in the primary sense; other things because they are quantitative determinations of what is a being in the core sense; still others because they are actions of what is a being in the focal sense.

So "being" like "healthy" has *pros hen* equivocity; but, Aristotle tells us, the case of "healthy" shows that there can be a single discipline concerned with all the things picked out by a *pros hen* term (1003b11–13). There is, after all, a single science dealing with all the things that are said to be healthy – the science of medicine or, perhaps, physiotherapy; and Aristotle thinks that what the example of that discipline shows us is that where a single discipline takes everything in the extension of a *pros hen* term as its subject, it makes the items picked out by the term in its primary use the focus of its investigation. Thus, while physiotherapy deals in complexions, diets, vitamins, and the like, the primary concern of the discipline is the metabolically sound organism. It deals with the other things called healthy only in so far as they are related to the focus of the discipline. But, then, there can be a single discipline concerned to investigate all the things that are; and while the discipline will deal with everything, it will have a focus – substance; and it will consider other things only in so far as they stand in some ontological relation to substance.

So we get the result that the science that investigates being is the science of substance; and Aristotle tells us that what follows is that the perennial metaphysical question "What is being?" turns out to be the question "What is substance?" (1028b2–4). Substances, we have implied, are the ontologically basic things. Accordingly, to attempt to answer the question "What is substance?" is to attempt to identify the things that do not depend on other things for their existence, but are such that everything else depends on one or more of them for its existence. That project was one that occupied the Aristotle of the early treatise, the *Categories*; and when, in Book VII, he turns to the question "What is substance?," he begins by examining the answer he gave to that question in the early treatise. The *Categories* tells us that the primary substances are those things that, while not predicated of anything else, are the subjects of which everything else is predicated. They are the ultimate subjects of predication, and the claim of the *Categories* is that it is the familiar particulars of common sense – things like "a certain man" and "a certain horse"–that are those ultimate subjects (2a11–13).

The *Categories*, however, does not confront the fact that familiar particulars are things that come to be and pass away. *Physics* I deals with the phenomenon of generation and corruption and argues that things that come to be have an internal structure (see *Physics* I, 7; in particular, 190b16–23). Thus, the musical man comes to be. According to *Physics* I, his doing so consists in the fact that some antecedently existing individual – the man – comes to have a form – musical – predicated of him; and once he has come to be, the musical man's continued existence consists in the continued obtaining of that same predication. To be, for the musical man, is for the man to be musical. Like the musical man, the man himself can come to be; and his doing so likewise consists in the fact that some antecedently existing thing – Aristotle calls it matter – comes to have some form – here, a substantial rather than accidental form – predicated of it; and once the man has come to be, his continued existence consists in the fact that his matter has the relevant substantial form predicated of it. So the familiar particulars of the *Categories* have an internal structure: they are matter/form composites, and the relationship between their matter and their form is that of subject and what gets predicated of it.

The Aristotle of *Metaphysics* VII, 3 argues that, in light of these facts, the *Categories'* criterion for substantiality fails to do what it was intended to do; it fails to identify familiar particulars like "a certain man" as the primary substances. Given that those particulars are matter/form composites, what turns out to be the ultimate subject of predication is a matter that "in itself is neither a particular thing nor of a certain quantity nor assigned to any other of the categories by which being is determined" (1029a 20–21). Aristotle thinks that we will agree that anything meeting that austere characterization is a woefully inadequate candidate for status as substance; and, consequently, he believes we will join him in rejecting the *Categories'* account of substance.

If we endorse the picture underlying the subject criterion of substantiality, we will think that what gets presented to us in experience is a kind of complex that includes a whole host of predicated features. On this view, the strategy for isolating substance is to engage in an abstraction in which we "strip away" (1029a11) from the complex anything that can be construed as something predicated of something else. What survives the abstraction, presumably, will be the "something else" of which all the features are predicated and, hence, by the early theory, an instance of primary substance. So we take the sort of thing we meet in our everyday encounters with the world – something like that pale, six foot, two hundred pound offspring of Diares; and we "think away" the qualitative features, the quantitative determinations, the relational properties, and so on. According to the author of the *Categories*, what remains is "a certain man"; a thing like that, he wants to say, is ontologically basic.

But is that right? It is true that the man provides a subject for the predication of all the accidents associated with him; but the man himself has a structure involving an ontologically more basic subject of predication. He is a thing that comes to be, so he is a matter/form composite; and his matter provides a subject for the predicated form. By the subject criterion, then, the matter constitutive of the man has a better claim than the man to status as substance. But, by that same criterion, there is something with a still better claim to that status. The matter constitutive of our man is, let us suppose, something like flesh and bones; but flesh and bones are themselves things that come to be, so they too must have a matter/form structure. Accordingly, we have some still more fundamental subjects of predication; and assuming the generability of those subjects, we are led on to even more basic subjects of predication. According to the chemical theory Aristotle borrows from Empedocles, this process of analysis continues until we reach the four elements (fire, earth, air, water). They are supposed to be the qualitatively most fundamental stuffs; but Aristotle takes it to be an empirical fact that they can be transformed into each other (see *De generatione et corruptione* II, 1, 329a24–329b3). So they too have a matter (it is called "prime matter"); but it appears at a level below that at which even the most primitive qualitative characterizations apply, so it is the sort of thing that conforms to Aristotle's austere characterization of the ultimate or final subject of predication; and what the Aristotle of VII, 3 is telling us is that anyone who endorses the *Categories'* criterion for substantiality is committed to making this matter substance.

But Aristotle takes this result to constitute a *reductio* of the subject criterion. He tells us that a constraint on our notion of substance is that what is ontologically primary must be a "this something" and separable (1029a27–28). These are not easy notions, but we can understand Aristotle's appeal to them as a gesture toward the notion of essence. The claim is that a substance is something with an essence. To say that a thing is a "this something" is to say that *what* it is is something like "this man" or "this horse" – something involving a determinate conceptual content that can be isolated and articulated ("separated") in a definition. And obviously a matter that falls under no category lacks that kind of conceptual content.

There is, then, a conflict between the subject criterion for substantiality and an essentialist interpretation of substance. Accordingly, if the critique of the early theory of substance is to be decisive, we need a clear-cut formulation and defense of substance essentialism. We get these things in VII, 6, where Aristotle argues for a very strong thesis about the connection between substance and essence (1032a5–6). What he tells us is that each primary substance is necessarily identical with its essence. So the primary substances do not have essences; they *are* essences – their own essences; and Aristotle defends this thesis (we can call it the VII, 6 Identity Thesis) not by reference to premises idiosyncratic to his own metaphysical theory. He argues that it is a constraint on any metaphysical theory – any attempt to identify the primary substances. To identify the primary substances, we have said, is to identify the ontologically basic things – those things that are prior to everything else. However, were it to be the case that a thing and its essence are always distinct and separate, then the attempt to identify the primary substances would be doomed from the start. Any entity one might want to select as ontologically primary would fail to have that status. Something else – its essence – would have a better claim to the status. After all, the essence of a thing is prior to that thing: it makes the thing be what it is. But given the separation of thing and essence, our new candidate for status as primary substance would likewise fail to be ontologically basic; for its essence would be prior to it. If thing and essence are always distinct, the primary substances would be forever elusive, and the central project of metaphysics – that of identifying primary substance – would be impossible. That project requires that there be things – the ontologically basic things – that just are their own essences. It requires that the VII, 6 Identity Thesis be true.

III

We have seen that one implication of VII, 3's critique of the subject criterion is that the search after substance cannot terminate in matter. A consequence of the VII, 6 Identity Thesis is that no concrete particular like the man or the horse of the *Categories* can be a primary substance. The Identity Thesis tells us that each primary substance is identical with its essence, but all the familiar particulars of a single kind or species exhibit the same essence. Accordingly, the claim that things like Plato and Socrates are ontologically basic commits us to holding that they are numerically identical with each other. More generally, the supposition that familiar particulars are primary substances yields the result that there is just one member of each species – a clearly unsatisfactory consequence. But if VII, 3 excludes matter from the inventory of primary substances and VII, 6 entails that no composite particulars are primary substances, the only things remaining as possible candidates for status as primary substances are the substantial forms of concrete particulars. And the fact is that from the early chapters of VII, Aristotle makes little secret of the privileged role that form will play in the theory of the middle books. It is not, however, until very late in VII and in VIII that we find Aristotle providing a formal statement and defense of the thesis that form is primary substance.

As he formulates the thesis, Aristotle uses the term "substance" in a special sense. In this sense, it functions as an abstract singular term, and its characteristic use is in the context "the substance of x." So the idea is that certain things have something else as their substance. Which things? In the middle books, Aristotle is interested in identifying the substance of the familiar particulars of the *Categories* – things, again, like "a certain man" and "a certain horse"; and the attempt to identify their substance is part of an explanatory project. As Aristotle tells us, the substance of a familiar particular is that constituent of the particular that is "the cause of its being" (1017b14–15); and in attempting to clarify what the search for such a thing consists in, Aristotle explicitly denies that the attempt to identify the substance of a thing, x, is the attempt to explain the truth of the bald existential claim "x exists" or the trivial identity claim "x is identical with x." It is rather the attempt to explain why some predication obtains (1041a11–17). Which predication? The predication that marks out x as *what* it is or as the kind of thing it is (1041b5–6). So what we seek to explain when we try to identify the substance of a familiar particular is a kind-predication like

Socrates is a human being

or

Secretariat is a horse;

and our explanation is to take a special form; we are to explain the kind-predication by reference to constituents of our chosen familiar particular. In our discussion of VII, 3, however, we have seen that what grounds the fact that an ordinary particular belongs to the kind it does is the fact that the substantial form associated with the kind is predicated of the matter constitutive of our chosen particular. So it is because the appropriate form-predication obtains that the relevant kind-predication obtains. And Aristotle tells us just that in VIII, 2:

> For example, if it is a threshold that is to be defined, then we should say, "Wood and stones lying in this way"; and if it is a house, we should say "Bricks and boards lying in this way"; and if it is ice, "Water frozen or solidified in this way. . . ." (1043a7–11)

The predication that does the explaining in each of these cases involves both matter and form; and both can be construed as constituents of the thing whose "being" we seek to explain. Accordingly, both its matter and its form should count as the substance of a familiar particular. And Aristotle concedes as much (1042a26–28). None the less, it is the thesis that substantial form is the substance of a thing that is the centerpiece of VII and VIII. It is not difficult to see why Aristotle construes form as pre-eminent here. What leads us on the search after the substance of a familiar particular is the fact that it fails to be what Aristotle calls a *kath hauto legomenon* – something "said to be what it is in its own right." Its being what it is depends on something ontologically more fundamental than it – the form-predication in question. But the matter constitutive of a familiar particular is no more a *kath hauto legomenon* than the particular itself. As we saw in our discussion of VII, 3, the matter making up an ordinary individual has an internal structure of its own; and its being what it is gets explained by reference to that structure. It is, recall, because some lower-level stuff has a form predicated of it that the matter constitutive of a human being is what it is – flesh or bones, say; and the analysis continues until we reach the matter for the four elements, what we called prime matter. That matter has no constituents on which it depends; but it has no *what* or essence either. There is no saying what it is; it is no *legomenon* at all, so it too fails to be a *kath hauto legomenon*.

But being a *kath hauto legomenon* is a requirement on anything that is to play the role of primary substance. Nothing can be a primary substance if it depends on something else for its "being," that is, for its being what it is or for its having the essence it does. But while he denies that anything that plays the role of matter satisfies this condition, Aristotle thinks that all substantial forms satisfy it. As he sees it, there is nothing external to a form that serves to explain why it is what it is; and he denies that substantial forms have any internal structure involving distinct entities standing in any kind of ontological relation. He has nothing like transcendental arguments for these claims; but he thinks that the central reason for attributing an internal structure to particulars and their matter does not apply here. It is because a thing can come to be and pass away that we take it to have a matter/form structure; but Aristotle insists on the ingenerability and incorruptibility of substantial form (1033b5–9); and he thinks that an examination of the procedures for defining forms confirms the absence of internal structure here (see *Metaphysics* VII, 10). Substantial forms are unanalyzable simples.

So substantial forms are *kath hauta legomena* – things whose "being" depends on nothing else; but the "being" of everything else depends on the predication of substantial form. Accordingly, substantial forms are the primary substances; and no sooner has Aristotle issued the formal statement of this thesis than he points out that the VII, 6 Identity Thesis holds for substantial form (1043b1). Each form just is its essence: the form is identical with what the form is.

IV

Although the claim that form is primary substance may be the central thesis of the middle books, its statement does not provide us with the culmination of Books VII and VIII. Indeed, its formulation only serves to give rise to what is the central problem occupying Aristotle in the middle books. What concerns Aristotle is the fact that in attributing this privileged status to substantial form, we seem to be undermining the core intuitions motivating the metaphysical theory of the *Categories*. There is a good bit of technical machinery at work in the early treatise, but that machinery is presented in the service of an intuition that is anything but technical; for what motivates Aristotle in the *Categories* is simply the belief that, despite the claims of his predecessors to the contrary, the familiar individuals of common sense (in particular, individual living beings) are fully real; and that belief gets expressed in the thesis that things like "a certain man" and "a certain horse" are the primary substances, the paradigmatic instances of things that are. In arguing that the matter and form constitutive of familiar particulars are prior to those particulars and in claiming that forms are the primary substances, however, the Aristotle of VII and VIII seems to be rejecting the core intuition at work in the *Categories*. He seems to be saying that the familiar particulars of common sense are just assemblages or heaps of ontologically more basic entities; and he appears to be telling us that, in the final analysis, the only thing that is genuinely real is substantial form. We have, then, what looks like a conflict between the ontological theory of the middle books and the common-sense conception of the world defended in the *Categories*. Books VII and VIII appear to be defending a reductionism about familiar particulars of precisely the sort that the Aristotle of the *Categories* sought to combat.

Now, some philosophers would not be concerned by the kind of conflict we appear to have here. They would not find a conflict between our metaphysical theory and our common-sense conception of the world problematic. But Aristotle is not one of these philosophers. He believes that there must be harmony between our philosophical theories and those pre-philosophical beliefs we find irresistible (see 211a6–11 and 1145b1–7). And, surely, the belief that things like cats, dogs, and human beings are fully real is irresistible. Indeed, *we* can make no sense of *our* denying the claim that *we* are real.

So for Aristotle at least, the possibility of a tension here is a serious problem; and a central aim of the middle books is to show that the tension is not real. Throughout VII and VIII, Aristotle is at pains to show that we can endorse the claim that form is primary substance while continuing to hold on to the beliefs motivating the *Categories*. Thus, he assures us that, despite the privileged status of substantial form, ordinary objects continue to be substances – real things; and he denies that this is a matter of mere stipulation (1042a24–32). Familiar particulars are, after all, things that are paradigmatically instances of the "this something" formula: each is a particular human being, a particular horse, or a particular oak tree. Furthermore, concrete particulars satisfy the other condition VII, 3 associated with substance. They are separable. Here, Aristotle insists on two different notions of separability. There is what he calls separability in formula and unqualified separability. To have the former is to have an essence that can be defined independently of a reference to anything else; whereas the latter is separability in existence or existential autonomy. And while only substantial forms have separability in formula, only familiar particulars have unqualified separability. They are things that come into existence at a time; they pass out of existence at a later time; and they enjoy a career in between, a career that makes up a chapter of the history of the natural world.

Forms, by contrast, do not enjoy this kind of existential autonomy. They do not come into existence or pass out of existence; and they do not undergo other kinds of change either. Accordingly, they do not have what we can think of as a career. They are essentially predicable entities. They do not exist independently; they exist merely as items predicated of something else. As Aristotle puts it, they are "such"es and not "this"es. They are not things that can be picked out and pointed to; they aren't objects of ostension in the way even that their matter is. They are, on the contrary, *how* some parcel of matter is, the way that matter is; and they can exist only if there is some matter that is that way. So while substantial forms have one kind of separability, there is another kind of separability that only the composite particular has; and that, Aristotle wants to say, warrants the claim that familiar particulars are full-blooded realities.

And they are genuine unities as well. On Aristotle's analysis, the matter and form constitutive of a familiar particular turn out to be categorically different kinds of things. The one is something suited to play the role of subject and the other, the role of predicated item. And Aristotle wants to insist that because they have these categorically different structures, they can constitute what is a unified subject of predication. Familiar particulars are not just piles or heaps of things that are connected by a merely additive process. They are rather predicative structures; and, for Aristotle, a predicative structure is more than a mere assemblage of nameable ingredients or what Aristotle calls elements (1041b12–13). To get a familiar particular, we need the appropriate material ingredients or elements, but we need more. Those material ingredients need to be put together in the right way; and their being so put together is not a matter of an additional ingredient. It is something categorically different from those nameable ingredients or "this"es; it is what Aristotle calls a principle (1041b30). It is the way those ingredients are structured or organized; and the relevant principle is form.

So matter and form are, so to speak, made for each other. They fit together in such a way that what they constitute is a substantial unity. Indeed, at the end of Book VIII, Aristotle tells us that what is unique about his hylomorphic analysis of the structure of familiar particulars is just that it leaves us with no problem about the reality and unity of those particulars (1045a23–25). By their very nature, matter and form are things such that the latter's predication of the former results in what is a genuine unity and a genuine reality. And if one has doubts about this, Aristotle implies, it is only because one supposes that being and unity are genera, that there is some one thing that is just plain being and some one thing that is just plain unity (1045b6–9). But there are no such properties. The only notions of being and unity that we have are those associated with kinds; and the pivotal kinds here are the kinds of substances, kinds like *human being*, *horse*, and *oak tree*. But where the appropriate form is predicated of the appropriate matter, that fact alone results in what is *one human being* and *a real human being*; *one horse* and *a real horse*; or *one oak tree* and *a real oak*. These sorts of things constitute the paradigmatic kinds of unity and reality; and matter and form are sufficient to deliver them.

V

In Book VI of the *Metaphysics*, Aristotle tells us that the science that studies being as being is distinct from physics only if there is what he calls separated substance, substance that exists apart from the material and sensible world of change. Aristotle, of course, thinks that there is such a separated substance – the Unmoved Mover he calls God. But the Prime Mover represents just one candidate for status as separated substance. The Platonist adds both forms and mathematical objects to the list. From the perspective of the middle books, the Platonic separation of form rests on a mistake, the mistake of construing a "such" as a "this" (1033b19–30). Although substantial form is separable in formula, no form is separable in existence. Forms are always predicable entities. For a form to exist is for it to be predicated of something else. As we put it, a form is *how* some matter is. It is a way matter is and exists only if there is some matter that is that way.

The case against the Platonic separation of mathematical objects is developed in *Metaphysics* XIII and XIV. There, we find that an important source of the view that mathematical objects are immaterial substances is the idea that no object in the material world matches the mathematician's characterization of the subject matter of geometry and arithmetic. As the mathematician describes them, geometrical objects and numbers are things whose only properties are those fixed by the axioms and theorems of geometry and arithmetic. Nothing in the sensible world, however, has geometrical or arithmetical properties and no others. Ordinary material objects have a host of properties over and above their specifically mathematical properties. They have colors, give off odors, undergo changes, and so on. Accordingly, the Platonist concludes that no ordinary objects can be the things arithmetic and geometry are about and posits immaterial substances with purely mathematical natures as the truth-makers for mathematical claims.

Aristotle thinks that this line of reasoning embodies a deep misunderstanding of the nature of science. The view is that for the propositions of a science to be true, there must be objects that have the properties specified in the axioms and theorems of the science and no other properties; and that view conflicts with what we know about the sciences (1077b17–31). What the Platonic view overlooks is the obvious fact that every science has a particular focus (1077b33–1078a2). A science selects certain features of objects for its investigation while prescinding from others. Accordingly, no object has only the properties constituting the focus of the science. The objects that have those properties have other properties that are not considered by the science; but despite that fact, those objects constitute the truth-makers for the science – the things the science is about. And that is how it is with both geometry and arithmetic. Neither science characterizes items separate from the sensible physical world. Both characterize ordinary physical objects, but they do so by focusing on selected features of those objects. As Aristotle puts it, both geometry and arithmetic deal exclusively with sensible objects, but neither science deals with them in so far as they are sensible. The two sciences examine sensible objects in so far as they exhibit, respectively, geometrical and arithmetical properties (1078a2–13). The geometrician deals with physical objects in so far as they have extension and are things like pyramids, cubes, and spheres. Arithmetic, by contrast, examines groups of physical objects from the perspective of their enumerability or countability.

Geometry, then, is the science of continuous quantities; and it is ordinary objects that are continuous quantities. Arithmetic is the science of numbers; and for Aristotle numbers are just countable pluralities or groups:

"number" means a measured plurality and a plurality of measures . . . The measure must always be some identical thing predicated of all the things it measures, e.g. if the things are horses, the measure is *horse*, and if they are men, *man*. If they are a man, a horse, and a god, the measure is perhaps *living thing* and the number of them will be a number of living beings. (1088a4–11)

So just as physical objects are continuous quantities, groups of physical objects constitute discrete quantities. The relevant quantitative features of those objects and groups of objects will, of course, be co-instantiated with all sorts of other properties; and the way the mathematician will proceed in characterizing the relevant objects and groups of objects is

by setting up by an act of separation what is not separate . . . For a man *qua* man is one indivisible thing; and the arithmetician supposed one indivisible thing, and then considered whether any attribute belongs to a man *qua* indivisible. But the geometer treats him neither *qua* man nor *qua* indivisible, but as a solid. (1078a21–26)

VI

So neither forms nor mathematical objects provide us with examples of separated substances. But the Prime Mover does. In Book XII, Aristotle arrives at this conclusion by reflecting on the nature of time. There is, he assumes, a single all embracing time, a time of which all other times are proper parts. That single temporal framework cannot, however, begin to apply or cease to apply (1071b6–8); for if time in general were to come into being, then it would be true that *before* it *came* into being there *was* no time. But that is incoherent. Accordingly, if we take time to have a beginning, then what we construed as time was not time, but rather a part of some longer time; and, of course, precisely the same argument applies in the case of that longer time. Similarly, if time were to cease to exist, then it would be true that *after* its corruption time *will* no longer exist. Again, we have incoherence, so that the period of time we took to be time was not time, but just a part of some longer time. Temporal facts cannot fail to obtain, and the times those facts import are necessarily parts of a single, all-embracing time. So we have to concede both that there is a single time with neither beginning nor end of which all times are interrelated parts and that this is necessarily the case.

Now, Aristotle thinks that what a time is is just the number of some change; it is what we count or measure in the change when we say how long the change takes. A time, then, is the duration of a change (219a3–8). Accordingly, for each stretch of time, there is some change whose duration that time is; and what holds the time together, what makes it one time, is just that it is the duration of some one change. So if there is to be a single all-inclusive time, there must be a single change whose duration it is; and if the single all-inclusive time is necessarily without beginning or end, then the one change whose duration it is must likewise be necessarily without beginning or end. Now, Aristotle holds that only one kind of change can, in the required way, be eternal – change in place of a circular sort (1071b10–11). All other kinds of change involve movement between contraries and so must come to an end; but in the case of circular motion, there are no states which, in a non-arbitrary way, can be said to initiate or terminate the motion. A body undergoing uniform circular motion is such that at any point in its motion what counts as completing the motion is always different; and if the change is eternally occurring, there is nothing that counts as its starting-point.

We can conclude, then, that necessarily there is at least one case of eternal circular motion; and since numerically one change is possible only if there is numerically one substance undergoing the change, we can conclude that there is at least one necessarily existent substance – the substance undergoing the eternally occurring change. All of this follows on strictly philosophical grounds, but Aristotle believes that the philosophical arguments have empirical confirmation in the never-failing regularity of the movement of the heavenly bodies (1072a22).

Now, Aristotle tells the story of the Prime Mover in terms of the model provided by Eudoxian astronomy. On this model, the heavenly bodies are attached to a series of concentric crystalline spheres with motion conveyed inwards from the outermost sphere. There are all kinds of complications involved in setting out the details of the model. We can, however, ignore these and focus merely on the motion of the outermost sphere – the "first heaven." That sphere moves the spheres within it, but it too undergoes a kind of change – the necessarily eternal circular motion of the outermost heavenly bodies, the fixed stars. So the first heaven is a mover that is itself in motion; and for Aristotle that entails that it is a moved mover; and although Aristotle would concede that, theoretically at least, it is possible that what moves the first heaven is itself another moved mover, he wants to deny the possibility of an infinite series of moved movers. He thinks that if each mover in the series were moved by a moved mover, there would be no First Mover and, hence, no motion at all (994a1–18). So there is an Unmoved Mover, something that "moves without being moved, being eternal, substance and actuality" (1072a24–26), and Aristotle, for his part, is satisfied that this Prime or First Mover just is the being that directly causes the first heaven to move.

There is, however, a problem here. The Prime Mover causes the locomotion of the outermost celestial sphere, but it is difficult to understand how anything could cause something else to move in place without being in some sort of physical contact with what it moves and, hence, without being itself affected or moved by the causal interaction. But if this is how it produces motion, then what was supposed to be the Prime or First Mover is not that at all. It is just another moved mover; and if there is no other way of producing motion, then the very idea of a First Mover seems to be threatened with incoherence. Toward showing that there can be something that causes change in place without being in contact with anything, Aristotle reminds us that "the object of desire and the object of thought move in this way"; they move without being moved (1072a26–27). So there is a familiar way things can cause motion without being moved or affected themselves. They can motivate by being objects of thought and desire; and Aristotle wants to claim that the causation of the First Mover is an instance of this form of causation. The First Mover "produces motion by being loved" (1072b3). None of the details of all this is spelled out precisely; but it seems, first, that Aristotle took the first heaven to be endowed with intelligence, to have some sort of cognitive access to the Prime Mover, and to find the Prime Mover a good worthy of emulation in the form of eternal rotatory motion, and, second, that since Aristotle took these facts to underlie the necessary motion of the celestial bodies, he construed them as holding of necessity.

VII

As we have already indicated, Aristotle characterizes the Prime Mover as "actuality." He denies that the Unmoved Mover has any unactualized potentialities: it actually is everything it can be. Given the connection between the concepts of matter and potentiality, it follows that the Prime Mover is entirely lacking in matter (1074a36); and Aristotle infers a number of claims from the immateriality of the Prime Mover. Since it is by way of matter that things with a single essence are diversified (1034b5–7), Aristotle concludes that there can be just one substance with the essence of the Unmoved Mover (1074a36–38). Furthermore, he invokes the immateriality of the Prime Mover to conclude that it is a being without parts, that it is through and through simple (1073a5–6). He does not, however, say that the Prime Mover is form; and it is no accident that he fails to invoke the familiar connection between actuality and form in his characterization of the Prime Mover. The Prime Mover agrees with substantial forms in being one with its essence; like those forms, it is separate in definition or essence. But unlike the forms of familiar objects, the Prime Mover is also separate in existence. It has the existential autonomy that forms lack: it is a "this" and not a "such." Accordingly, the Prime Mover is categorically a different kind of entity from any form.

So the Prime Mover enjoys both kinds of separability or independence; and this fact suggests that the ontological theory of Book XII enables us to resolve a nagging difficulty associated with the metaphysics of the middle books. In Books VII and VIII, we meet a gap between the things (substantial forms) that are independent or separate in essence and those (familiar particulars) that are existentially independent or separate in an unqualified way; and that gap can appear disconcerting. How can it be that the beings that are supposed to be the primary substances are not themselves things capable of standing alone, of existing in their own right? Book XII tells us that, in the final analysis, this cannot happen. It closes the gap between things that are separable in formula and separable in existence; for it tells us that when we look beyond the material world that provides the context for the middle books, we find a being that is at once independent in essence and independent in existence; and that being is the substance that is prior to everything else: it is the primary substance *par excellence*.

But what is this being? What kind of essence does the First Mover have? Aristotle's answer is that it is a being engaged in intellectual activity. It is a being that thinks. Indeed, he tells us that the Prime Mover just is its acts of thinking; and he argues that since thinking is a form of living, the Prime Mover is a living being, a being whose essence is to think and, therefore, to live. The Prime Mover, then, is alive; and since its life is the best life, the Prime Mover deserves the title "God."

So the Prime Mover is a living being whose life is the best any substance can aspire to; its life is a life of unchanging intellectual activity. What it thinks of is just itself. Accordingly, Aristotle claims, the Prime Mover or God is thinking that is thinking of thinking (1074b34). This characterization of the Prime Mover has been roundly criticized. Thus, we are told that Aristotle's God is narcissistic or that, since it focuses merely on itself, the Unmoved Mover's intellectual life is severely impoverished; and we meet with the more radical claim that Aristotle's description of God incorporates an incoherent conception of thinking. Thinking is essentially object-directed: for any act of thinking, there is some object that the thinking is about; and that object gives the act its character and identity. It is, however, unclear whether Aristotle's formula gives us any object for the Divine thinking. He claims that God is the act of thinking; but what is the thinking a thinking of? Aristotle's answer: the thinking that it is. But if the first use of "thinking" was problematic on the grounds that it failed to identify the object of the act we were attempting to pick out, Aristotle hardly helps things by identifying that object as what we initially picked out by the term "thinking."

These criticisms would be just were the claim that God is a thinking that thinks of thinking Aristotle's last word on God; but it is not. It is rather a template for an account of God's essence, a template offered as a solution to a problem about God's thought. If God's life is in the best kind of life and consists in intellectual activity, that activity must take the best thing as its object; but, then, it looks as though there is something more perfect than God – the object of God's thinking. We can avoid this conclusion, however, if we say that God is the object of God's thinking; and that is what Aristotle's formula tells us. But the formula needs an interpretation; and we meet with the required interpretation in a doctrine from the *De anima*, the idea that the act of thinking and its object are one and the same (430a3–5). The claim is that the intelligible in actuality just is the intellect in actuality. What the doctrine implies is that, in a way, every act of thinking is self directed. The intellect becomes its objects when it thinks, so every act of thinking is a case where the intellect in act is its own object (1075a1–4). But, then, the thinking that is God can grasp all the intelligibles there are and still be thinking of itself. We have, then, the interpretation of the formula and an answer to Aristotle's critics as well. God's thought encompasses all the essences or universals there are and is, none the less, a thinking of what is best.

But if we can make sense of Aristotle's characterization of the Divine thought, we need to realize that his conception of the Prime Mover is very different from the Judeo-Christian conception of God. It is, for example, doubtful whether the Prime Mover has cognitive access to the contingent particulars making up the material world; and it is fairly clear that Aristotle's Unmoved Mover is not a creator. The material world is eternal and uncreated. It can seem, then, that the dependence of the world on God is indirect and remote. It can seem that the physical universe is an independently existing, self-sufficient whole that merely needs to be kept moving. Some comments, however, at the end of Book XII suggest a deeper form of dependence:

> We must consider also in which of two ways the nature of the universe contains the good and the highest good, whether as something separate and by itself, or as the order of the parts. Probably in both ways, as an army does; for its good is found both in its order and in its leader, and more in the latter; for he does not depend on the order, but it depends on him. And all things are ordered together somehow, but not all alike – both fishes and fowls and plants; and the world is not such that one thing has nothing to do with another, but they are connected. For all are ordered together to one end . . . . (1075a11–19)

Here, Aristotle is saying that there is a universal order that ties the workings of the various natures together, and he is telling us that this universal order is like the order in an army. The order found in an army derives from the thought of its general; it is simply an expression of the overall strategic plan the general has formulated. The upshot of Aristotle's analogy, then, seems to be that the order or harmony he wants to impute to the natural world is an expression of the intelligible order and structure of the Divine Thought. He does not tell us just how the dependence of the natural harmony on God's thought works itself out. But if we pursue the analogy Aristotle offers, we will find it plausible to suggest that it is the movement of the first heaven that provides the causal mechanism for the expression of the natural order and harmony that originates in the Divine Thought. It is, after all, by the efforts of his subordinates that a general's strategic plan gets implemented.

It is tempting, then, to suppose that the first heaven grasps the intelligible order at work in the Divine Thought and moves as it does so as to realize that order in the natural world. But if something like this is what Aristotle means to be telling us, then even though his Prime Mover is not the creating God of the Judeo-Christian tradition, the dependence of the world on Aristotle's God is not the very remote sort of dependence it can seem to be. Aristotle does not see the world as an independently existing, self-sufficient whole that merely needs a "jump start" from an otherwise unrelated substance. The very order of the world – its general nature and structure – derives from God. That order is just a reflection or expression of the Divine Thought. It is because that order constitutes the intelligible content of God's thinking that it constitutes the intelligible structure of the world. So it is in a strong sense that the Prime Mover is "the first cause and first principle" of all things (981b29).

Bibliography

Editions and translations

Aristotle (1924) *Aristotle's Metaphysics*, 2 vols, ed. W. D. Ross (standard edition of the Greek text). Oxford: Oxford University Press.
Aristotle (1984) *The Complete Works of Aristotle*, 2 vols, ed. J. Barnes. Princeton, NJ: Princeton University Press.

Studies

Annas, J. (1976) *Aristotle's Metaphysics M and N*. Oxford: Oxford University Press.
Aubenque, P. (ed.) (1979) *Études sur la métaphysique d'Aristote*. Paris: J. Vrin.
Bostock, D. (1994) *Aristotle's Metaphysics Z and H*. Oxford: Oxford University Press.
Charlton, O. W. (1970) *Aristotle's Physics Books I and II*. Oxford: Oxford University Press.
Code, A. (1978) No universal is a substance: an interpretation of *Metaphysics* Z.13. *Paideia* (special Aristotle issue): 65–74.
Code, A. (1996) Owen on the development of Aristotle's *Metaphysics*. In W. Wians (ed.), *Aristotle's Philosophical Development*. Lanham, MD: Rowman and Littlefield.
Copleston, F. (1946) *A History of Western Philosophy*, vol. I. Westminster, MD: Newman Press.

Frede, M. (1987) *Essays in Ancient Philosophy*. Minneapolis: University of Minnesota Press (includes his "Individuals in Aristotle" [1983] and "Substance in Aristotle's *Metaphysics*" [1985]).

Furth, M. (1988) *Substance, Form, and Psyche*. Cambridge: Cambridge University Press.

Gill, M. (1989) *Aristotle on Substance*. Princeton, NJ: Princeton University Press.

Gotthelf, A. (1985) *Aristotle on Nature and Living Things*. Pittsburgh, PA: Mathesis.

Irwin, T. (1988) *Aristotle's First Principles*. Oxford: Oxford University Press.

Jaeger, W. (1948) *Aristotle: Fundamentals of the History of his Development*, 2nd edn, trans. R. Robinson. Oxford: Oxford University Press (first published in German 1923).

King, H. (1956) Aristotle without *prima materia*. *Journal of the History of Ideas*, 17: 370–89.

Lear, J. (1988) *Aristotle: The Desire to Understand*. Cambridge: Cambridge University Press.

Lesher, J. (1971) Aristotle on form, substance, and universal: a dilemma. *Phronesis*, 17: 169–78.

Lewis, F. (1991) *Substance and Predication in Aristotle*. Cambridge: Cambridge University Press.

Loux, M. (1979) Form, species, and predication in *Metaphysics* Z, H, and Θ. *Mind*, 88: 1–23.

Loux, M. (1991) *Primary ousia*. Ithaca, NY: Cornell University Press.

Loux, M. (1995) Composition and unity: an examination of *Metaphysics* H.6. In M. Sim (ed.), *The Crossroads of Norm and Nature*. Lanham, MD: Rowman and Littlefield.

Moravscik, J. (ed.) (1967) *Aristotle: A Collection of Critical Essays*. Garden City, NY: Doubleday.

Norman, R. (1969) Aristotle's philosopher-God. *Phronesis*, 14: 63–74.

Owen, G. (1986) *Logic, Science, and Dialectic*. Ithaca, NY: Cornell University Press (includes his "Logic and metaphysics in some earlier works of Aristotle" [1960] and "The Platonism of Aristotle" [1966]).

Owen, G. and Düring, I. (1960) *Aristotle and Plato in the Mid-fourth Century*. Goteburg: Studia Graeca et Latina Gothaburgensia, vol. 11.

Owens, J. (1963) *The Doctrine of Being in the Aristotelian Metaphysics*, 2nd edn. Toronto. Pontifical Institute of Medieval Studies.

Owens, J. (1979) The relation of God to the world in the *Metaphysics*. In P. Aubenque (ed.), *Etudes sur la métaphysique d'Aristote*. Paris: J. Vrin.

Ross, W. (1924) *Aristotle's Metaphysics*, 2 vols. Oxford: Oxford University Press.

Scaltsas, T. (1994) *Substances and Universals in Aristotle's Metaphysics*. Ithaca, NY: Cornell University Press.

Scaltsas, T., Charles, D., and Gill, M. (1994) *Unity, Identity, and Explanation in Aristotle's Metaphysics*. Oxford: Oxford University Press.

Sim, M. (ed.) (1995) *The Crossroads of Norm and Nature*. Lanham, MD: Rowman and Littlefield.

Wians, W. (ed.) (1996) *Aristotle's Philosophical Development*. Lanham, MD: Rowman and Littlefield.

Witt, C. (1989) *Substance and Essence in Aristotle*. Ithaca, NY: Cornell University Press.

Woods, M. (1967) Problems in *Metaphysics* Z. In J. Moravscik (ed.), *Aristotle: A Collection of Critical Essays*. Garden City, NY: Doubleday.

5

Aristotle, *Nicomachean Ethics* (367–323 BC)

A Sort of Political Science

T. H. Irwin

Aristotle's *Nicomachean Ethics* is one of the earliest and most influential treatises in moral philosophy. Aristotle (384–322 BC) begins by introducing the highest good, which he calls the "best good" (1094a22; all references are to the *Ethics* unless otherwise marked). This is the end that we pursue for its own sake only, while we pursue every other good for the sake of the highest good (1094a18–22). Knowledge of this highest good will have a significant influence on our lives because, if we know it, we will be like archers who have a definite target to aim at, and are more likely to organize our lives well (1094a22–4). Aristotle argues that the highest good, identified with happiness (*eudaimonia*), is activity of the soul in accordance with the best and most complete virtue in a complete life (1098a26–8). This account of the good leads us to discuss the virtues, in order to discover what happiness is in more detail (1102a5–7). Most of the following books of the *Ethics*, therefore, discuss the different virtues, and activities, states, and conditions connected with them (including continence, incontinence, pleasure, friendship, and theoretical wisdom).

We are probably not surprised that a treatise on ethics tries to describe the virtues, since a description of the virtues is a description of an admirable person with a good character, and that is what we expect to learn from ethics. We may be more surprised, however, that Aristotle embeds this description of the virtues in an account of happiness, and that he claims that this embedding is important for the conduct of our lives; the reason we examine the virtues is to find out about happiness.

Aristotle's claims about happiness might provoke us to ask two questions: (1) In what ways does his account of happiness influence his account of the virtues? (2) Is this influence good or bad? One step toward answering these questions is to understand what Aristotle is trying to do in the *Ethics*. If we have some idea of how he conceives ethical inquiry, we will be able to grasp some of the main points in his ethical argument. Perhaps we will then see the role he intends for his claims about happiness, and their intended influence on his account of the virtues.

Near the beginning of the *Ethics*, Aristotle describes ethical inquiry as "a sort of political science" (1094b11). This description of ethics also helps to explain why ethics is concerned with the highest good. Aristotle argues as follows:

1   Every productive and practical discipline aims at some end.
2   Since one end is subordinate to another, disciplines concerned with subordinate ends are subordinate to disciplines concerned with superordinate ends.
3   If there is a highest good, it is the concern of the highest science.
4   Political science is the science that prescribes the proper practice of the other sciences.
5   Therefore its end is all inclusive.
6   Therefore it is the highest science.
7   Therefore, if there is a highest good, it is the concern of political science.

The main point of this argument (which paraphrases *Ethics* I, 1–2) is to connect three claims about political science: (1) its supervisory role; (2) its all-inclusive end; and (3) its pursuit of the ultimate end. Aristotle argues that since it has a supervisory role, it must have an all-inclusive end, and this must be the ultimate end.

Political science examines other pursuits and disciplines concerned with various goods. It prescribes the proper extent of these pursuits, and the appropriate limit of acquisition of these other goods. Its prescriptions rest on some conception of the way of life that these other pursuits and these other goods ought to promote. The aspect of political science that occupies Aristotle in the *Ethics* tries to form a correct conception of the way of life, as defined by different traits of character, aims, and activities, that the other goods ought to promote.

Part of Aristotle's reason for thinking we ought to practice political science, as he understands it, is readily intelligible. The blind accumulation of assets or resources, without reference to any end for which we might use them, is likely to be harmful; we need some idea of what we want them for, and therefore some idea of how much of them we want. We may take one of Aristotle's own examples. If we make bridles with no idea of how many horses need bridles, or of what else we could do with the leather, we will waste our efforts. If, however, we plan to breed enough horses to use our surplus of bridles, our planning will be back to front.

In taking political science to have this supervisory function, Aristotle exploits a familiar idea about the virtues: that they ensure the good use of other goods (cf. Plato, *Euthydemus* 288d–291d). But in working out this idea, he faces some apparently serious objections. If we state and examine these objections, we may understand his whole theory better.

Political Science and the Apparent Limits of Deliberation

In claiming that the inquiry undertaken in the *Ethics* is a sort of political science, Aristotle implies that it is a deliberative science. He says it is the same cognitive state as prudence (*phronêsis*), which deliberates about what promotes happiness as a whole (1141b23–33). This feature of political science ought to help us to understand political science better; for since Aristotle offers an explicit account of deliberation, we might hope that if we apply this account to the questions that concern political science, we can understand how Aristotle intends his ethical inquiry to proceed. We may therefore turn to his explicit remarks on deliberation.

As Aristotle understands it, deliberation assumes some end and reasons about what has to be done to secure it. The doctor, he says, does not deliberate about whether to heal, nor the orator about whether to persuade; he begins from the relevant end, and looks for the means to it (1112b11–16). Once we have identified what we can do here and now to achieve our end, we make a decision (*prohairesis*, 1113a9–12).

Not every question about what to do to achieve some end is a question for deliberation. If we simply need to follow rules that provide an effective method for getting the right answer (such as the rules for spelling different words), our thought about how to get the right answer is not deliberation. We deliberate in cases where some question can reasonably be raised about how to achieve the end, and where potentially conflicting considerations need to be recognized in reflection on what to do (1112a34–b11).

This description of deliberation suggests an account of the procedure of political science. It should begin from a conception of its end; the end for political science – corresponding to health for medicine – is the highest good, which is happiness for individuals and communities. The proper task of political science is to find the various means that promote happiness. This is why it examines the virtues, since these are the states of character that promote the good of individuals and of the communities to which they belong (1102a5–13).

If the *Ethics* practices deliberative political science, so understood, we might reasonably infer that questions about the character of happiness are not its proper concern. It is not up to doctors to argue about whether we are healthier if we have a short life confined to a wheelchair and nourished by a feeding-tube than if we have a long life in which we can walk, run, and eat and drink without feeding-tubes; they simply presuppose that the second life is healthier than the first. Doctors who prescribed treatments that promoted the first kind of life rather than the second would not be promoting health, and it is no part of medicine to convince us that one kind of life is the healthy life. Similarly, we might infer, political science must presuppose some conception of happiness, and must confine its advice to people who already accept that conception of happiness. If we think happiness consists in pleasure, wealth, honor, moral virtue, or intellectual study, we will demand different sorts of advice from the political scientist.

Aristotle seems to recognize this restriction on the scope of deliberative political science. For he warns us that if we are to listen profitably to his lectures we must already have been well brought up and formed good habits (1095a2–11, 1095b4–6; cf. 1179b21–31; these passages need closer examination, since they may not all be referring to the same necessary condition for profitable study of political science). Since the result of good upbringing is the formation of the moral virtues, Aristotle might be taken to imply that we must have the virtues if we are to listen to political science. It is easy to understand his believing this. For if political science advises us on how to secure the way of life that promotes the conception of happiness accepted by the virtuous person, its advice is of interest only to someone who accepts that conception.

If political science presupposes that its students have the moral virtues, the deliberative aspects of political science cannot be part of the moral virtues. Virtuous people have reason to want to acquire political science, but Aristotle's remark about good upbringing suggests that this is an extra skill, not a prerequisite for virtue. Some deliberation is proper to the virtuous person, even if this account of virtue is correct. For such a person will often engage in low-level deliberation (for example, about how to patch up a quarrel with another person, once I have decided that this is what I ought to do). This does not mean, however, that virtuous people deliberate in very general terms about what contributes to the ultimate good.

Two aspects of Aristotle's description of the moral virtues seem to confirm this sharp separation between moral virtue and political science.

1   When Aristotle describes the moral agent, he emphasizes the cultivation of appropriate feelings, emotions, and habits. This feature of moral education is especially prominent in Book II (e.g., 1104a11–b3). The role of pleasure in moral education helps to explain the emphasis that the *Ethics* lays on pleasure (cf. 1104b3–26, 1152b1–8, 1172a19–27).
2   He marks a division of labor between virtue and prudence, so that virtue makes the end correct and prudence makes the means correct (1144a7–9; cf. a20–2, 1145a4–6). This division of labour is easily understood in the light of a deliberative conception of political science. The political scientist seems to take for granted the virtuous person's conception of the end.

If, therefore, Aristotle keeps his promise to practice political science in the *Ethics*, our expectations about the treatise should reflect his restricted conception of political science. If he presupposes moral virtue in his audience, he will not engage in the reasoning that is characteristic of the virtuous person, though he might well describe it. Nor will we expect him to argue for the specific conception of the end that the political scientist presupposes; such argument, even if it were possible, would apparently be outside the scope of political science.

An Expanded Conception of Deliberation

The conception of political science, and hence of the *Ethics*, that I have outlined fits some of Aristotle's remarks quite well. But it does not capture all his views. Some of what he says conflicts with the conception I have outlined.

He introduces deliberative political science as the line of inquiry (*methodos*) he will follow in the *Ethics*. But he does not begin the deliberation by taking a conception of the ultimate end for granted. On the contrary, his first question is about what the ultimate good is (1094a25–6, 1095a14–22). He pursues this inquiry dialectically (cf. 1145a1–7), following his own method of philosophical inquiry, adapted from Socratic cross-examinations (on dialectic in Aristotle's philosophy in general and in ethics in particular, see Irwin, 1988, sections 18–26, 34–6, 184–90). He sets out to examine the most common and most plausible beliefs that have been held about what happiness is (1095a28–30). His term "examine" (*exetazein*) is a standard dialectical term (Irwin, 1988: 493, n38); in using it he signals the fact that he will proceed dialectically in the deliberative inquiry that he has begun. The philosopher's question about the nature of happiness is part of the inquiry that belongs to deliberation.

The discussion of the nature of happiness shows that Aristotle does not intend to take any determinate conception for granted in his deliberative argument. He considers the three sharply different lives that are defined by their leading aims of pleasure, honor, and virtue, and argues that each conception of the best life is mistaken. He argues for his own candidate in I, 7, and at the end of his argument he claims to have said in outline what happiness is (1098a20–2; cf. 1094a25–6). Despite the limits that Aristotle imposes on deliberation by confining it to means to ends, he takes deliberative political science to argue about the nature of the end.

Deliberation and Prudence

We have noticed one aspect of Aristotle's claims about political science that does not seem to match his claim that it is a deliberative discipline concerned with means to ends. To grasp the significance of this difficulty, we ought to notice a further one. Though we saw some reason to believe that virtue of character is a prerequisite for, not a result of, political science, it is not clear that Aristotle really maintains this division.

To see the complexity of his position, we must return to the passage that seemed to say that a virtuous character is a prerequisite for learning political science (1095b4–6). On closer inspection, the passage does not say this at all. It says that a good upbringing is needed if we are to learn political science, but it does not say that this good upbringing must have produced the virtues in us. Aristotle claims that his inquiry is seeking principles that will provide the "because" or the "reason why" for our moral convictions. To begin the inquiry we need the belief "that" various things are good or bad, right or wrong, but we do not need the "why" or "because." To understand the relation between virtue and political science, then, we must ask whether virtue requires only the "that" or also the "why."

If we attend to the features of Aristotle's account of virtue that we have previously mentioned, we have a reason for saying that virtue does not require the "why" and the principle. In Book II, Aristotle emphasizes the importance of habituation, beginning in early childhood, and especially of habituation in pleasure and pain, for the formation of a virtuous character. We might well conclude that the virtues of character are the result of the process that he calls "good upbringing," which produces only the right convictions (the "that") without a grasp of their underlying principles (the "why").

This, however, is a quite misleading summary of Aristotle's account of virtue of character. To see this, we must consider his rather complex views about the intellectual virtue of prudence (Burnyeat, 1980: 74; Sorabji, 1980: 205). He defines virtue of character as lying in a "mean" or "intermediate state" that is defined by reason and the reason by which the prudent person would define it (1106b36). Virtue is a state that involves right reason, and right reason is prudence (1144b27; on the interpretation of this passage see Hardie, 1980: 237–9). Hence virtue of the proper or full sort requires prudence (1144b1–16).

This connection between virtue and prudence is relevant to questions about the role of political science in the *Ethics*, because prudence requires deliberation about happiness (1140a25–8; an interpretation of this passage that differs from mine is offered by Broadie, 1991: 211). In that case, moral virtue requires the sort of deliberation that is characteristic of political science, and the two points of view are not to be sharply distinguished.

This leads us to a further question. Does the prudence of the virtuous person include the aspect of political science that inquires into what happiness is and reaches some reasoned answer to the question? Aristotle takes prudence to be a correct apprehension of the end (1142b31–3; Hardie, 1980: 386ff). If it is correct to assume that, as Aristotle says, the procedure of prudence is deliberative, we might infer that its deliberative procedure reaches a correct conception of the end. In finding this correct conception of the end, it also finds the principle which, in Aristotle's view, appears only to the virtuous person (1144a31–6).

This deliberative virtue of prudence is needed to satisfy the condition that the virtuous person must decide on (*prohaireisthai*) the virtuous action (1104b31–2, 1106a3–4). Since Aristotle identifies virtue with a state that decides (*hexis prohairetikê*), a clearer understanding of his view requires some grasp of his conception of decision. The relevant point for present purposes is that decision is the product of wish and deliberation. Since excellence in deliberation is the mark of prudence, Aristotle believes that the right decision requires prudence (1145a4–6). He gives us further reason to suppose that he makes correct deliberation and prudence necessary for virtue of character.

In connecting virtue with deliberation, he raises a further difficulty for himself. For his claims about decision ought to explain how the virtuous person decides on the virtuous action for its own sake (1105a32; cf. 1144a19). This demand expresses the ordinary expectation that the just or generous person acts appropriately without the incentive of some further gain. Such a demand, however, seems difficult to capture within Aristotle's conception of decision. For decision depends on wish and deliberation; but deliberation, and hence decision, is concerned, not with ends, but with things contributing to ends (1112b1). To say that the virtuous person decides on an action for its own sake is, apparently, to contradict Aristotle's explicit description of deliberation. His position would be intelligible if deliberation could result in the conclusion that something is to be chosen for its own sake; but such a result seems to conflict with his explicit description of deliberation.

Deliberation about Ends

We can solve some of these puzzles about deliberation if we return to some of Aristotle's initial remarks about happiness. He distinguishes the sort of deliberation that is characteristic of a productive craft from the sort that is characteristic of virtue. This distinction emerges from a distinction between ends that he alludes to at the beginning of the *Ethics* (1094a3–5). In saying that some ends are the activities themselves, Aristotle implies that we do not pursue these ends purely as means to further ends. The distinction alluded to here is not explained until Book VI, where Aristotle distinguishes production (*poiêsis*) from action (*praxis*). Action, in contrast to production, is to be chosen for its own sake, not simply for the sake of some result beyond the action (1140b6–7). This action chosen for its own sake is the special concern of prudence, which deliberates about action, and not about production.

Aristotle recognizes that political science is concerned with non-instrumental goods.

It supervises the "practical" sciences – those concerned with *praxis* rather than *poiêsis*. It considers how far each of the other sciences ought to be practiced; and so its end includes the ends of the other sciences (1094b5–7). The highest good is comprehensive because it includes the different goods that are worth pursuing for their own sakes. In identifying these goods, and the appropriate pursuit of them, we are deliberating about what promotes happiness.

Aristotle takes deliberation about what promotes happiness to include consideration of what happiness is. He makes this clear when he begins his deliberative inquiry by attending to the question about what happiness is. He implies that the two questions "What promotes happiness?" and "What is happiness?" will be answered by an account of what happiness consists in. The three lives of pleasure, honor, and virtue provide wrong answers, but answers of the appropriate form, to these two questions; in I, 7, Aristotle claims to provide the right answer.

The claim that these inquiries belong to deliberation is more plausible if we agree that deliberation about what promotes an end includes deliberation about what the end consists in. This is sometimes expressed as the claim that "means" to ends include "constituent" as well as "instrumental" means (the significance of this broad conception of "means" is clearly explained by Wiggins, 1980: 221–7, and Cooper, 1975: 22). We need to keep this claim about "means" in mind when Aristotle contrasts happiness with honor, pleasure, understanding, and every virtue. He says that we choose these non-ultimate goods both for their own sake and for the sake of happiness (1097b2–5; I generally follow the account of this passage given by Ackrill, 1980: 20–2, which is opposed by Kraut, 1989: 230–2). He returns to the issue that he discussed in I, 1–2, about the relation of non-instrumental goods to the ultimate good. He argued there that even disciplines concerned with action rather than production are subordinate to an architectonic discipline that coordinates and regulates them; in that case, he claimed, the end of the architectonic discipline includes the ends of the subordinate disciplines. The non-instrumental goods pursued by the subordinate disciplines must, then, be parts of the ultimate good that includes them.

We now see why choosing non-instrumental goods for the sake of happiness does not amount to choosing them simply for the sake of some result that comes about from them – some end that is wholly external to them. In choosing them as non-instrumental goods and for the sake of happiness, we choose them as parts of a whole.

This composite conception of happiness explains how happiness can embrace the different forms of *praxis*, non-instrumental action chosen for its own sake. In one respect, deliberation cannot be about ends; for it must begin with some end in view. None the less, what deliberation finds to contribute to that first end is also an end in itself, if deliberation has found that it is a component of the first end. In the particular case of moral deliberation, we begin with some concept of happiness, and then we deliberate until we find the states of character that are components of happiness. If we deliberate correctly, we find the moral virtues, and we decide on these for their own sakes. To attribute these tasks to practical reason and deliberation is to assert that practical reason can properly claim to support one choice of ultimate ends rather than another.

Once we notice that deliberation about happiness includes reflection on what happiness is, and not simply on what causally results in happiness, we can also understand

Aristotle's claims about the role of deliberation and decision in virtue of character. Virtuous people decide on the virtuous action for its own sake because their deliberation about what constitutes happiness leads to the conclusion that this sort of action is worth choosing for itself.

A Useless Conception of Deliberation?

I have argued that Aristotle takes political science and moral virtue to be more closely connected than we might at first have supposed. The crucial connection presupposes that happiness is a composite end composed of non-instrumental goods, and that we can discover its components by deliberation. Deliberation leading to a choice of non-instrumental goods is the mark not only of the political scientist, but also of the virtuous person; for both of them need prudence to carry out this deliberative task.

If Aristotle conceives his ethical inquiry as primarily deliberative, does anything interesting follow? Does he simply stretch the notion of deliberation to include his procedure in the *Ethics*, so that we learn nothing further by being told that this procedure is deliberation? The aspect of deliberation that Aristotle especially emphasizes is its teleological character; it takes an end for granted, and deliberates about the means to it. If he also claims that inquiry into what the end is belongs to deliberation about the means to the end, what is left of the claim that deliberation takes the end for granted and seeks the means to it?

We can sharpen this question by considering what we need to show in order to demonstrate that something is a part or component of happiness. Aristotle seems to regard happiness as a composite of non-instrumental goods that are worth choosing for themselves. We might reasonably infer that our reasoning about parts of happiness must begin from a list of non instrumental goods. But in that case, the most controversial steps seem to have been taken before deliberation even gets started. If we take virtue, honor, and pleasure to be non-instrumental goods, our views on the composition of happiness will be different from the views we will accept if we think pleasure is the only non-instrumental good. But if Aristotle identifies his ethical argument with deliberation, the list of non-instrumental goods must apparently be fixed before we start ethical argument. This is an unwelcome result; for we might reasonably hope that ethical argument will tell us whether or not pleasure is the only non-instrumental good.

Moreover, this seems to be not only our hope, but also Aristotle's. For he does not take it for granted that there are non-instrumental goods other than pleasure. He argues for this claim in his examination of pleasure (1173b31–1174a8). Similarly, he argues that virtue alone is not complete enough to constitute happiness all by itself (1095b31–1096a2, 1100a4–9, 1153b14–25). Apparently, then, he cannot believe that ethical deliberation simply takes an agreed list of non-instrumental goods for granted.

Must we conclude, then, that the identification of non-instrumental goods belongs to an aspect of ethical argument that falls outside the deliberative conception that we have ascribed to Aristotle? Or does it somehow fit within the deliberative conception? We must try to see whether the deliberative conception really makes a significant difference to Aristotle's argument.

Deliberation and Non-instrumental Goods

The first step in understanding Aristotle's claims about deliberation is to recognize that the teleological structure of deliberation applies to the discussion of non-instrumental goods. In claiming that happiness is composed of some specific non-instrumental goods, Aristotle does not mean that it is simply their sum. He does not believe, therefore, that if we recognize one or more non-instrumental goods, we have thereby recognized an ultimate good as the basis for deliberation (contrast Ackrill, 1980: 26; Engberg-Pederson, 1983: 17–21). Recognition of an ultimate good introduces some structure into our pursuit of non-ultimate goods, and thereby gives us some basis for regulating our pursuit of them. This is why the understanding of the ultimate good that is the object of the superordinate discipline of political science is meant to make a significant difference to our lives, and to provide us with a target to aim at (1094a22–4).

We can easily understand this claim about structure and regulation if we apply it to productive crafts aiming at some result that is external to their exercise. If we are trying to make a table, we have a reason for trying to make all the legs the same length. We do not aim at legs of equal length simply for its own sake, or simply to display our skill as carpenters; we want the legs to fit into the table that we aim at as the external result.

Reference to an external result provides a clear example of regulating actions through some goal-directed structure, but it is not necessary for this sort of regulation; for we can regulate actions with reference to an end even if the end is not an external result. If we are trying to dance a particular step for its own sake, we want the component motions to fit one another, so that collectively they count as dancing a step.

This aim of fitting actions to one another applies to actions that we value individually for their own sakes. To value an action for its own sake is not to value it without reference to its relation to other things that we value for their own sakes. If we think of individual actions as parts of a whole, we can try to regulate each of them by reference to their tendency to make other non-instrumentally valuable activities easier or more difficult, or a more or less significant part of our lives.

This mutual adjustment of components of an end does not presuppose some result external to them, to which they are merely instrumental. But it requires our conception of the end to have some structure. We cannot adjust individual movements in a dance or a symphony to one another unless we have some idea of the whole in which these individual movements have a specific role. If, then, Aristotle has some useful work for deliberation, he must apparently have some sufficiently clear structural conception of the end to which the various non-instrumental goods belong.

Aristotle tries to provide the appropriate structural conception of the end. He presents it in three stages: (1) in the first part of I, 7, he presents two formal conditions for the final good, requiring it to be complete and self-sufficient; (2) in the second part of I, 7, he argues that this complete and self-sufficient good must include a dominant role for the realization of the capacities of human beings as rational agents; and (3) in I, 13, he argues that the realization of human capacities requires a life in which one's non-rational motives are regulated by, and agree with, practical reason.

Do these claims present enough structure in the final good to make it worth our while to deliberate about the components of the good? Deliberation would have nowhere to start unless it could begin with some initial convictions about which goods are non-instrumental; it must rely on some intuitive views. But it does not simply take over these intuitive views without question. For when we compare these intuitive views with the structure of the final good, we may discover reasons for modifying our initial list of non-instrumental goods. For one thing, we may find that our initial list was incomplete, once we see that some human capacities are not realized in the goods that we initially recognized. Again, we may find that a specific good is more or less important than we initially recognized, once we see how it interacts with other non-instrumental goods. We may even come to believe that we were wrong in our initial belief about some non-instrumental good; perhaps it is only good as an instrumental means.

This is just a sketch to show that Aristotle has some reason to claim that deliberation is the right way to think about the ultimate good and its components. It is a further question whether this deliberative conception makes any significant difference to the argument of the *Ethics* as a whole. We must now indicate how one might try to answer that question.

Deliberation and the Virtues

According to Aristotle's general account of the virtues of character, each virtue lies in a mean determined by the reason by which the prudent person would determine it (1106b36–1107a2). In describing a virtue of character as a mean Aristotle implies that it is a particular way of harmonizing the aims of the rational and the non-rational part of the soul under the direction of practical reason. Each virtue achieves this harmony in relation to its own particular range of non-moral goods and evils: the goods and evils proper to bravery are those that involve danger; those proper to temperance are those that involve the satisfaction of appetites, and so on.

These different goods and evils are "non-moral" because they are genuine goods that appear good apart from the outlook of the virtuous person. Aristotle calls these "unqualified" goods, meaning that they are good for us not in all circumstances, but in normal circumstances, where "normal" circumstances are those of the virtuous person. They are not good for everyone because they can be misused by everyone except the good person, who is the only person for whom they are genuinely good (1129b1–6). The outlook of the virtuous person identifies the extent to which it is reasonable to pursue each of these non-moral goods.

This role for the virtuous person in relation to non-moral goods recalls the role assigned to political science in I, 2. As a superordinate science, political science considers how far each of the subordinate sciences and pursuits should be practiced. To explain how it considers this question, we might reasonably refer to the teleological character of deliberation. To pursue one non-instrumental good beyond the point where it starts to interfere with others is to neglect the character of happiness as a whole. The different virtues guide our pursuit of non-instrumental non-moral goods with reference to the demands of the other virtues, which impose the appropriate shape and structure on the agent's life as a whole.

A few examples will illustrate the ways in which this deliberative pattern applies to

Aristotle's description of the individual virtues of character. One might be inclined to recognize bravery in bad causes as well as good. But Aristotle rejects this inclination. He sees genuine bravery only in actions that one undertakes for the sake of some worthwhile goal. Risking one's life for the sake of a trivial gain is the mark of a fool-hardy and misguided person, not of a brave person. Aristotle assumes that the brave person's assessment of the relevant costs and benefits is guided by the outlook of the other virtues. We need this outlook to identify the results that make it reasonable to face one or another danger.

In his discussion of magnanimity, Aristotle has to deal with a common conception of the magnanimous person as one who thinks highly of himself, ignores the criticisms of other people, and demands honor from them. These features of the common conception are present in Aristotle's description, but they are modified by the demands of the other virtues. The magnanimous person does not count honor as the greatest good; it is simply the greatest external good, and so it is inferior to virtue. That is why he is not unduly disturbed by the loss of external goods through ill fortune. Since it is never reasonable to act viciously for the sake of external goods, the magnanimous person's reactions rest on the correct belief that he or she is better off having made the virtuous choice, even at the cost of external goods.

These features of Aristotle's description of the virtues show how the deliberative pattern influences his views. Since he takes his task to be the deliberative one of finding the states of character and the actions that promote happiness, he looks for the virtues that achieve the appropriate non-instrumental goods in the appropriate proportion and combination. The ways in which the requirements of the different virtues determine the requirements of each virtue reflect the structure of happiness, as Aristotle conceives it. We cannot, therefore, expect him to give an account of one virtue without reference to the other virtues. If bravery or magnanimity is a genuine virtue, rather than a tendency that needs to be regulated by virtue, it must be guided by the demands of happiness, and hence by the demands of the other virtues. The teleological aspects of Aristotle's conception of happiness also influence his conception of deliberation, as he applies it to the virtues. (Aristotle affirms his belief in the reciprocity of the virtues at 1144b32–1145a2.)

This deliberative account of the virtues has two roles in the argument of the *Ethics*. First, it explains why we treat these states of character as virtues. Aristotle recognizes that we have incomplete success in identifying and naming the genuine virtues. In some cases we have no distinct name for the mean state that is the virtue because we do not clearly distinguish it from the extreme states that are readily confused with it (1125b17–29, 1126b16–20). In other cases, we identify the virtue correctly, but Aristotle has to modify the common conception of it; he argues, for instance, that many states commonly recognized as bravery are not the genuine virtue of bravery. Aristotle expects us to accept: (a) his account of happiness; (b) his demand to harmonize our views of the virtues with our view of happiness; and (c) most of his account of the individual virtues. In that case, it is also reasonable for us to accept his modifications of common views of the virtues. Second, it also explains why these are virtues, not only why we treat them as virtues. The states of character that we identify by deliberation about the composition of happiness are the ones that have the best claim to be the virtues.

Aristotle does not sharply distinguish these two explanatory functions of his account of the virtues. This is not surprising, since he proceeds on the assumption that ordinary beliefs are on the right track, and that we are ready to revise them appropriately, once we see that they need revision.

Deliberation, Moral Theory, and Moral Virtue

So far I have considered the relation between deliberative political science and moral philosophy. The questions I have addressed are philosophical questions about what makes something a virtue and about how the different virtues should be understood. The fact that they are philosophical questions does not make them of purely theoretical interest; for the conclusions that I have mentioned are also relevant to questions about what states of character we should try to cultivate in a society, what we should emphasize in moral education, and the other issues that concern Aristotelian political science. We must now grasp the connection between these questions and the ones that the virtuous agent can be expected to consider.

Some familiar facts about the virtues suggest that the deliberative approach cannot be the virtuous agent's own approach. (1) The sort of deliberation that I have described may seem to be more explicit and elaborate than anything we could reasonably demand from a virtuous person; brave, considerate, and honest people do not seem notable for their capacity to deliberate about the issues that concern Aristotle in the *Ethics.* (2) A virtue of character is valuable partly because it inculcates a tendency to react immediately without elaborate preparation. This is most obviously true in the case of emergencies where a pause for deliberation would make us miss the right moment. (3) Even apart from questions about urgency, it seems desirable for a virtuous person to be rigid in certain ways, and to be unwilling to entertain the sorts of questions that might be answered by deliberation. If, for instance, some people need to deliberate from first principles about whether to act honestly here and now, that seems to be a reason to question their honesty, since it seems to mark an unstable commitment that is liable to shift in the face of apparently plausible objections.

These familiar facts about virtuous people constitute reasons for being surprised that Aristotle takes prudence to be necessary for any virtue of character, given that he takes prudence to be a deliberative virtue that deliberates about "living well as a whole," and about action rather than production. This description suggests that we cannot confine the virtuous person's deliberation to restricted questions about how to perform a virtuous action; on the contrary, Aristotle's description of this virtue recalls the type of deliberation that – as we have seen – he undertakes in the *Ethics* as a whole. What place can we find for such deliberation within a plausible conception of a virtuous person?

In Aristotle's defense one might point out that we expect a virtuous person to have some idea of the point of a particular virtue. Virtuous people need not always be thinking about this, and they need not obtrude it into their thoughts about particular situations. But they should regard it as a non-arbitrary matter that they have these states of character rather than others. If people thought that their sense of certain actions being required of them was simply the product of their upbringing, with no further rational basis, that would be a shortcoming that would affect their claim to have the relevant virtues, not simply their claim to understand them.

This demand for some grasp of the point of a virtue appears still more reasonable once we notice that it does not simply affect how virtuous people look at their virtues, but may also affect what they do. Though it is often inappropriate for a brave person to count the cost before facing a danger fearlessly, it is not always inappropriate (the difference between these two situations is suggested in Luke 9: 62; 14: 28). Sometimes we have an opportunity to count the cost, and we ought to count it, in the light of our grasp of the different goods and evils at stake. Aristotle does not recommend that we should always restrict ourselves to noticing that there is a danger to be faced and assuming that a brave person must face it fearlessly. To grasp the point of a virtue is to see how it fits the demands of the other virtues, and how it contributes to the life that the virtues collectively aim at; we see all this as a result of deliberation about happiness.

Some of Aristotle's comments on conflicts or apparent conflicts of moral requirements show that he expects virtuous people to grasp the point of their virtues. (1) In discussing equity, he insists that we must look behind the actual formulation of the law to see what the legislator had in mind (1137b14–24). Once we see the point of the law, by seeing what end it is intended to secure, we see why we ought not to follow the formulation of the law, if we can secure its point only by acting differently. (2) In discussing casuistical problems in friendship, Aristotle recognizes that we have to consider the claims of a creditor against the claims of a friend, and the claims of one friend against another (1164b30–1165a14). We will not be able to do this unless we have some conception of the point of accepting these claims, and of how the acceptance of one of these claims affects our acceptance of another.

Without going into the details of these examples, we can extract the main argument, that recognition of the point of a given virtue is sometimes relevant to particular decisions that are expected of a virtuous person. More specifically, this recognition of the point of a particular virtue requires some understanding of its connection with the demands of the other virtues, and of the relative significance of these different demands. This is the sort of understanding that Aristotle expects us to acquire from the deliberation that is characteristic of the prudent person. It is intelligible, therefore, that he demands prudence, and so demands deliberation about the components of happiness, from the virtuous agent, no less than from the political scientist and the moral philosopher.

Bibliography

Editions and translations

Aristotle (1890) *Aristotelis Ethica Nicomachea*, ed. I. Bywater (standard edition of the Greek text). Oxford: Oxford University Press.

Aristotle (1980) *Nicomachean Ethics*, trans. W. D. Ross, rev. by J. L. Ackrill and J. O. Urmson. Oxford: Oxford University Press.

Aristotle (1984) *The Complete Works of Aristotle*, 2 vols, ed. J. Barnes. Princeton, NJ: Princeton University Press.

Aristotle (1999) *Nicomachean Ethics*, 2nd edn, trans. T. H. Irwin (with introduction, notes, and glossary). Indianapolis: Hackett.

Studies

Ackrill, J. L. (1980) Aristotle on *eudaimonia*. In A. O. Rorty (ed.), *Essays on Aristotle's Ethics*, pp. 15–33 (first pub. 1974). Berkeley, CA: University of California Press.

Broadie, S. W. (1991) *Ethics with Aristotle*. Oxford: Oxford University Press.

Burnyeat, M. F. (1980) Aristotle on learning to be good. In A. O. Rorty (ed.), *Essays on Aristotle's Ethics,* pp. 69–92. Berkeley, CA: University of California Press.

Cooper, J. M. (1975) *Reason and Human Good in Aristotle*. Cambridge, MA: Harvard University Press.

Engberg-Pederson, T. (1983) *Aristotle's Theory of Moral Insight*. Oxford: Oxford University Press.

Hardie, W. F. R. (1980) *Aristotle's Ethical Theory*, 2nd edn. Oxford: Oxford University Press.

Irwin, T. H. (1988) *Aristotle's First Principles*. Oxford: Oxford University Press.

Kraut, R. (1989) *Aristotle on the Human Good*. Princeton, NJ: Princeton University Press.

Rorty, A. O. (ed.) (1980) *Essays on Aristotle's Ethics*. Berkeley, CA: University of California Press.

Sorabji, R. R. K. (1980) Aristotle on the role of intellect in virtue. In A. O. Rorty (ed.), *Essays on Aristotle's Ethics*, pp. 201–19 (first pub. 1973). Berkeley, CA: University of California Press.

Wiggins, D. (1980) Deliberation and practical reason. In A. O. Rorty (ed.), *Essays on Aristotle's Ethics*, pp. 221–40. Berkeley, CA: University of California Press.

6

Lucretius, *De rerum natura* (ca. 99–55 BC)

Breaking the Shackles of Religion

David Sedley

De rerum natura (henceforth *DRN*) is a classic didactic poem in six books, written in Latin hexameters. The title means "On the nature of things" or "On the nature of the universe." Its author Titus Lucretius Carus, known only for this one composition, appears to have been a Roman who died in the 50s BC (albeit open to dispute, his generally adopted dates are ca. 99–55 BC). Although his poem became widely known, influencing Virgil and other Latin poets, virtually no uncontested facts about the author's life have been preserved. The story of his insanity and eventual suicide, related by St Jerome, is widely considered a hostile fabrication, and the once popular fashion of detecting confirmatory signs of insanity in the poem has waned. Even the poem's dedication to a prominent Roman, Gaius Memmius, tells us very little about its author's social, political, or geographical background.

What is certain is that Lucretius was an Epicurean, a committed follower of the philosophy taught by the Greek thinker Epicurus (341–271 BC). The *DRN* is, as a whole, an exposition of Epicurean physics. Its debt to Epicurus' magnum opus *On Nature* (*Peri physeos*), whose title its own echoes, is profound. This now largely lost work was probably Lucretius' immediate source, and, if not, then certainly the ultimate source of his doctrines and arguments. The *DRN* therefore should not be assumed to be, taken as a whole, a philosophically original work, even though its author has demonstrably reordered the material he found in Epicurus, has undoubtedly personalized it in many other ways, and in places may well have effected more radical transformations. The *DRN*'s standing as a classic of Western philosophy rests partly on its author's poetic brilliance, and partly on the fact that, by an accident of survival, it is by far the fullest exposition we now possess of the Epicurean worldview.

The later books of the poem show signs of incomplete reworking, and it has often been doubted whether the transmitted ending – a graphic description of the great plague at Athens – can fully represent its intended closure. Hence one biographical detail reported by Jerome, namely that Lucretius' poem was edited and published posthumously (by none other than Cicero, it was claimed), has won some credence among scholars. Nevertheless, the six-book structure does appear to be, broadly speaking, a carefully planned one. The poem falls into three matching pairs of books:

I   The permanent constituents of the universe: atoms and void
II   How atoms explain phenomena

III   The nature and mortality of the soul
IV   Phenomena of the soul

V   The cosmos and its mortality
VI   Cosmic phenomena

The sequence is one of ascending scale: the first pair of books deals with the microscopic world of atoms in its own right, the second with human beings, the third with the cosmos as a whole. And within each pair of books, the first explains the basic nature of the entity or entities in question; the second goes on to examine a range of individual phenomena associated with them. A further symmetry lies in the theme of mortality, treated by the odd-numbered books. Book I stresses from the outset the indestructibility of the basic elements, while Books III and V in pointed contrast give matching prominence to the perishability of, respectively, the soul and the cosmos.

Alongside this threefold division into pairs of books, the poem can also be seen as constituted by two balanced halves, orchestrated by the themes of life and death. The poem opens with a hymn to Venus as the force inspiring birth and life. The first half closes, at the end of Book III, with a long and eloquent denunciation of the fear of death. And the poem as a whole returns at its close to the theme of death, with the disquieting passage on the Athenian plague: whether or not this, as we have it, is in its finished form (see above), there can be little doubt that the placing of its theme itself somehow represents the author's own orchestration.

The celebrated opening hymn to Venus calls upon her to intercede with her lover, Mars, and to inspire Lucretius' poetry. For all its magnificence, it makes a puzzling beginning to an Epicurean poem, since Epicureans – Lucretius himself included – made the gods' sublime detachment from our world a cardinal tenet. To some extent the hymn is Lucretius' homage to his great Greek forerunner Empedocles, himself the author of a hexameter poem on physics much admired and emulated by Lucretius: for Empedocles' own poem was built around two cosmic forces, Love and Strife, whom he identified with Aphrodite (= Venus) and Ares (= Mars). But the apparently un-Epicurean theology is actually not so alien to Lucretius' subsequent poetic presentation of Epicureanism, in which he frequently represents Nature as a personified and craftsmanlike force, despite his school's strong opposition to creationism and to teleological modes of natural explanation. Arguably this is one manifestation of how the demands of poetic convention and those of Epicurean orthodoxy could on occasion pull in opposite directions.

It has even been maintained, albeit on inadequate evidence, that in setting out to write poetry in the first place Lucretius was already being untrue to the teachings of his master, who had been inclined to associate poetic persuasion with the abandonment of rational thought. Lucretius' own explicit justification for writing in verse is that, although his argument will benefit readers by liberating them from their fears of death and of the gods, following it through to the end requires perseverance, and the charm of poetry will keep them from flagging. In a celebrated simile, he compares the function of his verse to the honey which doctors spread on the rim of a cup of bitter medicine, to lure children into drinking it for their own benefit.

Lucretius' proems to his six books probably contain the most original thought in the *DRN*. Some (II, VI) are primarily ethical, eloquently advocating the somewhat ascetic brand of hedonism espoused by the Epicureans. But those to Books III and V also develop the theological thinking initiated in the first proem. In the proem to Book III, Epicurus himself begins to take on the profile of a divinity, and in the proem to Book V his divinization is completed: he is declared the greatest god among those who were held by a recent rationalizing tradition (known as Euhemerism) to have been deified for their benefactions to mankind. Here once more the strict canons of Epicurean theology appear to have been put on hold.

At II, 655–60 Lucretius comments on the popular tendency to divinize natural entities: what ultimately matters is less the nomenclature you choose than the avoidance of contaminating the mind with vile *religio* ("religion," "superstition"). In his estimation (especially I, 62–79), breaking the shackles of *religio* was among Epicurus' greatest benefactions to mankind.

We may turn now to the poem's main argument. The central aim of Book I is to sketch the underlying constituents of the universe. It consists of absolutely indestructible primary components, identified with atoms and void. Atoms have an almost miraculous generative power, which Lucretius frequently compares to the capacity of a small stock of alphabetic letters to constitute, by their rearrangement, an endless variety of words. In stark contrast, a series of rival theories of the elements, drawn from the Greek philosophers of the fifth century BC, are exposed for their inadequacy. At the end of the book the infinity of the universe – both the void space, and the atoms which occupy it – is argued at length, and Lucretius attacks the inward-looking centripetal view favored by rival schools, whereby matter is gathered around an absolute center occupied by a spherical earth.

Book II moves on to the behavior of atoms when they combine to constitute macroscopic objects. All atoms, even those in compounds, are in constant high-speed motion – compared, in an exquisite image, to motes of dust dancing in a sunbeam – and the appearance of stability in solid objects merely reflects the patterns of motion into which the constituent atoms have settled. The latter fact is illuminated by the comparison of a flock of moving sheep seen on a distant hillside, so far removed as to coalesce into a stationary white blob. These are among the analogies for which Lucretius' poetry is especially famous.

One significant detail of Book II's account of atomic motion is its critique of determinism. Lucretius postulates, besides weight and collisions, a third principle of atomic motion, the notorious "clinamen" (swerve). Atoms may, "at no fixed place or time," deviate fractionally from their trajectories. This addition of a minimal degree of physical indeterminism serves (a) to explain how atoms can ever collide to initiate the formation of worlds, rather than drifting downwards for ever in parallel lines at equal speed; and (b) to permit the "free will" (*libera voluntas*) which visibly, Lucretius insists, enables living beings to embark on new and unpredetermined patterns of motion. Lucretius' exposition of (b) has often been hailed as the first-known argument for free will. Although there can be little doubt that the basic theory derives from Epicurus, Lucretius' is the only detailed account of it to come down to us.

Lucretius goes on to argue for the wide but finite range of atomic shapes as a necessary postulate in order to account for the observed degree of phenomenal variety in the world. He has surprisingly little to say, however, about just how the different atomic shapes generate the various macroscopic properties – much less, in fact, than he then proceeds to tell us about why atoms must themselves *lack* all phenomenal (as well as mental) properties. To close Book II, he turns to the traditional atomist doctrine that our world is just one of many – a horizon-expanding theme which matches and reinforces the arguments against a finite universe at the end of the preceding book.

Book III is devoted to the soul and its mortality. Analyzed into a rational mind (*animus* or *mens*) and a spirit or life-force (*anima*), the soul is argued to be itself a special atomic compound, which therefore must, like all compounds, eventually disintegrate. Its survival after the body's death is argued, in a long series of proofs, to be an impossibility. Rather, death is nothing more nor less than annihilation. Accordingly, the diatribe which rounds off the book is an impassioned denunciation of the fear of death as groundless: "Death is nothing to us." The dead can experience nothing, good or bad, and it is irrational to fear something which will not, when it happens, be bad for you. Being dead will in reality be no worse than it was, centuries ago, not yet to have been born (Lucretius' much-debated "symmetry argument"). Fear of punishment in the afterlife not only is unfounded, but originates in our own moral malaise: the mythical tortures of fallen heroes in Hades are a projection of the distress caused by greed, ambition, and other moral failings in this life.

Book IV concentrates on explaining individual psychological functions, starting with sense perception. The volatile *simulacra* or images which stream from the surfaces of objects and enter either the eye, to produce sight, or the mind, to provide the stuff of imagination or dreams, play a central role in the account. Although Lucretius includes a lengthy discourse on the causes of all kinds of optical illusions, he nevertheless stoutly defends Epicurean empiricism: the senses are the proper foundation of knowledge. Skeptics, who dismiss such knowledge claims, are condemned to self-refutation, he argues, since they deny themselves the right to assert their own position as a justified and true one. The final major section of the book is on love; after accounting for the causes of the sex drive, it culminates in an impassioned diatribe about the perils of enslaving oneself to sexual passion.

Book V starts with an account of the cosmos, both its origin and its arrangement, notably including celestial phenomena. A primary goal is to show that all the apparent evidence of design in the world can be comfortably explained away in terms of atomic interaction. This motivation continues in the second half of the book, in which the origins of life and the development of human civilization are reconstructed. One much admired feature is the principle of the survival of the fittest, on which Lucretius leans in order to explain the origin of species. While he has no Darwinian notions of gradual evolution and adaptation, he does exploit the associated insight that species which originated more or less at random will then have had to compete for survival, a competition in which only those with the ability to reproduce, added to further advantages such as speed, cunning, or usefulness to mankind, were able to achieve permanence.

This insight owed something to his poetic forerunner Empedocles, but had also become a key element in the Epicureans' own campaign against natural teleology.

Naturalistic explanation remains a keynote of the ensuing history of civilization, where innovations such as the discovery of fire and the advent of language are attributed to initially accidental or natural causes, on which human rationality then built and elaborated. This history of civilization is also a deeply moralizing one, and has often been scoured for an answer to the question whether Lucretius is a "primitivist" or a "progressivist" – whether, that is, he considers the advance of civilization to have yielded a net gain or loss for human happiness. His emphasis, however, is on bringing to light in every advance both some gain and some matching loss: the discovery of metal, for example, brought new comforts and conveniences, but also hastened the growth of warfare. The real message is that the fundamental causes of human unhappiness are simply not addressed by the conventionally recognized benefits of civilization. This message is eloquently reinforced in the immediate sequel to Book V, the proem to the sixth and last book, where Lucretius praises Athens for its unrivalled contribution to human civilization, but adds that none of its other benefactions begins to compare with its gift to us of Epicurus and his philosophy, which alone can aspire to cure our real ills.

Book VI works through a long series of natural phenomena, ranging from thunder to disease. These were traditional explananda in cosmological treatises, and Lucretius' own primary aim is to show that they can be explained comfortably – usually, indeed, in a wealth of alternative ways – without postulating divine intervention. Theological explanations are in fact not just redundant, but also deeply implausible, he maintains. For example, if thunderbolts are expressions of divine wrath, as typically held by the opposing school of thought, why does the god responsible for them so often miss his target and waste ammunition, or even, on occasion, use it to demolish his own temples? Here as always, establishing the hard scientific truth has an intimate bearing on human happiness: the misleading image of interventionist and even malevolent deities is one which Epicurean physics alone can expunge from our minds, and until we have replaced it with the true image of god as the blessedly detached being that he really is we have no chance of living on tranquil terms with the world.

The aspiration to obliterate his readers' fears of both death and the gods is Lucretius' guiding ambition throughout the poem. He compares human beings to children trembling in the dark. Just as the children's terror can be dispelled by the arrival of light, so too our fears of the universe and of the apparent threats it poses to our well-being will yield to scientific illumination – a benefaction which Epicurean philosophy alone can offer.

One long-standing debate concerns the relation of Lucretius to the mainstream Epicurean tradition. Does the *DRN*, philosophically speaking, look back to the work of his school's revered founder, dead for over two centuries? Or was Lucretius *au fait* with current developments in the Epicurean school, which was well established and influential in Italy, and which in competing with rival schools such as the Stoics had undergone significant internal developments? Although the latter option may be what one would predict, it has proved surprisingly difficult to substantiate. It remains a serious possibility that Lucretius learned Epicurus' philosophy from direct reading of his writings, without the influence of any living teacher. This question of Lucretius' intellectual milieu and background is one of many on which, unless new biographical evidence turns up, consensus is unlikely to be achieved.

The *De rerum natura* has, for two millennia, retained its deserved status as a classic. It has inspired innumerable readers, kept the flag of ancient atomism flying among the pioneers of early modern science, and set a standard for philosophical poetry that has rarely if ever been equalled since.

Bibliography

Editions and translations

Lucretius (1947) *Titi Lucreti Cari De rerum natura libri sex*, 3 vols, ed. C. Bailey. Oxford: Clarendon Press.

Lucretius (1975) *De rerum natura*, trans. W. H. D. Rouse, rev. M. F. Smith (with new text, introduction, notes and index). London: Loeb Classical Library.

Studies

Algra, K. A., Koenen, M. H, and Schrijvers, P. H. (eds) (1997) *Lucretius and his Intellectual Background*. Amsterdam: Royal Netherlands Academy of Arts and Sciences.

Boyancé, P. (1963) *Lucrèce et l'épicurisme*. Paris: Presses Universitaires de France.

Classen, C. J. (ed.) (1986) *Probleme der Lukrezforschung*. Hildesheim: Olms.

Clay, D. (1983) *Lucretius and Epicurus*. Ithaca, NY: Cornell University Press.

Fowler, P. G. and Fowler, D. P. (1996) Lucretius. In *Oxford Classical Dictionary*, 3rd edn, pp. 888–90. Oxford: Clarendon Press.

Furley, D. J. (1989) *Cosmic Problems*. Cambridge: Cambridge University Press (chs 16: Lucretius and the Stoics; 17: Lucretius the Epicurean: On the History of Man).

Gale, M. (1994) *Myth and Poetry in Lucretius*. Cambridge: Cambridge University Press.

Sedley, D. (1998) *Lucretius and the Transformation of Greek Wisdom*. Cambridge: Cambridge University Press.

Segal, C. (1990) *Lucretius on Death and Anxiety*. Princeton, NJ: Princeton University Press.

West, D. (1969) *The Imagery and Poetry of Lucretius*. Edinburgh: Edinburgh University Press.

7

Plotinus, *Enneads* (250–270)
A Philosophy for Crossing Boundaries

Dominic J. O'Meara

The Making and Unmaking of a Classic

If we suppose that a philosophical classic is a work which is fairly complete in itself, which speaks to different readers of different periods and cultures (and is therefore translated into various languages), having a wide and lasting appeal, then Plotinus (205–270 AD) himself wrote his work in a very different spirit. He put down in writing the results of discussions that took place in his Platonist philosophical school in Rome in the 250s and 260s, results which took the form of texts of very varying length, having no titles, written sometimes in a crabbed and barely grammatical Greek reminiscent more of Aristotle than of Plato, dealing in no particular order with a range of subjects as they came up in discussions in his school throughout the years. Plotinus had to be encouraged to write and was in any case very reluctant to allow his work to circulate beyond a narrow circle of close pupils and colleagues. This somewhat random and difficult collection of texts was transformed by another, at a later date, into a "classic" of Western philosophy, the *Enneads*. Before returning to Plotinus himself and his work, we need first to look briefly at this making of a classic, and its unmaking in a more recent period.

Plotinus died in 270. However, it was about thirty years later that one of his most devoted pupils, Porphyry, made public his edition of the master's writings, the edition that we still use, the *Enneads*. In editing Plotinus' writings, Porphyry first divided some of them so as to bring their number up to a total of fifty-four treatises, i.e. the sum of 6 × 9, six indicating (in numerological terms) perfection, nine completion: from an open-ended and somewhat disorderly collection a perfect corpus was born! Porphyry then arranged the fifty-four texts thus obtained into six sets of nine ("nines," *enneades*) such that the first group of nine (*Ennead* I, 1–9) contains treatises in which are to be found what he considered to be "more ethical" matters, whereas the next two groups (*Enneads* II and III) each include nine writings relating to physics, the remaining three groups (*Enneads* IV–VI) containing texts dealing with soul, Intellect and the One, i.e. divine transcendent realities, the domain of the science of the divine, "theology." P. Hadot (1979), who has pointed out this arrangement by Porphyry of Plotinus' works in terms of a division of sciences (ethics, physics, theology), notes that the division is a scale intended to lead the soul of the reader from lower to higher forms of knowledge and of life, a scale leading to the ultimate goal, the One, the absolute Good, a subject discussed in the last treatises of *Ennead* VI. Porphyry thus completely rearranged his collection of Plotinian texts so as to make of it what, in *his* eyes, would be a perfect and complete course of philosophical instruction bringing the reader from ordinary life to union with the absolute transcendent Good. Porphyry also added titles for the treatises, probably corrected the Greek text (lightly, it seems), added explanations (these are lost) and prefaced the edition with a *Life of Plotinus*, which provides much fascinating biographical information, including a chronological listing of the treatises, an explanation of Porphyry's editorial approach, and especially a portrait of Plotinus as the ideal sage, a figure whose wisdom and perfection of life cannot but inspire the reader who goes on to begin a reading of the *Enneads*. Such is the power of this portrait and of the new structure given to Plotinus' writings that, even today, both continue to condition the reader's approach to Plotinus. Porphyry had made of Plotinus' texts a "classic."

Why did Porphyry publish his edition so long after Plotinus' death? Thirty years seems a rather long delay, and it is difficult not to think that new factors emerging at the beginning of the fourth century stimulated Porphyry in such a way that his edition is a reaction to these factors. It has been suggested (Saffrey, 1992) that the new element is a former pupil of Porphyry, Iamblichus, who had set up a successful philosophical school in Apamea (Syria), who was virulent in his criticisms of Porphyry and of Porphyry's teacher, Plotinus, insisting that the Platonic philosophy which he taught had far more ancient roots, in the thought of Pythagoras, the Egyptians, and Chaldaeans. The *Enneads* would then have emerged at the turn of the fourth century in the context of a struggle between Porphyry and Iamblichus over claims to Plato's heritage.

Porphyry's edition of Plotinus had some success. The *Enneads* were commented on by Proclus, head of the Neoplatonic school of Athens in 437–485, a distinction reserved otherwise for canonical authors such as Plato and Aristotle. (Only a few fragments survive of this commentary.) A Latin translation of Plotinus (also now lost) was published by Marius Victorinus in the fourth century and was read by Augustine at a crucial time in his intellectual development, prior to his conversion to orthodox Christianity in 386. An Arabic version of *Enneads* IV–VI, the *Theology of Aristotle*, was produced in the circle of al-Kindi in ninth-century Baghdad and became an influential text in Islamic philosophy, being read, for example, by al-Farabi and Avicenna, who commented on it.

In 1492 Marsilio Ficino published his Latin translation of the *Enneads* in Florence, the first translation to appear in the Latin West since that of Victorinus (whose translation does not appear to have survived into the Middle Ages). Although Ficino's Plotinus translation came out after the publication of his great translation of Plato (1484), in fact Ficino had already read and used Plotinus while working on Plato in the 1460s, and indeed his approach to Plato was conditioned by Plotinus (whom Ficino regarded as a second Plato) and other ancient Neoplatonists. The publication of the *Enneads* (and of Plato) in Latin responded to concerns which would have been very foreign to Plotinus and Porphyry (both of them pagan and Porphyry certainly very critical of Christianity): the replacement of medieval Aristotelianism, a threat, Ficino felt, to Christian faith, with Platonism, a philosophy far more in harmony, Ficino claimed, with an "ancient theology" of which Christianity was the culmination. The *Enneads* thus became a classic in the service of a new cause and as such had considerable success in Renaissance Europe, its impact extending to the Cambridge Platonists of the seventeenth century and to Schelling and Hegel at the beginning of the nineteenth century (O'Meara, 1992).

German Idealist sympathy with Plotinus' ideas encouraged German scholarly work on the Greek text of Plotinus and on his sources and context. The development of historical methods in the nineteenth century meant also, however, the growth of a tendency to read the *Enneads*, no longer as the expression of some timeless truth, but as the product of particular historical conditions, an approach leading to the effort to see Plotinus and his writings independently of their interpretation in the editions published by Porphyry (the *Enneads*) and by Ficino. A major moment in this unmaking of a "classic" was R. Harder's publication of the treatises in the chronological order of their composition, not in the enneadic ordering (1930–37, 2nd edn 1956–62). In Anglo-American philosophy, the *Enneads* ceased to have a place in the canon for most of the twentieth century for a number of reasons: an historical prejudice against the post-classical period of antiquity, a theological rejection of the mixing of religious faith and philosophy (such as Ficino had attempted), a philosophical rejection of Hegelianism (which had been strong in England) and of metaphysics. However, modern efforts to free Plotinus from the use made of him by Porphyry, Ficino, and Hegel, greater appreciation of the interest and importance of late antiquity, and more openness to metaphysical discussions should help give Plotinus' writings, if not the status of a classic, at least (and better) the title of works worth reading.

The Context of Plotinus' Works

Born in 205, perhaps in Egypt, where, in Alexandria, in 232–42, he studied with the Platonist philosopher Ammonius Sakkas (about whom we know very little), Plotinus, after taking part in a failed military expedition of the emperor Gordian III against Persia, settled in Rome in 244 where, hosted by an aristocratic lady (Gemina), he founded an unofficial philosophical school or circle. With the assistance of committed pupils such as Porphyry, and attended by a regular circle of men and women from the upper levels of Roman society, senators, writers, doctors, coming from different parts of the Roman Empire, the sessions of the school followed the general pattern of philosophical teaching at the time: authoritative texts were read, normally those of the founder of the philosophical movement to which the school adhered (be the founder Plato, Aristotle, Epicurus, or Chrysippus); these texts were explained with reference to earlier or recent interpretations of them; more thematic discussions of specific philosophical problems would arise, perhaps in connection with textual interpretation. The authoritative texts in Plotinus' school were the dialogues of Plato. Plotinus was sensitive to the difficulties of determining Plato's position on various problems (cf. e.g. *Enn.* IV, 8, 1) and well aware of the diverging interpretations among his Platonist predecessors and contemporaries. In contrast to modern scholars, Plotinus sought an interpretation of Plato that was satisfactory, not for historical reasons, but because it represented the correct treatment of the philosophical question at issue in Plato's text, his assumption being that whatever Plato's position might be, it should correspond to the truth. This, a philosopher's approach to Plato, meant also that Plotinus took issue, not only with what he regarded as incorrect Platonist readings of Plato, but also with other philosophies, Epicurean, Skeptic, Stoic, and Aristotelian, where they held theses with which he disagreed. He also criticized the ideas of a religious movement of the time, Gnosticism (see below), since he believed that it seriously and misleadingly perverted Plato's ideas. In effect, then, the whole heritage of classical Greek and Hellenistic philosophy was involved in Plotinus' effort to develop a true reading of Plato, that is a true philosophy. The breadth of this ambition, and the imaginative and bold way in which it was realized, explain to some extent, perhaps, Plotinus' wide and continuous appeal.

Plotinus' writings arose, not so much from the interpretations of texts which primarily occupied his school, but from the thematic discussions that accompanied text interpretation. However, in discussing directly a philosophical problem, for example that of the relation between soul and body, Plotinus included passages from Plato, as expressing the problem or as containing or confirming the solution Plotinus wished to propose. The list of problems discussed in Plotinus' treatises is extensive. A long series of works deals with the soul: its nature, its immortality, its relation to the body, its relation to other souls, its functions of memory, perception, and so on. Plato's forms are also discussed: their nature, their relation to intellect, their extent, their relation to numbers, and to particular things. A major question concerns the ultimate principle of all things and how all is constituted from this ultimate principle. The making of the world and of time, matter, fate, and its relation to free will are examined. The Aristotelian and Stoic theories of categories receive an extensive and technical discussion, which proposes a Platonic approach. Evil, beauty, human nature, the virtues, eros, happiness, and the role of philosophy in reaching the human good are also given attention, among other themes. The following selection from these themes may give an impression of Plotinus' distinctive approach and some of his more striking ideas.

The Making of the World

The genesis of the world is described in Plato's *Timaeus*, a description which, despite its richness, leaves much unclear and open to interpretation. Plotinus' Platonist predecessors of the second century usually identified three principal causes in the cosmology of the *Timaeus*: (a) transcendent, eternal, immaterial models of the world, Plato's forms; (b) a divine craftsman (the "demiurge"), or intellect, who is inspired by the models in bringing order to (c) a pre-existent matter, the result being the world. Most of these Platonists felt that the world was eternal and that the account of the genesis of the world was merely a way of bringing out the different causes eternally constitutive of the world. This interpretation gives rise to further questions and difficulties: what is the divine demiurge? How does this demiurge relate to the highest principle mentioned in Plato's *Republic* (509c), the form of the Good? What is the demiurge's precise relation to the forms? Are the forms the thoughts of the demiurge (like the project conceived by a craftsman, who then realizes it in matter)? What precisely is the demiurge's organizing activity? What is the matter that he organizes? How does this happen eternally? In dealing with these questions, Plotinus identifies three primary causes of the world: (1) soul, (2) Intellect, and (3) the One (*Enn.* V, 1). How this result is reached and how it responds to the questions at issue might be sketched briefly as follows.

(1) The constituted world, in Plato's *Timaeus* (30b–d), is represented as an organic unity, a cosmic living being structured, vivified, unified by a world-soul. The Stoics also saw the world as an organism, identifying two primary constitutive cosmic causes, the immanent active living force ("god," *logos*) permeating things and the passive matter elaborated by *logos* into a rational, diversified and coordinated whole, the world. Plotinus too sees the world as an organic whole, dependent for its structure and life, following the *Timaeus*, on world-soul. Where Plotinus disagrees with the Stoics, where his world-soul differs from the Stoic immanent life-force, is when he denies that soul is of a corporeal nature (on the critique of Stoicism, see Blumenthal, 1971: ch. 2). Bodies are composites, as such tending to decomposition, occupying specific places and having mass. If soul is to fulfill its cosmic function, however, it promotes unification and structure, not dissolution and disorder, it is capable of being present, as one, in different places of the body and thus has no mass such as to be subject to fragmentation in extending to different places. Contrary to Stoic claims, therefore, body depends for its existence, for its order and life, on soul which is not body. In this sense soul is the constitutive cause of body.

In arguing this point against the Stoics in *Enn.* IV, 7, Plotinus derives the conclusion that soul is not subject to bodily death: soul is immortal. Plotinus is thinking not only of world-soul, but also of individual souls, the souls of individual bodies. Souls of both types are of an incorporeal, purely intelligible nature, causally prior to body and independent of body. What is the relation between world-soul and individual souls? Sharing the same nature, they relate to each other in a way other than the way in which bodies interrelate: souls are one and many prior to and independently of the way bodies are one and many. Souls are not separated from each other by place and quantity and can thus be both one with each other and distinct from each other in a manner of which bodies are incapable.

(2) If soul in effect organizes the world, it does this in a rational way: soul acts with intelligence, with a rational "art" or knowledge which seems acquired rather than intrinsic: soul comes to know and can lose its knowledge, presupposing thus an independent and prior source of knowledge which has knowledge intrinsically. Plotinus identifies this source with Plato's demiurge, or divine intellect, and the knowledge it possesses with the transcendent Platonic forms (*Enn.* V, 1, 3–4). The forms are therefore the thinking of a transcendent Intellect (*Nous*), which inspires soul's organization of body. This identification of the forms as the thinking of a divine intellect was a disputed thesis among Platonists and within Plotinus' school: his reasons for defending it and his understanding of it will be considered below in the context of epistemology. At any rate, what applies to the unity and multiplicity of soul holds also and even more so for the unity and multiplicity constituted by Intellect and the forms: they make a multiplicity at an even higher degree of non-spatial, non-quantitative unity than souls.

(3) A divine Intellect occurs also in Aristotelian cosmology, in the form of the "Unmoved Mover," an immaterial pure act of self-thinking on which ultimately depend all movements in the world (Aristotle, *Metaphysics* XII, 6–10). Although much influenced by the Aristotelian conception of this Intellect, Plotinus does not accept that it can be causally ultimate. As he sees this Intellect (a unity of intellect and its thinking, the forms), it is unified multiplicity, the multiplicity of forms and the duality of subject and object of thinking. As such it is composed and requires a principle of unity constitutive of it and prior to it (*Enn.* V, 1, 4–5). Prior then to Intellect, Plotinus postulates as the truly ultimate cause a principle of unity which is not itself composed, not a unified multiplicity of any sort, an absolute non-multiple, in this sense "One." This "One" Plotinus identifies with the "Good" which is described as being "beyond being in dignity and power" in Plato's *Republic* (509b).

In interpreting the cosmology of Plato's *Timaeus*, Plotinus' Platonist predecessors tended to see the three primary causes they identified (forms, demiurge, matter) as equally pre-existent and coming together to produce the world. Such is Plotinus' approach, however, that, in the last analysis, there is really only one primary cause: body presupposes soul, which presupposes Intellect, which presupposes the One. All is therefore constituted (outside time), by stages, from the One. Plotinus therefore finds himself confronted by what he regards as a classic problem of Greek philosophy, which goes back to its pre-Socratic origins, the question of how the many comes from the One (*Enn.* V, 1, 6). In Plotinian terms, this question becomes: how, in successive order, does Intellect come from the One, soul from Intellect and the world from soul?

The first stage in the eternal derivation of things from the One, the derivation of Intellect, involves difficulties in that it concerns realities beyond the reach of human thought processes and language (see below). However, generative stages at lower levels of reality suggest images. Thus substances, considered as inherent activity, give rise to secondary external activities (e.g. sun and light, fire and heat). In organisms, this productivity consequent on the intrinsic activity of a substance is associated with biological maturity (procreation). From this Plotinus supposes that a substance reaching perfection in its activity gives rise to a secondary external activity which images it; in other words, that whatever is perfect or good gives or communicates of itself. If then the One is absolute perfection of existence (as prior to all composition and dependence), it can be supposed to produce a secondary activity. This secondary activity constitutes Intellect as a potentiality for intellection rendered determinate, defined, articulated intellect, in relation to the One, thus becoming an expression or image, in intelligible multiplicity, of the One (*Enn.* V, 4, 1–2; Lloyd, 1987; Bussanich, 1988). Plotinus approaches the question of the derivation of soul in a like manner: Intellect produces soul as a secondary activity of it, a further articulation of it, and expression of it (*Enn.* V, 2, 1).

The derivation of the world from soul involves particular problems. The cosmology of the *Timaeus* can be parodied (as it was by Aristotelians, Epicureans, and Stoics) so as to make of Plato's cosmic demiurge a laboriously calculating and toiling workman. Worse still, the Gnostics considered the world to be the evil product of an ignorant and erring god who made the world in rejection of a superior world of light and knowledge. In this evil world the Gnostic felt exiled, a fragment of light seeking return to the higher world through special knowledge (*gnosis*). Plotinus reacted very strongly against this way of seeing the world and its genesis, a perversion in his view of the *Timaeus*, devoting a long work to criticism of the Gnostic approach, a work which Porphyry, in his edition, cut into four treatises, *Enn*. III, 8; V, 8; V, 5; II, 9. In *Enn*. III, 8, Plotinus suggests a very different way of seeing the production of the world. In reflecting on the relation between contemplation (knowing), action and production, he regards action and production, in the human sphere, as related to contemplation either as a by-product of, or substitute for, contemplation: we act and produce either as an expression of what we know, or to replace (and compensate for) lack of knowledge. In the structure of reality, soul is the product of the perfect knowledge in Intellect and soul in turn, a further expression of knowledge, produces the world as an expression of its knowledge (as the geometer, to use Plotinus' image, draws figures as precipitates of his thinking). The world is not an aberration, a fabrication of some ignorant and evil demon: it is the continual expression of knowledge (Deck, 1967), indeed itself a form of unconscious knowledge. More specifically, soul generates matter (*Enn*. III, 4, 1; O'Brien, 1991), a sort of ultimate indeterminacy on which soul projects intelligible structures at various levels corresponding to the levels of organization of inorganic and organic life.

The Relation between Soul and Body

Within the overall scheme of things sketched out above, we may choose a number of specific themes as examples characteristic of Plotinus' thought. In a worldview such as his, where there is so much emphasis on immaterial transcendence, an obvious problem concerns the relation between soul and body, or, more generally, the relation between intelligible and corporeal reality. Both relations are sources of difficulties in Plato's dialogues, the latter, involving the relation between the transcendent forms and the concrete things participating in the forms, appearing in the eyes of Aristotle and other critics of Plato to be an insurmountable and fatal weakness in Platonic metaphysics.

Plotinus discusses the question of the relation between soul and body in *Enn*. VI, 4–5 (see Emilsson, 1994), another treatise divided by Porphyry. Plotinus relates this question to the larger issue of the relation between intelligible and material reality and notes the error in supposing that if soul is present as one throughout extended body, if form (e.g. the form of beauty) is present as one in different (more or less beautiful) particular things, soul or form must be present *in the mode of a body* in various bodies. If soul (or form) were a body, then indeed it could not be present throughout a body or bodies without being fragmented and losing its unity. Critics of Platonism make the false assumption that soul or form is present in body in the way body is present in another body, claiming then that they cannot see how soul or form can be present in bodies. Removing the false assumption means removing the criticism. However, the question remains how soul or form is present integrally in a non-corporeal mode throughout body. Reversing perspectives, Plotinus suggests that body is present in soul (as an object is present in a hand which holds it [*Enn*. VI, 4, 7], or a net in the sea which carries it [*Enn*. IV, 3, 9]), in the sense that body is causally dependent on soul, sustained by soul, such that body shares in its different parts in the one soul or form to the extent that these parts represent different capacities for reception of the various powers or activities united in soul or form (*Enn.* VI, 4, 12).

Epistemology

The relation between divine Intellect (or Plato's demiurge) and the forms, in Plato's *Timaeus*, produced much debate among Plotinus' Platonist predecessors and contemporaries (Armstrong, 1960). If the forms are, as some supposed, the thoughts of Intellect, then this appears to rob the forms of the independent reality that Plato gives them. But if forms are separate from Intellect, as either prior or posterior to it, then this externality of the forms to Intellect raises questions as to how Intellect comes into contact with the forms. Plotinus took the position that the forms had to be the thinking of Intellect since otherwise the claim of this Intellect to complete and unerring knowledge would be undermined. In *Enn.* V, 5, 1–2, again as part of the large-scale critique of the ignorant and erring demiurge of the Gnostics, Plotinus argues this point by making use of the arguments of Skepticism as follows. If, in perception, the object is external to the perceiver, then this object is known through the mediation of sense-images whose reliability it is impossible to verify: we know things outside us as they appear to us, not as they are in themselves. The same holds if the object of thought is external to the thinking subject, which reaches this object through images. To know something, as it is in itself and without error, the object of knowledge must then be internal to the knower, identical with the knower, such that this knowledge is self-authenticating: "what it says, it is, and what it is, it says" (*Enn.* V, 5, 2, 18–21; Emilsson, 1996). Thus Intellect must be its objects of thought, the forms: the forms are the activity of Intellect, Intellect is the activity of forms. Plotinus' use of Skeptical arguments to reach a self-authenticating intellectual knowledge is found again in Augustine and in Descartes's *cogito* (O'Meara, 2000). His argument also concludes that the only form of true, infallible knowledge is the self-knowledge of Intellect (*Enn.* V, 3): other forms of knowledge, perceptual knowledge, knowledge of things external to us, have claim to knowledge to the extent that they are grounded ultimately in the absolute knowledge that is Intellect.

Ineffability

Human souls know things external to them through perceptual images, through the concepts they derive from Intellect, and through processes of reasoning, using series of premises and conclusions, which can be described as "discursive" reasoning. Intellect, as identical with its objects (the forms), has no need of images or reasonings: it has a form of thinking superior to (fallible) discursive reasoning, knowing its objects immediately, totally, unerringly. The One, as the ultimate principle presupposed by the unified multiplicity that is Intellect, is prior to and beyond the highest level of knowledge and of the knowable. The One is not a determinate multiplicity such as must be any knowable object. Unknowable as such, the One must also be ineffable, if speech is a (multiple determinate) expression of knowledge. Although the notion of an "unknown god," an ineffable Absolute, is not uncommon among Platonists and religious thinkers of his time (Mortley, 1986), Plotinus gives this notion an explanation of unprecedented clarity.

He also proposes a solution to the dilemma that ensues: how can it be that the unknowable and ineffable is, in some way, known and spoken? Plotinus interprets language about the One as language that in fact describes our own experience. Our knowledge of contingency, of dependent multiplicity, of profound need is expressed in negations of this condition, the non-multiple (the "One"), the non-needy (the "Good"), as referring to our awareness of what might ground contingency, what might fulfill our need (*Enn.* VI, 9, 3–4; V, 3, 14). We know and speak of ourselves when we speak, it might seem, of the Absolute. The same applies to accounts of the perfect knowledge possessed by Intellect: here also it is human discursive thinking that is described in its deficiency, the negation of which suggests a higher mode of knowing, non-discursive knowing unseparated from its objects. Philosophy in general, then, in dealing with questions concerning higher forms of existence and ultimate principles, works with ordinary experience which furnishes multiple images and signs of what is higher and more fundamental: the world itself is an expression of the transcendent. Language communicates discursive knowledge among souls who are puzzled, confused, misled; there is no need of language when the knowledge possessed by Intellect is reached.

Evil

"Whence come evils?" This question occurs very frequently in philosophy and in religious thought in Plotinus' period. Gnosticism provided a dramatic and radical answer: an evil god made this world in which we live exiled in it as fragments of the good. The position in Plato seemed unclear. Some of Plotinus' Platonist predecessors found an evil world-soul in Plato; others, encouraged by Aristotle's reports, saw matter as the source of evil. Plotinus argues for the latter position in *Enn.* I, 8. If the concept of "good" is to be identified with what is non-deficient, perfect, then there is no evil (the opposite of the good) in the One, in Intellect and in soul prior to its presence in the world. Matter, however, as the absolutely indeterminate, deficient as such of all form and structure, corresponds to the notion of evil. Matter thus is primary evil. Secondary evils (natural and moral) derive from matter, as source of deficiencies of form (natural evils, such as diseases) or as the source of soul's infatuation with what is inferior to it.

Plotinus' Platonist successors in late antiquity on the whole rejected his answer to the question of evil, which involved, it seemed, major problems (O'Brien, 1996): how, for example, could matter, as absolute evil, be also the product of soul, itself deriving from the absolute Good, the One? How could soul be corrupted by what is inferior to it? What of soul's freedom? These questions were posed in particular by Proclus (412–85), whose work *On the Existence of Evils*, transmitted in various versions and excerpts in the Middle Ages, became a major source in debates over the problem of evil.

Beauty

At the end of *Enn*. I, 8, Plotinus insists that if matter is absolute evil, it is nevertheless covered in golden chains, i.e. overlaid with forms, with the diversified and rational structure that makes the world. We are surrounded by beauty that reminds us of the Good. As a Platonist, Plotinus is deeply interested in the phenomenon of beauty, in our reaction to beauty, and in what this means for human existence (Armstrong, 1975). In his first writing (*Enn*. I, 6), he criticizes the Stoic claim that what makes something beautiful is a symmetry of parts with the addition of good color, on the grounds that there can be "simple" beauties (sounds, colors) not involving symmetry. For him, what makes something beautiful is form, all form as present in matter. Form present in matter derives from soul inspired by the transcendent forms, which therefore correspond, for Plotinus, to what beauty in itself is. We notice that he does not speak of a form of beauty, as does Plato, but of all transcendent form as beauty, of Intellect as beauty. This he argues in particular in *Enn*. V, 8, again in opposition to Gnostic attitudes. The strength of our reaction to the presence of beauty, the love that it inspires, expresses, as in Plato, soul's recollection of a higher life and desire for it. In the experience of perceptible beauty, soul discovers itself, since it also originates from Intellect which is the forms. Artists can express in their work their knowledge of the beauty that is Intellect (*Enn*. V, 8, 1).

What is the relation between beauty and the Good? Another characteristic problem in the interpretation of Plato, this question finds a clear answer in Plotinus' approach: if beauty is the forms, then beauty is subordinated (since Intellect is) to the Good (the One). However, Plotinus avoids separating too strongly the beautiful from the good, describing beauty as the light, the "grace" of the Good (*Enn*. VI, 7, 22, and 32). Our love of what is beautiful is thus, more profoundly, the desire of the Good as it manifests itself in the light of the forms and in their presence in formed things in this world.

The Descent and Return of the Soul

Plato's dialogues seem to suggest different ways of seeing the descent of soul in the body and presence in the body. On the one hand, soul seems, in the *Timaeus*, to have a positive role in organizing body, giving it order and value. On the other hand, the descent of soul, in the *Phaedo* and *Phaedrus*, seems to be regarded in a negative way, as a fall, a punishment, and imprisonment of soul. Plotinus emphasizes (*Enn*. IV, 8) the positive role of soul in the world (both world-soul and the souls of individual bodies): it is characteristic of soul to seek to express its knowledge in giving order to matter. However, souls can also "fall," in the sense that, forgetting their origin and source of inspiration (Intellect), to which they remain linked, even if unconsciously (*Enn*. IV, 8, 8), they can become infatuated with lower things, material products to which they assign value although this value derives from soul. Such souls Plotinus compares to Narcissus, in love with his own image in water (*Enn*. I, 6, 8). Forgetting its own nature and value, soul assimilates itself to what is inferior. The "self," a theme developed by Plotinus (O'Daly, 1973), is mobile (*Enn*. III, 4): it can fix itself at different levels depending on the life it chooses, a higher life, that of Intellect, or a degrading life tending to the nothingness and obscurity of matter.

The task of philosophy is to bring soul back, through discursive reasoning, to an awareness of its origin and value. The problems discussed in philosophy reflect soul's confusion and ignorance about itself and the world; clearing up these problems means changing soul's relation to itself and its surroundings, a stage in a return of soul to what can respond to its needs and desires, the life of Intellect and, ultimately, union with the One. However, reasoning is not enough. Plotinus speaks also of the need for "civic" virtues, i.e. the four cardinal virtues (wisdom, courage, moderation, and justice) of Plato's *Republic* (428b–444a), which he interprets as concerning the appropriate relation of soul to its bodily affairs, a relation requiring practice (*Enn.* I, 4). Beyond these virtues Plotinus describes "purificatory" virtues (cf. Plato, *Phaedo* 69b–c) which concern soul's turning towards a higher life, a life on the level of Intellect. Once such a life is achieved (he refers to his living it in *Enn.* IV, 8, 1), these virtues are no longer required, no more than philosophical (discursive) arguments leading toward knowledge are required, since the life of Intellect is a life of perfect knowledge. However, since Intellect derives its perfection and value from the One that transcends it, Plotinus refers also to a transition to an ultimate state of unification with the One, a state beyond description and thought in which the desire of the Good is fulfilled supremely (*Enn.* VI, 7, 34, and 36). Plotinus' reflection on the ascent of the soul, through stages, to union with the Absolute had considerable impact, in its ideas and language, on later writers who gave expression to religious mysticism. We should however note that, for Plotinus, this ascent required philosophy, even if philosophy must in turn be transcended.

Bibliography

Editions and translations

Plotinus (1956–62) *Plotins Schriften*, 2nd edn, ed. R. Harder, R. Beutler, and W. Theiler. Hamburg: Meiner (the treatises published in chronological order, with a good German translation).

Plotinus (1966–88) *Plotinus*, ed. A. H. Armstrong. Cambridge, MA: Harvard University Press (complete Greek text with English translation in seven vols; vol. I contains Porphyry's *Life of Plotinus*).

Individual treatises published separately, with commentary, include at present (in English): III, 5 (by A. Wolters, 1984), III, 6 (by B. Fleet, 1995), IV, 3, 1–8 (by W. Helleman-Elgersma, 1980), V, 1 (by M. Atkinson, 1983), V, 3 (by H. Oosthoot, 1991) and VI, 9 (by P. Meijer, 1992); (in French) I, 8 (by D. O'Meara, 1999), II, 4 (by J-M. Narbonne, 1993), II, 5 (by J-M. Narbonne, 1998), III, 5 (by P. Hadot, 1990), V, 3 (by B. Ham, 2000), VI, 6 (by J. Bertier et al., 1980), VI, 7 (by P. Hadot, 1988), VI, 8 (by G. Leroux, 1990), VI, 9 (by P. Hadot, 1994); (in German) III, 7 (by W. Beierwaltes, 1967), V, 3 (by W. Beierwaltes, 1991), VI, 4–5 (by C. Tornau, commentary only, 1998).

Studies

Armstrong, A. H. (1960) The background of the doctrine "that the intelligibles are not outside the intellect." In A. H. Armstrong, *Plotinian and Christian Studies*, study IV. London: Variorum, 1979.

Armstrong, A. H. (1975) Beauty and the discovery of divinity in the thought of Plotinus. In A. H. Armstrong, *Plotinian and Christian Studies*, study XIX. London: Variorum, 1979.

Armstrong, A. H. (1979) *Plotinian and Christian Studies*. London: Variorum.

Blumenthal, H. J. (1971) *Plotinus' Psychology*. The Hague: Martinus Nijhoff.

Bussanich, J. (1988) *The One and its Relation to Intellect in Plotinus*. Leiden: Brill.

Deck, J. (1967) *Nature, Contemplation and the One*. Toronto: Toronto University Press.

Emilsson, E. (1988) *Plotinus on Sense-perception*. Cambridge: Cambridge University Press.

Emilsson, E. (1994) Plotinus' ontology in Ennead VI, 4 and 5. *Hermathena*, 157: 87–101.

Emilsson, E. (1996) Cognition and its object. In L. Gerson (ed.), *The Cambridge Companion to Plotinus*, pp. 217–49. Cambridge: Cambridge University Press

Gerson, L. (1994) *Plotinus*. London: Routledge.

Gerson, L. (ed.) (1996) *The Cambridge Companion to Plotinus*. Cambridge: Cambridge University Press.

Hadot, P. (1979) Les divisions des parties de la philosophie dans l'antiquité. *Museum Helveticum*, 36: 202–23.

Lloyd, A. (1987) Plotinus on the genesis of thought and existence. *Oxford Studies in Ancient Philosophy*, 5: 155–86.

Mortley, R. (1986) *From Word to Silence*. Bonn: Hanstein.

O'Brien, D. (1991) *Plotinus on the Origin of Matter*. Naples: Bibliopolis.

O'Brien, D. (1996) Plotinus on matter and evil. In L. Gerson (ed.), *The Cambridge Companion to Plotinus*, pp. 171–95. Cambridge: Cambridge University Press

O'Daly, G. (1973) *Plotinus' Philosophy of the Self*. Shannon: Irish University Press.

O'Meara, D. (1992) Plotinus. In F. Cranz and P. O. Kristeller (eds), *Catalogus translationum et commentariorum*, VII: 55–73. Washington, DC: The Catholic University of America Press.

O'Meara, D. (1993) *Plotinus: An Introduction to the Enneads*. Oxford: Clarendon Press.

O'Meara, D. (2000) Scepticism and ineffability in Plotinus. *Phronesis*, 45: 240–51.

Rist, J. (1967) *Plotinus: The Road to Reality*. Cambridge: Cambridge University Press.

Saffrey, H-D. (1992) Pourquoi Porphyre a-t-il édité Plotin? In L. Brisson, J-L. Cherlonneix et al. (eds), *Porphyre la vie de Plotin*, II: 31–64. Paris: Vrin.

8

Augustine, *On Free Choice of the Will* (388–395)

Evil, God's Foreknowledge, and Human Free Will

Gareth B. Matthews

The philosophy of religion, as Western philosophers conceive it today, begins with Augustine (354–430 AD). True, earlier philosophers had had interesting things to say about God, or the gods. Plato's "*Euthyphro* problem," for example, and Aristotle's proof of an Unmoved Mover certainly belong in a modern course on the philosophy of religion. But it was Augustine who first framed a whole set of interesting philosophical issues in such a way that they apply directly to the three great monotheistic religions of the West: Christianity, Judaism, and Islam.

If Augustine is the first philosopher of religion, in the modern Western sense, *On Free Choice of the Will* (or *De libero arbitrio*, hereafter *DLA*) is, one could add, the first treatise in the philosophy of religion. It remains relevant to issues covered in any standard course on the subject today, but especially to these three: (1) the problem of evil; (2) arguments for the existence of God; and (3) the problem of God's foreknowledge and human free will.

Augustine's discussion of these three topics is not the only thing that marks off *DLA* as a remarkably "modern," treatise. When Antoine Arnauld wanted to show that Descartes, in his *Meditations*, had "laid down as the basis for his entire philosophy exactly the same principle as that laid down by St Augustine," he backed up his claim with the following précis of *DLA* II, 3:

> First, if we are to take as our starting point what is most evident, I ask you to tell me whether you yourself exist. Or are you perhaps afraid of making a mistake in your answer, given that, if you did not exist, it would be quite impossible for you to make a mistake? (Descartes, 1984: 139)

The similarities and differences between Descartes's *cogito*-reasoning at the beginning of his *Second Meditation* and Augustine's *si fallor sum* ("If I am deceived, I am"; *City of God* XI, 26) are striking, but also difficult to be clear about (see Matthews,

1999: chs 2 and 3). Nor is its *cogito*-like reasoning the only feature of *DLA* that initiates what we think of as typically Cartesian ways of thinking about the mind. Thus a little later in *DLA* Augustine asks his interlocutor, Evodius, "Do you see [that everyone wants to be happy] in the same way that you see your own thoughts, of which I am completely ignorant, unless you disclose them to me" (*DLA* II, 10). Here we have the Cartesian idea of what has come to be called "privileged access," the idea that each of us has direct access to our own thoughts and feelings, but no such direct access to the thoughts or feelings of others.

Still, interesting as the Cartesian aspects of *DLA* are, its most significant contribution to philosophy lies in the way it takes up the three topics listed above. To them we now turn.

The Problem of Evil

The biblical Book of Job tells the story of an exemplary man, who comes to suffer the loss of his flocks and his children and, finally, to become afflicted with painful boils. This book cries out for a *theodicy* in the original sense of the word, that is, an explanation of how it can be that God is just (*theos*, God; *dikê*, just). Not only does Job himself suffer quite unjustly (after all, God had attested to Job's uprightness before the sufferings were allowed to begin), but Job also speaks movingly of the common human experience that bad things happen to good people and good things happen to bad people.

The problem of evil in Job, we could say, is a distribution problem. How can God, who is just, be in charge of things when the distribution of earthly goods and evils seems so poorly coordinated with human desert? There is here no question about how evil came to exist in the first place. The question that plagues Job is why people do not get what they deserve.

When we turn to Book II of Plato's *Republic* we find Socrates concerned about the mere existence of evil in the world. Here, for the first time, we have a discussion of what we might call "the metaphysical problem of evil." The metaphysical problem does not arise unless one takes a general, or cosmic, perspective, and supposes that there is some agent or principle that is responsible for everything. If that agent or principle is all good, how can there even be such a thing as evil?

Plato has his character, Socrates, solve the metaphysical problem by denying that God is responsible for everything. "Since a god is good," Socrates says,

> he is not, as most people claim, the cause of everything that happens to human beings, but of only a few things, for good things are fewer than bad ones in our lives. He alone is responsible for the good things, but we must find some other cause for the bad ones, not a god. (*Republic* II, 379c, trans. Grube)

Augustine, in his twenties, found very congenial to his own thinking a solution to the metaphysical problem of evil very much like the one Plato has Socrates suggest in the *Republic*. Augustine found this solution in the teachings of the Manicheans, who supposed there is a principle of good, or light, and a principle of darkness, or evil, and that what goes on in this world is a conflict between these two, equally potent, principles. As he tells us in Book VII of his *Confessions* and in the first book of *DLA*, the need to find a solution to the metaphysical problem of evil consonant with Christian teachings held up his acceptance of the Christian faith. As he also says in his *Confessions*, the Neoplatonist idea of evil as a deficiency, or lack, helped him to work his way through this problem.

In philosophy classes today the problem of evil is often presented as a "consistency problem." Thus it has seemed to many philosophers that the conjunction of these statements forms a contradiction:

(1)   God is all good.
(2)   God is all powerful.
(3)   There is evil.

If the conjunction of (1), (2), and (3) is indeed a contradiction, then, to speak coherently, we must give up at least one of these statements. The Manicheans can be understood to have given up both (1) and (2) by supposing that there are two equally powerful cosmic principles, one of good and the other of evil. The Hellenistic philosopher, Plotinus, and his followers, the Neoplatonists, with their idea that evil is not a "substance" but only a deficiency, a lack, can be understood to have given up (3). (Christian Scientists today seem to make a similar move.)

Some philosophers have pointed out that there really is no formal contradiction in the conjunction of the three statements above. To get a contradiction we need to add a "bridge principle," such as this one:

(4)   If there were an all-good and all-powerful being, there would be no evil.

Is (4) true? To defeat the problem of evil, construed now as the claim that (1), (2), (3), and (4) are jointly contradictory, it would be sufficient to make plausible the suggestion that even an all-good, all-powerful being might have had sufficient reason to allow the existence of evil. Taking a cue from Augustine's *DLA*, some have suggested "the free-will defense." The idea is that even an all-good, all-powerful being might conceivably want to create moral agents who have "free choice of the will," and hence the opportunity to make evil choices, as well as good ones. So long as this is a conceptual possibility, (4) is not a conceptual truth and so the Consistency Problem is dissolved.

The problem of evil is Augustine's major preoccupation in *DLA*. Evodius begins the dialogue with the request, "Tell me whether God is not the author [or cause, *auctor*] of evil." Not surprisingly, Augustine insists that

(5) God is not the cause of evil.

Yet he and Evodius agree that

(6)   Everything that exists, is from God.

Assumed throughout is this:

(7)   Evil exists.

If, now, (6) means the same thing as

(6*)   God is the cause of everything that exists

we can conclude:

(8)   God is the cause of evil

which contradicts (5). To avoid this unwanted conclusion Augustine tries to show how we might accept (6) and reject (6*) by appeal to this idea:

(9)   An act of free will is sometimes the uncaused cause of sin, and so, of evil in the world.

He argues most directly for (9) near the end of Book III in this passage: "But what cause of the will could there be, beyond the will itself? The cause is either the will itself, and it is not possible to go back to the root of the will, or else it is not the will, and there is no sin" (III, 17). Still, one might ask, why might God, an all-good and all-powerful being, allow there to be free will, if it is sometimes the uncaused cause of sin? The answer has to be that

(10)   Free will is a good.

In Book II at 19.50.192 Augustine argues for (10) by developing the idea of an "intermediate good" (something necessary for right living, that, however, can also be used for evil). It is this "free-will defense," as it is called today, that gives Augustine a principled way to deny the "bridge principle," (4), and, in this way, to dissolve the problem of evil.

Arguments for the Existence of God

Why should anyone want to offer an argument for the existence of God? Pascal thought it a blasphemy even to try. Other philosophers have puzzled over whether finding a successful proof would make faith unnecessary, and whether a failure to find a successful proof would make persisting faith unreasonable.

Quoting Isaiah 7:9 as "Unless you believe you shall not understand," Augustine develops the influential idea that a philosopher who is also a religious believer might have "faith in search of understanding." (This phrase, *fides quarens intellectum*, although apparently coined by Augustine and used by him several times, is most famous from its use by Anselm in his *Proslogion*.) Applied to the project of proving the existence of God, Augustine's idea is that one first has faith that God exists and then one sets out to show, if one can, that one's faith can be backed up by a rational proof.

The argument Augustine comes up with in Book II of *DLA* is an ancestor of Anselm's deservedly much more famous "ontological argument." Like Anselm's reasoning, Augustine's is purely *a priori*. Thus, it makes no appeal to any empirical premise, such as Aquinas's premise, "We see that some things that lack knowledge act for an end." Again, like Anselm's argument, Augustine's begins with a definition-like characterization of God. But, whereas Anselm begins with the idea that to be God would be to be *something than which nothing greater can be conceived*, Augustine begins with this claim: "God is something higher than our minds, which is also something than which nothing is higher still" (*DLA* II, 6).

Anselm argues by *reductio ad absurdum* to the conclusion that God is something that exists in reality, as well as in the understanding. By contrast, Augustine's proof is a constructive one. It begins by establishing, by reflection, that truth is more excellent than our minds. Augustine concludes that God exists, since either God is truth itself, or, if there is something even more excellent than truth, that will be God (*DLA* II, 6).

Augustine fails to discuss the possibility that there could be an endless succession of entities, each more excellent than its predecessors, and all more excellent than our minds. Otherwise the proof is successful, at least in its own terms. Still, it is worth reflecting on why the proof is less satisfying than Anselm's ontological argument, which, no doubt, it helped inspire.

Anselm's powerful characterization of God, "something than which nothing greater can be conceived," invites subsidiary proofs that God has all the "infinite attributes" (omnipotence, omniscience, omnibenevolence, etc.) traditionally assigned to him. By contrast, Augustine's proof leaves open the possibility that God is simply truth, which seems rather less satisfying. Christians may point out that Jesus, the Son of God, said he was the truth. But what he is reported to have said is more fully, "I am the way, and the truth, and the life" (John 14:6).

Still, despite the rather unappealing character of Augustine's proof, his idea of faith in search of understanding is a powerful one. Moreover, his audacious project of developing purely *a priori* reasoning to establish God's existence might have seemed even more impressive if it had not been so obviously improved on by Anselm.

God's Foreknowledge and Human Free Will

Perhaps the most richly argued issue in *DLA* is a problem raised by Evodius near the beginning of Book III. It is the problem of how anyone, say, Adam, can sin of his own free will, if God knows already beforehand that he will do so. Although this problem has antecedents in worries about prophecy and free will known to Augustine through Cicero, it is Augustine himself who establishes this difficulty as a primary problem in the philosophy of religion. Moreover, Augustine's discussion of the problem and his suggestions of possible ways of handling it are so fertile that they foreshadow many of the subsequent attempts to deal with it in the ensuing sixteen centuries.

Evodius begins the discussion by pointing out, quite reasonably, that, unless the movement of one's will to a given object of desire were voluntary and within our power, one would not earn praise for turning to a higher object of desire, or deserve blame for turning toward a lower object (*DLA* III, 1). But since God foreknew, he continues, that Adam would sin, "what God foreknew must necessarily come to pass." He adds: "How then is the will free when there is apparently this unavoidable necessity?" (III, 2).

Here is one way of reconstructing Evodius's reasoning:

(11)   Adam is not blameworthy unless Adam sinned of his own free will.
(12)   God foreknew that Adam would sin.
(13)   If God foreknew that Adam would sin, then Adam did not sin of his own free will.

Therefore,

(14)   Adam did not sin of his own free will.

Therefore,

(15)   Adam is not blameworthy.

Augustine sums up the problem this way: "You wonder how it can be that these two propositions are not contradictory and incompatible, namely that God has foreknowledge of all future events, and that we sin voluntarily and not by necessity" (III, 3).

To this problem Augustine mounts a number of ingenious and important responses. Here are some of them.

(a) *What about God's foreknowledge of his own actions?*

Evodius says that he has even greater confidence that God knows of his own future deeds than that he has foreknowledge of ours. If God's foreknowledge of Adam's actions precluded Adam's acting of his own free will, God's foreknowledge of his own acts should equally preclude their being free. But surely God does act freely.

In response to this further problem Evodius tries out the suggestion that God, being eternal and immutable, does not act in time at all. But then God, being outside time, would not really have *fore*-knowledge.

Evodius seems not willing to accept this solution. God "eternally had that foreknowledge," he says, "but I agree that he has it now, if indeed it is to happen so" (III, 3).

(b) *God can foreknow that we have free will to do something*

Perhaps Augustine's most ingenious response to the problem of God's foreknowledge and human free will begins with the claim that having free will is just having within ourselves the power to will (III, 4). Now God, Augustine goes on, also has foreknowledge of our power to will. "My power," he concludes, "is not taken from me by God's foreknowledge. Indeed I shall be more certainly in possession of my power because he whose foreknowledge is never mistaken, foreknows that I shall have the power" (III,

3). This move is brilliant. Instead of letting God's foreknowledge be a threat to human free will, Augustine argues that it can be a guarantor of the free will. If God foreknew that Adam would sin of his own free will, then his free will was actually vouchsafed by God's foreknowledge!

(c) *Necessity* de re *and necessity* de dicto

In *DLA* III, 4, Augustine suggests an interesting analogy between (veridical) memory and foreknowledge. Just as my recollection that something happened does not compel it to have happened, he says, so God's foreknowledge that something will happen does not compel it to happen either. The idea seems to be that, even though there is a necessary connection between veridically seeing that an event has actually happened or will actually happen and its actually happening, the sight itself does not turn the event seen into a necessary happening. This analogy may suggest to the reader a distinction that Boethius introduces into the discussion of foreknowledge and free will just over a century later. We can illustrate the distinction this way:

(16)   Necessarily, if God foreknows that Adam will sin, then Adam will sin.
(17)   If God foreknows that Adam will sin, then, necessarily, Adam will sin.

The difference between (16) and (17) can be displayed by affirming this as well:

(18)   God foreknows that Adam will sin.

From the conjunction of (17) and (18) we may validly infer:

(19)   Necessarily, Adam will sin.

And (19) certainly seems to rule out Adam's sinning of his own free will. By contrast, the conjunction of (16) and (18) yields only

(20)   Adam will sin

which is no problem for Adam's free will.

When the necessity operator governs the whole conditional, as in (16), what the conditional expresses is a necessary connection between the antecedent and the consequent. The idea is that the antecedent cannot be true unless the consequent is also true. Later medieval philosophers called this necessity *de dicto*. But when the necessity operator is placed inside the conditional, so that it governs the consequent in particular, the whole conditional tells us that some necessary state of affairs will hold, provided that the antecedent is satisfied. Later medieval philosophers called this necessity *de re*.

What Boethius sees clearly, but Augustine only begins to see, is that one can accept a doctrine of divine foreknowledge and suppose that it yields only statements of *de dicto* necessity, and not statements of *de re* necessity, where *de dicto* necessity is, apparently, no threat to human free will at all.

Bibliography

Editions and translations

Augustinus (1956) *De libero arbitrio libri tres*, ed. Guilemus M. Green. *Corpus scriptorum ecclesiasticorum*, vol. 74. Vienna: Hoelder-Pichler-Tempsky (the best Latin text available).
Augustine (1984) *City of God*, trans. H. Bettenson. Harmondsworth: Penguin.
Augustine (1993) *On Free Choice of the Will*, trans. Thomas Williams. Indianapolis, IN: Hackett.

Studies and references

Descartes, René (1984) *The Philosophical Writings of Descartes*, vol. 2, trans. J. Cottingham, R. Stoothoff, and D. Murdoch. Cambridge: Cambridge University Press.
Fischer, John Martin (ed.) (1989) *God, Foreknowledge, and Freedom*. Stanford, CA: Stanford University Press.
Matthews, Gareth B. (1992) *Thought's Ego in Augustine and Descartes*. Ithaca, NY: Cornell University Press.
Matthews, Gareth B. (ed.) (1999) *The Augustinian Tradition*. Berkeley, CA: University of California Press.
Oppy, Graham (1995) *Ontological Arguments and Belief in God*. Cambridge: Cambridge University Press.
Peterson, Michael L. (ed.) (1992) *The Problem of Evil: Selected Readings*. Notre Dame, IN: University of Notre Dame Press.
Plato (1992) *Republic*, trans. G. M. A. Grube, rev. C. D. C. Reeve. Indianapolis, IN: Hackett.
Stump, E. and Kretzmann, N. (eds) (2001) *The Cambridge Companion to Augustine*. Cambridge: Cambridge University Press.

9

Augustine, *Confessions* (ca. 400)

Real-life Philosophy

Scott MacDonald

In the *Confessions* we meet a great mind in an extraordinarily personal way. The intimacy of the encounter and the passion, energy, and humanity of the man it reveals have drawn readers to the *Confessions* in every generation since Augustine's own. Augustine (354–430 AD) wrote the work sometime between 397 and 401, in his mid-forties, just a short time after becoming Bishop of Hippo in northern Africa. Reflecting on the work thirty years later he tells us:

> The thirteen books of my *confessions* concern both my bad and my good actions, for which they praise our just and good God. In so doing they arouse the human mind and affections toward him. As far as I am concerned, they had this effect upon me in my writing of them, and still do when I read them now . . . The first ten books were written about myself; the last three about holy scripture. (*Retractationes* II, vi, 32; in Augustine, 1997: 36)

Augustine's Life Story: Books I–X

In Books I–IX Augustine records the story of the first thirty-three years of his life, from his birth in 354 until the death of his mother shortly after his baptism as a Catholic Christian in 387. It is largely a record of intellectual and spiritual restlessness. Augustine portrays himself as the prodigal son of the gospel story. He turns his back on God and wanders far from his true home in search of a life of his own making. It is a life – as he describes it in retrospect – given over to sensual pleasures and personal ambitions, a life in which he finds worldly success but ultimately only confusion and emptiness. Like the prodigal, he finally returns, broken and humbled, to the loving God whom he had forsaken but who had never let go of him.

The wanderings and return of the prodigal Augustine provide a general account of his first thirty-three years: his early education at home in Thagaste (Book I), his secondary schooling, adolescence, and early adulthood in Madaura and Carthage (Books

II–III), and his career as a teacher of rhetoric, first in north Africa and then at Rome and Milan (Books IV–VIII). They describe his love of the poetry of Virgil (Book I), the passion for philosophy that Cicero inspired in him (Book III), his decade-long commitment to but eventual disaffection for the Manichean religion (Books III–V), his encounter in Milan with the preaching of Ambrose and with Platonist philosophy (Books VI–VII), and his conversion to Catholic Christianity and his reading of the apostle Paul and the Psalms (Books VII–IX).

Against this backdrop of occupations, travels, and literary encounters Augustine tells the story that really interests him: the story of his own inner intellectual and spiritual journey. The telling of his life story is dominated by introspective examination of his beliefs, desires, motivations, questions, difficulties, and longings. Indeed, many of the events in his narrative seem to have been included not primarily because of their importance in the grand scheme of his life but because of what they can be made to reveal about the state of his soul at particular times or about the human condition in general. He tells a story of stealing pears from an orchard as an adolescent in the company of a group of boys. The description of the event itself is brief and colorless, and to all appearances the thievery is a relatively harmless piece of adolescent mischief. Augustine uses it, however, to introduce a brilliant and searching examination of his own motives at the time and, more generally, of the kinds of motivation that cause and explain human behavior, especially morally bad behavior (II, iv, 9ff; unless indicated otherwise, all references hereafter are to the *Confessions*).

Similarly, Augustine tells us of the death of a friend in Thagaste near the beginning of his teaching career. We learn very little about the person – Augustine does not even mention his name – but Augustine provides a detailed and moving account of his own grief and subsequent depression. Moreover, his scrutiny of his own despair at the time leads to a more general discussion of the nature of human companionship, the psychological and moral roles it plays in human life, and the corresponding depths and perversities of the love it can elicit (III, iv, 7ff).

It is no doubt this relentless and sometimes ruthless soul-searching that leaves us feeling as if we are acquiring a deeply personal and intimate understanding of Augustine himself. The stance Augustine has chosen to take as author heightens the sense of intimacy the text conveys. The *Confessions* are addressed to God; they are Augustine's confessions *to God*. Prayerful confession before God is by its very nature intensely private. In the *Confessions*, then, Augustine invites us to be silent observers of his most intimate conversations with God about the most personal matters in Augustine's life. We are allowed to be, perhaps even lured into being, voyeurs. And once we have watched these confessions, we feel as if we know Augustine in ways that one rarely knows another human being.

The narrative of Augustine's life story ends in Book IX with events that occurred in 387. He has become a Catholic Christian and been baptized into the church. He has been granted a momentary vision of the eternal blessedness that awaits those who will enter into eternal life in God's presence. The prodigal son has returned home. The restless heart has found rest in its creator, in the God in whose image Augustine himself has been made. In many ways it is a fitting ending to the story, except for the fact that these last events occur when Augustine is only thirty-three years old. That is to say, the narrative of Augustine's life ends before his return to Africa to establish a monastic community, before his ordination to the priesthood, and before his elevation to the bishopric at Hippo – a full decade before the writing of the *Confessions*.

It would be a mistake, however, to conclude that our acquaintance with Augustine is thereby limited to his first thirty-three years, for two main reasons. First, although Book X contains no narrative account of events in Augustine's life from the years following the vision at Ostia, Augustine clearly intends in that book to bring the story of his life up to date. He does that, characteristically, not by describing activities in his present life but by revealing the present state of his soul. "My love for you, Lord, is not an uncertain feeling but a matter of conscious certainty" (X, vi, 8; Augustine, 1991: 183). But Augustine is still a pilgrim and still in need of God's help:

> When at last I cling to you with my whole being there will be no more anguish or labor for me . . . But now it is very different . . . Joys over which I ought to weep do battle with sorrows that should be matter for joy, and I know not which will be victorious . . . This is agony, Lord, have pity on me! It is agony! See, I do not hide my wounds; you are the physician and I am sick; you are merciful, I in need of mercy. (X, xxviii, 39; Augustine, 1997: 262)

Over the last dozen or so chapters of Book X Augustine goes on to examine himself and confess both the sins with which he continues to struggle and the mercy of God in which he finds hope: "Many and grave are [my] infirmities, many and grave; but wider-reaching is your healing power" (X, xliii, 69; Augustine, 1997: 283).

Second, the *Confessions* reveals the Augustine of his mid-forties in so far as it is he who has been our guide through the life of the younger man. Augustine's depiction of his life story is never merely descriptive: in every scene and at every stage of the account, he explores, explains, and evaluates his former life from the perspective and with the knowledge and commitments of the older person he has become. As a result, by the end of Book X we have come to understand the man who is telling the story as much as we have the man on whom it has focused. We know what and how the Augustine of the late 390s thinks, we know his loves and his longings, his fears and his frustrations. Over the course of these ten books we have come to see the world through the older man's eyes.

Life Story Put to Good Purpose

What strikes us first about the *Confessions* is the life story. But Augustine writes about himself not merely to tell us who he was or what he has now become. As he tells us in the *Retractationes*, he intends the account of his good and bad actions to arouse the human mind and affections – his own mind and affections and those of his readers – towards God. Of course he is aware that these confessions are not private. They are, then, an acknowledgment before others of God's merciful and providential activity on his behalf.

In a spirit of thankfulness let me recall the mercies you lavished on me, O my God; to you let me confess them. May I be flooded with love for you until my very bones cry out, "Who is like you, O Lord?" Let me offer you a sacrifice of praise, for you have snapped my bonds. How you broke them I will relate, so that all your worshippers who hear my tale may exclaim: "Blessed be the Lord, blessed in heaven and on earth, for great and wonderful is his name." (VIII, i, 1; Augustine, 1997: 184)

Augustine sees another kind of instrumental value in the telling of his story: he intends to be helping us to uncover, and see clearly, deep and unchanging truths about the nature of reality. He intends his life story to be a vehicle for philosophical and theological reflection. These reflections emerge both in relatively brief, narrowly focused vignettes and in broad themes and arguments that span the entire work.

Particular events in his life are occasions for exploring particular philosophical issues: the theft of the pears introduces perplexing questions about human motivations and the sources of human action (Book II); his encounter with academic skepticism leads to an examination of the nature of knowledge and belief (Books V–VI); his encounter with Platonism prompts metaphysical and cosmological reflection (Book VII); his climactic moral struggle in the Milanese garden evokes a profound account of the nature of the will and of moral identity in the face of inner conflict (Book VIII). These vignettes and many of the others that are sprinkled throughout the *Confessions* stand as compelling pieces of philosophical analysis, each in its own right. If the *Confessions* were no more than a collection of these pieces, it would have significant philosophical value.

But the *Confessions* is not merely a collection of philosophically charged vignettes. Augustine believes that in his own experiences and in God's persistent and merciful dealings with him one can discern the story of God's relation to all people, indeed to all of the vast created universe. His own life is a microcosm of the universe and, as such, can be a vehicle for expressing a broad and integrated philosophical account of reality.

Augustine begins the *Confessions* with the idea that will be the dominant theme of the work: "You stir [human beings] to take pleasure in praising you, because you have made us for yourself, and our heart is restless until it rests in you" (I, i, 1; Augustine, 1991: 3). Wandering, confusion, discord, dissipation – restlessness is the human condition apart from God. That restlessness grounds the universal human desire for happiness: everyone seeks happiness by seeking to obtain the highest good. But not all discover what the highest good is, where it is to be found, or how to attain it. In Augustine's own case, the search for happiness is deliberate and overtly intellectual. At eighteen years of age he read Cicero's *Hortensius* and reports having been set ablaze by it with a love for wisdom (III, iv, 7–8). As he conceives of it, wisdom is the key to happiness – it is the truth about the highest good, the knowledge and possession of which constitute the happy life. Cicero inspires Augustine to love wisdom and to seek it – to be a philosopher.

Augustine first believed that he would find wisdom in Manicheanism, and he later considered seriously the claims of academic skepticism and Platonism. It is finally in a Christianity imbued with Platonism that he found it (VII, x, 16ff). But to have discovered that wisdom is to be found in Christianity is to have become convinced that

Christianity's understanding of the fundamental nature of reality and the place of human beings in it is the correct one. Augustine's intellectual journey essentially consists in his coming to understand and articulate for himself a compelling Christian cosmology, metaphysics, epistemology, and ethics.

Augustine's Understanding of Reality

Augustine's search for wisdom was driven primarily by three related questions: (1) What is the nature of the divine? (2) How are human beings related to it? And (3) what explains the existence of evil in the world? Part of the attraction of Manicheanism for the young Augustine was its tidy answers to these questions. The Manichees were cosmological dualists. They held that ultimate reality consists of two divine beings, the highest, good god and an opposing force of darkness and evil. In a primal cosmic conflict, the evil force captured a portion of the good god's substance and trapped it in matter, thereby bringing into existence the corporeal world. Human beings, too, are a result of this conflict: they contain within themselves a portion of the good god's substance but are also partly constituted by and instruments of the evil force that battles the good. According to Manicheanism, therefore, evil is part of the deep and enduring fabric of the cosmos, and the moral evil in human lives is an unavoidable part of their very nature as corporeal beings.

Over time Augustine became dissatisfied with this account and, finally, with the help of Platonist arguments, he came to see it as demonstrably false. Only that which is the highest good, that than which nothing better can be thought, can be god; and only that which is incorruptible and inviolable can be the highest good. The Manichean concept of a god who is the highest good but who is also subject to attack and corruption at the hands of an opposing force is incoherent (VII, i, 1–ii, 3). In a dramatic series of intellectual breakthroughs Augustine comes to see that only that which truly *is*, the being of which is utterly self-sufficient, independent, unchanging, and the source of all existence that is distinct from itself, can be incorruptible. Only that which truly *is*, therefore, can be the highest good; the supreme being and the highest good must be one and the same. Augustine came to believe that that being is the god identified and described in the Christian scriptures, the god whose name is "I am who am (*ego sum qui sum*)" (VII, x, 16ff).

Augustine's new-found Christian Platonism therefore gave him a defensible and deeply explanatory cosmology and metaphysics. God is being itself (*esse ipsum*), the single self-sufficient, eternal, and immutable ultimate reality. Everything else in the universe is created by God out of nothing and depends on God for its being. There can be no ultimate reality in the universe opposed to God nor any independent material on which God relies in creating other things – since God is being itself, anything distinct from and independent of God would have to be non-being, that is, non-existent, nothing at all. Human beings, therefore, are creatures and as such are mutable and hence corruptible; they are not themselves divine and possess no portion of the indivisible divine substance.

This sort of cosmological monism that sees God as the single ultimate source of all reality allowed Augustine to escape the incoherence of Manichean dualism and provided him with an alternative understanding of how human beings are related to the divine. But it might seem to have made his goal of explaining the existence and origin of evil unattainable. If everything that exists either is God or comes from God, and if God is the highest good and so neither does nor makes anything evil, then it seems that there can be no evil. Augustine, who never doubted that there is evil in the world, seems to have found this the most troubling difficulty of all (VII, iii, 4–5).

His resolution of the difficulty depended on his working out two of his most famous philosophical views. First, he argued that evil is not a substance or nature but a corruption or a privation in a nature. God creates substances or natures, and each substance or nature is good in so far as it exists. This allowed Augustine to claim that evil was no part of God's original creation. But if God did not create it, how did evil arise? Augustine claims that evil first arose as a result of the free choices of rational creatures, free choices that are disordered acts of will and corruptions in the rational natures in which they occur. All evil, he maintained, can be understood as either sin (evil free choice) or the consequences of sin, which include both God's just punishment of sin and sin's own debilitating effects on individual sinners and the human race (VII, iii, 5ff; xii, 18ff).

On Augustine's view, the debilitating effects of sin include difficulty in discerning what is good and, when human beings succeed in discerning the good, inability to do it. Augustine's own experience illustrates these points. On the one hand, his intellectual confusion about the divine nature is deeply rooted and the source of virtually all his philosophical and moral struggles (V, x, 19). That confusion is finally remedied only when God actively comes to his aid. "When I first came to know you, you raised me up to make me see that what I saw was Being" (VII, x, 16; Augustine, 1991: 123). On the other hand, having seen God and become certain that happiness is to be found with him, Augustine finds himself unable to remain stable in his love for God until finally he casts himself on God's grace, and God responds by healing and strengthening his will (VIII, xi, 27ff). God's grace made available to human beings through the incarnation of the second person of the Trinity, the divine wisdom itself, is the path that leads prodigal sinners back to God.

The Rest of the *Confessions*: Books XI–XIII

Augustine's claim in the *Retractationes* that the last three books of the *Confessions* are about holy scripture might seem overly general. They are in fact about only the first thirty-four verses of the book of Genesis (1: 1–2: 3). Augustine assigned profound significance to the opening chapters of Genesis. Over the course of his life he undertook five major treatments of them (*De genesi contra manichaeos* [written 388–90], *De genesi ad litteram imperfectus liber* [begun in 393–4 but left incomplete], *De genesi ad litteram* [401–15], Books XI–XIV of *City of God* [417–18], and these three books of the *Confessions*). He is convinced that they can shed crucial light on the divine nature, the divine purposes in creation, the nature and structure of the created world, the origins of evil in creaturely free choices, and ultimate human destiny.

The effect in the *Confessions* of Augustine's reflections on Genesis is to demonstrate that the outlines of God's nature and purposes that can be discerned in Augustine's life story are identical to those that are revealed to the careful interpreter of God's own word spoken through prophets and recorded in the Bible. God has made known in the scriptures and made available to everyone the very things Augustine has discovered through his own prodigal wanderings. God is the eternal and immutable source of all being. God brings the universe into existence out of nothing, simply by his own will and word. All things other than God are good but depend on God for their being; all things are therefore mutable, and, left to themselves, are subject to decay and corruption. The ultimate good for creatures with rational souls is union with God, the highest good, in love. Moreover, God provides the means whereby sinful creatures can be reconciled with God and return to the presence of their creator where they will find true fulfillment and rest.

Augustine no doubt also intends these reflections on Genesis to constitute for his readers a kind of primer in hermeneutics: he wants to show the Christians in his care how to read the scriptures and mine their rich but often hidden veins. He was convinced by his own experience of the critical importance of method and technique for interpreting the Bible. He tells us that as a youth he turned away from Catholic Christianity precisely because his first reading of the Bible had been hopelessly simplistic and had left him with only a crude and unattractive caricature of Christianity (III, v, 9). Moreover, his eventual return was made possible in large part by his learning from Ambrose and other Christian intellectuals how to distinguish various kinds and levels of meaning in the biblical text (VI, iv, 6). The holy scriptures are a repository of divine truth, but they must be read with care, sophistication, and humility.

Confessions XI–XIII are a *tour de force* of Augustine's hermeneutical dexterity and resourcefulness. He reads the text of Genesis with a keen eye both for the puzzles and difficulties that might arise for a philosophically minded reader and for indications of the lineaments of the systematic doctrine – the divine truth – that he believes underlies and unifies all of scripture and makes Christianity the true wisdom. For example, virtually all of Book XI is given over to a brilliant series of reflections prompted by the first clause of Genesis's first verse: "*In the beginning* God created heaven and earth." Augustine imagines an intelligent reader wondering what God was doing *before* he made heaven and earth. Augustine takes the puzzle seriously and proposes what he takes to be a philosophically satisfying reply. God is eternal and hence cannot be said to exist temporally prior to his creating of heaven and earth.

> It is not in time that you precede times . . . In the sublimity of an eternity which is always in the present you are before all things past and transcend all things future . . . Your "years" neither go nor come. Ours come and go so that all may come in succession. All your "years" subsist in simultaneity. (XI, xiii, 16; Augustine, 1991: 230)

In fact, time is among the things that the eternal and immutable God creates; it is a creature just as the things that exist in time are, things whose being is consequently unstable and mutable. Augustine goes on to inquire about the nature of time. "What is time? Who can explain this easily and briefly? Who can comprehend this even in thought so as to articulate the answer in words?" (XI, xiv, 17; Augustine, 1991: 230). Augustine's elaborate development of the puzzles surrounding the nature of time and temporal experience is justifiably among the most famous pieces of philosophical reflection in all of his writings.

In Book XIII Augustine's reading of the opening verses of Genesis in light of Christian doctrine allows him to find levels of meaning that might otherwise go unnoticed.

> Here in an enigmatic image I discern the Trinity, which you are, my God . . . Where the name of God occurs, I have come to see the Father who made these things; where the "Beginning" is mentioned, I see the Son by whom he made these things. Believing that my God is Trinity, in accordance with my belief I searched in God's holy oracles and found your Spirit to be borne above the waters. There is the Trinity, my God – Father, Son, and Holy Spirit, Creator of the entire creation. (XIII, v, 6; Augustine, 1991: 276)

Augustine goes on in Book XIII to develop an elaborate allegorical reading of the six days of creation that presents God's creation of intellectual creatures, their fall into sin, God's plan for their reclamation and healing through the church and the sacraments, and their final salvation.

These books on holy scripture – and the *Confessions* as a whole – close with Augustine's reflection on the Sabbath rest that follows God's six-days' labor (Genesis 2: 2–3).

> This utterance in your book foretells for us that after our works which, because they are your gift to us, are very good, we also may rest in you for the sabbath of eternal life. (XIII, xxxvi, 51; Augustine, 1991: 304)

Augustine's life, and all human lives, in his view, begin in restlessness and attain complete and final rest only when they enter eternal life in God's presence.

Augustine's Legacy

Augustine's philosophical outlook has exercised as profound an influence in the Western world as that of any thinker. His account of the divine nature, human freedom, and the nature and origin of evil, and his pioneering explorations of the human mind and its inner-most motivations, have set many of the enduring problems with which philosophers in the West have continued to struggle and shaped the way in which they have thought about them. As importantly, Augustine's thought transformed Christianity. He was not the first to defend Christianity as the true wisdom sought by philosophy. But he was the thinker who, above all, and at a critical historical moment demonstrated that Christianity could be mined for philosophical insight, made to answer philosophical questions in philosophically sophisticated ways, and presented as a philosophically satisfying worldview rivaling pagan philosophical systems.

The *Confessions* is just one of many important works in which Augustine articulates his views and develops his methods and arguments. But the *Confessions* in particular helps us to see why Augustine's influence should have been so deep and lasting. The *Confessions* reveals to us not only Augustine's abstract understanding of the world. It reveals to us Augustine the thinker and Augustine immersed in the activity of thinking. The *Confessions* invites us to share in an intellectual life, to travel along with Augustine through his puzzles, difficulties, confusions, and struggles, as well as through his meandering reflections, his focused investigations, his formulating, reformulating, and fine-tuning his arguments, and his moments of discovery and illumination. Indeed, Augustine's philosophical conclusions in the *Confessions* often seem secondary in comparison with the power, honesty, and creativity of his search for them. He finds the allure of philosophical puzzles and problems irresistible. He teases them out with subtlety and flair. He patiently explores their intricacies, sources, and implications. Augustine is at his best and his most stimulating when his mind is unsettled and his thought is still in progress, when he is in the midst of philosophical inquiry and not yet at its end. The *Confessions*, with Augustine's intellectual life story at its center, allows this side of Augustine to emerge as perhaps none of his other works does. For that reason, the *Confessions* is Augustine at his best.

Bibliography

Editions and translations

Augustine (1981) *Confessiones libri XIII*, ed. L. Verheijen. *Corpus Christianorum series latina*, vol. 27. Turnhout: Brepols.

Augustine (1991) *Saint Augustine: Confessions*, trans. H. Chadwick. Oxford: Oxford University Press.

Augustine (1992) *Augustine: Confessions*, vol. 1: *Introduction and Text*, ed. J. J. O'Donnell. Oxford: Clarendon Press.

Augustine (1997) *The Confessions*, trans. M. Bouldin. Hyde Park, NY: New City Press.

Studies

Brown, P. (2000) *Augustine of Hippo: A Biography*, 2nd edn. Berkeley, CA: University of California Press.

Clark, G. (1993) *Augustine: The Confessions*. Cambridge: Cambridge University Press.

Courcelle, P. (1963) *Les Confessions de saint Augustin dans la tradition littéraire*. Paris: Études Augustiniennes.

Courcelle, P. (1968) *Recherches sur les Confessions de Saint Augustin*, 2nd edn. Paris: Boccard.

Kirwan, C. (1989) *Augustine*. London and New York: Routledge.

O'Connell, R. (1969) *St Augustine's Confessions: The Odyssey of the Soul*. Cambridge, MA: Belknap Press of Harvard University Press.

O'Donnell, J. J. (1992) *Augustine: Confessions*, vols 2–3: *Commentary on Books I–VII and Commentary on Books VIII–XIII*. Oxford: Clarendon Press.

Rist, J. M. (1994) *Augustine: Ancient Thought Baptized*. Cambridge: Cambridge University Press.

Stump, E. and Kretzmann, N. (eds) (2001) *The Cambridge Companion to Augustine*. Cambridge: Cambridge University Press.

10

Boethius, *The Consolation of Philosophy* (ca. 525)

How Far Can Philosophy Console?

John Marenbon

No classic of philosophy, with the possible exception of Plato's *Phaedo*, has a more dramatic setting than Boethius' *Consolation of Philosophy* (*De consolatione philosophiae*; henceforth *DCP*). As in the *Phaedo*, a philosopher is in prison, awaiting execution. But, whereas the *Phaedo* is dramatized biography, the *Consolation* is autobiographical. It is Boethius, the author himself, who is about to be put to death – and, indeed, after he had finished the work (ca. 525), he was executed. Boethius was an aristocratic Roman, who lived at a time when Italy was ruled by Theodoric, king of the Ostrogoths. Boethius was also a Christian, like everyone in the Italy of his time (although there remained some pagan philosophers in the schools of Athens and Alexandria). Born ca. 480, his education made him master of Latin literature and of Greek philosophy as it was practiced in the Neoplatonic schools of his day. After a life mostly devoted to scholarship and writing (especially translating Greek logical texts into Latin and providing them with commentaries, and also producing some short theological works on current controversies), Boethius became one of Theodoric's highest officials in 522. Not long afterwards came the false accusation of treason, which led to his imprisonment and death.

At first sight, the overall plan of the *Consolation* seems straightforward. Boethius begins by representing himself (henceforth "Boethius" will mean the character Boethius) as utterly dejected by his sudden change in fortune, when there enters into his prison cell a personification of Philosophy. Book I is mainly occupied by Boethius' account of his downfall; it gives him the chance to set the historical record straight and show that he has been an upright official, wrongly accused by wicked men seeking his downfall. Philosophy's task in Books II and III is to console Boethius in the accepted ancient sense of this word: not to provide sympathy but to show that the evils of which he complains are not real evils at all. By Book IV, she is able to address Boethius' specific complaint. Boethius never doubts that there is a God who rules over the universe he has established. But, at the beginning of the work (*DCP* I, pr[ose] 6, 4; Boethius, 1957: 14.6–15.10), he complains that human beings have been left outside God's rule: whereas everything else in nature follows its appointed plan, among humans the good are oppressed and the wicked triumph unpunished (*DCP* I, metrum 5). In Book IV, Philosophy explains why, despite appearances, the wicked do not prosper and the good are not oppressed. By the fifth and final book, Philosophy is ready to turn and consider a difficult and technical problem which testifies to Boethius' lifelong interest in logic: whether God's prescience is compatible with human free will.

Since the arguments in Books I–IV are mostly neither original nor, in the form they are given, very powerful, the status of the *Consolation* as a philosophical classic seems to be taken by most commentators to rest mainly on the intricate discussion in Book V, and also on the vast influence of the work on medieval philosophers and on writers such as Dante and Chaucer (for Boethius' medieval influence, see Courcelle, 1967; Gibson, 1981). Yet there may be reasons to think that the *Consolation* is less straightforward than modern readers have usually thought. They are connected with the juxtaposition of the arguments, the casting of the work in prose with verse interludes (a prosimetrum or Menippean satire) and its apparent omission of anything specifically Christian, despite its author's religious beliefs. They will be discussed after a more detailed look at the arguments of the *Consolation*.

The Argument of Books I–IV

The consolatory section of Philosophy's argument has four main phases: the first three (Phase 1: *DCP* II, pr. 1–4; Phase 2: II, pr, 5–8; Phase 3: III, pr. 1–9) are presented as increasingly powerful and harsher remedies for the sickness which Boethius is suffering as a result of his sudden downfall. The fourth phase (III, pr. 9–12) supposedly leads on from the third, but seems in fact to move in a different direction.

In Phase 1, Philosophy does not yet claim that what Boethius has lost is not valuable. Rather, she points out that he has no good grounds for complaint against fortune. Fortune, by its very nature, is unstable: Boethius had previously enjoyed good fortune and now, as to be expected, he has met with bad fortune (II, pr. 1). All in all, despite his dire circumstances now, he will have done better from fortune than most people (II, pr. 4).

So far, the only flaw Philosophy has pointed out in the goods of fortune is that they do not last (see esp. II, pr. 4, 24–9; Boethius, 1957: 25.69–88). In Phase 2, however, she goes on to give a set of arguments showing that the goods of fortune, such as riches, high office, power, and fame, are not of much value at all. Her central point is that such goods are external, by contrast with internal goods, which are qualities of a person, such as virtue or knowledge.

In Phase 3, Philosophy advances an argument which is superficially like that of Phase 2: it involves going through a list of goods of fortune (the same as before, but with pleasure added), but turns out to be different and more complex. Everybody, Philosophy claims (III, pr. 2, 2; Boethius, 1957: 38.2–6), has a natural desire for true goods and wishes to gain true happiness (*beatitudo*), the state in which he possesses every good. But, as a result of error, people try to gain the true goods by seeking in each case a corresponding false one. Sufficiency, respect, power, fame, and joy are true goods: people mistakenly seek riches, thinking that thereby they will gain sufficiency, high office in order to win respect, and so on. Philosophy supports her argument by examining each of the pairs of true and false goods in turn and showing how, in practice, people fail to gain the true good they desire by seeking and obtaining the corresponding false good.

Phase 4 is presented by Philosophy as the positive inference which can be drawn from the negative discussion of Phases 1–3. In fact, the argument here is hardly compatible with what has been said before. Philosophy now claims that there are not really a number of different true goods, which would, when combined as the parts of a whole, bring happiness. "Sufficiency," "respect," "power," "fame," and "joy" are different names for one thing (III, pr. 9, 15; Boethius, 1957: 50.35–8): people err not, as she argued earlier, by seeking a false good instead of a corresponding true one, but by seeking a plurality of goods when they should be trying to gain a single, highest good which alone will give them happiness. This one highest good, and true happiness, is God. Since he is that than which nothing better can be conceived, he is perfect good (III, pr. 10, 7–9; Boethius, 1957: 53.20–9).

Philosophy now turns to answer Boethius' initial complaint. She has already established that gaining happiness is identical to gaining goodness, and that evil people fail to gain the goodness which they naturally desire. It is easy for her, therefore, following Plato's *Gorgias*, to show that the wicked, despite appearances, lack power, because they cannot gain what they really desire, and that, just because they are wicked, they are unhappy (IV, pr. 2–3). She also, however, advances a theory of punishment which is rather different from anything in the *Gorgias*. There Socrates argued that the purpose of punishment is rehabilitation: by making wicked people better, it also makes them happier. In the *Consolation*, however, Philosophy does not suggest that punishment rehabilitates, but argues, rather, that simply by its very goodness, just punishment adds something good to evil people and so makes them happier (IV, pr. 4, 13–20; Boethius, 1957: 74.37–75.51). Philosophy also contends that the evil punish themselves, simply by being evil (IV, pr. 3, 11–12; Boethius, 1957: 70.27–71.34).

Philosophy's approach does not, however, seem to convince Boethius (IV, pr. 5), and she abandons it for a different explanation (IV, pr. 6–7). God's providence – the unfolding of which in time is called "fate" – arranges all things justly, although they may not seem to be just when judged according to humans' limited knowledge. When the wicked prosper, it is for a reason: perhaps to prevent their being more wicked, perhaps to encourage them to be better. Similarly, the oppression of good people is allowed by God when it strengthens their virtues or keeps them from vice (IV, pr. 6, 35–49; 1957: 82.118–83.164). Philosophy does not seem troubled by the deterministic implications of this approach, although she does remark that (IV, pr. 6, 16; Boethius, 1957: 80.67–9), by clinging to the center of things, God, a mind can free itself from the necessity of fate. She goes on (V, pr. 1–2) to explain that, although chance is really the unexpected coincidence of two separate causal chains (cf. Aristotle's *Physics* 2.5–6, 196b10–198a12; Aristotle, 1984: vol. 1, 335–8), the human will is not causally determined.

Divine Prescience and the Contingency of the Future (V, pr. 3–6)

There is another threat to human free will, however. Boethius points out to Philosophy (V, pr. 3) that God's prescience of the future is not compatible with it. As he puts the argument: if God foresees everything and cannot be mistaken, then what his providence foresees will happen necessarily. As a result, our wills are not free, because we are not able to will anything but what God has foreseen. Boethius goes on to make clear that the problem at issue is not that God's knowledge causes future events: even if it is granted that the events are the cause of God's knowledge, the fact that he knows what will happen in the future is enough to destroy contingency.

The main part of Philosophy's reply (V, pr. 4, 24–pr. 6, 24; Boethius, 1957: 96.64–103.83) is an ambitious argument, based on God's nature and eternity, according to which God's foreknowledge of the future is not like our knowledge of the future but like our knowledge of the present. This view is based on the principle (V, pr. 4, 25; Boethius, 1957: 96.66–97.68) that beings with different cognitive capacities will cognize the same object in different ways: for instance, an irrational animal will be limited to sense-impressions, whereas a human will be able to grasp a thing as a universal. God differs from all other things in being eternal (V, pr. 6, 2–4; Boethius, 1957: 101.5–8) – where "eternal" means, not that his existence lacks beginning and end, but that he "possesses unending life entirely and perfectly and at once." God therefore exists in an eternal presentness, and sees all things, past, present, and future, as we see what is happening at the present moment.

The *Consolation* has had a deep influence on approaches to the problem of divine prescience and human free will from the Middle Ages until today, and many analyses suggest a closer continuity between its arguments and current discussions than, perhaps, they should. One central distinction in presenting the problem is that between

(1)   Necessarily (If God knows E [an event] will happen, then E will happen)

and

(2)   If God knows E will happen, then necessarily E will happen.

(1) is true, in virtue of the meaning of "knows," but it does not entail that E happens necessarily – that is to say, it allows God's knowledge to be compatible with the contingency of what he knows; (2) by contrast, asserts that an event God knows is necessary, not contingent. But there is no reason to accept (2). Some scholars have credited the author Boethius with making the distinction between (1) and (2) when Philosophy contrasts conditional with simple necessity. Their position, however, is implausible. (1) and (2) are confused in Boethius' initial presentation of the problem, and Philosophy never tries to correct this confusion. Moreover, she argues that if something is conditionally necessary then it *is* necessary, although in a way which does not threaten freedom; by contrast, in (1), no necessity is attributed to E. Indeed, it is unlikely that Boethius had the grasp of propositional logic which would have enabled him to see a distinction such as that between (1) and (2).

This distinction does not, in fact, solve the problem of divine prescience and human free will. The real difficulty of the problem lies in the time difference between knowledge and event involved in the notion of *pre*science. Since God *fore*knows that E *will* happen, when E does take place, it will be true to say that he already *knew* it would happen. That God already *knew* this is a fact about the past which is unchangeable and so, many would argue, necessary in a special "accidental" sort of way. From

(1*)   Necessarily (If God knew *E* will happen, then *E* will happen)
and (3)   Necessarily (God knew *E* will happen) [necessarily, because it is a fact about the past and cannot be changed]

it does follow that

(4)   *E* will happen necessarily.

Since the Middle Ages, a favorite way of tackling this powerful version of the problem is by appealing to Boethius the author's view of God's eternity. He is supposed to have held that God is a-temporal: no facts about an a-temporal God are facts about the past, and so his knowledge (which cannot properly be called *fore*knowledge) is not accidentally necessary. Yet it is not completely clear that the idea put forward in the *Consolation* of God's eternal present, in which he lives his whole life at once, does amount to divine a-temporality. God is not envisaged as something like a number, to which temporal qualifications are (arguably) entirely inapplicable: he is eternal, rather, because his life does not take place sequentially through time. In any case, Boethius himself was not tackling a modal argument based on accidental necessity – a formulation which was not devised until about seven hundred years later.

Interpreting the *Consolation*

It is perfectly reasonable to read the *Consolation* in a straightforward way, as a series of arguments presented in an attractive literary form. Such a reading would point out that Philosophy gradually leads Boethius to enlightenment: the arguments earlier in the work do not give the whole truth and might be expected to conflict with those put forward later.

Nevertheless, there are grounds for thinking that Boethius' intentions were more complicated (see Marenbon, forthcoming a, b). First, there is his Christianity. The *Consolation* makes one or two implicit allusions to the Bible, but nothing it says is explicitly Christian, and some passages seem to accept doctrines which Christians reject. In particular, Book III, metrum 9 – the most solemn of all the poems, placed at the center of the work – is an epitome of Plato's *Timaeus* and, if read literally, accepts the doctrine of reincarnation. Why did a Christian writer so thoroughly exclude his religion from a work written when he was facing death? Second, there is the form of the work. Menippean satire – the mixture of prose and verse – was a genre which had been used before Boethius almost always for works which, to some extent, satirized the pretensions of learning (see Relihan, 1993). Third, there are the incongruities between the different arguments, which perhaps cannot all be explained away in terms of the character Boethius' growing understanding. As remarked above, Phase 4 of the consolatory argument is not in accord with Phases 1–3, and there is an about-turn in Book IV on the oppression of the good and the success of the wicked. The intricate argument of Book V, which is supposed to vindicate human free will, is undercut by Philosophy's final claim that God is causally responsible for everything that happens. Given these considerations, perhaps the *Consolation* should be read as a work in which Boethius the author puts forward, in good faith, the best consolation which philosophy can offer, but is aware of philosophy's limitations, and wishes his readers to be so too.

Bibliography

Editions and translations

Boethius (1957) *Philosophiae consolatio*, ed. L. Bieler. Turnhout: Brepols (*Corpus Christianorum, series latina* 94) (critical edition; a slightly revised version was issued in 1984).

Boethius (1973). *The Theological Tractates: The Consolation of Philosophy*, ed. H. F. Stewart, E. K. Rand, and S. J. Tester. Cambridge, MA: Harvard University Press (Latin text with parallel translation).

Boethius (1991) *Cicero: On Fate (*De fato*) and Boethius: The Consolation of Philosophy IV. 5–7, V (*Philosophiae consolationis*)*, ed. R. W. Sharples. Warminster: Aris and Phillips (Latin text, parallel translation and detailed commentary).

Boethius (2000) *De consolatione Philosophiae, Opuscula theologica*, ed. C. Moreschini. Munich/Leipzig: Saur (new critical edition).

Studies and references

Aristotle (1984) *The Complete Works of Aristotle*, 2 vols, ed. J. Barnes. Princeton, NJ: Princeton University Press.

Chadwick, H. (1981) *Boethius: The Consolations of Music, Logic, Theology and Philosophy*. Oxford: Oxford University Press.

Courcelle, P. (1967) *La Consolation de philosophie dans la tradition littéraire*. Paris: Études Augustiniennes.

Gibson, M. (1981) *Boethius: His Life, Thought and Influence*. Oxford: Blackwell.

Gruber, J. (1978) *Kommentar zu Boethius De Consolatione Philosophiae*. Berlin/New York: De Gruyter.

Marenbon, J. (forthcoming a) *Boethius*. New York/Oxford: Oxford University Press.

Marenbon, J. (forthcoming b) Interpreting Boethius: rationality and happiness in *De consolatione philosophiae*. In Jiyuan Yu and Jorge J. E. Gracia (eds), *Rationality and Happiness: From the Ancients to the Early Medievals*. Rochester, NY: University of Rochester Press.

Obertello, L. (1974) *Severino Boezio*. Genoa: Accademia Ligure di Scienze e Lettere.

Relihan, J. (1993) *Ancient Menippean Satire*. Baltimore, MD: Johns Hopkins University Press.

11

Anselm of Canterbury, *Proslogion* (ca. 1078)

On Thinking of That-than-which-a-Greater-Cannot-Be-Thought

Jasper Hopkins

In the history of Western philosophy no written work has proved more enticing and intriguing than has Anselm of Canterbury's (1033–1109) *Proslogion* (cited as *P*). Written, perhaps, during the time span 1077–8, it became in Anselm's own day a work of considerable controversy, being attacked by Gaunilo, a French monk of the abbey of Marmoutier. Yet, this short work, whose main argument was rejected by Thomas Aquinas, seems to have influenced Descartes and (in one way or another) Leibniz, before being indirectly attacked anew by Kant (and by a myriad of philosophers since Kant), although Hegel paid it respect. In 1960 interest in the *Proslogion* was rekindled by the publication of Norman Malcolm's essay "Anselm's Ontological Arguments." This article provoked a plethora of responses, given that Malcolm defended, as being sound, a reconstructed version of Anselm's central argument.

The title *Proslogion* means "An Address." It is a soul's meditative and prayerful addressing of God – an intoning that is reminiscent of Augustine's entreating of God in the *Confessions*. Yet, amid Anselm's sacred invokings and his quotations of scripture, there resides a philosophical argument that is both penetrating and pithy. The aim of Anselm's argument is set forth in his preface: namely, by making use of a single consideration (*unum argumentum*) to prove both that God exists and that he is of such a nature as Christians believe. Anselm makes clear that he is aiming to arrive at the same conclusions as he had set forth more elaborately in 1076 in his treatise the *Monologion*, a title meaning "Soliloquy," or "Monologue." And, additionally, he makes clear, in his *De incarnatione verbi* 6, that the orientation of the *Proslogion* parallels the orientation of the *Monologion*, inasmuch as the argument of each work proceeds by appeal to reason rather than to scriptural authority. So, in spite of the fact that the original title of the *Proslogion* was "*Faith Seeking Understanding*" (*fides quaerens intellectum*), a title drawn from the wording of Isaiah 7: 9 in the Old Latin Bible, Anselm does not (in the *Proslogion* any more than in the *Monologion*) appeal to his faith in support of his extended argumentation. Rather, he proceeds *sola ratione* and *Christo remoto*, the respective watchwords of the *Monologion* and the *Cur Deus homo*.

Accordingly, in the *Proslogion*, as its preface tells us, Anselm sets out first to prove the existence of God and subsequently to demonstrate truths about God's nature. The reasoning about God's existence is found in chapters 2–4, with the purported proof-of-existence located specifically in chapter 2. Chapter 3 then explains that not only does God (who is described as "Something than which a greater cannot be thought") exist but that he exists so really and truly that he cannot even be consistently thought not to exist. Chapter 4 then elucidates an attenuated sense in which someone who does not rightly conceive of God (as Something than which a greater cannot be thought) can, albeit improperly, conceive that he does not exist. Chapters 5–26 continue by drawing inferences about God's nature and about the relationship of human beings to God.

The fact that Anselm himself viewed the *Proslogion* as divided into these two major sections is evident not only from his preface but also from his biographer Eadmer's account, which tells us that Anselm, at a later period, gave instructions (a) that chapters 2–4 be copied together with Gaunilo's critique and with his own response to Gaunilo and (b) that these items be appended to the end of the *Proslogion* proper. An acceptable re-statement of the argument of *Proslogion*, ch. 2 is the following:

	(1)	Whatever is understood is in the understanding.
	(2)	If one understands what is being spoken of when one hears of Something than which nothing greater can be thought, then Something than which nothing greater can be thought is in the understanding.
But:	(3)	When one hears of Something than which nothing greater can be thought, one understands that which is being spoken of.
Thus:	(4)	Something than which nothing greater can be thought is in one's understanding.
	(5)	Either That than which nothing greater can be thought is in the understanding only, or That than which nothing greater can be thought is in the understanding and exists also in reality.
Assume:	(6)	That than which nothing greater can be thought is in the understanding only.
	(7)	If anything is in the understanding only and does not exist also in reality, then it can be thought to exist also in reality.
So:	(8)	That than which nothing greater can be thought can be thought to exist also in reality.
	(9)	Whatever does not exist in reality but can be thought to exist in reality can be thought to be greater than it is.
So:	(10)	That than which nothing greater can be thought can be thought to be greater than it is.
Thus:	(11)	That than which nothing greater can be thought is That than which something greater can be thought – a contradiction.
Hence:	(12)	Something than which nothing greater can be thought is in the understanding and exists also in reality.

The core strategy of the argument is that of a *reductio ad absurdum*: it enumerates two alternatives that exhaust the universe of discourse. From asserting the one alternative, it derives a contradiction, so that the other alternative must be asserted – from the asserting of which no contradiction, or logical absurdity, follows. This *reductio* strategy lends itself also to reasoning about God's nature. For example, Anselm purports to establish the fact of God's omnipotence by means of parallel reasoning (implicit in *P*, ch. 5). In short, by means of his *reductio* strategy Anselm concludes that Something than which a greater cannot be thought – i.e. God – is "whatever it is better to be than not to be" (*P*, ch. 5; this and all other citations of *P* are taken from Anselm, 1986), so that God is just, truthful, blessed, omnipotent, omniscient, omnipresent, merciful, eternal, incorporeal, simple, infinite, and so on. Indeed, he is even greater than can be thought (*P*, ch. 15), since that which is so great that it is not essentially comprehensible to finite minds is ontologically better than is that which is great in such a way that its greatness *is* essentially comprehensible to finite minds. Anselm thinks of God as conceivable but as imperfectly conceivable (cf. *Reply to Gaunilo* 8). In chapter 5 Anselm argues for that which he was already presuming: namely, that Something than which nothing greater can be thought is a unique being, since unless it alone existed *per se*, with all else existing through it, it could be thought to be greater, etc.

In spite of the fact that in the *Proslogion* Anselm seeks to arrive at the *Monologion*'s conclusions by employing a simpler and more powerful line of reasoning than he had used in the *Monologion*, there are important differences between these works. Two differences are especially striking: (1) whereas in the *Monologion* Anselm takes himself to have proven that God is Triune, he does not in the *Proslogion* argue for Triunity but merely presupposes it in chapter 23; and (2) whereas in the *Monologion* he argues for the doctrine of man's immortality, he makes no attempt to argue this point in the *Proslogion*, where he simply accepts it without discussion (*P*, ch. 25).

We see, then, that Anselm's line of reasoning in the *Proslogion* presupposes certain theological doctrines – doctrines that were, however, argued for in the *Monologion*. On the other hand, in the *Proslogion* Anselm also raises certain puzzles that were not raised in the *Monologion*. For example, he broods over the conundrum of why God mercifully elects some men to salvation, while justly letting others waywardly rush headlong unto damnation. And in the course of doing so, he endeavors to show that God's mercy is not incompatible with his justice. Yet, in order for him successfully to explain God's justice, he needs (but does not at that point have) the soteriology contained in his later *Cur Deus homo*.

In the first section of his concise line of reasoning, Anselm presupposes that existence is a perfection, so that a being that exists only in our understanding exists less perfectly than it would if it existed also in reality. This presupposition was also made in *Monologion* 36 and 31. Now, just as in the first section of the *Proslogion* Anselm makes the foregoing metaphysical presuppositions, so also in the second section he makes certain psychological, moral, and theological presuppositions that are essential to the continuation of his reasoning. For example, in chapter 9 he morally presupposes that "someone who is good both to those who are good and to those who are evil is better than someone who is good only to those who are good. And someone who is good by virtue of both punishing and sparing those who are evil is better than someone who [is good] by virtue merely of punishing [them]." Similarly, in chapter 25 he accepts as a psychological truth the tenet that "each person rejoices in another's good [fortune] to the extent that he loves this other"; and he supposes that this is as it ought to be. Likewise, in chapter 26 he lays down the theological assumptions that in the next life (a) each of the blessed will rejoice in the degree that he loves God and that (b) each will love God to the extent that he knows God.

All of the foregoing testifies to the fact that Anselm, in attempting to prove "by compelling reasons" (*necessariis rationibus*), makes no pretense of being able to proceed presuppositionlessly. Rather, he proceeds *sola ratione* in so far as he makes only those suppositions that he presumes would doubtlessly be granted by any rational man.

Other Interpretations

The foregoing understanding of the *Proslogion* is a traditional understanding, as derived from the *Proslogion* itself, including its preface, and from such cognate sources as Anselm's *De incarnatione verbi* 6, Gaunilo's *Pro insipiente* and Eadmer's *Vita Sancti Anselmi*. Yet, in the twentieth century alone, a myriad of other interpretations of the *Proslogion* were propounded, both before and after Norman Malcolm, who regarded Anselm as having two different but not clearly distinguished arguments for the existence of God. Malcolm purports to untangle these arguments, the one of which is deemed to occur in chapter 2, the other in chapter 3. Malcolm regards the one in chapter 3 as the more significant one, once it is reconstructed. For in chapter 3 Anselm (says Malcolm) presupposes that *necessary* existence is a perfection ("What exists necessarily is more perfect than it would be if it existed non-necessarily"); and this, he thinks, is a more defensible assumption than is the assumption that mere existence is a perfection ("What exists is more perfect than it would be if it did not exist"), since it does not involve (a) comparing a state of existing with a state of not-existing and (b) alleging that the former state is, somehow, the more perfect. Such a comparison Malcolm regards as philosophically bizarre.

Subsequently to Malcolm's article, George Nakhnikian (1965) claimed to identify four different ontological arguments within the *Proslogion*. By contrast, Richard La Croix (1972) contended that not just chapter 2, or chapters 2 and 3 together, but rather the whole of the *Proslogion*, together with the whole of the *Reply to Gaunilo*, are required for extracting Anselm's one and only ontological argument. By still greater contrast, G. E. M. Anscombe (1985) conceded that Anselm has an argument for God's existence, but she contended that it is certainly not an *ontological* argument and is certainly not one that involves the dubious assumption that existence is a perfection. For, as she maintains, Anselm in chapter 2 is not reasoning in such a way as to be saying, in one step of the argument: "For if it [i.e. That than which a greater cannot be thought] were only in the understanding, it could be thought to exist also in reality – something which is greater [than existing only in the understanding]." Rather, what he is there saying is: "For if it is only in the intellect, what is greater can be thought to be in reality as well" – a construal that is presumed better to accord with the Latin (*Si enim vel in solo intellectu est, potest cogitari esse in re, quod maius est*), once the editorially inserted comma before *quod* is expunged (Anscombe, 1985: 36–7). Holding a still different view is Richard Campbell (1976), who claimed that in the *Proslogion* Anselm is involved in working out the logic of the concept of God and is not involved in offering a proof of God's existence in any traditional sense of "proof." Thus, Anselm's key point is said to be that anyone who understands God to be Something than which a greater cannot be thought cannot think and speak of him without thinking and speaking of him as existing, for it makes no sense to deny his existence. Yet, Campbell insists (a) that one does not need to think or to speak of God at all and (b) that from one's thinking or speaking of God – necessarily, as existing – it does not follow that God does exist, any more than from one's not being able to think of God as not existing, it thereby follows that he does exist.

Even before Malcolm's article appeared, there was dispute over just what Anselm was aiming to do in the *Proslogion*. Not everyone agreed that Anselm was at all intent upon proving God's existence *qua* existence. Indeed, A. Stolz (1933) construed Anselm as wanting to show not that God exists but that God exists in a certain manner – to show, namely, that he alone exists truly and necessarily. For only a Being (a) that alone exists through itself and not through another and (b) that alone is a Necessary Being can rightly be said to exist truly, so that in comparison with such a Being all else can be said not to exist and not to be anything of itself (*P*, ch. 22; *M*, ch. 28). Consequently, on Stolz's interpretation, the *Proslogion* is an exercise in mystical theology, whereby Anselm so exalts the being of God that the contemplating human soul is filled with awe and with a sense of its own nullity apart from God, so that thereby some souls are moved to draw mystically nearer to God, with the assistance of a divinely infused heightened love of God.

Just as there is disagreement about how many existence arguments are contained in the *Proslogion* and about what kind of existence is being putatively proved, so also there is controversy about whether Anselm is at all offering a defensible proof. William Rowe (1976) regards the alleged proof – in any of its plausible formulations – as question-begging. Richard Campbell (1976) sees it as a "proof" only within the community of faith. Karl Barth (1931), too, emphasizes that Anselm's argument stems from the religious community and is not a neutral argument that will appeal to the natural reason of unbelievers; at most, it is confirmatory of faith, never instigating of faith, as Anselm himself is said to have recognized. Over against these interpretations, F. S. Schmitt (1968), the editor of the critical editions of Anselm's Latin texts, holds the view that even in the *Proslogion* Anselm aims to exhibit that a man of ordinary intelligence will have to say to himself after reading the *Proslogion*: "I now understand to such an extent that even if I do not want to believe that God exists, I cannot fail to understand that He exists" (cf. *P*, ch. 4).

Exegetical Problems

Philosophical interest in the *Proslogion* has focused mainly on section 1 (in particular, chapters 2–4), since if the argument there is unsound, then the continued argument in section 2 (i.e., chapters 5–26) will be insignificant. However, a prerequisite to assessing the soundness of the argument in section 1 will be the articulating of a reliable version of the argument. Yet, such an articulation will be linked to just how one understands the Latin text. Let us look briefly at six focal issues. (a) In the opening sentence of chapter 2 Anselm uses the words "*sicut credimus*," in the sentence traditionally translated as (something like): "Therefore, O Lord, You who give understanding to faith, grant me to understand – to the degree You know to be advantageous – that You exist, as we believe [*sicut credimus*], and that You are what we believe [You to be]." However, we have already seen that Richard Campbell (and others such as Stolz) translate this passage as (something like): "Well then, O Lord, You who give understanding to faith, give me, so far as You know it to be beneficial, to understand that You are just as we believe [*sicut credimus*] and that You are what we believe." (b) The expression "*unum argumentum*," in the preface, has sometimes been construed as "a single argument," rather than as "a single consideration," namely, the consideration that God is Something than which a greater cannot be thought. (c) We have already seen disagreement about the construal of "*quod*" in chapter 3, where Anscombe translates it differently from the traditional way. (d) Similarly, the word "*probare*," used by Anselm both in the preface and in the *Reply to Gaunilo*, has sometimes been taken by interpreters to mean only "to demonstrate as contextually valid," so that what counts as a proof from the point of view of believers will not count as a proof from the point of view of unbelievers. (e) Some translator-interpreters take a sentence toward the end of chapter 4 ("*Qui ergo intelligit sic esse deum, nequit eum non esse cogitare*") as "Thus, whoever understands that God exists in such a way cannot think of Him as not existing," whereas certain others construe it as "Therefore, anyone who understands that God is such [a being] cannot think that He does not exist." (f) Finally, is the second sentence of chapter 3 ("*Non potest cogitari esse aliquid, quod non possit cogitari non esse* . . .") to be understood as "For there can be thought to exist something which cannot be thought not to exist . . ." or as "For it [i.e., That than which a greater cannot be thought] can be thought to be something which cannot be thought not to be . . ."? Interpreters of the *Proslogion* will have to settle for themselves these and other such translation issues, each of which is highly disputable.

Conceptual Problems

Similarly, an interpreter will have to come to terms with a multitude of conceptual issues that relate both to articulating the argument and to evaluating it. Let us here likewise single out six such sample issues. (a) Can one legitimately substitute for Anselm's word "*cogitare*" ("to think," "to think of," "to conceive") the expression "to be logically possible," so that the entire argument can be re-stated in terms of possibility and impossibility, as Malcolm and others re-state it? According to Gareth Matthews (1961) this substitution is not allowable, since it will not work in chapter 15, where for the clause "You are also something greater than can be thought" one would have to read "You are also something greater than is logically possible" – a reading that is philosophically preposterous and that subverts the logic of Anselm's reasoning. (b) Is the expression "Something than which a greater cannot be thought" a *definition* of God, or is it a *description*? According to Richard La Croix (1972) and others it cannot be a definition because Anselm states in *Reply to Gaunilo* 7 that one might not understand the meaning of the word "God" but would still understand the meaning of the longer expression. However, if the expression were definitional, then the meaning of the word "God" would be understood in understanding the expression. (c) Would Anselm, then, be prepared to treat the expression "Something than which a greater cannot be thought" as an *indefinite* description and to treat the expression "That than which a greater cannot be thought" as a *definite* description? Or is the former expression a disguised definite description, or is, rather, the latter expression a disguised indefinite description? (d) What justifies Anselm in identifying God as Something than which a greater cannot be thought? Does this identification come solely from his faith, so that in this way his reasoning is faith-dependent and not *sola ratione*? (e) Is Anselm's putative reconciliation of divine justice with divine mercy by deriving them both from divine goodness an acceptable reconciling step, or does his reasoning at this point break down? (f) Are all the perfections that Anselm's method allows him to ascribe to God perfections that are compatible, or compossible? For example, some philosophers have questioned whether omniscience is compatible either with immutability or with omnipotence.

Because of the many exegetical and conceptual intricacies that confront readers of the *Proslogion*, philosophers have found this opuscule to be intellectually challenging in fascinating ways, so that, as Richard Campbell insightfully acknowledges, "A confrontation with a thinker of Anselm's penetration and insight can lead to the exposing of our own intellectual inadequacies. But since this process of dialogue is living and dramatic in character, neither I nor anyone else can fairly claim to have said the last word" (Campbell, 1976: 227).

Bibliography

Editions and translations

Anselm of Canterbury (1968) *Sancti Anselmi opera omnia*, ed. F. S. Schmitt. Stuttgart-Bad Cannstatt: Frommann Verlag.

Anselm of Canterbury (1986) *A New, Interpretive Translation of St Anselm's Monologion and Proslogion*, trans. J. Hopkins. Minneapolis, MN: Banning.

Anselm of Canterbury (1998) *Proslogion*, trans. M. J. Charlesworth. In B. Davies and G. R. Evans (eds), *Anselm of Canterbury: The Major Works*. New York: Oxford University Press.

Anselm of Canterbury (2000) *Complete Philosophical and Theological Treatises of Anselm of Canterbury*, trans J. Hopkins and H. Richardson. Minneapolis, MN: Banning.

All of Anselm's major works are freely available on the Internet (http://www.cla.umn.edu/jhopkins/).

Studies and references

Anscombe, G. E. M. (1985) Why Anselm's proof in the *Proslogion* is not an ontological argument. *The Thoreau Quarterly*, 17 (Winter–Spring): 32–40.

Barth, K. (1931) *Fides quaerens intellectum. Anselms Beweis der Existenz Gottes im Zusammenhang seines theologischen Programms* [*Faith Seeking Understanding: Anselm's Proof of God's Existence in the Context of his Theological Program*]. Munich: Evangelische Buchhandlung Zollikon.

Campbell, R. (1976) *From Belief to Understanding: A Study of Anselm's Proslogion Argument on the Existence of God*. Canberra: Australian National University Press.

Eadmer, monk of Canterbury (1962) *Vita Sancti Anselmi*, ed. and trans. R. W. Southern. New York: Thomas Nelson.

Hopkins, J. (1976) *Anselm of Canterbury*, vol. 4: *Hermeneutical and Textual Problems in the Complete Treatises of St Anselm*. Toronto: Mellen.

La Croix, R. (1972) *Proslogion II and III: A Third Interpretation of Anselm's Argument*. Leiden: Brill.

Malcolm, N. (1960) Anselm's ontological arguments. *Philosophical Review*, 69 (January): 41–62.

Matthews, G. B. (1961) On conceivability in Anselm and Malcolm. *Philosophical Review*, 70 (January): 110–11.

Nakhnikian, G. (1965) St Anselm's four ontological arguments. In W. H. Capitan and D. D. Merrill (eds), *Art, Mind, and Religion*, pp. 29–36. Pittsburgh, PA: University of Pittsburgh Press.

Rowe, W. (1976) The ontological argument and question-begging. *International Journal for Philosophy of Religion*, 7: 425–32.

Stolz, A. (1933) Zur Theologie Anselms im Proslogion [On Anselm's theology in the *Proslogion*]. *Catholica*, 2 (January): 1–24.

12

Averroës, *The Incoherence of "The Incoherence"* (ca. 1180)

The Incoherence of the Philosophers

Deborah L. Black

Ibn Rushd, known to the Latin West as Averroës (1126–1198), was the last of the great Aristotelian philosophers of the medieval Islamic world. The majority of Averroës' philosophical writings consist of commentaries on the texts of Aristotle, many of which were translated into Latin in the thirteenth century. These works had a profound impact on the course of Western thought in the later Middle Ages, and Averroës became known in the Latin West by the epithet "the Commentator" because of his importance as an interpreter of Aristotle's works.

The *Incoherence of "The Incoherence"* was probably one of Averroës' last works, written around 1180, and it is intimately connected to Averroës' avocation as an interpreter of Aristotle. It follows the pattern of a "long" or "great" Aristotelian commentary, but in this case the text under consideration is the *Incoherence of the Philosophers* by the theologian and Sufi, al-Ghazali (1058–1111), to which Averroës' *Incoherence* offers a point-by-point reply. In his *Incoherence* Averroës displays the same unwavering commitment to the principles of Aristotelian philosophy that is expressed in his commentaries, and the same zeal to defend that philosophy not only against Ghazali's attacks, but also against the Neoplatonic innovations of his philosophical predecessors, al-Farabi (ca. 870–950), and especially Avicenna (Ibn Sina, 980–1037).

In the *Incoherence of the Philosophers*, Ghazali had attacked the views of the philosophers from the perspective of the Ash'arite school of theology. The Ash'arites (so-called after their founder, al-Ash'ari, d. 936) emphasized divine omnipotence and held that God must be understood as the sole cause and creator of all things, including human acts. In support of this they upheld a metaphysics of atoms and accidents held together at every moment by God, and they denied the reality of secondary causality in the natural world. Ghazali assailed the internal consistency of the Aristotelian–Neoplatonic synthesis that had been forged by Farabi and Avicenna, and he charged that three of their doctrines constituted heresy or unbelief, a serious charge under Islamic law, punishable by death. In responding to Ghazali's attacks on his philosophical predecessors, Averroës often accuses Ghazali of misunderstanding or misrepresenting the philosophers, and he mounts an especially strong counter-attack against those arguments of Ghazali that depend upon Ashʿarite principles. But oftentimes Averroës will accept Ghazali's contention that a philosophical position upheld by Farabi or Avicenna is unsound.

The arguments of Averroës' *Incoherence* are organized around a list of twenty metaphysical and physical propositions of the philosophers which, according to Ghazali, contravene Islamic belief. Seventeen of these twenty are deemed by Ghazali to be mere innovation, that is, deviations from the mainstream of orthodox belief that had, however, been upheld by other Muslims sects, in particular the rival theological school known as the Muʿtazilites. But three of the core doctrines of Islamic Aristotelianism are identified by Ghazali as beliefs that place their upholders outside the pale of Islam. They are: (1) the assertion of the world's eternityin the past, which entails a denial of the belief that God voluntarily created the world out of nothing; (2) the denial that God's providence extends to individuals; and (3) the denial of bodily resurrection. Of the twenty propositions discussed by Ghazali, sixteen are drawn from metaphysics: these include the doctrine of the eternity of the world as well as a number of propositions pertaining to other aspects of the philosophers' conception of God and his relation to the world. In the area of the physical sciences, which in an Aristotelian system includes psychology, Averroës and Ghazali are at odds over a number of propositions regarding the immateriality of the soul, the resurrection of the body, and the reality of necessary causal connections.

Metaphysics

The first three discussions in the metaphysics section of the *Incoherence* address the philosophers' thesis of the eternity of the world. The first and longest considers four philosophical proofs for the world's eternity in the past, and the second pertains to the world's future incorruptibility, both positions upheld by Aristotle himself. The third discussion pertains to the Neoplatonic doctrine of emanation adopted by Farabi and Avicenna, according to which the world is the necessary and eternal creation of God. Since emanation represents a departure from Aristotle, who considered God to be only a final and moving cause of the world, not its creator, in this case Averroës rejects both the arguments of his predecessors and the counter-claims of Ghazali.

The first of the philosophers' proofs for the eternity of the world is based upon the premise that it is impossible for an eternal God to produce a temporal effect. Since causes necessarily entail their effects, according to the philosophers, it follows that the effect proceeding from an eternal, necessary, and all-powerful God will likewise be eternal. Ghazali, however, rejects the model of causality underlying the philosophers' argument, and appeals instead to the very different conception of divine agency upheld by the Ashʿarites. On this model, we can conceive of an eternal God producing a temporal effect without this entailing any corresponding change in the creator himself. While God's act of willing is immutable and eternal, the *effect* of his act is temporally specified – God simply decrees from all eternity that the world will begin to exist at a particular time. To illustrate this, Ghazali draws on the famous example of a man pronouncing a decree of divorce against his wife, but stipulating that it take effect only upon the realization of some future event.

Ghazali's basic objection against the philosophers' arguments for the world's eternity thus rests upon the conception of the divine will that they presuppose. In reply, Averroës argues that Ghazali's own model of the divine will is flawed. Since God is omniscient and his will is all powerful, God's eternity and immutability render absurd all attempts to explain why God would prefer to create the world at one time rather than at another. Such a choice on God's part would be irrational and arbitrary: "For two similar things are equivalent for the willer, and his action can only attach itself to the one rather than the other through their being dissimilar" (Averroës, 1954: 20). On Averroës' view, then, the will is a power to choose the better of two dissimilar alternatives, and when there is neither any principle of differentiation, nor any limitation on the willer's knowledge or power, voluntary acts proceed ineluctably from his will. Ghazali, by contrast, defines the will precisely as a power to impose a differentiation on two identical and indiscernible alternatives, and for him both divine and human wills manifest this capacity. In another famous example, Ghazali alleges that if two similar dates are placed before a hungry man, he will not starve because he is unable to choose between them: "He will inevitably take one of them through an attribute whose function is to render a thing specific, [differentiating it] from its like" (al-Ghazali, 1997: 23). But Averroës rejects this clever example as being inapplicable to an omnipotent willer. For there *is* a difference for the human agent in this case, not between the two dates, but between satiety and hunger. It is this difference that forces the human agent to act at all, even though it may be incidental to the fulfillment of his purpose which of the two dates he eats. But the important point for Averroës is that the choice imposed upon the human has no parallel for God, since there is no possible lack or imperfection in God that the choice to create the world would remedy.

Conflicting models of divine agency are also at the core of the third discussion, which pertains to the Islamic philosophers' emanational account of creation. For Ghazali, emanation is a theory of creation that is at best metaphorical, and at worst utter nonsense, since it renders meaningless the claim that God is truly the "agent and maker" of the world. Ghazali charges that the basis for the philosophers' errors in this case is their confusion of the concepts of causality and agency: for not every cause is an agent, but rather, an agent is "one from whom the act proceeds, together with the will to act by way of choice and the knowledge of what is willed" (al-Ghazali, 1997: 57). Since the theory of emanation makes God's production of the world a necessary effect of his nature, emanation falls outside the definition of agency. The philosophers, then, have made God into an inanimate natural cause, like the sun, and robbed him of any claim to be the paradigmatic case of a free and rational agent.

In responding to Ghazali on this point, Averroës continues to charge Ghazali with offering an anthropomorphic account of divine attributes such as will and knowledge. But in this case he is also highly critical of Avicenna and Farabi and anxious to separate their Neoplatonic account of emanation from the authentic views of Aristotle himself. In particular, Averroës takes issue with the basic premise upon which Avicenna's adherence to the theory of emanation is based, namely, that "from the one insofar as it is one, only one can proceed," against which many of Ghazali's arguments are directed. Averroës reverts to a purer Aristotelian view, in which God's agency is to be understood as his ability to move the world as its end or final cause: "And it is evident to the philosophers that he who bestows on the immaterial existents their end is identical with him who bestows on them their existence, for according to them form and end are identical in this kind of existent, and he who bestows on these existents both form and end is their agent" (Averroës, 1954: 138). That such an "agent" is no longer a creator or an efficient cause at all, however, is a consequence to which Averroës prefers not to draw attention.

In discussions four to sixteen of the *Incoherence*, Ghazali takes issue with numerous other aspects of the philosophical conception of God. He claims that the philosophers' rational proofs for the existence of God are ineffectual, and he rejects the self-evidence of one of the fundamental principles of those proofs in the Aristotelian tradition, the impossibility of an actually infinite regress of causes. Here, too, while he is swift in his defense of this central Aristotelian principle, Averroës rejects Avicenna's proof of God as the Necessary of Existence, noting that it represents a departure from the traditional Aristotelian proofs for the existence of God from motion, and questioning the coherence of Avicenna's use of the modal notions of possible and necessary existence as the foundation for his argument. Averroës' disagreement with a number of Avicenna's metaphysical principles surfaces as well in his response to Ghazali's attacks on the philosophers' accounts of the divine attributes of unity and knowledge. In the course of his consideration of divine unity, Averroës rejects Avicenna's famous distinction between essence and existence, in particular what he takes to be Avicenna's claim that existence is an accident added to the essence of things.

On the question of God's knowledge, however, Averroës is somewhat more cautious in his replies to Ghazali's attack on the notorious Avicennian thesis that God knows particulars "in a universal way." According to this thesis, God knows individuals only in so far as they are contained under genera and species; for example, he knows Socrates and Plato only as "animal" and "human," not as discrete individuals. It was on the basis of this thesis that Ghazali raised one of his charges of unbelief – the rejection of God's providence over particulars – against the philosophers. Averroës rebuts this charge by arguing that it represents yet another instance of Ghazali's anthropomorphism, "making God an eternal man" (Averroës, 1954: 256). None the less, Averroës finds Avicenna's own analogy between God's knowledge of particulars and human knowledge of universals unsatisfactory. Averroës takes refuge instead in Aristotle's description of God's activity as a "thinking of thinking," a form of self-knowledge. Properly speaking, then, God's knowledge is *neither* universal nor particular, since these descriptions pertain only to human knowers. Human knowledge is passive, and caused by the objects known; divine knowledge admits of no such passivity, but rather, God knows all beings in so far as he is their cause, and the primary and most perfect exemplar of being *qua* being.

Physics

The most famous exchange between the two *Incoherences* of Ghazali and Averroës occurs in the seventeenth discussion, the first of four pertaining to the physical sciences. This discussion contains Ghazali's refutation of the philosophers' concept of causality based on the principles of Ash'arite theology, a refutation often viewed as a forerunner of David Hume's skeptical arguments against causality. Like Hume, Ghazali's strategy is to show that the claim that we have certain and infallible knowledge of necessary causal relations is supported neither logically nor empirically. Unlike Hume, however, Ghazali's main motive for denying that the connection between cause and effect is a necessary one is his desire to defend the possibility of miracles.

According to Ghazali, careful consideration will show us that "the connection between what is habitually believed to be a cause and what is habitually believed to be an effect" is not a matter of logical entailment or implication (al-Ghazali, 1997: 170). While eating usually produces satiety and decapitation usually produces death, it remains possible to conceive of one of these "causes" occurring without its effect ensuing. These things usually coincide only because God habitually chooses to create them concurrently. Ghazali's favorite illustration of his point is that of the burning of a piece of cotton when it comes into contact with fire. God is the true agent of the burning and of the blackness and disintegration that the fire appears to produce. Ghazali also offers an epistemological argument for this claim, based upon the limitations of our actual observation of the causal nexus. All we actually see is the simultaneous concurrence of the two events, contact with fire and burning. But, Ghazali urges, "existence 'with' does not prove that it exists 'by' it," for we can perfectly well imagine cotton and fire coming into contact without burning, or decapitation occurring without death (al-Ghazali, 1997: 171).

In keeping with the epistemological tenor of Ghazali's attack, Averroës points out the consequences that a denial of causal connections has for the possibility of human knowledge. Averroës contends that knowledge is nothing but the recognition of real causal connections in the world around us, and thus to reject causality is to reject reason: "Denial of cause implies the denial of knowledge, and denial of knowledge implies that nothing in this world can really be known" (Averroës, 1954: 319). Averroës' point rests on the fundamental Aristotelian principle that things have real natures or essences which define what they are and what they can do. Hence the essences of things are knowable only through the causal powers that they display. The nature of "fire" is nothing but its capacity to burn, and we would have no grounds for identifying a substance as fire if, when it touched cotton, it failed to burn it. For this reason, Ghazali's attempts to undermine our confidence in the reality of causal connections cannot even get off the ground, just as the denial of a necessary logical principle like that of contradiction cannot get off the ground. To deny the reality of causal connections is to deny that things have the essential natures that make them what they are and distinguish them from other things. And unless we can identify and distinguish things from one another, we cannot even talk about them in order to raise skeptical doubts.

Ghazali concludes his attacks on the philosophers by challenging Avicenna's many attempts to prove the immortality and immateriality of the human soul. That a theologian should attack a philosopher for upholding the immortality of the soul may seem odd, especially since Avicenna was one of the few Islamic philosophers explicitly to champion personal immortality. But most of the Islamic theologians were metaphysical atomists who upheld a materialist view of human nature, and Ghazali reflects their traditional focus on the resurrection of the body rather than the immortality of the soul. Hence the twentieth and final discussion in the *Incoherence* consists of a series of arguments designed to show that, despite the philosophers' denials, bodily resurrection and corporeal reward and punishment in the afterlife are logically possible.

Here, too, Averroës accepts many of Ghazali's attacks on Avicenna's belief in the personal immortality of the soul, but he declines to discuss in any detail Ghazali's third principal charge of unbelief against the philosophers, namely, that they deny bodily resurrection. Instead, he is content with the disclaimer that "this is a problem which is not found in any of the older philosophers" (Averroës, 1954: 359). None the less, Averroës asserts, all philosophers believe in bodily resurrection as the foundation for religious law and political society. That is, unless a state is founded on a religious law which holds out the promise of eternal reward or misery in the afterlife, there will not be sufficient order and virtue in the citizens of that state to enable it to thrive. The belief in the resurrection of the body, then, is a part of political philosophy inasmuch as it is a religious tenet that the mass of citizens must be induced to accept in order to ensure their compliance with the laws of their city. But it is not something that forms a part of the philosophers' own system of reasoned, theoretical beliefs.

Conclusion

Averroës' evasiveness on the question of bodily resurrection highlights the difficulties that have faced many commentators in determining the degree to which both his *Incoherence* and Ghazali's reflect their authors' personal intellectual commitments. Both men characterize their approach in these works as dialectical, Ghazali because his aim is merely refutation and destruction, and Averroës because his task is simply to reply to Ghazali and to correct his misconceptions. None the less, most of Ghazali's attacks on the philosophers reflect the presuppositions of the Ash'arite school to which Ghazali belonged for part of his life, and whose tenets he espoused in other works. As for Averroës, it is clear that his reticence on issues such as bodily resurrection reflects his firm belief that theoretical matters are not to be discussed openly for mass consumption, lest they undermine the simple faith of ordinary believers. But there is no reason to believe that Averroës' affirmation of the practical benefits of religious belief is insincere. Moreover, Averroës' disclaimers throughout the *Incoherence* that his arguments are not technical demonstrations should not detract from their intrinsic value nor from their ability to illuminate what Averroës says in his mature Aristotelian commentaries. To call a work such as the *Incoherence* "dialectical" does not mean that it fails to reflect Averroës' own philosophy, but rather that, given its polemical context, Averroës is not always in a position to explain fully all of the presuppositions of an argument, nor to present premises in their proper logical order or omit extraneous considerations. His presentation is guided by Ghazali's attack, and not merely by the truth of the matter. But the *Incoherence* remains a valuable guide to Averroës' philosophy and to the general conflicts between philosophers and theologians in medieval Islam, as well as an impressive philosophical *tour de force* in its own right.

Bibliography

Editions and translations

Averroës (1930) *Tahafut al-tahafut*, ed. Maurice Bouyges. Bibliotheca Arabica Scholasticorum, Série arabe, vol. 3. Beirut: Imprimerie Catholique.

Averroës (1954) *Averroës' Tahafut al-tahafut* [*The Incoherence of the Incoherence*], 2 vols, trans. Simon Van Den Bergh. London: E. J. W. Gibb Memorial Trust (reprinted as one volume, 1978).

Studies and references

Al-Ghazali (1997) *The Incoherence of the Philosophers*, ed. and trans. Michael E. Marmura. Provo, UT: Brigham Young University Press.

Druart, Thérèse-Anne (1995) Averroës on God's knowledge of being *qua* being. In Paul Lockey (ed.), *Studies in Thomistic Theology*, pp. 175–205. Houston, TX: Center for Thomistic Studies.

Ivry, Alfred (1972) Towards a unified view of Averroës' philosophy. *Philosophical Forum*, 4: 87–113.

Kogan, Barry (1985) *Averroës and the Metaphysics of Causation*. Albany, NY: State University of New York Press.

Leaman, Oliver (1988) *Averroës and his Philosophy*. Oxford: Clarendon Press.

Marmura, M. E. (1962) Some aspects of Avicenna's theory of God's knowledge of particulars. *Journal of the American Oriental Society*, 82: 299–312.

Marmura, M. E. (1965) Ghazali and demonstrative science. *Journal of the History of Philosophy*, 3: 183–204.

13

Maimonides, *The Guide of the Perplexed* (ca. 1190)

The Perplexities of the Guide

Alfred L. Ivry

Moses Maimonides (1138–1204) is the most celebrated and influential Jewish philosopher of the Middle Ages. He wrote a number of definitive rabbinical works in which he expresses philosophical ideas in summary form, but his major philosophical work is *The Guide of the Perplexed*. Maimonides composed the *Guide* in the five-year period 1185–90, purportedly in the form of chapters sent to a prize pupil in Asia Minor. Written in Arabic with Hebrew letters (Judeo-Arabic, ed. Kafih, 1972), as was customary among Jews living in the Islamic world, the *Guide* quickly received two Hebrew translations for the benefit of Jews living in Europe. The first Latin translation, commonly referred to as *Dux neutrorum*, was composed in the 1220s, affording Christians the opportunity to read a work which was prompting a strong reaction – both positive and negative – among its Jewish audience. The *Guide* had a marked influence upon Thomas Aquinas and other medieval philosophers, more so than any other Jewish philosophical work. The *Guide* has been translated into a number of Western languages in modern times, and there exists an exemplary English translation (Maimonides, 1963).

The *Guide* evoked considerable controversy among Jewish readers, leading to prolonged disputes and even public book-burning in Paris in the thirteenth century. Maimonides was regarded by many as a dissembling Aristotelian, his philosophy an elaborately disguised form of deism. Indeed, Spinoza can be seen as deriving much of his inspiration from Maimonides, though fundamentally differing on the necessity of maintaining Jewish law, the *halakha*.

Maimonides' supporters accepted his declaration that he wrote the *Guide* to show the compatibility of Judaism with philosophy, and believed that he did so in good part by showing the limitations of philosophy. Some Maimonideans of the late Middle Ages like the fourteenth-century Moses of Narbonne read the *Guide* as a radically Aristotelian work, akin to those of Averroës. The *Guide* to its admirers took on the challenge of science and philosophy as then conceived, and paved the way ever after for Jews to partake in these endeavors.

Modern scholars are still debating Maimonides' true positions in the *Guide*. Leo

Strauss (1984) believes the book reinforces Maimonides' views on the differences, not similarities, between Jerusalem and Athens. Strauss (1987) and others (Pines, 1979; Kreisel, 1999) regard the work as essentially political. Pines (1979) believes the *Guide* shows Maimonides ultimately to be an agnostic, while Stern (2000) takes him as a skeptic. Fox (1990) regards Maimonides as a pious Jew who mastered philosophy in order to expose its weaknesses, offering a philosophical defense of Judaism.

Esotericism Rationalized

A major reason for the divergent interpretations of Maimonides' thought lies in what may be seen as his declaration of disinformation, proffered in the introduction to the book. Maimonides gives the reader to understand that he will be anything but candid, indeed, that he will contradict himself deliberately, and that the reader must be alert to that and be prepared to navigate around the contradictions. Maimonides does little to help the reader in this task other than to describe the seven (!) kinds of contradictory or contrary statements which can be found "in any book or compilation," and to single out two which are particularly present in this work (*Guide* I: Introduction, Maimonides, 1963: 20; hereafter all references are to this translation).

The reason Maimonides gives for his unusual methodology appears straightforward, namely, to dissuade the reader who has not already studied philosophy from attempting to make sense of the book. Such an "ignoramus" must be kept at arm's length, even if (especially if) he is learned in the religious sciences, that is, in the Bible and Talmud. Such a person has either a literal understanding of the Bible or mistakes its midrashic dimensions, opposed to the sort of philosophical midrash which Maimonides proposes. Introducing such a person to philosophy can only have deleterious results for the individual and the community (as well as the author).

Midrash, a homiletically oriented interpretation of the words of scripture, was developed by the rabbis as a way of expanding upon the perceived multivalent meanings of the biblical text. Through midrash, the rabbis implicitly proposed an open-ended, relatively inchoate theology. Maimonides' midrash pours new wine into old bottles, discovering in the Bible views usually identified with Aristotle, Plato, and Plotinus.

The secrecy with which Maimonides cloaks his teachings has another cause, which he offers as his main reason for adopting an esoteric style of writing. It is that the Jewish tradition dictates such a course of action, the sages of the Talmud allegedly having forbidden public discourse of physics and metaphysics (*Guide* I: Introduction, 1963: 6). Maimonides makes this claim by identifying the Talmudic "Account of the Beginning" with "natural science," or physics, and the "Account of the Chariot" with "divine science," or metaphysics.

The rabbis had discouraged the teachings of these "accounts" as part of their struggle in late antiquity with mystical and pagan, probably Gnostic, thought. They are said to have permitted the teaching of the "Account of the Beginning" to a select few, while restricting the teaching of the "Account of the Chariot" only to a single person, one who could understand a subject from the "chapter headings" alone.

The rabbis' animus to classical philosophy can be surmised by its absence from the Talmud. Maimonides is not far off the mark, therefore, in seeing the exoteric teaching of philosophy as not part of the Jewish tradition. He is, however, thoroughly – and thrillingly – off the mark in claiming that the esoteric teaching of philosophy has rabbinic sanction, and is mandated by a proper understanding of the Bible.

This claim allows Maimonides to write as he wishes, concealing his views behind an elaborate artifice of conflicting statements. His point of departure is philosophy, however, for the purpose of the book is to guide the person who is attracted to the teachings of philosophy and perplexed by its seeming conflict with the claims of the Bible and of rabbinic Judaism. Frequently, however, Maimonides emphasizes the limitations of philosophical inquiry, leading many readers to believe that the *Guide* essentially is either a repudiation of metaphysics and/or a defense of Judaism against the challenge of reason.

The Structure of the *Guide*

This approach is supported by the external, formal structure of the book, upon which Maimonides places great significance (Strauss, 1963: xi–xiii). He would have us believe that every word of his text is deliberately chosen and placed, every contradiction and anomalous statement intentional (*Guide* I: Introduction, 1963: 15).

Maimonides surprises the reader who is prepared by the preface and introduction for a dense philosophical tome, by offering a plethora of mostly exegetical chapters in *Guide* I: 3–49. They are devoted to a dogmatic denial of the literal understanding of anthropomorphic depictions of God in the Bible. Having insisted first upon the incorporeal nature of God, Maimonides turns in *Guide* I: 50–70 to inveighing against the notion of multiplicity or composition in God, really the basis for denying God physical attributes. Here the discussion turns analytical and linguistic, as Maimonides investigates the problem of predicating anything of the One, and propounds a doctrine of negative attributes.

The philosophical tenor of the book is sharpened in *Guide* I: 71–II: 31, where Maimonides describes and critiques arguments for the existence, unity, and incorporeality of God as developed by the *mutakallimûn*, the Muslim theologians, and by Aristotle and his disciples. This involves arguments for and against the eternity of the world, an issue which Maimonides believes has not been conclusively decided (Davidson, 1987: 5).

Prophecy is the next topic which Maimonides discusses (*Guide* II: 32–48), a standard medieval topos in which Aristotelian psychology is read into the prophet's experience. The subtext, however, is political philosophy, as Maimonides distinguishes between Moses' prophecy and that of all other prophets, with corresponding claims made for Mosaic law.

Maimonides returns exegetically in *Guide* III: 1–7 to cosmological themes in discussing the "Account of the Chariot," the theophany reported in Ezekiel l. If Aristotle and Ptolemy are Maimonides' main sources here for delineating the cosmos, Plotinus is ultimately the main inspiration for *Guide* III: 8–24. In this section Maimonides offers his view of matter and evil, divine omnipotence and omniscience.

Guide III: 25–54 returns the reader to a theological form of discourse, Maimonides arguing dialectically for the essentially rational nature of Mosaic law. This is important to Maimonides both as a theologian and as a political philosopher.

The closing section of *Guide* III: 51–4 has Maimonides move from the collective to the personal sphere, offering his view of the ideal for which one must strive. While individual conjunction with the divine realm is the goal of philosophical striving, Maimonides concludes on a Platonic as well as Jewish note, saying that the person who reaches the highest levels of knowledge should act on his wisdom to lead society to acts of loving kindness, judgment, and righteousness.

Theology and/or Philosophy

While Maimonides' approach is often theologically oriented, he was critical of Muslim theologians for letting their faith dictate their understanding of nature. "[They] did not conform in their premises to the appearance of that which exists, but considered how being ought to be in order that it should furnish a proof for the correctness of a particular opinion, or at least should not refute it" (*Guide* I: 71, 1963: 179). In contrast, Maimonides intended his own faith to conform to the "appearance of that which exists" and to be guided by what he saw as the ensuing dictates of science, to the degree it offered incontrovertible knowledge.

It is this scientific standard, this apparently empirically based approach, which Maimonides acclaims in writing the *Guide*. Yet it must be noted that Maimonides himself did very little empirical investigation of his own, and that he relied almost entirely on the scientific (and not so scientific) observations of Aristotle, supplemented by those of Ptolemy (Kraemer, 1989: 56, 77). Where he is critical of Aristotle, he bases himself on the astronomic observations of Ptolemy and later Muslim astronomers (*Guide* II: 24, 1963: 325). His own skill as a philosopher emerges in the way in which he organizes and presents his material, the logical manner, contradictions notwithstanding, in which he makes his argument.

This is another one of the ironies of the *Guide*, however; for while Maimonides, like other medieval philosophers, hails the apodictic syllogism as the hallmark of philosophical investigation, he himself (again, like most other medieval Islamic and Jewish philosophers) makes little use of it in this book. His argument is more commonly dialectical (where it is not rhetorical) (Hyman, 1989: 45). Dialectic, however, is the *métier* of the theologians, even as rhetoric is that of statesmen, as he is aware. Significant parts of the *Guide* should thus be recognized as belonging to these genres, less compelling philosophically than Maimonides would have wanted.

Maimonides thus has much in common with the Muslim theologians or *mutakallimûn* (Schwarz, 1991, 1992–3). Yet so determined is his opposition to them, both to their methodology and to their doctrines, that it does him a disservice to place him in their company. The *Guide* is at once a work of philosophy and theology, of scriptural exegesis and political statesmanship, its beliefs both conventional and highly unconventional. It is a work of contradictions, both intended and not intended.

Metaphor and Allegory

Before and besides alerting the reader to the unique methodology of his composition, Maimonides declares in the introduction to the first part of the *Guide* that his purpose in writing the book is to explain the language of the prophets, both their words and parables.

It is thus that the first forty-nine chapters of the *Guide* are mostly devoted to a philosophically oriented exegesis of biblical terms and events, Maimonides consistently allegorizing their literal meanings (Harvey, 2000: 181). Accordingly, all descriptions of God which have him moving in any direction at all are explained as ways of expressing the prophet's awareness of the divine presence (*Guide* I: 10, 23, 24), while depictions of God as being in any one unmoving position, e.g., sitting or standing, are seen as pointing to the deity's unchanging nature (*Guide* I: 11–13). The "heart," "soul," and "spirit" of the Lord really indicate for Maimonides the will of God, as do all speech acts attributed to him (*Guide* I: 29, 40, 41, 68). Lastly, the sensory activity which the prophets attribute to God, such as his many alleged acts of seeing and hearing, are all taken as metaphors for intellectual apprehension (*Guide* I: 44, 45).

The message of these early chapters of the *Guide* is unmistakable. God is not to be conceived in corporeal terms, and he never really was, by the prophets (nor, Maimonides adds with some justice, by the rabbis of the Talmud). This Maimonides firmly believes, and wants us to believe. He feels Moses and the prophets presented their understanding of the deity in anthropomorphic terms because of popular religious conceptions that they could not contravene. "The Torah speaks in human language," Maimonides says (*Guide* I: 53, 1963: 120), it being the tactic of scripture, of God's own "wily graciousness," to wean the people gradually from their primitive beliefs (*Guide* III: 32, 1963: 526). Indeed, the main teachings of the Torah for Maimonides, which he locates in the first two of the ten commandments (the only ones which he considers knowable by demonstration), assert the existence and unity of God (*Guide* II: 33, 1963: 364). So strongly does Maimonides believe in this that he says that one who denies either belief deserves to die, belief in the composition and hence corporeality of God being a form of idolatry (*Guide* I: 36, 1963: 84).

The Ambiguities of Attribution

Maimonides' campaign against idolatry goes much further than debunking biblical anthropomorphisms, however. He is led, by his conception of God as a uniquely unified being whose essence is solely existence, to deny any kind of positive attribution to God. Such attribution, distinguishing between the subject and its predicate, introduces multiplicity and hence composition into the singular oneness of God, and accordingly is not to be allowed. God must be pure simplicity of being to avoid an infinite regress of causes in a futile attempt to account for the composition.

Maimonides says therefore that the denial of essential attributes to God (let alone accidental attributes) is a "primary intelligible" (*Guide* I: 51, 1963: 112), in that the attribute, however essential, is distinct from the subject and modifies it in one way or another. If, however, the attribute is simply another word for the subject, the attribution being a tautology, then Maimonides accepts it. It is thus that he allows it to be said that God "has" (i.e., is) existence, power, wisdom, and will. These terms as predicated of God are "absolutely equivocal" in meaning as used otherwise, not standing for anything other than the being of God.

Maimonides is not prepared to deny these traditionally core divine attributes, but he cannot affirm them in any non-tautologous sense without destroying the logic of his belief in God. To alleviate this problem (but not resolve it), he turns to the doctrine of negative attribution, responding with greater logical precision to previous formulations of this concept in Muslim thought (Wolfson, 1977: 199). Maimonides believed that in negating the privation of an attribute, in asserting what God is not, one avoids false affirmations; thereby obtaining some understanding, however oblique, of the divine nature. All positive attributes are thus to be understood as negations of their privations (*Guide* I: 58, 1963: 135), the positive affirmation itself totally equivocal. Accordingly, "God is living" means God is not dead; "powerful" means not powerless, "knowing" not ignorant, "willing" not inattentive or negligent.

As Maimonides proceeds, however, he identifies each attribute with more than just the negation of its privation. Thus, the statement "God exists" means more than the negation of his non-existence. It means, he claims, that God's non-existence is impossible, that his existence is eternal, uncaused, and the cause – through an orderly emanation – of other existents.

Similarly, denying powerlessness to God also signifies for Maimonides that God is responsible for bringing other things into existence; God's "lack of ignorance" is taken as a sign of his apprehension and life; and his "not being inattentive or negligent" is held as indicative of the order and governance in the world, of which he is the cause. Maimonides actually compares this state of affairs to that of "all the things [which] are generated that a willing being governs by means of purpose and will" (*Guide* I: 58, 1963: 136).

It does not matter that Maimonides follows that sentence with the statement that "we apprehend further that no other thing is like [God's] being"; for we have been given to understand a good deal of God's nature, more than Maimonides' logic should have allowed. The one God emerges as more Neoplatonic than Aristotelian in his attributes, the cause through emanation of an orderly, providentially governed universe.

This treatment of the "essential" attributes thus leaves the reader in less darkness than he or she may at first have feared. God's nature becomes intelligible in broad but comprehensible terms. This is particularly reassuring, for it comes after Maimonides' treatment of the attributes of action, the only other form of predication concerning God which he allows (*Guide* I: 52, 1963: 118). Maimonides discusses the attributes of action after his unambiguous rejection of non-essential attributes. He believes with certainty that God has no qualities (active or passive) and no dispositions or affects (*Guide* I: 52, 1963: 115), for all such entail composition. Nor can God be said to have a relation with anything else, to be implicated in any way and made correlative to anything else. God's unique being, his uniquely necessary existence, has nothing in common with other existents.

Maimonides must realize this teaching leaves God unrelated to the world, beyond space and time and all within it, and it is therefore completely contrary to popular religious belief. Thus, he states that "indulgence should be exercised if [a relational attribute] is predicated of God" (*Guide* I: 52, 1963: 118), claiming that it does less damage to the true understanding of God's nature than other forms of attribution. As we have seen, he himself relates God to the world in the way he expands upon the meaning of the essential attributes.

At first, Maimonides' acceptance of attributes of action seems to further undermine his thesis, for here we have a multiplicity of acts in the world which are said not to affect God's essence, but which do bring him into relation with the world. As Maimonides proceeds, however, it becomes clear that it is we who view the one action of God in the world (the emanation of his being or existence, and cf. *Guide* I: 63, 1963: 154) in many ways, attributing diverse actions to the one unchanging activity of being (*Guide* I: 53, 1963: 121).

Maimonides brings biblical proof-texts, citing as attributes of action the thirteen attributes which Judaism sees revealed in the theophany of Exodus 33 and 34 (*Guide* I: 54, 1963: 124). God is essentially described there as merciful and gracious, long suffering and forbearing, though also, when necessary, punishing (*Guide* I: 54, 1963: 127). These are not to be seen as moral qualities, but as actions "resembling the actions that in us proceed from moral qualities." It is we who attribute diversity to God's action, to his being, and who project on to it moral qualities and distinctions. For Maimonides, Moses is depicted as instructed in God's "ways" in order to know how best to govern. The people are presented with an image of God in human terms, both politically and ethically, which it behooves the wise ruler to emulate. The attributes of action thus are important for political purposes, even as the essential attributes have metaphysical significance, in Maimonides' thought.

The Calamity of *Kalâm*

Maimonides' proofs for the incorporeality of God depend on his argument for the unity of God, and that in turn depends upon his arguments for the existence of God. He engages the views advanced by Muslim theologians (the *mutakallimûn*) first, and takes the opportunity as well to survey and critique their main tenets (*Guide* I: 73, 1963: 194). He rejects their *Kalâm* notion of atomism and Occasionalism, which sees objects as having no permanent properties, constituted each moment by a divinely ordained combination of a property-less atom of matter and whatever accidental properties God wills. Continuity in nature, the very idea of nature, is seen as an illusion, created as well by God's inscrutable will.

This view thus denies the validity of sense perception and the judgments based upon them. Anything that can be imagined is possible in *Kalâm* thought, as long as the proposition asserting it is not self-contradictory (*Guide* I: 73, 1963: 206). Nature has no claims on God's power or will, there is no necessity in nature.

It is a measure of Maimonides' dedication to philosophy that he is repelled by this argument, however attractive theologically. Yet, for him, the testimony of the senses is self-evident, nature is coherent and predictable, and God acts through natural intermediaries. Maimonides realizes, however, that the premises of his and of *Kalâm* thought concerning possibility and necessity, the realms of imaginative and rational, demonstrative thought, are irreconcilable (*Guide* I: 73, 1963: 211; Ivry, 1982: 76).

Invoking Aristotle and Plotinus

Maimonides is on stronger ground in rejecting the *Kalâm* arguments for the nature of God, seeing them as based on their arguments for creation, an issue he considers not at all proved (*Guide* I: 71, 1963: 180). It is best, he believes, to argue for the existence of God and all that follows from that on the basis of Aristotle's belief in the eternity of the world, since *a fortiori* believers in creation would have no reason to reject the conclusions of such proofs.

Accordingly, Maimonides introduces the second part of the *Guide* with an apparently original summary of Aristotelian physics, given in the form of twenty-six "premises," all but one of which he believes are demonstrated beyond any doubt (*Guide* II: Introduction, 1963: 235). The premises with which he fully concurs refer to the impossibility of an (actual) infinite magnitude, and to Aristotle's conceptions of potentiality and actuality, change, essence and accident, time, motion and body, matter and form, and causation. The twenty-sixth premise is that of the eternity of the world, which Maimonides grants without much discussion at this point. For his purposes, Aristotle has proved even without this last premise that the world needs a first mover, which must be an immaterial separate being (*Guide* II: 1, 1963: 245).

Maimonides employs a number of arguments based on Aristotle's cosmology to make this same point, that there exists one being separate from matter in which there is no possibility whatever, no potentiality, no corporeality and no multiplicity; a being which exists solely in virtue of its essence, uncaused, non-contingent. This, Maimonides says, "is the deity" (*Guide* II: 1, 1963: 249).

We know, however, from the *Guide*'s prior discussion of attributes, that Aristotle's conception of God as the Unmoved Mover is not sufficient for Maimonides. His deity reflects as well Plotinus' One, the unknown source that endows the world with the forms of being, the source from which our souls ultimately derive, and to which they yearn to return. Aristotle has helped Maimonides ascend philosophically to God, Plotinus is essential in bringing this God down to earth, in relating him to us. It is through an unspecific, general process of emanation that Maimonides posits a providential God (Ivry, 1991: 127).

Maimonides' God, accordingly, is anything but simple conceptually, and contains contradictory modalities. The God whose existence he accepts as proved, and on the basis of which he can insist upon divine unity and incorporeality, is not the God who is concerned with humanity, even in the most general way. The willing and caring God is taken on faith, faith buttressed by a philosophical tradition of realism far removed from the Peripateticism that Maimonides lauded. Having criticized Aristotle's cosmology on the basis of its inadequate explanation of the physical phenomena of the heavens, Maimonides must have known he was going beyond the evidence in presenting this other image of God.

It is thus an open question whether Maimonides as a philosopher is speaking more than rhetorically when he involves God in the world. Certainly, even on the Plotinian model, God is not personal, and it is often apparent that neither is Maimonides' God. He may be the creator of a finite world, as Maimonides may wish to argue, but that is only because the astronomical evidence of the day did not support Aristotle's view of the perfectly circular motion of the spheres, and hence of the unceasing, eternal motion of the world (*Guide* II: 11, 1963: 273). Maimonides argues for the possibility of *creatio ex nihilo*, knowing he has no empirical evidence for it, and that therefore it is, in the logical terms he normally insists upon, unintelligible (Ivry, 1982: 79).

Creation, Revelation, and Personal Perfection

Maimonides acknowledges that he needs a traditional creator God to establish the possibility of miracles, particularly the miracle of revelation at Sinai, which in turn establishes the legitimacy and necessity of maintaining Jewish law. Other miracles, such as those recorded by the prophets, are acknowledged to be the products of their inspired imaginations. The prophet has the gift to interpret universal truths in specific depictions which capture the people's imagination and attention. This gift, like all else, is divine in that it ultimately comes from God, the source of all being. Hence, belief in creation, as tied to belief in revelation and itself a product of biblical revelation, serves in part to instill belief in an ideal polity, established by God and ruled by his ministers.

This political reading of the *Guide* should be balanced by the poignant striving of Maimonides to bring the reader toward a religiously existential fulfillment, a "perfection of the soul." Maimonides is less explicit than most other medieval philosophers concerning the development of an individual's intellect from potentiality to actuality. However, from scattered remarks in the *Guide* and elsewhere, it is apparent that he accepts Aristotle's views on the soul, as modified by Alexander of Aphrodisias and Muslim philosophers. The widely held doctrine understood that the perfected intellect, having moved from potentiality to a state of acquired true cognitions, conjoins thereby with the (proximate) ontic source of true propositions, their formal and efficient cause, the universal and eternal Agent Intellect. This separate immaterial intelligence is akin to Plotinus' Universal Soul, and, like it, is part of the eternal and hence divine realm.

For Maimonides, then, the mastery of science, in particular metaphysical knowledge, as much as can be known, has the effect of joining one's individual intellect with the universal Agent Intellect. In this conjunction lies the possibility of immortality of the soul, which Maimonides affirms. Yet it is really immortality of the intellect only, an immortality that has no distinctive individual characteristics, conjunction being with universal truth and being. Maimonides admits this in passing, and is not deterred by it at all (*Guide* I: 74, 1963: 221). The felicity to be experienced in joining in the divine realm, in coming as close to God as human beings may expect, is sufficient for him.

In one of the most striking passages of the book (*Guide* III: 51, 1963: 625) Maimonides claims that a person who reaches this level of spiritual bliss suffers no harm or evil. This person has moved to another level of being almost, aware that his or her physical body is inessential and insignificant. It is part of the material realm of change and corruption, and is identified with potentiality and privation, the antithesis of all that is eternal and truly existent. Matter is real only to the extent that it serves to support and enhance form, immaterial being. In itself, matter has no being, it is pure privation, not real to man or God.

This raises questions concerning Maimonides' supposed belief in creation from nothing, where nothing, absolute nothing, is actually and literally called "privation" (*'Adam* in Arabic, translated in *Guide* II: 13, 1963: 283–5 as "non-existence"). God, in creating "after" or "from" absolute privation, would presumably have to relate to that which is totally foreign to his being, and thus beyond his control. Were he successful in doing so, he would then be responsible for a world in which evil and suffering would be all too real.

Accordingly, Maimonides' doctrine of providence and evil fare better in a Platonic or Neoplatonic eternal universe. Maimonides admits he could find accommodation between Judaism and Platonic doctrine if convinced of the latter (*Guide* II: 25, 1963: 328). Thus his strong attempt to argue for *creatio ex nihilo* may be another example of his deferral, or seeming deferral, to popular opinion.

Bibliography

Editions and translations

Maimonides, Moses (1963) *The Guide of the Perplexed*, trans. Shlomo Pines (English trans.). Chicago: Chicago University Press.

Maimonides, Moses (1972) *The Guide of the Perplexed*, ed. Joseph Kafih (Arabic text and Hebrew translation, reprinted 1991). Jerusalem: Mossad HaRav Kook.

Studies

Davidson, Herbert (1987) *Proofs for Eternity, Creation and the Existence of God in Medieval Islamic and Jewish Philosophy*. New York: Oxford University Press.

Fox, Marvin (1990) *Interpreting Maimonides*. Chicago: Chicago University Press.

Harvey, Warren Zev (2000) On Maimonides' allegorical readings of Scripture. In Jon Whitman (ed.), *Interpretation and Allegory*, pp. 181–8. Leiden: Brill.

Hyman, Arthur (1989) Demonstrative, dialectical and sophistic arguments in the philosophy of Moses Maimonides. In Eric L. Ormsby (ed.), *Moses Maimonides and his Time*, pp. 35–51. Washington, DC: The Catholic University of America Press.

Ivry, Alfred (1982) Maimonides on possibility. In Jehuda Reinharz and Daniel Swetschinski (eds), *Mystics, Philosophers and Politicians*, pp. 67–84. Durham, NC: Duke University Press.

Ivry, Alfred (1991) Neoplatonic currents in Maimonides' thought. In Joel Kraemer (ed.), *Perspectives on Maimonides*. Oxford: Oxford University Press.

Kraemer, Joel (1989) Maimonides on Aristotle and scientific method. In Eric L. Ormsby (ed.), *Moses Maimonides and his Time*, pp. 53–88. Washington, DC: The Catholic University of America Press.

Kreisel, Howard (1999) *Maimonides' Political Thought*. Albany, NY: State University of New York Press.

Pines, Shlomo (1963) The philosophic sources of *The Guide of the Perplexed*. Translator's introduction to *The Guide of the Perplexed*, trans. S. Pines, pp. lvii–cxxxiv. Chicago: University of Chicago Press.

Pines, Shlomo (1979) The limitations of human knowledge according to Al-Farabi, Ibn Bâjja and Maimonides. In Isadore Twersky (ed.), *Studies in Medieval Jewish History and Literature*, vol. I, pp. 82–102. Cambridge, MA: Harvard University Press.

Schwarz, Michael (1991, 1992–3) Who were Maimonides' *Mutakallimûn*? Some remarks on *Guide of the Perplexed*, part I, chapter 73. In Arthur Hyman (ed.), *Maimonidean Studies*, vol. 2, pp. 159–210; vol. 3, pp. 143–72. New York: Yeshiva University Press.

Stern, Joseph (2000) Maimonides on language and the science of language. In Robert S. Cohen and Hillel Levine (eds), *Maimonides and the Sciences*, pp. 173–226. Dordrecht: Kluwer.

Strauss, Leo (1963) How to begin to study *The Guide of the Perplexed*. In *The Guide of the Perplexed*, trans. S. Pines, vol. I, pp. xi–lvi. Chicago: University of Chicago Press.

Strauss, Leo (1984) Jerusalem and Athens. In *Studies in Platonic Political Philosophy*, pp. 147–

73). Chicago: University of Chicago Press.

Strauss, Leo (1987) *Philosophy and Law*, trans. F. Baumann. Philadelphia: Jewish Publication Society.

Wolfson, Harry A. (1977) Maimonides on negative attributes. In Isadore Twersky and George H. Williams (eds), *Studies in the History of Philosophy and Religion*, vol. I, pp. 195–230. Cambridge, MA: Harvard University Press.

14

Thomas Aquinas, *On Being and Essence* (ante 1256)

Toward a Metaphysics of Existence

Jorge J. E. Gracia

Written almost eight hundred years ago (before 1256), when Aquinas (ca. 1225–1274) was just over thirty years old, *On Being and Essence* is still one of the most important and original books of metaphysics ever written and continues to attract attention and controversy. One may disagree with the views it presents, but this should not be an obstacle to the recognition of its status as a classic. When compared with other well-known books in the discipline, its value easily stands out. In contrast with Aristotle's disorganized and perhaps even inconsistent *Metaphysics*, it is a marvel of systematic unity and coherence; its conciseness recommends it over Suárez's over-extended and plodding *Metaphysical Disputations*; to Spinoza's contrived and artificial method in the *Ethics*, it contraposes an easy and natural exposition and argumentation; next to Descartes's presumptuous *Meditations*, it is a lesson in intellectual humility; and compared with the obscurity of Hegel's *Logic* and Heidegger's *Introduction to Metaphysics*, it is a paradigm of clarity. These qualities, joined to the originality of the ideas it puts forth and the tightness of the arguments with which it supports them, explain its extraordinary influence in the history of metaphysics and ensure for it a permanent place in philosophy.

In spite of its extreme brevity – no more than thirty pages in standard type – the book is packed with original metaphysical doctrines and subtle philosophical arguments. Its central doctrine is a revolutionary existential conception of being as an act which turns on its head the classical Platonic–Aristotelian essentialistic conception that has dominated Western metaphysics from antiquity. Why? Because most philosophers before and after the publication of *On Being and Essence* hold one or more of three views, all of which are challenged by Aquinas's position. These three views may be expressed in a variety of ways, but let me describe them as follows:

1   Essence precedes existence. This means that in the metaphysical order, to be a kind of thing, or have an essence, is more fundamental than to exist.
2   To exist is nothing other than to be a kind of thing. Sometimes this is understood metaphysically to mean that there is no real distinction between existence and

essence. To exist and to be a kind of thing are in fact the same. This may be expressed in terms of the denotation and connotation of terms. The denotation of a term consists of the things of which the term is truly predicated. Misifuz, Minina, and every other single cat are part of the denotation of "cat" because this term can be truthfully predicated of all of them. The connotation of a term, on the other hand, consists of the features that are associated with the things of which the term is predicated. Thus rationality and animality are part of the connotation of "human". Now, we can express the metaphysical doctrine that there is no real distinction between essence and existence by saying that "being" and "essence" have the same denotation, even if they have different connotations; the terms are truthfully predicated of the same thing even though the features they connote are different. At other times, however, the claim that to exist is nothing other than to be a kind of thing is understood not just metaphysically, but also logically to mean that no cogent distinction between existence and essence can be made. "Being" and "essence" not only denote, but also connote the same thing.

3   Perfection is always associated with essence and never with existence. Something can be more or less perfect than something else but only because they are both kinds of things, that is, because of their essences. It makes no sense to say that something is more perfect merely in virtue of its existence, nor does it make sense to say that existence is a perfection, perfects essence, or is the source of a thing's perfections.

The revolutionary character of Aquinas's *On Being and Essence* rests in part on the fact that it lays the groundwork for a challenge to these common views by arguing that:

1'   Existence metaphysically precedes essence. To be is more fundamental than to be a kind of thing. This is expressed by Aquinas by saying that to be (*esse*) is the actuality of essence (ch. 4, §8).
2'   Existence is distinct from essence (ch. 4, §6). In *On Being and Essence*, the nature of this distinction is not specified, although in later works Aquinas makes clear it involves not just logic, but also metaphysics. The distinction between essence and existence is real, not just conceptual (*De veritate* 27, 1, ad 8).
3'   Perfection is associated with both existence and essence, and in fact existence turns out to be the very perfection of essence. Although this view is not explicitly articulated in *On Being and Essence*, it is implied by some of the things Aquinas says in it. For example, he claims that the root of all of God's perfections is precisely his existence (ch. 5, §3), and this implies that there is a direct connection between perfection and existence. In later works, he was more specific, noting that existence is the "actuality of all acts and perfection of all perfection" (*De potentia* 7, 2, ad 9).

This is the core of what some have called, with reason, Aquinas's existentialism, but which, in order to distinguish it from recent views with which this term is connected, should perhaps be more appropriately called "metaphysical existentialism." Apart from this doctrine, *On Being and Essence* introduces many other related views worthy of consideration. Three of the most provocative are the following: God is a pure act of existence; natures considered as such are neutral with respect to being or unity; and the principle of individuation of material entities is designated matter.

Aquinas supports these doctrines with philosophical arguments independent of faith or philosophical authority; the views of other authors are used merely to help and illustrate, rather than as argumentative props. *On Being and Essence* is a book of philosophy, not of theology or history, and its sources are primarily the Islamic and Jewish philosophers of the Middle Ages, particularly Avicenna and Averroës, although the presence of Aristotle is obvious and there are references to other authors as well.

The treatise is divided into six chapters, preceded by a brief preface. The latter explains that the overall purpose of the book is to explore the meaning of "a being" (*ens*) and "an essence" (*essentia*), how being and essence are found in different things, and their relation to the logical notions of genus, species, and difference. The first chapter is propaedeutic and clarifies the terminology of being and essence. "Being" had been a subject of controversy in that the term is used to refer both to things that exist, such as a cat or a color, and to things that do not exist, such as blindness. To say that blindness exists in the eye, or that an eye is blind, seems to generate a contradiction, for blindness is nothing but a lack of sight. This had puzzled many philosophers before Aquinas, but he dissolves the puzzle by drawing a distinction between two senses of "a being" (*ens*). In one sense it means whatever is classifiable into the Aristotelian categories, such as substance, quality, relation, and so on. Later he makes clear that being in this sense is not to be understood as a genus, but rather analogically (ch. 6, §9). But in another sense "a being" refers to the truth of propositions. If this distinction is kept in mind, then it is clear that one can say that blindness is in the eye, in the second sense of "a being" without falling into the contradiction implied if the claim concerned the first sense.

With respect to "an essence" (*essentia*), which applies only to the things that are beings in the first sense, the difficulty arises because of the confusion in the usage of this term and the terms "quiddity" (*quidditas*), "form" (*forma*), and "nature" (*natura*), introduced into the West as a result of the recently made available translations of Greek and Arabic works into Latin. The problem consisted in that all four terms were interchanged in some contexts and not in others. So how are we to make sense of this? Aquinas argues for a solution in which these terms are taken to refer to the same thing but in different ways. Using the terminology introduced earlier, we could say that these terms have the same denotation but their connotations differ. "Essence," "quiddity," "form," and "nature" denote the same thing, but "quiddity" connotes it as what (*quid*) makes a thing to be what it is, "form" connotes it as what determines it to be so, "nature" connotes it in terms of its direction to an specific operation, and "essence" connotes it as that through which a thing has being (*esse*).

Because essence (and the same goes for quiddity, form, or nature, in so far as these are in reality the same thing) is primarily found in substances, chapter 2 takes up the question of the meaning of an essence in them. Aquinas finds that there are also two senses of it. In one, "an essence" means everything that is expressed in the definition of the substance in question; this is why it can be predicated of the individuals who have such an essence. Accordingly, the essence of man embraces everything that is part of the definition of man, including materiality. In another sense, however, "an essence" means just the form that, united to matter, constitutes the individual substance. Accordingly, the essence of this man, for example, refers only to the form of this man, which joined to this matter constitutes the individual man. Aquinas calls the first *forma totius* – generally translated as "form of the whole," but better expressed as "the whole form" – and the second *forma partis* – again generally translated as "the form of the part," but better expressed as "the form that is a part." The status of the second is quite clear, for it is the individual essence of an individual being (*ens*). The status of the first, however, is unclear, so Aquinas addresses this question in chapter 3.

The problem this question poses is known in the literature as *the problem of universals*. Aquinas raises it by asking about the kind of unity and being (these are the two key elements of what we might today call ontological status) that the essence considered as a whole has. The traditional answers to this question are gathered under three major divisions: realism, conceptualism, and nominalism. The first holds that an essence (e.g., man) exists as one outside the mind, in addition to existing in the mind as a concept (e.g., the concept man) and as a word (e.g., "man"). Conceptualism holds that an essence exists only as a concept in the mind (e.g., the concept of man) and as a word (e.g., "man"). And nominalism holds that an essence exists merely as a word (e.g., "man").

Aquinas's answer cuts the Gordian knot that had plagued this issue by arguing that an essence can be taken in two senses: absolutely in itself, and in relation to something else. Absolutely, an essence is neutral with respect to being and unity because its definition contains no reference to either of these; only what is included in the definition can be truthfully predicated of it. Thus, the essence "man" is neutral with respect to being and unity because the definition of man (i.e., rational animal) does not refer either to unity or being. For this reason, essences considered absolutely cannot be said to be one or many, or to exist in individual things or in the mind (the two modes of existence Aquinas is willing to accept). We cannot say that man, considered absolutely, that is *qua* man, is one or many, exists or does not exist. But this does not preclude that essences be one or many and exist in the mind as universals and in individuals as individuated. They can acquire these different modes of unity and being only when they are considered not absolutely, but in relation to something else, namely the mind or the world of individuals outside the mind. Man, considered in relation to the mind, is both predicable of many (i.e., universal) and exists in it as a concept. And man, considered in relation to the world of individuals, is one in each and every man (i.e., individual) and exists as individuated.

Having offered a solution to the problem of universals, Aquinas turns to the central topic of the treatise, the ultimate nature of reality (*res*) and how essence and being are found in it, first in substances (chs 4 and 5) and then in accidents (ch. 6). In order to understand Aquinas's view, however, we need to clarify further the language of being and how it relates to essence. The key terms Aquinas uses are *ens* and *esse*. The first is the participial form of the verb "to be" and is appropriately translated by the English expression "a being." The second is the infinitive form of the verb and has no precise counterpart in English. It can be translated roughly by either "to be" or "existence." Now, a being (*ens*) is something like this cat or this white, but existence (*esse*) is the very act (in later works Aquinas refers to it as *actus essendi* [*De veritate* 1, 1]) whereby this cat or this white exists. He argues that this means, first, that there is a distinction between what this cat is (i.e., its essence) and the act whereby the cat exists (i.e., its *esse* or existence), and, second, that there is a composition of essence and existence in this cat. Aquinas's argument for this is that an essence can be understood without knowing anything about whether it exists or not. "I can know, for instance, what a man or a phoenix is and still be ignorant whether it has being in reality . . . [and] from this it is clear that being is other than essence . . ." (ch. 4, §6).

Now we are ready to look at the comprehensive picture of reality Aquinas paints for us. According to it, reality is divided into several levels which are distinguished and arranged hierarchically. At the very top of this hierarchy is God. He is different from everything else in that he is the only being whose essence consists in his existence. He is a "to be" (*esse*), an act of pure and simple existence (*esse tantum*), which is in turn the source of all his perfections. Aquinas does not deny that God has an essence, but he interprets this essence in a non-essentialistic way. At bottom, God is not a kind in the way other things are kinds, for God's essence is radically different from the essences of everything else. Moreover, there can be only one thing whose essence is its existence, and thus God's individuality is explained by his existential uniqueness.

The next level of reality is occupied by spiritual substances that are neither divine nor related to matter in any way. These substances are distinguished from God in that they are composed of their essences and the acts whereby they exist. They are, therefore, neither simple, nor pure existence. Moreover, their existence is derived and can come about only as a result of participation in the divine act. These entities are distinguished from each other by both their individual acts of existence and their essences, for each of them is a unique kind of thing. This means that there is no multiplication of individuals within their kind; each of these substances comprises a single species.

Next come spiritual substances whose essence includes matter and therefore are united to matter. This is where human beings belong. Their composition is twofold: of essence and existence, and of form and matter. The composition of form and matter distinguishes them from purely spiritual substances and explains their individuality and multiplication within the same species. Humans are individuated by designated matter (*materia signata* or *designata*), that is, matter considered under determined dimensions. In spite of its connection with matter, however, the human soul – which is part of a man, not the whole man, and the same as a man's form – is able to exist independently of matter after death because its primary function, which is to know, is immaterial. Moreover, once individuated by matter, the soul can maintain its individuality even after its separation from the body in death.

The world below humans is composed of substances whose essences are inherently bound up with matter. The composition of these beings, just like that of humans, is double: of essence and existence, and of form and matter. However, their form cannot survive outside of matter because its functions are not independent of matter.

On Being and Essence closes with a chapter on accidents. The world is composed not just of substances, but also of the accidental features that attach to substances, so it is necessary to make clear how being and essence are related to them. Just like substances, accidents exist and therefore must have essences which can be defined. Their being differs from that of substances, however, in that it is not independent of the being of the substances in which they are found, for accidents exist only in substances. This is clear in their definitions, for these are incomplete without reference to a substance.

There is much that is remarkable and revolutionary in *On Being and Essence*. Most revolutionary is the existential understanding of being that it presents, for although there are antecedents to it in the work of some Arabic and Latin writers who preceded Aquinas (e.g., al-Farabi, Avicenna, and William of Auvergne), it is only in this book that we find this intuition made into the centerpiece of an overall view of reality. Most remarkable is that Aquinas is able to present and develop this intuition and apply it comprehensibly in the few pages that compose this very brief book. Only a handful of philosophers have ever been able to accomplish as much in such a limited space, and the views of only a very few of those have survived beyond a century. In contrast, the views put forth in *On Being and Essence* are still the source of intense debate nearly eight hundred years after they first appeared.

Bibliography

Editions and Translations

Aquinas, Thomas (1965) *Aquinas on Being and Essence: A Translation and Interpretation*, trans. Joseph Bobick. Notre Dame, IN: University of Notre Dame Press.
Aquinas, Thomas (1968) *On Being and Essence*, 2nd edn, trans. Armand Maurer. Toronto: Pontifical Institute of Mediaeval Studies.
Aquinas, Thomas (1976) *De ente et essentia*, ed. Fratrum Predicatorum. In *Opera omnia*, vol. 43, pp. 369–81. Leonine Edition. Rome: Editori di San Tommaso.
Aquinas, Thomas (forthcoming) *On Being and Essence*, trans. Peter King. Indianapolis, IN: Hackett.

Studies

Chenu, M. D. (1964) *Toward Understanding Saint Thomas*, trans. A. M. Landry and D. Hughes. Chicago: Regnery.
Davies, Brian (1992) *The Thought of Thomas Aquinas*. Oxford: Clarendon Press.
Davies, Brian (2002) *Thomas Aquinas: Contemporary Philosophical Perspectives*. New York: Oxford University Press.
Gilson, Étienne (1952) *Being and Some Philosophers*, 2nd edn. Toronto: Pontifical Institute of Mediaeval Studies.
Gracia, Jorge J. E. (1994) Cutting the Gordian knot of ontology: Thomas's solution to the problem of universals. In D. Gallagher (ed.), *Aquinas and his Legacy*, pp. 16–36. Washington, DC: The Catholic University of America Press.
Maritain, Jacques (1948) *Existence and the Existent*, trans. L. Galantière and G. B. Phelan. New York: Pantheon.
Owens, Joseph (1963) *An Elementary Christian Metaphysics*. Milwaukee, WI: Bruce.
Owens, Joseph (1968) *An Interpretation of Existence*. Milwaukee, WI: Bruce.
Wippel, John (2000) *The Metaphysical Thought of Thomas Aquinas*. Washington, DC: The Catholic University of America Press.

15

Thomas Aquinas, *Summa theologiae* (ca. 1273)

Christian Wisdom Explained Philosophically

James F. Ross

The *Summa theologiae* is more than a philosophical work. It is a systematic exposition (written ca. 1266–73) of a whole Christian conception of the world within philosophical principles and concepts. The work is clear, compressed, and explicitly reasoned, with vivid examples. It is arranged into questions, answers, objections, and replies. Its structure, nevertheless, seems complex, like cathedral architecture; the analytic tables in most English editions help one to locate and see the order of issues. The organization is not according to philosophical priorities, but, rather, theological ones, so there is not a formal rationale and defense of its underlying philosophical skeleton. The scholarly reader has to extract that, supplementing it from Aquinas's (ca. 1225–1274) other works. This book explicitly addresses the vast Western literature from ancient times. It still stands, nearly eight hundred years later, as the single most comprehensive exposition of the whole of Latin Christian wisdom. Because of the book's massive scope and detail, this survey has to be restricted to some major topics.

Some Facts

The *Summa* (the conventional short name for the book) is in three parts (the second being divided into two sub-parts), with 512 questions, 2,669 articles, and about 10,000 objections and replies, overall about 1.8 million words, nowadays in nearly 3,000 double-columned pages. It was written in about five years, along with major commentaries on Aristotle and on scripture. It is usually reprinted now, in English translation, in five paperback volumes (see bibliography).

References to the *Summa* are made by numbered part, question, article, and reply to objection. The name of the book is often left out or abbreviated as *ST*; and it is typically cited like this, say: "I, 21, 3, ad 4," to read "Part I, Question 21, Article 3, Reply to objection 4" (the Latin *ad* means "to"). The questions on a single major topic are grouped by editors into "Treatises"; for instance, "The Treatise on God" (I, 1–26), "The Treatise on the Trinity"(I, 27–43), "The Treatise on Man" (I, 75–102), "The Treatise on Law" (I-II, 90–108).

It has three main parts. Part I: The Being and Nature of God, including the Trinity of Divine Persons, the creation of the cosmos, the origins of good and evil, and the creation and nature of angels and of man, and, finally, the divine governance of the world, about 600 pages, in 119 questions.

Part II has two sub-parts: I-II ("the First Part of the Second Part") treats human happiness and fulfillment and the means to it, the nature and components of human acts, particularly, freedom and the voluntary, the passions, emotions, feelings and habits, and the principles regulating human actions: (i) internally, namely, the virtues and vices; and, (ii) externally, law and divine grace, about 500 pages. Included there is the vastly influential Treatise on Law (I-II, 90–108), which contains the foundation for moral law, and then for civil law, the limits on government power, and the rights of rebellion (against tyranny), civil disobedience and just war, and a commentary on ancient Hebrew law and its relationship to the New Testament. It concludes with six questions on divine grace.

Part II-II ("the Second Part of the Second Part") is a full-scale, applied moral philosophy, organized under the theological virtues of faith, hope, and charity (love), and the natural virtues of prudence, justice, temperance, and fortitude, exploring the vices opposed to each by excess and deficit, and their sub-divisions, along with four questions (II-II, 67–71), on the obligations of judges, attorneys, witnesses, and defendants in legal actions. The classification and rationales for the virtues and vices are extensive, learned in ancient and Roman thought, and have had immense influence, notably, upon Dante's *Commedia*, and on Milton, Chaucer, and Shakespeare, and the rest of Western and Russian literature and art.

Part III is almost exclusively concerned with the supernatural events about Jesus: the incarnation, redemption, resurrection, and the sacramental aids to individual humans, though it is expressed and explained in the philosophical categories and principles that are threaded throughout the whole book, sometimes expanded for the context, for instance, the distinctions in the notions of "necessity" found in III, 46, 1. Thomas died in 1274 at the age of forty-nine, before finishing the treatment of sacraments, so the rest of his plan for Part III, covering the end of the world, the general resurrection and final judgment was filled in by his medieval editors with material from his other works, particularly from his commentary on the *Sentences* of Peter Lombard.

The overall plan is on the "origin–return"(*exitus / reditus*) pattern of (i) one source of all being, differentiating into everything else, and (ii) the eventual return (or renewal, III, 91, 1, ad 4, suppl.) of all things to their source (cf. I, 102, 2), found in Plotinus (ca. 250), and others. But Aquinas reinterprets that outline and fills it in with (i) the philosophical story of a divine first, free, cause of all other things, including the stars and all life and especially of humans, overlaid and intertwined with (ii) the Judeo-Christian story of creation, sin, redemption, and the promise of eternal life with bodily resurrection, along with (iii) a divine law for humans and a divine plan for a future but certain everlasting Kingdom of God beginning on the earth. He contemplates the end of the earth and of the stars, but without the destruction of the creation as a whole, and, instead, with its everlasting renewal.

How to Read the Work

The three parts are divided into questions. Each question is divided into component articles, as sub-questions. Each article begins with a succinct statement of key objections to the expected answer, and a paragraph "On the Contrary" citing scripture or some major thinker like Aristotle or a Father of the Church, expressing the general sentiment of Aquinas's answer. Next is a section beginning, "I answer that," known variously as "the answer," "the reply," or "the corpus" (Latin *corpus*: body) of the article, giving Aquinas's position and reasons; that is followed by his numbered replies to the objections.

Every article of the book follows the same order. Even the longest answers, like I, 2, 3 (part I, question 2, article 3), which gives the five proofs for the existence of God, and I, 76, 1, on the union of soul and body, are no more than 1,500 words, and answers are often only 200 words; similarly, replies to objections are usually brief, the longest perhaps 200 words. The questions are organized so that the general explanatory principles for the later articles under each question are laid out in the first article, with more particular principles being added in the following articles. Nevertheless, later articles under a question often contain the key philosophical issue: as do I, 2, 3, and I, 75, 2 (proof of subsistence of the soul); and sometimes replies to objections do as well. The reader should explicitly decide whether the answer to each question is "yes" or "no," and what is the key philosophical (or other) reasoning on which the answer rests.

Aquinas answers questions, even the most particular ones, by placing them in a broad context, often of large-scale philosophical conflicts, say of Democritus, Plato, and Aristotle (I, 84, 6) and of Plato and Avicenna (e.g. I, 88, 1), but concisely; and sometimes the philosophical reasoning is detailed, but brief, as on "whether the intellectual principle is united to the body as its form" (I, 76, 1). Some of the most important philosophical theories are developed in densely religious contexts, as when he develops the theory of relations and of names in his exposition of the Trinity of Divine Persons (I, 32, 2). For his overall task involves philosophical exposition and grounding of the elements of the Christian faith amidst what is known by philosophy and other human inquiry as well.

Faith and Reason

There are two basic sources of knowledge, that is, of "rational certainty as to what *is* so": human understanding and divine revelation (I, 1). Understanding is the source of what we know for ourselves by reason, and revelation is the source of what we know by divine faith, that is, by divinely gifted trust in God's word (I, 1, ad 1). The items can variously overlap for different people (II-II, 5). There is, of course, human faith, namely, all the forms of natural trust; that is, rational reliance upon others and upon the regularities of experience that makes the fabric of human thinking (and is subject to the vices of superstition and obduracy, lying, boasting, and the like, e.g. II-II, 109–111).

Some of the things known by divine faith (revealed) are also accessible to our figur-

ing them out, and even proving them on our own, such as the existence of one immaterial God, that humans have free choice, and even the immortality of the human soul
(*psyche*). But, as to the rest, Aquinas says, "we must not attempt to prove what is of the
Faith, except by authority alone and to those who receive the authority; while as regards others, it suffices to prove that what the Faith teaches is not impossible" (I, 32,
1; and I, 1, 8).

There can be no conflict between faith and reason (natural knowledge or successful
science) because whatever is divinely revealed must be true and whatever is actually
found out by human reasoning is also true. There are often *apparent* conflicts, partly
from misunderstandings of what is revealed and partly from errors or inadequate reasoning or information in natural inquiries; proposed science is constantly revised.
Moreover, humans are prone to take the objective appearances of things for the explanatory reality and, thus, to confuse what they understand partly for the whole of
what needs to be known (I, 70, 1, ad 3); this happens in the conflict of untutored
experience with science (I, 67, 3, Moses "out of condescension to their weakness . . . put
before them only such things as are apparent to sense"), often preventing real belief in
the science and, reciprocally, inviting false reverence for its unstable speculations.

Philosophy and Theology

The intellectual disciplines, philosophy and theology, do not divide from one another
exactly as do the sources of human knowledge, faith and reason, for theology involves
both, whereas "philosophical science built up by reason," although prompted and
urged by religious faith, as it is by other pre-scientific convictions, is "finding out on
our own" – what Aquinas called "truth such as reason can discover" (I, 1) and truth
"known by natural reason." It does not rest on authority from outside the community
of science. Philosophy belongs to human science and consists of those things whose
rationale humans can figure out entirely on their own, and includes all of the specialized sciences, as well as what we are rationally certain about that has not yet been
organized into science, and/or is unsuitable for it, like politics (statecraft) and art.

Theology, the science of things divine, has both revealed beginnings (e.g. that there
is only one God, maker of all else, who is a Trinity of Persons, and who participates in
human history, etc.) and philosophical beginnings (e.g. to establish that there is one
God, creator of all things, and that the physical world is a complex of form and matter,
and of act and potentiality, that there are four sorts of causes, that act is prior to
potentiality, etc.). So the content of theology is mixed, where elements of revealed
religious faith, which are its very first principles, are expounded and elaborated philosophically, and philosophical discoveries are adapted, complemented, and supplemented
with divine revelations (e.g. about the persons of God and the ultimate destiny of
humans as individuals and as a species) to make up the one "wisdom above all human
wisdom" (I, 1, 6), which is "divine science" (*scientia divina*). Philosophy consists only
of what can be found out by unaided human inquiry.

The overall Christian story that Aquinas underpins with his philosophical worldview can be summarized in nine points: (1) Humans sinned, in some aboriginal catas-
trophe, the Fall, plunging all humans into a vortex of evil, both individual and corporate,

for which no forgiveness was available to mankind before Christ's sacrifice. (2) In time, God the Father made a gift of his Son to be a human, Jesus, (3) who, by a perfect act of love of all humans and of obedience to his Father's will, offered his own life, taken by judicial murder, as a sacrifice (a key element of worship from the time of the children of Adam, and foreshadowed by Abraham's offering Isaac), that made forgiveness available to all humans, and who rose by his own power from the dead, as the "first born of a new generation," thereby offering all humans (4) who accept faith in Jesus the Redeemer, the prospect of life forever with God, and (5) establishing an earthly institution, his Church, the People of God, to continue offering that sacrifice, and sharing in the Bread of Life, and in the aid of the Sacraments, (6) working for human society in accord with divine love, (7) until the "Second Coming," the return of the Redeemer, the resurrection of all who have died, and a final judgment of all mankind, and (8) the establishment of the divine community of humans (the Kingdom of God), and (9) the "life of the world to come."

That story, with elaborate details and interpretations of past and future human history, is embedded by this work in the philosophical conceptions of Aquinas's philosophy, to make one overall fabric of human wisdom, that is, one overall account of the nature of reality, of man's place in it, and of the course and outcome of human history: the story of God and man. That is what is presented with detailed rationales in this book, though, of course, not all the details, even all the ones Aquinas worked out elsewhere, are contained in it.

The Philosophical Sources

Aquinas is usually regarded as an Aristotelian, having been one of the major interpreters and adapters of all of Aristotle's philosophy, and central to its introduction to the Latin West in the mid-thirteenth century. And, indeed, the overall outlines of his philosophical scheme, and most of the content and of the explanatory general principles he uses, are adapted right from Aristotle. But there are crucial alterations in Aristotle's presuppositions, some to fit the demands of Christian belief (such as a temporal beginning of the world and personal immortality), and some original and basic philosophical changes, particularly his notions of being and existence.

Some of those changes, especially in the metaphysics of transcendental being, have Platonic and Neoplatonic origins (in Philo, Plotinus, Porphyry, [pseudo-] Dionysius, Augustine, and twelfth-century writers, like the School of St Victor); and some have Stoic sources, especially concerning the passions and moral virtues, while others originate in Roman law (elements of his theory of law) and in sacred scripture (about 100,000 citations), Boethius and the early Fathers, such as his notion of divine persons. Others still, like the absolutely basic claim of a real distinction between essence and existence in all finite things, originate in response to the Islamic philosophers of the ninth to the thirteenth centuries, Avicenna particularly, while still others come from Moses Maimonides and other Jewish thinkers, and many, many more come from Augustine, Boethius, Abelard, and other medieval Latin philosophers (about 5,000 other works are cited overall).

The philosophy of the *Summa* is not a *mélange*, a salad of others' ideas; it is an original and unified construction, like a cathedral with many integrated styles and influences, but one overall plan. The crucial architectural elements show up right in the beginnings, in the Treatise on God (I, 1–26), and are elaborated in all that follows: that there must be one thing that exists on account of itself, in which being and essence are the same. The overriding philosophical theme is that God is *ipsum esse subsistens*, the one and only self-subsistent being. That all other being is caused, dependent, and is both actuality and potentiality in various respects; that all finite being is made and sustained by God, aimed at God as its final cause, and that humans, the highest animal creatures, are by nature aimed at happiness, which, however, cannot be concretely and perfectly achieved without divine supernatural intervention.

On God's Existence and Nature

Like Augustine (ca. 400) and others, Aquinas expands the ancient Greek idea of a divine being that is the divine ultimate *explanatory* principle of all being into a notion with elaborate *religious* content: the Judeo-Christian belief that there is a loving, omnipotent, and free being, the one *object of worship and sacrifice*, who gives a divine law for mankind, and has an indefeasible plan for human history and for each human.

The key philosophical step is to show that, besides being a logically necessary *explanatory* condition for the existence of all things perceived, the divine being must be intelligent, free, good, and loving, in order to cause and sustain the universe (cosmos, world) that might not have been at all (i.e., that exists contingently). So the essential departure from ancient necessitarian views is that everything of the perceivable world might not have been at all, and that the ancient materialists (Democritus, Empedocles) were wrong too, just as Plato and Aristotle had thought as well, to suppose that the perceivable world originated by chance from necessarily existing particles. The result is that there must be a cause of being that exists necessarily and acts freely: otherwise there could be no contingent being at all. For whatever a necessarily existing being causes by nature, exists necessarily as well, even if not on its own account (as Avicenna, ca. 980 had explained). From that base, the more "personal" attributes are then deduced, and religious features are anchored to it.

Such freedom to create the perceived universe logically requires intelligence, omniscience, omnipotence, freedom of action, moral agency, goodness, love, and willing conservation to keep all else in being. Aquinas provides the argumentation to establish each of these outcomes as a necessary condition for the existence of anything other than the divine being (God). The key step, once the existence of some primary being (God) is established, is for him to show that what-it-is (its essence) cannot be in any way different from its being (*esse*): it exists on account of what-it-is.

Aquinas disposes of whether it is self-evident that God exists by saying "Not to us," though if we knew by direct acquaintance "what" God is, as we know by perception what a triangle is, then God's existence would indeed be evident, just the way "a triangle is three-sided" is evident from perception. But we don't perceive or intuit God.

However, the existence of God can be demonstrated (proved); but not *a priori*, that is, not from something explanatorily prior to the conclusion. Rather, it is proved *a posteriori,* as a reality required for perceived effects that are experienced by us: motion, change, causation, contingency, and order. Such are the perceptions from which we begin to inquire: namely, the things in the perceived universe that might not have existed at all; for nothing comes to be without a cause.

So the "proofs" consist in identifying realities that logically require a cause, or broadly, an explanatory condition, and showing that the required kind of cause is something "everybody calls God." Thus, first he tells how to prove the *existence* of a cause that *is* the divine being, and is commonly called that. Then he tells how, further and formally (I, 2–26), to *identify* that being by its attributes as the God of religious worship and faith. He does the existence proofs in one article of about 1,200 words. (This may be the origin of the phrase, "a proof, one, two, three" for quick decisive argument; for the article is I, 2, 3.) The divine nature, however, takes twenty-five questions (about 140 pages).

Aquinas calls the existential proofs "ways" because he is sketching classic reasoning, found in Aristotle, Plato, Avicenna, and Maimonides, not providing all its details; for instance, the argument to a first cause of cosmic motion is found lengthily in Aristotle's *Physics.* We summarize the "third way," the contingency argument here:

> Some things exist that might not have existed at all (contingently). But it is impossible that everything be like that. For on that supposition, there *might* (possibly) have been nothing at all. But, if there had been nothing at all, nothing would have been possible. But something *is* possible, because things are actual. So there can be (could be) no condition under which nothing is possible. Thus, the supposition that *everything might* not have been, conflicts with a self-evident truth, that something is possible (exists). Therefore, not everything "might not have been at all": so, there must be something that cannot not-exist, namely something that exists necessarily. But that is the thing people call "God."

The objectors primarily say "maybe things really did come from nothing," and "maybe each thing might not have been, but not all of them, altogether." The latter, raising the "fallacy of composition" objection, is irrelevant because Aquinas is using the modal logical principle that any conjunction with a contingent member, even only one, is contingent and, therefore, might not have been so. So any conjunction of contingent beings, no matter how many, as a whole, might not have been at all. And thus an explanation is needed for its being.

And the former denies the obvious. Aquinas thinks "no thing [say a star] comes to be without a cause" is known *for certain.* Nothing comes from nothing. Thus, those objections simply suppose what we *know* not to be so, and are thus contradictory to known truth. (Of course, Avicenna [ca. 1000] thought the order of apparent causes emanates necessarily from the being of God, and so nothing is contingent as Aquinas and the Christians supposed: basically Avicenna denied that it is evident that if a thing does not exist on account of what-it-is, it might not have existed at all.)

The second of his "ways," that the beginnings-to-be of contingent things require an unproduced originating cause, is like the one above. The other arguments for the existence of a First Being are structurally similar, though the general premises, that cosmic motion/change has to have a, relatively, unmoving cause (Aristotle), that less perfect things are explained by more perfect ones (Neoplatonism), and that the intelligible order of nature must have an intelligent explainer (Augustine and, perhaps, Aristotle), are more contentious and specialized, and may involve cosmic analogies. But the basic reasoning is that it is impossible that we have a universe such as we perceive unless there is a necessary being, a first cause of whatever begins to be, a cause of the diverse degrees of perfection, and a designer of the intelligible order of all of nature. Just consider the last one: if the cosmos is inexhaustibly intelligible, yet might not have been at all, then whence the intelligibility, and whence the laws of nature?

As to change (cosmic motion) and coming-to-be, Aquinas says an infinite regress of all-together causation is impossible. His reason is that you would never get to "here," to any particular perceived case now, if you had to run through an *unending* (infinite) sequence of predecessors; that is transparent because by supposition it is not ever completed (any more than you could have arrived at a particular coin flip by going through an infinite run of prior flips because you would not, ever, have arrived "here," always having further to go).

The Divine Nature

Aquinas provides a far more elaborate inquiry (I, 2–25) into the nature of the divine being. The question, "what features are required on the part of a necessary being to explain the existence of contingent being?" is common to each stage, and the form of argument each time is "indirect proof," namely, to deduce an inconsistency between denying the proposed divine attribute and the conclusions already established.

Simplicity

A basic common premise in those steps is that "whatever is a composite of actuality and potentiality, is contingent, causable, and in need of an explanation." Thus, a First Being cannot be composite in any way: of parts, of components, of multiplicity, or even of really separate traits, like knowledge and power, or knowing and choosing. Rather, such a being is entirely *simple*: it must not be a composition of distinct *act and potency* (that is, of capacity and its realization, or of ability and its exercise, or of possibility and actuality) in any way whatever because that would defeat its existing on account of itself (already established by I, 2, 3). For what exists on account of itself exists *because* of what-it-is, without any further explanatory feature.

We can know that God exists on account of what-God-is, without being able to know what-God-is (the divine essence); for God is incomprehensible to any creature – not that God is unintelligible, for we can understand a great deal about God; but we cannot know, as we can, say, with a triangle or a chemical element, what-it-is.

Being and essence

In everything else, what-the-thing-is is really distinct from its being (existing) because a separate cause is required to make it come to be. But in God's case, being and essence are really the same: there is no additional explanatory factor. That is sometimes called, misleadingly, nowadays, "identity of essence and existence"; but, of course, what Aquinas meant was *not* the *de dicto*, "everything true of the divine being is true of what-God-is" (for we know that God exists and do not know what-God-is); but, rather, *de re*, there is no difference of reality at all between what God is and that God is, because there is no additional explanatory factor for the divine being. With everything else, there is a real distinction between *what*-a-thing-is (essence) and *that*-it-*is* – namely, that there must be an additional explanatory factor for there to be such a thing, a cause; for instance, no dog exists on account of being canine but, instead, each requires a producing cause.

From the denial of any difference between the being and essence of God, the major elements of the divine nature follow: simplicity, first, as above, and then, immutability, intelligence, will, freedom, power, omniscience, omnipotence, and eternity, each *by indirect proof*. For, supposing the denial of any of those contradicts the real sameness of the divine being and essence by requiring some additional explanatory factor and some composition of (unfulfilled) potentiality with actuality.

The apparent multiplicity of divine attributes is entirely the result of the human manner of conception and definition based upon physically perceived things: "we always name a thing as we understand it" (I, 32, 2). Divine attributes are multiplied according to the plurality of human conceptions, not according to distinctions of divine being. In fact there is no difference in reality among God's knowledge, power, being, will, and any other divine perfection. So that opens the question (I, 13) of the meaning of the words applied both to creatures and to God. Are they different in meaning?

Analogy of Meaning

All words that apply to God, like "knows," "loves," and "judges," are captured in meaning by the context of divine being and, though remaining the same in word-definition (idea), in contrast to different words (the way "loves" contrasts with "knows"), the *manner* of meaning (Latin: *modus significandi*) contrasts with the application of the same word to any finite thing. It is somewhat the way *waited for* differs in "they waited for the dawn" and "they waited for the bus" and *turned red* contrasts in "the sky turned red at the sunset" and "he turned red with embarrassment." There is contextual adaptation of what is meant to the different sorts of things involved (I, 13, 5).

Thus, no word is univocal (exactly the same in meaning) between finite things and God; but the difference is systematic and not haphazard as it is with equivocals like "bank" (for money) and "bank" (for turn). Moreover, that linguistic phenomenon, contextual adaptation, is very general in our languages, and has several other linguistic forms, as in *healthy*/dog; *healthy*/diet, as well as metaphor, *sowing*/seeds; *sowing*/lies. Both Aquinas and Aristotle make analogy of meaning a central tool everywhere in their philosophy, apart from its religious applications.

The analogy of word meanings tracks the analogy of beings (of reality), through our analogous thinking (Latin: *analogia rationis*) – the sort of thinking tested nowadays by Millers Analogies Tests. Aquinas reasons that a creature cannot be said to exist in the same sense as God does, because its being is derived, participated (I, 44, 1), whereas God is what-is-because-of-itself (*ens per se subsistens*).

The underlying idea is that human concepts are abstractive responses to realities, and as the realities differ proportionally in manner of being and causation, so do our conceptions for them; and since the meanings of words *are* concepts, the meanings differ as the concepts adjust. Thus analogous realities are thought of with analogous concepts.

So Aquinas does not think all words applied to God, like "loves," and "understands," apply only negatively to eliminate the error of saying the opposites (Maimonides) (I, 13, 2); or, that when they are used positively, they apply only "symbolically" or "metaphorically" (Maimonides) (I, 13, 3), as in "God is the lion of Judah"; but many apply literally, but analogously to other literal applications to things we can perceive (as with "turned red" above). That is, it is literally, but analogically true that God exists and knows and loves the world (I, 13, 3); and God is correctly characterized *reciprocally* from relations things in the world bear to God (I, 13, 7, ad 4), but without standing in any real relationship to the world (I, 44, 3). That deserves a pause.

Real Relations to God but not Vice Versa

This is a central idea, one that eliminates many apparent paradoxes about God's permanence, knowledge, will, and timelessness. Other things are *really related* to God: as effects, as dependent, imperfect, created, temporally ordered, foreknown, willed, planned, etc. But God stands *in no real relations to other things at all*. Not even by creating, sustaining, and governing the world.

Now the thirteenth-century notion of a *real relation* involved much more than that a relational word truly applies to some group of objects, say "being near," "being married to," "being a child of," "being the square of," or "being known by." Some of those are real relations, and some are merely "rational" or "logical." A thing has to begin to be, cease to be, or change to come into a real relation to another (I, 46, 3, ad 1); all change, beginning and ending, is in things other than God (I, 45, 3).

The same holds for divine knowledge, foreknowledge of what is future to us, and predestination, providence, and even final judgment: the reality of divine activity is in the humans being judged (and rewarded or punished), known and made; *they* undergo a change. There is no future to God who is unchanging, omnipresent by being and power and will, and to whom all is present at once. It is all his present, and his doing, just as your present consciousness, and all its contents, is yours, continuously dependent on you, and would all disappear instantly with a change of your attention. Aquinas quotes Augustine, who says: "if the ruling power of God were withdrawn from His creatures, their natures would at once cease, and all nature would at once collapse" (I, 104, 1).

Divine conservation is sometimes also called "continuous creation" for the act is the same, except in definition of the word, as to make things be at all. Aquinas does not, however, reject the pious practice of believers who describe God as if God had already seen (in a common time) what will happen, and already decided (as if in our past) who is to be saved, etc. Yet Aquinas is very clear that in the science of God, God does not change, does not have any temporal relation of past, or future, to anything else at all.

It would, perhaps, have helped the perplexities of believers, if Aquinas had said that, strictly, such claims about foreknowledge and predestination are not true, as his theory requires. It seems that he allows the discourse of piety as discourse according to the objective appearance, but not the science, of things (cf. I, 67).

God knows whatever can be known, all together in one awareness, but not with knowledge caused by things, as what *we* see is caused by the things we see; rather God's knowing causes things to be ("the knowledge of God is the cause of things": I, 14, 8); for God's will and knowing are really the same. So, too, all our future, as all our past, is relative to the temporality of human experience and also to the physical succession in nature (cf. III, 91, 2, ad 8). But, for God, it is all "now!" "God knows contingent things not successively, as they are in their own being and as we do; but all at once"(I, 14, 13). So divine *fore*knowledge is a description of God's knowledge from *our* vantage in experience; so is *pre*destination. So puzzles arise from confusing our progressive experience with God's awareness. God knows whatever *is*, and so knows what *will be for us*, but not "now" because God does not, by nature, share a "now" with us.

The Goodness of God and the Origin of Evil

In so far as anything has being it is intelligible ("true"), and suitable for rational desire, and so, ontologically "good," as both Plato and Aristotle held, as well. The ontological goodness of things is their rational desirability. Therefore, an evil is "a missing good," a privation (I, 48, 1), the absence of good that "ought," either naturally or morally, to be there. It is privation, like blindness in a person, not mere absence like blindness in a stone. Natural evils, like animal blindness, suffering and death, lethal earthquakes, tornadoes, and the like, are only incidentally evil, that is, locally and relatively undesirable by affected creatures (if they are not caused, like some plane crashes, say, by immoral acts).

Nothing, in so far as it has being, is or can be evil. It is not possible for God to make something that is less than it "ought" to be. For in so far as it is made, the thing is rationally desirable. "Nothing can be essentially bad" (I, 49, 3). Further, there is nothing that absolutely ought not to be, not even the worst evil actions of free rational creatures. Still (I, 49, 2), God can be the cause of what ought not to be, by causing a *penalty* fitting to justice (I, 49, 1), for creaturely wrongs, but never can, as angels can (I, 63, 1), and humans can, cause evil by *fault* (I, 48, 5). "Every evil in voluntary things is to be looked on as pain or fault" (I, 48, 5).

Aquinas reasons that it is within the perfection of a divine agent to make a created order in which the natural and imperfect causes produce effects that people deem evils, like plagues, pestilences, bugs, and beasts that harm us; for, of course, finite causes will be imperfect agents. Therefore, the "order of nature requires that some things can, and sometimes do, fail" (I, 49, 2). At I, 22, 2, ad 2, he says, "hence, corruption and defects in natural things are said to be contrary to some particular nature; yet they are in keeping with the plan of universal nature"; and he reasons that "a lion would cease to live if there were no slaying of animals," thus acknowledging that biotic life requires death, that it is not a defect for God to create carnivorous and vicious animals, and poisonous snakes. Human suffering and death is another matter because it is the result of Adam's sin which incurred the loss of an extra-natural divine protection in which human persons were first created (I, 97, 1).

So, genuine evil requires what ought not to be *from that cause*. But God's will is the *cause* of good in all things, because being and goodness are the same (I, 20, 2), and things are good because God loves them, not vice versa: "the love of God infuses and creates goodness." But "it is of the essence of evil that it is the privation of a good" (I, 14, 10). Hence God cannot be the cause of evil as such. "Evil can only have an incidental cause; hence reduction to any *per se* cause is impossible"; so, there is no intrinsic principle of evil, no anti-god; even Lucifer (Satan) is a creature gone wrong. And moral evil is caused incidentally by created free agents acting for what they deem to be goods, angels acting to enjoy pride; or humans, acting for pleasure.

And furthermore, no one rightly says such freedom ought not to be at all, because without freedom, nothing among creatures could be right or praiseworthy. And there is no evil from which God cannot bring divine good: forgiveness, redemption, and salvation. The innocent (e.g., Abel, Genesis 20) cannot be really harmed, but are in the bosom of God, while the evil-doer faces eternal death, repudiation forever by God, destroying himself.

Which is better: for there to be no evil by there being no creature able to fall from the good, by misusing the ability to do good, or for God to bring good out of evil, no matter what humans do? "Christ's passion was sufficient and superabundant atonement for the sin and debt of the human race" (II, 48, 5), not just for the fall of Adam, but for all the terrible evil of mankind, ever to come. The latter is Aquinas's conviction: that divine forgiveness and the gift of eternal life "makes good" out of all the evil there will ever be. The human measure of divine mercy is the magnitude of human evil.

Aquinas, like Augustine, thinks it is contradictory to say a creature has freedom but can do no evil in its earthly condition, even given that it has a divinely assisted holy will; for that would take away the indeterminacy of the agent between what is good and what is not, and so, would have to presuppose the presence of a completely fulfilled will that is not naturally possible.

In addition, Aquinas envisions a cosmic drama, larger than earth's history, involving evil among the angelic spirits (demons), e.g. Satan (Lucifer), "for the motive of pride is excellence"(I, 63, 8) and is "worst among the best" (I, 63, 7), as dramatized by Milton, and painted, for instance, by Pieter Bruegel (ca. 1560), *The Fall of the Angels*. He treats the earth's story of salvation as one that displays the perdition of the demons by their evil agency (I-II, 80), their envy of humans for God's incarnate love, by their exacted and frustrated faith (II-II, 5, 2), and by their participation in human evil (I, 104–14).

Angels

Prompted by Aristotle's speculation that the stars are moved by intellectual spirits, by Platonists (cf. I, 63, 7) who believed in supra-earthly beings, by scripture (e.g. Daniel 7: 10), and by spiritual writers like (pseudo-) Dionysius, Aquinas wrote (I, 50, 3) that there are innumerable created immaterial spirits (angels). Just as "the heavenly bodies . . . exceed corruptible bodies almost incomparably in number; for the entire sphere of things active and passive is very small in comparison with the heavenly bodies," so also, "immaterial substances [intelligences] exist in exceeding great number, far beyond all material multitude" even of the heavenly bodies. For, "the more perfect things are, in so much greater an excess are they created by God."

From the twenty-four questions on angels (I, 50–74), already mentioned, and the later exploration of angelic being, of their being human guardians, and of the agency of demons (I, 104–14), it seems that Aquinas considers the earth to be a small part of the natural drama of the cosmos, just as it is of the created things of the cosmos. But from a supernatural religious standpoint, the earth is the locus of a most extraordinary, personal, and permanent divine activity: the special creation of man, the fall, incarnation, redemption, and salvation of humans, with the coming Messianic kingdom, and a universal judgment and transformation of humans forever.

But such entirely immaterial things, the angels, must be intelligences with free choice, and, furthermore, cannot differ from one another materially, and so, have to differ in species (I, 50, 4). Therefore, one angel differs from the next as much as a human differs from a dog: "it is impossible for two angels to be of the same species"; "all the angels differ in species according to the degrees of intellectual nature" (I, 50, 4, ad 1). The innumerable angelic species indicate how far God's being exceeds anything humans can perceive. Aquinas draws out his philosophical principles to answer questions about their powers of understanding and will, their memory, knowledge of one another, communication, the relation of such spirits to bodies, to movement, place and time, and to error, wrongdoing, and its relation to human evils (I-II, 80, 2, and I, 106–14).

Man: Human Nature, Powers, and Fulfillment

All material things of any kind are composites of form (structure) and matter (stuff out of which). The form determines the "what" and (internally) causes the thing to exist (as a shape causes a statue to be, until it melts), and the matter, the stuff, clay or gold, limits and individuates it. So a crystal may consist of molecular parts (matter) structured (formed) to behave a certain way chemically, like salt. Form, structure, is the intelligible feature of the physical – what can be understood and represented by humans in a formula – and is the explanation of what each thing is able and disposed to do. Thus, as we know now, there can be "on-off switches" mechanically, electrically, magnetically, and molecularly and even biologically, and, so, in principle, can be such computers. The form "on-off switch" is realized in each: as Aristotle said, "the same form can be received in many kinds of matter."

All earthly *living* things, plants and animals, are composites of a form capable of causing life and action, called "soul" (*psyche*), operating in matter suitable for life (say, carbon molecules). Humans are a special case of living things: rational animals who are persons. Thus, they are a composite of soul (*psyche*) and body. But people are not two conjoined things; for rationality is not *added* to animality as a power of it, as Locke later supposed, but is a *manner of animal being*. Being human is a kind of being animal.

A human is a composite of a material basis (Aquinas called it flesh and bone; nowadays, perhaps, "cells"), organized by *psyche* (spirit/soul) into a single animal that is able to understand and to choose its actions. "The first thing by which the body lives is by the soul" (I, 76, 1). When Aquinas says "man is a composite of soul and body," he means "body" as "matter capable of human life," not, "living thing with organs" that already supposes a soul. And he is speaking of soul (as it were, software) as the organizing form that makes the human alive and operate as one single thing, a thinking animal. (What was for centuries hard to grasp is commonplace now: software that makes a thing what it is, and do what it does: that is form. And soul is a kind of form.)

He thinks the soul not only provides the composite with abilities, like a program with sub-capabilities, but in humans the soul also has its *own* manner of being, "subsistent being," which it "communicates" to the composite. The being proper to the soul *is* the being of the composite. (In other living things, the soul is the formal cause of the being of the composite, but has no being of its own; it is "hard wired" and destroyed with the composite, as is the shape with the triangle.) When a human dies, as with animals, it dies all over at once; but the human soul is separated and not destroyed, because it has existence on its own.

Why is the human soul subsistent (actively existent on its own) (I, 75, 3)? That manner of being is *required* for the defining operations of the intelligent soul, understanding and choice (I, 75, 2). Aquinas thinks the immateriality, and thus immortality, of the human soul is proved from the fact that "understanding is not possible through a corporeal organ" (I, 76, 1). The understanding has to be actively able to be in an unlimited (infinite) variety of states (say, to understand any one of an infinity of arithmetical truths, or sentences of one's language) and so cannot be restricted to the physical states of any bodily organ. For no material power, sight, hearing, imagination, or the like, *can* be in an unlimited variety of states. Aristotle formulated that reasoning (*De anima*, iii.4). Thus, the understanding can do what cannot be done physically. Therefore, the *psyche* "has an operation and a power in which corporeal matter has no share whatever" (ibid.).

His reasoning is this: "It is impossible for it [the soul] to understand by means of a bodily organ since the determinate nature of the organ would impede the knowledge of all bodies"; "therefore, the intellectual principle which we call the mind, or the intellect, has an operation *per se* apart from the body. Now only that which subsists [exists on its own] can have an operation *per se*" [that is, by itself and on account of itself]. Why must the immaterial soul have subsistent being? Because the manner of being must explain the manner of a thing's operation (I, 75, 3). If it acts on its own, it must exist on its own. Otherwise, something comes from nothing.

All the powers of a living thing have the soul as their one explanatory source; otherwise, there would not be one, single life. Such a program must have many sub-parts, because the "powers" or "faculties" are distinct. Aquinas distinguishes and determines the order and causal interactions of such "powers" (see below); that is, his cognitive psychology. Some abilities are found in all living things (nutrition, growth, reproduction), and others are found in animals generally (sensation, imagination, memory, perception, and action from desire). But some are definitive of humans, like understanding (intelligence) and will. Intelligence transforms all the animal powers (even aspects of the nutritive, reproductive, and growth powers), by unifying them into one intelligent life.

The powers of understanding and will are also affected and incidentally limited by the bodily states of the human, e.g., its health, pains, pleasures, hunger, passions, suffering, and death. One can't think of much else, if hungry enough. And one can be absorbed in thought. The living body *is* the human, the person. Aquinas is thus not an Augustinian or Cartesian dualist.

The causal chain in human knowing

Basically, I, 75–90 is "generative" cognitive psychology; that is, it is "black box" reasoning, mostly taken from Aristotle, to determine the abilities and their intermediate causal connections and outputs (e.g. "sensible species": appearances) that are required for animals, and particularly humans, to behave as they observably and introspectively do.

So we count the external senses of animals from their discriminatory response abilities, to color, taste, touch, smell, and sound, and count the internal senses from the distinct abilities required for perception and action, namely, imagination, memory, coordination of senses, and estimative ability. Those are needed to do what animals do and what we can tell we do: remember, imagine, unify multiple sensations into one appearance (the "common sense," *sensus communis*), and gauge and proportion the motion of limbs, eyes, muscles, etc., and intuitively estimate strength and effort to be expended, as in a horse's jumping a fence (estimative/cogitative power). Natural estimative abilities are also subject to learning in higher animals, and to feedback from understanding in humans. All those abilities amount to the perceptual and behavioral abilities of animals.

The "representationalism" of Aquinas belongs only to the conjectured stages of the causal chain from physical objects to perception and understanding (and back). But the output of perception is the *presence* of things to animals: hawks see *mice*, by means of representations ("sensible species"), not by seeing representations of mice and somehow "inferring" to the world.

The outcome of cognitive psychology for Aquinas is direct realism about animal perception and human truth: namely, what animals, normally, see and hear and taste and touch, is what is real. And, most importantly, when what we think is true, what we know *is* what is so. With Aristotle he holds, not what is nowadays called a correspondence theory of truth (though he describes the *causal* process that way, as a series of causes and effects, producing resemblances, e.g., I, 85, 5), but an *identity* theory of truth for the outcome: the understanding *becomes what it knows:* "as regards things actually understood, the intellect and what is understood are the same" (I, 87, 2). And in I, 79, 5, ad 2, he quotes Aristotle with approval: "Knowledge in act is the same as the thing." What we understand, when we are right, *is* what is so: when I know you are here, what I know is that very reality.

In animals and, so, humans, there are drives called appetites. One is a constant bias causing pleasure and avoiding pain (the "concupiscible" appetite), and the other, in crises, directed by instinct, overrides the first, and causes flight or fight to preserve the animal ("irascible" appetite). These are constant causes of all animal action, whether perception, movement, or even sleep and dreaming, and determine the operation of the senses as well as behavior.

Every sense is a form of pleasure (and displeasure, as well): every sense is a mode of love. Perception, which is more than sensation because it is a presence of "the other" to the animal, requires imagination (of things sought or feared), and memory of the expectations aroused. Imagining is not typically by picturing, but is a particular readiness that perception of the object relieves, as when something lost is sought. So imagination does not require belief, but is expectation, readiness of a certain sort.

The normal living of animals is active, from the pleasure in the acting, and avoiding pain, and fulfilling desire (which requires imagination). Mice scurry because they can; animals eat because the want to. Higher animals, like horses and dogs, are said by Aquinas to have an "imperfect voluntary": that is, such animals do what they *want* to do because they want to, but, unlike humans, without any grasp of *why* they are doing it or awareness that they want to. They act with "imperfect knowledge" of the end for which they act, "through their senses and estimative powers," "without knowing it under the aspect of an end" (I-II, 6, 2), and so, without any control over what they want (I-II, 6, 2, ad 2). Still, in the training and use of animals, it is their "imperfect voluntary" that is habituated by rewards and aversions. In humans, the animal desires and powers can be corrupted by human intelligence, as well (e.g., into greed, lasciviousness, perversity, bestiality, cruelty, etc.). In humans it is not the animal powers that corrupt, but reason that corrupts the animal inclinations.

Human reason

The rationality of humans consists of three basic abilities, three powers of the *psyche*, whose operations are (i) conception, (ii) judgment and reasoning, and (iii) choice. The first is the "abstractive" understanding, variously called "the active intellect" (*intellectus agens*), or the "making intellect," because it *makes* conceptions out of sensation; it is the active, always "on" ability to separate the forms, the intelligible structures, of things from their particular matter, making conceptions. Thus a human does not see an object *just* as a physical particular, under no interpretation at all; even in a flash, it is a "what?" Active conceptualization, the first step of understanding, is something humans do, willingly, but by nature and always.

Judgment

The second constant intelligent activity is judgment, typically the combining of conceptions into commitments to perceived reality, for example, "that house has red woodwork," or "there isn't anyone standing in front of the house." The most basic form of judgment is a constant reality commitment, an existential commitment, usually accompanied by habitual affirmation of appearances. (Aquinas does not discuss the varying vividness of such commitment or its willing suspension, for stories.)

The ability to make judgments and to reason with conceptions, in response to reality presented by appearances, or imagined or remembered, is called, by awkward translations from the Greek and the Arabic, *the possible intellect* (sometimes, by Arabic writers, also "the potential intellect"), roughly, "the capable understanding." Such judgmen-

tal understanding is also "always on," requiring only conceptions, along with sensation, for its activity. Its states are our beliefs, our convictions, and our reasoning. When
true, the content of the states is the reality known.

Will

The third intellectual power is the rational appetite (will): the will is the constant cause
of activity in pursuit of something wanted (some "good"). It is causation that consists
of a constant leaning to satisfaction from what we choose (e.g., to get the thing you
choose). Abstractly, that bias is toward fulfillment, toward what Aristotle called
"happiness."

But that inclination is opaque, to get what one decides on. It is without a concrete
object; and so, it is dependent upon our appraising the promise of options "to which
the will is indifferently disposed" (I-II, 6, 2, ad 2). Thus, an unlucky person can be
constantly mistaken in what he seeks. A vicious person, rancorous, or badly trained can
constantly mistake relief of desire for satisfaction, like a person imprudently scratching
an itch he makes worse.

About options to which the "will is indifferently disposed" (I-II, 6, 2, ad 2), a
person can *deliberate*. And one typically terminates deliberation by decision: that ability to reach decision from indifferent options is freedom of will. Such decision aimed at
"getting one's way" can, and will if repeated, originate patterns, habits, of action,
either in accord with reason (virtues) or opposed to it (vices). "Those actions are
properly called human which proceed from a deliberate will" (I-II, 1).

Freedom of choice, as an ability, is both a necessary condition of action in accord
with understanding and for the fact that humans, unlike animals, are subject to moral
praise and blame (I-II, 6, 2 ad 3), that is, to judgment as to whether they act rightly or
wrongly, in contrast to merely well or badly, as with horses or dogs.

Do humans seek happiness? In the abstract, yes, because they always want what they
choose. But do they always want something? Yes. "All human actions must be for
some end." But is there *one* end for which humans always act? Yes, Aquinas says, all
human action is essentially ordered toward one end, happiness; that is because "*to
desire happiness is nothing other than to desire that one's will be satisfied*" (I-II, 5, 8),
which we do by nature in whatever we do. So, he reasons, "it is impossible that one
man's will be directed at the same time to diverse things as last ends" (I-II, 5). Even
what is in other respects evil is always chosen under some respect in which it is a good:
for pleasure, power, excellence. And anything sought as a good is either sought as a
good in itself or as an intermediate to some good (I-II, 1, 6). So there must be a last
end that is the aim of appetite and that is the aim of all intermediates: happiness, a state
of having one's will fulfilled. Opaquely it is what ends the constant pursuit (I-II, 2, 7),
namely, *that our wills be satisfied*.

Such a satisfaction has to be permanent, and consist in active understanding and
enjoyment. So it is not naturally available. Only life with God is happiness, and it is
attained, by those who do, by knowing and loving God (I-II, 1, 8), not by any created
good (I-II, 2, 8); it is the direct vision of God (I-II, 3, 8) that causes delight (I-II, 3,
4, ad 5). The present life is limited to various forms of flourishing, and that is uncertain
and transient (III, 75, 1).

Immortality and the possibility of resurrection

Immortality, as indestructibility of the soul, is *not sufficient* for human personal survival of death. For the soul, even though *per se* existing, is *not* the person (III, 75, 1, ad
2), but a part, requiring individual embodiment for a complete human. "Abraham's
soul properly speaking is not Abraham himself, but a part of him . . . there needs to be
a life in the whole composite, soul and body" (III, 75, 1, suppl. ad 2). So, it has to be
possible that humans are resurrected for it to be possible for humans to survive death.
Since possibility does not follow from conception alone, such a possibility cannot be
demonstrated by appeal to God's omnipotence, but rather is presupposed by it.

Aquinas does not offer reasoning that is independent of revelation to establish the
possibility of resurrection. His philosophical reasoning goes only this far: the human
spirit (cf. I, 97, 3) is incorruptible and naturally immortal, and the soul (spirit) is not the
person (III, 75, 1, ad 2). And, also, that it would be incoherent for a part of persons to
survive, forever naturally incomplete, and not suitable for the rewards and punishments
fitting for one's life but belonging only to the composite substance (III, 75, 1, ad 3).
That amounts to a weak likelihood. The rest has to be settled by divine revelation; for
such a vast material change, from dust, mud, or ashes, or from parts of cannibals, to a
restored living body, lies only in the miraculous power of God (III, 75, 3). He seems to
take it as sure that such a transformation is not within the power of nature, as is meta-
morphosis. Nevertheless, as theologian, relying upon scripture, he concludes, "the soul
cannot have the final perfection of the human species so long as it is separated from the
body. Hence, no soul will remain forever separated from the body" (III, 75, 2).

Man: The Regulation of Human Conduct

Internal

The morality of human actions depends on their being voluntary (done from desire in
the absence of defeating ignorance, fear, violence, or passion); voluntary actions are
either habitual or deliberate (chosen). The measure of *objective* moral permissibility
(right or wrong, not tied to the praise or blame of the agent) of a *sort* of action is
whether such an action is in accord with reason used rightly. The same test applies
objectively to the intention, circumstances, and foreseeable consequences of the act.
The measure of *subjective* moral permissibility (praiseworthiness or blameworthiness
of the agent) is: a permitted intention, and a reasonable belief that the action is right in
itself, and under the circumstances and in its consequences. The overall "goodness"
(rightness) of action is from an "integral cause," that is, from its being both objectively
and subjectively good; (i) the intention, (ii) that *sort* of act (objectively described), (iii)
its circumstances, and (iv) its consequences, all have to be in accord with right reason,
both objectively and subjectively.

And the content of right reason as to action and its circumstances is determined by
a fit between human nature, one's circumstances, resources, and aims, all measured by
human reason. That fit is objectively regulated by moral law; hence, Aquinas's philosophical moral theory is called "natural law morality" (see below).

Virtues and vices

Human action is typically habitual, though the most important acts, including the ones that initiate habits, are deliberate choices. Habits are constant tendencies to action, a constant causation; some are natural, like bold temperament, or timorousness; some are acquired, by training, or by self-discipline, like studiousness; others, by self-indulgence, like pride and gluttony.

Habits in accord with right reason are called "virtues" and others, acquired from impermissible choices or from bad training, bad example, or by self-indulgence, are persistent inclinations toward action contrary to right reason and are "vices," like greed, covetousness, and envy. Aquinas sorts and orders the wisdom of the Greeks and of the Stoics, as well as the content of Roman law, into an elaborate classification and analysis of the virtues and the vices, arranged under the classical "cardinal [hinge] virtues," of prudence, justice, temperance, and fortitude, and, further, with religious inspiration, under the theological virtues of faith, hope, and charity. Those are just the headings; the classification is detailed and full of examples.

In each case, he considers the opposed vices, employing Plato's and Aristotle's scheme that the virtues are the habits lying in the mean between too much (excess) and too little (deficit), like proper weight, between corpulence and anorexia (e.g., II-II, 10, 5); so justice is giving others what is their due, while profligacy is giving too much, and stinginess is giving less than what is reasonable. And courage is the active propensity to act against obstacles, when reasonably afraid of the danger, while cowardice is losing action to the fear, and rashness is the tendency to act, underrating the danger.

Aquinas elaborates on whether the defects and excesses are from deficiencies of understanding, weakness of resolution, distraction, and the like. Even the modes of habits are detailed, for example, virtuous anger (in defense of the innocent, or in self-defense) is distinguished from the many sorts that are evil: rage, wrath, ire, revenge, sullenness, indignation, contempt, vindictiveness, and rancor (II-II, 158). For instance, his descriptions of human passions and emotions distinguish feelings, like the "fervor," "languor," and "melting" effects of love (I-II, 28, 5), and the pleasure, both in presence and in memory, caused by sadness (I-II, 32, 4), as well as by rage.

External: The Treatise on Law (I-II, 90–108)

Law, both human and divine, is an external explanatory feature of human action because it regulates it. This treatise is one of the most influential documents in Western legal history. It is part of Aquinas's general *natural moral law theory*, basically that the general principles of morality are known by human understanding and experience of what it is *in accord with rightly used reason for a human being to do*. There is a basic principle, evident from human nature, "act in accord with reason." All the rest of the principles are specifications of it, some obvious in themselves and others through experience.

Theologically, such moral law is a human cognitive participation in the divine regulation of the universe (Eternal Law, I-II, 93, 6, God regulated the universe by divine governance and positive law). This presupposes that all human beings form one real kind of thing that does not vary in essentials with history or environment, race or culture, and is the foundation of universal moral principles.

The very basic moral principles are self-evident, that is, evident just from a consideration of them. However, Aquinas acknowledges that the self-evidence of some propositions is accessible only to the educated (I-II, 94, 2). But the most basic "first principles" are obvious to everyone: as "do good and avoid evil," "act in accord with reason," "do not do what you believe to be wrong," "preserve your own life," "care for human beings" (I-II, 94, 2).

There are equally obvious "secondary principles" that fill out and apply the primary ones, like "do not harm others" (I-II, 94, 5, ad 3), but involve more particular circumstances, such as the Ten Commandments of biblical law (I-II, 100), prohibiting idolatry, murder, rape, torture, theft, and commanding worship of God and respect for parents. They belong to the natural moral law as well as to divine positive law (the revealed Commandments).

Then for circumstances more complex, more qualified, but still general, other principles are required by reason, such as "help the afflicted," "educate your children," "return things left with you for safe-keeping," "pay back what you borrow," which are subject to particular qualifying conditions or conditions of application that vary and can't be settled by a list of exceptions in advance of cases, e.g. "but you don't give weapons back to a now mad-man . . . *and so on.*"

And then there are even more particular, but general rules, like "care for your parents," "get medical care for sick children," that have qualifications, as reason accommodates to one's particular situation. He says, "in matters of action, truth or practical rectitude is not the same for all as to matters of detail, but only as to general principles; and where there is some rectitude in matters of detail it is not equally known to all." (I-II, 94, 4). So it might not be surprising that, unless one were specially trained, one might not know what reason requires in the way of transferring real property to another, or how to care for the dying or how to relieve pain, or whether a lawyer can present a witness he knows will lie, what punishments are fitting for offenses, and how such ideas are conditioned by local custom that can amount to law (I-II, 97, 3).

So Aquinas claims that there are simple, obvious, absolutely certain, unchanging moral principles for all times and circumstances that are the bedrock of morality, but that the more particular principles become, the less certain and the less universal they may be, depending on various factors, as do the usages of war, on the customs and abilities of times, persons, and places, and, when proportionality or special sorts of issues (I-II, 95, 4) are involved (see below), they may be subject to uncertainty and variability.

Thus, the widespread picture of his natural moral law theory as conservative, static, authoritarian, and *a priori*, distorts it. For it is empirical, adaptive, and, when applied to civil law, is the origin of the first general account of the invalidity of legislation, and of insuperable rights of conscience against the state. It even has revolutionary consequences, as when Aquinas argues (II-II, 66, 7), "Hence whatever certain people have in superabundance is due by natural law to the purpose of succoring the poor" and, in some cases, may be taken away by force. He also speaks of "things which are of human right" (ibid.), e.g., by law, as being subordinate to the natural and divine law: "that man's needs have to be remedied by those very things" that someone else claims are his.

Moreover, natural law can change by accretion and adaptation (I-II, 95, 5 and 97–104). The primary and very general secondary principles do not change. But the content of natural moral law, both requiring and prohibiting things, can grow as circumstances change, and some requirements may not continue for every case, as when there are special causes hindering the observance of such precepts (e.g., the despotic suppression of religion might abate the requirement of public worship for a time). He does not discuss whether something thought permissible in the past may be found, in new circumstances, impermissible (e.g. executions or slavery), or something previously thought contrary to reason, may later be found to be required by reason, say, equal political status for all the governed, or population control over the whole earth. But it seems that his moral theory requires both changes by contraction and expansion. For what reason requires and prohibits is a function of human nature and the conditions of human life, mediated by human experience.

Foundations of civil law

Aquinas's overall scheme is that the main fabric of civil and criminal law (and of the judicial system) is an application and particularization of natural moral law.

He observes that society is cooperative, and aimed at things that are important goods for everyone that cannot be reliably achieved by mere cooperation, without entrusting what otherwise would be individual rights of defense and coercion to a common source. So, government is coercive power (i.e., for taxation, war, police, and regulated commerce) toward the common good of everyone (e.g., II-II, 66, 8), under public rules that must meet certain conditions to be civil law, and thus morally as well as effectively binding upon everyone.

Aquinas derives the justified coercive power and existence of the public legal institutions of both civil and criminal law from the consent of the governed; that is, from a people's grant, directly or indirectly by custom, of what would otherwise be inefficient, and perhaps excessive, individual coercive power, to a ruler for their common well-being. In fact, law is defined as: "regulation (ordinatio) in accord with right reason, by the one charged with care of the community [ruler], aimed at the common good and promulgated" (I-II, 90, 4). "Coercively" is implicit in "regulation." The definition specifically requires (1) jurisdiction (both personal and over subject matter), "charged with . . ."; (2) a public objective, "aimed at the common good," not private enrichment or privilege of the few or the rulers; (3) in accord with right reason: nowadays phased: "reasonably related to legitimate public objective"; and (4) promulgated: that regulations be made known to those governed (no secret or *ex post facto* laws). In the absence of any of these conditions, a general command is not law: it is void. Historically, this is the first general philosophical theory of the invalidity of legislative enactment.

Aquinas identifies further conditions of legislative invalidity: acts "beyond the power committed to the legislator"; burdensome schemes of unjust enrichment, "directed to the cupidity and vainglory of rulers" (I-II, 94, 4), and schemes so burdensome as to destroy the common good (e.g., individual expression); and unequal burdens imposed, even for legitimate public aims, upon the community (equal protection under law) (I-II, 95, 2). "The like are acts of violence rather than laws" (I-II, 96, 4). These criteria have survived into the body of current American and many other nations' constitutional law.

Moreover, legislative power does not extend to prohibit private vices, or intentions, or inner vices (I-II, 96, 2), only public ones affecting others; or allow the law to require all virtues, even useful ones, unless needed for the common good (I-II, 96, 3). And the law may be disobeyed, morally, when the burden is imposed unequally on the community, unless the danger of scandal forbids it. And, of course, enactments contrary to divine law "are in nowise to be obeyed." "Law that conflicts with the law of nature is no longer a law but a perversion of law" (I-II, 95, 2).

Disobedience is also permitted in a variety of circumstances, for instance when reasonable disregard of the letter of the law is needed to attain the very purpose of the law (e.g., public safety) (I-II, 96, 6), but with limitations (ibid., ad 2 and 3); and when there are special dispensations that are permitted by law, and when there are differences of legitimate status under law (I-II, 98, 4, ad 2).

The basic scheme of justified civil legislation is application of natural moral law to public acts for public objectives, by what he calls (i) "conclusions of natural law," with extensive (ii) "determinations" settling what is indeterminate in moral law, but needed for an orderly body of law. So if natural morality requires (as a conclusion from "do not harm others") building codes for public safety, then the particular standards, which could reasonably be different, are "determinations" within the wisdom and discretion of legislators. The same would apply to traffic patterns, zoning laws, tax codes, trade regulations, food safety, and thousands of other elements of public safety and convenience and commerce, though the legal systems of his time were much simpler; and he might generally be found on the side of legislative minimalists; for he also proposed that persons harmed by changes of law for the better should be compensated (I-II, 97, 2).

He briefly sketches "law of nations" (*ius gentium*), combining some principles of natural law (e.g., for just payments for trade) and some agreements by sovereigns, that (I-II, 95, 4), anchored in the Roman tradition of law for the provinces and conquered people, became the schema of sixteenth-century and later theories of international law. He says that such law, even though "natural to man," is nevertheless distinct from natural law (I, 95, 4, ad 1), mainly because it is sketchy, and by the agreement of sovereigns.

He offers a theory of just war (II-II, 40) on principles of self-defense, which implies the principles of insurrection (overthrow of tyrants), and of civil disobedience, partly to be found in the conditions stated (I-II, 96, 4 and 6) and by analogy from the principles of conflict. The basic principles of these theories are: (i) proper public authority to act; (ii) moral necessity to act against a wrongdoer or aggressor; (iii) a permissible intention (e.g., not just vengeance) and reasonable prospect of success; (iv) proportionality in the losses in relation to the gains; (v) only incidental and not great harm to non-participants (not disproportionate collateral damage); and (vi) no targeting or aimed injuring of the innocent (in a word, no terrorism). The latter provisions (iv, v, and vi) have been culled by commentators from other places in his moral theory, and from his other writings. These ideas have reverberated in legal systems ever since. So too have the questions (II-II, 67–71) on judges, prosecution and accusation, defense, witnesses, and counsel in judicial proceedings.

Aquinas did not offer a theory of individual human "demand rights" against government; his was a theory of the nature and limitation of public legislative coercion against the governed, with some development of the moral right to resistant, disobedient and interpretative (I-II, 97, 6, ad 2 and 3) acts. Individual rights theories came later.

Finally, Aquinas, like Augustine, regarded coercive power as a necessity arising from the sinful condition of mankind in which conflicts and crimes arise. All such coercive law will be abrogated as unnecessary with the establishment of the Kingdom of God. From the principles of natural philosophy, Aquinas speculated, but did not attempt to prove, that the sun will die and the stars go out, and the earth will be destroyed, but "the substance of the creation will endure forever," and on religious grounds he affirmed that all humans will be resurrected and be finally judged and granted everlasting happiness in life with God, or condemned in everlasting rejection and separation from God.

Conclusion

The work is dominated and organized by the task of providing a unified conception of the origin and destiny of the world, and of individual life, within the framework of the Catholic Christian faith. The philosophical underpinning of it all, and the detailed explanation of the religion in a unified philosophical system and with explicit philosophical reasoning, distinguished this book from any prior comprehensive Christian work; and its excellence as philosophical craftsmanship established it as one of the classics of the history of philosophy and one of the most influential works of Western literature.

Bibliography

Editions and translations

Aquinas, Thomas (1882–) *Sancti Thomae de Aquino opera omnia*, vols 4–12: *Summa theologiae*. Leonine Edition. Rome: Editori di San Tommaso.

Aquinas, Thomas (1946) *The Summa theologica of Saint Thomas Aquinas*, 5 vols, trans. the Fathers of the English Dominican Province (Christian Classics). Available on the Internet (http://www.newadvent.org/summa/).

Aquinas, Thomas (1964–81) *Summa theologiae*, 61 vols, ed. T. Gilby (Latin and English, with notes and introductions). London: Blackfriars; New York: McGraw-Hill.

Aquinas, Thomas (1989) *Summa theologiae: A Concise Translation*, selected, trans. and ed. Timothy McDermott. Westminster, MD: Eyre and Spottiswoode.

Studies

Anscombe, G. E. M. (1982) *Ethics, Religion and Politics*. Oxford: Blackwell.

Anscombe, G. E. M. and Geach, P. T. (1961) *Three Philosophers*. Oxford: Blackwell.

Copleston, Frederick (1993) *History of Philosophy*, vol. II: *Medieval Philosophy, Augustine to*

Scotus. New York: Image Books.

Davies, Brian (1992) *The Thought of Thomas Aquinas*. Oxford: Clarendon Press.

Davies, Brian (2002) *Aquinas*. New York and London: Continuum.

Gilson, Étienne (1955) *A History of Christian Philosophy in the Middle Ages*. New York: Random House.

Gilson, Étienne (1956) *The Christian Philosophy of Saint Thomas Aquinas*. New York: Random House.

Henle, R. J. (1956) *Saint Thomas and Platonism*. The Hague: Martinus Nijhoff.

Kenny, A. (1980) *Aquinas*. Oxford: Oxford University Press.

Kenny, A. (1993) *Aquinas on Mind*. London: Routledge.

Kretzmann, N. and Stump, E. (eds) (1993) *The Cambridge Companion to Aquinas*. Cambridge: Cambridge University Press.

Lysska, A. (1996) *Aquinas's Theory of Natural Law*. Oxford: Clarendon Press.

Lyttkens, H. (1952) *The Analogy between God and the World*. Uppsala : Almqvist and Wiksells.

MacIntyre, A. (1990) *Three Rival Versions of Moral Inquiry*. Notre Dame, IN: University of Notre Dame Press.

Pope, S. J. (ed.) (2002) *The Ethics of Aquinas*. Washington, DC: Georgetown University Press.

Sillem E. (1961) *Ways of Thinking about God*. London: Darton, Longman and Todd.

Torrell, J-P. (1996) *Saint Thomas Aquinas: The Person and His Work*, vol. 1. Washington, DC: The Catholic University of America Press.

Weisheipl, J. (1983) *Friar Thomas d'Aquino, his Life, Thought and Work*, rev. edn. Washington, DC: The Catholic University of America Press (originally pub. 1974).

Wippel, J. (1984) *Metaphysical Themes in Thomas Aquinas*. Washington, DC: The Catholic University of America Press.

Wippel, J. (2000) *The Metaphysical Thought of Thomas Aquinas*. Washington, DC: The Catholic University of America Press.

16

John Duns Scotus, *Questions on the Metaphysics of Aristotle* (ca. 1300)

A New Direction for Metaphysics

Timothy B. Noone

The text of Scotus's *Questions on the Metaphysics* (henceforth *QM*) is composed of chronologically disparate layers. Some sections are original to the first composition, while other elements are added later and denoted as "extras" or "additions." Under lying both of these textual features is the historical origin of the text. According to the research presented in the introduction to the critical edition (Scotus, *Quaestiones*, 1997: xiv–xv; xxviii–xxxvii; xlii–xlvi), Scotus's *QM* has its historical origin as lectures, repeated several times in the Franciscan houses of study, to the younger friars studying philosophy. Since Scotus (1265–1308) himself would have been pursuing his studies in theology or perhaps (depending upon which section of the text one wishes to consider) have already attained his mastership, the questions presume extensive acquaintance with theological disputations and works wherein many of the metaphysical themes of the Aristotelian *Metaphysics* are employed.

While the *Metaphysics* of Aristotle may be the focal point for many of the questions discussed by Scotus, the reading of the *Metaphysics* proposed in them is done through the lens of the Islamic commentators, Avicenna and Averroës, as well as the various Latin commentators, especially Roger Bacon, Albert the Great, Thomas Aquinas, and Giles of Rome. The questions discussed, accordingly, belong to the tradition of difficulties raised among commentators and the continuing dialogue in the Latin West regarding the adaptation of Aristotelian metaphysical principles to philosophical perspectives essentially alien to that of the Stagirite as well as their appropriation into theological discourse. Salient among the themes treated in the work are the ones upon which we shall focus in the following: the subject of metaphysics, being and its transcendental properties, the problem of universals, and the problem of individuation.

The Subject of Metaphysics

The Islamic commentators Avicenna and Averroës set the background to the questions that discuss this issue in Scotus's *QM*, namely Book I, q. 1, Book IV, q. 1, and Book VI, q. 1. Avicenna had concluded that the only way to reconcile the criteria for scientific knowledge laid down in Aristotle's *Posterior Analytics* with the descriptions given and the procedures followed by Aristotle in the text of the *Metaphysics* was to take the subject of investigation within metaphysics to be being as being. In proposing this manner of understanding the subject of metaphysics, Avicenna showed how only being as being could fit the Aristotelian requirements for scientific knowledge (Aristotle, *Posterior Analytics* I.10, 76a31–76b23; I.28, 87a38–87b4), the range of subjects treated in metaphysics (truth, goodness, and unity; cause/effect; substance and accident; act and potency, as well as necessary and possible being), and, above all, the metaphysical proof of God's existence and the divine attributes (Avicenna, *Metaphysics*, I.1.1 [IV 4: 64 – 5: 81]; I.1.2 [IV 12: 14–22]). Fundamentally, Avicenna reasons that, since no science can prove the existence of its subject, if God's existence is shown in metaphysics, that science cannot have God as its subject.

Adopting the opposing standpoint, Averroës argued that, since no science proves the existence of its own subject, metaphysics must be about God as First Form and Substance or Last End. God's existence is not, contrary to Avicenna's claim, shown within metaphysics but in physics or natural philosophy and its treatment of the Unmoved Mover. Metaphysicians begin, then, with the proof of God's existence afforded them by the natural philosopher and hence the range of being displayed before them: material and immaterial being. What metaphysical analysis strives to indicate is how all the beings of our experience are related to the First Form or God by way of final causality, while also attempting to show how we may meaningfully attribute certain properties to God (Averroës, *Physics* I, t. 83 [1550, 22vb–23ra]; Averroës, *Metaphysics* IV, t. 6 [1562, 145vM–146vM]; IV, t. 2 [71vG–M]).

Scotus's discusssion in Book I, q. 1 involves a protracted treatment of the two Islamic interpreters and their conflicting claims. Though this particular question is one in which there are layers of revision on Scotus's part and, at times, the discussion is a strain to follow, the gist of Scotus's successive views becomes clear. In the earliest view expressed in the primitive text, Scotus held ultimately that metaphysics is a science that has being as being in the sense of substance as its subject (*Questions* I, q. 1, n. 91–2; 1997: 38–9). At this stage of his career he could see no greater unity to the concept of being than that of the ten categories of being and among these there is only a unity of attribution of the nine accidental categories to the category of substance. Since there is no common notion under which the full range of being can be treated, Scotus opted for the primary subject of the science as substance with the properties of accidents being treated in so far as they are dependent upon and exist for the sake of substance.

When we turn to the extras and additions found in Book I, q. 1, we encounter the more mature and developed position that is assumed in the later books of the *QM* and expounded at even greater length in Scotus's theological writings. The concept of being is univocal not only to the whole of categorial being, the being of substance and the nine accidents, but to being as considered prior to its modal differentiation into finite being and infinite being. Such a notion allows God to enter into metaphysical discourse as something falling under disjunctive propositions such as "Every being is either First or not-First" or "Every being is either in act or in potency" and hence under the disjunctive properties of being "finite/infinite" and "act/potency" respectively (*Questions* I, q. 1, n. 156–7; IV, q. 1, n. 45; 1997: 57–8, 264). This position is one that engenders its own difficulties, troubles that would cause Scotus to continue to struggle with the senses in which being can be predicated of its own differences and would lead to conflicts among his followers for a considerable period of time after his premature death (Dumont, 1987); subsequent refinements of the position aside, however, the position itself was attractive to contemporaries because of its ability to explain both the transcendental and theological dimensions of metaphysical discourse within the same framework.

Metaphysics: The Science of the Transcendentals

In the prologue to his *QM* (Scotus, *Questions* I, prol. n. 18; 1997: 7–8), Scotus announces that the science of metaphysics needs to treat the common features of being (*communissima*) and, to the extent that it does so, it is the universal science, studying the transcendental features of being; it is, as it were, a science of transcendentals (*quasi transcendens scientia, quia est de transcendentibus*). The notion of transcendental employed in this text and its parallels throughout the *QM* is that of a property of being that is really identical to being, yet not the same as being in meaning or formally speaking. Such a property of being transcends the being that is divided up into the categories since, unlike the being of, say, substance, it can be found in more than one category (we may speak of the unity of a substance or the unity of an accident, for example) and may also be found in things transcending our experience (we may say, in a meaningful sense, that both man and God are good or one).

Two points are noteworthy in connection with Scotus's doctrine of the transcendentals in the *QM*: (1) Scotus tries to describe the sense in which the transcendentals are distinct from each other in a more refined way than his predecessors on this score (Avicenna, Averroës, and Henry of Ghent); and (2) he expands the list of transcendentals covered within metaphysics to include disjunctive attributes, insisting that they are transcendental because of the universality and comprehensive character of the disjunction despite the limited applicability of each of the disjuncts.

Let us turn to the first of these points. In question 2 of Book IV, Scotus frames his treatment of the question "whether being and unity signify the same nature" against the disagreement of Avicenna and Averroës along with the ancient monism of Parmenides: Avicenna had argued in his own *Metaphysics* that "being" and "unity" are only one in reference to the same concrete, ontological subject of which they are predicated (Avicenna, *Metaphysics* VII, c. 1); Averroës, on the other hand, had argued that the two terms "one" and "being" signify the exact same nature, but do so in different ways (Averroës, *Metaphysics* IV, com. 3; 1562, 32ra–b). Problems are raised on both sides: Avicenna seems to be at a loss to explain the convertibility of the two transcendental terms "being" and "unity" since, according to his analysis, the two terms do not signify the same nature, whereas Averroës is equally at a loss to account for how we can meaningfully predicate both terms of the same object and express different notions.

How, then, do unity and being differ if they are truly convertible, that is, if every thing of which "unity" is predicated "being" is also predicated? Following Avicenna, Scotus suggests that unity and being differ in their very notion: "being" signifies that the thing is, whereas "unity" signifies that the thing is undivided in itself and distinct from all others. That is why "being" and "unity" cannot be predicated of each other or of the same nature in the same respect. But they can be predicated of the same concrete object and that is the sense in which they are convertible: if a thing is such that it can have "being" predicated of it, it can also have "unity" predicated of it. The two notions, being and unity, differ, then, in that they pick out different formal features of a concrete thing; these formally distinct features are such that they are both equally and necessarily predicable of the thing that is (*id quod est*) – which contains them unitively in its ontological structure – but are not the same as each other, differing as two perfections constitutive of the thing (*Questions* IV, q. 2, n. 143–4; 1997: 307–9).

In one of his arguments for the formal distinction between unity and being, Scotus mentions the second point worthy of our attention: his systematic inclusion of the disjunctive attributes of being among the transcendentals. The argument in question is that being cannot be completely identical to unity and unity to being, for, if they were altogether identical, no plurality of beings would be genuinely possible. Since plurality is an evident fact of our experience, being must be something different from unity. Commenting upon this line of reasoning, Scotus argues that unity is really part of a disjunctive pair of concepts applicable to things, one whose opposite, multiplicity, is also found in reality (*Questions* IV, q. 2, n. 66; 1997: 290). Nor is the pair "unity/multiplicity" alone in this regard; Scotus lists elsewhere the pairs "act/potency," "necessary/contingent," and "infinite/finite" among the disjunctive transcendentals. His explanation of how they are transcendental is as well expressed here as anywhere else in his works. Instead of being co-extensively convertible in the way that goodness, or truth, is co-extensive with being (to the extent that something is good it is and to the extent that something is it is good), the disjunctives exhaust the range of being taken precisely as a logical disjunction: every being is either one or many; every being is either in act or in potency; every being is either necessary or contingent; and every being is either finite or infinite. As Scotus points out (*Questions* IV, q. 2, n. 66, n. 81; 1997: 290, 294–5), neither member of the pair, severally taken, is convertible with the totality of being, but the disjunction is convertible in so far as every being must fall under one of the two disjuncts (here Scotus's reasoning clearly trades on the logical principle that a disjunction is true just in the case that either one of its disjuncts holds true).

The Problem of Universals

Medieval discussions of the problem of universals originated, historically speaking, in the classical text of Porphyry that served as an introduction to the *Categories* of Aristotle, the *Isagoge*. In that text, Porphyry had raised three questions regarding the status of universals: whether they are in things or only in the mind; assuming they are in things, whether they are corporeal or incorporeal; and whether they are only in sensible things or even exist apart from them. Yet the growing acquaintance with Aristotle during the twelfth and thirteenth centuries had focused matters considerably for later medieval philosophers. By the time of Scotus's *QM*, the Latin tradition had largely absorbed the Aristotelian notion of substance along with its concomitant critique of the Platonic theory of forms and had advanced to the stage where the precise ontological commitment to universals somehow existing in things had to be reconciled with the Aristotelian position that every substance that exists in the world is a singular thing. Discussions of the issues arising out of Aristotle's *Metaphysics* had been focused through the assimilation of the works of Avicenna, whose attempt to work out the ontology implicit in the doctrines of being and form in the central books of Aristotle's *Metaphysics* had resulted in a new set of terms and distinctions regarding the problem of universals. This set of terms and distinctions dominated treatments of the problem throughout the thirteenth century and well into the fourteenth.

Scotus's treatment of the problem of universals occurs mainly in questions 13, 17, 18, and 19 of Book VIII of his *QM*. Scotus's concern in all these texts is twofold: first, he wishes to uphold the reality of common natures as somehow prior to the individual things in which they are found; second, he wishes to recognize the ultimately irreducible character of individual things. The second concern entails for Scotus that individual things enjoy a perfection that cannot be found in another – their irrepeatability – and that, being unknowable by us in the present life, they are none the less intelligible in principle.

If we start with the analysis of Scotus's views on universals, we understand better the self-imposed constraints under which he operates in the case of the problem of individuation. Scotus begins his *ex professo* treatment in Book VII, q. 18 with the classical figures Plato and Aristotle. Though he expresses doubts and hesitation regarding whether the interpretation of Plato by Aristotle is entirely correct and whether, absolutely speaking, the Platonic position is impossible, he restricts the discussion of the problem of universals to the Aristotelian framework. Within this framework, those setting the terms of discussion are, as usual, Avicenna and Averroës: Avicenna is depicted as the figure defending the reality of extramental universals, whereas Averroës is construed as arguing that universals come to be only in and through the operations of the human mind (*Questions* VII, q. 18, n. 10, n. 34; 1997: 291–2, 297). Yet there were more recent representatives of the respective positions than the Islamic commentators: an extreme realism is discussed that originates from the position of the Franciscan scientist and philosopher Roger Bacon and a proto-nominalism is mentioned that comes from the school of the Franciscan theologian Peter John Olivi. The former view locates universals primarily in things and only secondarily in the mind; universal things are predicated of particular things on this score. The latter view locates universals primarily in the mind and only secondarily, if at all, in things (*Questions* VII, q. 18, n. 17–20, n. 26–8; 1997: 293–4, 296).

Scotus strives to carve out a position intermediate between the two extremes. In response to proto-nominalism, Scotus uses reasoning similar to that often seen on the same problem in his theological writings. Universals are what make individuals to be of a kind; the singular is only a "such and such" by reference to a kind of which it is an instance. Were there only singulars each absolutely singular through and through, it is not clear how things could be of a kind. Nor is it clear how the intellect could cause universals to characterize things in regard to their substances since the intellect only causes its own acts, which are accidental features belonging to it and not to things outside the mind.

But the most telling arguments brought forth by Scotus are in regard to why the natures found in things cannot be singular. If all universals or natures were singular, they would only have numerical unity and this, Scotus thinks, leads to impossible consequences. The three consequences worthy of mention are: (1) all things would be equally different from each other since they are equally numerically one and thus our minds would not be any more disposed to acquire the specific concept of white from white things than they are in fact disposed to acquire a specific concept from black and white things combined; (2) things would not be genuinely the same in species apart from the consideration of the human mind and hence all so-called opposites of a kind would only be numerical opposites, something that would destroy the basis for natural science at least in its Aristotelian version; and (3) neither the object of the sense nor the object of the intellect would have the kind of unity required for the types of cognition they produce since the object of the sense can move only in so far as the same kind of feature recurs in a numerically distinct thing, while the intellect can issue in understanding only in so far as the sense operates properly and the nature informs its act of understanding (*Questions* VII, q. 18, n. 1–9, n. 29–37; 1997: 289–91, 297–8).

Having arrived at the intermediate ground of moderate realism, Scotus must articulate a view of universals as found in things. Like Avicenna, Scotus distinguishes the nature from the concrete objects outside the mind in which the nature is found and the presence of the nature in the mind in the form of a universal concept. Unlike Avicenna, however, Scotus is much more precise on what a universal is, or rather what being universal involves, in its various stages and what status the nature enjoys when it is considered as such. The universal may be said to be the concept that is both found in many and predicable of many; as such the universal is fully such (*complete universale*) and it enjoys this form of existence only in the human mind. The universal may also be said to be apt to be found in many and apt to be predicable of many, having a being of identity in terms of its content and being of itself not-this. A universal considered in this way is incompletely such (*incomplete universale*) since it fails to verify the severally necessary and jointly sufficient conditions for universality: being found in many and being predicable of many. It is in this latter sense that natures are universal since they are both apt to be predicable of many and apt to be found in many no matter whether they are present in the mind or found in extramental reality (*Questions* VII, q. 18, n. 38–43; 1998: 298–9).

The being of the nature is then a kind of identity in indetermination; the nature is, contrary to Avicenna, such that it enjoys its own unity, called a minor unity (*unitas minor*) in contrast to the major or numerical unity found in an individual substance. Moreover, the nature is either further determined by the principle of individuation that contracts it to being just this item in the world, say this humanity, or rendered even more indeterminate by the activity of the intellect so that it can be predicated of many items outside the mind. But, in itself, the nature is an entity, that is an ontological principle, that both causes things to be of a certain kind outside the mind and thoughts to have the contents that they do within the mind, although it is not entirely identical to either a concrete substance or a given thought. In short, the nature is what binds the mind to reality and allows reality to inform the mind.

The Problem of Individuation

Obviously, in light of his commitment to the doctrine of the common nature, Scotus needs a theory of individuation. His theory is laid out in what became a classic text in the history of the problem of individuation, Book VII, q. 13. The overall structure is that of asking whether the principle of individuation is something negative or positive, and, assuming that it is positive, examining how the principle will be accounted for in terms of the Aristotelian ontology. The latter entails asking whether the principle of individuation belongs to the category of substance or one of the nine accidents. The framing of the question against a strict dichotomy of a negative or positive principle is one of the achievements of Scotus's *QM* and represents a real economy of analysis compared to his earlier writings (Dumont 1995; Noone, 1995).

Scotus first expresses his opposition to the view of Henry of Ghent that describes the principle of individuation in terms of two negations: the denial that the individual is like the species and further divisible into subjective parts and the denial of identity between any two individuals within a species. Scotus's line of criticism is quite predictable. The negations Henry proposes, taken as logical expressions, simply describe aspects of an individual's individuality; they do not uncover what makes individuals have those features. If the negations, however, are meant as ontological principles, they must be positive, or be meant to point to something positive, since the numerical unity and indivisibility into subject parts that they are trying to explain are positive features of things (*Questions* VII, q. 13, n. 56–9; 1998: 206–8).

Eliminating any negative principle of individuation, Scotus considers the range of alternatives on the side of a positive principle: quantity, matter, *esse*, or the relation to the agent that produced it.

What is common to all these theories, in Scotus's view, is that they all appeal to something accidental in order to explain the individuation of substances. (Scotus focuses on the individuation of substances, believing that the individuation of accidents is to be explained with reference to the substances in which they adhere.) After his general line of criticism against accidentalist accounts, Scotus raises objections to each of the particular ways of explaining individuation mentioned. Since space does not allow for anything more than a summary treatment of these, I shall only mention the more important ones. Against the quantity thesis, Scotus reasons that the quantity is either *terminata* (quantity with definite and distinctive dimensions) or *interminata* (quantity with indefinite and generic dimensions). If the latter, the quantity precedes and succeeds the given physical individual; hence, it cannot be what accounts for the uniqueness of the individual. Alternatively, if the quantity is *terminata*, such definite dimensions are the expression of the substantial form of the individual and depend upon it for their entity, not the converse. Regarding the materialist thesis on individuation, one of Scotus's favorite criticisms is that matter, as a principle of potentiality, is ill suited to function as the source of determination and actuality for the individual thing. For positing matter as the principle of individuation seems to entail locating the source of the greatest unity (*unitas maxima*) and actuality in a principle that is ordinarily the source of multiplicity and potentiality. Scotus has two chief criticisms of the *esse* theory of individuation. The first is that, although the theory is correct to seek a source of actuality as the principle of individuation, *esse* would seem to lack the characteristic of determination also required in the individuating principle, in so far as *esse* receives its determination from the essence which it actuates. The second is that, if *esse* functions as the principle of individuation, nothing can, properly speaking, be individual if it does not actually exist, in that it lacks precisely what constitutes it as individual. The latter claim would seem to rule out possible individuals and would call into question the possibility of God knowing individuals prior to their actual existence. As to the theory that individuals are such thanks to the relation that they have to the agent who produces them, Scotus points out that substance is absolute and prior to any relation; hence it cannot be made "this" by a relation (Scotus, *Questions* VII, q. 13, n. 50–1; 1998: 204–5).

We should now pause to see what we have learned from Scotus's criticism of alternative solutions to the problem of individuation. First, in seeking to explain the individuation of substances, Scotus wishes to discover what principle would account for the most telling feature of their individuality as he conceives it, non-instantiability. Second, Scotus faults the theses we have been considering for failing in various ways to come to grips with the depth of the problem of individuation in the case of substances, since in each case an appeal is made to the order of accident as the ultimate ground of substantial individuation. Third, we know by implication what we are looking for in a principle of individuation through reflecting on the strengths and weaknesses of the alternative positions. We are searching for a principle that is a positive element in the individual thing which must have the following characteristics: it must be substantial (to avoid the flaw of appealing to accidental being); it must be actual (failure to appeal to such a principle is what is mistaken in the materialist theory, whereas positing such a principle is the virtue of the *esse* theory); it must be determinative (failure to add this feature is what mars the *esse* theory); and, finally, it must be individual of itself, not needing further individuation in turn (this is the virtue of the quantitativists' account, since quantity, as the source of parcels, is individual of itself).

In many ways we have already arrived at Scotus's own position, since what he proposes as the principle of individuation is a principle that is, in the main, a theoretical construct fitting the requirements just mentioned. Scotus compares the determining role of the individuating principle, as he conceives it, to a specific difference's interrelation to other items on the Porphyrian tree: the specific difference may be compared to what is below it, what is above it, and what is adjacent to it on the Porphyrian tree. If the specific difference is viewed in reference to what is below it, namely the specific nature, the specific nature determined or informed by the specific difference is such that it is no longer open to multiplicity at the specific level; it is determined to be that species and no other. Likewise, the individual difference determines the individual in such a way that it is no longer open to further numerical multiplicity but is determined to be this individual and no other, i.e. it is non-instantiable. If the specific difference is viewed in reference to what is above it, we may say that it contracts the genus to the species, as act relative to the potency represented by the genus. So, too, we may say that the individual difference functions in like fashion with respect to the specific nature, yet with an important and noteworthy qualification. In the case of the specific difference and the genus a formal determination is added to a formal determination, but in the case of the individual difference a form is not added to a form. Rather the addition is from the very reality of the form itself – the individual entity is the ultimate expression of the thing's form – and the resulting composite is not constituted in quidditative (or essential) being but in what Scotus calls material being or contracted being. Finally, if we compare the specific difference to the items adjacent to it on the Porphyrian tree, namely other specific differences, we may say that every ultimate specific difference, while simultaneously giving the items in the species a certain distinguishing feature and consituting the items in the species in the being they have, is none the less diverse from other differences. Consequently, if we ask what is common to rational and irrational as they divide animal, the proper response is that they share in nothing but are simply diverse, if we wish to avoid an infinite regress. Likewise, the individual differences are primarily and simply diverse, although the individuals constituted by those differences are items sharing the same specific nature, just as the items in the different species share in the genus despite the fact that they are each constituted in their respective species by differences that are primarily diverse (*Questions* VII, q. 13, n. 115–64; 1998: 224–37).

Two problems arise immediately regarding Scotus's account of individuals. First, how are the common nature and the individual difference distinct in the individual thing? Second, how can the nature as contracted retain its minor unity which is indifferent to being just this, when it is contracted to being just this through individual difference? Are we not saying that the nature has two contradictory properties, minor unity and numerical unity? Scotus's reply to the first problem is that the common nature and the individuating difference are formally distinct while they are really identical. What this means is that, to the extent that the two principles could be given logical descriptions, the common nature would not be included in the description of the individual difference and vice versa, yet they both are constitutive parts of one thing (Gracia, 1996).

The second problem is a bit more thorny. Scotus suggests that, although the nature as contracted is one in number, it is only denominatively so, i.e. just as Socrates may be called white, but not properly "whiteness," so too the nature may be said to be numerically one in that the subject in which it is found is numerically one, but only improperly so, since it enjoys its own minor unity in its own right. In the *QM*, he supplements the appeal to denominative predication through the doctrine of unitive containment. Humanity does not include the individual difference of Socrates nor does Socrateity include humanity essentially. Socrates, however, unitively contains both human nature and Socrateity and they are both essential to him (*Questions* VII, q. 13, n. 131; 1998: 229–30).

In his discussion of all of these problems in the *QM*, Scotus in effect sets a new direction for metaphysical discussions. The science of metaphysics would henceforth be a transcendental science concerned to articulate transcendental notions and their interrelation, though it would have a theological goal as well. Furthermore, through his extensive treatment and his linkage of the problems of universals and individuation, Scotus assured that these problems would steadily occupy the attention of metaphysicians well into the modern period.

Bibliography

Editions and translations

Scoti, B. Ioannis Duns (1997) *Quaestiones super libros Metaphysicorum Aristotelis*, 2 vols, ed. R. Andrews, G. Etzkorn, G. Gál, R. Green, F. Kelley, G. Marcil, T. Noone, and R. Wood. St Bonaventure, NY: The Franciscan Institute.

Scotus, John Duns (1997–8) *Questions on the Metaphysics of John Duns Scotus*, vols I and II, trans. Girard J. Etzkorn and Allan B. Wolter. St Bonaventure, NY: The Franciscan Institute.

Studies

Boulnois, Olivier (1992) Réelles intentions: nature commune et universaux selon Duns Scot. *Revue de métaphysique et de morale*, 1: 3–33.

Dumont, Stephen D. (1987) The univocity of being in the fourteenth century: John Duns Scotus and William of Alnwick. *Mediaeval Studies*, 49: 1–75.

Dumont, Stephen D. (1995) The question of individuation in Scotus's *Quaestiones super Metaphysicam*. In Leonardo Sileo (ed.), *Via Scoti: Methodologica Joannis Duns Scoti*, vol. I, pp. 193–227. Rome: PAA-Edizioni Antonianum.

Gracia, Jorge J. E. (ed.) (1994) *Individuation in Scholasticism: The Later Middle Ages and the Counter-Reformation, 1150–1650*. Albany, NY: State University of New York Press.

Gracia, Jorge J. E. (1996) Individuality and the individuating entity in Scotus's *Ordinatio*: an ontological characterization. In Ludger Honnefelder, Rega Wood, and Mechthild Dreyer (eds), *John Duns Scotus: Metaphysics and Ethics*, pp. 229–49. Leiden: Brill.

King, Peter (1992) Duns Scotus on the common nature and the individual differentia. *Philosophical Topics*, 20 (2): 51–76.

Noone, Timothy B. (1995) Individuation in Scotus. *American Catholic Philosophical Quarterly*, 69: 527–42.

Wolter, Allan B. (1946) *The Transcendentals and their Function in the Metaphysics of John Duns Scotus*. St Bonaventure, NY: The Franciscan Institute.

17

William of Ockham, *Summa logicae* (ca. 1324)

Nominalism in Thought and Language

Claude Panaccio

Ockham's *Summa logicae* was intended as a handbook of logic in the medieval sense. Its professed goal was to provide students and scholars with a useful apparatus of concepts and rules for distinguishing truths from falsehoods, and good arguments from bad ones. What gives it a unique place in the history of Western philosophy is that it steadfastly follows what we would today term a *nominalist* approach. Meaning, truth, and validity are accounted for without acknowledging in the world anything but individuals, and generality is treated as a purely semantical affair. The book thus offers a far-reaching theory of how language, thought, and reality fit into each other.

William of Ockham (ca. 1287–1347) was an English Franciscan friar, whose thought soon became influential, and quite controversial. As far as we can guess from scanty evidence, he had previously taught theology at the University of Oxford in the late 1310s, and logic and physics at the Franciscan convent in London in the early 1320s. Along with the *Quodlibetal Questions*, the *Summa logicae* is one of his mature works in philosophy. It was written somewhere between 1323 and 1327. The modern editors date it more precisely from the summer of 1323, but the arguments for that remain slim. Given the size of the book (850 pages in the modern edition) and its astonishing density, it seems more probable that all or most of it was composed after the summer of 1324, while Ockham was in Avignon where he had been summoned by Pope John XXII to answer charges of heresy. He stayed there for four years, presumably without teaching, before fleeing to the Emperor Louis of Bavaria's court and turning to political writings until his death in 1347.

Ockham's Program

Logic, in the universities of the time, was the basis of all training in philosophy and theology. For the most part, it consisted of the material covered by Aristotle in his

Organon, complemented by the so-called terminist logic which had developed since the twelfth century and which mainly had to do with the semantical properties of terms (see Kretzmann et al., 1982: pt IV). Ockham, in the *Summa*, skillfully integrates and develops all these various components within a unified presentation, adopting as a general framework his own nominalist reinterpretation of the new terminist semantics. The basic organizing idea remains traditional: "All those who treat of logic," he writes in the first sentence of the first chapter, "try to show that arguments are composed of propositions and propositions of terms" (*Summa logicae*, ed. Boehner et al., 1974: 7; hereafter *SL*). Ockham, however, takes this compositional principle with the utmost seriousness and the *Summa*, accordingly, is divided into three main parts: the first deals with terms (seventy-seven chapters), the second with propositions (thirty-seven chapters), and the third with arguments (173 chapters, distributed between four sub-divisions).

The nominalist ontology which constrains the enterprise is considered as a matter for metaphysics to discuss, rather than logic itself. Ockham had lengthily argued for it in his large commentary on Peter Lombard's *Sentences* and he is content in the *Summa* with a short – but very sharp – review of his main arguments for rejecting the reality of universals (*SL* I, 15–17; 1974: 50–62). Two basic sorts of individuals are admitted: singular substances, such as a given man or a given horse (along with their essential parts: forms and pieces of matter); and singular qualities, such as the whiteness of a given horse, or its degree of warmth. General terms and sentences are not dismissed as misleading or arbitrary for all that, but they are not supposed to refer in the end to anything but such substances and qualities (or their parts).

Ockham's theoretical strategy for building an acceptable semantics on the basis of this rarefied ontology can be said to rest upon two main guiding principles: semantical atomism on the one hand, and a mental language approach to cognition and reasoning, on the other. The first of these requires that the semantical properties of arguments and propositions all ultimately depend upon the signification (*significatio*) that their constitutive terms are held to possess by themselves prior to being inserted within propositions. The second principle is that spoken and written words belonging to particular idioms of communication receive whatever meaning they have by being conventionally subordinated to mental representations, called "concepts." These representations are taken to be natural signs of things, and to be combinable by the mind into mental propositions just like external words can be combined into spoken or written sentences. The program, then, is to build a compositional semantics for this postulated universal mental language, without supposing anything but singular significates for its basic units; and to account from there for the overt particularities of spoken languages.

Terms

Part I of the *Summa* is organized around a central distinction between two sorts of semantical properties of terms (whether mental, spoken, or written): those that the term possesses before entering propositional combinations, and those it acquires only within such complexes. The former are discussed under the general label of signification (*significatio*) in the first sixty-two chapters, and the latter form the topic for Ockham's famous theory of supposition (*suppositio*) introduced in the last fifteen chapters.

Signification is understood as a relation between a sign and a number of individual things in the world, without general properties or abstract entities being required as intermediaries. It comes in two main varieties: primary signification and secondary signification (also called "connotation"). The primary signification of a sign *S* is the relation between *S* and whatever individual things *S* happens to be true of: thus "horse" primarily signifies anything which is a horse, and "white" primarily signifies anything which is white. Secondary signification, on the other hand, is a relation between certain signs and some individual things that these signs indirectly call to mind, usually without being true of them. Take "white" again: it calls to mind not only the white things themselves, but also their (singular) whitenesses, albeit indirectly. Some terms – whether mental or conventional – have only a primary signification, and some have both a primary and a secondary signification. Ockham calls the former "absolute terms"; they are what contemporary philosophy calls "natural kind terms": "horse," "man," "animal," "flower," "water," and so on. And he calls the latter "connotative terms," including among them all concrete qualitative terms such as "white," "warm," etc., and – more saliently – all relational terms ("father," for example, primarily signifies all fathers and secondarily signifies all children). This is a crucial distinction for Ockham's nominalism, and it looms large all through the *Summa*, allowing for a unified account of a wide variety of semantical and cognitive phenomena without supposing the existence of general or abstract objects out there in the world.

Ockham's detailed treatment of the Aristotelian categories in chapters 40–62 is a case in point. Aristotle, as is well known, listed ten basic categories of simple items acknowledged by his logic: substance, quantity, quality, relation, location, time, position, possession, action, and passion. What these are exactly is one of the most vexing – and most discussed – questions of the age-old tradition of Aristotelian scholarship. Ockham, for his part, offers a straightforward nominalist interpretation, based on his theory of connotation. The ten Aristotelian categories, according to him, are categories of simple meaningful terms in our mental language. A corresponding complexity, however, is not posited among real things: Ockham, as we saw, admits only of singular substances and qualities in his ontology. Connotation is precisely what accounts for this lack of isomorphism between the order of basic meaningful terms and that of external things: "all the expressions in the categories other than substance and quality," Ockham says, "are connotative names, and even some of those that belong to the genus of quality" (*SL* I, 10; 1974: 38). Thus, a relational term such as "father" need not refer to a special relation of fatherhood. Its adequacy as a sign requires only that it be endowed with a complex internal semantical structure: it primarily signifies certain singular substances (the fathers) and secondarily signifies more singular substances (the children), and that is all there is to it. Quantities, places, times, and so on are similarly reduced to singular substances and qualities through the virtues of connotation theory.

A number of other devices and distinctions introduced in the first chapters of Part I also play a significant role in Ockham's project. The distinction between categorematic and syncategorematic terms in chapter 4 is a good example. Properly speaking, Ockham says, only the former have signification. The latter – terms like "every," "no," "some," "except," "and," "or," "if," and so on – neither primarily nor secondarily signify anything of their own. They simply modify in determinate ways the signification, supposition, or syntactic role of the categorematic expressions they are combined with. Thus no special logical objects are called for to account for their semantics. Other fascinating examples are to be found in Ockham's treatment of abstract terms – such as "animality," "convexity," or "freedom" – in chapters 5–9 (the upshot of which being, unsurprisingly, that no special abstract objects are needed), and in his interpretation of terms such as "species" and "genus," in chapters 18–25, as being meta-linguistic in character rather than metaphysical: they are held to signify special sorts of signs rather than special sorts of things.

When a term is used as subject or predicate of a proposition (whether mental, spoken, or written), it thereby acquires, according to Ockham's theory, a new semantical property called "supposition" (*suppositio*), which is discussed in Part I of the *Summa* from chapter 63 on. Supposition is defined as "a sort of taking the place of another" (*SL* I, 63; 1974: 193). It is, in other words, the referential function of the term within the context of a proposition. Supposition has to be distinguished from signification for three reasons. First, a term occurring within a proposition does not always refer to its significates: it can be used to stand for itself as a spoken or written word, as "horse" does in "horse is an English word" (this is what Ockham calls "material supposition"); or it can be used to stand for the mental concept which it is subordinated to, as in "horse is a natural kind concept" (this is "simple supposition"). In such cases, the term does not loose its significates, but the sentence, nevertheless, is not *about* them. Secondly, even when it does stand for its primary significates – which is what Ockham calls "personal supposition" – it frequently stands only for some of them (e.g. for those that exist at the time of utterance if the main verb is in the present tense). Thirdly, whereas signification remains constant, the modes of reference can vary from one context to another ("horse," for example, does not supposit in the same way in "all horses are animals" and in "Bucephalus is a horse"). Displaying the array of possible referential functions for a given term, then, allows for an elucidation of many contextual semantical phenomena. What is important is that in all cases the referents are but individuals: singular tokens of (mental, spoken, or written) signs in the case of material and simple suppositions, and singular primary significates of the term in all variants of personal supposition.

Propositions

Supposition, moreover, plays a decisive role in the theory of propositions that Ockham develops in Part II of the *Summa*. A proposition, in his vocabulary, is a structured sequence of terms – whether mental, spoken, or written – which is either true or false. In its elementary form, it has a subject, a tensed copula, and a predicate, both the subject and predicate being either singular or general terms endowed with a supposition. The largest portion of Part II (chapters 2–29) is dedicated to such elementary propositions, while the last eight chapters (30–37) cursorily deal with more complex ones (conditional, conjunctive, disjunctive, causal, and temporal). The most striking and original development in this part has to do with the truth-conditions of non-modal elementary propositions in chapters 2–8. It is in this context that supposition turns out to be most useful as an intermediate semantical property between the significations of terms and the truth-values of propositions.

Consider, for instance, the case of a singular affirmative proposition such as "Socrates is a man." One must not say, Ockham insists, that what is required for such a proposition to be true is that the subject be identical with the predicate (since they are different *terms*), nor that the predicate or its referent really inhere in the subject or be part of it. The correct truth-conditions, instead, must be formulated in terms of a relation between the supposition of the subject-term and that of the predicate-term: "it is sufficient and necessary," Ockham writes, "that the subject and predicate supposit for the same thing" (*SL* II, 2; 1974: 250). In the chosen example, the proper name "Socrates" supposits for Socrates himself. For the sentence to be true, then, this singular referent must also be among the individuals that the predicate "man" stands for, namely all the men that exist at the moment of utterance. Similarly, in the case of a negative singular proposition, such as "Socrates is not a donkey," the subject-term must not supposit for any of the referents of the predicate-term. Truth-conditions are also given along the same lines for particular affirmative or negative propositions, such as "a man is running" or "some horses are not black," and for universal affirmative or negative propositions, such as "all men are mortal" or "no horse is a man." It all comes down to this, in the end, that the truth-values of such propositions are always derived from the supposition of their terms (given the logical structure of the proposition). Since the supposition in turn is contextually derived from the signification of the terms, the truth-value of the proposition turns out to be a contextual function of the signification of the isolated terms, which, as we insisted, should involve nothing in the world but individuals.

There are more complicated cases, of course, and Ockham is well aware of it. Chapters 9 and 10, most saliently, are dedicated to the truth-conditions of modal propositions (including belief or knowledge ascriptions of the form "it is believed – or known – by *A* that *p*"); and chapters 11–20 deal with a rich selection of special cases. On each occasion, Ockham has intriguing and original proposals to offer, while scrupulously avoiding any departure from his nominalist ontological basis.

Arguments

Part III of the *Summa*, dedicated to arguments, is by far the longest. Yet, in the present state of our knowledge, it remains the least studied. It is subdivided into four sections. The first one, based on Aristotle's *Prior Analytics*, develops Ockham's own theory of the syllogism (68 chapters). The second one, based on the *Posterior Analytics*, deals with scientific demonstration, understood as syllogistic derivation from necessary premises (41 chapters). The third one, partly inspired by Aristotle's *Topics* and partly by recent developments in the so-called theory of "consequences," discusses non-syllogistic inferences (46 chapters). And the fourth one (18 chapters) reviews, in Ockham's characteristically original way, the various sorts of fallacies identified by Aristotle in his treatise *On Sophistical Refutations*.

It is here, of course, that the *Summa* comes closest to what we call "logic" today, namely the theory of valid inferences. Yet this is not formal logic as we understand it. In Ockham's view, the correctness of an inference rests, in most cases, upon the reference – or supposition – of its component terms rather than on purely formal features. This is especially true of the syllogism. The validity of any syllogistic inference, according to Ockham, ultimately hangs upon two – and only two – semantical relations.(*SL* III-1, 2; 1974: 362–3): the *dici de omni* ("being said of all") and the *dici de nullo* ("being said of none"), which both have to do with the supposition of the component terms of the syllogisms. And the non-syllogistic inferences dealt with in Part III-3 are also systematically treated as depending, for their validity, upon the supposition of their terms.

Part III of the *Summa*, like the previous ones, abounds with original doctrines, precise analyses, and exciting insights. One of its most striking achievements, for example, is that it develops, for the first time, a detailed modal logic, extensively dealing with all kinds of syllogisms from premises of the form "it is (not) necessary – or possible – that *p*" (*SL* III-1, 20–64; 1974: 411–97). The main thing, however, from a philosophical point of view, is that the reasoning never loses sight of Ockham's nominalist project. Inferential validity, just like truth and falsity, is ultimately made to rest upon the semantical connections between our mental concepts and some individuals in the world.

Bibliography

Editions and translations

William of Ockham (1974) *Guillelmi de Ockham: Summa logicae* (= G. de Ockham, *Opera philosophica*, vol. I), ed. Ph. Boehner, G. Gál, and S. Brown. St Bonaventure, NY: The Franciscan Institute.

William of Ockham (1974) *Ockham's Theory of Terms* (English trans. of Part I of *Summa logicae*), ed. M. J. Loux. Notre Dame, IN: University of Notre Dame Press.

William of Ockham (1980) *Ockham's Theory of Propositions* (English trans. of Part II of *Summa logicae*), ed. A. J. Freddoso and H. Schuurman. Notre Dame, IN: University of Notre Dame Press.

William of Ockham (1991) *Quodlibetal Questions*, 2 vols, trans. A. J. Freddoso. New Haven, CT: Yale University Press.

Studies

Adams, M. M. (1987) *William Ockham*, 2 vols. Notre Dame, IN: University of Notre Dame Press.

Kretzmann, N., Kenny, A., and Pinborg, J. (eds) (1982) *The Cambridge History of Later Medieval Philosophy*. Cambridge: Cambridge University Press.

Spade, P. V. (ed.) (1999) *The Cambridge Companion to Ockham*. Cambridge: Cambridge University Press.

18

Nicholas of Cusa, *On Learned Ignorance* (ca. 1440)

Byzantine Light *en route* to a Distant Shore

Peter Casarella

Nicholas of Cusa (1401–1464) lived during what is sometimes dismissed as a transitional period in Western culture, for his life and thought cross the epochal threshold that divided the still closed world of late medieval theology from the dawn of Renaissance humanism's infinite universe. During his lifetime, Cusanus (literally translated, "the one from the village of Kues") was acclaimed throughout Europe as a scholar, a lawyer and canonist, a collector of ancient manuscripts, a mathematician and philosopher of science, and a preacher. Twentieth-century scholarship frequently emphasized his affinity with the forerunners of modern science. The interpretation that follows shows that the cardinal's *philosophical* acumen was also an element of his religious beliefs.

On the dedication page of *On Learned Ignorance* (ca. 1440), Nicholas states that the inspiration for the work came while accompanying a group of Eastern Orthodox patriarchs back from Greece to the projected reunion council in Italy. The dedication is made to Julian Cesarini, an influential cardinal and humanist.

> Receive now, Reverend Father, what I have long desired to attain through the paths of diverse doctrines but could not until, while I was at sea *en route* back from Greece, I was led, as I believe, by a heavenly gift from the Father of lights, from whom comes every excellent gift, to embrace incomprehensible things incomprehensibly in learned ignorance and through a transcending of humanly knowable incorruptible truths.

These words summarize the purpose of the work. The reference to the "gift from the Father of lights" comes from the Epistle of James (1: 17) and is also the opening line of *The Celestial Hierarchy* of Dionysius the Areopagite. Shipboard Nicholas surveyed his own finite position against the boundless expanse of the sea, an element of epideictic rhetoric noted by O'Rourke Boyle (1991). Experiencing both the relativity of his own perspective and a genuine inspiration from above, Cusanus hit upon the central idea of the entire book: "in learned ignorance [*docta ignorantia*] . . . to embrace incomprehensible things incomprehensibly."

In the dedication he offers Cesarini things he desired in vain to attain by various doctrinal approaches, suggesting that Cusanus did not want to associate learned ignorance with the philosophy of the schools. Cusanus in fact mentions three sources for learned ignorance, all of which point to a more ancient and remote provenance: St Augustine, Dionysius the Areopagite, and the Islamic theologian Algazel.

What is "learned ignorance?" To know something ignorantly sounds like less than firm knowledge, a misperception Cusanus had to confront even in his own day. A clue arises in Cusanus' gloss on a simile in Aristotle's *Metaphysics* (II, 1933b 9–11): "Aristotle . . . asserts that in things most obvious by nature it is as difficult for us as for a night owl trying to look at the sun" (*Learned Ignorance* [hereafter *LI*] (1985) I, 1). As Aristotle suggests, one recognizes that what cannot be known or seen is intrinsically hidden. Learned ignorance describes the condition of the knower trying to know the infinite *as* infinite, thus linking the perspectival basis of all knowing with the very idea of the infinite (Harries, 2001). For Cusanus, learned ignorance is not just a way of saying that rational understanding has not yet completed its victory. Learned ignorance is the permanent condition of the finite knower facing the infinite.

Human knowledge proceeds, according to Cusanus, by way of comparative relation. The mind (*mens*) functions like a measure (*mensura*), for things are generally known as either more or less. Apart from mathematicals, nothing knowable in the finite world is intrinsically equal to something else. The infinite surpasses the world of comparative relations and can only be grasped through learned ignorance. *There is no comparative relation between the finite and the infinite*, a principle that has been termed Cusanus' principle of incommensurability.

Learned ignorance is both *docta* (learned) and *ignorantia* (ignorance). Without both aspects, learned ignorance becomes either self-refuting skepticism or an esoterism separated from all rational inquiry. To learn ignorance is, as it was for Socrates, to know oneself. To know oneself as a finite knower is to know that one's discursive reasoning is incapable on its own accord of leaping over the radical disproportion between the finite and the infinite. Learned ignorance begets not the methodical doubt proposed by René Descartes in his *Discourse on Method* but genuine certitude, albeit not of knowledge limited to discursive reasoning.

Cusanus returned from Greece seeking to know "incomprehensible things incomprehensibly." Learned ignorance is thus also the unknowing that makes way for what is beyond knowing and not knowing. In other words, his newly discovered path of learned ignorance arises out of philosophical wonder and leads ineluctably to the desire for sacred ignorance.

On Divine Names

The program of learned ignorance includes a re-examination of the divine names. In the Eastern Christian, Jewish, and medieval Western theology with which Cusanus was intimately familiar, treatises on the divine names were a recognized, although sometimes suppressed, genre. Cusanus, for example, acknowledges his debt to the contributions of Dionysius the Areopagite, Raymond Lull, Hugh of Strasbourg, and Moses Maimonides to this speculative tradition. His own personal path to the incomprehensible God, however, is no mere repetition of ancient formulae. Learned ignorance, he maintains, begins by looking beyond the expressions of other theologians and all other perceptible truths:

> Someone who desires to grasp their meaning must elevate his intellect above the meaning of the words rather than insisting upon the proper significations of words which cannot be properly adapted to such great intellectual mysteries. (*LI* I, 2)

Learned ignorance follows the way of negation, preferring the meaning of words to the speaking of words and the apprehension of ineffable mystery by the intellect to the grasp of perceptible truths by discursive reasoning.

Cusanus is not, however, fleeing linguistic forms altogether. In fact, the treatment of divine names begins with the way of affirmation. If affirmative names befit God, he says, they befit him only in relation to created things (*LI* I, 24). Attributes such as "truth," "justice," "virtue," are ascribed to God "in accordance with something found in created things" (*LI* I, 24). Neither human truth nor human justice is predicated of God, but rather an analogy drawn from created things. Positive names of God therefore derive from the created order of things.

Following the principle of incommensurability, Cusanus then contends that there is no comparative proportion between names drawn from created things and the name that can be properly ascribed to God. Accordingly, no name properly agrees with the "*unqualifiedly* Maximum, to which nothing is opposed" (*LI* I, 24) because names are bestowed on the basis of finite reasoning.

Two examples will illustrate this. Cusanus knew that the people of Israel signified God's unspeakable name with the four letters of the tetragrammaton, generally transliterated from Hebrew as "YHWH." The figure of the tetragrammaton befits God according to his essence and "not according to his relation to created things" (*LI* I, 24). The same, he states, can be said for the notion of oneness among the Neoplatonists. Neither term can be defined as that which stands opposed to created things. Neither the hidden God of Israel nor the Greek notion of incomprehensible oneness can be defined in purely negative terms.

Cusanus then fashions a definition of God's name that conforms to the Hebrew and Greek experience of God's incomprehensibility:

> If anyone were able to understand or to name such Oneness . . . he would attain to the name of God. But since the name of God is God, His name is known only by an understanding which is the maximum and is the maximum name . . . although "Oneness" seems to be a quite close name for the Maximum, nevertheless it is still infinitely distant from the true Name of the Maximum, which is the Maximum. (*LI* I, 24)

Although the name "Maximum" would be proper to God, it turns out not to be a name at all. In ordinary speech we can distinguish between names and what they name. The four letters "b-o-o-k" are not a book; they signify the book's name. The same is not true for the ineffable name of God. The truest spoken name of God is "the Maximum," but no finite speaker can comprehend that such a comprehension is at once a name and the thing named. In "the true name of the maximum which is the maximum," he states, there is no distinction between naming and being. To say that the name of God is God is equivalent to saying that no name *qua* name befits God.

By postulating the coincidence of naming and being in the name of the maximum, Cusanus questions whether God's true name signifies by representing some thing. In ordinary language, a name which is what it signifies cannot represent anything at all, for it is nothing other than itself. Rather than signifying, the name "Maximum" *instantiates* the negation of all names. This name turns that to which it is applied (e.g., God or Oneness) into a sign of its own otherness. For Cusanus naming that which is transcendentally signified involves a play of signs pointing to a kind of presence other than mere signification.

Cusanus concludes that although affirmative theology is appropriate to the language of worship, God is spoken of more truly through negation (*LI*, I, 26). In claiming that "in theological matters negations are true and affirmations are inadequate," Cusanus is not refuting the positive use of names but is contending that in learned ignorance affirmations about God drawn from created things play a role subordinate to that of negations.

Spoken names are removed from the divinity so that the one true ineffable name can shine forth in language. Cusanus' questioning of verbal signification leads to a symbolic view of language, whose context is faith's knowledge of the divine. After all discursive likenesses and metaphors are taken away, the "name" of God is not just a spoken word but something revealed through the eyes of faith. Cusanus contends that even though faith comes from hearing we still need to look for signs of divine presence. In the end, he states in a sermon from the same period, "we will see this Name to be the true and correct name . . . in which God the Father can be seen and understood" (Nicolai de Cusa, 1984, *Sermo* XXIV,12, 9–10).

In learned ignorance language about God no longer refers to a determinate thing that is signified (what the medievals called *res significata*) but discloses an infinite reality seen in a finite form. Like a mirror, the image of the truth about God can both deceive and reflect truly. According to Cusanus, when the intellect is able to focus on an undistorted image of the truth, it then beholds a reflection of the truth in the image as if it were looking face to face. Only later in *On Learned Ignorance* is the real name of the true image of the invisible God disclosed.

Learned Ignorance and Christ

Learned ignorance is a philosophy of Christ (Schönborn, 1979). Cusanus did not write the work as a learned defense of his religious beliefs or as a manual to instruct the faithful. His aim was to present a synthesis of religious and philosophical beliefs that also reflected the renewal of humanistic learning in quattrocento Italy that he himself had absorbed.

In Book III of *On Learned Ignorance* Cusanus considers the notion of the absolute maximum from a new vantage point. The absolute maximum is not the highest finite maximum in the world but the maximum *absolved* from all worldly opposition. There is no comparative relation between the absolute maximum *qua* absolute and the greatest maximum in the world. The absolute maximum cannot be named and is not fully comprehensible to finite reasoning.

The oneness of the absolute maximum none the less communicates itself in diverse ways in finite things. There is an *explicatio* ("unfolding") in the world of all that is a *complicatio* ("enfolding" or synthesis) in the oneness of the absolute maximum. The finite universe includes infinite diversity (a thought that inspired Giordano Bruno in the sixteenth century to hypothesize infinite worlds and cite Cusanus as an inspiration), without exhausting the possibilities enfolded in the absolute maximum itself. Even though the finite order admits of no absolute equality, the diversity of finite things in the created order already implies a gradation of visible perfections.

The idea of the absolute maximum can be thought even without full comprehension; therefore, Cusanus' argumentation proceeds as a hypothesis. One can conceive of the perfection of a maximal individual. From that one can conceive of the perfection of a maximal species. Finally, a maximum of humanity is also thinkable if it embraces everything that is already implied by the maximum of all possible individuals and all possible species. The maximum of humanity would not involve a mixture of the absolute maximum with the finite maximum. As the maximum of humanity, it would "enfold" within itself all finite natures.

This line of reasoning allows one to ask, "What if the hypothesis of maximum humanity were joined to the power of the absolute maximum itself?" The power of the absolute maximum is in itself without limitation. For a human nature to be elevated unto a oneness with this power could not involve a mixture of finitude with the infinite, for in that case the power of the absolute maximum would be limited by the admixture of finitude. To be absolutely maximum, human nature would need to be joined to the infinite power of the maximum without limiting or changing the maximum. This elevated human nature is a creature existing not in itself but in oneness with the power of the infinite. In other words, the absolute maximum of humanity would be joined in a single individual to the absolute maximum itself without separation or division.

This conclusion represents the full development of the hypothesis of maximal humanity up to the end of Book III, chapter 3 of *On Learned Ignorance*. In the next chapter, Cusanus no longer speculates about hypothetical knowledge. As Haubst demonstrates (1956: 143–57), the transition in the text marks the difference between a preliminary and hypothetical notion of the absolute maximum and the cognitive presupposition in faith that the absolute maximum of humanity is the human nature of Christ. Cusanus then states: "In Him humanity was united to his divinity in a Word so that the humanity existed not in itself but in the Word; for the humanity could not have existed in the supreme degree and in every plenitude except in the divine person of the Son" (*LI* III, 4). The notion of the " absolute maximum" thus prepares for *and* presupposes the Christian doctrine that human nature is united to the Word of God in Christ. Cusanus is not deducing the concept of maximal humanity from the fact of the incarnation. The hypothetical concept is meant to guide a reader of *On Learned Ignorance* already in possession of faith's knowledge (e.g. Cardinal Cesarini) to a preliminary understanding of what the incarnation would mean if it were to be understood in terms of the philosophy of learned ignorance.

The project of *On Learned Ignorance* is thus defined by what St Anselm had termed faith seeking understanding. Without the real knowledge that the humanity of Christ is united to the divine Word in one person and without separation or confusion, the logic of *On Learned Ignorance* begins to unravel. Without this knowledge, all finite modes of knowing the unnameable God would be of no consequence. The book that introduces the person of Christ thus discloses that the hidden God of the treatise's first book *is* the revealed God. Here the divinity who is only known conjecturally through images is truly disclosed in the image of the invisible God, i.e., Christ. God's relation to the world thus does not end with the abstract relation of God as the enfolding unity of that which is unfolded in the world. In the humanity of Christ, God's enfolding unity assumes the finitely maximal form of unfolded unity. Christ is the very medium of creation, for in Christ God has become man.

The deliberately theological affirmations of the third book add to the program of *On Learned Ignorance*. Here Cusanus reveals the one exemplary, saving name of Jesus which unifies and transcends all names. Through learned ignorance, faith and philosophy, two modes of thinking that Cusanus himself opposed to one another, coincide.

Conclusion

Cusanus did not view himself as a transitional figure standing between medieval and modern thought. The notion of "a middle age" had not yet been invented. The experience of a "gift from the Father of lights" recounted in the dedicatory letter ignited tinders of Eastern Christian thought that he had already encountered in Latin translation at the universities of Padua and Cologne and on the trip to Constantinople (Lohr, 1988: 548–58, 563–6). In *On Learned Ignorance*, Cusanus attempted to recover a more ancient approach to philosophical wisdom than was being taught in either the humanist or the scholastic centers of learning of his day. This particular blending of philosophical rigor and humanistic faith also remains radically other than the primary trajectories of modern Western thought. *On Learned Ignorance* defies labels such as ancient, medieval, or modern. Perhaps for that very reason the path of learned ignorance continues to provoke interest even today.

Bibliography

Editions and translations

Nicolai de Cusa (1932) *Opera omnia*, I: *De docta ignorantia*, ed. E. Hoffman and R. Klibansky. Leipzig/Hamburg: Felix Meiner.

Nicolai de Cusa (1984) XVI/4. *Sermones* I (1430–44), ed. R. Haubst and M. Bodewig. Leipzig/Hamburg: Felix Meiner.

Nicholas of Cusa (1985) *On Learned Ignorance: A Translation and Appraisal of De docta ignorantia*, 2nd edn, ed. J. Hopkins. Minneapolis, MN: Banning Press.

Studies

Harries, H. (2001) *Infinity and Perspective.* Cambridge, MA: MIT Press.

Haubst, R. (1956) *Die Christologie des Nikolaus von Kues.* Freiburg: Verlag Herder.

Lohr, C. (1988) Metaphysics. In Charles B. Schmitt and Quentin Skinner (eds), *The Cambridge History of Renaissance Philosophy*, pp. 537–638. Cambridge: Cambridge University Press.

O'Rourke Boyle, M. (1991) Cusanus at sea: the topicality of illuminative discourse. *Journal of Religion*, 71: 180–201.

Schönborn, P. C. (1979) "De docta ignorantia" als christozentrischer Entwurf. In Klaus Jacobi (ed.), *Nikolaus von Kues*, pp. 138–56. Freiburg: Verlag Karl Alber.

19

Niccolò Machiavelli, *The Prince* (1513)

Politics as the Pursuit of Power

Bjørn Thommessen

This short but potent book, written in 1513, has more than any other work made Niccolò Machiavelli (1469–1527) famous (or infamous, as some would have it) as a political thinker. *The Prince* (*Il principe*) has often been viewed as the source of Machiavellianism, a doctrine of political cynicism.

Spinoza, Rousseau, and Hegel are among those who have judged it a masterpiece of political theory, while others, such as Cardinal Reginald Pole (1500–1558) and the Huguenot Gentillet (1532–1588), considered it an almost satanic script. As early as 1557, *The Prince* was placed on the Index of Prohibited Books by the Catholic Church, not because it was deemed formally heretical, but rather because of the presumed immorality of its teaching. *The Prince* has indeed remained controversial up to this day.

The Prince is not Machiavelli's sole important work. His *Discourses on Livy* have also enjoyed wide recognition. In the latter, Machiavelli argues in favor of republican rule, all the while acknowledging that in many circumstances this rule can neither be established nor maintained. This, he believed, was certainly the situation confronting his native Florence at the time that he wrote *The Prince*.

What is Politics About?

Machiavelli gives us his brief answer to the question of what politics should be concerned with at the very outset of *The Prince*: "All the states and governments that ever had or now have power over men were and are of two sorts, either republics or princely states" (Machiavelli, 1992: ch. I, 4; all quotations from *The Prince* are taken from this edition). In either case, politics is about rule, the exercise of power over men.

There is, according to Machiavelli, in all human societies a natural tendency toward corruption and decay, that is, toward anarchy (*licenza*). Anarchy means lack of order, insecurity, lawlessness, and moral dissolution. Over the course of history, the various principalities and republics may all be seen as so many attempts at stemming this tide.

The Prince is about leadership exercised in the most precarious of political situations, that of a state teetering on the very edge of anarchy.

Anarchy, Machiavelli believed, is sometimes unavoidable. He inherited the Platonic–Aristotelian theory of cyclical change in regimes. In his version principalities follow upon anarchy, from principalities emerge republics (regimes of freedom), and from the freedom of republics, anarchy returns. The steps in this cycle are caused by the ineradicable conflict between the rich (*ottimati*) and the poor (*popolo*), a duality inevitably present in any society (*The Prince*, ch. IX, 27–8).

The contemporary situation in Italy seemed to him dangerously close to anarchy. The Italian city-republics and principalities were fighting each other; some of them even attempted to marshal the support of non-Italian powers. Italy thus became a battleground in which foreign powers – most notably France, Spain, and the German emperor – engaged in a struggle for hegemony. This situation prompted Machiavelli to search for a way to free Italy from the ravages of these intruders (*gli barbari*).

The Prince is dedicated to the one person Machiavelli considered a candidate to be the political savior of Italy: the Medici prince, Lorenzo. The dedicatory address and the last chapter of the book (*The Prince*, ch. XXVI, 69–72) urge Lorenzo to take on this task. Lorenzo, however, appears to have taken no notice of the book at all. It is doubtful whether he even read it.

Machiavelli the Political Realist

Machiavelli is reputed to be the pioneer political realist thinker of the modern period, and one of the founding fathers of modern political science. His realism can be recognized in the following passage from *The Prince*:

> since I intend to write something useful to an understanding reader, it seemed better to go after the real truth of the matter than to repeat what other people have imagined. A great many men have imagined states and princedoms such as nobody ever saw or knew in the real world, and there is such a difference between the way we really live and the way we ought to live that the man who neglects the real to study the ideal will learn how to accomplish his ruin, not his salvation. Any man who tries to be good all the time is bound to come to ruin among the great number who are not good. (ch. XV, 42)

Machiavelli obviously intends to write about people as they *really* are, not as we wish them to be. But how are we then – "really" – according to him? On Machiavelli's view, very few of us are good; in truth, most of us are bad: "For it is a good general rule about men, that they are ungrateful, fickle, liars and deceivers, fearful of dangers and greedy for gain." (*The Prince*, ch. XVII, 46). Machiavelli never justifies or discusses the truth of such statements. They are simply axioms, fundamental to all his political analyses and judgments. And it is this pessimistic anthropology which above all has given him the reputation for being a political realist. It is indeed a remarkable fact in our culture that the more one describes men as evil and wicked, the more realistic, that is, closer to reality, one's descriptions are considered to be.

As Machiavelli's prince has to act among such men, in a political world bordering on anarchy, he cannot avoid being cruel. To be sure, every ruler would prefer to be thought of as compassionate rather than cruel. But Machiavelli warns against too much compassion:

> People thought Cesare Borgia [one of Machiavelli's favorite contemporary princes] was cruel, but that cruelty of his reorganized the Romagna, united it, and established it in peace and loyalty . . . This prince was much more merciful than the people of Florence, who to avoid the reputation of cruelty, allowed Pistoia to be destroyed . . . He may make examples of a very few, but he will be more merciful in reality than those who, in their tenderheartedness, allow disorders to occur, with their attendant murders and lootings. (*The Prince*, ch. XVII, 45)

Machiavelli tells us that, in this somber world, princes are often in situations where they are obliged to choose between evils. There may be greater and lesser evils, but even the least is, of course, an evil. So an acting prince, especially a new one, cannot, if he does not wish to be destroyed himself, avoid doing ugly things – murder, fraud, breaking of faith, etc.

This is probably the background for Machiavelli's notorious advice to the prince that he must learn both the "way of law" and the "way of the animal" (*The Prince*, ch. XVIII, 47ff). The way of law cannot be adhered to under all circumstances. Therefore the prince must learn how to resort to the way of the animal. The animal he should imitate is the lion and the fox, the lion because of its force, the fox because of its slyness.

The way of law teaches that the prince should always keep faith. But, as Machiavelli puts it, "a prince who wants to keep his authority must learn how not to be good and use that knowledge, or refrain from using it, as necessity requires" (*The Prince*, ch. XV, 42).

Machiavelli is often accused of promoting political amorality. Some of his recommendations are certainly *immoral,* but it is doubtful whether one can term them *amoral.* He never stops calling what is cruel cruel, what is good good, and what is wicked wicked. He seems to keep the moral vocabulary intact and never abolishes the distinctions between the good and bad.

On the other hand, political justice, for Machiavelli, includes no inherent reference to moral (natural) law. This form of justice, on the contrary, must take its bearings solely from necessity. Machiavelli thus tells the Medici prince that he is lucky to have justice on his side, since "a war is just for those to whom it is necessary, and the arms are sacred when there is no hope except in arms" (*The Prince*, ch. XXVI, 70). The war to redeem Italy from *gli barbari* is necessary, and therefore just.

What is *The Prince* About?

Apparently, *The Prince* is about how *princely states* can be acquired, kept in hand – and how they can be lost. The book may be read as a "mirror of princes," but not of the conventional brand where the author counsels the prince to rule according to a moral ideal. Machiavelli's maxims are *strategic*, not moral rules. The reward for adopting them is power; the punishment for not adopting them is ruin and destruction, loss of power.

The book starts with a classification of principalities, obviously intended to be an analytical framework for the further treatment of subjects. There are various princely regimes, each with its peculiar problems. Some principalities are hereditary, principalities where the family of the ruler has been in control for a long time. These are the easiest to keep; it is simply a matter of not upsetting ancient customs, and accommodating oneself to new circumstances (*The Prince*, ch. II, 4). Only through excessive acts of force brought against these principalities may they be lost, and they can easily be regained as they have the legitimacy of tradition and custom behind them (ibid.).

Other principalities are new; these are the ones most difficult to establish and to preserve. Of the new principalities, some (termed "mixed") have been freshly joined through conquest or other means to a previously existing hereditary princedom. Others are completely new. Often it happens that the latter "are acquired with one's own arms and political virtue [*virtù*]," while in other cases they fall into the prince's possession by foreign arms or by good luck (*Fortuna*). Still others are acquired by cruelty or crime (*scelleratezze*).

In addition, there are also civil principalities, where "a private citizen becomes a prince in his native land, not through crimes or other intolerable violence, but by the choice of his fellow citizens" (*The Prince*, ch. IX, 27).

Lastly, Machiavelli writes about the ecclesiastical (papal) states, which stand undefended, and whose subjects who are "ruled by a heavenly providence to which human reason cannot reach," and hence enjoy a security and prosperity which they would otherwise not have. Machiavelli alerts the reader that he "shall say nothing of such states" (*The Prince*, ch. XI, 32). One senses the irony, for Machiavelli was indeed very critical of the secular, Italian politics of the Roman Church.

Machiavelli's interest in *The Prince* is primarily with completely new states, innovative projects where a prince has to make everything new. Such undertakings are always dangerous, for a new prince is bound "to offend some and disturb all," as he lacks the legitimacy of custom and tradition. Whether the new prince will succeed depends on his political virtue (*virtù*), and on good fortune (*Fortuna*). Although both factors may ease the project, "the less one trusts to chance, the better one's hope of holding it" (*The Prince*, ch. VI, 16).

Among the completely new states, those acquired by the prince's own arms and political virtue (*virtù*) stand out as truly paradigmatic. Historically speaking, some princes have succeeded through their political virtue (*virtù*) alone. The most admirable of these are Moses, Cyrus, Theseus, and Romulus. As founders of states their achievements will forever remain unsurpassed. They constitute the ideal standard of princely conduct; all others should seek to imitate them (ibid).

New princedoms acquired by the weapons of others and good luck (*Fortuna*) may be easily gained, but are almost impossible to maintain. Principalities acquired by pure luck (*Fortuna*) alone are indeed very easily won, but just as easily lost.

It is urgent for a prince not to make himself too dependent on factors beyond his control – for example on foreign troops, mercenaries, or more generally on Fortune.

On the contrary, he should always try to maintain his freedom of action as much as possible. This freedom of action is a function of his political virtue (*virtù*).

Virtù

Machiavelli's idea of political virtue is very different from the one found in Plato, Aristotle, or in medieval Christian thinkers. His term *virtù*, the literal meaning of which is *manliness*, designates the prince's ability to control factors relevant to establishing and maintaining a princedom. *Virtù* is a measure of the prince's active power, not of his moral goodness.

The *virtuoso* prince manifests his *virtù* in various ways: his prudence in choosing ministers, his ability to see through flatterers, his intelligence, courage, audacity, determination, and slyness, as well as his prowess in the art of war – the ability *sine qua non* for any successful prince – but almost never by his moral goodness. Nevertheless, Machiavelli emphasizes that the prince should always *seem* to have all the Christian (moral) virtues. Nothing is more important than this *appearance*.

It is necessary that the ruler understand how to disguise his animal nature and "know how to be a clever counterfeit and hypocrite" (*The Prince*, ch. XVIII, 48). If he has to be cruel, he must be so in a prudent way such that he does not arouse hatred in his subjects. He must avoid being cruel in such a way that he "must hold a knife in his hand all the time" (*The Prince*, ch. VIII, 27). Indeed, the hatred of his subjects he cannot control; it will always destroy him in the end. He must, in short, never lack the support of his subjects.

On the other hand, it is better for him to be feared than to be loved if he must choose between the two. The reason is the depravity of human nature. Love is unreliable, but fear can always be instilled in men at will.

Fortuna: The Limits of *Virtù*

The ruler's *virtù* notwithstanding, his control is never total or certain. Even the legendary founders of states mentioned above had to be *given the occasion* to act. Without the occasion, their *virtù* would have achieved nothing.

The scope of the ruler's power to act is certainly limited – not least by the agency of *Fortuna*. As Machiavelli puts it, "I think it may be true that Fortune may be mistress of one half of our actions" (*The Prince*, ch. XXV, 67). *Fortuna* is Machiavelli's key term for designating the uncertainty, unpredictability, and dependency of human affairs, especially of politics. Politics is always a risky business, full of contingencies.

Machiavelli betrays an almost religious relationship to this element. He imagines *Fortuna* as a powerful personified force, a goddess, always stronger than men. She may be influenced, even persuaded, to support us, but this may unpredictably bring about our ruin. Prudent princes can prepare themselves against her agency – to a certain extent. But without her support there is no hope. Those against whom she turns will always lose their power. The fate of Cesare Borgia is Machiavelli's sad example (*The Prince*, ch. VII, 19–24).

So we are to a large extent in the power of fortune (or chance). But Machiavelli stresses that we have scope for the use of our free will. As he puts it, God does not wish to do everything for us (*The Prince*, ch. XXVI, 70–1). To a certain extent, and to our honor as human beings, we can help ourselves.

War and Violence

Politics, as analyzed in *The Prince*, is essentially a warlike activity. The conditions of politics as Machiavelli conceives of them are very similar to the conditions of war. Under the circumstances dominating Machiavelli's Italy, this conception of politics may be easily understood. The prince he is addressing is supposed to "put an end to the devastation and plunder of Lombardy, to the robbery and ransom of the Kingdom [Naples] and Tuscany, and cure her [Italy] of those sores already long since festered" (*The Prince*, ch. XXVI, 70).

The parallel to war also discloses the ever-present reality of violence as an option for the ruler. The following statements sum up Machiavelli's problematic ethical stance in *The Prince*: "In the actions of all men, and especially of princes, who are not subject to a court of appeal, we must always look to the end. Let a prince, therefore, win victories and uphold his state; his methods will always be considered worthy, and everyone will praise them" (*The Prince*, ch. XVIII, 49).

In articulating this conception of violence and power, was Machiavelli a political cynic? This would indeed be so had he maintained that the *sole* end of politics is the conquest and maintenance of power (see Maritain, 1952). However – according to Machiavelli – the end is ultimately "the common good of a united and morally virtu-ous people," living in a free republic (*Discourses* I, 58). But this end, he acknowledges, may be very difficult to achieve.

Machiavelli always looks upon principalities as less perfect than free republics, al-though he is quick to add that in some circumstances the former may be the only workable possibility. A princely order – about which Machiavelli writes in *The Prince* – is inherently more unstable than the civic order which is maintained by a free republic. The former sort of regime is more prone to engender conflicts between the ruler and his subjects than is the latter sort (*Discourses* II, 2).

Machiavelli certainly looks upon tyranny as bad rule. For him (and his contemporar-ies) tyranny is a *lawless* rule, wherein a prince promotes his private interests at the cost of the common good (*Discourses* I, 2). It is, he thinks, a seriously defective form of rule, not because it is immoral, but because it is an extremely unstable form of govern-ance which readily shifts into anarchy.

A Classic of Western Philosophy

Machiavelli did not look upon himself as a philosopher, but rather as a man who, because of his long and varied experience as a working politician, and a careful study of classical literature, was able to think prudently and in a *new* way about politics (*The Prince*, dedicatory address to Lorenzo de Medici).

The answer to the question – why is this book a classic? – is bound up with the new way of thinking about politics that Machiavelli inaugurates in *The Prince*. The novelty of this approach consists in construing political philosophy as *strategic thinking* about power and survival, rather than as a moral discourse with the common good as its horizon. In this way it stands apart from the trajectory of political philosophy in the preceding classical and medieval periods.

In short, politics as conceived by Machiavelli is best understood as *poiêsis* (production), not *praxis* (action). In this way he departs from the Aristotelian conception of politics as an ethical science. From the outset this new doctrine was thought to be highly problematic, as the legacy of what we often term Machiavellianism demonstrates. That it is an important view is proved by modern power- and conflict-oriented political science, of which Machiavelli clearly stands as a founding father.

Bibliography

Editions and translations

Machiavelli, Niccolò (1983) *Il principe e discorsi*, ed. S. Bertelli. Milan: Feltrinelli.
Machiavelli, Niccolò (1986) *The Discourses*, trans. Leslie Walker. London: Penguin.
Machiavelli, Niccolò (1988) *Florentine Histories*. Princeton, NJ: Princeton University Press.
Machiavelli, Niccolò (1992) *The Prince*, ed. and trans. Robert M. Adams. New York: W. W. Norton.

Studies

de Grazia, Sebastian (1989) *Machiavelli in Hell*. Princeton, NJ: Princeton University Press.
Maritain, Jacques (1952) The end of Machiavellianism. In *The Range of Reason*, ch. 11, pp. 134–64. New York: Charles Scribner's Sons.
Skinner, Quentin (1981) *Machiavelli*. Oxford: Oxford University Press.
Viroli, Maurizio (1998) *Machiavelli*. Oxford: Oxford University Press.

20

Francisco de Vitoria, *De Indis* and *De iure belli relectiones* (1557)

Philosophy Meets War

Gregory M. Reichberg

There has hardly been a time when war has not cast its shadow over philosophical speculation. From Plato onwards, many a philosopher has felt compelled to reflect on the origin, practice, and consequences of war. Not, however, until Francisco de Vitoria (ca. 1492–1546) wrote the *De Indis* (On the American Indians), and its sequel *De iure belli* (On the Law of War), did the problem of war between nations become the express theme of a full fledged work by a philosopher of note. Delivered in 1539, and first published in 1557, the two lectures were destined to enjoy great notoriety. From Suárez and Grotius onwards, philosophers and jurists would use Vitoria's writings as an essential point of reference for normative thinking about international relations.

Spain's expansion into the newly discovered territories of the Americas had by Vitoria's time become a subject of heated debate. Reports of indiscriminate killing, forced labor, and confiscation of land had raised doubts about the fast-growing colonies. Most vexing was the issue of slavery. In the early years of the Spanish conquest it had been thought relatively easy to justify this practice by an appeal either to the Christian faith (the Amerindians were said to be enemies of the one, true religion) or to natural reason, since, in the light of the latter, it was considered manifestly evident that the natives of the Caribbean Islands, who appeared to lack all but the most rudimentary social development, were incapable of self-government. The views on natural slavery expressed by Aristotle in *Politics*, Book 1, chs 4–7, where he argues that some people, due to their inferior intelligence, are fit to be ruled by others with superior mental endowments, were adduced as theoretical justification for the enslavement of local populations.

However, by the early 1530s, with the discovery in the preceding decade of the great empires of Mexico and Peru, it had become increasingly difficult to allege cultural impoverishment as a basis for enslavement. Growing dissatisfaction with the putative reasons justifying enslavement prompted a storm of controversy among

Spanish intellectuals over the legitimacy of their country's colonization of the Americas. This controversy provided the setting for Vitoria's two lectures on the "affair of the Indies."

Relectiones

Vitoria was at that time a noted professor of theology at the University of Salamanca. A member of the Dominican religious order, he received his higher education in Paris, where he was schooled in the thought of Thomas Aquinas. There he was also exposed to nominalism, as well as to the new French humanism which was very much in vogue at the time.

Little of Vitoria's own teaching was published in his lifetime. Apart from several prefaces which were written for works that he edited, his writings have survived mainly in the form of notes taken down by university students, to whom he dictated lectures under two different rubrics. First, there were his lectures on Aquinas's *Summa theologiae*. The Spanish philosopher's predilection went to the "*Secunda pars*" of this work, which served as a vehicle for his systematic discussion of the principles of morality, as well as a platform for his ethical treatment of concrete social issues (relating *inter alia* to law, economics, and war).

Secondly, each academic year Vitoria would speak before the entire university community. Taking as his point of departure some passage which had already been covered in the regular course syllabus, this kind of address was accordingly named a *relectio* (a "re-reading"). At the beginning of the *De Indis*, Vitoria informs his audience that a question taken from Aquinas's *Summa theologiae* (II-II, q. 10, a. 2), "whether it is licit to baptize the children of unbelievers against the wishes of their parents," would serve as the springboard for a broad-ranging discussion of Spanish rule in the New World (*De Indis* [hereafter cited as *DI*], preface, in Vitoria, 1991: 233; all references to the two *relectiones* will be taken from this edition). Since it was by force of arms that his countrymen had come to exercise dominion over the indigenous peoples of the Americas, Vitoria would, in the course of his treatment, assess whether religious motives – for instance, a desire to convert the Amerindians to Christianity – could provide moral warrant for the employment of these coercive measures.

Vitoria divided his discussion into two parts, each representing a distinct *relectio*. First, under the heading (affixed by a later editor) *De Indis*, literally "*On the Indians*," Vitoria critically examines the reasons which apologists had put forward to justify "in the court of conscience" Spain's claim to dominion in the New World. "By what right (*ius*)," he asks pointedly, "were [these] barbarians subjected to Spanish rule?" (*DI*, preface; 1991: 233). Next, in the companion piece *De iure belli*, Vitoria discusses in more abstract terms whether military force can rightly be made to serve moral aims such as self-defense or sheltering the innocent from harm. This line of inquiry traditionally goes under the heading of *ius ad bellum*. Likewise, Vitoria also gives some consideration to the sort of behavior that should be observed in wartime (*ius in bello*): the differentiation between combatants and non-combatants, the legitimate means of warfare, treatment of prisoners, and so forth.

Ius Gentium

Engaging in a form of philosophical discourse that we would today term "applied ethics," Vitoria deliberately side-steps the perspective of civil law (*leges humanae*), which he deems inapplicable in the present case. The whole problem was to decide in the first place whether the Amerindians had rightly been made subject to the laws of the Spanish Crown, given that, prior to the conquest, they appeared to be self-governing. Ecclesiastical law, likewise, was of little use in settling this question, since church authorities in his opinion had no legitimate temporal jurisdiction over these non-Christians (*DI*, q. 2, a. 2; 1991: 261–4). Moreover, few if any positive international laws had yet been codified to regulate the nascent relations between European states, on the one hand, and the autochthonous peoples of Africa, the Americas, and the Far East, on the other. To determine the normative principles which ought to govern Spain's expansion into the New World, Vitoria accordingly appealed to the precepts of an unwritten law which, in accordance with ancient Roman and medieval tradition, he termed "*ius gentium*" (the law of nations).

On Vitoria's understanding, *ius gentium* designates a set of moral requirements which are binding within and between all nations that have achieved a modicum of social organization. While these norms are reflected in the customs of diverse peoples and in the agreements reached between them, they ultimately derive their authority from the pre-given dictates of natural law (*lex naturalis*). As articulated by Vitoria and other Scholastics, *natural law* signifies a set of moral imperatives which, though unwritten, stand as the normative basis of all human laws. Rooted in a divinely ordained human nature, hence in a source antecedent to human deliberation and choice, the precepts of natural law were said to be known naturally (*naturaliter*) rather than learned by study or inference. Hence the most elemental of these precepts were held to be knowable by all human beings, regardless of their cultural setting. Moreover, this was a moral instruction that did not inherently depend upon special religious revelation.

Borrowing from Thomas Aquinas's treatment of this theme (*ST*, II-II, q. 57, a. 3), Vitoria notes that the requirements of *ius gentium* are one step removed from natural law in so far as they involve contingent conditions which must first be met in order to be made applicable in concrete circumstances. Private property, for example, is not an unqualified exigency of natural law; certain rudimentary forms of society can exist without it. At a certain stage of development, however, private ownership of goods cannot be disallowed without grave detriment to the peace of civil society, one of the chief goods promoted by natural law. Despite the contingent conditions which attach to *ius gentium*, this law, Vitoria observes, nevertheless confers upon its recipients determinate rights and obligations. As examples, he cites internationally recognized standards of conduct such as the inviolability of ambassadors and freedom of navigation on the seas (*DI*, q. 3, a. 1; 1991: 280–1; cf. Vitoria, "De jure gentium et naturali," in Scott, 1934, appendix E, pp. cxi–cxiv).

Furthermore, Vitoria observes that the precepts of *ius gentium* are of two kinds. Some derive directly from natural law and are *ipso facto* binding upon all humanity. Other precepts do not follow directly from natural law, yet, because they enjoy the "consent of the greater part of the world" and "are for the common good of all men," they may rightly be deemed "to have the force of law" (*DI*, q. 3, a. 1; 1991: 281).

Often Vitoria frames *ius gentium* in terms of moral precepts which are binding across different cultures. At other times, he speaks of it as a set of obligations that nations are duty-bound to observe in their dealings with individuals (*DI*, q. 3, a. 1; 1991: 284–7). On still other occasions he alludes to it as a moral law that governs relations *between* all nations, *inter omnes gentes* (*DI*, q. 3, a. 1, in Truyol y Serra, 1987: 261–4; Vitoria, 1967: 78; Simon, 1992: 150–5). Essential to Vitoria's conception was the idea that *ius gentium* constituted a universal order of right from which the leaders of sovereign nations were to take their bearings and to which they were expected to conform their decisions. Alongside the asymmetrical relations of power which *de facto* existed between states, *ius gentium* established these same states as juridical equals. While familiar to us now, the idea of legal equality between states was quite new at the time, and has merited for Vitoria the title (albeit contested by some; see Muldoon, 1972) "founder of the modern law of nations" (Scott, 1934: 288).

Structure of the *De Indis*

Working from the premise that Spain and the pagan nations of America were common participants in *ius gentium*, Vitoria divided his *De Indis* treatment of the Spanish occupation into two sets of arguments, one dealing with *illegitimate* titles of conquest and the other with possible *legitimate* titles.

The discussion of these titles is preceded by consideration of the question whether or not the American natives should be viewed as fit to govern themselves. The problem revolves around the issue of rights. If it could be shown that the inhabitants of the Indies were incapable of self-rule, the Spanish Crown would then not be obliged to deal with their leaders on an equal footing. By contrast, if these peoples could be shown to possess true dominion, the ensuing analysis of legitimate and illegitimate titles of conquest would have to proceed on the assumption that the Amerindians were bearers of substantive rights that would have to be respected by the European newcomers.

Opting for the latter alternative, Vitoria inveighed against the view that the natives' state of unbelief would prevent them from owning property and exercising self-rule. The main thrust of his rebuttal consists in arguing that dominion derives not from profession of the Christian faith (a view he ascribes to some Protestant reformers) but rather from natural law. Since unbelief does not cancel out entitlements received from natural law, neither does it cancel out dominion (*DI*, q. 1, a. 3; 1991: 243–6). Moreover, to the contention that the Amerindians lacked the requisite mental capacity to govern their own affairs, Vitoria cites empirical evidence to the contrary. These natives, he says, "have order (*ordo*) in their affairs; they have properly organized cities, proper marriages, magistrates and overlords (*domini*), laws, industries, and commerce . . . [T]hey likewise have a form of religion, and they correctly apprehend things which are evident to other men, which indicates the use of reason" (*DI*, q. 1, a. 6; 1991: 250).

Illegitimate Titles of Conquest

Turning next to the central issue of the titles "by which the barbarians of the New World passed under the rule of the Spaniards," Vitoria first exposed as "irrelevant and illegitimate" seven attempts at justification (question 2). Of these, three were based on *a priori* claims (on the legal terminology of *a priori* and *a posteriori* claims to dominion, see Fisch, 1986): that the Holy Roman Emperor (then Charles I of Spain) possessed dominion over the whole world (art. 1), that the Pope had conferred these lands on the Spanish Crown (art. 2), and that possession of the said territories had devolved to Spain by right of discovery (art. 3). Dismissing the last as manifestly invalid – discovery grants title only when a land is uninhabited – against the first two claims Vitoria argues at some length that neither the Emperor nor the Pope enjoyed secular jurisdiction over the non-Christian world. The question of sovereign rights over America could only be decided on the basis of natural, not divine, law.

The remaining illegitimate titles postulated on *a posteriori* grounds that territorial sovereignty in America had been ceded to Spain as a consequence of the Amerindians' misconduct. Deriding as preposterous the contention that on first encountering representatives of the Spanish Crown the natives had recognized this sovereign as their rightful ruler – this consent if ever given would have been uttered under invalidating circumstances of fear and ignorance (art. 3) – Vitoria instead focused his attention mainly on two sorts of claims: that the Amerindians had refused to accept faith in Christ (art. 4), and that their culture was rife with violations of natural law (art. 5). With respect to the latter claim, he maintained that even if all adults could be deemed to have a knowledge of natural law sufficient to hold them accountable before the full range of its precepts (this he doubts), it still would not follow that violations of this law in one nation may rightly be punished by high-minded leaders in another. If allowed, this would greatly imperil the good of peace ("since every country is full of sinners, kingdoms would be exchanged everyday," q. 2, a. 5; 1991: 274). Similarly, apropos the former claim, Vitoria argued that even if the Christian faith had been adequately presented to the Amerindians in a form that they could understand (this too he doubted), rejection of it would still not provide a legitimate ground for conquest. "Difference of religion cannot be a just cause of war," Vitoria stated emphatically in a parallel passage of the *De jure belli* (q. 1, a. 3; 1991: 301, henceforth cited as *DIB*). Written on the eve of the sectarian strife that was soon to engulf Europe, Vitoria's disquisition against religiously motivated warfare would have a formative influence on the development of the modern, post-Westphalian conception of the legitimate use of force by sovereign states, wherein the *ius ad bellum* (the right to go to war) is framed in terms of secular rather than religious reasons.

Legitimate Titles of Conquest

Vitoria's presentation of the *legitimate* titles of conquest (q. 3) is formulated in conditional terms as a set of valid reasons by which "the Spaniards could (*potuerunt*) have seized the lands and rule of the barbarians" (*DI*, q. 3, a. 1; 1991: 283; Vitoria, 1967:

86). Nowhere does Vitoria assert that these precise reasons actually motivated the Spanish military initiatives in the New World. He reminds his countrymen of the obligation "to remove any cause of provocation" (*DI*, q. 3, a. 1; 1991: 281), cautioning them against "trickery or fraud" and "inventing excuses" to make war on the Amerindians (*DI*, q. 3, a. 1; 1991: 284). Moreover, Vitoria insists that any show of force by the Spaniards must be preceded by sincere negotiations (*DI*, q. 3, a. 1; 1991: 282).

In the terminology laid out by Aquinas in his seminal discussion of the just war (*Summa theologiae* II-II, q. 40, a. 1), political leaders who cite a "just cause" (*causa iusta*) when resorting to the sword will do so with a "right intention" (*intentio recta*) only when their actions are motivated by that precise cause, and not by some ulterior motive – enlargement of empire, the personal glory or convenience of the prince, and so forth. The same principle also carefully limits "what, and how much, may be done in a just war" (*DIB*, q. 1, a. 4; 1991: 304). Likewise, Vitoria invokes the possibility of "simultaneous ostensible justice" (the idea that a war may appear *just* in the eyes of a belligerent who, *de facto*, is possessed of an unjust cause, thereby producing a situation wherein each side simultaneously believes it is in the right) to urge restraint upon the parties at war (*DI*, q. 3, a. 1; 1991: 282; Johnson, 1975: 175–95).

The key tenet that overarches Vitoria's ethics of military force is the idea that "the sole and only just cause for waging war is when harm has been inflicted." There can be "no [just] vengeance," he adds, "where there has not first been a culpable offense." Yet "not every and any injury gives sufficient grounds for waging war" (*DIB*, q. 1, a. 3; 1991: 303–4). Armed force may justifiably be applied solely in response to injuries that endanger social values of the highest sort. Even then, not anything whatsoever may be done in a just war. Direct targeting of non-combatants, killing enemy prisoners after victory has been achieved, are the sort of acts Vitoria deemed impermissible (*DIB*, q. 3; 1991: 314–26). The list has been considerably expanded in modern times, with the Geneva Conventions, for example. The *De jure belli* nevertheless represents an early attempt at systematizing guidelines for right and wrong conduct in war (*ius in bello*). In sum "the prince should press his campaign not for the destruction of his opponents, but for the pursuit of the justice for which he fights" (*DIB*, q. 3; 1991: 327).

Applied to the case of the Spanish invasion of America, Vitoria identifies a number of *possible* just causes, *inter alia* (*DI*, q. 3; 1991: 278–91): the Amerindians' (1) denial of the natural right of free travel and free trade (essential, he thought, to the building up of friendship between peoples); (2) unwillingness to permit the preaching of the Christian faith and conversion to that faith; (3) allowance of tyrannical rule; and (4) the practice of nefarious customs or rites (for example, human sacrifice). As a further possible ground for conquest, Vitoria mentions the pedagogical value of colonial rule ("these barbarians, though not totally mad . . . are unsuited to setting up or administering a commonwealth both legitimate and ordered in human and civil terms"), although this he is unable to assert "with confidence," listing it solely "for the sake of argument" (*DI*, q. 3, a. 8; 1991: 290).

Although some if not all of these rationales might seem dubious today, much of enduring value can be gleaned from the systematic way in which Vitoria structures the question of just (and unjust) causes of war. In this respect his work has served as a model for later research in this field. Vitoria is one of Western philosophy's most articulate exponents of the idea that force – applied with restraint and for the right ends – can be made to serve the higher interests of justice. For this reason he remains a potent voice within contemporary discussions of the ethics of war and peace.

Bibliography

Editions and translations

Vitoria, F. de (1917) *De Indis et De iure belli relectiones*, ed. E. Nys; trans. J. P. Bate. Classics of International Law. Washington, DC: Carnegie Institution.

Vitoria, F. de (1967) *Relectio de Indis*, ed. L. Pereña and J. M. Perez Prendes. Corpus Hispanorum de pace V. Madrid: Consejo Superior de Investigaciones Científicas.

Vitoria, F. de (1981) *Relectio de iure belli; o, Paz dinámica*, ed. L. Pereña, V. Abril, C. Baciero, A. Garcia, and F. Maseda. Corpus Hispanorum de pace VI. Madrid: Consejo Superior de Investigaciones Científicas.

Vitoria, F. de (1991) *Political Writings*, ed. A. Pagden and J. Lawrance. Cambridge: Cambridge University Press.

Studies

Fernández-Santamaria, J. A. (1977) *The State, War and Peace: Spanish Political Thought in the Renaissance 1516–1559*. Cambridge: Cambridge University Press.

Fisch, J. (1986) International law in the expansion of Europe. *Law and State*, 34: 7–31.

Haggenmacher, P. (1986) La place de Francisco de Vitoria parmi les fondateurs du droit international [The place of Francisco de Vitoria among the founders of international law]. In Antonio Truyol y Serra et al. (eds), *Actualité de la pensée juridique de Francisco de Vitoria*, pp. 27–80. Brussels: Bruylant.

Johnson, J. T. (1975) *Ideology, Reason, and the Limitation of War: Religious and Secular Concepts 1200–1740*. Princeton, NJ: Princeton University Press.

Muldoon, J. (1972) The contribution of the medieval canon lawyers to the formation of international law. *Traditio*, 28: 483–97.

Pagden, A. (1982) *The Fall of Natural Man: The American Indian and the Origins of Comparative Ethnology*. Cambridge: Cambridge University Press.

Pangle, Thomas L. and Ahrensdorf, Peter J. (1999) *Justice among Nations: On the Moral Basis of Power and Peace*. Lawrence, KN: University of Kansas Press.

Reichberg, Gregory (2002) Just war or perpetual peace? *Journal of Military Ethics*, 1(1): 16–35.

Scott, J. B. (1934) *The Spanish Origin of International Law: Francisco de Vitoria and his Law of Nations*. Oxford: Clarendon Press.

Simon, Y. R. (1992) *The Tradition of Natural Law*. New York: Fordham University Press.

Truyol y Serra, A. (1987) *La conception de la paix chez Vitoria et les classiques espagnols du droit des gens* [The idea of peace in Vitoria and the Spanish classics on the law of nations]. Paris: Librairie Philosophique J. Vrin (orig. pub. 1961).

21

Francisco Suárez, *Metaphysical Disputations* (1597)

From the Middle Ages to Modernity

Jorge J. E. Gracia

Francisco Suárez's (1548–1617) *Metaphysical Disputations* (hereafter *DM*) first appeared in print at the end of that philosophically ambiguous period we know as the Renaissance, and thus stands at the crossroads between the Middle Ages and modernity. It is the last great medieval *summa* in so far as it summarizes and evaluates medieval metaphysical thought, and to this day remains the most complete exposition of scholastic and Aristotelian metaphysics ever produced. But it is also a modern work in that it is the first systematic and comprehensive treatise on metaphysics composed in the West that is not a commentary on Aristotle's *Metaphysics*. Indeed, its fifty-four disputations constitute a veritable encyclopedia of all metaphysical topics and opinions that preceded its publication, from the nature of metaphysics to the status of mental beings. This does not mean, however, that it is a mere compendium of previous views, or even, as some have claimed, that in it Suárez aims merely at developing an eclectic position that harmonizes the opinions of preceding scholastics. On the contrary, Suárez is moved by the search for truth and departs substantially, whenever he deems it appropriate, from the views of Aristotle and his medieval predecessors, even though he takes them into account in working out his own position.

The *Disputations* first appeared in 1597 and underwent at least seventeen editions outside the Iberian peninsula within the next forty years. By comparison, Descartes's *Meditations* were edited only nine times in the sixty years that followed their publication, a measure of the extraordinary popularity of Suárez's work.

The impact of Suárez's treatise can be detected in some of the major figures of modern philosophy, such as Descartes, Leibniz, Spinoza, Wolff, Berkeley, and Schopenhauer among others, in spite of the conscious efforts of some of them to play down their sources. Indeed, the very language used by some of these authors can often be traced to terms which are found in Suárez's work. The influence of Suárez's *Disputations* is evident in German philosophy before Kant, particularly among the so-called German scholastics, and in Catholic philosophy up to, and including, the nineteenth century. Suárez's metaphysical views, often misunderstood, permeated Catholic thinking to such an extent that they became the filter through which the doctrines of other scholastics were sifted. As a result, Suárez was blamed, by neo-Thomists like Gilson and Maritain, for many of the excesses of scholastic manuals. In Latin America, Suárez's *Disputations* dominated metaphysical discussions well into the nineteenth century, and were to some extent responsible for a continued scholastic emphasis.

Suárez's sources are vast, ranging from antiquity to his own contemporaries, but it is in Aristotle and Aquinas that he most frequently finds inspiration. Suárez's position in the history of philosophy is often disputed. Some historians locate him firmly in the medieval tradition, claiming that he should be considered as perhaps the last world-class figure of that tradition, before modern philosophy changed the philosophical direction of the West. Others, however, see Suárez as a precursor of modern philosophy. Both opinions contain some truth.

Suárez has a rigorous view of the distinction between metaphysics and theology and of his own role as philosopher and theologian. In the *Disputations*, he explicitly calls himself a philosopher, avoids arguments based on faith, and apologizes for dealing, even incidentally, with theological matters. Moreover, he abandons the standard medieval scholastic literary genres used in works of metaphysics. Medieval authors generally presented their metaphysical views in commentaries on Aristotle, which were sometimes internally organized in *quaestiones*; or they presented them in the course of theological works, such as theological *summae* or commentaries on the *Sentences* of Peter Lombard. Occasionally, short didactic or polemical tracts (*opuscula*) were also composed. But no systematic and comprehensive metaphysical treatises were produced. Suárez, however, adopted precisely this format.

This does not entail, however, that Suárez abandons the view of philosophy as a handmaiden to theology. On the contrary, he sees his work in metaphysics as propaedeutic to theology and his philosophy as eminently Christian: "philosophy should be Christian, and serve divine theology" (*DM, Ratio et discursus totius operis*).

At the center of Suárez's *Disputations* is an analysis of the nature of metaphysics. This is an issue that became a subject of philosophical discussion immediately after the appearance of Aristotle's *Metaphysics*, and which to this day continues to attract attention and disagreement (Gracia, 1999). In the Middle Ages, it became a point of intense debate after the translation of ancient and Islamic texts into Latin in the twelfth and thirteenth centuries.

Like previous scholastics before him, Suárez conceives metaphysics as a science in the Aristotelian sense of a discipline of learning whose procedure is deductive, but he adds that metaphysics is also perfect and *a priori*. Something is perfect if it is complete, that is, if it lacks nothing required for it to be the sort of thing it is (*DM* 10, 1, 15). Thus a perfect science is a science that lacks none of the conditions required of sciences. Such conditions stipulate that sciences provide certain and evident knowledge of the objects they study through knowledge of the properties, principles, and causes of those objects (*DM* 1, 3, 2, and 1, 1, 27). Moreover, because metaphysics is an *a priori* science, such knowledge is not based on experience. In this sense, metaphysics is quite unlike today's empirical sciences.

Metaphysics includes the study of immaterial substances such as God, angels, and souls, and the real accidental features of immaterial substances (e.g., knowledge of grammar). It excludes, however, the study of mental beings (*entia rationis*) and of beings which are completely accidental, and it abstracts from all matter (*DM* 1, 1, 26). Mental beings have no status outside the mind, existing only as objects of thought (54, 1, 5 and 6). They include negations (e.g., a cat's inability to fly), privations (e.g., a cat's blindness), and mental relations (e.g., a cat being the same as itself).

The most serious controversy concerning Suárez's conception of metaphysics arises from his characterization of its object of study. He describes this object in two ways, as "being insofar as it is real being" (*ens in quantum ens reale*) (*DM* 1, 1, 26) and as "the objective concept of being" (*conceptus objectivus entis*) (*DM* 2, 1, 1), and he conceives this objective concept in analogical (Aquinas) rather than univocal (Scotus) terms. These characterizations have been two of the sources of the charge that Suárez contributed to the mentalization of metaphysics. By the mentalization of metaphysics is understood the view that metaphysics does not study extra-mental reality but rather concepts, ideas, mental images, and the like. Metaphysics does not study the world as it is in itself, but only the perceptions or conceptions humans have of it. Versions of this position are found throughout modern philosophy, from Descartes and Kant to Strawson. Opposed to it is the Aristotelian-inspired view according to which metaphysics studies realities that are mind independent. This position is often described as a form of realism.

Suárez's claim that the object of metaphysics is the objective concept of being may be interpreted as implying mentalism because objective concepts, *qua* concepts, presumably cannot be anything but mental. The notion of objective concept is one of two members of a distinction widely used by later scholastics. The other member is the formal concept (*conceptus formalis*). The *formal concept*, according to Suárez, is an act of our minds whereby we conceive something, and as an act of the mind, it is a quality and thus an accident of the mind. The formal concept is called "formal" because it informs the mind in the way any form informs its subject. It is by means of the formal concept that the mind knows a thing, for the formal concept represents the thing known to the mind (*DM* 2, 1, 1).

The *objective concept*, on the other hand, is what is represented in the act, or quality, which is the formal concept. The objective concept is not a concept in the way a formal concept is such, namely as a form that modifies the mind. Indeed, it is called a concept only derivatively because of the relation it has to the formal concept. It is objective in so far as it is the object with which the formal concept is concerned; it is not objective in the sense of being an image or representation of something else. The objective concept is what is represented by the formal concept and "the thing signified" (*res significata*) by it (*DM* 29, 3, 34).

In short, the distinction between the objective concept and the formal concept is the distinction between what I think about (objective) and that through which I think it (formal). So, whereas "the formal concept cat," for example, is the mental act whereby I think of "cat," "the objective concept cat" is what I think about when I think of "cat," namely cat.

Now, what we think about is not always concepts, ideas, or mental images but such things as cats and dogs. And when we think about being, the object of study of metaphysics, what we think about is not always something in the mind, for not all being is in the mind. So it is a mistake to conclude from Suárez's characterization of the object of study of metaphysics as the objective concept of being, that metaphysics studies only what is in the mind.

Suárez's other claim concerning metaphysics, namely, that it studies being in so far as it is real being, does not seem *prima facie* to support the charge that he contributed to the mentalization of metaphysics. However, matters are not so simple, for Suárez's conception of real being is idiosyncratic. For him, real being need not be actual; it can be possible, and thus encompasses both actual being (e.g., my existing cat Hunter) and possible being (e.g., my non-existing cat Misifus). The difference between non-real beings and possible beings is that possible beings have an aptitude for existence, even though they do not exist, whereas non-real beings do not. A possible being, like Misifus, has an aptitude such that it could exist even if it does not; but a non-real being, like a goat-stag, lacks such an aptitude and neither exists nor can exist (*DM* 31, 2, 10).

Real being, then, includes possible, unactualized essences in addition to actualized ones (*DM* 31, 2, 10). This conception of metaphysics, as the study of not only actual essences but also possible essences, has been identified as one of the sources of mentalism; for possible being, so the argument goes, can be nothing but mental, and thus the door is open to a conception of metaphysics as a science of the mental.

Although this conclusion is disputable, in so far as possible being for Suárez is not equivalent to concepts, ideas, or mental images, still it is reasonable to think that Suárez's statements may have contributed to the mentalization of metaphysics. A superficial reading of Suárez can lead to the conclusion that for him metaphysics studies what is in the mind rather than what is outside it.

It has also been argued that Suárez contributed to metaphysical mentalism by his use of the formal concept to explain the process of cognition, in so far as the formal concept is a mental representation of what is known. This concept could be interpreted as an intermediary between the mind and what the mind knows, opening in this way the doors to the view, adopted by many modern philosophers, according to which the only things the mind knows directly are mental entities.

The function of the formal concept in the process of cognition, however, does not imply a tendency toward mentalism as long as this concept is not conceived as the object of knowledge. In fact, nowhere does Suárez tell us that what we know in metaphysics is the formal concept of real being. The formal concept is merely the act whereby we know real being – it is the act of knowing, if you will – and not the object of knowledge, that is, real being. In this sense, Suárez's doctrine is not different from the doctrines of such lean metaphysicians as Ockham, for even Ockham accepted that knowing implies an activity (*Ordinatio* 2, 8, *prima redactio*, in Ockham, 1957: 41–5).

Is Suárez's metaphysics, then, realistic or mentalistic? There is nothing in the definition that Suárez gives us of metaphysics that suggests that it is not realistic. True, Suárez (1) identifies the object of metaphysics with an objective concept; (2) conceives real being in such a way that it includes the possible; and (3) uses the notion of formal concept. But, for him, not all objective concepts and possible beings are mental and, although the formal concept of real being depends on the mind in so far as it inheres in it, it is not – *qua* formal concept – the object of study of metaphysics. Besides, in so far as objective concepts derive their ontological status from what is known, and for Suárez what is known in metaphysics is real being, the objective concept metaphysics studies is real. Indeed, as a science, metaphysics treats only of what is real (*DM* 31, 2, 10), so that the objective concept studied by metaphysics cannot be mental. The use of the term "concept" in the expression "objective concept" is unfortunate and produces confusion, to the extent that it suggests something mental. For Suárez, the object of metaphysics is being considered as real and not as something mental, for the objective concept of being is neither a concept (in the strict sense of the term) nor a mental representation (formal concept).

This does not mean, however, that these notions, as used by other scholastics, did not have mentalistic connotations, or that modern philosophers did not interpret them mentalistically, even in their understanding of Suárez. My thesis is only that Suárez's ontology about objective concepts, his understanding of real being as including possible beings, and his use of the notion of a formal concept in the process of cognition, do not justify a mentalistic interpretation of his metaphysics. The Suárezian conception of metaphysics follows, rather, the medieval Aristotelian tradition of realism, and is opposed to the metaphysical mentalism which characterizes modern philosophy.

So much, then, for the nature of Suárez's views on metaphysics and their place in history. Now, we may ask: what can Suárez's *Disputations* say to us that is of more than antiquarian interest? Let me mention five things in closing. First: the very conception of metaphysics. Suárez walks a fine line between the mentalism that characterizes much metaphysics from the sixteenth century onward and the naïve realism of some Aristotelians. By making real being the proper object of metaphysics he separates himself from mentalism, but by including possible being in real being, he acknowledges that most metaphysics has to do with possibility rather than actuality, opening the doors to a more sensible and accurate description of the discipline. Second: methodological rigor. There are very few books of philosophy that are as rigorous and carefully argued as Suárez's *Disputations*. In an age where obscurity and dilettantism permeate much of philosophy, this book serves as an example of what a serious philosophical inquiry should aspire to be. Third: ruthless honesty. There is no fudging in the *Disputations*. Suárez calls the shots as he sees them, making clear what he means, what he claims, what he is certain of, and that of which he is not. He never hides behind faith or obscurity. Fourth: the systematic approach. In an age where the short article and the philosophical sound-bite are frequently *de rigueur*, the systematic and comprehensive nature of the *Disputations* might look out of place. Yet, the very systematic and comprehensive approach that this book displays shows how in metaphysics everything is related to everything else, and therefore, the solution of one problem depends also on the solution to others. If this is so, then it should be clear that more than the piecemeal and dilettantish approach common among many contemporary philosophers is needed. Fifth, and finally, the *Disputations* are rich not only in novel philosophical positions, but also in subtle arguments that merit our attention and from the consideration of which any philosopher can profit. In short, this book has much to offer to the serious contemporary philosopher. Those who wish for a quick fix, however, should look elsewhere.

Bibliography

Editions and translations

Suárez, Francisco (1597) *Disputationes metaphysicae*, ed. C. Berton, vols 25 and 26 of *Opera omnia*. Paris: Vivès, 1866; reprint in Hildesheim: Georg Olms, 1965.

Suárez, Francisco (1597) *Metaphysical Disputation V: Individual Unity and its Principle*, trans. Jorge J. E. Gracia. In Jorge J. E. Gracia, *Suárez on Individuation*. Milwaukee, WI: Marquette University Press, 1982.

Suárez, Francisco (1597) *On Formal and Universal Unity*, trans. James F. Ross (of *Metaphysical Disputation VI*). Milwaukee, WI: Marquette University Press, 1964.

Suárez, Francisco (1597) *On the Various Kinds of Distinctions*, trans. Cyril Vollert (of *Metaphysical Disputation VII*). Milwaukee, WI: Marquette University Press, 1947.

Suárez, Francisco (1597) *Metaphysical Disputations X and XI and Selected Passages from Disputation XXIII and Other Works*, trans. Jorge J. E. Gracia and Douglas Davis. In Jorge J. E. Gracia and Douglas Davis, *The Metaphysics of Good and Evil According to Suárez*. Munich and Vienna: Philosophia Verlag, 1989.

Suárez, Francisco (1597) *On the Formal Cause of Substance: Metaphysical Disputation XV*, trans. John Kronen and Jeremiah Reedy. Milwaukee, WI: Marquette University Press, 2000.

Suárez, Francisco (1597) *On Efficient Causality: Metaphysical Disputations 17–19*, trans. Alfred J. Freddoso. New Haven, CT: Yale University Press, 1994.

Suárez, Francisco (1597) *On the Essence of Finite Being as Such, On the Existence of that Essence and their Distinction*, trans. Norman Wells (of *Metaphysical Disputation 31*). Milwaukee, WI: Marquette University Press, 1983.

Suárez, Francisco (1597) *On Beings of Reason: Disputation LIV*, trans. John Doyle. Milwaukee, WI: Marquette University Press, 1995.

Studies and references

Copleston, F. C. (1953) *A History of Philosophy*, vol. 3: *Ockham to Suárez*. London: Newman Press.

Courtine, Jean-François (1990) *Suárez et le système de la métaphysique*. Paris: Presses Universitaires de France.

Cronin, Timothy (1966) *Objective Being in Descartes and Suárez*. Rome: Gregorian University Press (repr. New York: Garland, 1987).

Fichter, Joseph (1940) *Man of Spain: Francis Suárez*. New York: Macmillan.

Gracia, Jorge J. E. (ed.) (1991) *Francisco Suárez*, issue of *American Catholic Philosophical Quarterly*, 64(1).

Gracia, Jorge J. E. (1999) *Metaphysics and its Task: The Search for the Categorial Foundation of Knowledge*. Albany, NY: State University of New York Press.

William of Ockham (1957) *Ordinatio*. In *Philosophical Writings*, ed. and trans. Philoteus Boehner. London: Thomas Nelson.

22

Francis Bacon, *New Organon* (1620)

The Politics and Philosophy of Experimental Science

Robert K. Faulkner

Francis Bacon's (1561–1626) *New Organon* (1620) is the seminal attempt to replace pre-modern modes of inquiry with a science governed by experimental method. The work appeared before the *Discourse on Method* (1637) of Descartes, who had elsewhere praised "the method of Bacon" as a model. The father of modern chemistry, Robert Boyle, could call Bacon the "founder of natural history" in general, and Bacon's imprint is on the Royal Society of London (1663) and all the other seventeenth-century scientific institutes that turned "from Words to experimental Philosophy" and to "useful knowledge." A century later, the philosopher-scientist Jean-Jacques Rousseau could even rank Bacon as the "greatest, perhaps, of philosophers." Nevertheless, a disdain for Bacon's works arose in the nineteenth century with historical explanations of science and of the Enlightenment generally. Only recently have a few scholars unequivocally corrected this. They contend that Bacon's experimental method prescribes more than the collection of observations; it recasts physics to require hypothesis and mathematics. His science is not the product of an age; it is part of a comprehensive plan for progress (Urbach, 1987; Faulkner, 1993).

"Organon" is Greek for "instrument." Aristotle's *Organon* comprised his logical treatises, which showed how to make a sound argument in any science or art. Bacon's *New Organon* replaces a logic of words and syllogisms with a method to get at natural processes, that is, to devise effective formulas for describing and producing them. One sees in it a mixture of critique and constructivism: the critical thinking about ordinary reasoning, and the controlled outlook on the world, that is near the core of much science since. The implications go beyond natural science. For the sake of human power Bacon aimed to transform all knowing, including the human outlook as to ethics, politics, and God.

The *New Organon* alludes to a vast purpose from the start: it is for those "who would conquer nature in action" (preface; this and all other citations of the *New Organon* are from Bacon, 1994, although the translations are occasionally altered).

The conclusion too is portentous: Bacon can now "hand over to men their fortunes" (II, 52). The very titles become more radical as the volume proceeds. The half-traditional "New Organon" is dropped, as well as references to "intellect" and the "true," and the re-titlings call the new method an "art," an "art of interpretation." The last title, of Book II, equates the art of interpreting nature with "The Kingdom of Man."

Even the literary context of the work bespeaks its ambition. Bacon explicitly published the *New Organon* as one part of his *Great Instauration*, which is both his systematic literary plan and the corresponding stages of a vast project of reform. In its first edition the *New Organon* began with a "Preface" and "Plan" to the *Instauration*; these little sketches, especially the "Plan" (*distributio*), remain the best introduction to this whole project. There are six parts. The first is the *Advancement of Learning* (especially the Latin version), which proceeds to recast all the arts and sciences. It prefigures the reforming encyclopedias to come, notably Diderot's famous *Encyclopédie*, the literary megaphone of the French Enlightenment. There follows the *New Organon* itself, the second part, and then three parts that show how to exploit the new method so as to get the greatest flood of discoveries and inventions. The secret is an ever-growing "natural history," that is, a progressive accumulation of scientific formulas of natural processes (part three). In turn, the secret of this mining of nature's powers is a rhetoric of science, an appeal that can win the cadre of busy experimenters, theorists, and technologists now familiar (parts four and five). While Bacon leaves the labor of particular experiments largely to the scientists he induces to follow, he published many "preparations" and illustrations and casts himself as "trumpeter" to help raise such a following. The way to persuade is to show the uses of the new science. Exhibit examples of the whole procedure from experiment to invention (part four); indeed, publicize the most appealing inventions whether or not derived from the procedure (part five). Part six then shadows forth the greatest use, the culmination of the new learning in the new power of man over the universe. It is Bacon's "philosophy" established, together with "the real business and fortunes of the human race, and all power of operation." This is a heady appeal indeed. To be sure, such a future cannot "easily be conceived or imagined." Still, Bacon may allude even here to his little fable *New Atlantis* (1626), which does the hard work of conceiving and imaging forth a scientific future.

The *New Atlantis* is perhaps the first science fiction in the modern sense. We are shown not a golden age of milk and honey, bestowed by God or nature, but a progressive land of Gatorade and laboratories, bestowed by scientists and inventors. A scientific-technological institute manages the new society, in cooperation with a knowing economic elite and a knowing officialdom. We see a scientific civilization that masters man and nature both. In his *Essays* of 1625 Bacon outlined the practical side. The political–economic vehicle of progressive civilization is to be an industrious, secular, growth-oriented, and rather republican nation-state.

Nevertheless, many recent scholars have doubted whether Bacon is a thorough innovator. And he himself suggests at times that his humane science follows on Christian charity, only complements the ancient philosophers, and devotes itself to contemplative knowing. But are these bows to traditional teachings more than rhetorical? When Bacon discussed literary artfulness (in the *Advancement*), he expressly advised that new wine should be put in old bottles. Use "similitudes" when introducing "knowledge which is new, and foreign from opinion received." He designed the *New Organon*, in particular, to be accepted "without strain into men's minds (however strangely they are already occupied and obstructed)" (preface). Its very style bespeaks such rhetorical concerns. The *New Organon* is introduced as not a "regular treatise" but a summary in "aphorisms," and aphorisms, according to the *Advancement*, are particularly suited for innovation. Aphorisms are compressed and scattered sentences, lacking explanatory connection. Thus they disguise as well as provoke. They direct, but reserve the meaning and implications of the direction "for wits sharp enough to pierce the veil." "Nature to be commanded must be obeyed," to take a key example from the *New Organon*, "and that which is in contemplation as the cause is in operation as the rule" (I, 3). In short, the *New Organon* innovates while so clothing its innovations as to avoid offending traditional beliefs. Bacon may parade the Platonic-sounding doctrine of "form," for example, but only because "familiar" (II, 2); under the old name "form," he installs a new doctrine of formulas or laws of action (I, 51). He may allow to ancient philosophers the sphere of "discourse" and "civil business" (preface), but in effect he removes it. The Socratic tradition's reliance on primary notions and opinions is baseless and misleading, and their remedy of dialectic comes too late (preface; I, 14–16, 30). Eventually Bacon sweeps ethics, politics, and all logic under the purview of the new science (I, 127).

The *New Organon* begins by reshaping the whole human orientation and only then sets forth its new method. The first book is to "prepare the mind" (preface); the second, to set forth the art of command over nature and direct it to the most important battlefields. Since "preparing" requires confronting old ways as well as persuading to new, the radicalism of Baconian enlightenment is most visible in Book I. Besides, the first book has the decisive task of command: it shows how to master "assent," that is, human belief. And he who can master belief can master human nature. The decisive portion of the decisive modern work on method ends by insisting on an intellectual dictator (I, 92, 97, 124).

Mastering men involves mastering their opinions, and the art of mastery by enlightenment mixes skepticism, about the old ways, with optimism, as to hopes from the new. The skepticism is novel and directed at the old reverence for nature and especially for human nature. "The root cause of nearly all evils in the sciences is the admiration of the mind" (I, 9). Critique of Aristotle's logic, then, is but part of an expurgation of the intellect directed at all Socratic philosophy, indeed at all philosophy hitherto, indeed at all thinking hitherto. The radicalism shows in the very form of the attack. Bacon refuses even to consider arguments on the other side. For that would defer to the tribunal he rejects, the tribunal of argument. Instead, his critique is by "signs" and "causes" (I, 115). There are two decisive signs that the old ways have failed: endless quarrels among philosophic sects, and lack of progress in useful inventions. Philosophy hitherto provides for neither human agreement nor human necessities; Bacon's new philosophy will provide for both. The causes of failure hitherto involve a naïve reliance upon sense and intellect, a reliance that, according to Bacon's psychology, leads necessarily to distortions and wishful thinking.

The perfected rhetorical formula of Bacon's skeptical psychology is the famous doctrine of the "Idols of the Mind" (I, 38–68). The four idols are of the Tribe, Cave, Market-place, and Theater. They indict in turn intelligence, the soul, speech, and all the great philosophies and theologies. Such things may have been thought wonderful, worthy of reverence, even divine. But they are all merely visions of false gods. Here is a disenchantment of the world. Bacon's purgation prepares the later critical doctrines of epistemology, subjectivity, social construction, and cultural domination.

The "Idol of the Tribe" is the distortion inherent in human nature, especially its reliance upon "sight and intellect" (I, 45–52). Seeing and conceiving merely surfaces, we miss the subtle particles and hidden processes that make up nature. Our common-sense world of species and other primary notions is therefore illusory; any awe before natural kinds (beet, racoon), and a natural order (vegetable, animal), is radically misplaced. The "Idol of the Cave" refers to the distortions from every individual's peculiar spirit (*animus*, not *anima*: soul) and ingenuity (*ingenium*) (I, 53–8). Moved restlessly by desire, especially by pains and fears, each seeks ultimates or rest, and each supposes more help from an orderer of nature than is there. Still, as a Socratic might ask, what of the *logos* or order of speech that we seem by nature to share? That is a third idol, Bacon would reply, that of society or "the Market-place" (I, 59–60). Words are merely signs, inventions provoked by mutual need and someone's governing will. Accordingly, and finally, all philosophies are but "Idols of the Theater" (I, 61–5). They are stage-plays produced out of "intellectual ambition." In the two central aphorisms of the first book (I, 65, 66), Bacon announces that "the greatest harm" has come from "theology," and that philosophers hitherto (such as the Socratics) have been partly at fault. They too were contemplative rather than oriented to human needs. They looked in wonder at the quiescent principle, rather than in humanity to moving or productive causes. They sought imaginary *archai*, fundamental truths, rather than "utility." Bacon, by contrast, means to prepare "the entry into the kingdom of man, which is founded on the sciences" (I, 68). Those sciences will not harbor the old causes of failure, which are absence of the true goal ("new discoveries and powers" for human life; I, 81), disdain for "great enterprises" (I, 88), and lack of popular honor for the ingenious minds who can advance science (I, 91). The Baconian redirection points to utility, conquest of suffering and nature, and Nobel prizes.

The key to the project's victory is the victory of a discipline, even a violent authority, over the mind (*mens*, rather than *intellectus*, intellect; I, 97). Expurgation of "all sciences and their authors" has to be mixed with a new law: the mind can only pass judgment by Bacon's new experimental form of induction. Why might potential followers of experimentalism entertain hopes for the victory of this intellectual razor? The most promising sign is the presence of a masterful leader who can impose it. Book I's preparing the mind turns political and personal. Bacon compares himself not only to Columbus, as the cause "of great events" (I, 92), but also to Alexander the Great, in sweeping away old arrangements (I, 97). One can "win the kingdom of nature" because a master is available to conquer the old awe before nature and intellect, and to fix a new "end and mark" for thinking (I, 124). Book I closes by showing the motive of a Bacon. He can win supreme honor from mankind in return for the supreme art of discovering all other discoveries – and thus the power of mankind over "the whole universe" (I, 129).

Book II is dense, and it begins with ten direct but difficult aphorisms that set out the new "mark of doctrines" (*doctrinae scopo*; II, 10). "It is the task and purpose of human power," for example, "to generate and superinduce a new nature or new natures on a given body" (II, 1). Equivocations elsewhere disappear here. The scientist is to take his bearings from what is useful in practice, not from a desire for knowledge as such. Hence the need for laws; that is, formulas as general as possible. Seek directions that are "certain" and give "freedom" in selecting materials, as well as being "directed to action" (II, 4). Look, too, to the underlying unity of nature – to particles and motions and not to the heterogeneity of things that we see. This is power. This is also truth. Nature *is* a complex of simples, a complex joined by "processes" that link the effects we see with "latent" causes. To analyze such material causes and effects, be exact. Physics should be "bounded by mathematics" (II, 8).

After this initial reform of the end and content of learning, the second book becomes a how-to-do-it manual for getting at the actual powers of nature and especially the most useful powers. In general, rely on controlled experiment rather than experience, and look for general laws and motions of particles rather than natural kinds (II, 11–20). Look especially for the "predominant" processes, those likely to be most powerful (II, 22–44) and thus most useful (II, 45–52).

In particular, the scientist should look to the effects or "natures" sought (such as heat), and to the underlying process beneath an apparent cause (motion of particles, say, beneath the rubbing). Hence the need for artificial experiment that both vexes nature and controls the looker. Nature has to be forced to reveal processes not on the surface, and human nature has to be forced to look for them. Accordingly, the experimenter should collect apparently heterogeneous instances of an effect (such as flame and rubbing) and should exclude causes that contradict one another. Such generalizing frees the mind from a tendency to abstractions (to explain things, for example, by species) and concentrates it upon fundamental and underlying causes. Indeed, "natures" or "effects" *are* merely the underlying process. The appearance to us ("hot") is but an image. Accordingly, Bacon introduces a "more powerful aid" to the investigator: an affirmative hypothesis that the process sought is simply a special motion of particles (II, 20). Nature as particles in motion: with that "universal philosophy" the scientist is to approach all particular processes.

Most of Book II consists in directions to predominant processes in nature. Yet these directions too are also calculated to force the scientist to control his own nature. One set of "instances" counters especially the natural tendencies of mind (II, 22–37); another, the natural tendencies of the senses (II, 38–43). The first few instances focus on isolating a cause of production from existing compounds ("concretes," II, 22–6). In this context Bacon urges the investigation of memory, taste, and even "communication of quality" – as if bodily motions. So much for any non-bodily element in spirit, intellect, or soul. The next few instances withdraw the mind from familiar kinds of things and focus it on formulas, which can transform familiar things and produce even "miracles" (II, 27–31). The upshot is a direction to treat nature as common processes useful for human arts, and to treat the arts, not natural forms, as one's model. Other discussions explain further the new universals (II, 32–7). Seek especially the correlations between cause and effect that produce absolute possibilities of power, such as the heaviest material or the fastest body. Concentrate on cases where the greatest masses are moved by the smallest force, as gunpowder by flame, or whereby great heat, which Bacon seems to regard as the most powerful force for transformation, can be most easily produced. As to the senses (II, 38–44), Bacon's corrections go much beyond his recommendation of microscope, telescope, and exact measurement. For the senses, too, go fundamentally wrong when they rely on themselves. The "grand deception of the senses," which is to "draw lines with respect to man, not the universe," is to be corrected by "universal philosophy." Accordingly, anything insensible is to be understood as sensible. Hypothesis corrects radically what eyes see and ears hear. Life and "spirit," in particular, are but "action" or rather "motion" of invisible bodies.

The *New Organon* culminates in the seven "operative" instances that most cause a "magical" outpouring of discoveries and inventions. The first few concern revisions in mathematics (II, 45–8), and the others, "practical" direction of the sciences (II, 49–51). Bacon calls for new modes of measuring the relations between forces and bodies, such as the analytic geometry and calculus that Descartes and others soon invented. He calls especially for measuring the most important forces: fundamental motions (II, 48). This discussion is the longest in the book, and the title, instances "of wrestling or predominance," alludes to the book's thematic search for the predominant or most powerful powers. The scientist is directed to the forces struggling in a compound, and especially to the "royal or political" motion that enforces the equilibrium that is the compounded body. This is a "sketch of natural science," at least "of no small part." It might seem the volume's culmination. Yet the language here, of "royal or political" motion, intimates the primacy of human force in setting up such a science to move the human compound. The final aphorisms, the "practical" aphorisms, are the true culmination. They direct the governor of science to look for profound arts of many uses (II, 50), such as our electronics, and for profound sciences that can, like "magic," transform the world (II, 51). Bacon hints here at new sciences of fundamental particles, of chemistry, and of forces such as magnetism. He directs above all to researches that intimate "what is advantageous for man" (II, 49). For the scientist needs a "human chart," a "chart of things to be wished for" (*chartae optativae*). "It is the role of science both to seek and to desire not foolishly" (*non inepte*; II, 49). The direction of natural science rests finally with moral and civil science, such as the pictures in *New Atlantis* and *Essays* of the humane, industrious, and technological societies to be wished for.

It has become a question whether mastery of nature and of man is not exploitation and repression. It is also a question whether Bacon's insistence on knowing through method is consistent with his reliance on a pre-methodical psychology and a "universal philosophy" of nature. It is certainly a question whether his doubts about knowing wholes permit him to speak of desire and wise desire, or even of man, nature, human nature, and "values" altogether. But this is not the place to explore the problems in Bacon's project of human power and amelioration, upon which subsequent developments in modern science and modern philosophy are a kind of commentary.

Bibliography

Editions and translations

Bacon, Francis (1861) *New Organon*, in *The Works of Francis Bacon*, ed. and trans. James Spedding, Robert Leslie Ellis, and Dennis Denon Heath. London: Longman.

Bacon, Francis (1889) *Bacon's Novum Organum*, ed. Thomas Fowler. Oxford: Clarendon Press (Latin text).

Bacon, Francis (1989) *New Atlantis and The Great Instauration*, rev. edn, ed. Jerry Weinberger. Wheeling, IL: Harlan Davidson.

Bacon, Francis (1994) *Novum Organum*, ed. and trans. Peter Urbach and John Gibson. Chicago and LaSalle, IL: Open Court.

Studies

Faulkner, Robert K. (1993) *Francis Bacon and the Project of Progress*. Lanham, MD: Rowman and Littlefield.

Peltonen, M. (ed.) (1996) *The Cambridge Companion to Bacon*. Cambridge: Cambridge University Press.

Urbach, Peter (1987) *Francis Bacon's Philosophy of Science*. LaSalle, IL: Open Court.

23

René Descartes, *Meditations on First Philosophy* (1641)

Thought, Existence, and the Project of Science

Emily R. Grosholz

In his *Meditations on First Philosophy*, René Descartes (1596–1650) offers philosophy a fresh beginning that owes nothing to the past and might free philosophy from the disputes that have for so long obscured and misguided its investigations. No philosopher before or since has had the audacity to invent the starting-point for philosophy in such a radical way, setting aside all the content of earlier philosophy so as to leave thought, or consciousness, free to contemplate itself. From this transparent starting-point, unclouded by the world and its prejudices, Descartes hoped to secure truth by demonstrating the objective validity of clear and distinct ideas and locating the limits of human reason; to set natural science on a sure path; and to revisit conclusively the question of the existence of God. Willy-nilly, he also detached theology from natural science, and made consciousness itself for the first time a topic of philosophical reflection. We may dispute whether or to what extent Descartes was entitled to his claim about the radical nature of his starting-point, and whether he succeeded in the projects, explicit and tacit, that flowed from it. But we cannot dispute the dramatic effect of the *Meditations*: after Descartes's great thought experiment, European philosophy was forever changed.

The Context for the *Meditations on First Philosophy*

In 1600, philosophy was still dominated by scholasticism; at the century's end, philosophy stood on the threshold of the Enlightenment. Thus in a sense the philosophers of the seventeenth century invented modernity; and no text seems more essential to this development than the *Meditations*. One might suggest Galileo's *Dialogue Concerning the Two Chief World Systems* or Pascal's *Thoughts* or Hobbes's *Leviathan* as important harbingers of the new relation between thought and world that we call "modern." But each of these is too tied to a specific subject matter (physics, mathematics, politics) and still too entangled in medieval modes of thinking (Aristotelianism, Catholicism, monarchism) to claim priority as a catalyst; and none has the requisite kind of philosophical offspring. The *Meditations*, by contrast, results from a methodological and metaphysical decision to stand beyond subject matter, and the manner in which Descartes makes this departure also tears him away from medieval habits of construing reality. There is, moreover, no important philosophical book of the seventeenth century that does not pay homage to the *Meditations*. Malebranche, Spinoza, Locke, and Leibniz choose to characterize their systems precisely by the way in which each veers off from the assumptions of the *Meditations*.

Descartes begins the *Meditations* with a philosophical act which he invites the reader to re-enact with him: he sets aside everything except his awareness of his own awareness. This is an act without precedent, which affects everything that follows from it in Descartes's opus: traditional elements are metamorphosed by it, and novel elements are rendered almost occult, so that many successive generations of thinkers are then required to plumb their novelty. The project of thought thinking only itself makes the dogmatic Aristotelian adequation of assertion and thing impossible, by the simple expedient of removing the things. In its stead, Descartes puts his awareness of his own powers of construction, guided by the criterion of the clear and distinct, and – as his constructive powers readmit them in order – of the organization of things as simple or increasingly complex. Thus, truth becomes an adequation of thought (ideas of things) and the canon of construction (Belaval, 1960: ch. 1; Vuillemin, 1984: ch. 7). We can determine the limits of human knowledge by reconstructing the realm of objective validity out of clear and distinct simples combined in the proper order: thus Descartes's path, where we are supposed to walk alongside him, is constructivist, intuitionist, finitist, and reductionist. The idealism of the late eighteenth century and the subjectivism of the late twentieth century are still far in the future, but Descartes has made them intelligible possibilities, as they were not before. Before Descartes, philosophers asked: *what must the world be like for it to be intelligible?* After Descartes, that question is balanced, or submerged, by another: *what must the mind be like for the world to be intelligible to it?*

Descartes's thought experiment also reveals certain possibilities of disjunction. Consciousness which has set everything aside is susceptible to new anxieties. The most salient is whether the world as we think it resembles the world as it is; and a related though distinct worry is: does the world as we perceive it resemble nature? Even Epicurus, that constructivist–intuitionist of classical antiquity, could not carry his questioning so far: his canon of construction was based on perception. Descartes introduces further disjunctions between the study of God, the study of nature, and the study of human nature, though his methodology holds them in a kind of juxtaposed order. And, finally, Descartes poses between one human being and another "the unplumbed, salt, estranging sea" of isolated consciousness, which understands its fellow only by the postulate of analogy, and construes polity only as the sum of individual atoms. As Matthew Arnold's poetry attests, these disjunctions have all proved to be a mixed blessing for the modern age.

Our estimation of the novelty of the *Meditations* must, however, be tempered by a recognition that – to instantiate Descartes's own precept that something cannot spring from nothing – no philosophy arises outside of a tradition. Descartes's belief in the autonomy of his system was perhaps necessary in order for him to give full range to his unrivaled powers of philosophical invention; and psychologically it was linked to his own hermit-like personality, so unlike that of the thoroughly political Locke or Leibniz. The treatment of the *Meditations* by mid-twentieth-century Anglo-American philosophy often seemed to take Descartes's claim of autonomy at face value, assessing the text solely from within and accusing it at various points of logical inconsistency. (See, for example, the many journal articles on the Cartesian Circle, or on the logical status of the *Cogito,* collected or cited in Doney, 1967, and Hooker, 1978; as well as, more generally: Beck, 1965; Kenny, 1968; Frankfurt, 1970; Williams, 1978; Wilson, 1978.) But the more robust twentieth-century tradition of Descartes scholarship in France never lost sight of his location in the philosophical disputes of his day, and his various debts to neo-Scholasticism, the Epicurean materialism and Skepticism lately revived by the Renaissance, and that Augustinian upstart, Jansenism (see Gilson, 1930; Laporte, 1945; Alquié, 1950; Gueroult, 1953; Gouhier, 1958; Vuillemin, 1960; Rodis-Lewis, 1971; Marion, 1975; Beyssade, 1979). Over the past few decades, Anglo-American scholars have been increasingly influenced by the French tradition, and the tendency to set Descartes back in his historical context has been intertwined with another, which reconnects Descartes's metaphysical program more closely with his scientific program. Current scholarship makes use of the history of philosophy and the history of science, as well as close reading of the text itself; and it increasingly emphasizes the importance of the *Objections and Replies,* and Descartes's correspondence, as well as the *Geometry, Principles,* and *Treatise of Man,* to an understanding of the *Meditations.* (This influence is clear in the essays collected and cited in Gaukroger, 1980; Cottingham, 1992; and Ariew et al., 1998; as well as in Curley, 1978; Jolley, 1990; Grosholz, 1991; Garber, 1992; Grene, 1985; Des Chene, 1996; Ariew, 1999.)

Indeed, the *Meditations* first appeared in print with their philosophical context conspicuously attached to them in the form of the *Objections and Replies.* Well before their publication in Latin in Paris on August 28, 1641, they were circulated to a group of scholars with the help of Descartes's friend Marin Mersenne, a monk who occupied the center of some of the most important circles in the intellectual life of Paris (and therefore of Europe). Objections to the argument of the *Meditations* were contributed by great, subtle, and well-schooled philosophical minds: Mersenne, Arnauld, Morin, Hobbes, Gassendi, and Bourdin (as a representative of the Jesuits); and Descartes replied to all of them in wider or narrower compass. Did Descartes view these additions as essential to the original text of the *Meditations*? This is a point of dispute. Stephen Gaukroger claims that Descartes appended the *Objections and Replies* on mostly prudential grounds: "Descartes did not take kindly to objections, and was inclined to be dismissive of them" (Gaukroger, 1995: 354). By contrast, Jean-Luc Marion disputes the "legend" of Descartes as a solitary thinker: "Cartesian reason is communicative, precisely because truth manifests itself by a display of evidence; indissolubly, at one and the same time, it is to one's own reason and to the community of those looking on that the thing appears" (Marion, 1995: 10–11). Examining the role played by objections in the transition from the earlier *Discourse on Method* (where the argument of the *Meditations* is given in the nutshell of Part IV) to the *Meditations,* he concludes, "Cartesian thought, insofar as it obeys a logic of argumentation, is inscribed in its very origin in the reponsorial space of dialogue" (Marion, 1995: 20).

Descartes could not in fact escape his philosophical and scientific context. Moreover, he could not pursue the order of reasons in the strict sense, because its dogmatic reductionism cannot be sustained. Descartes presents both his choice of the simple and the means of concatenation for reproducing the complex as if they were transparent to reason. One of the first and most influential of the modern reductionists, he asserts in metaphysical, scientific, and (by implication) social contexts that the complex can be recovered as a concatenation of the simples, which are taken to be fully homogeneous with the complex. But the evidence of the sciences (and, I would argue, metaphysics) as they develop in the post-Cartesian age is that the choice of analytical simples and means of concatenation is the outcome of reflection, and subject to revision; and that the simple and complex remain heterogeneous (Grosholz, 1991). Thus, the project of the *Meditations* in retrospect appears impossible. And yet, his glorious attempt to liberate philosophy from the past, from subject matter, from doubt and dissent, was precisely what allowed Descartes to guide philosophy up and over the watershed of modernity. Attempting the impossible at the appropriate stage in history often leads to unexpected and fundamental discoveries: consider the fruitfulness of efforts to square the circle, build a perpetual motion machine, disprove the divine right of kings, codify logic in a single system, or provide mathematics with a fixed foundation.

The *Meditations* is a response to the three great social changes (and the books that articulated them) whose joint imperative is that the old order must be reimagined: the Renaissance, the Reformation, and the scientific revolution. The Renaissance revived pagan doctrines that had been suppressed by medieval Christianity, in particular, the materialism of Democritus, Epicurus, and the Roman Lucretius, as well as the skepticism of Sextus Empiricus. Descartes uses skeptical methods to block the skeptical assault (characteristic of Montaigne) on objectively valid knowledge claims, and invents a metaphysical dualism that can reinstate the important projects of materialism (most importantly, the investigation of the "machine" of the human body) alongside the moral education of Christian souls. He takes over the model of knowledge presupposed in the writings of Luther, Calvin, and the Augustine soon to be adopted by the Jansenists, where an individual soul, sufficiently prepared by careful divestment of prejudice and distraction, can hear the still, small voice of (in this case) reason. The democratic thrust of the model is only latent in the writings of Descartes, which lack altogether a political dimension; but a generation or so later it is elicited by Locke in his equation of reason and freedom, and returns home when the *Two Treatises of Government* is translated into French. The scientific revolution also looms large in the *Meditations*, which can be read as the plan for a metaphysics that will not just tolerate, but resolutely spur, scientific research. In January 1641, Descartes wrote to Mersenne, "I may tell you, between ourselves, that these six *Meditations* contain all the foundations of my physics . . . I hope that readers will gradually get used to my principles, and recognize their truth, before they notice that they destroy the principles of Aristotle" (*Oeuvres de Descartes*, ed. Adam and Tannery, III: 297–8). Thus, at least in part, the *Meditations* is designed to legitimate and undergird Descartes's scientific projects, in particular his exposition of matter, motion, and force in the *Principles of Philosophy*, whose publication in 1644 followed three years after that of the *Meditations* (Garber, 1992: chs 1 and 3; Gaukroger, 1995: chs 7–9). The trajectory of thought from the pure recognition of the *cogito* to the determinate projects of natural philosophy is long and marvelous: we will now pursue it.

The Argument of the *Meditations on First Philosophy*

Descartes begins the *Meditations* with a brief summary of the account of his early life that takes up so much of the *Discourse on Method*:

> Some years ago I was struck by the large number of falsehoods that I had accepted as true in my childhood, and by the highly doubtful nature of the whole edifice that I had subsequently based on them. I realized that it was necessary, once in the course of my life, to demolish everything completely and start again right from the foundations if I wanted to establish anything at all in the sciences that was stable and likely to last. (I, 17; all citations are from Descartes, 1985: vol. II)

The rest of the *Meditations* is the record of Descartes's once-in-a-lifetime and solitary attempt to begin from the very beginning by rejecting, not just all obvious falsehoods, but everything that might possibly be doubted. Yet it is not altogether solitary: his writing (and rewriting) of this famous thought experiment is also a re-enactment that the reader, by reading attentively, is to share. Dante to Descartes's Virgil, the reader must actively experience clear and distinct thought, learn to distinguish it from thought that is confused and obscure, and thereby progress along "the order of reasons." And indeed, the opening pages of the *Meditations* are mildly hellish: the reader is swept up by a whirlwind skepticism that seems to demolish every truth, and haunted by "some malicious demon of the utmost power and cunning [who] has employed all his energies in order to deceive me" (I, 23).

The *First Meditation* is a sequence of skeptical arguments, each more potent than the last. The first is drawn from the canon of skeptical arguments; similar examples can be found in the *Outlines of Pyrrhonism* of Sextus Empiricus. The first argument notes particular instances where the senses deceive us (the stick submerged in water seems to be broken; the distant square tower appears round), and then asserts that in any given instance, we cannot be sure that the senses do not deceive us: "it is prudent never to trust completely those who have deceived us even once" (I, 18). Descartes counters himself with the objection of common sense: to doubt the evidence of the senses in such a global way is to be mad. But then he brings forward a second argument, also drawn from the skeptical canon. In particular instances, we may think we are having a certain experience, but are in fact dreaming; thus, in any given instance, we cannot be sure that we are not dreaming, and this is not madness. And yet, Descartes observes, there seem to be some truths that remain intact whether I am waking or sleeping, truths that pertain to mathematics, and to "corporeal nature in general and its extension" (I, 20). To sweep these remaining truths away, Descartes invents a skeptical argument that goes far beyond what ancient skepticism and Christian theology (even late medieval voluntarism) were able to frame. If God allows me to be deceived sometimes, he wonders, why is it not at least possible that he allows me to be deceived all the time? Or, perhaps what we believe about God's omnipotence and goodness is a fiction? Or (backing off from the hint of heresy or atheism) perhaps my thoughts are controlled by "some malicious demon of the utmost power and cunning" (I, 22) who deceives me in all things, even possibly the simple truths of arithmetic? This supposition is so dizzying that the first *Meditation* breaks off there.

The *Second Meditation* begins in vertigo: "It feels as if I have fallen unexpectedly into a deep whirlpool" (II, 24). But this total loss of orientation is ultimately instructive, for if there is anything at all that can be saved from such philosophical chaos, it may prove to be the "firm and unmoveable point [Archimedes demanded] in order to shift the entire earth" (II, 24). The argument that follows is one of the most poignant in Western philosophy, the utterance of a small human flame lighting the maelstrom. And its use of the first person singular is essential: supposing I am deceived in all things, I am still aware that I am, and that I am aware. "Let him deceive me as much as he can, he will never bring it about that I am nothing so long as I think that I am something. So that after considering everything very thoroughly, I must finally conclude that this proposition, *I am, I exist*, is necessarily true whenever it is put forward by me or conceived in my mind" (II, 25). The significance of this moment for the *Meditations* is that the reader, re-enacting while reading it, experiences what it is to have a clear and distinct idea, immune from doubt; thereafter, Descartes can say with confidence, now the reader and I know what a clear and distinct idea is: not the logician's third person proposition on the page, but a certain lived apprehension. This is why Descartes is called an intuitionist. The significance of the moment for the history of philosophy is that the propositions *I am, I exist*, and finally *I think* are simply affirmations of an awareness without content, thus opening the door to the study of consciousness as such: Leibniz's *Monadology*, Kant's *Analytic*, Hegel's *Phenomenology*, Husserl's own *Meditations*.

The economy of Descartes's argument in the remainder of the *Second Meditation* is admirable, for he uses the malicious demon argument and its sweeping agnosticism to clarify the meaning of the *I am* in such a way that the introduction of scientific method at the end of the *Meditations* is inevitable, as well as the transition from the *Second* to the *Third Meditation*. Since there are as yet no grounds for trusting the evidence of the senses or imagination, the *I am* cannot be identified with a body located in external nature; indeed, externality cannot be affirmed. Instead, the *I am* recognizes itself in its activity of thought, an activity that – for reasons still unknown – has proved over the course of two *Meditations* to be inflected: "But what then am I? A thing that thinks. What is that? A thing that doubts, understands, affirms, denies, is willing, is unwilling, and also imagines and has sensory perceptions" (II, 28). With this claim, Descartes identifies himself with his soul, thinking substance, and not the machine of his body, extended substance; and he has, by implication, announced his dualism.

Thus I may doubt what I seem to perceive, but I cannot doubt that I seem to perceive it; sense perception is just one modality of awareness, and awareness holds true independent of its ability (or inability) to furnish an object. Descartes makes this claim even more radical by going on to consider the case of an alleged object of sense perception, a piece of wax "just taken from the honeycomb; it has not yet quite lost the taste of the honey; it retains some of the scent of the flowers from which it was gathered" (II, 20). This passage too has its pathos, for it is the only place in the *Meditations* where the sensory riches of nature are acknowledged, but – as in Plato's

Phaedrus – they are introduced only to be set aside. Descartes argues that since thought is an inflected unity, the piece of wax is not merely sensed and imagined, but also always *thought*, that is, understood or reasoned upon. What I can *think* about the piece of wax as it melts in my hand is what remains constant under all the transformations, and that is just what is quantifiable, falling under the categories of extension and motion. The sweet qualities delivered by sense perception and imagination introduce me to an object of knowledge that is obscure, changing without pattern; but reason offers an object that can be known distinctly. What really constitutes the wax is thought rather than sensed. "The perception I have of it is a case not of vision or touch or imagination – nor has it ever been, despite previous appearances – but of purely mental scrutiny" (II, 31).

To say that sense perception is best understood as a modality of thought in 1641 is astonishing. Aristotelian epistemology assumed that all knowledge begins in sense perception, that sense perception is our conduit to external things, and that knowledge depends on the adequacy of thought and things. Even Neoplatonists, insisting that the intelligible dimension of things is the key to their truth, supposed that knowledge begins in the sensible realm and that the sensible mirrors the intelligible. By contrast, Descartes proposes in the *Second Meditation* that if it should turn out that the *I am* can know objects, it must learn to *think* them first of all, and only turn to the senses subsequently with the greatest mistrust, poised to abstract from and correct them in light of the constructions of reason. If there are external objects, they will be the objects of science, and reason, not empirical judgment, will pronounce on them first. Thus the malicious demon argument turns out not to be merely negative; it is also a version of the new scientific method that enjoins us both to quantify everything, and to try to think the world as a rational system independent of the accidents of human sense perception.

Because sense perception is a modality of awareness, and awareness cannot furnish its own object via sense perception, at the end of the *Second Meditation* Descartes (and the reader) must reinstate the object of knowledge in a novel way. Awareness also cannot be its own object, for that is just to repeat itself: my awareness of my awareness is just my awareness. Descartes and the reader have already secured the *I am, I think*. The problem is, how to move on and "out" to something else. (This could not have been a philosophical problem for Aristotle, or for Plato.) Thus we arrive perforce on the threshold of the *Third Meditation*; there is nowhere else to go.

Besides its inflection into doubting, affirming, denying, understanding, not understanding, willing, not willing, imagining and sensing, the *I think* has a further articulation into what might be called the images or qualities of "external" objects, should they be shown to exist. Descartes calls them ideas. An idea has a double reality, because on the one hand it is a mode of my thought, and on the other hand it is representative of an object (should objects exist). Descartes uses, and transmutes, scholastic vocabulary to express this distinction: the former is the formal reality of the idea, the latter its objective reality. Descartes observes that taken as a formal reality, an idea cannot be false, for considerations of truth and falsity only arise over the objective reality of an idea, when something is predicated of it in a judgment. Two questions must then be considered: what caused the idea? And does it resemble the object that caused it?

Because the hypothesis of the malicious demon is still in effect, because my consciousness of objects is so far only my consciousness, there seems to be no good reason to refer the cause of the objective reality of my ideas to anything but their formal reality, as modes of my consciousness; and then we would have to admit that most ideas do not resemble their cause. (What would it mean, to resemble a consciousness?) But among all the ideas that Descartes – and the reader – survey, there is one exceptional idea whose objective reality prevents it from being merely a mode of my consciousness, that is, whose object and cause could not be me. It is the idea of God, distinguished from all the rest by its infinity and perfection. Here again, the economy of Descartes's argument is admirable: because I doubt, I know that I am imperfect; because I am so far painfully aware of the small compass of what I can know, my knowledge is not infinite. Thus the cause of this infinite and perfect idea must be something that is not my awareness; whatever is caused by my thought must be, at best, finite and imperfect. Descartes puts it this way:

> Now it is manifest by the natural light that there must be at least as much reality in the efficient and total cause as in the effect of that cause. For where, I ask, could the effect get its reality from, if not from the cause? And how could the cause give it to the effect unless it possessed it? It follows from this both that something cannot arise from nothing, and also that what is more perfect – that is, contains in itself more reality – cannot arise from what is less perfect. And this is transparently true not only in the case of effects which possess actual or formal reality, but also in the case of ideas, where one is considering only objective reality... in order for a given idea to contain such and such objective reality, it must surely derive it from some cause which contains at least as much formal reality as there is objective reality in the idea. (III, 40–1)

Moreover, since the idea of God is unique as well as infinite and perfect, it must resemble its cause. Nothing short of God could produce the idea of God.

> The unity, the simplicity, or the inseparability of all the attributes of God is one of the most important of the perfections which I understand him to have. And surely the idea of the unity of all his perfections could not have been placed in me by any cause which did not also provide me with the ideas of the other perfections; for no cause could have made me understand the interconnection and inseparability of the perfections without at the same time making me recognize what they were. (II, 50)

So there it is: Descartes (like the reader) finds in his thoughts an idea that must have originated elsewhere. He has discovered an Other for an object of thought; however, it is important to note that this Other is not Out There, for no externality has yet been established, only alterity. "It only remains for me to examine how I received this idea from God. For I did not receive it through the senses" (III, 25). The order of reasons requires that Descartes locate an object of thought, apart from thought itself, and that the conduit to that object not be sense perception. Descartes fulfills that demand, and in so doing both proves the existence of God (at least to his own satisfaction) and finds an idea that must be true. Thus he and the reader enjoy another instance of a clear and distinct idea, which in this case comes along with an object that it truly represents. Now Descartes and the reader can proceed to consider truth at greater length, and get on with the projects of mathematics and natural science.

But the transition to the "external world" is not easily made. Descartes has acquired a method; surprisingly, the skeptical method has been transmuted, tilted on the Archimedean fulcrum of the *I think* into a positive way of proceeding. In a letter to Mersenne, Descartes calls it the order of reasons, the stepwise linkage of truths from the simpler to the more complex, in which nothing is accepted which is not "clear and distinct." Descartes has also acquired an object (God) without the mediation of sense perception; surprisingly, the *I think* has discovered innate to itself the trace of an Other, qualitatively and quantitatively distinct in virtue of its perfection and infinity, "the mark of the craftsman stamped on his work" (III, 35). But Descartes has yet to elucidate the relation between method and object, a task that requires two more *Meditations*. That relation is circular, but the circle is – I would argue – interpretative and explanatory rather than vicious. The *Fourth Meditation* shows that the vision of God underwrites thought's best construction (understanding and organization) of its own activity, that is, method. And the *Fifth Meditation* shows that the exercise of method is the best way to focus, assess, and extend our vision of God. Moreover, taken together they provide the reader with meditative exercises that strengthen the ability to "[turn] the mind away from imaginable things and towards things which are objects of the intellect alone and are totally separate from matter" (IV, 53).

The *Fourth Meditation* begins with the vision of God: "And now, from the contemplation of the true God, in whom all the treasures of wisdom and the sciences lie hidden, I think I can see a way forward to the knowledge of other things. To begin with, I recognize that it is impossible that God should ever deceive me" (IV, 53). Thus Descartes is finally able to set aside the hypothesis of the malicious demon. In the *Second Meditation*, that hypothesis forced Descartes to cut off his contemplation of the piece of wax, for he could not be sure that his subjective certainty about the "clear and distinct" (quantitative) features of the wax was not an illusion: global illusion made it impossible to distinguish between truth and error in reference to his ideas. Now that the shadow of the demon has been shortened to the vanishing point by the sun of God's perfection, Descartes (and the reader) can raise the issue of truth and error; error, unlike global illusion, can be diagnosed and treated. The diagnosis stems from what the inflection of my thought has come to mean in light of God. God has given me a faculty of knowledge which constructs judgments from ideas; perfect in itself, it is however finite. And he has given me a faculty of willing, which is not only perfect but also infinite, since I can freely choose to exercise it about anything, undetermined by any external force. The mismatch between the finitude of the intellect and the infinitude of the will is the source of error:

> The scope of the will is wider than that of the intellect; but instead of restricting it within the same limits, I extend its use to matters which I do not understand. Since the will is indifferent in such cases, it easily turns aside from what is true and good, and this is the source of my error and sin. (III, 58)

When the intellect has not made a matter sufficiently clear and distinct, the will may leap to ill-judged conclusions; the treatment of this intellectual malady is proper method, which can be described negatively as the stepwise avoidance of precipitancy, and positively as keeping one's attention fixed on the clear and distinct.

> If, whenever I have to make a judgment, I restrain my will so that it extends to what the intellect clearly and distinctly reveals, and no further, then it is quite impossible for me to go wrong. This is because every clear and distinct perception is undoubtedly something, and hence cannot come from nothing, but must necessarily have God for its author. (IV, 62)

Thus the avoidance of error is also the pursuit of truth; and truth and existence are coupled, as they were in the realization that the *I am* is necessarily true every time I think it.

What Descartes means by the claim that every clear and distinct perception is undoubtedly *something* is illustrated at the beginning of the *Fifth Meditation* by the things of mathematics. His fresh insight into "what to do and what to avoid in order to reach the truth" leads him to reconsider the array of his ideas. As in the *Second Meditation* but now with renewed insistence, the ideas of extension, figure, and number seem particularly significant. They are imagined, but they are distinctly imagined; they are "remembered" – in an evocation of Plato's anamnesis – rather than discovered, and are therefore innate; they are not outside me or discovered by sense perception, yet they exist in so far as they have "their own true and immutable natures" independent of my whims or wishes. My awareness of the things of mathematics is an illustration of the indissoluble link between truth, the clear and distinct, and existence; and the linkage so illustrated brings Descartes (and the reader) back to the consideration of God.

In the *Third Meditation* Descartes showed that the idea of God must be caused by something other than the *I think*, and must resemble its cause; the idea is treated in terms of its objective reality (its reality *qua* representation) and the question of existence is referred to its cause. But the *Fifth Meditation* reveals another dimension of the idea of God, for it turns out to be the best, most robust illustration – one might call it the archetype – of the indissoluble link between truth, the clear and distinct, and existence. The existence of God is entailed not only by the finitude of the frail human flame, the *I doubt*, but is also expressed directly in the idea of God, once that idea is methodically inspected. Existence belongs to the sum of God's perfections even more clearly and distinctly than the property that its three internal angles equal two right angles belongs to the triangle.

> As regards God, if I were not overwhelmed by preconceived opinions, and if the images of things perceived by the senses did not besiege my thought on every side, I would certainly acknowledge him sooner and more easily than anything else. For what is more self-evident than that the supreme being exists, or that God, to whose essence alone existence belongs, exists? (II, 69)

The *Fourth* and *Fifth Meditations* are a kind of spiritual calisthenics to strengthen the habit of putting first things first, in particular, of putting things of the spirit before things of the body. In the utterance of the *I am*, in the objective idea of God, and in the things of mathematics, clarity and distinctness announce truth, and truth and existence arrive together. The soul is now as well prepared as possible to turn its attention, finally, to material things, confident that extension, figure, and number will serve as the bridge to the external world – the machines of nature.

And yet, at the beginning of the *Sixth Meditation*, Descartes still hesitates. He reminds the reader that our awareness of mathematical things involves, once again, an inflection of thought – this time into intellection and imagination – which in turn requires an account of what this inflection means. I can think mathematical things clearly and distinctly that I cannot imagine: a case in point is the chiliagon, which I simply cannot picture as I can the triangle or pentagon. How are we to explain this constraint upon imagination, which seems to be different from the constraint of finitude? Descartes explains (as a "probable conjecture") that, when we imagine, thought "turns towards the body and looks at something in the body which conforms to an idea understood by the mind or perceived by the senses" (VI, 73). Thus the very inflection of the mind suggests that body exists.

Moreover, there is more to corporeal nature than its quantifiable properties, the way it instantiates the things of mathematics, the extent to which it can be known clearly and distinctly. In fact, knowledge of material things always also involves "colors, sounds, tastes, pains, and so on," qualities that seem incurably confused and unclear: such stubborn cloudiness must be accounted for. Descartes surmises that, like imagination, sense perception involves the body. Indeed, the cogency of skeptical arguments based on errors of the senses is best explained by supposing that we think in the mode of sense perception by making use of the machine of the body, in order to know other bodies. Descartes is using the inflection of thought to work his way "outwards," as it were, from intellection to imagination to sense perception. However, up till now the question of existence has been answered by the link between existence, truth, and clarity and distinctness; but here on the threshold of externality, the clouds of sense perception will never part. Descartes has thoroughly revised epistemology by asking what we can know when sense perception is not taken to be the primary conduit to what we know. In particular, he has revised our approach to the things of nature by showing, in the *Second* and *Fifth Meditations*, that whatever sense perception seems to offer us must first be understood in terms of extension, figure, and number. And yet, there is more to nature than mathematics, just as there is more to thinking than intellection. He must address this "more," and it cannot be addressed solely in terms of the criterion of clarity and distinctness.

Descartes announces that it is time for a review.

> To begin with, I will go back over all the things which I previously took to be perceived by the senses, and reckoned to be true; and I will go over my reasons for thinking this. Next, I will set out my reasons for subsequently calling these things into doubt. And finally I will consider what I should now believe about them. (VI, 74)

Why, before the project of the *Meditations*, did it seem as if the senses were a conduit to the truth? Sensory ideas seem to arrive willy-nilly, and they are more "lively and vivid" than ideas merely imagined or remembered; thus they seem to be caused by external objects. We also use our senses before we use our reason: so genetic priority suggests logical priority. Finally, nature teaches that bodily sensation is connected in regular and predictable ways with sensory objects and action.

Then came the moment of doubt: doubt stemming from errors made by the senses, doubt from errors made while dreaming, doubt from the deception of the malicious demon. *Meditations Three* and *Five* dispelled the latter, and *Meditations Four* and *Five* showed "that everything that I clearly and distinctly understand is capable of being created by God so as to correspond exactly with my understanding of it" (VI, 78). Thus I can infer that the inflection of my thought into the faculties of intellection, imagination, and sense perception indicates a real distinction between myself as a thinking thing (what I am essentially, and therefore necessarily) and the embodiment that also seems to be mine, though only probably. Since God is not a deceiver, since these ideas arrive (often against my will) via an embodiment that is passive, and since God has given me a strong natural inclination to believe that these ideas are caused by and resemble external objects, my doubt from errors made by the senses is defeated.

Moreover, my new understanding of nature in terms of extension, figure, and number – that is, as a collection of machines – reinforces this conviction. For nature also teaches me "that I am not merely present in my body as a sailor is present in a ship, but that I am very closely joined and, as it were, intermingled with it, so that I and my body form a unit" (VI, 81); and if my body is a well-constructed machine it will sometimes lead me astray. First, any good machine is built for certain kinds of circumstances and not others; when placed in an exceptional situation, it may misfire. Second, a machine is a system of *partes extra partes*; the transmission of intention and interpretation along its pathways may go astray. As to the doubt that stems from dreams, it is easily dismissed: for dreams do not have the systematic unity of reality. Since I can trust in the clear and distinct dimension of what I know, not only in the present but in the past as well, I can gauge the difference between the piecemeal fantasies of dreams, and the whole fabric of the real world. Thus the end of the *Meditations* restores the world of sense perception – though now transformed into the object of natural science – and dispels the doubt that opened them in one and the same conclusion.

The Reception of the *Meditations on First Philosophy*

The reception of the *Meditations* began even before it was published. Descartes first sent the text to two Dutch friends who forwarded it to Caterus, a Catholic archpriest who was rather precariously holding his office in Holland; then he forwarded it, with Caterus' objections and his own reply appended, to Mersenne. Mersenne in turn circulated it, Descartes responded to the objections amassed, and the edition of the *Meditations* published in 1641 included six sets of *Objections and Replies*, from Caterus, Mersenne (and probably a Professor Morin), Thomas Hobbes, Antoine Arnauld, Pierre Gassendi, and a group of "various theologians and philosophers" put together by Mersenne. The second edition of 1642 also included a seventh set, from Pierre Bourdin. Thus the *Meditations* made its first public appearance already embedded in a scholarly discussion, which has continued unabated up to the present day.

The *First* and *Seventh Objections and Replies* set the *Meditations* in relation to scholasticism, raising various theological and methodological issues: how God could be the cause of his own existence, how a finite being might know the infinite, how the distinction between body and soul is to be understood, whether the method of doubt brings assumptions in by the back door, and whether after all it can lead beyond itself. The *Second* and *Sixth Objections and Replies* set the doctrines of the *Meditations* in relation to Mersenne's circle, and elicit from Descartes an often-quoted pronouncement on the organization of his *Meditations* (*Second Replies*, 155–60). Distinguishing between analysis and synthesis, Descartes writes of the analytic format of the *Meditations*:

> The order consists simply in this. The items which are put forward first must be known entirely without the aid of what comes later; and the remaining items must be arranged in such a way that their demonstration depends solely on what has gone before . . . Analysis shows the true way by means of which the thing in question was discovered methodically and as it were [prior in the order of discovery], so that if the reader is willing to follow it and give sufficient attention to all points, he will make the thing his own. (*Second Replies*, 155)

None the less, Descartes ends the *Second Replies* by rewriting his argument in synthetic or "geometrical form," that is, arranged in Euclidean fashion as definitions, postulates, axioms, and derived propositions (for more detail, see Ariew and Grene, 1995).

But the two most philosophically compelling exchanges are those with Arnauld and Gassendi, the *Fourth* and *Fifth Objections and Replies*. (The *Third Objections*, written by Hobbes, is disappointing. Hobbes addresses the *Meditations* in a rather piecemeal and superficial way, opposing his own materialism to what he views as Descartes's "immaterialism," and Descartes replies in kind.) Arnauld was quite a young man when he wrote his *Objections*; this is perhaps why he doesn't attack Descartes's system externally, from an already completed position, but tries to understand it, as it were, from the inside. His objections are for the most part attempts to reconcile what he sees as discordant claims or unnoticed circularity; he notes as a problem, for example, a version of the "Cartesian Circle": "I have one further worry, namely how the author avoids reasoning in a circle when he says that we are sure that what we clearly and distinctly perceive is true only because God exists. But we can be sure that God exists only because we clearly and distinctly perceive this. Hence, before we can be sure that God exists, we ought to be able to be sure that whatever we perceive clearly and distinctly is true" (*Fourth Objections*, 214).

But Arnauld's deepest objections have to do with the theory of ideas, to which he would devote the great book of his maturity, *On True and False Ideas*, written when he had avowedly become both an Augustinian and a Cartesian. Arnauld wonders, for example, whether Descartes's knowledge of himself in the *Second Meditation* can be taken as adequate and complete, as well as clear and distinct. Descartes is certain that he is a thinking thing: does this entail that he is not also an extended thing? For, as Arnauld observes, he might just as well have reasoned thus about the right triangle:

> I clearly and distinctly perceive . . . that the triangle is right-angled; but I doubt that the square on the hypotenuse is equal to the squares on the other two sides; therefore it does not belong to the essence of the triangle that the square on its hypotenuse is equal to the squares on the other sides. (*Fourth Objections*, 202)

How, asks Arnauld, is my perception of the nature of my mind any clearer than my perception of the nature of a triangle? Arnauld also raises important questions about the truth and falsity of ideas (apart from the judgments in which they stand), and about the very pertinence of the idea of cause to God, for whom "there is no past or future, but only eternally present existence" (*Fourth Objections*, 211) (see Nadler, 1989).

In sum, Arnauld's *Objections* are his inauguration into the philosophy of Descartes. The first of Descartes's great seventeenth-century disciples, Arnauld was also the most faithful: he defended Cartesian dualism against Malebranche's immaterialism and radical occasionalism, and later against Leibniz's attempt to modernize the Aristotelian–Scholastic notion of substantial form. Descartes repaid his admiration. Arnauld's *Objections* are the only ones that inspired Descartes to modify and add to the text of the *Meditations* when it was reprinted; Arnauld seems to have persuaded Descartes to take a second look at Augustine; and Descartes publicly acknowledged his admiration of the young man: "I could not wish for a more perceptive or more courteous critic of my book" (*Fourth Replies*, 218). Descartes's treatment of Gassendi was entirely otherwise; indeed, the *Fifth Objections and Replies* records a bitter altercation that was settled only in 1648, beside Gassendi's sickbed.

Gassendi was a Catholic priest who introduced the atomist doctrines of Epicureanism into seventeenth-century European philosophy by recommending a modified version of it, consistent with Christian doctrine. For Descartes, the stakes are very high in the *Fifth Objections and Replies*, for he is dealing with a mature philosopher whose presuppositions are radically opposed to his own, and who demands a systematic confrontation. Indeed, this set is more than twice as long as any other; Gassendi prolonged it in a book entitled *Disquisitio metaphysica* where he appended *Rebuttals* to his original *Objections*; and Descartes responded to the latter with an *Appendix* to the *Fifth Objections and Replies* in the first French edition of the *Meditations*, published in 1647. Once again, the central issue is the cogency of Descartes's claims about his two initial clear and distinct ideas, those of the self and of God. But whereas Arnauld seemed only to be asking for further clarification, Gassendi attacks Descartes's basic assumptions. In particular, he questions the claim that "the essences of things are indivisible. An idea represents the essence of a thing, and if anything is added to or taken away from the essence, then the idea automatically becomes the idea of something else" (*Fifth Replies*, 371). Since the idea represents the essence of what is referred to, it determines reference. Gassendi holds, on the contrary, that ideas give us only the accidents – not the essences – of things, and is furthermore skeptical about whether there are in fact any essences to be known. In the wake of this dispute, Arnauld and Malebranche take the part of Descartes, but Locke's position is very much like Gassendi's, for he claims that our knowledge of nature is restricted to congeries of sense data and thus to "nominal essences." Locke doubts that we will ever arrive at knowledge of "real essences" because of the relativity of sense perception: the human mind is not the measure of reality (see Lennon, 1993).

The common wisdom that professors of philosophy dispense to undergraduates is that late seventeenth- and early eighteenth-century philosophy can be tidily dichotomized into Continental rationalism and British empiricism, whose exponents – misled in two different ways by dogmatic metaphysics – framed a series of puzzles that was then settled by Kant. But if we view the same period as a collection of philosophers trying to deal with the legacy of Descartes's *Meditations*, it looks quite different. First of all, the family resemblance between, for example, Malebranche and Berkeley, or

Locke and Leibniz, is much more striking than the rifts that divide them; the resemblance is built not only upon shared presuppositions (some blend of Cartesianism and what is left of medieval philosophy) but upon shared problems. Second, the metaphysical experimentation these figures carried on offers us unexplored possibilities that were foreclosed precisely because of the success of Kant's system, but whose revival might be quite useful in the context of philosophical debate at the beginning of the new millennium. Descartes is responsible for much of the family resemblance, and much of the foment.

One important problem is the relation between form and matter, or – taking man in analogy with cosmos – soul and body. Descartes throws into question the accepted Scholastic account of this relation: the soul is the form of the body, whose matter individuates the form (this is the Aristotelian doctrine of substance), and both soul and body are revived at the Last Judgment (this is the Christian way of insuring personal immortality). By contrast, Descartes asserts that there are two kinds of substance, thinking substance and extended substance, and that they are radically different in kind. To thinking substance belongs activity, unity, and "inwardness"; to extended substance belongs passivity, divisibility (and so multiplicity), and the exteriority of *partes extra partes*. A human being is a compound or "substantial union" of thinking substance and extended substance: "Nature teaches me that I am not merely present in my body as a sailor is present in a ship, but that I am very closely joined and, as it were, intermingled with it, so that I and my body form a unit" (VI, 81). The advantage of Descartes's account is that it offers a metaphysical basis for the scientific study of the "machine of the body" on the one hand, and on the other for the philosophical study of consciousness as such.

The disadvantages are twofold. In the short run, within Descartes's own system, he has created for himself the (insoluble) problems of how to account for the unity of body, and how to explain the individuation of souls, in particular, how to keep souls whose essence is thought from Averroistically melting back into God. In the long run, he leaves behind him the problem of the relation of body and mind in human beings, and (by analogy) matter and spirit in the universe. Malebranche addresses the problem with his doctrine of occasionalism, which Berkeley further rarifies by getting rid of matter altogether in his theory of ideas; Spinoza proposes that the causally disjoined congeries of bodies and congeries of ideas making up a person are just two sides of the same coin: a mode of God, the sole substance; Locke takes the common-sense view that matter and spirit are causally related, since I (my soul) can obviously cause my arm to lift, although I know not how; and Leibniz attributes the relation to pre-established harmony, God's benevolent coordination of the perceptions of monads in the creation of the world. Leibniz (and Newton) also address the cosmological version of the problem within mechanics, where matter is re-imagined as mass and force is introduced mathematically, and the notions of energy and work begin to emerge. Kant accounts for the free eruption of spirit into deterministic material nature – ruled by the category of cause – in terms of his distinction between the phenomenal and noumenal realms. The scientific investigation of nature in the ensuing centuries has enlarged our vision of the mechanisms of nature and how they help to determine human action, and at the same time made the very notion of mechanism less deterministic; and the problem of how to relate constraint and spontaneity remains unresolved.

A second important problem has been mentioned in relation to Gassendi: to what shall we attribute the unity of thoughts and things? Once again, Descartes throws into question the medieval account which held that the unity of our thoughts is to be referred to the unity of things, which God and our sense perception reliably deliver to be known. For Descartes, sense perception is no longer a reliable guide to what exists, but must be constantly corrected by reason; rather, it is the clarity and distinctness of an idea that attests to the unity of what it represents, since to know a thing clearly and distinctly is to grasp its essence. For Gassendi and Locke, by contrast, our ideas are just compendia of simple ideas, from whose "nominal essence" the unity of an existing referent cannot be read off. For Spinoza, the unity of my thoughts is not, like the Christian soul, something already given, but rather the result of my active striving to organize them; and my self-organization is equally and isomorphically spiritual and mental. For Leibniz, the unity of things is referred to their intelligibility, for to exist (as something either actual or possible) is to be one, and to be intelligible; thus the unity of a thing, while encountered in thought, must always be investigated in a search for its conditions of intelligibility. The unity of things, obviously, has been thoroughly problematized. Kant's reaction to this situation is to refer unity to the transcendental structure of the human mind: the unity of consciousness, so structured, becomes the source of the unity of things, concepts, and judgments. The unity of things is only the unity of thought. The dogma, more Kantian than Cartesian, that all unity must be referred first of all to the mind is one that deserves to be re-examined. So too does the dogma, more Cartesian than Kantian, that all knowledge ought to constitute a single homogeneous whole.

Bibliography

Editions and translations

Descartes, René (1964–76) *Oeuvres de Descartes*, 12 vols, ed. C. Adam and P. Tannery. Paris: Vrin.

Descartes, René (1985) *The Philosophical Writings of Descartes*, 2 vols, trans. J. Cottingham, R. Stoothoff, and D. Murdoch. Cambridge: Cambridge University Press.

Studies

Alquié, F. (1950) *La Découverte métaphysique de l'homme chez Descartes*. Paris: Press Universitaires de France.

Ariew, R. (1999) *Descartes and the Last Scholastics*. Ithaca, NY: Cornell University Press.

Ariew, R. and Grene, M. (eds) (1995) *Descartes and his Contemporaries: Meditations, Objections, and Replies*. Chicago: University of Chicago Press.

Ariew, R., Cottingham, J., and Sorell, T. (1998) *Descartes' Meditations: Background Source Materials*. Cambridge: Cambridge University Press.

Beck, L. J. (1965) *The Metaphysics of Descartes: A Study of the Meditations*. Oxford: Oxford University Press.

Belaval, Y. (1960) *Leibniz, critique de Descartes*. Paris: Gallimard.

Beyssade, J-M. (1979) *La Philosophie première de Descartes*. Paris: Flammarion.

Cottingham, J. (1992) *The Cambridge Companion to Descartes*. Cambridge: Cambridge University Press.

Curley, E. (1978) *Descartes against the Skeptics*. Oxford: Blackwell.

Des Chene, D. (1996) *Physiologia: Philosophy of Nature in Late Aristotelian and Cartesian Thought*. Ithaca, NY: Cornell University Press.

Doney, W. (ed.) (1967) *Descartes: A Collection of Critical Essays*. New York: Doubleday.

Frankfurt, H. G. (1970) *Demons, Dreamers, and Madmen*. Indianapolis: Bobbs-Merrill.

Garber, D. (1992) *Descartes' Metaphysical Physics*. Chicago: University of Chicago Press.

Gaukroger, S. (ed.) (1980) *Descartes: Philosophy, Mathematics and Physics*. Sussex: Harvester.

Gaukroger, S. (1995) *Descartes: An Intellectual Biography*. Oxford: Oxford University Press.

Gilson, E. (1930) *Études sur le role de la pensée médiévale dans la formation du système cartésien*. Paris: Vrin.

Gouhier, H. (1958) *Les Premières pensées de Descartes*. Paris: Vrin.

Grene, M. (1985) *Descartes*. Minneapolis, MN: University of Minnesota Press.

Grosholz, E. (1991) *Cartesian Method and the Problem of Reduction*. Oxford: Oxford University Press.

Gueroult, M. (1953) *Descartes selon l'ordre des raisons*. Paris: Montaigne.

Hooker, M. (ed.) (1978) *Descartes: Critical and Interpretive Essays*. Baltimore, MD: Johns Hopkins University Press.

Jolley, N. (1990) *The Light of the Soul: Theories of Ideas in Leibniz, Malebranche, and Descartes*. Oxford: Oxford University Press.

Kenny, A. (1968) *Descartes: A Study of his Philosophy*. New York: Random House.

Laporte, J. (1945) *Le Rationalism de Descartes*. Paris: Presses Universitaires de France.

Lennon, T. M. (1993) *The Battle of the Gods and Giants: The Philosophical Legacy of Descartes and Gassendi, 1655–1715*. Princeton, NJ: Princeton University Press.

Marion, J-L. (1975) *Sur l'ontologie grise de Descartes*. Paris: Vrin.

Marion, J-L. (1995) The place of the "Objections" in the development of Cartesian metaphysics. In R. Ariew and M. Grene (eds), *Descartes and his Contemporaries: Meditations, Objections, and Replies*, pp. 7–20. Chicago: University of Chicago Press.

Nadler, S. (1989) *Arnauld and the Cartesian Philosophy of Ideas*. Princeton, NJ: Princeton University Press.

Rodis-Lewis, G. (1971) *L'oeuvre de Descartes*. Paris: Vrin.

Vuillemin, J. (1960) *Mathématiques et métaphysique chez Descartes*. Paris: Presses Universitaires de France.

Vuillemin, J. (1984) *Nécessité ou contingence*. Paris: Les Editions de Minuit.

Williams, B. (1978) *Descartes: The Project of Pure Inquiry*. Atlantic Highlands, NJ: Humanities Press.

Wilson, M. D. (1978) *Descartes*. London: Routledge.

24

Thomas Hobbes, *Leviathan* (1651)

The Right of Nature and the Problem of Civil War

Henrik Syse

Thomas Hobbes (1588–1679) advocated monarchical government, opposed the separation of powers, and denied that citizens should have a right to freedom of speech or worship. Furthermore, he was a thoroughgoing materialist, and in his own time was considered by many a religious heretic if not an atheist. Hobbes is also one of the most influential political philosophers of all time. Indeed, along with Locke, Montesquieu, Rousseau, and Mill, he is looked upon as one of the founders of modern, mainstream liberalism. How can this be, considering the facts mentioned above? This chapter will attempt to analyze Hobbes's most famous work, *Leviathan*, with the aim of explaining how Hobbes developed concepts and ways of thinking that have come to constitute an integral part of liberal political thought. The main Hobbesian ideas to be focused on in this discussion are the human being's *right of nature*, and the concept of a *social contract*.

Hobbes and his Times

Upon his death at the age of 91, Thomas Hobbes was indeed an old man even by our standards. Most of his philosophical works were written and published at a stage in his life when, by the standards of his own time, he would have been expected to have been long gone. However, even if he had died in, say, 1638, at the age of fifty, before any of his famous political works had been published (*Elements of Law* in 1640, *De cive* in 1642, and *Leviathan* in 1651), he would very likely have been remembered, at least among philologists, for his translation (published in 1628) of the classic work on the Peloponnesian War by the Greek historian Thucydides. Indeed, Hobbes was a versatile and knowledgeable man, publishing a translation of Homer at the age of eighty-five, and showing a deep interest in language, politics, theology, metaphysics, geometry, and the natural sciences.

Hobbes's views on politics were formed during the Thirty Years' War in Europe

(1618–48). This was the last phase of a hundred-year period of violence that had revolved around claims to religious rights and state sovereignty in the wake of the Protestant Reformation. This period also coincided with the English Civil War (1642–60), which was the bloody culmination of a long struggle between the king and parliament.

Hobbes himself hated war. In a famous autobiographical statement he makes it clear that he considered himself fearful, timid, and no friend of conflict, having been born as his mother heard the frightful news that the Spanish Armada was nearing the shores of England:

> And hereupon it was my mother dear
> Did bring forth twins at once, both me and fear
> (Hobbes's Verse Autobiography, reprinted in *Leviathan*, 1994 edn, p. liv)

Hobbes spent much of his career as a writer and thinker arguing that society must be organized so that *civil* (if not all) war becomes obsolete. He was firm in his belief that no one as yet had managed to construct a political theory that could show the way to a lasting civil peace.

In Hobbes's long list of the dangerous and erroneous ideas fostering civil war, he singled out three for special attention: (a) all kinds of separation of powers; (b) most variants of democracy; and (c) the separation of church and state. All of these ideas, according to Hobbes, would, if carried into practice, create division and strife.

According to Hobbes, right and peaceful rule must be based on the rights of the people, but at the same time sovereign power must be unified in a single ruler (possibly an assembly) who (which) must carry the full, undivided, and unlimited authorization of the people to rule. The following remarks aim to explain how Hobbes reached this conclusion, which on the one hand takes the rights of individuals as a central premise, and on the other appears to deny these individuals any real rights at all.

Leviathan: **Structure of the Work**

"Leviathan" is a Biblical image of a monster described in the book of Job (40: 25). Hobbes uses the image to depict the awe-inspiring nature of sovereign power. He does not, however, begin his work with a description of what this Leviathan should look like. Rather, he opens with a long discussion (chs i–xi) of human nature. And even when we get to his description of political authority and the state (chs xvii–xxxi, based on the theoretical underpinning of chs xiii–xvi), we find that it does not constitute the largest section of *Leviathan*. Indeed, the bulk of the work is devoted to religion and biblical exegesis (chs xii, xxxii–xlvii). However, both the anthropology and the theology of *Leviathan* serve the same purpose: to show that Hobbes's construction of political society is rational and, indeed, constitutes the only possible construction if one is to avoid civil war.

With this, we can sense a basic method used by Hobbes: to marshal a plurality of arguments, with the aim of demonstrating that they all converge upon the same conclusion. No matter whether one starts from physics, biology, anthropology, geometry, moral philosophy, or theology, Hobbes's theory of the Leviathan is presented as the only viable solution to the problem of civil war. The reason for this convergence, it seems, is that all of these disciplines are essentially reducible to the unitary science of matter and motion.

Matter, Motion, and Fear

In long-winded, complex discussions of difficult subject matters, we often feel like exclaiming: "Get to the point!" Such a phrase very much sums up, however colloquially, the attitude that Hobbes adopts in the first chapters of the *Leviathan*. He insists that much of earlier philosophy has failed to "get to the point" and has instead fallen into what he calls "insignificant speech" and "abuse of words" (*Lev.*, 1994: i, 5, p. 7 and viii, 2, p. 46; henceforth all citations will be taken from this edition). It has multiplied concepts, conjured up confused images and ideas, created empty distinctions, and produced notions that are not only false but plainly dangerous.

Now, in the midst of war and unrest in England and in Europe, it is high time, according to Hobbes, to get to the point! His first attempt to do this can be found in his description of life as "but a motion of limbs" (*Lev.*, Introduction, 1, p. 3), and his insistence that all reality is made up of one and only one substance, namely, matter. Traditional Christianity – and under its influence much of Western thought, even in our day – has seen matter and spirit as two different, albeit complementary and co-existing, aspects of the world. One of Hobbes's contemporaries, the very influential René Descartes, was even more radical and portrayed matter and spirit as two entirely different substances, the meeting and combination of which constitute a key to understanding man.

For Hobbes, by contrast, there is only *one* substance, *one* reality: matter. Hence, speech about incorporeality or spiritual beings is nothing but vain and useless imagery. All that exists, even God, is matter. Life is matter in motion. Perception occurs when matter moving through space is received into our sense organs. In turn, these perceptions move us to formulate concepts and put them into speech, so that we may give voice to what we have sensed. These sensations may be combined in different ways, even to the point of producing images and ideas of things that do not exist (such as "incorporeal body," *Lev.*, vi, 21, p. 21).

Already we discern why in his own day Hobbes was considered a radical and controversial thinker. Reducing all of life to matter and motion, he equates human thoughts and passions with mere reactions to physical stimuli. All the words we use and judgments we make are based on our reactions to matter in motion. Similarly, the emotions of love and hatred, pleasure and displeasure, belief and disbelief, arise when motions in the body combine with motions outside of the body. The *political* problem – which Hobbes aims to solve in *Leviathan* – consists in understanding and actively organizing these motions so that they do not lead to unrest and war.

Hobbes observes in his *Leviathan* – and likewise in the shorter Latin work *De cive* – that many of our passions, especially those associated with personal glory and religion, easily lead to violent disagreements. The prospect of these disagreements provokes fear. *Fear* is in many ways the cornerstone of Hobbes's political theory (see *Lev.*, xiv,

31, p. 88). It is this passion that creates war, yet understood and utilized rightly, it can also lead human beings to peace. Hobbes even discerns the origin of religion in *fear*, rather than in love or a desire for goodness (see *Lev.*, xii, 5–6, pp. 63–4), and he wants to channel this fear into deeds that are productive of peace, not war.

Individualism in a Universal System

Before we strike to the core of Hobbes's political theory, we should note that his mechanistic philosophy produces an interesting amalgamation of two seemingly contradictory perspectives. On the one hand, Hobbes's epistemology is individualistic to the extreme. There is no truth or falsehood, no good or bad, apart from what each individual perceives and opines. My own desires, passions, sensations, reactions, and fears effect how *I* understand and view the world, and this alone can be my basis for judging good and bad, right and wrong (*Lev.*, vi, 7, pp. 28–9). The problem, as Hobbes sees it, is the fact that my desires – my "motions," so to speak – are never-ending. I am never at rest; Hobbes speaks of a "continual progress of the desire, from one object to another" (*Lev.*, xi, 1, p. 57) and a "restless desire of power after power, that ceaseth only in death" (*Lev.*, xi, 2, p. 58). He presents us here with an image of restless individuals, each seeking after his own incomplete good. Until death comes, we can never become satisfied, because for every desire sated and every fear conquered new desires and fears are always lurking in the background, waiting to come forward.

On the other hand, in the midst of this rampant and pessimistic individualism, Hobbes lays the groundwork for a rigid and universal system. Since anything thought by human beings is ultimately reducible to matter in motion, it is also possible to formulate universal *laws* that can govern and direct this motion. In short, if it is possible to understand motion properly, it will likewise be possible to make predictions and thereby order events in conformity with laws of motion.

In the end, the philosopher can construct laws for political society that will ensure peace and stability. Thus, individuals may be brought into line, and their fears and restless competition for power, glory, and truth may finally be dissolved, or at least kept in check so that peace will follow.

The State of Nature

Chapters xiii–xv of the *Leviathan* are, politically, the most important part of this work. Here we find first (ch. xiii) a description of the state of nature. Hobbes's intention in conjuring up this unpleasant image of a savage society is to portray what human existence would be like in the absence of a common sovereign. It follows from his physics and his anthropology that human beings are condemned to live in fear of each other. Human existence is therefore a continuous striving after security, survival, and power.

On the one hand, the state of nature is introduced as an hypothesis – it is a reconstruction of how human beings may have lived in an imaginary and distant past when there was no political society. On the other hand, it represents something very real and present, as Hobbes sees it: the relations which hold between independent nations (see

Lev., xiii, 12, p. 78; see also Tuck, 1999: 135–8). Nations are perpetually at odds because there exists no common, acknowledged sovereign to pronounce judgments putting an end to their disagreements. And, indeed, even in civil society we can see residual elements of such a state of nature. For is it not true that we lock our doors, we arm ourselves (or at least take precautions) when we are out traveling – in short, we display constant distrust and fear of our fellow human beings (see *Lev.*, xiii, 10, p. 77)?

Hobbes's point is that if people who live in civil society regularly show such distrust, how much more radical and violent would such distrust be in the state of nature, where there is no common sovereign at all. He avers that whenever human beings have reason to feel unsure about the presence (or efficiency) of a common political power, capable of making laws, judging, and punishing, they will immediately distrust their fellow men and show hostility toward them. Hobbes thereby concludes that the state of nature is a state of war, or at least a state of constant readiness for war: "Hereby it is manifest that during the time men live without a common power to keep them all in awe, they are in that condition which is called war, and such a war as is of every man against every man" (*Lev.*, xiii, 8, p. 76). This passage (many others could be cited) reflects a bleak view of human nature. It is undoubtedly inspired by Christian theology – not least the belief in original sin, which Hobbes knew well from Augustine and John Calvin. On the other hand, it is also strikingly *different* from the standard Christian view, according to which man's original state – symbolized by the Biblical Garden of Eden – is, after all, good. Hobbes's state of nature is no Eden; quite the contrary, it is the state of fallen nature.

Based on his description of the state of nature, we may safely say that Hobbes has little faith in the ability of human beings to live in lasting peace without a common power to enforce that peace. His thesis, amply substantiated by the wars of his own time, is that human society will, if not governed rightly, degenerate into disorder and war. And in such a state of war, life is bleak and empty, with no industry, no invention, no learning, and no true society. Indeed, one will experience "continual fear and danger of violent death," and thus the life of man will be, in one of the most famous lines of all of philosophy, "solitary, poor, nasty, brutish, and short" (*Lev.* xiii, 9, p. 76).

The way out of this misery is through a contract. The individuals who live in the state of nature come together in order to erect and submit to a common sovereign power, thus putting an end to the constant fear and warfare which had previously disrupted and destroyed their lives. To understand how the social contract makes possible the transition from the natural condition of perpetual war to the peaceful condition of civil society, we must first consider Hobbes's teaching on natural law. On his account, the precepts of this law constitute the crucial building blocks of the transition from civil war to civil peace.

Natural Law and the Right of Nature

In the Christian, scholastic tradition, modified but not rejected by the Protestant Reformers, natural law (*lex naturalis*) represented the law of God, as it is made knowable to men naturally, independently of divine revelation in sacred scriptures. This idea, with roots in Plato, Aristotle, and Cicero, stands opposed to moral and legal positivism, that is, the idea that morality and law are purely and simply man-made. The natural law tradition teaches that certain tenets of morality and law are natural and thus not changeable by human volition. There are, in other words, norms of justice which stand above the human sovereign and political laws. This *natural justice*, which is an expression of natural law, goes under the name of *ius naturale* ("natural right" or "the right of nature"), a term that Scholastic authors frequently used as nearly equivalent to natural law.

Hobbes makes a frontal attack on the natural law idea, insisting at once that no higher law overarches politics, and that no humanly knowable good or right stands prior to human volition. Yet, strangely and strikingly, he embraces the language of natural law, and indeed helps inaugurate a whole new tradition of natural law. In this way he may be said to *subvert* the natural law tradition, daringly filling its terminology with new content. (Some influential interpretations, it should be noted, have tried to place Hobbes closer to a more traditional view of natural law, esp. Taylor, [1938]1965 and Warrender, 1957, but against this see Strauss, 1953.) Let us now investigate step by step how Hobbes effects the transformation of natural law.

First, Hobbes says that there is indeed a "right of nature," commonly termed *ius naturale*. This, however, is not a norm of natural justice, but rather

> the liberty each man hath to use his own power, as he will himself, for the preservation of his own nature, that is to say, of his own life, and consequently of doing anything which, in his own judgment and reason, he shall conceive to be the aptest means thereunto. (*Lev.*, xiv, 1, p. 79)

In Hobbes's hands, *ius* no longer refers to *something due in justice* (as it did for the Scholastics); instead it signifies *a right claimed*. The latter signification had already surfaced among canon lawyers in the early thirteenth century, and had been developed by, among others, William of Ockham in the fourteenth century and later by Francisco Suárez and Hugo Grotius in the seventeenth. Legal scholars in the European Continental tradition often call this the *subjective* as opposed to the *objective* meaning of *ius*. Taken in this juridical (not epistemological) sense of *subjective*, *ius* denotes a right under the aspect of its being owned by an individual (a *subject*), while the older, *objective* meaning focused on the item thus owed (the *object*).

Natural law theorists prior to Hobbes had emphasized that rights (*iura*), in the sense of powers or claims, were derivative upon an objective standard of right. One could be possessed of a right only *vis-à-vis* that which was authentically just or good. Hobbes, however, dramatically turns this picture on its head. This reversal he attempts to conceal from the reader, by misleadingly suggesting that "right" taken in the subjective sense was what his predecessors primarily meant by this term (*Lev.*, xiv, 1, p. 79). But Hobbes certainly knew that the mainstream Christian natural law tradition had taken the term *ius naturale* to mean natural (objective) justice, not subjective rights.

On Hobbes's rendering, natural law (*lex naturalis* – translated by Hobbes as "law of nature") no longer signifies "man's participation in God's eternal law," as Thomas Aquinas had earlier defined it in *Summa theologiae* (I-II, q. 91, a. 2). Rejecting the medieval understanding of natural law as that which is right or wrong according to man's highest good, Hobbes declares that, "there is no such *Finis ultimus* (utmost aim) or *Summum Bonum* (greatest good) as is spoken of in the books of the old moral philosophers" (*Lev.*, xi, 1, p. 57). Instead, the law of nature is nothing more than a "precept or general rule, found out by reason" (*Lev.*, xiv, 3, p. 79), by which a man discerns what is apt to preserve his life and what may destroy it.

In still another departure from the preceding tradition, wherein *ius* and *lex* were so closely intertwined they seemed nearly synonymous, Hobbes concludes that these are in fact two very different concepts. *Ius* in his philosophical lexicon denotes liberty of action, while *lex*, by contrast, denotes a principle that determines, binds, and holds men in its grip.

Hobbes is thus able to conclude that the right of nature (*ius naturale*) permits human beings to take whatever steps they deem necessary to defend their lives from harm. This right, however, proves to be self-defeating. Each individual's exercise of reason in the state of nature breeds collective irrationality, a war of all against all. The assertion of individual rights, while beneficial in the short term, provokes disaster in the long term, the loss of precisely those goods – life, peace, and security – that our "right of nature" was originally meant to help us secure. To exit this unfortunate condition, Hobbes sees no other solution than giving up, or rather giving away, the right of nature. The rules which guide the surrender and transfer of individual rights, Hobbes designates by the general term *lex naturalis*, thereby giving the venerable expression an entirely new meaning.

The foregoing analysis implies that (a) society is entirely a human construction; (b) its laws are based on individual calculation of what serves one's most basic interests; and (c) these interests are properly speaking each individual's right of nature.

Hobbes's subversion of the natural law tradition made the *Leviathan* one of the pivotal works of Western political philosophy. In a radical departure from the earlier tradition (though, some would argue, anticipated by Hugo Grotius), Hobbes states that natural rights (today we would undoubtedly speak in terms of "human rights") are prior to natural law, and as such they are the essential building blocks of human society. All human beings are in possession of a natural right to do whatever they judge necessary to preserve life and limb, and this right is not circumscribed by any law. This "right of nature" is surely not a right in the full legal sense, since we have already seen that in the state of nature there is no common authority to enforce it, and thus we end up with a war of all against all – a terrible conundrum to which the laws of nature represent the only possible solution.

The Laws of Nature

The first law of nature – Hobbes enumerates nineteen in all in *Leviathan* – states "*that every man ought to endeavour peace, as far as he has hope of obtaining it, and when he cannot obtain it, that he may seek and use all helps and advantages of war*" (*Lev.*, xiv, 4, p. 80, emphasis in original). This first law is followed by a second law, which in essence gives form to the social contract: each and every human being should agree (when others do the same) to give up the natural right of unfettered self-protection, which is essentially what the right of nature is.

Up to this point, Hobbes's conception of rights may not look very different from the social contract theory of John Locke, formulated fifty years later, which became so influential, not least on the American continent. However, between the two thinkers there are several crucial differences.

According to Locke and other Enlightenment liberals, individuals are allowed to keep their natural right(s) in civil society – indeed, civil society is erected to protect them, with the exception of the right to be a judge in one's own case. Hobbes, by contrast, requires that individuals give up nearly (the one exception will be discussed below) all of their original right of nature. If there is to be a stable peace and the state of nature is to be avoided once and for all, it is incumbent upon all individuals to transfer their entire natural freedom to a single sovereign.

As I have already noted, the social contract theory of Hobbes is based on individual self-interest. Unlike Locke and later Immanuel Kant, who premised their theory of the contract on the equal dignity of all human beings, Hobbes thinks that calculated self-interest, not charity or justice, should be the motivating principle behind the social contract. On this understanding, the contract exists to serve rational self-interest. It is not postulated as an instrument for preserving the moral worth of human beings (see Hampton, 1993: 385; according to some interpretations, such as Leo Strauss's, 1953, John Locke in essence shared this view; for a defense of Hobbes's social contract logic on this score, see Gauthier, 1988).

Finally, in contradistinction to later social contract theories, for Hobbes there can be no original contract between the sovereign (a monarch or a legislature) on the one side, and the citizens on the other. The individuals who exit the state of nature enter into a contract *solely amongst themselves*. The sovereign cannot be a party to this contract, otherwise disputes could arise between him and the individuals under his rule. Such disputes would imperil the very peace for the sake of which the contract was entered into in the first place. The sovereign is the arbitrator and *not* a contracting party.

Are there, then, no limits to the sovereign's power? Can he do *anything* in the name of keeping society out of the state of nature? At first glance, it certainly seems so. But, upon closer inspection, there is a limit to the sovereign's power even in Hobbes's rigid system.

First of all, Hobbes's laws of nature include several formulations strongly reminiscent of the Christian natural law tradition – concerning equity, the avoidance of revenge, the importance of goodwill, and the obligation to negotiate conflicts peacefully (see *Lev.*, xv, pp. 89–100). The cultivation of these virtues by the citizens will, Hobbes thinks, promote a lasting peace. *Ipso facto*, we can assume that the imperative to cultivate and exercise these virtues applies to the sovereign as well.

In the end, however, the laws of nature are not legally or politically binding upon the sovereign. Hobbes is emphatic on this score (*Lev.*, xviii, pp. 110–18): the sovereign is himself the arbiter of law, and for that reason he cannot at the same time be bound by it. If the sovereign is bound by the law in any way, this will be in conscience only, which, in Hobbes's authoritarian system, amounts to a politically impotent concession.

There is, however, one more possibility of constructing a limit on the sovereign's power. We must remember that the sovereign, even if not a party to the contract, has an office to execute, namely, that of preserving the lives of citizens and maintaining peace among them. The contract was instituted to defend the right to live in peace. From this it follows that no one is obliged willingly to undergo death at the command of the sovereign. Such a command would violate the natural imperative of self-protection for the sake of which the original contract was instituted in the first place. This is the sole right of nature that remains in effect within the state of civil society. In practice, however, this limit placed on the sovereign's legitimate exercise of power is worth little, since one individual can do little but protest and shout as he is drawn to the gallows. But this limitation is none the less significant. It shows how, within the logic of Hobbes's theory, there is a possible basis for civil disobedience (*Lev.*, xiv, 29, p. 89 and xxi, 11–16, pp. 141–3).

Paradoxically, then, the sovereign has the right to take the life of his subjects, and the subjects have the right to resist in order to defend their lives. While Hobbes nowhere says so explicitly, we may infer that a ruthless tyrant, who foments unrest by oppressing significant numbers of his subjects, may rightly be deposed, since he fails in his task of keeping the peace. In effect, such a sovereign will have turned society back to the state of nature.

Unsurprisingly, Hobbes never speaks of a right of resistance against tyranny. While seemingly implied by the logic of his theory (see, in particular, *Lev.*, xxi, "the liberty of subjects"; cf. Hampton, 1986: 197–207), the outright assertion of such a right would cut too sharply across the grain of his political ethos for him to have contemplated it explicitly.

The Social Contract: its Authors and Actors

In *Lev.*, xvi, Hobbes maintains that each individual who has (hypothetically) left the state of nature and is now living under a sovereign, is in effect an *author* of the social contract. By contrast, the person who, under the terms of this contract, receives authorization to engage in a certain range of actions, is termed an *actor*. This latter role, for Hobbes, is filled by the sovereign, who, depending on the type of political regime adopted, will either be a monarch or an assembly. Essential to this theory is the idea that the citizens, as authors of the social contract, are contractually bound by the deeds of the sovereign. When the authorization is of the sort that the law of nature demands, everything accomplished by the sovereign (the *actor*) may be formally attributed to his corresponding *author*(s). In the same way that stage actors are not the authors of their own lines and movements, but simply re-enact a pre-arranged script, likewise the sovereign acts through the original authority of his subjects. Consequently, his deeds are their deeds. Everything done by *him* is also imputable to *them*.

As a result, any subject who comes to the sovereign and accuses the latter of wrongful execution of his office, in essence raises a self-accusation. However, unlike an ordinary stage-play, in Hobbes's philosophical drama the citizen-authors may never issue a complaint against a sovereign-actor who deviates from his script. The former have given the latter free rein in the interpretation and execution of their "script." Hence they must assume full responsibility for all that he has enacted.

Religion

As already indicated, Hobbes accords the theme of religion a prominent place in the *Leviathan*. Hobbes knew that his book would be seen as going against the grain of earlier Christian political thought, first in claiming a purely human (not divine) origin of authority, and secondly in denying any role for an ecclesiastical power independent of the state.

Hobbes insists that secular power must rule in all matters of religion. If differences in religion often account for war and unrest, such absolute secular rule over religion is indeed very much called for – it is, after all, the secular power's office to avoid war. Hobbes does not think that the exercise of secular authority over religion will in any way prejudice the right of subjects to pursue their salvation. Nor does he think that there is any inconsistency in allowing this authority to impose a church (or system of religious beliefs) upon recalcitrant citizens. The aim of Christianity is peace. Thus, the sovereign, in taking whatever steps are necessary to ensure peace, will, Hobbes argues, never conflict with the tenets of true Christianity (see *De cive*, iv, 3). Moreover, even if the sovereign should establish a religious institution which conflicts with the conscience of certain subjects, the latter can still maintain their original faith in their hearts, and merely conform to the officially sanctioned religious practices in public. They thereby in no way endanger their salvation (see *Lev.*, xxxi).

Hobbes knew, of course, that this argumentation was controversial, to say the least. However, his aim was to show how any interpretation of the Bible that denied the full plenitude of the sovereign's power, or that gainsaid the true laws of nature, was inconsistent with the achievement of peace: (on his reading) the chief end promoted by Holy Writ. Thus, he insisted that he did not challenge or prejudice the Christian faith. Judging by the debate surrounding Hobbes ever since the first appearance of the *Leviathan*, few seem to have agreed with him on that score.

Conclusion

Without doubt, Hobbes remains one of the most important philosophers of all time. Not only did he address crucial questions about God, political society, the rights of human beings, war and peace, and free will. He also wrote a prose which is clear and concise, cunning and manipulative, yet beautiful and rich. If for no other reason, *Leviathan* deserves to be read by every new generation of philosophers as an authentic masterpiece. In philosophy there are few of this distinction.

Acknowledgment

Credit goes to my colleague Gregory Reichberg for formulating several passages in this chapter.

Bibliography

Editions and translations

Hobbes, Thomas (1946) *Leviathan; or, The Matter, Forme and Power of a Commonwealth, Ecclesiasticall and Civill*, ed. Michael Oakeshott. Oxford: Blackwell.
Hobbes, Thomas (1968) *Leviathan*, ed. C. B. Macpherson. Harmondsworth: Penguin.
Hobbes, Thomas (1991) *Leviathan*, ed. Richard Tuck. Cambridge: Cambridge University Press.
Hobbes, Thomas (1994) *Leviathan: with Selected Variants from the Latin Edition of 1688*, ed. Edwin Curley. Indianapolis, IN: Hackett.
Hobbes, Thomas (1998) *On the Citizen* (*De cive*), ed. and trans. Richard Tuck and Michael Silverthorne. Cambridge: Cambridge University Press (orig. pub. 1642).

Studies

Brown, Keith C. (ed.) (1965) *Hobbes Studies*. Oxford: Blackwell.
Flathman, Richard E. (1993) *Thomas Hobbes: Skepticism, Individuality and Chastened Politics*. Newbury Park, CA: Sage.
Gauthier, David (1988) Hobbes's social contract, *Nous*, 22: 71–82.
Hampton, Jean (1986) *Hobbes and the Social Contract Tradition*. Cambridge: Cambridge University Press.
Hampton, Jean (1993) Contract and consent. In Robert Goodin and Philip Pettit (eds), *A Companion to Contemporary Political Philosophy*. Oxford: Blackwell.
Macpherson, C. B. (1962) *The Political Theory of Possessive Individualism*. Oxford: Oxford University Press.
Overhoff, Jürgen (2000) *Hobbes's Theory of the Will*. Lanham, MD: Rowman and Littlefield.
Riley, Patrick (1982) *Will and Political Legitimacy*. Cambridge, MA: Harvard University Press.
Rogers, G. A. J. and Ryan, Alan (eds) (1988) *Perspectives on Thomas Hobbes*. Oxford: Clarendon Press.
Sorell, Tom (ed.) (1996) *The Cambridge Companion to Hobbes*. Cambridge: Cambridge University Press.
Strauss, Leo (1938) *The Political Philosophy of Hobbes*, trans. Elsa Sinclair. Chicago: University of Chicago Press.
Strauss, Leo (1953) *Natural Right and History*. Chicago: University of Chicago Press.
Syse, Henrik (forthcoming) *Natural Law, Religion, and Rights*. South Bend, IN: St Augustine's Press.
Taylor, A. E. (1965) The ethical doctrine of Hobbes. In Keith C. Brown (ed.), *Hobbes Studies*. Oxford: Blackwell (orig. pub. 1938).
Tuck, Richard (1988) *Hobbes*. Oxford: Oxford University Press.
Tuck, Richard (1999) *The Rights of War and Peace*. Oxford: Oxford University Press.
Warrender, Howard (1957) *The Political Philosophy of Thomas Hobbes*. Oxford: Clarendon Press.
Zagorin, P. (2000) Hobbes without Grotius. *History of Political Thought*, 21: 16–40.

25

Benedict de Spinoza, *Ethics* (1677)

The Metaphysics of Blessedness

Don Garrett

Benedict (Baruch) de Spinoza (1632–1677) composed the philosophical classic *Ethica ordine geometrico demonstrata* (*Ethics Demonstrated in Geometrical Order*) over the course of more than a decade while earning his living primarily as a lens-grinder in his native Holland. Although he was rightly cautious about disseminating his radical views – indeed, he traveled to Amsterdam in 1675 to arrange for the publication of the *Ethics*, only to change his mind in response to rumors about the book's "atheism" – he shared his work in draft form with a circle of close friends, who arranged for the publication of the *Ethics* as part of his *Opera posthuma* in 1677, following his death at the age of forty-four from respiratory disease. The *Ethics* challenged many traditional philosophical conceptions and offered a bold philosophical system – at once a naturalization of the divine and a divinization of nature – that shocked many of his contemporaries but has nevertheless provided intellectual stimulation and inspiration to generations of readers. It remains, more than three centuries later, one of the most remarkable philosophical treatises ever written.

The most immediately striking feature of the *Ethics* is its axiomatized "geometrical" format. Spinoza sought to demonstrate his doctrines not only in proper order (that is, in such a way that a conclusion is never employed until the arguments for it have been presented), but also in what he called the "geometrical style." Accordingly, the book is a deductive structure essentially composed – much like Euclid's *Elements of Geometry* – of numbered definitions, axioms, propositions, corollaries, and demonstrations. Within this structure, *definitions* state the intended meanings of key terms; *axioms* state fundamental doctrines proposed for acceptance without demonstration; *propositions* and *corollaries* (which differ only in that the latter are treated as subsidiary to the former) state theses for which *demonstrations* are provided that appeal (almost always) to previously stated definitions, axioms, propositions, and corollaries. These logical elements are fleshed out by prefaces, notes (*scholia*), and appendices. Spinoza did not always expound his views in the geometrical style; aside from the *Ethics*, he used it extensively in only one of his other works (his first published work, a geometrical reconstruction of parts of Descartes's *Principles of Philosophy* which established his credentials as an interpreter of Descartes). Nor was Spinoza the first to apply this style to philosophical writing; on the contrary, he was inspired to use it at least partly by Descartes's sample geometrical treatment, in his *Objections and Replies*, of some key doctrines of the *Meditations*. The *Ethics* remains, however, the only original philosophical work of the first rank written "geometrically."

The geometrical format of the *Ethics* serves several closely related purposes for Spinoza. In theory, if not quite always in practice, it imposes a rigorous discipline on the author, requiring him to identify his presuppositions explicitly as axioms and to propound no claims other than these axioms without explicit proof. At the same time, the format imposes a corresponding discipline upon his readers: if they accept the definitions and axioms, and cannot identify a specific fallacy or defect in the reasoning, then they are bound to accept the propositions and corollaries as well, no matter how unpopular those doctrines might be or how strange they might seem. Moreover, the format's demand for austere reasoning – instead of emotional appeals or rhetorical flourishes – helps Spinoza and his readers alike to maintain his desired stance of detached scientific objectivity in considering "human actions and appetites just as if it were a Question of lines, planes, and bodies" (*Ethics*, Part 3, preface; all quotations of this work are taken from Spinoza, 1985).

Even more remarkable than the format of the *Ethics*, however, is its scope. Divided into five parts – "On God," "On the Nature and Origin of the Mind," "On the Origin and Nature of the Affects," "On Human Bondage, or the Powers of the Affects," and "On the Power of the Intellect, or on Human Freedom" – it begins with a proposition about the metaphysical and conceptual priority of a substance over its modes and concludes with a proposition about the nature of blessedness itself. Spinoza's ambition was nothing less than to deduce the nature of blessedness ("man's highest happiness") and the path to it by demonstrating a science of ethics ("knowledge of the right way of living") from the fundamental structure ("metaphysics and physics," as he wrote to a correspondent) of the universe itself. Thus, the metaphysics of Part 1 is meant to support the general theory of matter and mind of Part 2, which supports the account of human nature and the emotions (i.e., "affects") in Part 3; and this account of human nature and the emotions, in turn, supports the ethical theory of Part 4, which supports the explanation of what blessedness is and how it is possible in Part 5. In fact, the *Ethics* offers what might be called a "metaphysics of blessedness" in two quite distinct senses: its metaphysics provides the intended *foundation* for an understanding of what blessedness is and how it is possible; and, in addition, this blessedness turns out to *consist* largely in understanding that very metaphysics and its many consequences.

Spinoza's Approach to Philosophical Understanding

In order to understand the system that Spinoza proposes, it is helpful first to understand his conception of the nature of *understanding* itself, for it is a conception that underlies his entire approach to philosophy. Spinoza is deeply and irrevocably committed to the idea that all facts in reality can in principle (though not, of course, all within a finite human mind) be conceived or understood through their necessitating causes. This commitment is embedded in axioms 2–4 of Part 1 of the *Ethics*:

> Axiom 2: What cannot be conceived through another, must be conceived through itself.

> Axiom 3: From a given determinate cause the effect follows necessarily; and conversely, if there is no determinate cause, it is impossible for an effect to follow.

> Axiom 4: The knowledge of an effect depends on, and involves, the knowledge of its cause.

Axiom 2 entails that every aspect of reality is conceivable – that is (as Spinoza makes clear), knowable or capable of being understood. Axiom 3 characterizes the causal relation as one of necessitation, in which effects are necessitated by causes and are impossible without them. Finally, Spinoza intends the distinctive axiom 4 to require that every aspect of reality can be known or understood only through it causes (for although axiom 4 explicitly applies only to "effects," his use of the axiom shows clearly that he regards all states of affairs as "effects"). Thus, Spinoza holds that everything can be understood, and can only be understood, by understanding the causes that necessitate its being just as it is. Falling within the scope of this principle are not only all facts about what exists but also all facts about what does not exist. Accordingly, Spinoza writes in his demonstration of the existence of God (proposition 11 of Part 1): "For each thing, there must be assigned a cause, *or* reason, as much for its existence as for its non-existence." That he neglects to cite axioms 2–4 – or any other axiom, definition, proposition, or corollary – as support for this premise of the demonstration is an indication of just how deeply embedded in his thinking the principle is.

An adequate understanding of things through their causes demands, in Spinoza's view, the use of what he calls the *intellect*. He thus distinguishes between two different kinds of ideas or mental representations. Whereas ideas of the *imagination* are like sensory images – indeed, for Spinoza, sense perception itself is classified as a kind of imagination in this broad sense – ideas of the *intellect* constitute a higher, more adequate, and non-imagistic form of understanding. Although the distinction between intellect and imagination dates back to the ancient Greeks, its significance was particularly emphasized by those early modern philosophers (including Descartes, Malebranche, Spinoza, and Leibniz) who are now commonly classified as "rationalists," and it was disparaged or ignored by those early modern philosophers (including Locke, Berkeley, and Hume) who are now commonly classified as "empiricists." For Spinoza, one of the chief aims of philosophical method is to develop reliance on the intellect in preference to the imagination; indeed, one of his earliest works was an unfinished *Treatise on the Emendation of the Intellect*. Precisely because he believes that the intellect provides the mind with a higher and more adequate form of understanding than does the imagination, he holds that sensory observations alone provide an inadequate basis for one's theories; rather, principles derived from the intellect can and must be used to determine the proper interpretation of what would otherwise be highly inadequate, confused, and unreliable sensory observations. This is one sense, at least, in which Spinoza is indeed a "rationalist."

Metaphysics

Spinoza employs a substance/mode metaphysics. According to this general metaphysical scheme, the fundamental entities that constitute the universe are *substances*, which are the entities capable of existing independently of other things. Each substance has or is constituted by an *essence* that makes the substance the thing that it is; thus, a substance exists only so long as it retains its essence, and it is best understood through an understanding of that essence. This essence consists of an essential or principal attribute – which Spinoza calls simply an *attribute*. As an expression or further qualification of its essential attribute, each substance has *modes*, which are the qualities or characteristics of the substance; these are all to be understood as determinate modifications of, or particular ways of instancing, the substance's essential attribute – in the way, for example, that spherical shape is a determinate modification or particular way of instancing spatial dimensionality (which Spinoza calls *extension*). Modes can exist only *in* the substance of which they are modes. It should be emphasized, however, that the relation of *being in* that holds between modes and substances is not a relation of spatial containment nor of parts to wholes; rather, it is intended to be a metaphysical relation of dependence that is exemplified (among other ways) in the relation between qualities of things and the things of which they are qualities.

Although Descartes and many other early modern philosophers also employed this general metaphysical scheme, Spinoza's unique transformation of it provides much of the initial impetus that his philosophy derives from the definitions and axioms of Part 1 of the *Ethics*. For Spinoza, the relation of *being in* necessarily runs in parallel with the relation of *being conceived through*, so that the order of dependence among ideas in thought must correspond precisely to the real order of ontological dependence among the intended objects of thought. Since Spinoza holds (in axioms 1 and 2 of Part 1) that each thing must be in and conceived through something, and since substances are not in anything other than themselves, he defines a *substance* as that which is *in itself* and *conceived through itself* (definition 3 of Part 1). He defines a *mode*, in contrast, as whatever is *in* another and *conceived through* that other (definition 5 of Part 1). He defines an *attribute* (i.e., an essential attribute, or what Descartes called a *principal attribute*) as "what the intellect perceives of substance as constituting its essence" (definition 4 of Part 1). From the doctrine of axiom 4 of Part 1 (already cited) that things must be conceived through their causes, together with the doctrine of the parallelism of the relations of *being in* and *being conceived through*, it follows that whatever is *in* something is also *caused by* it. Hence, for Spinoza, modes must be caused by the substances of which they are modes, and substances themselves must be self-caused.

Perhaps the best-known and most important metaphysical doctrine of the *Ethics* is Spinoza's conclusion that there is only one substance, God. His argument for this conclusion in the demonstration of proposition 14 of Part 1 invokes two previous propositions of Part 1:

Proposition 5: In nature there cannot be two or more substances of the same nature or attribute.

Proposition 11: God, or a substance consisting of infinite attributes, necessarily exists.

Proposition 11's characterization of God as a substance of infinite attributes is just an application of Spinoza's definition of *God* at the beginning of Part 1:

> Definition 6: By God I understand a being absolutely infinite, i.e., a substance consisting of an infinity of attributes, of which each expresses an eternal and infinite essence.

Spinoza's definition of the *infinite* (definition 2 of Part 1) entails that whatever has *infinite attributes* must have all possible attributes. Hence, the argument runs, since God exists (proposition 11), all attributes are already present and realized in God; and since substances cannot share attributes (proposition 5) but must each have some attribute (to serve as its essence), no substance can exist other than God.

The soundness of this demonstration largely depends, of course, on the two propositions (propositions 5 and 11) that serve as its premises. The demonstration of proposition 11 offers several different proofs of God's necessary existence; the first and simplest, however, applies, to the special case of God, proposition 7's claim that "it pertains to the nature of substance to exist." By this, Spinoza means that every possible substance must have a nature such that it could not possibly fail to exist, so that the existence of any possible substance follows immediately and with logical necessity from any definition of the substance that properly states its nature or essence. That this kind of necessary and eternal existence must indeed be a feature of any possible substance can be seen most easily from the fact that every substance is, by definition, conceived through itself and so also the cause of itself; for a thing could cause itself (as definition 1 of Part 1 affirms) only if it pertained to the thing's own nature to exist, so that its non-existence would be inconceivable and impossible. Of course, since it pertains to the nature of any possible substance to exist, and since no substance other than God actually exists, according to Spinoza, it follows for him that no other substance than God is really even so much as possible; any attempted definition of another substance must contain either an explicit or a hidden contradiction, consisting in the attempt to specify something as *substance*, and so entirely independent of other things, while nevertheless limiting its number of attributes and hence also its power.

Spinoza's demonstration of proposition 5 (that substances cannot share attributes) is highly compressed. Its strategy, however, is reasonably clear: to argue that there could be no *conceivable* – and hence no *genuine* – distinction between two substances sharing the same attribute, on the grounds that they could be distinguished as two different substances sharing that attribute neither by appeal to the attribute itself (which by hypothesis is the same in each) nor by appeal to any difference in their modes of that attribute. They could not differ in their modes because modes are subsequent (by proposition 1 of Part 1) to the substance of which they are modes. That is, they are entirely in and conceived through (by definitions 3 and 5), and hence entirely caused by (in consequence of axiom 4), the substance of which they are modes. But to be conceived through and caused by a substance is to be conceived through and caused by its attribute. Accordingly, there could be no conceiving of a difference of modes that did not require conceiving a pre-existing difference in the attribute of which they were modes. In thus denying that two substances could share an essential attribute, Spinoza is rejecting a key part of Descartes's metaphysics. According to Descartes, all human minds are substances that share the essential attribute of *thought* (understood broadly enough to include emotion and volition), and all bodies are substances that share the essential attribute of *extension* (i.e., spatial dimensionality). Descartes could allow that there are substances that share an essential attribute yet differ in modes partly because he accepted the possibility of causal interaction between substances, so that the modes of a substance need not all be causally determined entirely by their substance's own essential attribute; Spinoza's conception of substance requires that he deny the possibility of such interaction and hence also the possibility of such a resulting difference of modes.

In traditional Western philosophical theology, God is regarded as a substance or being distinct from the natural world, which consists of God's many creatures. Spinoza's *substance monism* – the doctrine that there is only one substance – demands a different account of the relation between God and nature in general and a different account of the relation between God and his creatures – including individual minds and bodies – in particular. In the context of his substance/mode metaphysics, Spinoza's doctrine that God is the only substance entails that everything that exists is either God or a mode of God; thus, as Spinoza expresses it in proposition 15, "Whatever is, is in God, and nothing can be or be conceived without God." It follows that if nature is to be conceived as a substance, nature must be identical with God – hence Spinoza's famous phrase "God, or Nature" (*Deus, sive Natura*), a phrase that has contributed to the common, but obstinately reactionary, imputation of concealed atheism to the *Ethics*. Since particular things are not themselves individually identical with God, for Spinoza, they must be modes of God, as he explicitly confirms in the corollary to proposition 25 of Part 1: "Particular things are nothing but affections [i.e., qualities or modifications] of God's attributes, or modes by which God's attributes are expressed in a certain and determinate way."

Understandably, Spinoza's assertion that human beings and other particular things are not really substances in their own right but are instead modes of substance evokes approval from some readers and consternation from others. Edwin Curley (1969, 1988, 1991) has sought, in his interpretation of the *Ethics*, to reduce the element of consternation by emphasizing the cause/effect implications and minimizing the subject/quality implications of the substance/mode relation. Nevertheless, it is very difficult to avoid reading the *Ethics* as claiming that modes of extension, including particular bodies, are ways in which God is extended and that modes of thought, including particular minds, are ways in which God is thinking. Jonathan Bennett (1984, 1991, 2001) has argued that one should see Spinoza's assertion that particular things are modes of a single substance as an early forerunner of the "field metaphysic" of contemporary physics – that is, the view according to which the universe is not, at the ultimate level, a composite of ontologically independent elementary particles but is instead a unitary being, a medium in which particular individual "things" arise as and ultimately consist of varying and moving distributions of different forces, properties, or fields that qualify or modify regions of that permanent medium.

Spinoza's view of the relation of God to nature is often characterized as *pantheism* – that is, as the doctrine that everything is God. This characterization is not unwarranted, for Spinoza does hold that every substance is God. Some commentators, however, have preferred to call his doctrine *panentheism*, intending by this coinage to emphasize his doctrine that everything (including God Itself) is *in* God, so that different particular things are only modes of God and are not themselves identical with God. Although Spinoza is also often described as holding that everything is a part of God, this characterization is not accurate, since for him modes are not parts: wholes are ontologically dependent on the existence of their parts, which bring wholes into existence by composing them; a substance, in contrast, is ontologically prior to its modes, which are modifications, or "affections," of the substance that follow from its essence.

Spinoza's re-conception of the relation between God and nature demands a reconsideration of the question of how God acts. Traditional Western philosophical theology holds that God (i) created a world distinct from himself, (ii) choosing to do so without acting from necessity, (iii) in order to achieve some good. As has already been observed, Spinoza denies the first element of this theory. According to him, all of God's causal activity is *immanent* causation (proposition 18 of Part 1): the production of modes that are *in* rather than external to God. According to Spinoza, some of these modes – the *infinite modes* – are pervasive and eternal features of God; the others, including such individual things as human beings, are *finite modes* that exist locally rather than pervasively, and come into and pass out of existence. While all modes of God have real causal power, in Spinoza's view, their causal power is not distinct from or in addition to God's own infinite power, since they are not themselves substances external to God.

Spinoza equally rejects the second element of the traditional theory of God's causal activity, for he denies that God *chooses* to act and affirms that God acts from absolute necessity. Spinoza's God does not in any sense choose from among alternatives, for his God conceives of no alternatives. Because he holds that everything must be conceivable through necessitating causes, Spinoza is a *necessitarian*; that is, he holds that everything true is so necessarily, and that nothing could possibly have been otherwise than it is. God could not possibly have had an essence different from the essence that God actually has, he argues; for God is by definition the absolutely infinite or unlimited substance, and it necessarily pertains to the nature of just such a substance to exist with the most unlimited nature or essence. Furthermore, everything that is genuinely conceivable or possible must follow with absolute causal necessity from that essence (propositions 16, 29, and 33 of Part 1, with demonstrations and *scholia*), for an absolutely infinite nature must cause everything that is possible to exist, and causes necessitate absolutely. Despite this, however, God is *free* in Spinoza's own sense of the term, according to which a thing is free if it "exists from the necessity of its nature alone, and is determined to act by itself alone" (definition 7 of Part 1). God satisfies this definition, for Spinoza, because the causal necessity by which God exists and acts is entirely internal to God's own essential nature; indeed, there is nothing outside God by which it could be imposed.

Spinoza rejects the third element of the traditional theory of divine causal activity as well: his God acts for the sake of no end or good. If God were to act in order to achieve some end, Spinoza argues in the appendix to Part 1, that would only show that God desired something that he lacked and so (contrary to definition 6 of Part 1) was not absolutely infinite. For Spinoza, all goodness is relative: something is *good for* a thing if it benefits that thing. Since nothing can benefit or harm God, it follows that nothing is good or evil for God – even though many things are, of course, good or evil for human beings. Because Spinoza's God has no desires and acts with no end in view, his God does not act in order to benefit human beings, is neither pleased nor displeased by their actions, and has no interest in being worshipped by them. Although Spinoza's God is an infinite thinking – and also an infinite extended – thing, his God is in no sense a *person*. Accordingly, the traditional problem of how a perfectly benevolent God could permit evils to befall human beings simply does not arise for Spinoza.

Theories of Matter and Mind

In Cartesian metaphysics, extension and thought are each essential attributes – some created substances (*bodies*, in the broad sense encompassing all physical objects) have the former, and other created substances (*minds*) have the latter. Descartes's God thinks but is not extended. If there is only one substance, as Spinoza maintains, then what is to become of thought and extension as essential attributes? Spinoza's bold answer is that they are *both* essential attributes of the one substance, God. Spinoza conceives of thought and extension as two fundamentally different aspects of God's being; that is, as two fundamentally different manners in which God, the absolutely infinite being, exists. Just as God is an infinite thinking being whose thinking nature is expressed through the being of infinitely many – that is, all possible – modes of thought, so God is also and equally an infinite extended being whose extended nature is expressed through the being of infinitely many – that is, all possible – modes of extension. God is thus both *res extensa* (*the extended thing*) and *res cogitans* (*the thinking thing*). The essence of *res extensa* is extension; the essence of *res cogitans* is thought; extension and thought are each the essence of God, in so far as God is conceived in the one manner or the other. In fact, God's attributes are not limited to extension and thought, in Spinoza's view, for God has, by definition, infinite attributes. All possible attributes of God must also be possessed and conceived by God; however, Spinoza maintains that no attributes in addition to extension and thought can be conceived by a human mind. Because every attribute is a fundamental manner of being, none can be conceived through the conception of any other, and no mode of one can be conceived through any mode of any other; the attributes are conceptually, and hence also causally, closed and self-contained. Thus, for example, each fact of extension is conceived through and caused only by facts of extension, not by facts of thought; and each fact of thought is conceived through and caused only by facts of thought, not by facts of extension (propositions 5 and 6 of Part 2).

Since Spinoza's God is an infinite thinking thing, however, there is nevertheless in God an actual idea of each thing that actually exists; and since each thing must be conceived through its causes (axiom 4 of Part 1), the causal order of dependence among things is mirrored by the causal order of dependence among their ideas. Thus, Spinoza affirms a strict but non-causal parallelism between things and ideas: "The order and connection of ideas is the same as the order and connection of things" (proposition 7 of Part 2). Nor is this all; he holds not only that a mode of extension is always paralleled by a corresponding mode of thought having that mode of extension as its object; he also holds that a mode of extension is *identical* with the mode of thought that has it as its object (*scholium* to proposition 7 of Part 2). Thus, just as extension and thought are two different manners of being through which one and the same substance, God, causes Itself to exist and conceives Itself, so also they provide two different manners in which each particular mode of God is caused to exist and can be conceived.

This theory of the relation between extension and thought in general provides the basis for Spinoza's account of the relation between the human body and the human mind in particular: the mind of a human being is the complex idea having that human being's body as its object, and hence the human mind and the human body are the very same thing, expressed under different attributes. The human body is a local and temporary aspect of God's own infinite extension; and the human mind is the corresponding, and indeed identical, local and temporary part of God's own infinite thought. Spinoza's substance monism entails that the human mind is not a substance in its own right, engaged in thinking ideas that are numerically distinct from God's ideas; instead, Spinoza holds that each human mind is a complex idea contained within God's infinite intellect (corollary to proposition 11 of Part 2), so that ideas in a human mind are literally shared with God. The human mind is, as it were, some of God's own knowledge – namely, God's knowledge in so far as it constitutes knowledge specifically of that human body, or God's knowledge of things from the limited perspective of that human body. When a mind has ideas of things together with the ideas of their causes, the mind has ideas that are *adequate* and *true* – ideas of the intellect – and it understands in just the same way that God does. When the mind has ideas of things without the ideas of their causes, it has *inadequate* and *false* ideas, ideas of the imagination, and the mind's understanding is mutilated and confused in comparison with God's more comprehensive and complete understanding, which does include ideas of these causes. All ideas by their nature involve an affirmation of their content, according to Spinoza (proposition 49 of Part 2). He therefore denies Descartes's doctrine that a mind can sometimes choose whether to affirm or deny the content of its ideas; instead, the mind will necessarily affirm that content unless it also has other ideas that necessarily lead the mind to reject it.

Human Nature and the Emotions

Spinoza's account of human nature and the emotions is the result of conjoining his general conception of the nature of finite beings with his theory of the distinguishing features of human beings. This account is often called his "psychology," and this designation is not entirely erroneous; but it is misleading if it is taken to imply that his account concerns only the mental, or the realm of thought, for on Spinoza's conception of the emotions, they are equally modes of thought and of extension (definition 3 of Part 3).

Although Spinoza asserts clearly and emphatically that there is only one genuine substance, he does not deny that some modes of this substance, including human beings, are what we may also properly call *things* – that is, proper subjects for the ascription of qualities in their own right. Modes of God qualify as *things* to the extent that they constitute (finite) approximations to the nature of a (necessarily infinite) substance. Since substance is, for Spinoza, entirely self-caused, something is a *thing* to the extent that it approximates to being self-caused, i.e., to the extent that it constitutes the sufficient necessitating explanation for its own existence. Of course, no finite mode is eternal, and so every finite mode must be brought into existence originally by something other than itself; but a finite mode can none the less be a cause of its own *continued* existence to the extent that it exerts causal power to *maintain* itself in existence. Hence, as Spinoza claims in proposition 6 of Part 3, "Each thing, insofar as it is in itself, strives to persevere in its being." His argument for his doctrine that all things have a striving (*conatus*) for self-preservation offers a good example of his "rationalistic" method. He justifies the doctrine not on the basis of extensive observation, although he no doubt thinks that it is confirmed by observation, but rather on the basis of a consideration of the conditions for being a *thing* – that is, for being *substance-like* – at all. The more something constitutes a finite approximation to a genuine infinite substance, the more power it will have and exert to preserve itself in being. For a finite thing truly to *act* (i.e., to be active) is to be the cause of effects through its own essential endeavor to persevere in being (definition 2 and proposition 7 of Part 3).

Like all things in nature, human beings strive to persevere in their being, according to Spinoza; but they differ from most other things in three related respects. First, like some other animals but unlike other beings, they have highly complex bodies that are capable of forming, retaining, and utilizing (for purposes of self-preservation) relatively distinct *images* of things. That is to say, they have highly developed sense organs that provide them with imaginative (including sensory) representations of the world. These representations, considered as modes of the attribute of thought, are ideas of states of the human being's own body, states that owe a considerable part of their natures to – and hence also represent, although incompletely and inadequately – states or qualities of external things. Second, because human beings are such complex mechanisms, they are not only capable of exerting considerable power for self-preservation, they are also capable of undergoing increases and decreases in the amount of power for self-preservation they possess. Third, and most distinctively, as they increase their capacity for active self-preservation, they are capable not only of imagination but also of a considerable degree of conscious intellection – that is, of consciously forming adequate ideas of things.

The nature of human beings thus makes them susceptible to three basic emotions, or *affects*, which are "affections of the Body by which the Body's power of acting is increased or diminished, aided or constrained, and at the same time, the ideas of those affections" (definition 3 of Part 3). The first of these basic emotions is *desire* (*cupiditas*), which is the basic endeavor toward self-preservation as it becomes directed toward some particular object that a human being represents to itself. The second is *joy* (*laetitia*), which is an increase in self-preservatory power for action. The third is *sadness* (*tristitia*), which is a decrease in self-preservatory power for action. Desires and joys can be either passions or active emotions, but sadness can only be a passion. Spinoza catalogs and explains the enormous variety of other human emotions as particular combinations or kinds of these three basic emotions in so far as they have various causes and objects. Whenever an emotion is caused by external forces of one kind or another, it is a *passion*; when it results entirely from the human being's own power, it is an *active emotion*.

Ethical Theory

This description of human nature and emotions raises, and at the same time provides Spinoza with much of his basis for answering, the question of what the right kind of life for a human being is. He firmly rejects legalistic conceptions of ethics, according to which the right way of living is determined by conformity to a code specifying that some actions or omissions of actions are obligatory while others are impermissible: "Absolutely, it is permissible for everyone to do, by the highest right of nature, what he judges will contribute to his advantage" (article 8 of the appendix to Part 4). Although citizenship is properly concerned with obedience to laws enacted by the state, ethics for Spinoza is concerned not with edicts of permission and obligation but with discovering the *best* way of living. Popular religion, he believes, errs in conceiving of ethics as a matter of obedience to the *positive commands* of an anthropomorphized and monarchical God, when in fact true ethics requires an understanding not of divine commands but rather of the *natural laws* governing human well-being or advantage. For the *best* way of living is that which maximizes one's advantage – that is, one's good – and thereby achieves that for which (as Spinoza has argued in Part 3 of the *Ethics*) every human being naturally and necessarily strives: namely, the preservation of his or her being. Since the preservation of one's being must be everyone's goal as a matter of metaphysical necessity, no one can consistently deny that it constitutes his or her good. Accordingly, there is no need for an ethics that externally commands or enjoins; for to know ethics is simply to understand adequately where one's true advantage or good lies (i.e., what will truly preserve one's being), and the very ideas that constitute this true knowledge will necessarily also constitute emotions of desire for what is known to be one's good. Spinoza does not, of course, deny (indeed, he emphasizes) that human beings frequently desire what is not really good for them; but he does hold that this occurs only through their having inadequate ideas of things, ideas which manifest their own lack of power to understand more adequately. Such desires are passions, external perversions of the natural direction of human *conatus*. Subjection to passions is what Spinoza calls *human bondage*; and it is the task of ethics to show how such bondage may be overcome.

Spinoza uses four closely related concepts to express his specific ethical doctrines. The first of these is the concept of *the good* – that is, the concept of that which is useful in the endeavor to persevere in one's being (definition 1 of Part 4), or (equivalently for Spinoza) that which aids one in "approaching the model of human nature that we set before ourselves" (preface to Part 4). The second concept is that of *virtue*, which he regards as identical to that of *power* (definition 8 of Part 4). The third concept is that of *guidance of reason* or *dictate of reason*, which signifies what one does in so far as one understands things adequately. The fourth is the concept of *the free man*, which is the concept or model of human nature that we properly strive to exemplify. Part 4 of the *Ethics* offers a number of specific claims about what is good or evil, what one does from virtue, how one acts under the guidance of reason, and (in its final propositions) the nature and behavior of the free man. The last three concepts are, in fact, practically equivalent. Although only God absolutely satisfies Spinoza's definition of *freedom*, human beings can approximate more or less closely to being free: to act freely – that is, to be determined from one's own nature alone – is to be the adequate cause of one's own perseverance in being. To whatever extent human beings act freely, however, they also exert their own power – that is, their virtue. Moreover, one acts freely, or from one's own power or virtue, just to the extent that one has adequate ideas and so is guided by reason, for only to the extent that one's ideas are adequate are they the result of one's own power rather than one's weakness and the impositions of external forces. The good is therefore equivalently whatever enables us to become free, virtuous, or guided by reason.

Although its basis is undeniably egoistic, the ethical theory that Spinoza provides in these terms is nevertheless a cooperative rather than a competitive one. This is because "knowledge of God is the Mind's greatest good" (proposition 28 of Part 4), and this good "can be enjoyed equally by all" (proposition 36 of Part 4), for someone's acquiring it leaves no less for others. On the contrary, Spinoza holds that nothing is more useful to a human being in the pursuit of knowledge than the genuine friendship of other human beings. Spinoza argues that knowledge is the highest good on the grounds that what each individual thing strives to achieve in order to persevere in being must be its good, and the human mind's endeavor to persevere in its being is nothing other than its endeavor to realize understanding (demonstration of proposition 26). For Spinoza, of course, *knowledge of God* is not distinct from knowledge of other things; because God is the only substance, all knowledge is really knowledge of God.

The content of Spinoza's ethical theory thus emphasizes the joy (i.e., increase in self-preservatory power for action) that consists in the achievement of adequate – that is, intellectual – understanding, understanding that allows one to acquire further adequate understanding and to live freely and virtuously under the guidance of reason. Those who come to understand the divine nature as it manifests itself in the natural world and in human life will remain undisturbed by reverses, Spinoza thinks, and will not be tormented by "what ifs," for they will understand that what occurs must occur of necessity and could not have failed to occur. Blame and disapprobation for others are species of hatred, which is a form of sadness; hence, those who are virtuous and free are less subject to these passions and instead pursue the joy of understanding in fellowship through the resources provided by the knowledge that they already enjoy. To the extent that they are virtuous and free, they also do not feel pity, humility, or repentance, for these, too, are all species of sadness. They do not even fear their own dissolution, for "a free man thinks of nothing less than of death, and his wisdom is a meditation on life, not on death" (proposition 67 of Part 4).

Blessedness

As will be apparent from the foregoing sketch, Spinoza seems to provide two quite different and seemingly conflicting conceptions of the nature of the good for a human being. On the one hand, it consists, as it does for all things, in persevering in existence – that is, in not ceasing to exist (as is confirmed in proposition 39 of Part 4). On the other hand, it consists in adequate understanding (as emphasized in proposition 27 of Part 4). Yet humans and other beings often continue in existence for many years in relative ignorance; and adequate understanding of things, while sometimes useful in avoiding or forestalling death, is nevertheless frequently accompanied by an early demise – as it was in Spinoza's own case. Part 5 of the *Ethics* serves, in part, to reconcile these seemingly conflicting conceptions by showing how adequate understanding constitutes a higher kind of perseverance in being even when it does not lengthen the duration of one's biological life. In doing so, it also explains what true blessedness is and how it is possible that human beings achieve it.

Because of his doctrine that the human mind is identical with the human body, Spinoza's philosophy offers no prospect of an afterlife in which an individual human mind continues to experience and remember its earlier experiences without the existence of its body; the death of the finite body must equally be the death of the finite mind. Nevertheless, he argues that an important *part* of the human mind is eternal (proposition 39 of Part 5). This part is the intellect (corollary to proposition 40 of Part 5). For the intellect, as distinguished from the imagination, consists of adequate ideas of pervasive and eternal aspects of the universe that are not dependent on the particular perspective of a particular human being. These very ideas (and not merely ideas similar in content) are therefore in God, not only in so far as he constitutes a particular human body, but also eternally and pervasively. They did not come into existence with a particular human being, and they will not go out of existence with that human being. Rather, some of the very ideas that are eternal in God's infinite intellect come also to be included, with greater or less conscious power of thinking, in the mind of a particular human being during that human being's lifetime. The greater the extent to which the intellect dominates the imagination of a particular human being, the more he or she understands the universe from an eternal, rather than a local, perspective, and the greater the part of his or her mind that *remains* – although not, of course, *as* his or her mind – after death. Eternal life is not, for Spinoza, something that a human being achieves after death; rather, it is an eternal way of being in which the intellect allows a human being to participate while he or she is alive. Yet, because it is at once the maximization of one's present being and a participation in the eternal, it constitutes the highest kind of perseverance in being of which human beings are capable.

To improve one's intellect is to participate in God's eternal intellect, in Spinoza's view, but it is also something more: it is to participate in God's blessedness itself. Whenever a human being acquires adequate understanding, this event is an increase in his or her power for action (because it facilitates further understanding) and so constitutes active joy while at the same time giving power over the passions. To the extent that one understands that God is the ultimate cause of this joy, it will be (by the definition of *love* in the *scholium* to proposition 13 of Part 3) a *love of God*. This intellectual love of God, like everything else that exists, must itself be in God; and hence there is, in some sense, an "emotional" as well as an intellectual aspect to God's thought. Speaking loosely, Spinoza states that this intellectual love of God is a share of the very love with which God (through a mode constituting a human being) loves Itself (proposition 36 of Part 5) and with which God loves (as modes of Itself) human beings (corollary to proposition 36). But the emotion that human beings experience as love cannot literally be joy or love *to God* as God, since God is eternally and absolutely perfect; an increase in power for action on the part of a finite mode of God is not an increase in God's own power for action. God's eternal perfection, of which human joy is a temporally occurring manifestation, is what Spinoza calls "blessedness." To the extent that a human being participates in the eternal perspective, not merely *increasing* knowledge and power but enjoying its already eternal perfection, he or she participates in divine blessedness. This blessedness is not, as popular religion would have it, an externally bestowed reward for obedience and restraint of our corrupt natures; as Spinoza says in the final proposition of the *Ethics*, "Blessedness is not the reward of virtue, but virtue itself; nor do we enjoy it because we restrain our lusts; on the contrary, because we enjoy it, we are able to restrain them" (proposition 42 of Part 5). The achievement of Spinozistic blessedness consists in adequate philosophical and scientific knowledge of God-or-Nature, including the very kind of knowledge that makes it possible to understand what blessedness is and how it is possible. It is a fitting kind of salvation for a philosopher who sought, above all, to break down the dichotomy between the natural and the divine.

Bibliography

Editions and translations

Spinoza, Benedict de (1925) *Spinoza opera*, 4 vols, ed. Carl Gebhardt. Heidelberg: Carl Winter.

Spinoza, Benedict de (1928) *The Correspondence of Spinoza*, ed. and trans. A. Wolf. London: Allen and Unwin.

Spinoza, Benedict de (1985) *The Collected Works of Spinoza*, vol. 1, ed. and trans. Edwin Curley. Princeton, NJ: Princeton University Press.

Spinoza, Benedict de (1989) *Tractatus theologico-politicus*, ed. and trans. Samuel Shirley. Leiden: Brill.

Spinoza, Benedict de (2000) *The Ethics*, ed. and trans. G. H. R. Parkinson. Oxford: Clarendon Press.

Studies

Allison, Henry (1987) *Benedict de Spinoza: An Introduction*, rev. edn. New Haven, CT: Yale University Press.

Bennett, Jonathan (1984) *A Study of Spinoza's Ethics*. Indianapolis, IN: Hackett.

Bennett, Jonathan (1991) Spinoza's monism. In Y. Yovel (ed.), *God and Nature: Spinoza's Metaphysics*. Leiden: Brill.

Bennett, Jonathan (2001) *Learning from Six Philosophers*. Oxford: Oxford University Press.

Curley, Edwin (1969) *Spinoza's Metaphysics: An Essay in Interpretation*. Cambridge, MA: Harvard University Press.

Curley, Edwin (1988) *Behind the Geometrical Method*. Princeton, NJ: Princeton University Press.

Curley, Edwin (1991) On Bennett's interpretation of Spinoza's monism. In Y. Yovel (ed.), *God and Nature: Spinoza's Metaphysics*. Leiden: Brill.

Curley, Edwin and Moreau, Pierre-François (eds) (1990) *Spinoza: Issues and Directions*. Brill's Studies in Intellectual History, vol. 14. Leiden: Brill.

Delahunty, R. J. (1985) *Spinoza*. London: Routledge and Kegan Paul.

Della Rocca, Michael (1996) *Representation and the Mind–Body Problem in Spinoza*. New York: Oxford University Press.

Donagan, Alan (1988) *Spinoza*. Chicago: University of Chicago Press.

Garrett, Don (1991) Spinoza's necessitarianism. In Y. Yovel (ed.), *God and Nature: Spinoza's Metaphysics*. Leiden: Brill.

Garrett, Don (ed.) (1996) *The Cambridge Companion to Spinoza*. New York: Cambridge University Press.

Garrett, Don (2001) Spinoza's *conatus* argument. In O. Koistinen and J. Biro (eds), *Spinoza: Metaphysical Themes*. Oxford: Oxford University Press.

Grene, Marjorie (1973) *Spinoza: A Collection of Critical Essays*. New York: Anchor/Doubleday.

Gueroult, Martial (1968–74) *Spinoza*, 2 vols. Paris: Aubier.

Hampshire, Stuart (1951) *Spinoza*. New York: Penguin.

Koistinen, Olli and Biro, John (eds) (2001) *Spinoza: Metaphysical Themes*. Oxford: Oxford University Press.

Mason, Richard (1997) *The God of Spinoza*. Cambridge: Cambridge University Press.

Matheron, Alexandre (1969) *Individu et communauté chez Spinoza*. Paris: Les Editions de Minuit.

Parkinson, G. H. R. (1954) *Spinoza's Theory of Knowledge*. Oxford: Clarendon Press.

Wolfson, Harry Austryn (1934) *The Philosophy of Spinoza*, 2 vols. Cambridge, MA: Harvard University Press.

Yovel, Yirmiyahu (1989) *Spinoza and Other Heretics*, 2 vols. Princeton, NJ: Princeton University Press.

Yovel, Yirmiyahu (ed.) (1991) *God and Nature: Spinoza's Metaphysics*. Leiden: Brill.

26

John Locke, *Essay Concerning Human Understanding* (1690)

An Empirical View of Knowledge and Reality

Vere Chappell

Locke's *Essay* is the most important book of philosophy ever written by an Englishman. Its importance is twofold: it is full of original doctrine and argument on central issues in epistemology and metaphysics; and it had a major role in shaping the thought of subsequent philosophers, not only in Britain but on the European continent. The *Essay* is famous, above all, for its statement and defense of empiricism. Locke (1632–1704) was not the first philosopher to stress the importance of sense experience in the acquisition of knowledge. But in the *Essay* he worked out a more detailed, more comprehensive, and more convincing form of empiricism than any of his predecessors had done.

Locke says that his purpose in the *Essay* is "to enquire into the Original, Certainty, and Extent of humane Knowledge; together, with the Grounds and Degrees of Belief, Opinion, and Assent" (I, i. 2: 43; references to the *Essay* cite book, chapter, section, and page in Locke, 1975). This makes it sound as if his subject is epistemology, the theory of knowledge, and nothing more. But in fact the *Essay* is at least as much a work of metaphysics, the theory of reality. This is obvious from the specific topics that are treated: besides knowledge and its surrogates, these include substance, modes, and qualities; space, time, and number; bodies, minds, and persons; existence and identity; God, freedom, and immortality.

A casual reader might wonder whether the order in which these topics are treated in the *Essay* is controlled by any systematic plan, so loose and rambling and uneven does the discussion sometimes appear. Locke does have some trouble staying on the paths he sets for himself; he is a frequent and voluminous digresser. He is also wont to go over the same ground several times: he himself apologizes for the "repetitions" to be found in his text (epistle: 8). But the *Essay* does have a controlling plan, one that, besides being coherent, is quite highly structured.

At its most general level, the plan of the *Essay* is dictated by Locke's general conception of knowledge. Knowledge, he holds, is a complex achievement of the human mind, not something we simply find in ourselves but a product of the mind's activity. The mind does not fashion knowledge out of nothing; it must use pre-existing materials. These materials are the various *ideas* it has within itself. How then do these ideas get into the mind? Locke has both a negative and a positive answer. His negative answer is that ideas are not "innate" in the mind, any more than knowledge is. That is, they are not in it from birth, as part of its natural or God-given endowment. This is Locke's anti-innatism. His positive answer is that all ideas come into the mind, after birth, from experience. This is his empiricism.

Locke undertakes to prove the truth of his anti-innatism; that is, he offers arguments by which, he maintains, innatism is conclusively refuted. He makes no comparable claim to prove his empiricism. This positive doctrine is incompatible with innatism, but is not simply equivalent to its denial: other options are available to the anti-innatist. Hence the arguments designed to refute innatism do not themselves serve to establish empiricism. And in fact Locke offers no arguments directly in support of empiricism. What he does is try to show that all the ideas we have can be accounted for on empiricist grounds, as having come into our minds from experience. Success at that venture will justify empiricism, not by proving it true or its denial false, but by demonstrating its explanatory adequacy.

Locke's central task, then, is to carry out this empiricist program, to show how the ideas we have arise in our minds from experience. Or rather, this is the first part of his central task, for he has also to show how the mind, its materials given, proceeds to produce knowledge out of them. Locke devotes the second of the four books of the *Essay*, entitled "Of Ideas," to this first part of his task. The second part is then taken up in the fourth book, "Of Knowledge and Opinion," although it turns out that Locke says relatively little, there or anywhere, as to how knowledge is generated. What he does discuss in Book IV is the general nature of knowledge, its various characteristics, and its limitations, along with the nature and strengths of its surrogates, judgment, probable opinion, and faith. Together these two books, II and IV, contain the heart of the *Essay*.

What then of Books I and III? Book I, "Of Innate Notions," is devoted to Locke's arguments against innatism. These arguments are meant to prepare for the constructive work of Book II, but are not themselves part of it. Book III, "Of Words," is also not part of Locke's main line of inquiry, starting with ideas and proceeding to knowledge; it is, strictly, a digression from that. But because of the close "connexion" between ideas and words, Locke says, "it is impossible to speak clearly and distinctly of . . . Knowledge . . . without considering, first, the Nature, Use, and Signification of Language" (II, xxxiii. 19: 401).

Let us move now to a more detailed survey of the *Essay*. First comes Locke's attack on innatism in Book I. His initial target is the doctrine of innate knowledge: that there are certain "principles" which are, as it were, inscribed on the mind at its inception, such that they can be apprehended without effort and are incapable of being doubted. Locke distinguishes between two applications of the doctrine, one to theoretical or "speculative" principles, the other to action-oriented or "practical" ones, and brings several arguments against each of them. In the final chapter of Book I he turns to the doctrine of innate ideas, which holds that whether or not there is knowledge that is innate, some of the materials of knowledge – that is, some ideas – are. He then marshals a new set of arguments against this second form of innatism. His conclusion at the end of the book, as he puts it at the beginning of Book II, is that the human mind is "white Paper" at birth, "void of all Characters" (II, i. 2: 104). It is thus, as he thinks, ready and waiting to be written upon by experience.

In Book II Locke takes up his main positive task, the first part of which is to show how the ideas we possess all have their origins in experience. He begins by distinguishing two forms of experience, sensation and reflection. Sensation is sensory experience, involving the five external senses; reflection is the awareness of the processes occurring within our minds. Some of our ideas, Locke says, arise from one of these sources, some from the other, and some from both. He next introduces a distinction between simple and complex ideas. Simple ideas come directly from experience and the mind is purely passive in receiving them. Complex ideas are those which the mind has an active role in producing, constructing them out of simple ideas which it already possesses. Locke then puts the two distinctions together, thereby generating a scheme by which all the ideas we have can be classified. It turns out that most of the ideas that are divided according to origin, those from sensation, or from reflection, or both, are simple ideas. Simple ideas of sensation are then subdivided into those which come through a single one of the external senses, and those which come through more than one. As for complex ideas, they fall into three groups: modes, substances, and relations (or, as Locke sometimes says, ideas of modes, of substances, and of relations); and modes are further subdivided into simple and mixed modes. (Although Locke does not divide complex ideas in general according to origin, he does seem to apply this division to simple modes: the ideas of distance and of remembering are both [ideas of] simple modes, but the former is an idea of sensation, while the latter is an idea of reflection.) The whole scheme is shown figure 26.1, which also gives some examples of specific ideas that Locke places in the resulting categories.

This scheme largely determines the organization of Locke's presentation in Book II, though he does not always follow it perfectly. The book as a whole consists of thirty-three chapters. After an initial chapter, in which he sets up his inquiry and contrasts his conception of mind and thinking with that of the Cartesians, four chapters deal with the various kinds of simple ideas of sensation; the next briefly introduces the two basic simple ideas of reflection; the next after that lists a few simple ideas conveyed into the mind "by all the ways" of both sensation and reflection; chapter viii presents "some farther considerations concerning our simple ideas"; and chapters ix–xi examine perception or thinking and a few of its specific modes, the ideas of which are ideas of reflection.

Locke then turns to complex ideas and, after a short introductory discussion in chapter xii, spends fourteen of the next sixteen chapters examining various subcategories thereof: simple modes compounded of certain simple ideas of sensation (chapters xiii–xviii), simple modes of thinking (chapter xix), mixed modes (chapter xxii), (ideas of) substances (chapters xxiii–xxiv), and relations (chapters xxv–xxviii). In the remaining two of these chapters, he discusses – out of order – the ideas of pleasure and pain (chapter xx) and that of power (chapter xxi); these discussions are out of order because these three ideas are not only not simple modes, they are not even complex ideas: they are rather simple ideas of both sensation and reflection.

Simple ideas	
Of sensation	
Of one sense	
Of sight	Colors (e.g. red)
Of hearing	Sounds (e.g. that of a bell)
Of taste	Tastes (e.g. that of wormwood)
Of smell	Smells (e.g. that of a rose)
Of touch	Heat, cold, solidity
Of more than one sense	Space, figure, motion
Of reflection	Perception or thinking, volition or willing
Of both sensation and reflection	Pleasure, pain, existence, unity, power
Complex ideas	
[Of] modes	
[Of] simple modes	Distances, durations, numbers
[Of] mixed modes	Obligation, drunkenness, a lie
[Of] substances	Individual bodies, finite spirits, God
[Of] relations	Causation, identity, moral rectitude

Figure 26.1   Locke's classification of ideas in Book II of the *Essay*

At the end of this survey of complex ideas, Locke devotes four chapters (xxix–xxxii) to various properties that may be attributed to ideas of all categories, simple or complex, of sensation or of reflection. These properties come in pairs, of which there are five: clarity–obscurity, distinctness–confusedness, reality–fantasticalness, adequacy–inadequacy, and truth–falsity. The final chapter of Book II takes up the association of ideas; this chapter in fact was not included in the *Essay* until its fourth edition, so that in the first three editions Book II ended with chapter xxxii.

Although Locke's stated purpose in Book II is to explain how the ideas in each of the categories he distinguishes originate in our experience, he often stops to consider these ideas themselves, that is, their content as opposed to their genesis. Otherwise (though equivalently) put, he stops to examine the natures of the things or phenomena which these ideas are the ideas of. Thus in chapter viii he points out that the simple ideas of sensation that he has been presenting are ideas of the qualities of physical objects existing outside our minds, whereas ideas themselves are entities existing within our minds. He then launches into a discussion of qualities, in the course of which he draws and defends his famous distinction between primary and secondary qualities. In chapter ix Locke turns to ideas of reflection, beginning with that of perception or thinking. But instead of examining how we acquire this idea, he details the nature of perception itself, and what the mind does when it performs this operation. In the two following chapters he does the same for several other mental operations – remembering, discerning, comparing, abstracting, and such – barely noting that the ideas of these operations are ideas of reflection. And in later chapters of Book II this same pattern recurs. In chapter xxi Locke moves from a discussion of the idea of power to a searching analysis of one specific power, that of free action on the part of a human being; he even lays out a positive theory as to how such action is motivated. In chapter xxiii he starts with the idea of substance and proceeds to discuss the nature, first of an individual substance such as a horse or a stone, and second of a sort of component or ingredient that he claims every such substance must contain. The latter he also calls "substance," though he sometimes calls it "substratum" or "pure substance in general" to distinguish it from substance in the first sense of the word. And in chapter xxvii, where the official subject is identity conceived as one specific (idea of) relation, Locke's main concern is to establish wherein identity through time consists for different kinds of entity, including especially persons.

It is in these accounts of the things that our ideas represent that much of Locke's metaphysical doctrine is contained. These are also the parts of the *Essay* that have most attracted the attention of commentators and critics: the secondary literature is dominated by discussions of Locke on three topics: qualities, substance, and personal identity.

Locke's distinctive contribution on the subject of qualities is, first, a general definition of qualities as powers to produce ideas in our minds, and, second, an account of the distinction between primary and secondary qualities. The primary qualities (of a body) are those which, as he says, "are utterly inseparable from" it (II, viii. 9: 134); secondary qualities are those which "are nothing in the objects themselves but powers to produce various sensations in us by their primary qualities" (II, viii. 10: 135). Critics from Berkeley onward have attacked Locke's position, especially the distinction he draws. Either there is no such distinction, they have argued, or, if there is, Locke has radically mischaracterized it.

Locke's discussion of substance, in chapter xxiii, has also drawn fire from critics, more perhaps than any other topic in the *Essay*, and he himself seems unusually uncertain in the course of it, appearing to speak now on one side, now on the other, of several issues. The basic problem is that, on the one hand, Locke is convinced that an individual body is more than the sum of its qualities, that there must be something else which unites these qualities and in which they inhere – the substance of the body in question. And yet, on the other hand, the idea he has of this substance seems utterly devoid of content, which ought not to be possible given his theory of ideas and his empiricist doctrine as to their origins.

Locke's account of personal identity, presented in chapter xxvii, has also been a focus of particular interest on the part of Locke's readers, but in this case the response has not been so uniformly negative. Many philosophers have borrowed from Locke's account in their own efforts to deal with the "problem of personal identity," which "problem" indeed was first discovered by Locke. The problem is set by the fact that persons change from one moment to the next, and yet retain their identities – continue to be the same persons – through extended periods of time. Locke's question is: what makes someone the same person through time? And his answer is: sameness of consciousness, which usually boils down to memory. Person *A* existing now is the same person as person *B*, who existed at an earlier time, just in case *A* can be conscious of doing and experiencing at least some of the things that *B* did and experienced, in the same way that *B* was conscious of doing and experiencing them at the time – just in case, that is, that *A* can remember doing and experiencing those things. Note that

Locke makes no mention either of human bodies or of souls in his account: the criterion of identity he appeals to is purely psychological.

In Book III, Locke's general target is language. His treatment of it can be divided, roughly, into three parts. In the first, comprising chapters i and ii, he presents a general theory of "the signification of words." In the second, consisting of the next six chapters, he considers different categories of words: "general terms" in iii, "names of simple ideas" in iv, "names of mixed modes" in v, "names of substances" in vi, "particles" in vii, and "abstract and concrete terms" in viii. And in the third part, which covers the three final chapters, Locke examines various defects in language and its use. Some of these are natural "imperfections of words"; these are described in chapter ix. Some are the product of "wilful faults and neglects" on the part of language users; these "abuses of words" are taken up in chapter x. Finally, in chapter xi, Locke suggests a number of "remedies" of the imperfections and abuses lately catalogued.

The things in Book III that have most attracted the attention of scholars are, first, Locke's theory of signification, and second, his discussion of general terms and essences. Locke's theory of signification is encapsulated in two well-known formulas: first, that "Words in their primary or immediate signification, stand for nothing, but the ideas in the mind of him that uses them" (III, ii. 2: 405); and second, that though the words speakers use immediately signify their own ideas, "yet they in their thoughts give them a secret reference to two other things," namely "ideas in the minds also of other men, with whom they would communicate," and "the reality of things" outside the mind (III, ii. 4–5: 406–7). But it is far from obvious just how these formulas are to be understood, especially in view of other doctrines Locke professes, and there has been a good deal of controversy over the proper interpretation of them.

Locke's account of general terms and essences is presented in chapter iii of Book III. He begins by noting that most of the words we actually use are general words, applying not to single individuals but to multitudes, or rather to kinds, of things, and he asks how it is that "general words come to be made." This is a question for him because he takes it for granted, not only that "all things that exist are only particulars," but that the first words a child learns are words standing for particulars. Locke's answer is that "words become general by being made the signs of general ideas," and that the mind makes general ideas from particular ones "by separating from them the circumstances of time, and place, and any other ideas that may determine them to this or that particular existence" (III, iii. 6: 410–11). This separating process is "abstraction," which he has already described in Book II as one of the operations by which the mind constructs complex ideas from simple ones. The upshot is that "general and universal belong not to the real existence of things, but are the inventions and creatures of the understanding, made by it for its own use, and concern only signs, whether words or ideas" (III, iii. 11: 414). This is Locke's response to the traditional "problem of universals" – a version of conceptualism.

Locke then proceeds to ask what general words stand for, "what kind of signification" they have. His answer is that a general word signifies "a sort of things" – that is, a species or kind – and that it does so by signifying an abstract idea in the mind of the speaker or hearer of it. Since what determines the extension of a sort, and which individuals belong to it, has traditionally been said to be the essence of (the things of) that sort, Locke thinks it appropriate to speak of the abstract ideas that are signified by general words as essences too (III, iii. 14: 416). But then, noting that the word "essence" has had other connotations for its traditional users, beyond that of determining sort membership, he proposes that his abstract ideas be called nominal essences, and that the contrary term "real essence" be applied to "the real internal . . . constitution of things, whereon their discoverable qualities depend." For it is (probably) this, according to Locke's corpuscularian theory of (at least physical) reality, that most closely answers to the formula, "the very being of any thing, whereby it is what it is," by which the term "essence" has traditionally been defined (III, iii. 15: 417).

Having thus distinguished these two kinds of essence, real and nominal, Locke goes on to say quite a lot about both of them in the next three chapters of Book III. This discussion has been another main focus of interest on the part of Locke scholars.

As we have seen, Locke's treatment of language and essences in Book III is a digression from the main line of inquiry in the *Essay*, from ideas to knowledge. In Book IV he returns to that main line and takes up the subject, first, of knowledge, and second, of various surrogates of knowledge – judgment, opinion, belief, and faith – and matters related thereto – reason, probability, and error.

The discussion of knowledge extends through the first thirteen chapters of Book IV. The first four of these concern the nature of knowledge and some of its properties. In the first chapter Locke states his famous definition of knowledge: "the perception of the connexion and agreement, or disagreement and repugnancy of any of our ideas" (IV, i. 2: 525). He then distinguishes four "sorts" of agreement or disagreement: "identity or diversity," "relation," "co-existence or necessary connexion," and "real existence." In chapter ii, he lists three "degrees of our knowledge," which he labels "intuition", "demonstration," and "sensitive knowledge of particular existence." These labels are misleading, since what they connote are different ways or means of achieving knowledge, not variations in the knowledge achieved. Furthermore, that which admits of degrees, strictly speaking, is not knowledge but the certainty or evidence which necessarily attaches to it; for a perceptual or cognitive state of mind which lacks certainty, or at least a high degree of it, is not knowledge at all, but opinion.

In chapter iii, on the "extent of human knowledge," Locke considers the limitations on our knowledge, stressing that, despite our pretensions, we know relatively little. It is in this chapter that he makes his two startling pronouncements about scientific knowledge, that is, knowledge that is completely certain and fully general: on the one hand, that "morality is capable of demonstration," so that a science of morals is possible for us (although no one has yet achieved it); and that, on the other hand, physical science, a science of bodies, is not possible for us. It is also here that Locke raises the "scandalous" question of thinking matter. For all that we know, he says, there is no reason why God should not, "if he pleases, superadd to matter a faculty of thinking" (IV, iii. 6: 541). Locke does not of course think that God does or will do this; but merely suggesting the possibility of it was enough to call forth charges of blasphemy and even of atheism against him. In chapter iv Locke undertakes to show how it is that, even though "all knowledge lies only in the perception of the agreement or disagreement of our own ideas," some knowledge is none the less "real," that is, conversant with real beings existing apart from our ideas.

The next seven chapters of Book IV (v–xi) deal first with truth, and then with propositions, propositions being both the bearers of truth and the proper objects of knowledge. Locke begins with universal propositions, treating them generally in chapter vi and then examining two special types of them, "maxims" and "trifling propositions," in chapters vii and viii. He then takes up particular propositions in chapters ix–xi. These all turn out to be propositions which affirm or deny existence of particular things, for universal propositions, he says, "concern not existence" at all. There are only three things, Locke believes, whose existence can be known. We have intuitive knowledge of the existence of our own selves, demonstrative knowledge of the existence of God, and sensitive knowledge of the existence of (some) bodies. In chapter x, he presents a demonstrative argument for the existence of God; and in chapter xi briefly considers skeptical worries about our knowledge of the existence of material objects. Rounding out Locke's treatment of knowledge in Book IV are two shorter chapters, xii on the "improvement of our knowledge" and xiii on "some farther considerations concerning" it.

There is a great deal of interesting material in Locke's discussion of knowledge, but scholars have been quite selective in their study of it. One question that has been addressed is that of the proper interpretation of Locke's definition of knowledge, especially as it applies to the case of "real existence." The problem here is obvious: how can knowing that something really exists be a matter of perceiving a relationship between two or more ideas? Real existence is surely not itself an idea, nor is there any pair of ideas the perception of whose connection would count as the knowledge of real existence. The conclusion some critics have reached is that the most Locke is entitled to claim is that we have probable opinion about real existence, and not knowledge.

Having finished with knowledge, Locke devotes the remaining eight chapters (xiv–xxi) of Book IV to cognitive states other than knowledge. He first considers judgment in chapter xiv. Judgment is a mental operation "whereby the mind takes its ideas to agree . . . without perceiving" that they do (IV, xiv. 3: 653). The products of judgment are beliefs or opinions, and these, like knowledge, "consist in propositions." Unlike knowledge, however, beliefs and opinions are characterized by probability rather than certainty. In chapter xv Locke discusses the nature of probability and how it is (or ought to be) determined, and in xvi he considers the different "degrees of assent" that correspond to the different degrees of probability that we assign to our beliefs. Then in chapter xvii he turns to reason, which might seem surprising in view of the traditional tendency to associate reason exclusively with knowledge. Locke, however, is quite deliberately flouting tradition, here and throughout this part of the *Essay*. Reason is a faculty, he makes clear, that is capable of producing probable belief as well as certain knowledge. Locke does not quite explicitly draw the distinction between deductive and inductive reasoning that later philosophers were to do, but he does seem to be working toward it.

Next comes chapter xviii on "faith and reason," where by "faith" is meant "religious faith." This chapter is appropriate here because faith is a form of belief or assent, although it is different not only from knowledge but also from empirically justified opinion: its basis is revelation by God. Locke's position is that reason and faith have "distinct provinces," but that, although there are truths of religion which go "beyond reason" and which it is legitimate for us to assent to "on faith," there are no truths on any subject which go "against reason." The next chapter, on "enthusiasm," was not part of the original *Essay*; Locke added it to the fourth edition. Its subject is a third supposed "ground of assent" pertaining to matters religious, distinct both from reason and from (legitimate) faith. "Enthusiasm," as the term was used in the seventeenth century, is a form of feeling or experience; and for the followers of certain religious sects this was the best or even the only proper means of discovering truths of religion. For Locke, however, enthusiasm really consists in "the ungrounded fancies of a man's own brain" (IV, xix. 3: 698). Chapter xix is a vigorous attack on those who rely on it.

Book IV concludes, finally, with a substantial chapter (xx) on "wrong assent or errour" and a short one (xxi) on "the division of the sciences"; these were chapters xix and xx in the *Essay*'s first three editions. Despite the variety and richness of the material contained in the last half of Book IV, scholars generally have given scant attention to it, apart from a few studies on the topic of reason and faith. The situation may now be changing, however, thanks in part to the work of Owen (1993) and Wolterstorff (1996).

Locke's achievement in the *Essay* as a whole has been variously judged. The book's impact on his immediate successors in Britain was enormous: college curricula were altered to reflect, not only its teachings, but its "plain, historical method," and the conception of philosophical inquiry it exemplified. In France, the *Essay* was a major factor, throughout the eighteenth century, in advancing the Enlightenment. In the nineteenth century, its reputation waned, as empiricism and analytic thinking generally came under attack: Locke's work was dismissed by Hegelian speculators as shallow and pedestrian. More recently, the pendulum has swung back, and the *Essay* is again in favor, the object both of scholarly study and of philosophical engagement. There is probably no contemporary philosopher who thinks that Locke told the exact truth and nothing else on any subject in the *Essay*. But there are many who credit him with being broadly right much of the time.

Acknowledgment

An earlier version of some parts of this chapter was included in the Introduction to Chappell (1998). This material is used here by permission of Oxford University Press.

Bibliography

Editions

Locke, John (1690) *An Essay Concerning Human Understanding.* London: Elizabeth Holt.
Locke, John (1975) *An Essay Concerning Human Understanding*, ed. Peter H. Nidditch. Oxford: Clarendon Press.

Studies

Aaron, Richard I. (1971) *John Locke*, 3rd edn. Oxford: Clarendon Press.
Ayers, Michael R. (1991) *Locke*, 2 vols. London: Routledge.
Chappell, Vere (ed.) (1994) *The Cambridge Companion to Locke.* Cambridge: Cambridge University Press.

Chappell, Vere (ed.) (1998) *Locke*. Oxford: Oxford University Press.

Cranston, Maurice (1985) *John Locke: A Biography*. Oxford: Oxford University Press (orig. pub. 1957).

Hall, Roland (1970–2000) Recent publications. *Locke Newsletter*, 1–31.

Hall, Roland (2001–) Recent publications. *Locke Studies*, 1– .

Hall, Roland and Woolhouse, Roger (eds) (1983) *80 Years of Locke Scholarship: A Bibliographical Guide*. Edinburgh: Edinburgh University Press.

King, Peter (1830) *The Life of John Locke*, 2 vols. London: Colburn and Bentley.

Lowe, E. J. (1995) *Locke on Human Understanding*. London: Routledge,

Mackie, J. L. (1976) *Problems from Locke*. Oxford: Clarendon Press.

Owen, David (1993) Locke on reason, probable reasoning, and opinion. *Locke Newsletter*, 24: 35–79.

Tipton, I. C. (ed.) (1977) *Locke on Human Understanding*. Oxford: Oxford University Press.

Wolterstorff, Nicholas (1996) *John Locke and the Ethics of Belief*. Cambridge: Cambridge University Press.

Woolhouse, R. S. (1983) *Locke*. Brighton: Harvester.

Yolton, Jean S. (1998) *John Locke: A Descriptive Bibliography*. Bristol: Thoemmes.

Yolton, Jean S. and Yolton, John W. (1985) *John Locke: A Reference Guide*. Boston: Hall.

Yolton, John W. (1956) *John Locke and the Way of Ideas*. Oxford: Oxford University Press.

Yolton, John W. (1970) *Locke and the Compass of Human Understanding: A Selective Commentary on the Essay*. Cambridge: Cambridge University Press.

Yolton, John W. (1993) *A Locke Dictionary*. Oxford: Blackwell.

27

George Berkeley, *Three Dialogues* (1713)

Idealism, Skepticism, Common Sense

George Pappas

George Berkeley's (1685–1753) *Three Dialogues between Hylas and Philonous* was first published in 1713. It was his third major book in just four years, having been preceded by the *Essay towards a New Theory of Vision* (1709), and the *Principles of Human Knowledge* (1710). (All references to the author's works will be to Berkeley, 1948–57, citing volume number and page.) It was the poor reception of the *Principles* that seems to have led Berkeley to compose the *Three Dialogues*. The former work met with some ridicule, and some went so far as to question Berkeley's sincerity with regard to the book's doctrines, and even to doubt Berkeley's sanity. Philosophically, it was thought that Berkeley denied outright the existence of all physical bodies, and that his position encouraged skepticism and a departure from common sense (see Bracken, 1965, who notes in detail how the *Three Dialogues* did not fare much better on this score than the *Principles*).

Since it is cast in dialogue form, the *Three Dialogues* differs markedly from the *Principles*. However, there are also differences in content. There is hardly any discussion of abstract ideas in the *Three Dialogues*, while the entire introduction of the *Principles* concerns abstraction. However, perhaps the most important differences are these: the *Three Dialogues* adds critical arguments for Berkeley's philosophy of immaterialism that were omitted from the *Principles*; also, in the *Three Dialogues*, Berkeley tries to show that the immaterialist doctrine is consistent with common sense, and that the materialist doctrines of Locke and others are not. Such a concern was present but in a muted form in the *Principles*. Finally, Berkeley argues in the *Three Dialogues* that his immaterialist doctrine provides for a refutation of skepticism concerning the existence and nature of physical bodies. Nevertheless, these differences of content aside, the core doctrines in Berkeley's immaterialist philosophy are the same in both works.

Immaterialism

Immaterialism is a thesis about physical objects and about perceivers who experience them. Any physical object, such as a chair, has a range of properties or what Berkeley would have called qualities. The chair will have some shape, and color, and surface texture, for example, and of course other qualities as well. The immaterialist thesis about objects is that they are identical to the collection of these qualities they are said to have. There is no material substratum or substance in which these qualities inhere, according to immaterialism; the object just *is* the set of qualities. More exactly, Berkeley identifies the object with the collection of its sensible qualities, i.e. the qualities of bodies one typically encounters in sense perception. Material substance, construed as a substratum of qualities, simply does not exist.

Berkeley develops this immaterialist view further into a version of idealism because he identifies each sensible quality with a sensible idea. Sensible ideas for Berkeley are phenomenal entities that are present in all cases of perception, after the fashion of what Locke termed "ideas of sensation." The idealist version of immaterialism about objects, then, is just that each object is nothing more than a collection of sensible ideas. Often Berkeley expresses this point by saying that anything sensible exists only in the mind. What this provocative claim comes to, however, is just that such entities exist if and only if they are perceived.

Perceivers, in contrast to things perceived, Berkeley regards as simple spiritual substances. They are simple in so far as they have no parts, and they are spiritual in so far as they are essentially Cartesian minds that are wholly non-material in nature. Minds are active in that they engage in acts of willing, imagining, remembering, reasoning, and perceiving. However, it is not true that minds exist only when they perceive or otherwise act. On this point Berkeley follows Locke, in opposition to what both took to be the Cartesian position.

Persons Berkeley regards as finite perceivers, here taking perceiving in the broad Cartesian sense to include all mental activity. There is, too, a unique infinite perceiver, namely God. Further, it is God to whom Berkeley adverts when he tries to explain how sensible physical objects and their qualities can exist when not perceived. The chair in the office continues to exist at night when there is nobody perceiving it because it is perceived at all times by God. In this way Berkeley can uphold the common-sensical claim that unperceived entities exist – they are not perceived by any *finite* perceiver – whilst at the same time he defends the general thesis that all sensible things exist if and only if they are perceived.

Is this *all* that exists in Berkeley's immaterialism, just various perceived things and finite and infinite perceivers? One might well wonder, what about unperceivable features of objects such as their micro-structure, and the micro-particles that enter into those structures; and about relations between objects both sensible and not perceivable; and about other sorts of properties such as moral properties; and about universals, and also abstract entities such as numbers and classes? Space considerations rule out a full discussion of these important topics. Briefly we can say that, for micro-particles and their properties and structural combinations, Berkeley defends an instrumentalist picture, according to which these posits are useful explanatory fictions. Relations

Berkeley seems to regard as in some way mind-dependent, though he says very little on the matter. Universals such as multiply instantiated properties Berkeley rejects outright; everything that exists both in the world and in the mind is particular. Numbers, and one suspects classes as well, Berkeley regards as mind-dependent constructions. Interestingly, however, Berkeley does seem to have felt that there are moral properties, though they are not perceived. This is based on the scattered remarks Berkeley makes about ethical theory; he never finished the projected part three of the *Principles*, which was to take up moral theory (see Olscamp, 1970).

Philosophy in the *Dialogues*

The first dialogue is concerned with the immaterialist account of objects, and simultaneously with criticism of an alternative position. To this end, Berkeley argues through his spokesman, Philonous, first that each sensible quality is an idea that exists only in the mind. He proceeds by enumeration, using arguments for sensible qualities taken one at a time. This set of arguments constitutes a major difference between the *Principles* and the *Three Dialogues*. In the former work, Berkeley assumed that each sensible quality is an idea (for example at *Principles* 5 [*Works*, II, 42–3]), both an untenable and an unwise move on his part.

For the heat and cold said to be in bodies Berkeley uses what we can call the *heat–pain* argument. A great heat, such as one gets by being too close to a fire, is a distinctive pain. Pains, Berkeley notes, exist only in the mind, and so he has Hylas, the other discussant in the dialogue, concede that "A very violent and painful heat cannot exist without the mind" (*Works*, II, 177). Berkeley is aware that the first premise in this argument needs defense, and he has Hylas distinguish between the heat in the body and the pain one feels. Berkeley argues, through Philonous, that when one experiences the heat of the fire and feels the pain, one experiences just one simple idea, so that

> Seeing therefore they are both immediately perceived at the same time, and fire affects you only with one simple or uncompounded idea, it follows that this same simple idea is both the intense heat immediately perceived and the pain; and consequently, that the intense heat immediately perceived, is nothing distinct from a particular sort of pain. (*Works*, II, 176)

Hylas tries to argue, naturally enough, that what holds for intense heat need not hold for very modest heat. It might well exist without (outside of and unperceived by) the mind. In reply Berkeley argues that modest heat generally is a pleasure, and certainly pleasures cannot exist without a mind.

A second argument is used for heat and cold together, namely an argument based on perceptual relativity. When one hand is cold and the other warm, and then both are put in water presumed to be of a uniform temperature, one hand will feel cold and the other hot. We cannot say that the water is both hot and cold, and so we ought to conclude that the principles that seem to generate that result are false. Those principles belong to Hylas, namely that qualities such as cold and heat are in the water. By concession, Hylas says: "I am content to yield this point, and acknowledge, that heat and cold are only sensations existing in our minds: but there still remain qualities enough to secure the reality of external things" (*Works*, II, 179). This comment by Hylas launches a series of relativity arguments, all aimed at the different sensible qualities: taste, odors, sounds, and colors. These are all conceded to exist only in the mind. However, these are all the so-called *secondary* qualities, and it occurs to Hylas that perhaps the *primary* quality should have a different status. Berkeley's strategy on this point is to argue that the primary qualities are no less subject to perceptual variability, and so are really just ideas in the mind. Taking extension as an example, Philonous asks

> Phil.:   Was it not admitted as a good argument, that neither heat nor cold was in
>   the water, because it seemed warm to one hand, and cold to the other?
> Hyl.:   It was.
> Phil.:   Is it not the very same reasoning to conclude, there is no extension or figure
>   in an object, because to one eye it shall seem little, smooth, and round, when
>   at the same time it appears to the other, great, uneven, and angular? (*Works*,
>   II, 189)

These relativity arguments show nothing about extension in general (while Berkeley makes full use of relativity arguments here in the first dialogue, he denied that they were quite so forceful in *Principles* 15; on this, see Winkler, 1989: 172ff). Extension in general, or extension considered merely as a determinable, might well exist outside the mind for all these relativity arguments show. Berkeley is thus led to tackle the question of extension in general. He notes first that the reality of extension in general conflicts with the thesis that everything that exists is particular which, he says, is a "uniformly received maxim" (*Works*, II, 192). Second, Berkeley argues that we cannot have an idea of extension in general. It would have to be an idea of extension, but no particular extension, neither large nor small, nor any specific extension between these two. He concludes that, if Hylas cannot have such an idea, "it will be unreasonable on your side to insist any longer upon what you have no notion of" (*Works*, II, 193).

An alternative position to Berkeley's thesis that all sensible qualities are just ideas would be that real sensible qualities inhere in material substance, and some of our ideas represent by resembling these qualities. The concept of material substance as a substratum of qualities is ridiculed, for it amounts to something like material substance standing under and supporting the qualities. This would require that material substance is extended, when *ex hypothesi* a substratum for qualities itself has no qualities, but serves merely as the bearer of them. The resemblance thesis is rejected on two grounds. First, our ideas are constantly changing in character, while real sensible qualities are supposed to be fixed. One would have to explain how the variable can resemble the fixed, or else show that some select members of the ideas have the resemblance. In the latter case, we would have no basis for making the selection. Second, Berkeley invokes what has come to be called *the likeness principle* (so named by Cummins, 1966: 63–9; Winkler, 1989: 141–8, criticizes Cummins's account and proposes an alternative), viz., the claim that an idea can only be like, or resemble, another idea. If this principle is correct, it seals the fate of the alternative account.

Berkeley's immaterialist account of objects is incomplete by the end of the first dialogue. It is not till the third dialogue that we find him identifying objects with collections of ideas. He has Philonous say, "I am not for changing things into ideas, but rather ideas into things; since those immediate objects of perception, which according to you, are only appearances of things, I take to be the real things themselves" (*Works*, II, 244). He does not mean that each idea itself is a thing; instead, it is certain groups of ideas that make up things. As he says:

> I see this *cherry*, I feel it, I taste it: and I am sure *nothing* cannot be seen or felt or tasted: it is therefore *real*. Take away the sensations of softness, moisture, redness, tartness, and you take away the cherry. Since it is not a being distinct from sensations; a *cherry*, I say, is nothing but a congeries of sensible impressions, or ideas perceived by various senses. (*Works*, II, 249, emphasis in original)

Berkeley is thus not denying the existence of physical bodies, as many have supposed, but rather identifying them with sets of ideas.

What, though, explains these ideas we experience? One *natural* explanation would be that independently existing bodies provide the explanation. We experience the ideas by means of causal interactions with these bodies. Such a position, held by Locke and many others, Berkeley thinks is unsatisfactory. If these bodies partially consist in material substance, then the position is inconsistent because material substance is supposed to be causally inert. Also, the position is extravagant. A much simpler hypothesis, Berkeley argues, posits just *one* cause of these ideas, namely God. The existence of God and the rest of Berkeley's account of objects, is thus secured via an appeal to explanatory simplicity. (The discussion of God as the explanation for ideas occurs in the third dialogue, *Works*, II, 236. This is not Berkeley's only reason for thinking that God exists. He gives a different argument in the second dialogue, *Works*, II, 212ff.)

Skepticism and Common Sense

Berkeley argues in the third dialogue that his account of objects paves the way for a rejection of skepticism and also for a vindication of common sense. We may think of the discussion of skepticism as having three parts. First, the alternative account of objects one finds in Locke, and which is defended by Hylas, leads to skepticism. The root problem there is that the alternative account distinguishes between appearances (ideas) and real things. Then objects are never immediately perceived; we can only infer their existence and nature from the appearances and such an inference is precarious at best. Second, rejection of this alternative account removes the support for skepticism about bodies. By itself this does nothing to refute skepticism; it merely removes part of the support for skepticism. The refutation requires something additional. Berkeley nicely conveys this needed element in this passage:

> Wood, stones, fire, water, flesh, iron, and the like things . . . are things that I know . . . And I should not have known them, but that I perceived them by my senses; and things perceived by the senses are immediately perceived; and things immediately perceived are ideas; and ideas cannot exist without the mind; their existence therefore consists in being perceived; when therefore they are actually perceived, there can be no doubt of their existence. Away then with all that scepticism, all those ridiculous philosophical doubts . . . I might as well doubt of my own being, as of the things I actually see and feel. (*Works*, II, 230)

This passage indicates that Berkeley thinks that bodies and their qualities are immediately perceived, and that this fact allows us to have knowledge of such objects. Indeed, he sometimes says that the knowledge thus gained is immediate or, in the language of Locke, intuitive. He says, "I am the farthest from Scepticism of any man. I know with an intuitive knowledge the existence of other things as well as my own soul. This is w^t [*sic*] Locke nor scarce any other Thinking Philosopher will pretend to" (*Philosophical Commentaries* no. 563, in *Works*, I, 70). His idea is that since objects and their qualities are among the things we immediately perceive, we thereby acquire immediate, or intuitive, knowledge of such objects. Berkeley is actually being loose in his usage of the term "intuitive knowledge" here. As this term occurs in Locke, it is restricted to knowledge that has the highest degree of certainty, that is, where one cannot be in error. Berkeley does not claim anything of that sort for what *he* calls intuitive knowledge.

We might ask, however, how it is that objects count as immediately perceived things. The answer goes back to Berkeley's account of objects. These are reckoned collections of ideas. Then, by immediately perceiving some of the constituent ideas included in a given collection, one thereby immediately perceives the collection which is the object (on the immediate perception of objects and its connection to skepticism, see Glauser, 1999; Pappas, 2000).

At the very end of the third dialogue, Philonous says:

> I do not pretend to be a setter-up of *new notions*. My endeavors tend only to unite, and place in a clearer light, that truth which was before shared between the vulgar and the philosophers: the former being of the opinion, that *those things they immediately perceive are the real things;* and the latter, that *the things immediately perceived, are ideas which exist only in the mind.* Which two notions put together, do in effect constitute the substance of what I advance. (*Works*, II, 262, emphasis in original)

This makes it clear that in Berkeley's view a key element of common sense is the claim that physical objects are immediately perceived. No doubt he would also include the claim that we gain immediate knowledge of such objects in perceptual contexts as an element of common sense as well. Points such as these lead Berkeley to say a bit earlier in the third dialogue that it is his own immaterialist position that is "most agreeable to common sense, and remote from *scepticism*" (*Works*, II, 259; emphasis in original; Pappas, 2000, ch. 8). This very fact, he maintains, is one piece of evidence that immaterialism is correct.

Bibliography

Editions

Berkeley, George (1948–57) *The Works of George Berkeley*, ed. A. A. Luce and T. E. Jessop. Edinburgh: Thomas Nelson.

Berkeley, George (1979) *Three Dialogues between Hylas and Philonous*, ed. Robert Adams. Indianapolis, IN: Hackett.

Berkeley, George (1998) *Three Dialogues between Hylas and Philonous*, ed. Jonathan Dancy. New York: Oxford University Press.

Studies

Bracken, Harry (1965) *The Early Reception of Berkeley's Immaterialism*, rev. edn. The Hague: Martinus Nijhoff.

Cummins, Philip (1966) Berkeley's likeness principle. *Journal of the History of Philosophy*, 4: 63–9.

Glauser, Richard (1999) *Berkeley et les philosophes du XVIIe siècle: perception et scepticisme.* Sprigmont, Belgium: Mardaga.

Olscamp, Paul (1970) *The Moral Philosophy of George Berkeley.* The Hague: Martinus Nijhoff.

Pappas, George (2000) *Berkeley's Thought.* Ithaca, NY: Cornell University Press.

Pitcher, George (1977) *Berkeley.* London: Routledge.

Stoneham, Tom (forthcoming) *Berkeley's World.* London: Oxford University Press.

Winkler, Kenneth (1989) *Berkeley: An Interpretation.* Oxford: Clarendon Press.

28

G. W. Leibniz, *Monadology* (1714)

What There Is in the Final Analysis

Robert Sleigh

Those who offer survey courses on early modern philosophy have little difficulty in selecting texts for most of those regularly surveyed, e.g., Descartes, Spinoza, Malebranche, and Locke. The obvious and appropriate choices are, respectively, *The Meditations*, *The Ethics*, *The Search* (or, perhaps, *The Dialogues on Metaphysics*) and *The Essay*. By contrast, Leibniz (1646–1716) presents a problem. He published but one book on philosophy during his lifetime, *The Theodicy*. It is a work devoted primarily to offering purported solutions to various problems posed by the existence of evil. In fact, it does contain brief outlines of various of Leibniz's philosophical views outside the confines of philosophical theology. Those brief outlines contained in *The Theodicy* led some to request that Leibniz write out a summary of the leading ideas of his philosophical system. In response, in 1714, just two years before his death, he wrote two distinct such summaries in French: *Principles of Nature and Grace*, and a longer and more sophisticated summary, which is now known under a title he did not give it, the *Monadology*.

The *Monadology* is the subject of this chapter. It is as good a summary of his final views on metaphysics as is available in a single short work by Leibniz. None the less, there are surprising lacunae. Important aspects of his natural philosophy are never mentioned, e.g., his theory of space and time, and his account of force. Important aspects of his theory of knowledge are among the missing, e.g., his commitment to innate ideas, and his complex theory of truth. In metaphysics proper, his theory of free choice and his conception of well-founded phenomena are not explicitly mentioned.

In addition to lacking discussion of some crucial aspects of Leibniz's philosophy, some have claimed that the *Monadology* is just what you would expect of a summary written for political figures – superficial and inaccurate. I disagree with this assessment. My view is this. In the *Monadology*, Leibniz offered formulations of many of his fundamental metaphysical theses, as well as arguments in support of those theses in a number of cases. The charge of superficiality and inaccuracy is off target in the case of Leibniz's formulations of his fundamental metaphysical theses in the *Monadology*, but there is something to be said for the charge in the case of the arguments mustered therein in support of those theses.

My point may be illustrated by the first three sections of the *Monadology*, of which the first two are:

> The Monad, which we will discuss here, is nothing other than a simple substance; simple, i.e., without parts.

> And there must be simple substances, since there are composites; for the composite is nothing other than a collection or aggregate of simples.

Someone peculiarly prone to avoiding controversy might want to provide a metaphysically innocent reading of both these sections, taking the first as providing no more than a definition of "monad" and the second as providing no more than a definition of "composite," coupled with the weak claim that there are such. But there is no long-term relief from controversy available, since in section three Leibniz added the following: "these monads are the true atoms of nature, and, in a word, the elements of things."

In the first three sections of the *Monadology* Leibniz presented his major ontological thesis, formulated succinctly in a letter to De Volder of June 30, 1704, as follows: "Indeed, considering the matter carefully, it may be said that there is nothing in the world except simple substances, and, in them, perception and appetite." The idea is this: in a proper ontology, i.e., account of what there really is, there is need to commit oneself to the existence of monads, but there is no need to commit oneself to any other kinds of individuals. Since monads are simple, i.e., without parts, they are immaterial entities, which are mind-like in some sense. Hence, "considering the matter carefully," there is no need to commit oneself ontologically – not at the deepest level – to material objects.

So the first three sections accurately present Leibniz's major ontological thesis. But the reasoning in its favor offered by section two is weak, and masks an area of investigation to which Leibniz devoted prodigious amounts of thought. Leibniz was well aware of the following alternative to his conception of what is ultimately real: there are individual substances, i.e., basic items in an acceptable ontology, that are material, and, hence, are not simple, that is, without parts; furthermore, although material substances are composed of parts, none of those parts is simple, since matter is infinitely divisible. So Leibniz was well aware that there were philosophers who would reject out of hand his claim that "there must be simple substances, since there are composites; for the composite is nothing other than a collection . . . of simples."

Reconstructing Leibniz's deepest reasons for believing that, in the final analysis, there is no need to commit oneself to any individuals other than monads, is a daunting, deep, and continuing task of Leibniz scholarship. Some of the most useful material is to be found in his *Discourse on Metaphysics*, a summary of his then current metaphysics prepared in 1685 for Antoine Arnauld, and in the correspondence between Leibniz and Arnauld that ensued (see Sleigh, 1990). In section 12 of the *Discourse* Leibniz claimed that "the notions of size, shape, and motion are not as distinct as is imagined . . . and that is why qualities of this kind cannot constitute any substance." Spread throughout Leibniz's writings are arguments intended to establish that shape, infinite divisibility, and even extension, turn out on probing metaphysical analysis to be attributable only to phenomena, i.e., entities that are not to be admitted into the basic ontology, but rather are to be logically constructed from entities in the basic ontology, i.e., the monads. Since these arguments are not found in the *Monadology* they will not be pursued here. Suffice it to say that behind a number of them is the idea that it is a basic feature of any acceptable candidate for inclusion in an acceptable ontology as a basic individual that there be well-defined, non-conventional criteria for ascribing numerical identity over time to such individuals, coupled with the claim that individuals whose basic features are size, shape, and motion do not make the grade.

Sections four to six of the *Monadology* draw consequences from the thesis that the ultimate individuals are simple, and, hence, immaterial. The basic claim therein is that monads can begin only by creation and end only by annihilation, since the alternative beginning and ending, i.e., generation and corruption, applies only to composite entities. Section seven introduces the next major claim; namely, that there is no causal interaction among created monads. One might suppose that Leibniz was on his way to something like Malebranche's occasionalism, where only God (in Leibniz's scheme, the uncreated monad) has any real causal power. But section eleven makes clear that Leibniz was no occasionalist; therein, he claimed that "the natural changes of monads come from an internal principle that can be called active force. . . ." By "the natural changes" Leibniz meant those that are non-miraculous, thereby intending to leave room for one form of causal interaction between diverse monads, i.e., divine intervention.

Section seven accurately presents Leibniz's denial of causal interaction among created substances. But, similar to what we have seen in connection with sections one to three, the reasoning Leibniz offered in seven for its thesis is not Leibniz at his best. It is based on the idea that since monads are simple, there can be no replacement of parts that could account for changes in a monad; moreover, "accidents cannot . . . wander about" from one substance to another. Leibniz summarized his reasoning in a famous remark: "Monads have no windows through which something can enter or leave them." Catchy, but limp. Leibniz was aware that part-replacement and accident travel did not exhaust the possible accounts of causal interaction among substances. Reconstructing Leibniz's deepest reasons for believing that there can be no causal interaction among created substances is yet another daunting, deep, and continuing task of Leibniz scholarship. I suggest that the heart of the matter is Leibniz's belief that non-conventional identity over time in the case of individual substances is inconsistent with the idea that there is causal interaction between created substances. This conclusion allowed him to characterize numerical identity in the case of created substances as follows: substance x at t' is numerically the same substance as y at t (t' later than t) just in case there is some state of x at t' caused by some state of y at t. In any case, I am quite confident that Leibniz's deepest thinking on this subject is not captured by his rejection of "wandering accidents" and "windowed monads."

In the first eighteen sections of the *Monadology* Leibniz presented an account of the salient features of all monads, followed in sections nineteen to thirty by an account of three significant classes of monads: "bare monads," souls, and spirits. Much of the general account of monads concerns a description of the kinds of properties that they are capable of possessing, given that they are immaterial entities. Leibniz preceded this description with an important thesis concerning monads and their properties; namely, what has come to be called the identity of indiscernibles; i.e., the thesis that, for any monads *x* and *y*, if for any intrinsic feature *f*, *x* has *f* if and only *y* has *f*, then *x* = *y*. Note that this is a powerful principle; it is not a logical truth consequent upon an acceptable notion of numerical identity. What makes this thesis powerful (and controversial) is the claim that if *x* and *y* are different monads then there must be some *intrinsic* feature with respect to which they differ. Obviously, the exact content of this thesis turns on how the notion of an "intrinsic feature" is explicated.

Leibniz claimed that there are two basic types of properties possessed by monads – perceptions and appetitions. The latter consists in an action that accounts for change of perception in a monad. Hence, we may focus on Leibniz's account of perception. It should be noted initially that in the *Monadology* Leibniz appears to have assumed that, given that monads are immaterial substances, they must be mind-like, a conclusion that makes it plausible to assume that monads have perceptions as basic features. But surely there are other candidates, e.g., numbers and sounds. Leibniz was committed to a version of Cartesian dualism; namely, that the only viable candidates for types of individual substances, i.e., basic individuals in an acceptable ontology, are mind and body. As we have noted, although body makes the short list, ultimately it does not make the grade. The "short list" thesis is one for which Leibniz provided argumentation, although not in the *Monadology*. Leibniz's conception of perception is worth some scrutiny. It is this: a perception is a state of a simple entity that represents a multiplicity. It is typical of Leibniz's creative philosophical imagination to offer a general account of a phenomenon his contemporaries took as primitive. Leibniz noted that this account of perception left room for the possibility of a monad having perceptions of which it was not aware. And in the *New Essays* he provided arguments intended to prove that there are such, contrary to most of his contemporaries. The varying relations of a monad to its perceptions provided Leibniz with a basis for classifying them: bare monads are those not conscious of any of their perceptions; souls are monads with both consciousness and memory; spirits (the category that includes us) are monads with consciousness, memory, and the knowledge of necessary truths, which is the basis of reason, according to Leibniz.

This categorization of spirits provided Leibniz with an opportunity to introduce some of the lead elements of his theory of knowledge in sections thirty-one to thirty-six. Leibniz claimed therein that:

> Our reasonings are based on two great principles: the *principle of contradiction*, in virtue of which we judge to be false that which contains a contradiction, and to be true that which is opposed or contradictory to the false; and that of *sufficient reason*, in virtue of which we consider that no fact can be real or actual, and no proposition true, without there being a sufficient reason for its being so and not otherwise.

Leibniz then proceeded to claim that there are two kinds of truths – those of reasoning, and those of fact, i.e., necessary truths and contingent truths. It is natural, but misguided, to suppose that he took the law of contradiction to be the principle of necessary truths, and the principle of sufficient reason to be the principle of contingent truths. The first claim holds, although it needs detailed explication not to be found in the *Monadology*. The second claim does not hold. Leibniz held that every true proposition, necessary or contingent, has a sufficient reason, although in the case of the most basic necessary truths, e.g., *A* is *A* – what Leibniz termed identities – the sufficient reason is just their form. One would expect that in a scheme as well articulated as Leibniz's philosophy there would be a special principle for contingent truths, and, indeed, section forty-six tells us what it is – the principle of *fitness* or best. We will take note of some of the relevant points when we consider Leibniz's famous thesis that this is the best possible world.

For Leibniz, a proposition is a necessary truth just in case it may be reduced to an identity via a finite analysis, i.e., by a process of substituting *definiens* for *definiendum*. What is not stated in the *Monadology* is Leibniz's striking claim that some such account must also hold in the case of contingent truths. Roughly, the account comes to this: a proposition is a contingent truth just in case it is not a necessary truth, i.e., it is not provable via a finite analysis of the sort just described, but none the less there is an analysis of its subject and predicate concepts that approaches an identity as its limit. Why Leibniz believed this, and the nature of the analysis he thought held in the case of contingent truths, are outstanding problems of Leibniz scholarship.

In section thirty-seven Leibniz made use of his principle of sufficient reason in order to provide what purports to be a proof of the existence of God. In sections thirty-eight to fifty-five Leibniz outlined his beliefs concerning the nature of God and his creation of contingent things, culminating in the thesis that this is the best possible world. The alleged proof of God's existence in section thirty-seven brings out what appears to be an ambiguity in Leibniz's conception of a sufficient reason. The discussion in preceding sections would tempt one to offer some such account as this: α is a sufficient reason for the obtaining of β if and only if α obtains in conditions such that α's so obtaining is a sufficient condition of β's obtaining. Suppose, as Leibniz did, that there are infinitely many contingent items in the world, then the requirement that there be a sufficient reason for the obtaining of each such item might be satisfied in virtue of each contingent item having some other contingent item as its sufficient reason, given the account just noted. But sections thirty-seven and thirty-eight suggest a somewhat different conception of a sufficient reason; namely, a truly sufficient reason is one that not only provides a sufficient condition, but also does not, in turn, require a reason of the sort that it provides. This leads Leibniz to the conclusion that there must be a sufficient reason for the entire series of contingent things, which is not itself a member of that series – a necessary substance, i.e., God.

Leibniz articulated a conception of God as the being having all and only perfections – the unique perfect being. Three items introduced by Leibniz in the sections devoted specifically to God are especially noteworthy. First, there is the claim that essences, possibles, eternal truths, and the like depend for their reality on God's understanding, but not on God's will. The thesis that eternal truths, for example, do not depend on God's will is explicitly aimed at Descartes. The claim that such items none the less depend on God's existence in a way in which his existence does not depend on them is absolutely standard fare among Leibniz's contemporaries. I am not aware of a plausible account of it. Second, there is Leibniz's short summary in section forty-five of the ontological argument for the existence of God, together with an equally short summary of Leibniz's reasons for accepting a lemma, which he took to be his unique contribution to this grand old argument. Section forty-five reads, in part:

Thus only God, or the Necessary Being, has this privilege, that it is necessary that he exists, if it is possible. And since nothing can prevent the possibility of that which contains no limits and no negation, and consequently no contradiction, this by itself suffices to establish the existence of God *a priori*.

The first sentence formulates what Leibniz took his predecessors to have established; namely, it is necessary that God exists, if it is possible that God exists. The second sentence formulates the lead idea of Leibniz's reasoning in support of his lemma; namely, that it is possible that God exists (for further textual sources relevant to Leibniz's lemma and related matter, and a marvelous discussion thereof, see Adams, 1994: chs 4–8).

And, third, there is Leibniz's effort to establish that this is the best possible world. The argument goes this way. The context in which God makes a choice to create one of the infinitely many possible worlds or not to create at all includes God's omniscience, omnipotence, and perfect goodness. Like any choice of any agent, this choice is subject to the principle of sufficient reason. Given God's perfect goodness, the only relevant reason must have to do with the goodness of the state of affairs that would ensue were a given choice actually made. Given this as background Leibniz concluded that God would create no world were there not a unique world better than any other, i.e., a unique best possible world. But there is a world; and there would be none were God not to create a world. QED – this is the best possible world.

Leibniz was well aware that the orthodox position on this matter was the position formulated by Thomas Aquinas in article six of question twenty-five of the first part of the *Summa theologiae*. It amounts to this. Given the context of choice previously noted, we are assured that God has created a very good world. Indeed, we have reason to believe that God would have created the best possible world, were there such. But there is not, since any possible world may be improved by adding good individuals to it, thus creating a yet better world. It is this last claim that Leibniz rejected. His confidence that God would create no world were there none best displays his commitment to the principle of sufficient reason, and, more generally, to the primacy of metaphysics, in an especially transparent manner. Leibniz's reasoning in favor of the thesis that this is the best possible world generated a problem concerning necessitarianism with which he wrestled throughout his philosophical maturity. Necessitarianism is the view that all true propositions are necessarily true. This is a view Leibniz rejected. Here is a sketch of an argument for necessitarianism that may appear to contain premises to which Leibniz was committed. God is necessarily morally and epistemically perfect; whoever is necessarily morally and epistemologically perfect necessarily makes the best possible choices; hence, necessarily, God chooses to create the best possible world. Necessarily, in virtue of his necessary omnipotence, what God chooses to create, he creates. Whatever possible world is best, is so necessarily. Any state of affairs that obtains in a possible world necessarily obtains in that possible world, since possible worlds are defined by the states of affairs that obtain in them. Hence, any state of affairs that actually obtains does so necessarily. Therefore, all true propositions are necessarily true. Just what Leibniz ultimately rejected in this argument is an outstanding question in Leibniz scholarship. Although Leibniz did not dwell on the problem of necessitarianism in the *Monadology* the tension is on display. There is no doubt that in formulating the principle of contingent truths in section forty-six Leibniz meant to imply that there are some contingent truths. Yet, in concluding his discussion of God's choice of a world to create in section sixty, he wrote: "Moreover, one sees in what I have just discussed the *a priori* reasons why things cannot be otherwise than they are."

Sections sixty-one to eighty-four concern composite entities, and, in particular, the relation of the soul to the body. The closing sections of the *Monadology*, sections eighty-five to ninety, concern God's special relation to spiritual monads (us and angels). Before turning to these sections, we need to note what Leibniz wrote in section forty-nine:

> A created being is said to act externally insofar as it has perfection and to be passively affected by another insofar as it is imperfect. Thus *action* is attributed to the monads insofar as it has distinct perceptions, and *passivity* insofar as it has confused perceptions.

This is an example of what might be termed a "replacement analysis," with which Leibniz's philosophy abounds. Recall that in his scheme there can be no causal interactions among created entities. In this "replacement analysis" Leibniz set out to explain what transpires at the level of ultimate reality – the monadic level – when we assert that one created entity is causally efficacious with respect to another. In assessing the acceptability of Leibniz's proposed analysis it is important to bear in mind that it is no part of his thesis that the analysis offered provides a correct account of the ordinary meaning of what is being analyzed.

We begin a survey of what Leibniz offered in the relevant sections concerning composite entities with the main theses. Leibniz held that there is a decomposition of the created world into corporeal substances, each of which consists in a body whose entelechy – soul in the case of animals – is a monad, which is said to dominate its body. Moreover, each created monad has a body, although the components of the body may alter over an interval of time during which the corporeal substance remains numerically the same. What are we to make of this? According to Leibniz, there are no bodies at the level of ultimate reality. So the bodies that are noted in his discussion of composite entities must be logical constructions based on monads, since there is nothing else on which they could be based. It is sometimes useful to reason as if a corporeal substance consisted in a dominant monad functioning in a soul-like way with respect to an infinite collection of other monads. That cannot be quite right; a body, in this scheme, is a logical construction from monads, and is not identical with some collection thereof. What sort of logical construction Leibniz envisaged is yet another open question of Leibniz scholarship (see Adams, 1994). And another open question is the proper account of domination, which is crucial to Leibniz's account of corporeal substances. Obviously the account must be in terms of the relative clarity of the perceptions of the monads involved, but the details are elusive.

Section seventy-eight applies a general theory about inter-monadic behavior to the case of the mind–body relation, a topic of considerable significance in seventeenth-century thought. Leibniz therein wrote:

> These principles provide me with a way of explaining naturally the union, or rather the conformity, of the soul and the organic body. The soul follows its own laws, and the body likewise its own, and they accord in virtue of the *harmony pre-established* among all substances, since they are all representations of one and the same universe.

The doctrine of pre-established harmony (pre-established by God) provided Leibniz with material for a solution to the mind–body problems under consideration in the seventeenth century, which he took to be preferable to what he saw as the main competitors, i.e., Descartes's "change the direction of motion" view, and Malebranche's occasionalism. Problems of interpretation surface here, however. In section seventy-eight Leibniz implies that the pre-established harmony is a logical consequence of the thesis that each monad in a possible world is a representation of that world, and, hence, expresses every other monad in that world. But Leibniz's formulations of the doctrine of universal expression make it appear to be a necessary truth; whereas, his formulations of the doctrine of the pre-established harmony (relative to the monads in this world) make it appear to be a consequence of divine activity that could have been otherwise. There are a number of open questions in this area that confront Leibniz scholarship.

Leibniz closed the *Monadology* by noting some crucial relationships between God and spiritual monads, i.e., those capable of moral reflection. He characterized the City of God, constituted by God and the spiritual monads, as a moral world within the natural world – a realm of grace within a realm of nature. Consideration of God's activity in the realm of nature and his activity in the realm of grace, and the resulting harmony of the two, permitted Leibniz the opportunity to express his piety, the sincerity of which one cannot doubt.

Bibliography

Editions and translations

Leibniz, G. W. (1875–90) *Die Philosophischen Schriften von G. W. Leibniz*, 7 vols, ed. C. I. Gerhardt. Berlin: Weidmann (reprinted Hildesheim: Georg Olms, 1965).

Leibniz, G. W. (1954) *Principes de la nature et de la grâce / Principes de la philosophie ou monadalogie*, ed. André Robinet. Paris: Presses Universitaires de France.

Leibniz, G. W. (1969) *Philosophical Papers and Letters*, trans. Leroy E. Loemker. Dordrecht: D. Reidel.

Leibniz, G. W. (1984) *Philosophical Essays*, trans. Roger Ariew and Daniel Garber. Indianapolis, IN: Hackett.

Leibniz, G. W. (1991) *G. W. Leibniz's Monadology: An Edition for Students*, trans. Nicholas Rescher. Pittsburgh, PA: University of Pittsburgh Press.

Studies

Adams, Robert Merrihew (1994) *Leibniz: Determinist, Theist, and Idealist*. New York and Oxford: Oxford University Press.

Broad, C. D. (1975) *Leibniz: An Introduction*. Cambridge: Cambridge University Press.

Rutherford, Donald (1995) *Leibniz and the Rational Order of Nature*. Cambridge: Cambridge University Press.

Sleigh, Robert (1990) *Leibniz and Arnauld: A Commentary on their Correspondence*. New Haven, CT: Yale University Press.

Wilson, Catherine (1989) *Leibniz's Metaphysics: A Historical and Comparative Study*. Princeton, NJ: Princeton University Press.

29

Giambattista Vico, *The New Science* (1730/1744)

The Common Nature of Nations

Donald Phillip Verene

What is commonly called Vico's *La scienza nuova* (*The New Science*) is the third edition of the work (first published in 1730), which Vico (1668–1744) was seeing through the press in his native city of Naples at the time of his death in January 1744.

Vico's Axioms and Method

Vico's work begins with an engraving and commentary in the Renaissance emblem tradition depicting the various elements of the life of nations as they develop in history. Vico says: "As Cebes the Theban made of moral, we present for view here a tablet of civil things, as will serve the reader to conceive the idea of this work before reading it, and to bring it back most easily to memory, with such aid as the imagination may afford after it is read" (par. 1). Vico's reference is to the Tablet of Cebes, which influenced the moral imagination of the Renaissance; it depicted a journey of the self, charting a course between virtues and vices upward toward the moral life. Vico employs this emblematic method, not in relation to the course of an individual's quest for virtue but in relation to the course of a nation's quest to develop itself in history. From this frontispiece Vico turns to a chronological table of the events of ancient nations, connected to a set of 114 axioms which provides the basis for his science of their histories.

The term Vico uses for axiom is *degnità*, which is a play on the Greek *axioma* that derives from *axios*, worthy. These axioms do not form a set of logically ordered elements as do the axioms of Spinoza. They do not appear on their surface to present immediate and self-evident truths as are claimed for axioms of geometry. They vary from such odd, particular, and seemingly empirical assertions as "The Phoenicians were the first navigators of the ancient world" (par. 302, axiom 101) to maxims such as "Honor is the noblest stimulus to military valor" (par. 277, axiom 89) and propositions such as "Uniform ideas originating among entire peoples unknown to each other must have a common ground of truth" (par. 144, axiom 13).

Vico was professor of rhetoric at the University of Naples and an expert on jurisprudence and Roman law. This must always be kept in mind when approaching his work. His *New Science* has the character of a complete speech about the nature of the human world which includes indications of the principles by which the reader can come to make this speech. The axioms are like commonplaces or *topoi* that the mind needs as points of thought in order to put the details of the histories of nations into the universal pattern of three ages that Vico calls *la storia ideale eterna* (ideal eternal history). He attributes the conception of these three ages to the Egyptians, as reported by Varro. Each nation originates in an age of gods, in which all the world is formed as full of gods, which passes into the age of heroes, in which the virtues and wisdom for the ordering of society are embodied in the personalities, traits, and deeds of heroes. This age finally passes into the purely secular age of humans, in which written law replaces natural custom and rational thought reduces the world to abstract orders, pushing into the background the great images of religion and the heroes. Thus the axioms are the most worthy thoughts, the keys to comprehending human history. They are what "dignify" or make sense of the civil world.

Vico claims that one thing is certain: that the world of nations has been made by humans. Since this world has been made by us we can know its truth. In this sense human making imitates divine making; God makes by knowing and knows by making. Vico's principle of the convertibility of true and made (*verum ipsum factum convertuntur*) is the basis of his conception of science. *Scienza* requires this convertibility. There can be a science of mathematics because mathematical truths are true because we make them, and a science of history because we make history. Natural science for Vico is not truly science but *coscienza*, a kind of consciousness practiced on the natural world because the objects to be known are not made by us. Not being their cause, we cannot fully know their being.

Vico's science of the world of nations requires philosophy to examine philology. Philosophy, which formulates the universals of experience, must find these as constant features or trues of the certains of the histories of nations that philology studies, that is, the customs, laws, languages, and deeds of peoples at peace and in war. Philosophical knowledge and philological knowledge are brought together by looking at history through the axioms. When we do this we will see what God has wrought in history; that is, we will make for ourselves the providential order that consists in the cycles of the three ages of ideal eternal history. We will see the providential design of the "great city of the human race," a term with which Vico plays on Augustine's city of God and city of man.

Vico says "he who meditates this Science narrates to himself this ideal eternal history so far as he himself makes it for himself by that proof 'it had, has, and will have to be'" (par. 349). The proof of the new science is for the reader to meditate (*meditare*) and to narrate (*narrare*) the ideal eternal history. This meditation is not Descartes's rational reflection to arrive at the principles of first philosophy because Vico's meditation takes the form of narrative, the form of thought natural to history and genetic understanding. Vico's method is modeled on the power attributed by Hesiod and tradition to the Muses, who could sing of what was, is, and is to come. The mother of the Muses, who are said to govern the arts of humanity, is Mnemosyne or Memory. Vico's proof rests on an art of memory, but one that shows the causes or necessary order of events, as Vico transforms the phrase describing the attributes of the Muses into the imperative "had, has, and will have to be" (*dovette, deve, dovrà*).

Poetic Wisdom and the True Homer

To make the true narration of the world of nations requires a doctrine of origin. As Vico says: "Doctrines must take their beginning from that of the matters of which they treat" (par. 314, axiom 106). All mentality and social order, Vico claims, are originally rooted in *la sapienza poetica* (poetic wisdom). At the beginning of all human experience is the myth. According to Vico, the "first science to be learned should be mythology or the interpretation of fables" (par. 51).

Vico says that the "master key" to his science was the discovery that the origins of both languages and letters rests on the fact that the first peoples were poets who spoke in poetic characters (par. 34). These *caratteri poetici* are the basic forms of human *fantasia* (imagination). They contain what Vico calls *universali fantastici* (imaginative universals). These universals are the elements of a pre-rational logic by which the first humans ordered their world. What Vico calls "poetic wisdom" is what in modern terms would be called "mythical thought." The first humans were unable to form abstract or rational universals, what Vico calls *universali intelligibili* (intelligible universals), so they formed the objects around them as gods; later they formed those human virtues necessary to civil society as the figures of heroes. Myths or fables are narrations of the gods and are the first histories of humanity. Vico thus alters Aristotle's claim that poetry is more philosophical than history because poetry treats of universals and history reflects particulars. Vico sees the first histories to be the myths, which are the products of *fantasia* as the primordial human power of thought.

Vico understands Jove as the first imaginative universal. In Vico's account, after the universal flood the world required two centuries to dry out. During that time the sons of Noah grew to the size of giants and roamed the great, placeless forests of the earth. When the atmosphere dried out sufficiently, the giants experienced entirely new phenomena – lightning and thunder. This caused them to experience for the first time fear or terror (*spavento*). They could not form the abstract notion of sky or thunder so they formed the thunderous sky as a giant body, an alter to their own, as the god, Jove. According to Vico, every people has its Jove, although it may go by other names. Once they could apprehend the sky as Jove they could separate sky from earth and nature from themselves. Having the power of the name, they named all things as gods. Due to their fear of Jove they fled into caves and formed marriages, out of sight of Jove, and established families, whereas formerly they fornicated as animals. Thus the second passion is their experience of shame. From the establishment of families comes burial. In clearings made in the great forest, the heads of families take the auspices of Jove's actions, from which they founded cities. Juno becomes goddess of marriage.

These original imaginative universals of gods are the means to form nature and basic social institutions. As society develops to the age of heroes, the peoples develop virtues in terms of their embodiment in heroic figures. Unable to form the abstract notion of the virtue of courage, they form this as Achilles; unable to form the virtue of wisdom or cleverness, they form this in the figure of Ulysses. Society is generated by the stories of the character and deeds of these heroes and around these stories an order of natural customs is formed. The heroic age gives way to the age of humans when the power of *fantasia* fades and the world is made intelligible in rational, abstract terms. Written law replaces custom; theories of natural events and human society replace the images of the gods and heroes. Instead of being regarded as storing great human truths, the myths and fables begin to be a logic of illusion or are said to have only aesthetic and not metaphysical meaning.

Vico regards Homer as a key figure in his conception of poetic wisdom. He claims to have discovered the "true Homer," which is the Greek people themselves. By this Vico means that Homer is not simply an individual poet. Homer is a summary figure that brings together the age of gods and heroes of the most ancient periods of the Greeks. After Homer, the age of purely human thought and human institutions, first formulated by the philosophers of Greece, begins. This age of human reason ends in the fall of the ancient world. This original *corso* of three ages results in a *ricorso*. From the ruins of the ancient world there is a return to religion. This proceeds to the Middle Ages, the age of heroes, of chivalry and knights. These two ages culminate in the poetry of Dante, whom Vico calls the "Tuscan Homer." After Dante arrive the philosophers of the Renaissance, who recollect the ideas of the Greeks and Romans as the basis of a new rationality. Vico finds himself in this third age of humans, the *ricorso* of Western culture.

In his doctrine of poetic wisdom, Vico offers a solution to Plato's quarrel between philosophy and poetry. Vico sees in poetry not a false philosophy but an original wisdom that is based on *fantasia* and images and which is required by philosophy as its own starting-point.

The Courses and Recourses of the Nations

Vico intends the *New Science* to be a new conception of natural law. Vico regards seventeenth-century natural-law theory, represented by Hobbes, Grotius, and Pufendorf, to be the "natural law of the philosophers." Against this Vico puts his conception of the "natural law of the peoples" (*il diritto naturale delle genti*). The natural law of the philosophers was conceived from the distinctions drawn by later Roman jurists between natural law, civil law, and the laws of nations (*ius naturale, civile,* and *gentium*). Natural law is a product of abstracting, the view that there are certain natural rights or laws that can be established by reason alone apart from historical conditions. Civil law is the positive law that is made through human choice based on civil authority. The law of nations or *ius gentium* in Roman jurisprudence is the basic "common" law to be found in most nations in contrast to their particular civil laws. It was also that part of Roman law that applied to citizens and foreigners alike. Vico conceives this as a form of natural law, as *ius naturale gentium*, which arises directly from the peoples (*genti*) themselves, and as being universal law, identical at a given stage of a society's development with that of any other society at a corresponding stage of its development. This is a sense of natural law that makes it not a rational ideal but an actual fact of the life of nations in the great city of the human race.

Vico's natural law of the peoples is grounded in his conception of ideal eternal history. Ideal eternal history conceives civil society as originating in the familiar and poetic or mythic wisdom of the age of gods and progressing in a cycle to the ages of heroes and humans. This is set against the conception of society as made up of individuals who emerge from an original state through a rational impulse to form a covenant among themselves by which to establish civil order. For Vico society is formed, not from individuals pursuing their own aims, but from the original social groups from which forms of social order develop in history. These are for Vico in the cycle of the development of all nations bound to the three ages of ideal eternal history. There are three kinds of natures, customs, natural law, governments, languages, written characters, jurisprudence, authority, reason, judgments, and kinds of epochs. In terms of natural law, the first kind is divine, derived from the gods, the second is heroic law – a law of force but controlled by religion – and the third is human law dictated by reason.

History is not progressive for Vico. All nations arise in a "barbarism of sense" (*barbarie del senso*) in which all is formed in terms of the passions and sensation. In the third age there develops a "barbarism of reflection" (*barbarie della riflessione*), in which humanity loses itself in an attempt to rationalize all forms of life into abstract orders. When custom, imagination, and religion fail, the nations finally disintegrate. Vico states this as: "men first feel necessity, then look for utility, next attend to comfort, still later amuse themselves with pleasure, thence grow dissolute in luxury, and finally go mad and waste their substance" (par. 241, axiom 66). The modern period or third age of any nation is one of rational madness. The collapse of any nation, unless conquered by another and absorbed by it (and it, too, in time will come to the point of collapse), results in a return to the forest, which establishes the condition for a *ricorso* built upon the memories and ruins of the previous *corso* of the nation.

Vico looks at history and sees that no nation masters history, that all nations rise, mature, and fall within history. Unlike eighteenth-century views of providence in which history is regarded as progressing toward a better state, Vico sees the stages of ideal eternal history as a providential order in which humanity is taught and retaught a lesson that it continually fails to learn. This eternal pattern of cycles holds true only for the gentile peoples, those which have arisen after the flood. Vico regards the sacred history of the ancient Hebrews as having a direct relationship to God. This sacred history does not undergo such courses and recourses.

Vico's new science might be seen in its largest terms as an attempt, not only to juxtapose the civil, natural, and divine worlds which he depicts in the frontispiece, but to combine in one extended oration the interconnections among the four terms of the Judeo-Christian and Greco-Roman worlds. In understanding how his own culture of the nations of the West has developed, Vico claims to have discovered the principles by which the world of nations itself develops, hence he has produced the first modern philosophy of history and human culture, based on his philosophy of mythology.

Bibliography

Editions and translations

Vico, Giambattista (1990) *Opere*, 2 vols, ed. Andrea Battistini. Milan: Mondadori.
Vico, Giambattista (1984) *The New Science of Giambattista Vico*, trans. Thomas Goddard Bergin and Max Harold Fisch. Ithaca, NY: Cornell University Press.

Studies

Berlin, Isaiah (2000) *Three Critics of the Enlightenment: Vico, Hamann, Herder*, ed. Henry Hardy. London: Random House.
Goetsch, Jr, J. R. (1995) *Vico's Axioms: The Geometry of the Human World*. New Haven, CT: Yale University Press.
Mooney, M. (1994) *Vico in the Tradition of Rhetoric*. Mahwah, NJ: Lawrence Erlbaum.
Pompa, L. (1990) *Vico: A Study of the "New Science,"* 2nd edn. Cambridge: Cambridge University Press.
Verene, D. P. (1981) *Vico's Science of Imagination*. Ithaca, NY: Cornell University Press.

30

David Hume, *Treatise of Human Nature* (1740)

A Genial Skepticism, an Ethical Naturalism

Fred Wilson

In early modern philosophy some, like Descartes and Leibniz, concentrated on ontology. Others, like Locke, concentrated on epistemology. But David Hume (1711–1776), like Spinoza, aspired to give a complete picture of human being and its place in the world. For Spinoza, however, the picture is that of the mystical rationalist, where for Hume the picture is thoroughly this-worldly and empiricist. It was in his *Treatise of Human Nature* that Hume gave his most complete account of human nature and of the world in which human being finds itself.

Hume locates his own work in the tradition of Locke. Like Locke he aims to find both the limits of human knowledge and the capacities that human beings have to know things. He takes for granted the success of Locke's argument against innate ideas: all our ideas, Hume agrees, come from sense experience or from inner awareness of our own conscious states. There are no other kinds of ideas, no innate ideas, that give us *a priori* access to a world beyond the world of ordinary experience. We have no innate knowledge of any metaphysical principles or entities, nor any innate knowledge of moral principles. As for Hume's moral theory, the tradition here is that of Locke's student Shaftesbury and Hume's teacher Francis Hutcheson.

This limiting by Hume of our knowledge to the world of ordinary experience has often led critics to characterize him as a skeptic. Certainly, relative to those who embrace religious claims about God and other beings that transcend the world of ordinary experience, Hume is a skeptic. And, of course, compared to Descartes or Spinoza, who claimed to have ideas of things that are far beyond any ordinary thing, Hume might again be called a skeptic. But given that he is prepared to argue that we have no ideas of such things, that they are not even genuinely thinkable, that they are the consequence of confused thinking, it is unfair to speak of skepticism: within his own terms, he is not a skeptic. Nor, when compared to Hobbes, is Hume a moral skeptic, though when compared to Aristotle he might be called a skeptic, though he again provides arguments why Aristotelian ethical positions are devoid of content.

Hume proposes to use the methods of the new experimental science of Newton to explore human nature. In this he is not going beyond what Locke envisaged. Except that Hume did not want to limit himself to human understanding, as Locke did, but aimed to make the whole of human nature his object of study. He aimed not merely to put the new science on a more secure footing by finding the nature and limits of human knowledge but equally to secure a sure foundation for a set of humane moral principles.

Besides taking for granted the Lockean empiricist framework, Hume assumes a fairly specific theory of the human mind and human behavior. He assumes, in the first place, that learning proceeds primarily by association. On this account of learning, if x and y are presented regularly as standing in a relation R, then a habit is formed in the mind so that the impression of x or the idea of x introduces the idea of y. He assumes, in the second place, a more or less Epicurean view of human motivation, that what primarily moves us to action is pleasure and the avoidance of pain. This is not to say that only pleasure is an end in itself. Rather, what is sought as an end is sought as part of one's pleasure.

The argument of the *Treatise* is divided into three books. Book I deals with the world and our knowledge of it. Book II deals with the human passions. Book III deals with moral philosophy, the nature of man in society. But the books are not independent. Here are three examples. Book I deals with the nature of the self from a metaphysical viewpoint. Hume here disagrees with the traditional account that would have the self be a simple substance; it is, rather, a complex entity, a series of connected impressions, ideas, and passions. But he does not address the issue of how we come to acquire the complex idea of the self until Book II. Again, parts of the account of knowledge in Book I presuppose that the mind is active in seeking out truth. But the passion of curiosity which moves and gives purpose to such activity is not discussed in detail until Book II. Finally, in Book I Hume deals with such issues as the rules of language or the rules by which to judge of causes and effects. But he does not discuss how such rules might acquire normative power until Book III. So, having read the *Treatise* through, one must, as it were, circle back and reflect upon the earlier parts in the light of the later. Unfortunately, Book I is often read in isolation from the others, and the same is true of the moral philosophy of Book III, while Book II is very often simply ignored. Such a partitioning of the *Treatise* into parts leads one to miss some of the important connections.

Impressions and Ideas

Hume begins his discussion with a distinction that would have been well known to his contemporaries, the distinction, as he calls it, between impressions and ideas. When we see a green apple, we are given a sensuous patch, which is green, and which we locate perceptually as that surface of the apple that is towards us; that sensuous patch is the impression of the apple. Derived from this impression is the idea of the apple; this idea is itself a sensuous object, an image. Hume holds, with Locke and Berkeley, that all our ideas derive from impressions.

With regard to the impressions, they are all separate and distinct. Ordinary objects are patterned collections of sensible events, some of which are sensed – those that we experience as sense impressions – others of which are not sensed. In particular, ordinary objects are not to be understood in the traditional way as involving a substantial particular that endures unchanged through the history of the object. However, unlike Locke and Berkeley, Hume makes no assumption that our sensory impressions of objects are somehow dependent upon the mind that experiences them.

It is in the context of his account of ideas as images that Hume addresses the issue of how it is that words become general. The traditional account had been that such terms were associated with abstract general ideas (often, as in Descartes, taken to be innate). Hume, however, accepts Berkeley's critique of such ideas: there are none. But that requires a different account of how words become general. Hume uses his associationist theory to provide an alternative to the traditional account, one that is compatible with empiricism.

The principle of association holds where we take the relation R to be the relation of resemblance: if x and y resemble or are similar to one another in some respect, then an association between them will be established in the mind, and the one will tend to introduce the other.

Now let the general term "red" apply to x and y by virtue of their resembling each other in respect of that color. It also applies to z, u, v, w, etc., *ad infinitum*. If the general term does not mean an abstract idea that stands for all these individuals, then it must mean these individuals directly as it were. Instead of the abstract idea being before the mind when one uses the general term "red," one must have this infinity of individuals before the mind when one uses the term. But our minds are finite; they do not have the capacity to hold before themselves at one time an infinity of ideas, that is, an infinity of particular images. This is the problem that seems to confront any account of thought that would do away with abstract general ideas.

Hume's solution is to argue on the basis of his associationism that something x which is red introduces by established custom or association the other particular ideas which resemble x in respect of being red. They are introduced by that custom, which we have acquired by surveying them. However, they are not actually all before the mind; they are there only potentially. Thus, on Hume's account, an abstract idea is a habit or custom.

But, of course, if something is before the mind only potentially then it is not really before the mind. So this cannot be the full story of abstract ideas. Hume completes his account of how words become general by making the word itself play a crucial role. On Hume's account, general words *mean* by becoming associated with some way or other in which things – impressions and ideas (images) – resemble one another. Thus, the general term "red" means things by virtue of becoming associated with that way of resembling that holds among stop lights, stop signs, fire trucks, and so on: it means just those things that resemble one another in this way. One has an impression or idea of x which is red. This introduces by association the word "red." This in turn introduces on the one hand some one or another of the various ideas of things which are red, together, on the other hand, with the custom, the tendency, or disposition of other such ideas to be available as it were for recall as fit.

To think in general terms, to use an abstract idea, is not just to have an association amongst ideas based on some relation of resemblance. That association will not by itself place a particular idea before the mind. What plays the role of introducing a particular idea before the mind when we think in general terms is the general term itself, by virtue of its association with the relevant relation of resemblance. And here what is crucial is not that the general term applies to all the particular impressions and ideas; what is crucial is the tendency or disposition of the mind to apply the term to those things. The meaning of a general term is a matter of the complex associations which link it and the members of a resemblance class of things, that is, of impressions and ideas or images. These associations are acquired, of course, when we learn language.

Hume now proceeds to explore the implications of the doctrine of ideas for a concept that more or less defined material things for the age. This is the property of extension. Descartes argued that this is the whole essence of material things; Locke and the Newtonians that it is at least part of the essence. Hume made a case for the empirical intelligibility of extension against, on the one hand, the Platonists and the Cartesians, who held that extension could be known only by innate ideas, and, on the other hand, Pierre Bayle, who had argued in his *Historical and Critical Dictionary* (Art. Zeno, Rem. G) that the concept of extension is inconsistent, concluding that material things are figments of the imagination.

Plato had argued in the *Phaedo* – the Cartesians offered similar arguments – that since we judge things given in sense experience to be inexactly equal we must have the concept of exact equality. But we cannot get that from sense experience, so it must be *a priori* and innate. This assumes that the idea of exact equality is positive. Hume argues to the contrary. The ideas that we obtain from sense experience are of things that are larger (or smaller) than others by a bit. We then notice that some other things are larger by even a smaller bit. The concept of exact equality is that of a thing which is larger than another by no bit. Contrary to what Plato argued, it is exactness that is the negative notion. The ideas of exact geometrical forms are based on our experience of ordinary things, arrived at by extrapolation. As for applied geometry, that is inevitably inexact.

Hume pointed out that things as presented in sense experience are extended and that this extension is divisible, but that there are limits to this divisibility: at some point we arrive at indivisible, that is, extensionless, points. Bayle had argued that extension cannot be divisible into extensionless points since these would be mere nothings, things without properties. Hume proposed that the extensionless points are to the contrary propertied. They are, for example, colored: that is how they are given in experience. Bayle's objection fails.

Hume's arguments regarding extension are as good as any of the age. But his arguments and claims are obscure owing to the fact that he had no clear account of the nature of relations. But neither did others, until Bertrand Russell much later made such things clear. There are several other points in his argument where a more adequate account of relations would have helped Hume defend the theses he was advocating.

Hume now goes on to the concept of reason itself. Reason, traditionally, was the capacity to grasp the reasons of things, that is, the causes of things. These causes are, for the Aristotelians and Cartesians, the essences or forms of things, entities explaining by lying beyond the sensible qualities of things. They provide the objective necessary connections that explain the regularities that we observe. Given Hume's empiricism, there are no such things: we have no ideas of them. Hume's account of reason is therefore very different from that of the tradition.

Causation

Hume's discussion of the concept of cause is perhaps his most well-known piece of philosophical analysis. He systematically attacks the position that there are objective necessary connections. Thus, Cartesians attribute all such objective necessary connections to the causal activity of the deity. But, Hume argues, all that we experience is regularity. It follows (assuming that Locke's case against innate ideas is successful) that we have no idea of an objective necessary connection. Since such an entity cannot be thought, it cannot be part of our ontology. In particular, since we have no idea of it from our impressions, there is no way we can think of God as producing objective necessary connections among things. Again, Locke argued that the principle that everything has a cause is an objective necessary truth which principle can, therefore, provide the backing necessary to transform a judgment of regularity into a judgment of objective causal necessity. But Hume argued to the contrary that the proposition that every event has a cause is itself contingent. Locke suggested that the contrary thesis, that nothing is a cause of something, is unthinkable: nothing cannot be a cause. Hume argued that this is to make an illegitimate substantive of the term "nothing": the real contrary of "every event has a cause" is "there is an event for which there is no cause," and that there is nothing contradictory or unthinkable about this. Hume does not deny the principle that every event has a cause. To the contrary, he clearly affirms it. But he denies its necessity. It is a contingent truth, established on the basis of our experience of having in the past been successful in discovering causes.

Hume concludes that when looked at objectively there is nothing more to causation than regularity. But this fails to capture the moment of necessity that distinguishes causal regularities from mere accidental generalities. Hume proposes that we can account for this feature of causal propositions in terms of the custom or habit that we have to use some regularities in inferences, and others not. A causal proposition is a generality "All *A* are *B*" such that the impression of *A* by virtue of that custom produces the idea of *B* and such that the idea of *A* produces the idea of *B*. The former case is that of predicting, the latter case is that of contrary to fact inference. In the case of "mere" or accidental regularities, we do not use propositions expressing them for prediction and contrary to fact inference. The necessity of causal propositions lies in this habit of thought.

This habit comes to be in the first instance through the mechanism of association. After repeatedly experiencing *A* and *B* conjoined, the habit is formed in us of connecting *A* and *B* in thought. But as we become reflective and self-conscious in our reasonings, if we are moved by the passion of curiosity or love of truth, then we can train ourselves to reason more effectively. Hume examines in detail a variety of rules and argues that some are to be preferred to others. The principle that the wish is the parent of the belief, the principle that because things are similar therefore they are causally related, even the principle of induction by simple enumeration, are all principles that lead often to false beliefs. Hume argues that the rules of experimental science, in effect the rules of eliminative induction, are the rules that so far as we can tell are the most effective in yielding beliefs that satisfy our love of truth. Science and superstition are both parts of human nature, but science is distinguished by these rules, conformity to which is most likely to lead to truth.

Skeptical Problems

Reason, that is, causal reason, has now been transformed by Hume from the grasp of timeless forms or essences, that is, entities outside the world of experience, to the grasp of timeless patterns of entities within the world of experience. But all we ever observe is a sample, while a generalization is about a population. On Hume's account of reason, then, there is always uncertainty attached to a causal inference; the incorrigibility sought by Plato and Descartes is simply not to be had. This has been taken by many to amount to skepticism about causal inferences. But Hume has in effect argued that the goal of incorrigibility is beyond our cognitive powers. He suggests that a reasonable person, once he or she finds a goal to be impossible of attainment, will give up that goal. So the reasonable person will rest content with fallible powers to know causes. This is not skepticism, just a reasonable view of human cognitive capacities.

But Hume does take up two skeptical challenges by reason to reason. On the first of these, reason reflects upon itself and realizes that there is some probability it made a mistake. That will diminish the probability of the original judgment. But this reasoning too might be erroneous. That diminishes the probability of the original judgment still further. And so on, until all probability reduces to the vanishing point. But this reasoning, too, is possibly wrong, so even this reasoning is undercut. The conclusion seems to be that all reasoning is weak including the reasoning that all reasoning is weak.

Hume draws an immediate inference from this. Even if this reasoning is valid, all that it shows is that we do not rely entirely upon reason in making our inferences. Nature has determined that we shall reason, and nature will triumph in spite of any inferences that we might make about the weakness of reason. But this is not all he has to say about this argument: he will return to the issue later.

The other challenge of reason to reason has to do with our perception of the world of ordinary experience. We have several sense impressions of a single object, but there are gaps between these impressions. On the basis of a habit of inference formed with the observing of gapless series, we fill in the gaps with the ideas of intervening sensible events. These ideas refer to unsensed sensible events. Although these fillings-in are more or less automatic in perception, none the less, one can recognize that they can be justified by the rules by which to judge of causes. But so firmly do we make the inference that there is a unified series that we as it were invent a unifying individual, present throughout the series, that provides the unity. Such an individual does not exist, on Hume's own grounds, where the temporally distinct impressions are in fact separate. That Hume must invent this fiction to provide unity is one of the grounds for the charge of skepticism; a more adequate account of relations among impressions and sensible events would have done as well.

This world that we perceive consists of objects that are connected patterns of sensible events, most of which are simply unsensed. Hume refers to this as the world of the vulgar. If, however, we notice certain generally ignored events, and pursue their causes moved by simple curiosity we arrive rationally at a very different world. While looking at a candle, put your finger to your eyeball and press: a second image appears. Since like effects have like causes, and one image is caused by the state of our sense organ, the other must also be caused by the state of our sense organ. Thus, sense impressions do not exist independently of the state of our organs, contrary to what is proposed in the system of the vulgar. We can form ideas of the events that cause the different states of our sense organs, but the ideas are abstract and general, and, moreover, only relative. What we can say, on the basis of the causal principle that all events have causes, is that there are causes of these events, but we cannot specifically identify how they are qualified, save negatively: they do not have those qualities we experience when we experience sense impressions. What we know of the world to which these scientific inferences lead us is simply structure, including spatial structure; but we know nothing of its qualitative aspects.

Hume refers to this world as the world of the philosophers. He is careful to point out that the dependence of sense impressions is a casual dependence on our sense organs, not an ontological dependence of impressions on a substantial mind. He will soon argue that there is no substantial mind, just as there is no material substance. There is nothing self-contradictory about sense impressions existing unperceived. Indeed, the system of the vulgar consistently maintains that view. But consequent to scientific investigation, we discover that in fact they do not, and that the world of science is very different from the world of the vulgar.

Hume now raises two concerns which seem to cast skeptical doubts on reason. The first is that he has relied on trivial properties of the imagination, the associative mechanisms, to provide us with an account of material objects. This is in contrast to Descartes, who relied on *a priori* metaphysical reasoning to prove that there were material objects, or Malebranche, who insisted that it could not be proved and had to be accepted as a matter of religious faith based on the Book of Genesis. How can something as simple as the imagination do the job that others thought required metaphysics or religious faith?

But, secondly, we have arrived at the conclusion that nature, in the form of perception, leads us to the world of the vulgar, but these inferences, when pursued in conformity with the rules by which to judge of causes, lead us to a very different world, and to conclusions that contradict the inferences of perception. Reason and nature come into conflict. This contradiction between reason and nature seems to provide a real ground for skepticism.

Hume goes on to examine the philosophical systems that have preceded his. He first considers the Aristotelian system, and simply rejects it as unreasonable, together with its assumption of primitive causal powers. The modern philosophy is more reasonable. It is close to what Hume has called the system of the philosophers. But it contains a substantial mind, and makes sense impressions ontologically dependent on this mind. What holds for secondary qualities holds also for primary qualities, including therefore all spatial properties. All material things, whether conceived as in the world of the vulgar or as conceived in the world of the philosophers, disappear into the mind: the world becomes mind-dependent, and there is no way out to a real world beyond the mind. The modern philosophy needs metaphysical proofs for the existence of ordinary things or an appeal to faith because it contains mental substance. Abolish that and the skeptical problems disappear, nor is there any need then for some grand proof of the material world: ordinary inferences will suffice.

Hume now turns to a detailed examination of the self. He concludes that he has no impression of a simple substantial self that remains unaltered through change. The self, like an ordinary material thing, is a bundle of impressions, including those impressions he calls the passions, together with ideas of the various impressions. This may seem paradoxical; certainly, it has also led to charges of skepticism. However, it is important to recognize that it is a connected bundle. There are the connections provided by the causal ordering of the self. Memory provides connections, and the gaps in our memory are filled in by the continuity provided by the body. Nor is it paradoxical to call a connected bundle a unity. Plants and animals change but are denoted the same; the parish church may change greatly over the years, but is the same parish church. The continuity here is provided by a teleological ordering: we find a similar ordering defining our selves in terms of our purposes and our social roles. This is not the whole story of the self, more will be said when Hume discusses the passions. But he is still puzzled by how exactly to account for self-identity in the absence of a continuing substance. Here again a more adequate doctrine of relations would have helped.

In any case, it is clear that this account of the self eliminates the basis on which a radical skepticism about the external world could be generated. There is nothing in Hume's account of the self and world that would lead it to collapse into skepticism and idealism.

To conclude his discussion Hume now turns to the apparent paradoxes into which reason has fallen, the infinite regress toward zero probability and the skepticism about the external world consequent upon science. He has in fact concluded from the former that we could never give up belief; the Cartesian method of doubting everything in order to begin a fresh start is incapable of withstanding the demand of nature that we make causal inferences. Radical skepticism, it seems, can have no effect. But further reflection reveals that this skeptical position is one that is indeed depressing for one concerned to find the truth: it seems that there is no way to achieve its goal. The depression itself is cured again by nature, which leads one out of the study to eat and make merry with one's friends. It seems that to avoid the depressing effects one should simply be indolent in the pursuit of truth, resolving to let no long set of inferences move one. But, unfortunately, this resolve is itself backed by a long set of inferences, so it undercuts itself. The problem with the infinite regress is that reason simply repeats itself, with no guidance. When reason is mixed with a passion, and in particular with the passion of curiosity or love of truth, reason will use a different strategy, one more conducive to the discovery of truth. One will more critically examine the grounds of one's inferences, rather than blindly letting reason undercut itself. As for the skepticism consequent upon science, one will recognize that the picture of the world to which reason leads us is indeed strange, but it is one that we can live with. We can recognize in it the limitations of perception and our human cognitive capacities. It is diffidence, not skepticism, that is called for. But it is less strange than the hypotheses of religion. And unlike the hypotheses of religion, it is not dangerous; it does not generate either superstition or enthusiasm. Hume thus resolves the skeptical challenges with a reasonable appeal to a reasonable reason, one actively guided by the passion of curiosity, the love of truth.

The Passions

Hume next turns, in Book II of the *Treatise*, to the passions. Just as he treated perception and reason in empiricist and associationist terms, Hume similarly treats the passions, including the will or volition. This assumes that the will has causes, such as the passions, and effects, and that these causal relations are understood in the way Hume has outlined in Book I. This means that the will is causally necessitated. But Hume distinguishes this sort of causal determinism from fatalism. Fatalism is the doctrine that things happen in spite of what we do; Hume's account of our actions insists that they happen, often enough at least, precisely because of our volitions. Hume's necessitarianism does not contradict moral responsibility for what we do; it is compatible with liberty. The opposite of liberty is not causal necessity but rather coercion, and it is clear that not all actions are coerced.

Central to Hume's discussion of the passions is his doctrine of sympathy, how we understand the feelings and passions of others. We first experience the outward signs of the passion. By virtue of a learned association between such signs and the passion, we form the idea of the passion that the other is experiencing. This idea is then converted into what amounts to an impression, something with the force and liveliness of our own passions. If the other person is connected to one's self by some relation, e.g., contiguity, resemblance, causation, nationality, family, then one's imagination will enliven the idea of the passion to the point where it becomes as motivating as the original passion itself.

Hume goes into considerable detail about a number of the passions. These details are important to his project of giving a scientific account of human nature. But they tend to obscure the overall thrust of his argument as he moves from Book I to Book III. Nor is the organization as pellucid as that of Books I and III; the discussion of liberty and necessity, for example, is awkwardly placed, and might in fact have found a better home in Book I. The outline of what Hume has to say is, however, clear, as is its relevance to completing Book I and preparing for Book II.

The central point about motivation, for Hume, is that all goods are pleasurable, all evils painful. The tendency to seek pleasurable things and to avoid the painful is native to one. This he endeavors to show in detail in Book II, through a systematic examination of all the passions. This point will be important for his discussion of morality in Book III. But so will his argument, again deriving from the discussion of Book II, that hedonism is false: pleasure (or pain) is connected with our ends, but in general is not in itself the end sought after (or avoided).

The first set of passions to be considered are those involved with natural appetites such as hunger, lust, parental love, and love of life. These impulses are basic, not further to be accounted for. Their objects are pleasing: thus, provided that we are hungry, food is pleasant. Such impulses do not aim at pleasure, though their objects are in fact pleasant. They are, in Hume's terms, primary in so far as they are not based on an antecedent perception of something pleasant. If we are hungry and food is perceived or imagined, then this creates a desire for that food. Such a desire is dependent upon the antecedent perception of something pleasant; it is therefore, in Hume's terms, a secondary perception or passion. Grief, joy, hope, fear, and despair are other secondary passions. So is volition. If we desire food, and it is perceived to be attainable, then this determines a volition which moves us to attain it.

The secondary passions divide into the direct and the indirect. The direct are not to be explained in terms of the mechanisms of association; they are primitive or native. The indirect passions can be accounted for in terms of an antecedent perception of pleasure (or pain) through association with other qualities.

The direct passions divide into the violent and the calm. The violent passions are desire, aversion, grief, hope, fear, despair, and volition. These are founded directly on the perception of pleasure (or pain) and move us directly to action. The calm passions, in contrast, are not sufficiently disturbing to move us directly to action. These passions are our sentiments of approval and disapproval. They arise from the mere contemplation of fitness or unfitness in thought or action or external forms. Among the calm passions are the moral sentiments, to which Hume will return in Book III of the *Treatise*.

Among the direct passions is curiosity or the love of truth. It operates where truth itself has come to be felt pleasurable, but it is from the action of mind in achieving truth that this pleasure derives. The indirect passions are pride and humility, passions directed at oneself, and love and hatred, passions directed at another. Here associations based on relations are relevant to explaining these passions. In the case of pride, there are two relations. (Humility is analogous.) The first is the relation R_1 of the cause to the self. Some of the things in which we take pride are simply qualities that we have as human beings, qualities of our mind and body, such as virtue as a quality of mind and beauty as a quality of the body. But we also take pride in things which are extrinsic to us and distant. Hume explains that this happens when external objects acquire some particular relation to ourselves and are associated or connected with us, and he gives as examples our houses or gardens, as well as personal merit and accomplishments. The quality in a subject evokes the feeling of pride; this is the cause of the feeling. But the object of the feeling is always the self.

In order to see how the mechanism of pride (and humility) works, we should consider a particular example, say pride in one's house. If one takes pride in one's house, then R_1 is the relation of ownership. The cause produces independently of the feeling of pride a feeling (in this case) of pleasure in the self. (In the case of humility, the cause produces feelings of pain in the self.) These feelings of pleasure stand in the relation R_2 of resemblance to the pleasant feeling of pride. If, then, one has an impression or idea of one's house, this produces feelings of pleasure. This impression or idea together with the feelings of pleasure jointly, by virtue of the two relations R_1 and R_2, introduce the feeling of pride with its two aspects of pleasantness, on the one hand, introduced by R_2, and, on the other hand, the idea of the self, the object of the passion, introduced by R_1.

The repetition that is necessary to generate the habit comes through sympathy. Hume notes how praise and pride go together, and discusses the importance of praise in generating pride. Praise is the expression of love. Love (and hate) run parallel to pride (and humility). Love has another as its object, where pride has oneself as its object. As before one must distinguish the cause from the object, and the cause is further distinguished into the subject and the quality that evokes the love. Thus, when David praises someone, Jones, say, for a quality, say the excellence of his house, then David loves that person in virtue of that quality. Jones, recognizing in the praise the outward signs of this love, forms the idea of that love, which in turn is, by means of the mechanism of sympathy, converted into the passion. Since David's love is directed at Jones, the passion that Jones comes to feel is likewise directed at Jones, i.e., at himself. Since David's love is pleasant, so is the passion that Jones experiences: he experiences a pleasant passion directed at himself. But David loves Jones by virtue of a quality that Jones has, or, more specifically, by virtue of another entity which has a certain quality and which stands in a certain relation R_1, in this case, that of ownership to another entity which in turn has the quality of excellence. This quality of excellence itself produces pleasant feelings in Jones, the owner, which pleasant feelings stand in the relation R_2 of resemblance to the feeling of pride. The mechanism of sympathy can thus produce repeated cases of pride. Once this has happened, the habit becomes established and begins to work as it were on its own, so that the Jones house alone when perceived or thought of produces the feeling of pride.

It is important to notice what else can become associated in this context. For, this completes the doctrine of the self that has been left incomplete since the discussion of personal identity in Book I. The cause of pride is repeatedly presented as standing in relation R_1 to the self. Thus, the idea of the cause, qualified in the appropriate way, and the idea of the self come themselves to be associated in the mind: the concept of the self is expanded and comes to have a further defining characteristic. In this way the concept of the self that a person has is generated by the passion of pride (and humility).

It might be argued that the notion of pride presupposes the notion of a self rather than accounts for it. The feeling of pride is of course owned by a self. But then there is also the self in the sense of self as a succession of related or connected ideas and impressions of which we have an intimate memory and consciousness. This is the bundle account of the self of Book I, but now Hume is attempting to say something important about the relations or connections that structure the bundle into a self. What are these connections? Clearly, there are the connections that are established by bodily continuity, and those established by memory. But Hume has in view other qualities that establish connections between the perceptions and give an enduring quality to the self. He points out that accidental blessings and calamities are in a way separated from us, for we never consider them as connected with our being and existence. Clearly, Hume has in mind that there are things which, in contrast to these accidental blessings and calamities, are taken to be a fixed part of oneself, and as connected with our being and existence: these stable characteristics define one as the individual that one and others conceive oneself to be and, to the extent that it is a characteristic peculiar to oneself, it determines one's individuality, how one and others distinguish one as a person from other persons. Hume distinguishes personal identity, as it regards our thought or imagination, which he discussed in Book I, and as it regards our passions or the concern we take in ourselves. He indicated in Book I how the latter sort of teleological unity is important for defining personal identity, but did not further explain it: he could not do so until he had discussed the passions which determine the ends at which we aim. We now see how identity as regards our passions and the concern that we take in ourselves comes to be: the qualities that enduringly through time define our being and determine our individuality become part of our self-concept through the mechanisms of pride and sympathy. In becoming part of our self-concept, part of the idea that we and others have of ourselves, they thereby become the relations that structure our perceptions into the self we and others conceive ourselves to be, the relations that as it were transform a mere bundle of impressions into a person.

Perhaps what is most important about this account of the self is that it involves social relations. Personal identity is not a matter of an underlying spiritual or mental substance. It is rather determined by our bodily identity and by the relations that connect us to others: the concept of oneself is a concept that we derive through social interaction with others. It is the self in this sense that is the moral agent which forms that background to the account of morality of Book III of the *Treatise*.

Traditional moral theory had rested on a metaphysical principle to the effect that each of us is a substance with an essence or form that naturally inclines toward certain moral ends. This essence or form both explains what we do and determines what we ought to do, determines the ends toward which we ought to strive. In this sense, our moral ends are given to us as part of the metaphysical structure of the universe and of human beings in that universe. The moral order is a metaphysical order. Reason as the capacity to grasp the reasons of things grasps this essence or form and is able to determine the means that are best to achieve our given moral ends. In this sense, as Aristotle insisted, we deliberate about means, not about (ultimate) ends.

Hobbes had used much the same sort of argument as Hume to deny that there are any such essences or forms. Both he and his critics inferred that human beings on this view have no moral ends. This meant, on the one hand, that human beings were intrinsically amoral or selfish, with no ends other than those required for material survival. It meant, on the other hand, that all apparently moral principles were merely prudential norms about how best to satisfy our material needs.

It was a bleak picture of human nature. Hume wished to argue much the same metaphysical thesis as Hobbes, that there are no such essences or forms as the traditional picture would have it. So morality is not part of the metaphysical structure of the universe: it is relative to purely human ends. In this sense Hume is, like Hobbes, a moral skeptic. At the same time, however, Hume also wanted to argue that there is more to human beings than the satisfaction of material needs. To be sure, there are norms such as those of justice or property which deal with the rights to the sorts of goods that are required for the satisfaction of our material needs. But these norms have more than a prudential justification; they also have non-prudential moral force. Thus, in contrast to Hobbes, Hume argues that there is something about human beings that enables us to draw a distinction between prudence, on the one hand, and moral norms, on the other hand. In this sense Hume is, unlike Hobbes, no moral skeptic.

Morality

Hume begins his discussion of morality in Book III of the *Treatise* by arguing against the traditional view, that morality is a matter of fact built into our metaphysical structure and that reason can discern the essence or form that inclines us toward our moral ends. Given that there are no essences or forms, there is no matter of fact of the traditional sort that inclines us toward virtue, nor are there metaphysical reasons that reason can discern that could so move us. Moreover, given the alternative account of reason Hume has developed in Book I, reason cannot incline us to action. Reason is a matter of discerning matter-of-fact truth and falsity. What moves us to action are passions, not reason. But the whole point of morality is to determine us to act: moral judgments are among the things that move us to action. Since reason cannot move us to action, such judgments must be passions rather than judgments in the strict sense. These passions are the calm passions of moral approval and disapproval. Precisely because they are calm, Hume suggests, they have been mistaken for deliverances of the equally calm reason.

Reason can, of course, discern the means available to achieve our ends, but it does not assign those ends. In this sense, there is logical gap between "is" and "ought": from the is-statements given by reason, we cannot derive a statement about what we ought to do or be. Those ought-judgments derive rather from our passions.

Thus, in human action, it is the task of reason to serve the passions, finding the means to the ends which the latter determine. This led Hume to comment that reason is the slave of the passions. Moreover, the argument of Book I was that reason ought to be guided in its work by the passion of curiosity or love of truth, and that if it is not so guided it tends to excess, including excessive skepticism. To avoid such excess, reason ought to be the slave of the passion of curiosity. So Hume added that not only is reason the slave of the passions but that it ought only to be such.

There is another point on which Hume wished to dissociate himself from Hobbes and in this case Locke also. Hobbes and Locke argued that the rules of society are prudential rules determined by a social contract or promise that members of society make with each other. This view, that social rules are the result of a social contract, Hume wished to dispute. They are, rather, matters of convention. Indeed, contracts or promises themselves presuppose conventions rather than account for their binding force.

Hume argues that we judge to be virtuous those sorts of behavior that produce pleasure either for the actor or for others. What makes sorts of action fit and the objects of our moral approval is their tendency to produce pleasure. And what makes them unfit and the object of our moral disapproval is their tendency to produce pain.

Hume divides the virtues into artificial and natural. The artificial virtues are those that depend on social convention: they would not be productive of goods in the absence of the generally binding convention. The natural virtues are those that we would have even in a situation where there was no need for social conventions to regulate behavior.

Consider first the convention of justice or property. This, he argues, is an artificial virtue. In so arguing he disagreed with the tradition that made it part of the essence or form of human beings that they ought to respect the property of others. He makes two points. First, given the wide variety of property rules in different cultures, it is manifestly absurd to think of them all as somehow built into our very human nature. Second, it is not hard to conceive of situations – contrary to fact, to be sure – in which there would be no need for rules of property. Consider, he suggests, a golden age when there was no scarcity of goods, when there was sufficient for everyone for the taking. In such a situation there would be no need to protect my goods against your encroachment, since there would be no need for you to encroach.

Notice that such things as parental love or a concern for the well-being of others would still be useful in a golden age in a way that the rules of property, the division into mine and thine, would not. That means that parental love and a concern for the well-being of others are natural virtues. But the rules of justice are not in the same way universal in human nature.

So if the rules of justice are not part of human nature, they must therefore be the result of human art, designed to meet certain needs that we have. To the extent that conformity to such rules is a virtue, it is an artificial virtue. But its justification is utility. In that sense such rules are in the first instance prudential, as Hobbes had argued.

In the real world, as opposed to a golden age, there are three special conditions. There is, first, the fact that material resources are scarce. There is, second, a rough equality amongst human beings. And there is, third, the fact that our sympathy is limited on the whole to those close to us, our family or tribe. If there was no scarcity, as in the golden age, there would be no need for rules of property. If one of us was very much more powerful that the rest, that person would divide the goods as he or she saw fit. And if there was shown to all the generosity that we show when we share without question within the family, then we would have no problem sharing limited resources. But given restricted sympathy or generosity and rough equality, there will be conflict with regard to the scarce resources, as each family or tribe tries to get as much as it can: there would be no security.

How much better it would be to cooperate. One might not get quite as much from the resources, but one would be compensated by security of ownership. Two persons in a row boat learn through trial and error to coordinate their strokes on the oars in order to achieve the shared goal. Similarly, two persons or two tribes can learn to coordinate their behavior with respect to scarce resources and limit themselves to allotted shares in order to achieve peace and security of possession. Indeed, in the latter case, there is a training ground for children within the context of the family: it is there, within the protective framework, that they learn the virtues of cooperation and sharing. For any person, it is in his or her interest that there be a rule to which all conform for sharing scarce resources. The interest that such a rule serves is that of providing security in possession. The end of security will not be served unless all conform to the rule, whatever it may be. Each person will therefore act in the appropriate ways to ensure that all conform, not only others, by appropriate reinforcement and training, but also his or her own self, through the appropriate self-discipline. As first conformity to the rule will be a means toward securing the desired end of security. But this means toward a pleasurable end will itself become associated with that pleasure, and become part of it. In that way conformity to the rule will become for each person an end in itself.

This is not to say that there will never be knaves who violate the rule, especially if they think that they will not be caught. For some, selfish short-term motives will be stronger. That is simply part of the complexity of human nature. But for many, if not most, concern for the approbation of others and for one's reputation will strongly urge conformity.

Notice that, contrary to the accounts of Hobbes and Locke of the norms of civil society, Hume is arguing that the norm is not the result of a contract among the parties bound by the norm. To be sure, everyone in a society is bound by it, and in that sense there is agreement. But it is not the result of *an* agreement, nor is it justified by virtue of people entering into a contract each with all. Its justification lies rather in the utility that results when there is universal conformity to it.

Notice, too, that the case that Hume presents is the case that there be norms of justice. This argument does not establish specifically what those norms ought to be. In fact, as an examination of various cultures makes clear, there are a wide variety of such norms. All are justified by Hume's argument, even though each set is in ways inconsistent with the other sets. These different sets of norms have grown up through the contingencies of the histories of different societies. Each is right for the society in which it holds. Each is a set of conventions, which is to say a set of settled habits. Such habits are not easily changed. If they are to be changed, incremental change is the only safe way to do it.

There is more to justice than a prudential norm, however. It is also a moral norm in the sense that actions in conformity with it are the object of moral approval, violations the object of moral disapproval. These feelings of moral approbation and disapprobation, whether directed at others or at oneself, strengthen the motivation to conform to the norm.

These moral feelings arise through our capacity to sympathize with those who suffer from violations of the norm. The knave takes another's property. In the absence of the norm the stranger is simply a stranger, and one has difficulty sympathizing with him or her: our sympathy is limited to the tribe, those who are related to us. But once the norm is instituted, the stranger like oneself becomes the owner of property, and this resemblance provides a quality that can enable us to extend our sympathies even to those outside the tribe or family. We therefore feel the pain of the person exploited by the knave. Since a virtue is productive of pleasure and a vice productive of pain, the action of the knave is viewed as unfit, and, when so contemplated, produces the moral sentiment of disapproval. Similarly, conformity to the norm produces pleasure; it is therefore viewed as fit, and, when so contemplated, produces the moral sentiment of approval. In this way the norms of justice, justified in the first instance on prudential grounds, come to be moral norms.

This provides an answer to the critics of Hobbes, who insisted that human beings have a moral sense over and above their concerns for material goods, and that the norms of justice are among the objects of this moral sense. Hume agrees, but has now made the case in a way that does not require the introduction of a metaphysical essence or form: the explanation of the morality of justice lies in the very human mechanism of sympathy. Justice is artificial, but the sense of its morality, Hume argues, is natural.

Hume has given in his discussion of justice the basic structure of how other artificial norms are to be justified. In particular, he mentions that the norms of language are to be understood and justified in the same way. (Hume mentions also the norms concerning the price of gold; these are conventional, and these norms play a role in his economic writings. But these implications lie beyond the argument of the *Treatise*.) That there be rules of language is justified on grounds of utility: general conformity to them throughout a society is useful. Various rules arise contingently in different societies; hence, the different languages of the world. These rules become normative through the mechanism of sympathy. These norms strengthen conformity to the rules.

Recall, now, that in Book I Hume had made language central to the formation of abstract ideas. There he simply spoke of association. But the picture is now completed. He has now shown how those rules can be given a justification in terms of their utility, and an account of how they acquire normative force. Only with this discussion in Book III, can one fully understand that on Hume's account of language and thought our capacity for abstract thinking depends upon our social being.

Hume's account of rules also clearly applies to the rules of experimental science, the rules by which to judge of causes and effects. Conformity to these rules, too, has utility, if only in satisfying the passion of curiosity or love of truth, though of course there is also the utility that comes from the results of applied sciences such as medicine. The rules then acquire normative force through the action of sympathy. Contrariwise, the norms of superstitious religion or enthusiastic religion have dangerous consequences and so conformity to them is cognitively and socially vicious. Recall from Book I the claim that the hypotheses of religion, in contrast to those of science, are dangerous.

The reference to language not only ties in with the discussion of Book I but also points forward to Hume's account of promising and contracts. Here, too, linguistic norms play a crucial role. Specifically, Hume here points to the performative role of sayings, that is, certain conventionally determined effects of what have been called speech acts of saying.

Hume argues that justice by itself is insufficient for human beings to obtain the full benefits of living in society. For that one needs division of labor and the exchange of goods, and, more strongly, the capacity to obtain at a later time compensation for goods delivered at an earlier time. For this one needs the convention of promising: if you do so-and-so for me now, I promise to give you such-and-such in return at a later time. Hume argues that what is crucial is a linguistic convention about the use of the words "I promise." The convention is this: *saying* "I promise . . ." creates in the promisor a new feeling of obligation that he or she do what is promised and creates in the promisee a new feeling of expectation that what is promised will be done. These feelings become moralized through sympathy and in a similar way so does the linguistic norm for the performative role of saying "I promise." Notice that, contrary to what Hobbes argued, it is not the promise or the contract which is basic, but the social convention. Contract presupposes rather than accounts for the social convention concerning saying "I promise . . . ."

Justice and contract enable one to develop an exchange economy to the material benefit of all members of society. Unfortunately, there are knaves who will violate the rules if they think that they can get away with it. It is in this context that the institution of the civil magistrate arises. The civil magistrate has the power to enforce through threats of punishment the norms of justice and contract. Such threats add to the likelihood that conformity to those norms will be universal.

That a person can legitimately use force to coerce others is a convention. Members of a society universally conform to this convention, which is to say that they conform to the deliverances of the civil magistrate. It is utility that justifies that there be a such a convention, that is, that there be a civil magistrate obeyed by all and empowered to enforce rules of justice and contract. Any such convention, once instituted, will become normative through the action of sympathy.

Different norms will develop in different societies: the standards for the behavior of the civil magistrate will vary from society to society. What counts as constitutionally legitimate in one country will not be the same in another country. What the French king or chief magistrate can legitimately do is different from what the British king can legitimately do. There is no absolute standard for constitutional legitimacy, no more than there are absolute standards for what counts as rightfully owned property or for what counts as the correct language. Just as there are no *a priori* cognitive standards, so there are no *a priori* constitutional standards. Indeed, to suppose otherwise, as for example the Lockeans did, can be socially hazardous. Constitutions are matters of habit, and to try on the basis of *a priori* theorizing to change them overnight in a radically complete way cannot undo but can dangerously confuse the established social habits. It has sometimes been argued that Hume's skepticism about an objective metaphysical foundation of morals led the way to the excesses of the French Revolution. The causal relation is unlikely, but in any case Hume can reply that it was the *a priori* theorizing by Robespierre and other revolutionaries about the perfect constitution and the perfect state that led to the excesses. Revolutions based on *a priori* political theory inevitably fail with disastrous consequences. This is not to say that social change is impossible, but the only way in which it can safely be done is incrementally.

Hume now moves on to a more detailed discussion of the natural virtues and vices. In the case of the artificial virtues of justice, promising, and allegiance to the civil magistrate, it is the convention which has the social utility, and it is possible that individual acts may in fact, in themselves, be less conducive to utility than their alternatives, as when a judge renders a decision which takes goods from a poor person and gives them to someone who is rich. But in the case of the natural virtues every act in itself has utility, as, for example, every case of generosity yields benefits. However, as in the case of the artificial virtues, the natural too are accounted virtues and receive our moral approbation on the basis of the mechanism of sympathy.

In this context Hume makes the important point that given that we sympathize with people to different degrees depending on their relations to us, moral sentiments will inevitably vary from person to person, and, moreover, the same person will judge similar cases differently depending on other relations. In effect, there will be contradictions in our moral judgments among different persons and even within oneself. This has also led to the charge of moral skepticism. Hume has a response, however. Such relativism is acknowledged as a possibility, but he argues that in moral practice it is minimized. In order to eliminate such conflicts and to make possible agreement in moral discourse the convention is established that we count as genuinely moral judgments only those which are made from a disinterested point of view, i.e., without reference to the observer's own special interest or own special perspective on the situation. This convention, like other conventions, is justified in terms of the social utility that arises from general conformity to it. Then it too becomes a moral norm through the action of sympathy.

What in the end recommends virtue, whether it be the cognitive virtues delineated in Book I or the moral virtues of Book III? There is in both cases, Hume has argued, social utility. There is also the approbation of others to recommend it to one: one values such esteem, takes pride in it. Finally, there is the internal sense of peace and satisfaction that comes from doing what is right and good. In this way, our long-run self-interest determines that we ought, if we are reasonable, to cultivate within ourselves an abiding attachment to virtue.

Bibliography

Editions

Hume, David (1978) *Treatise of Human Nature*, ed. L. A. Selby-Bigge, rev. edn P. H. Nidditch. Oxford: Oxford University Press.
Hume, David (2000) *Treatise of Human Nature*, ed. D. F. Norton and M. J. Norton. Oxford: Oxford University Press.

Studies

Árdal, Páll (1989) *Passion and Value in Hume's Treatise*, 2nd edn. Edinburgh: Edinburgh University Press.
Baier, Annette (1991) *A Progress of Passions*. Cambridge, MA: Harvard University Press.
Frasca-Spada, Marina (1998) *Space and the Self in Hume's Treatise*. Cambridge: Cambridge University Press.
Green, T. H. (1886) Introduction. In T. H. Green and T. H. Grose (eds), *The Philosophical Works of David Hume*. London: Longmans, Green.
Mackie, J. L. (1980) *Hume's Moral Theory*. London: Routledge and Kegan Paul.
Norton, D. F. (1982) *David Hume: Commonsense Moralist, Skeptical Metaphysician*. Princeton, NJ: Princeton University Press.
Popkin, R. H. (1966) David Hume: his Pyrrhonism and his critique of Pyrrhonism. In V. C. Chappell (ed.), *Hume*, pp. 53–98. Garden City, NY: Anchor Books.
Smith, N. K. (1941) *The Philosophy of David Hume*. London: Macmillan.
Wilson, F. (1997) *Hume's Defence of Causal Inference*. Toronto: University of Toronto Press.
Wright, J. (1983) *The Skeptical Realism of David Hume*. Minneapolis, MN: University of Minnesota Press.

31

Baron de Montesquieu, *The Spirit of Laws* (1748)

From Political Philosophy to Political Science

David W. Carrithers

Immediately upon its publication in 1748 *The Spirit of Laws* evoked an extraordinary amount of discussion and commentary. Fifteen editions appeared by 1757, and twenty-eight editions were published before 1789. No one with any pretense to political knowledge could remain ignorant of Montesquieu's new classificatory scheme of governments, including his attribution of virtue to republics, honor to monarchies, and fear to despotisms. Equally noteworthy were his incisive analysis of English politics and society, his appreciation of the crucial role of commerce in augmenting national wealth while simultaneously fostering peace, his persuasive arguments for moderating criminal law punishments, and his striking attribution of substantial influence to climate and other "physical causes" (*causes physiques*).

Montesquieu (1689–1755) chose as the motto for *The Spirit of Laws* a phrase from Ovid's *Metamorphoses*, "*Prolem sine matre creatam*" ("A child born of no mother"). He broke new ground by shifting the focus from the behavior of rulers or ruling classes to the broader question of the underlying structure and principles of various regimes. It was not just the specific laws of particular countries but rather the "spirit of laws" in general that served as his focus, freeing him to posit connections between laws and customs and the physical and moral causes influencing them. Moreover, as was typical of most *philosophes* of the Enlightenment, he adopted a mode of analysis and explanation at odds with religious orthodoxy. Rather than resorting to providential explanations of human actions and achievements, he pointedly explained to his readers that he was a political writer and not a theologian (*SL*, XXIV, 1; 1989: 459). Nor was he a neoclassical writer in the republican tradition repeating Aristotle's conviction that government is natural to man and provides the essential grounds for human flourishing. Rather, he was one of those modern inventors of a new science of politics.

The Spirit of Laws is a very ambitious work. The strict boundaries of political analysis are continually stretched as the analysis spills over into forms of discourse now labeled sociology, anthropology, political science, economics, and comparative politics. Above all, Montesquieu set out to explore the diverse influences shaping the content of laws. Thus his search for the "spirit of laws" became the central quest bestowing order on his treatise. Believing that very little in the world of man is the product of pure chance, he explored the basic causes underlying what exists. "Everything is closely linked together," he concluded (*SL*, XIX, 15; 1989: 316). Thus practitioners of the science of politics must seek the veritable "chain" linking one fact to all the others (*SL*, preface; 1989: xliv). Once this chain is discovered, what formerly appeared arbitrary and capricious – and therefore not subject to scientific analysis – will be seen to conform to "natural reasons" (*les raisons naturelles*). In an especially striking book (Book XIX) of his treatise he explored the complex relations between maxims of government, precedents, positive laws, customs, manners, climate, and religion jointly producing the "general spirit" (*esprit général*) of a nation. The content of a people's laws, he explains, will necessarily reflect the complex environmental and cultural situation in which they find themselves. The final result, he concludes, will be a nation's way of thinking (*SL*, XIX, 4; 1989: 310).

In proclaiming that "laws are the necessary relations deriving from the nature of things" (*SL*, I, 1; 1989: 3), he was suggesting that laws arise from underlying political, economic, psychological, and material conditions characterizing the life-pursuits of a given people. Far from being the arbitrary result of abstract ratiocination on the part of world-historical lawgivers, the proper laws for a given society await discovery by legislators capable of discerning the underlying nature of things. This appreciation of the context of human laws represented the modern side of Montesquieu's conception of law-making so greatly appreciated by Auguste Comte and Emile Durkheim. Combined with this viewpoint was a much more traditional outlook regarding laws as designed to reflect justice writ large in the universe. "Before laws were made, there were possible relations of justice. To say that there is nothing just or unjust but what positive laws ordain or prohibit is to say that before a circle was drawn, all its radii were not equal" (*SL*, I, 1; 1989: 4). Judged from this more classical perspective, the law-maker is conceived, not as an architect of regime stability seeking to impose a code of laws well suited to contextual conditions, but rather as a purveyor of justice conceived as a transcendent ideal that pre-exists political or legal arrangements.

Montesquieu resisted the positivist tendency to treat humankind as merely a laboratory for scientific, empirical analysis. If he was sensitive to the limits placed on human beings by the influence of such physical causes as climate, topography, and natural resources (*SL*, XIV–XVIII; 1989: 231–307), he was equally concerned to delineate a realm of human freedom in which mankind can seek to counteract physical causes affecting human potentialities. He was no relativist, if by that term one means being content to judge human practices without relying upon overarching, absolute standards of justice and morality.

No interpretations of Montesquieu are more erroneous than those suggesting that he was prepared to accept and defend whatever exists in a given society. In spite of attacks by Condorcet and others on what they perceived as his strong tendency to justify the historically shaped nature of things, he did not follow Machiavelli in ignoring how men should act in order to concentrate on how they do in fact act. The distinction between "is" and "ought" was fundamental to his project, as is revealed by his opposition to despotism, slavery, abortion, infanticide, homosexuality, and brutal punishments far in excess of the crimes committed. For all his intention to accurately describe the nature of various regimes, his reformist impulse was always present. He conceived the very purpose of enlightenment as revealing the proper path toward reform of whatever abuses mar a political system (*SL*, preface; 1989: xliv).

Montesquieu was nevertheless perceived by contemporary religious critics as demolishing the very standards of morality that he sought to uphold by tracing them back to nature. His critics interpreted the texts in Book XV of *The Spirit of Laws* as contending that whether or not multiple wives (polygamy) should exist, or multiple husbands (polyandry), will depend on whether the presence of unequal numbers of men and women in the population suggests the utility of such non-monogamous practices. Montesquieu himself no doubt contributed to this impression of a utilitarian calculus of morality by entitling the key chapter on this subject, "The Law of Polygamy is a Matter of Calculation" (*SL*, XVI, 4; 1989: 266). So severe were the attacks on him for appearing to "calculate" on the basis of gender ratios what forms of marriage should exist that he altered this chapter title to "On Polygamy, its Various Circumstances." Whatever the title, he never meant to imply that he was approving of either polygamy or polyandry. Rather he was merely describing the conditions under which such non-monogamous marriages are most likely to occur.

The Spirit of Laws and Modernity

Montesquieu was a key proponent of various trends commonly associated with the spirit of modernity. He cordoned off the classical *politeia* from modern times by stressing not only the minuscule scale of the ancient political playing field, but also the unnaturalness and unpleasantness of renouncing self-interest in order to produce the political virtue enabling citizens to place state needs over personal needs (*SL*, IV, 5; 1989: 35). He believed that the ancients had not understood the full dimensions of human liberty since they had attempted to control every aspect of human behavior. Thus he likened life in ancient Sparta to what Christian monks endure (*SL*, V, 2; 1989: 43). For Montesquieu and other moderns, liberty wore the crown once awarded to virtue. He envisioned liberty as carving out from the state's jurisdiction a large area for individual initiative and freedom. "The law," he remarked, "is not a pure act of power; things indifferent by their nature are not within its scope" (*SL*, XIX, 14; 1989: 316). His primary concern was not governmental fostering of virtue or excellence but rather the need to minimize governmental interference in an expanding sphere of activities regarded as private rather than public.

In modernity, the question of what human beings should do with their lives is addressed within the sphere of civil society – not government. Thus Montesquieu recommended that far from attempting to design a regime molding the citizens along distinctive lines aimed at achieving a supreme good, legislators should follow the "general spirit" of the people and conform their rules to the predispositions and general behavioral characteristics of the people they govern. Few, if any, political philosophers have had a higher regard for political and civil liberty than Montesquieu. "Liberty," he asserted, "[is] that good that renders us capable of enjoying other goods" (*Pensée*, 1797, in *Oeuvres complètes*, 1949–51, I: 1430).

Montesquieu abandoned the Platonic quest for the single best form of government since he believed several forms of constitutions are capable of generating good laws. He regarded various forms of moderate government as praiseworthy. He was more an expositor of various types of government in the tradition of political science than a political philosopher outlining the essentials of the single best regime that can be devised. Moreover, he considered the appropriate regime the one most in accord with the diverse array of societal components or influences making up the "general spirit" of a nation. Thus there entered into his thinking a sociological dimension contrasting with the more universalist viewpoint of the classical philosophers. "Perfection," he noted in one of the strikingly modern assertions of *The Spirit of Laws*, "does not concern men or things universally" (*SL*, XXIV, 7; 1989: 464).

Montesquieu undermined classical approaches by historicizing human goals. Rather than adopting a universalizing perspective, he suggested that each culture's "general spirit" produces a distinctive behavior. One people will value war, another will revere commerce, another will consider religion man's highest calling, and still another will consider liberty the essential human priority (*SL*, XI, 5; 1989: 156). This modern perspective so respectful of diversity contrasts sharply with the classical approach of positing a uniform and universal essence of human perfectibility.

In Montesquieu's discussion of governmental forms, the praiseworthy citizen or subject is that individual whose behavior conforms to and supports a particular regime. As long as a regime is moderate and avoids despotism – a very significant, normative qualification to be sure – a variety of human behaviors can be deemed praiseworthy. And to the extent that the quest for political and personal freedom rather than the classical quest for the supreme good has proved to be the driving force of modern politics, Montesquieu may be regarded as one of the patron saints of the modern city. He relied on institutional restraints such as checks and balances and an independent judiciary – not virtue – to check the human appetite for power, while relegating the project of instilling virtue through what he termed "singular institutions" to ancient states. While he felt compelled to study ancient political practices for what they reveal about small-scale republicanism based on citizen virtue and self-denial, he did not believe that the way in which the ancients had approached politics and political questions had any direct relevance to modern practices.

The Legacy of *The Spirit of Laws*

The Spirit of Laws is a veritable compendium of liberal principles, including the need to temper political power to avoid despotic rule; the necessity to abolish slavery and other forms of oppression incompatible with the needs of the human spirit; the requirement to oppose brutal, dehumanizing conquest and colonialism; the mandate to establish toleration for the sake of preserving peace; and the imperative to radically lessen the severity of punishments while also decriminalizing offenses again religious orthodoxy. All of the major Enlightenment conceptions regarding the freedom and dignity of human beings can be found in Montesquieu's great and abiding work. Clearly he envisioned his treatise, at least in part, as an enlightened breviary designed to explain to princes, or other law-makers, how they could best compose laws to achieve the moderation of power necessary for the protection of liberty and security. "By seeking to instruct men," he wrote in the preface to *The Spirit of Laws*, "one can practice the general virtue that includes love of all" (*SL*, preface; 1989: xliv).

Montesquieu was able to champion important liberal causes, however, while none the less displaying a profound distrust of wrenching, ill-considered change, an attitude which explains why Edmund Burke and other conservatives have often been drawn to his work. Perhaps the most revelatory sentence in the whole of *The Spirit of Laws*, therefore, is the passage in Book XIV where he likens politics to a "dull rasp" (*lime sourde*), which arrives only slowly at its ends (*SL*, XIV, 13; 1989: 243). He was very much in favor of implementing enlightened reforms where human freedom can thereby be advanced, but this essentially liberal outlook was balanced by his awareness that changing a key aspect of a government or legal system can have extremely destabilizing consequences.

Montesquieu believed that free states possess complex constitutional structures stemming from the conscious effort of law-givers to divide and balance powers. Despotic governments, on the other hand, spring spontaneously from the natural human instinct to dominate (*SL*, V, 14; 1989: 63). Constitutionalism therefore emerges as a key legacy of *The Spirit of Laws*. For a formula to achieve political liberty in France, Montesquieu relied on the presence of a complex array of intermediary institutions designed to balance the king's authority. Thus he flatly rejected the concept of what the physiocrats would later term "legal" despotism, and, unlike Voltaire, he opposed forms of enlightened despotism that would reduce the power of the *parlements* in France to act as "a depository of laws" (*SL*, II, 4; 1989: 19). Moreover, like Alexis de Tocqueville whom he substantially influenced, he had no more patience for the despotism of the many, exercised in an unmixed democratic regime, than for the despotism of a single individual pretending to a monopoly of wisdom (*SL*, II, 2; V, 7; VIII, 2–4; 1989: 10–15, 49–51; 112–15).

One of Montesquieu's key goals in *The Spirit of Laws* was to support a system of criminal punishment at once fair to the accused and productive of deterrence. He initiated intense public discussion of the proper scale of punishments that aroused Cesare Beccaria's interest in the subject, and his decriminalization agenda, which included an absolute prohibition on offenses against religion being considered criminal, influenced the French Declaration of the Rights of Man and of the Citizen (1789) and also the American Founders (*SL*, VI, 9–21; XII, 4–21; XXV, 12; 1989: 82–95, 189–207, 489).

His views on toleration were also of crucial significance to the liberal project of modernity. His scalding denunciation of the Spanish Inquisition (*SL*, XXV, 13; 1989: 490–2) and his argument that competing religious traditions must be tolerated once they gain a foothold in a state render him a key figure in the development of conceptions of religious freedom. Although he believed that the presence of a single religion augments regime stability, he was just as firmly convinced that wherever more than one religion has taken root, toleration of difference is not only just but necessary for peace to prevail (*SL*, XXV, 10; 1989: 488).

Montesquieu's ideas on commerce and economics are equally striking. He believed commerce substantially contributes to peace between nations (*SL*, XX, 2; 1989: 338; Hirschman, 1977), and he struck an important blow for economic liberalism in warning of the dangers of excessive taxation while at the same time linking willingness to pay taxes to the extent of liberty existing in a state (*SL*, XIII, 1; XIII, 12; 1989: 213, 220–1). He posited a connection between liberty and national wealth, contending that "countries are not cultivated in proportion to their fertility but in proportion to their liberty" (*SL*, XVIII, 3; 1989: 286–7). In addition, he suggested that self-interest is the best incentive for activating citizens to undertake activities that benefit, first themselves, and then the state of which they are a part (*SL*, III, 7; 1989: 27). It is for that reason that he regarded monarchy based on honor, rather than republics based on virtue, as the governmental form most likely to function smoothly in accord with the needs of human nature (*SL*, III, 5–7; 1989: 25–7).

Montesquieu was not a doctrinaire advocate of a single set of institutions or laws regarded as appropriate for all peoples regardless of their distinct histories, material circumstances, and aspirations. Rather, he believed that there exist multiple paths to political moderation, which he considered the ultimate goal of politics. Certainly he believed that there are some governments so despotic and abusive of human nature as to be in need of transformation, but identifying abuses to be repaired was not his primary focus. He saw himself first and foremost as an analyst of how things are linked together in a particular political, social, and economic system. His reformist impulses, though always present, were secondary to his more explanatory perspective. Thus we look to Voltaire for the language of outrage at the abuses of the *ancien régime* and to Montesquieu for the language of descriptive analysis that has proved so fruitful for modern social science.

Bibliography

Editions and translations

Montesquieu (1949–51) *De l'esprit des lois*. In *Oeuvres complètes*, 2 vols, ed. Roger Caillois. Paris: Bibliothèque de la Pléiade.

Montesquieu (1989) *The Spirit of the Laws*, trans. and ed. Anne Cohler, Basia Miller, and Harold Stone. Cambridge: Cambridge University Press.

Studies and references

Aron, Raymond (1965) *Main Currents in Sociological Thought*, vol. I. New York: Basic Books.

Beccaria, Cesare (1963) *On Crimes and Punishments*. Indianapolis, IN: Bobbs-Merrill (orig. pub. 1764).

Carrithers, David W. (1986) Montesquieu's philosophy of history. *Journal of the History of Ideas*, 47: 61–80.

Carrithers, David W. (1995) The Enlightenment science of society. In Christopher Fox, Roy Porter, and Robert Wokler (eds), *Inventing Human Science: Eighteenth-century Domains*. Berkeley, CA: University of California Press.

Carrithers, David W. (1998) Montesquieu's philosophy of punishment. *History of Political Thought*, 19: 213–40.

Carrithers, David W. and Coleman, Patrick (eds) (2002) *Montesquieu and the Spirit of Modernity*. Oxford: Voltaire Foundation.

Carrithers, David W., Mosher, Michael A., and Rahe, Paul A. (eds) (2001) *Montesquieu's*

Science of Politics. Essays on The Spirit of Laws. Lanham, MD: Rowman and Littlefield.

Comte, Auguste (1851–4) *Système de politique positive*, vol. IV: Appendix. Paris.

Courtney, C. P. (1975) *Montesquieu and Burke.* Newport: Greenwood Press (orig. pub. 1963).

Durkheim, Émile (1960) *Montesquieu and Rousseau as Forerunners of Sociology.* Ann Arbor, MI: University of Michigan Press (orig. pub. 1892).

Ehrard, Jean (1998) *L'Esprit des mots: Montesquieu en lui-même et parmi les siens.* Geneva: Droz.

Hirschman, Albert O. (1977) *The Passions and the Interests.* Princeton, NJ: Princeton University Press.

Larrère, Catherine (1999) *Actualité de Montesquieu.* Paris: Presses de Sciences Po.

Manent, Pierre (1998) *The City of Man*, trans. Marc A. LePain. Princeton NJ: Princeton University Press (orig. pub. 1994).

Manin, Bernard (1984–5) Montesquieu et la politique moderne. *Cahiers de philosophie du Centre de philosophie politique de l'Université de Reims*, 2–3: 157–229.

Pangle, Thomas (1973) *Montesquieu's Philosophy of Liberalism.* Chicago: University of Chicago Press.

Shackleton, Robert (1961) *Montesquieu: A Critical Biography.* Oxford: Clarendon Press.

Waddicor, Mark (1970) *Montesquieu and the Philosophy of Natural Law.* The Hague: Martinus Nijhoff.

32

Jean-Jacques Rousseau, *Of the Social Contract* (1762)

Transforming Natural Man into Citizen

Richard Velkley

Of the Social Contract (hereafter *Contract*) is Jean-Jacques Rousseau's most systematic treatment of politics, and the writing that most undergirds his reputation as a great political philosopher. But in a wider sense Rousseau (1712–1778) is one of the most extraordinary intellectual forces in Western history. His thought brings to a certain fruition early modern thinking on natural right, the origins of society in contract, and the non-teleological science of human nature in the tradition of Hobbes, Locke, and Montesquieu. At the same time, it argues against the utilitarian spirit of early modernity, and seeks to revive the aspirations of classical political and philosophic virtue. Rousseau's critique of the Enlightenment calls into question that movement's grounding of law and society in self-interested nature, and points toward the emphasis in later thought on history and on freedom interpreted as autonomy. Thus it is a primary source of later idealism – the rationalisms of Kant, Fichte, and Hegel that aimed at higher understandings of the Enlightenment – as well as of "Romantic"critiques of rationalism. Influential accounts of social life and civilization as alienating (as in Marx, Nietzsche, and Freud) owe deep, if not fully acknowledged, debts to Rousseau. His reflections on the historical and malleable essence of humans helped to instigate anthropological thinking about language, the arts, and what after him was termed "culture." His approach to history constitutes a new approach to the problem of "theodicy," or the justification of evil, since Rousseau proposes that the development of reason in man's abandonment of original pre-rational simplicity is the ground of all significant evil. Although it is hard to reconcile Rousseau's account of reason with a positive view of the future of humans, many – notably some of the leaders of the French Revolution – saw in his work the basis for programs of universal moral and political liberation. This interpretation overlooked, however, the profound ambiguity of Rousseau's thought and the central thrust of its opposition to the Enlightenment.

Born and raised in Geneva, Rousseau spent most of his turbulent adult life in France where the projects of the Encyclopedists were in full flower, and at first Rousseau found himself a contributor to their reformist causes. Remarkable for volatility of temper as well as for literary and philosophic gifts, Rousseau soon broke with his colleagues and was engaged for much of the remainder of his life in disputes with and accusations against his erstwhile friends. In his autobiographical *Confessions* Rousseau gives an account of a visionary experience which marked the beginning of his rejection of Enlightenment reformism. While walking to Vincennes in 1749 he read an announcement by the Academy of Dijon of a prize-essay topic for the following year: "Has the progress of the arts and sciences done more to purify or to corrupt morals?" Rousseau records that he was overwhelmed by a flood of thoughts supporting the idea that morals had been disastrously corrupted by progress. All of his writings thereafter, Rousseau avows, were a development of that theme. In this imposing corpus, which includes novels, dialogues, autobiography, plays, philosophical letters and essays, musical and scientific treatises, Rousseau gives the first fully philosophical analysis of the modern era. His exposure of hitherto unseen problems in this age prepared the way for more radical forms of modernity.

Contract was published in the same year (1762) as the educational novel *Emile*; both works were condemned and publicly burned in France and in Rousseau's native Geneva. They were preceded by two *Discourses: On the Arts and Sciences* or *First Discourse* (1751) and *On the Origin and Foundations of Inequality Among Men* or *Second Discourse* (1755). Taken together, these four pieces and the major autobiographical works (*Confessions* and *The Reveries of the Solitary Walker*) expound what Rousseau calls his philosophical "system." They present the same fundamental human problem from different standpoints; each work is an effort to solve that problem. The multiplicity of treatments suggests that none contains a wholly satisfactory solution. This does not mean that they simply express a series of trials, in which the author seriatim adopts a new approach after finding that each experiment fails. Rather, it means that Rousseau understands the fundamental problem to have an internal structure which discloses a small number of paths toward possible solutions. Each path ends in unresolved tension. Rousseau expects his readers, inspired by his wonderful eloquence, to pursue each path believing that it leads to an unproblematic conclusion. He thinks most readers will cling to that belief, in spite of each work's subversion of it. Readers of a philosophic bent – aware of the lack of direction of philosophic speech – will persist in the search for significance in the strange turns in the arguments. "I developed my ideas only successively and always to but a small number of readers" (Rousseau, 1997b: 110).

The peculiar character of Rousseau's thought and writing is often missed in interpretations of *Contract*. This work is commonly viewed as a celebration of popular sovereignty which treats "participatory democracy" as the highest form of political life. Surely it propounds a principle of popular sovereignty, but Rousseau does not identify that principle, "the general will," with democratic government. In his account, popular sovereignty is compatible with aristocratic and monarchical government. Rousseau, furthermore, claims that "a genuine democracy never existed and never will exist" since "it is against the natural order" (III, 4.3 in Rousseau, 1997a; all citations from this edition give the book of *Contract* in Roman numerals followed by the chapter and paragraph in Arabic numerals). It is also often thought that the tribute that Rousseau pays to citizen virtue in this work contradicts the positive account of the primitive state of nature in other writings. But Rousseau asserts that "everything that is not in nature has inconveniences, and civil society more than all the rest" (III, 15.10). Although Rousseau speaks of the "great advantages" that man has gained by leaving forever the natural state, he also says that man would "ceaselessly bless the happy moment" of that departure "if the abuses of this new condition did not often degrade him to beneath the condition he has left" (I, 8.1). In his view, political life, even in its best forms, cannot re-establish original human freedom and contentment. *Contract* does not ascribe to political life the highest human prospects, and only with trepidation may one read it as a practical recipe for politics. It is better read as a philosophical discourse on the inherent difficulties and limitations of political life. Here it is useful to recall what Rousseau said of *Emile*: rightly understood this book is not a practical treatise on education but "rather a philosophical work on this principle advanced by the author in other writings, that man is naturally good" (cited in Melzer, 1990: 8). The goal that *Emile* presents as eminently desirable – the education of social man that preserves original goodness – is shown to be, in practical terms, unattainable. A corresponding statement can be made about the political goals described in *Contract*.

This chapter offers a preliminary illumination of a few central issues in the argument of *Contract*, whose basis is laid in the first two books. Four topics are discussed: (1) original nature and human history; (2) slavery and legitimate rule; (3) the original contract and the general will; and (4) the original lawgiver and limits of the sovereign.

Original Nature and Human History

The tension between natural freedom and social-political life is announced early in the work: "Man is born free, and everywhere he is in chains" (I, 1.1). These chains cannot be removed; they adhere to humans as social beings, to kings no less than to their subjects. Rousseau claims to answer here the question "What can make this change legitimate?" He claims to be unable to answer the question "How did this change come about?" Yet he had elaborated a hypothetical answer to the latter question in the *Second Discourse*. Certain lacunae and apparent contradictions in *Contract* relate to its abstraction from the account of human history in the earlier work. Most centrally, the status of the original contract – whether it is the work of reason, appetite, chance, or some other cause – is intentionally left obscure in *Contract*. Hence some discussion of the state of nature and man's leaving it, and how history thus relates to the fundamental human problem, is indispensable for understanding *Contract*.

Rousseau's account of the state of nature is derived from the accounts of earlier modern philosophers, especially Hobbes and Locke. These accounts share a common premise: human nature has an original pre-social form, and the life of man as social and political arises out of that condition through calculation. The most fundamental intent of these accounts is to oppose the teleological thought of the tradition: man is not a rational animal whose rationality is ordered toward the attainment of certain perfections, the moral and the intellectual virtues which presuppose sociality. The modern philosophers of the state of nature are skeptics with respect to the powers of reason; they question whether reason is the authoritative power in the soul that rules appetite, and whether it is the theoretical power that grasps the natures of things. Their concern is above all to undermine claims to authority – political and religious – that are grounded in presumed metaphysical knowledge of the first principles of nature, being, and God. Yet Hobbes and Locke do not deny that man is a rational animal; they regard reason as subject to the authority of the passions, serving them in an instrumental capacity. This approach to reason is a component of a general philosophic account of nature in which "ends" and "perfections" play no causal role, being replaced by "laws of nature" as principles of necessary action holding in nature homogeneously, regardless of apparent differences of species and kinds. Thus the view that humans have a distinctive rational end becomes highly questionable.

Accordingly, social and political life arises out of natural necessities – the pre-social needs and passions – that compel humans to devise, in rational calculations, the best means to overcome the difficulties of original nature. In their first condition humans compete for the basic goods of life without settled law and recognized judges to resolve disputes, and without means to secure life and property from assault. Hence the creation of the original contract establishing general peace, and of sovereign powers to defend it. Political life comes into being as a means for the individual to improve his chances for self-preservation. The ground of political authority is the natural right of the individual to life, security, and the basic liberty required to pursue these ends. The ground is no longer the individual's need to participate in social-political life so as to attain rational ends, i.e., the virtues perfecting the rational powers. Rights and freedom replace duties and virtues as the central subjects of political philosophy.

Rousseau deepens this early modern skepticism about the power of reason and whether man is part of an intelligible whole, arguing that reason itself is an acquisition of the species. In his account of the history of the species the essence of humans is perfectibility, the capacity to acquire new faculties. The original condition of man is pre-passionate, since the passions rest on powers of forethought and comparison possessed only by rational beings. Accordingly, the first condition is one of peace; the first humans have simple needs that are easy to satisfy, and are different from other animals only in their relative lack of instinct and their need to imitate other animals. In the first age, they enjoy the tranquil pleasures of a feeling of existence. Rousseau offers a new account of the origin of peculiarly human ills: they are the result of the acquisition of thought which extends desires beyond simple needs, thus rendering an individual's powers inadequate to the satisfaction of passionate desires. From this disproportion arises the human need for cooperation and therewith the servitude (physical and psychic) that is alien to original nature. The new account of the origin of social life reverses the relative evaluations of the natural state and social life in Hobbes and Locke: the move from the one state to the other is not a progress, the amelioration of nature's harshness. Instead, the development of reason causes a decline of human freedom and contentment. This is the thought behind Rousseau's attack on hope for human improvement through advances in the arts and sciences – his criticism of "Enlightenment" that was so shocking to his contemporaries.

Philosophy is a product of human corruption by reason, but it is indispensable for corrupted humans for finding ways to restore, as much as possible, original nature. The goodness of man's original nature consists in its self-unity, in the lack of discord between desire and power. The whole problem of reform in social and political life is to recover such self-unity. "All institutions which put man in conflict with himself are worthless" (IV, 8.17). Man as social, especially the man of modern society who is not "citizen" but "bourgeois," lives neither wholly within himself nor in virtuous dedication to the common good. The concern with self-unity indicates the novelty of Rousseau's enterprise in *Contract*: he conceives the founding contract of society not as the overcoming of natural disunity (the natural state of war) but as the overcoming of rational-social life's disunity. The aim of the philosophic reform of politics is not the securing of independence in the form of protection of the private pursuits of life and happiness from the ambitions of rulers and the passions of fellow-citizens. It is rather the re-creation of original freedom through a new sort of unity with fellow-citizens who form the self-ruling sovereign. Rousseau inaugurates an era of political thought and practice in which political life takes on exalted redemptive functions. At the same time, Rousseau has, as we shall see, severe doubts about the attainability of the redemptive vision he puts forth.

The opening lines of the treatise point to the central difficulty. Rousseau says that his inquiry into "some legitimate and sure rule of administration" will consider "men as they are, and the laws as they can be"; it will "try always to combine what right permits with what interest prescribes" (I.1). "Men as they are" are governed by their passions; they are no longer natural men. A politics that accommodates their interests cannot be purely natural. The subtitle of the work is "principles of political right"; the theme is not natural right. The subject of right is treated as a problem of administration – the search for legitimate "rules." In these opening remarks Rousseau separates his argument from both the central subject of earlier modern political philosophy (natural right) and the central subject of ancient political philosophy (the regime that is best according to nature). *Contract* takes a decisive step away from grounding morality, right, and law in nature, toward regarding these simply as products of human will – a step that is historically of great moment for later European thought.

Slavery and Legitimate Rule

The second chapter of Book I raises the question whether any form of rule is legitimate by nature. Rousseau speaks of the family, "the most ancient of societies," as the only natural society, and of the natural bond between father and child; the child "owes obedience" to the father (I, 2.1). But family relations are based on utility alone, since the "first law" of man's nature is "to attend to his own preservation" (I, 2.2). Each human being becomes his own master when, at the age of reason, "he is the sole judge of the means proper to preserve himself." The natural authority of the parent is temporary, being based solely on the child's passing weakness. Men are not born free and equal; they are free and equal only as self-ruling adults in the state of nature. Clearly the father, the sole natural ruler, cannot be the model for rule of an adult multitude (I, 2.3, 2.9). Yet a certain weakness, not natural to men as adults capable of self-rule, now pervades the human condition. What is the ground of this strangely enduring and universal authority of civil society over humankind? Rousseau denies that there are natural slaves and natural masters; civil society did not arise through the enslavement of the naturally weak majority by the naturally strong few. There are natural inequalities of intelligence, strength, beauty, and so on, but they give no title to rule. The fact of slavery is indeed now common, but is not by right, being based only on conventional inequalities of power (I, 2.4–8). Rousseau implies that all distinctions of power prevailing in society are artificial and hence forms of slavery.

Did the universal servitude come about through a free and conscious act? It is contrary to human nature for one human being to give up his freedom to another, even for subsistence; to do so would be "absurd and inconceivable" for the individual thereby would gratuitously give up his power to benefit himself (I, 4.4). In other words, no favor or benefit from another can be commensurate in goodness to possessing the power of self-rule, and it is absurd to make an agreement knowing that one will suffer the worst thing from it. But slavery is a universal fact of social life; a situation exists that is contrary to human nature. It could have arisen only because human beings somehow abandoned their original nature. They clearly could not have done so by absurdly enslaving themselves in full knowledge of what they were doing. It must have been the case that self-enslaving human beings failed to see that their power of self-rule is an incomparable good or, if they did see this, they did not know that they were handing over this power to others. Such ignorant self-enslavement is the story of the *Second Discourse*.

In *Contract* Rousseau asserts that force is only physical power, and no morality or right can result from it (I, 3.1). But the account of human history in the *Discourse* describes a process in which human desires, through no human intention or plan, exceed individual forces; thereby unwittingly human beings gave up power, by growing weaker in relation to their own desires. They did not know at the time what true power is (the equality of desire and force) and they did not know that they were abandoning it by increasing their desires and by seeking help from others for their satisfaction. The first framing of society as described in the *Discourse* was therefore not an act of intelligent consent. *Contract* describes a compact which would be such an intelligent act; it would rectify the blindness of history. Yet it cannot conceal the role that force plays in this compact, and so it shows that morality in a decisive sense does arise from force. It shows how the force behind human self-enslavement can be made moral or just, if transformed through an original legislation into a universal and equal constraint on human willing. This demonstration is Rousseau's benefaction as lawgiver; the magnitude of his deed warrants Rousseau's description of the "great soul of the lawgiver" as "the true miracle" (II, 7.11) and his linking of that soul to "true genius, the kind that creates and makes everything out of nothing" (II, 8.5).

The Original Contract and the General Will

The problem of legitimate social order for Rousseau is man's recovery of natural self-unity, or the overcoming of the disunity of social man. But social man is permanently different from natural man, having *qua* rational acquired passions and therewith dependency on other humans. The recovery of unity can come about only through conventions. "The social order is a sacred right, which provides the basis for all the others. Yet this right does not come from nature; it is therefore founded on conventions" (I, 1.2). Through conventions the alien forces to which the individual has become permanently linked, and which thus enslave him, must somehow be made to serve his ends.

The gulf between the alien forces and his own forces must be overcome; the two forces must, if possible, become equal or the same. The contract which establishes that equality is called "original" by Rousseau, yet it clearly presupposes the departure from the natural state and the entry into social life. Even so, Rousseau writes in *Contract* as though the original contract is identical with the departure from the "primitive state" into social life. He assumes that men "reached the point where the obstacles that interfere with their preservation in the state of nature prevail by their resistance over the forces which each individual can muster to maintain himself in that state" (I, 6.1). Not being able to engender new forces, men were compelled "to form by aggregation a sum of forces that might prevail over those obstacles' resistance" (I, 6.2). Here Rousseau altogether ignores the *Discourse*'s account of human history, in which the new obstacles arise from the development of reason itself. He thus obscures the extent to which reason itself is the source of the problem that reason tries to solve. He thereby also makes it seem as though man enters into the social order through a rational calculation that fully serves his interests; the entry does not occur as an unknowing self-enslavement.

The contract solves this problem: how, in cooperating with others, can each man commit his own forces of self-preservation to the common force, without breaking the "first law" of caring for his well-being? The right form of association will establish a common force that defends and protects the person and goods of each member and "by means of which each, uniting with all, will nevertheless obey only himself and remain as free as before" (I, 6.4). The rational calculation is that if each member alienates all his forces without reservation to the whole, then no one has anything to fear from other members. No one retains special rights, so that "each by giving himself to all gives himself to no one" (I, 6.8). Each has reason to think that his individual force is identical with the common force.

But clearly this is not true, in a sense: the individual exists in the association as an "indivisible part of the whole" (I, 6.9; see I, 7.1, the final sentence). Natural man never had to think of himself as relating to a larger whole. Social man is compelled to think about how he relates to forces – the wills of others that both promote and oppose his desires – which tend to overwhelm him. The social contract is an attempt to conceive these forces as a constructed whole which immediately expresses the individual's will as the general will. Again, the project is to legitimate inevitable servitude. Although "slavery and right are mutually exclusive" (I, 4.13), the general will is the attempt to reconcile them. Nature is no longer available, human willfulness having replaced it. The general will and the state built on it are the constructions of an "art" (III, 11.2) which endows willfulness with the universality and necessity that earlier philosophy ascribed to natural law. Yet in order to conceive this construction as the beginning of social life, as Rousseau claims to do here, one must forget or ignore the whole truth about the beginning.

Rousseau writes that forming the social contract is the "act by which a people becomes a people," the foundation of society that establishes the principle of majority rule, thus preceding the formation of governments and the election of magistrates (I, 5.2–3). But he also says that the social contract "may never have been formally stated," and is "everywhere tacitly admitted and recognized" (I, 6.5). How much self-awareness is contained in this tacit performance? Once formed, the general will as the sovereign power and the source of laws for the common good allows no alienation of itself to another power, or any division within itself among conflicting interests. Indeed, the sovereign by definition cannot have any interest departing from that of the individuals that compose it, and hence "by the mere fact that it is, is always everything it ought to be" (I, 7.5). The general will cannot err (II, 3.1; II, 4.5); it is the coincidence of "is" and "ought." The individual as member of the general will is both a citizen who partakes in law-making and a subject under the laws he has made (I, 7.1). So it would seem that "the people" is a self-sufficient whole, both ruling and being ruled, not needing or even allowing guidance or correction from another power or authority.

The chapter on the sovereign (I, 7) concludes with a reminder of man's original condition. Because of the individual's "absolute and naturally independent existence," his particular will may be contrary to or different from the general will. He may be inclined to "enjoy the rights of a citizen without fulfilling the duties of a subject," since he may think of the "moral person" of the state as nothing more than a "being of reason" (I, 7.7). Thus the notion of the identity of his will with the general will comes not at all naturally to him. The sovereign (general will) must find means to ensure the fidelity of its members, who "shall be forced to be free" for the "operation of the political machine" (I, 7.8). Thereupon comes a chapter, "Of the Civil State" (I, 8), that brings into the open the precariousness of the whole notion of the original contract. This famous passage describes the "remarkable transformation" that occurs when man moves from the state of nature to the civil state: as man learns to substitute justice for instinct, and to consult his reason before acting, he becomes a different being altogether. "Out of a stupid and bounded animal" emerges "an intelligent being and a man" (I, 8.1). Natural freedom with its unlimited right to possess everything is replaced by civil freedom with the positive title to property granted by the general will. The second freedom rests on accepting the rule of law. Lastly, "one might add to the credit of the civil state" the instituting of "moral freedom" as a characteristic of the individual, whereby he ceases to be the slave of appetite and becomes master of himself (I, 8.3). Here then is the highest and most philosophical sense of freedom: "Obedience to the law one has prescribed to oneself is freedom." But although this topic is of first importance, Rousseau hastens to add that this philosophical meaning "is not my subject here."

This formula of freedom as obedience to self-imposed law was the inspiration for Immanuel Kant's conception of the moral will as a power of self-determination guided by the universal moral law (the categorical imperative). But Rousseau, unlike Kant, treats moral freedom as the creation of human institutions; for Kant it is an *a priori* principle essential to reason (more precisely, to the reason of a "finite rational being"). Rousseau's thought points to an obvious problem: the human beings who form the general will, and who establish the rule of law, are still under the rule of appetite, since only the habit of living under law creates moral freedom. The reader then has to wonder how pre-civil humans are capable of making the calculation of the original contract, since they have not yet benefited from living under laws. The men who formed a "people" were still somehow "bounded animals" for whom the "people" or general will could be at most unattractive abstractions. Rousseau has already pointed to this deep perplexity surrounding the original framing of social order, by declaring at the start of *Contract* his alleged ignorance of how man made the transition from nature to the civil state.

The Original Lawgiver and the Limits of the Sovereign

The subject of the second half of Book II is "the lawgiver." This figure – a founder of superior intellect and character, one belonging to the remote past for most peoples – enters unexpectedly, and seems to have a role that in some ways contradicts the preceding account of the sovereign. Rousseau has just defined "law" as the act that occurs "when a whole people enacts statutes for the whole people." "The people ought to be the author" of the laws which are the "conditions of civil association" (II, 6.4–10). Such acts of the general will must be universal in both their source and their object. Law as directed toward the common good never pronounces on subjects as individuals (by name) or actions as particulars. But Rousseau immediately exposes a difficulty: the people are not capable of authoring "the system of legislation" which is the condition for their own existence as a people. Whereas the universality of willing ensures goodness of intent, it by no means guarantees adequate vision. The people are a "blind multitude" (cf. the references to the prisoners in the Cyclops' cave at I, 2.8 and I, 4.3). "Individuals see the good they reject, the public wills the good it does not see" (II, 6.10). The wisdom required for the founding of a people must combine the different strengths of individual and people without their defects.

Thus the institution of a people is, after all, not an act of the people themselves but one of a wise original founder (II, 10.3–5). Indeed, as Rousseau proceeds to argue in detail, the individual who "dares to institute a people" (II, 7.3) undertakes a task of extraordinary complexity, and must have regard for an array of particular facts (a people's native character, population size, level of civilization, geography, climate, and so on) in order to produce laws most suitable for the given people. Above all, the original lawgiver gives to a people a fundamental set of customs, or morals, resting on divine sanctions, which his eloquence engraves "in the hearts of the citizens," and which secure the habits of living under law. On the strength of these moral laws "the success of all the other laws depends" (II, 12.5). The foundational customs are both highly particularized (crafted for the given people) and the condition for a people's acting universally. The people cannot pre-exist themselves, *qua* legislators, so as to be the founders of their moral life.

To grasp this difficulty it helps to think back to how the combination of individuals into a people arises to remedy the weakness of the solitary individual. The individual, in departing from pure nature, sees (and so desires) more than he can effect with his own forces. The social whole produces a new power based on general consent, and greatly enhancing its members' powers. Yet it lacks the sight of the individual; vision is by its nature the act of an individual. The human problem is that individual vision brings into being desires demanding expanded powers, and such powers tend to be blind. Human vision as perfectible gives birth to universals ("ideas") and therewith to desires for the whole. How can the creation and use of inherently visionless powers realize the visions of wholeness? The solution calls for the improbable: the formation of social powers must be designed and guided by one whose vision is vast and yet unclouded by the passions to which vision always gives birth. This quasi-mythical being can "see all of men's passions yet experience none of them" (II, 7.1). He cannot desire honor nor have political authority – for these bring the blindness of passion – and thus he can be neither magistrate nor sovereign (II, 7.4); his most important labor is done secretly (II, 12.5). He combines independence of others with willingness to care for them, the burden of a task beyond human force with lack of authority to execute it (II, 7.1; II, 7.8; cf. Plato, *Republic* 347a–e). Only such an individual is capable of, "so to speak, changing human nature; of transforming each individual who is by himself a solitary whole into part of a larger whole" (II, 7.3). But not only is the appearance of this human type a rarity; Rousseau also states that the lawgiver can successfully transform human nature only when fortune grants him circumstances (a people combining natural simplicity and docility with the needs of society) which are almost impossible to find (II, 10.5).

Rousseau's political philosophy, it can be concluded, has an optimistic practical surface concealing deep theoretical skepticism about ambitions to cure the human problems by political means. The intent of that skeptical teaching is not to induce despair, but rather, in the spirit of Plato, to lead the soul beyond hopes for attaining the highest good in the political realm by giving birth in the soul first to sobering recognition, then to delightful contemplation, of the wonderful and inescapable perplexities of being human.

Bibliography

Editions and translations

Rousseau, Jean-Jacques (1964) *Du contrat social ou principes du droit politique*, ed. R. Derathe. In J-J. Rousseau, *Oeuvres complètes*, vol. III, ed. B. Gagnebin and M. Raymond. Paris: Pléiade.

Rousseau, Jean-Jacques (1997a) *The Social Contract and Other Later Political Writings*, ed. and trans. V. Gourevitch. Cambridge: Cambridge University Press.

Rousseau, Jean-Jacques (1997b) *The Discourses and Other Early Political Writings*, ed. and trans. V. Gourevitch. Cambridge: Cambridge University Press.

Studies

Derathe, R. (1970) *Jean-Jacques Rousseau et la science politique de son temps*. Paris: Vrin.

Fetscher, I. (1960) *Rousseaus politische Philosophie*. Neuwied: Luchterhand Verlag.

Gildin, H. (1983) *Rousseau's Social Contract: The Design of the Argument*. Chicago: University of Chicago Press.

Halbwach, M. (1943) *Rousseau: du contrat social*. Paris: Aubier.

Masters, R. (1968) *The Political Philosophy of Rousseau*. Princeton, NJ: Princeton University Press.

Melzer, A. M. (1990) *The Natural Goodness of Man: On the System of Rousseau's Thought*. Chicago: University of Chicago Press.

33

Immanuel Kant, *The Critique of Pure Reason* (1781)

A Lawful Revolution and a Coming of Age in Metaphysics

Allen W. Wood

The Critique of Pure Reason is the most decisive work in Kant's career, and thereby also of the history of modern philosophy. It constitutes the point of division of philosophical modernity into its two phases. For, looking backward, the *Critique* constitutes the last great version of the Cartesian project of providing a philosophical foundation for early modern natural science; looking forward, it is the supreme expression of the spirit of the Enlightenment and the model for all subsequent attempts to determine the relation of philosophy to the empirical sciences. It transformed the conception of philosophical questions themselves, viewing them all as expressions of the human mind's activity and its endless struggle to come to terms with its own limitations, whether by resigning ourselves to them or by striving to transcend them.

In a well-known passage from the *Prolegomena to Any Future Metaphysics*, Kant (1724–1804) encourages the notion that his philosophical career may be divided into a "pre-critical" phase of Wolffian "dogmatic slumbers" and a "critical" phase in which alone he is to be regarded as truly himself (*Immanuel Kants Schriften* [hereafter Ak], 4: 260). But the notion is nevertheless false, since Kant had been a trenchant critic of Wolffian metaphysics at least since 1755, and the development of his "critical philosophy" proceeded through a number of stages both before and after *The Critique of Pure Reason* (1781), ceasing only when Kant's philosophical labors were brought to an end by old age and death.

The *Critique* even continues to shape our conception of the history of modern philosophy. For it is still customary to divide seventeenth- and eighteenth-century philosophers into "rationalists" and "empiricists," and to represent the former as guilty of metaphysical extravagances and the latter as threatened by skeptical doubts. Not only does such a picture originate in Kant's *Critique of Pure Reason*, but it also obviously serves far better to motivate Kant's philosophical project in that work than it does to provide an accurate portrayal of philosophy during the early modern period. Yet a second commonly accepted notion, encouraged this time not by Kant himself but by his nineteenth-century critics, has it that his philosophy, along with that of the entire Enlightenment, is basically lacking in historical self-consciousness (for the invention of which nineteenth-century thinkers were pleased to take all the credit). But this notion is even more fundamentally false than the first. For not only is Kant's project in the *Critique* quite explicitly motivated fundamentally by a certain conception of the history of metaphysics, but the Enlightenment also devised all those conceptual tools for whose invention the next century congratulated itself (as we have just observed, Kant is responsible for the very conception of the history of modern philosophy that we tend to take for granted down to the present day). Let us begin with the *Critique*'s historical self-conception, as explicitly presented in the two prefaces (of 1781 and 1787).

The Historical Self-conception of *The Critique of Pure Reason*

The monarchy of metaphysics and the critical revolution

Part of the complexity of *The Critique of Pure Reason* is due to Kant's intention to argue on several fronts against several different alternative positions current in modern philosophy generally, and within the German Enlightenment in particular. Perhaps his most fundamental aim (shared with modern predecessors such as Descartes, Locke, and Hume) is to rein in the pretensions of traditional metaphysics, which, for Kant, was represented by Christian Wolff (1679–1754) and his followers, chiefly Alexander Gottlieb Baumgarten (1714–1762) (see Beiser, 1987: ch. 7). In the first preface, "metaphysics" (feminine both in Latin and German) is called "queen of the sciences" but the legitimacy of this title of honor is called in question. Both Kant's own project in the *Critique*, and the various alternatives against which he wants to define it, are assigned metaphorical roles in a political drama surrounding the legitimacy of the reign of Queen Metaphysics (A, viii–xiii).

The position of Wolff and Baumgarten, which Kant calls "dogmatism," is likened to the despotic ministry of an absolute monarchy – capricious, opinionated, faction-ridden, and consequently unstable and open to the contempt of rational observers. The skepticism of Hume and his German followers is likened to a nomadic people challenging the very foundations of the civil state. The empiricism of Locke challenges the queen's right to rule by alleging that her ancestry can be traced to the "common rabble of experience." Yet another stance was one Kant calls *indifferentism*, which rejects not so much metaphysical assertions as the systematic form and rigorous method of argument. He has in mind chiefly the popular Enlightenment philosophers, who often agreed substantively with dogmatists on metaphysical issues, such as the existence of God and immortality of the soul, but rejected their propositions and proofs, resting metaphysics instead on "healthy understanding" or common sense. In the political metaphor, the indifferentists are depicted as a disgruntled faction which has no real allegiance to the queen but offers no significant alternative to the prevailing despotic regime. (On both Lockeans and popular philosophers – there was some overlap between the philosophers Kant characterizes in these two ways – see Beiser, 1987: ch. 6.)

A "critique" (as the etymology of the Greek name implies) is depicted metaphorically as a "court of justice" before which both the accusers of Queen Metaphysics and the defenders of the old regime are to present their cases. The judge in this court is the human faculty of reason, just as the claims to be decided by it, both those of metaphysics and those of its accusers, are made on behalf of reason. The knowledge most needed by reason is self-knowledge (A, xi); the genitive in the title of the work is therefore at once both subjective and objective. This court of reason is to determine both the monarch's rightful powers and the limits on them "not by mere decrees but according to its own eternal and unchangeable laws" (A, xi–xii). Kant's metaphor thus depicts a kind of political event which occupied the imaginations of many progressive thinkers during the Enlightenment: the revolutionary transformation of a despotism or absolute monarchy into a constitutional system of government, achieved in a just and orderly fashion, with both the procedure and the outcome dictated by the requirements of natural law. Lest we think that the metaphor is only that, Kant tells us in a footnote that "our age is the genuine age of *criticism*, to which everything must submit," including both religion and the state; any attempt to exempt themselves from criticism or to suppress the rational questioning of their claims, he says, only excites further just suspicions against them, and deprives them of "that unfeigned respect that reason grants only to that which has been able to withstand its free and public examination" (A, xi note).

Kant's *Critique of Pure Reason* is therefore self-consciously designed to respond to the needs of its own age in the critical spirit of its own age. It seeks to apply to the world of the sciences the same spirit and the same kinds of standards that apply to the political world; and it casts both itself and the various philosophical alternatives against which it argues in the light of players in such an historical struggle.

Kant's position thus requires him not only to undermine the arguments of traditional metaphysics, but also to put in their place a scientific metaphysics of his own, which limits what can be known *a priori* to that which is required for natural science. Kant must find a way of limiting the pretensions of the dogmatists while still defending systematic metaphysics as a science which is both possible (as is denied by the skeptics) and necessary (as is denied by the indifferentists). Kant needs not only to fight a war on several different fronts (to borrow a metaphor from Beck, 1978), but also to be prepared to defend parts of the positions he is attacking, such as the possibility of *a priori* cognition against both empiricists and skeptics, the unanswerability of many metaphysical questions against both dogmatists and empiricists. Also, while proving to the indifferentists that a science of metaphysics is important, he wants to embrace part of their position too, since he thinks that in regard to some insoluble metaphysical questions, we can defend a kind of common-sense belief (for instance in God, freedom, and immortality) in so far as our moral outlook has a stake in them.

The scientific revolution in metaphysics

The preface to the second edition of 1787 views the task of the *Critique* with an equally historical self-consciousness, but differently. This time, Kant's historical conception is not metaphorical, but depends on a conception of the kind of intellectual revolution that founds a genuine science, and attempts to display the critical philosophy as having all the marks of such a revolutionary event. Prior to this founding his-torical event, an inquiry takes the form merely of a "groping about." The "secure course of a science" is indicated by the absence of any need constantly to retrace its steps and make a new beginning, and by the unanimity of the various co-workers who develop the science (B, vii). By these standards, Kant thinks that there are three philo-sophical disciplines whose status as sciences is beyond question: logic, mathematics, and physics. He thinks the first two achieved this status in ancient Greece, logic at least from the time of Aristotle, and mathematics even earlier (perhaps from the time of Thales) (B, xi). Physics, by contrast, has achieved the status of a science only in moder-nity, since the age of Bacon and Galileo (B, xii–xiii).

In the case of logic, Kant attributes its scientific status to its self-imposed limitations, its restriction of itself to the formal activities of the understanding, and its success in bringing this subject matter to formal completion (B, viii). The scientific success of mathematics is to be explained by its willingness to restrict itself to what the mind of the mathematician actually represents in its objects, "ascribing to the thing nothing except what followed necessarily from what he himself had put into it in accordance with its concept" (B, xii). Strikingly, Kant attributes the success of modern empirical physics to a similar self-limitation, and a similar resolve to approach its subject matter actively and constructively. The founders of modern physics "comprehended that rea-son has insight only into what it itself produces according to its own design; that it must take the lead with principles of its judgments according to constant laws and compel nature to answer its questions, rather than letting nature guide its movements by keeping reason, as it were, in leading strings" (B, xiii). Adapting the judicial meta-phor from the preface to the first edition, Kant then restates this same idea in the following arresting manner:

> Reason, in order to be taught by nature, must approach nature with its principles in one hand, according to which alone the agreement among appearances can count as laws, and, in the other hand, the experiments thought out in accordance with these principles – yet in order to be instructed by nature not as a pupil, who has recited to him whatever the teacher wants to say, but like an appointed judge who compels witnesses to answer the questions he puts to them. (B, xiii)

The pre-modern attitude toward nature was one of childlike trust and uncritical recep-tiveness; the modern or scientific attitude is one in which the human mind, assuming the status of adulthood, liberates itself from tutelage to nature and adopts toward nature the attitude of a suspicious magistrate shrewdly cross-examining a possibly re-calcitrant and prevaricating witness. The role of experiment in science is precisely *not* that it frees our minds from preconceived theories and opens them to the data of experience. The role of experiment is rather to wrest from a reluctant nature the an-swers to questions we formulate in accordance with our theories. Experiments presup-pose a well-developed theory of nature projected by the experimenter, without which it would be impossible to inflict on nature the experimental inquisition of science.

As Kant presents it, metaphysics must imitate the tactics of its scientific predecessors if it is to achieve a similar status. Like logic, metaphysics must achieve scientific status by limiting itself. It must no longer claim to know anything *a priori* about objects except what our own faculties contribute to the constitution of these objects. And it must attempt to bring the knowledge so obtained to a systematic completeness, so that it exhausts what can be cognized of objects *a priori* and arranges these cognitions into a system, whose modesty is exhibited in its admission that there are many questions of vital interest to human beings that it cannot answer (B, xxiv–xxxi). The "architectonic" pretensions of the *Critique* are therefore indispensable to achieving Kant's aims in it. Like mathematics, metaphysics must consider its objects solely in terms of what is represented in them precisely as objects of our cognitive faculties. Finally, metaphysics must imitate both the doctrines and the methods of modern physics. Like modern science itself, metaphysics must conceive of nature according to a theoretical plan projected *a priori* by understanding and reason. Without this, our empirical knowledge can never amount to more than a groping about among accidental observations and can never achieve the status of a science. Kant proposes to rest his revolution in metaphysics on a startlingly counterintuitive hypothesis, analogous to Copernicus' heliocentric hypothesis concerning celestial motions: namely, the *transcendental idealist* hypothesis that instead of our cognitions always conforming to objects, we must suppose that in certain fundamental respects the objects (as appearances) must conform to our cognitions of them (B, xvi). In addition, certain concepts produced by pure reason – those of a beginning of the world in time, of its limit in space, of a simple substance, an uncaused cause and a necessary being – lead to apparent contradictions or "antinomies" – to arguments both that their objects must exist and that they cannot exist. These contradictions, Kant argues, are unavoidable as long as we assume that the objects of our cognitions are things existing in themselves, but once transcendental idealism is assumed, the contradictions disappear (B, xviii–xxi).

The fundamental task of the Critique

The Critique of Pure Reason argues on different fronts because it conveys a complex message: metaphysics can be a science, but only if its foundations are laid properly, and only if it accepts certain limitations on our rational powers that are understandably difficult for human beings to accept. There is a *positive* message: that metaphysics as a science is possible, which is presented mainly in the first three hundred pages or so; and also a *negative* message, which dominates the final three-fifths of the book: that metaphysics must limit its pretensions and resign itself to regarding many of its traditional aims as incapable of achievement – as fitter objects of practical concern and moral faith than of rational determination by theoretical arguments and evidence. Which message is the more basic one?

Owing to an unfortunate propensity of human nature to begin difficult tasks but then leave them unfinished, many classic works of philosophy are much better known for what is said in their early pages than for what they say as a whole. This is especially true of long books, conveying a complex and subtle argument. In many such works, what is said early is intended by the author only as a foundation for the more important message which is presented closer to the end. Suppose John Locke, for example, had begun his *Essay Concerning Human Understanding* with the Book Four exposition of his theory of knowledge (which is in agreement with Descartes's rationalism on all the main points) instead of with his Book One attack on innate knowledge (which

was not aimed primarily at Descartes, and represents a comparatively superficial disagreement with him, on an issue regarding which, in any case, philosophers generally
talk past each other more than they engage each other's real views). In that case it is
unlikely that the *Essay* would be regarded as setting forth a basic alternative to Cartesian rationalism. Or suppose that in *Capital* Karl Marx had consigned his highly technical and abstruse discussion of value (about whose excessive difficulty he warns us in
the preface) to an appendix, and begun his chief work instead with the kind of lively,
readily intelligible, and copiously documented indictment of capitalist exploitation
that occupies most of the rest of the book. If Marx had done this, then it would have
been more difficult for shameless apologists of exploitation to represent *Capital* as a
ponderous and forbidding text, whose argument is so esoteric and forbidding that it
must not even be named in a civilized language, so that even its title must always be
left untranslated (indicating a barrier between us and a set of thoughts we must not
allow ourselves to think).

We do not treat *The Critique of Pure Reason* as badly as we do *Capital*. But Kant's
chief classic has to some extent also fallen prey to the same failure to read all the way
through long books before deciding definitively what they are saying. Readers are
often so exhausted by the attempt to adjust to the transcendental approach to philosophy, decipher the meaning of transcendental idealism, and understand Kant's reply to
Humean skepticism that they fail to see that the chief point of the *Critique*'s positive
doctrine on these matters has been to prepare us to accept the painful limitations on
the powers of metaphysics entailed by it. Metaphysics is capable of theoretically supporting our capacity to do mathematics and empirical physics, but it can provide us no
consolation regarding the questions about our human condition and destiny that most
deeply engage us as human beings: the questions of God, freedom, and immortality of
the soul (B, xxx). The chief aim of the *Critique*, however, is not to deliver this bad
news, but rather to understand the reasons – the legitimate *theoretical* reasons, as well
as practical, moral, or religious concerns – why these unanswerable questions nevertheless occur to us inevitably, and how we are to come to terms with, and make some
positive use of, the metaphysical concepts and propositions which occasion the
insoluble problems.

Even those who study only the beginnings of books could have known what Kant's
chief concern was, since he states it with unmistakable clarity in the very first sentence
of the preface to the first edition: "Human reason has the peculiar fate in one species of
its cognitions that it is burdened by questions it cannot dismiss, since they are given to
it as problems by the nature of reason itself, but which it also cannot answer, since they
transcend every capacity of human reason" (A, vii). The detailed attempt to spell out
what is implied in the *Critique*'s opening sentence occupies Kant throughout the "Transcendental Dialectic," and the conclusions – both scientific and human – that are based
on the results of the dialectic are drawn in the last hundred and fifty pages of the book,
"Transcendental Doctrine of Method."

It is not as though we are not still grappling with the same problems. We continue
to be torn between a modern scientific worldview for which there seems to be compelling intellectual evidence but which we fear leaves us destitute of answers to the questions which most deeply concern our humanity. People still try to "supplement" or
"correct" what reason and science can give us – through some outworn metaphysics,

or traditional revealed religion, or pretended mystical epiphany. But they are always haunted by intellectual bad conscience, and the more honest among them know better than to think that anything significant for the collective life of humanity can ever be made to rest on any such rotten, worm-eaten foundations. The fundamental aim of Kant's *Critique of Pure Reason* was to face this predicament of ours both honestly and sympathetically, to *understand* why we are in it and why it necessarily troubles us, and to recommend a set of practices, not only for the activities of science, but also for the conduct of public argument and the formation of private conviction, that embody this hard-won self-understanding.

Metaphysics and the Possibility of Experience

"Metaphysics," as Kant understands it, consists of synthetic *a priori* cognition from concepts. As "cognition" (*Erkenntnis*), it consists of conscious representations brought under concepts and referred to objects. However, the reference to objects means for Kant that cognition must involve intuitions – or the immediate relation of a representation to its object in which the object is given. But for beings such as us, all intuitions are through sense, and involve being affected by the object. This makes it problematic how there could ever be any *a priori* cognition of objects at all, that is, any cognition of them that is independent of sensible experience. Yet the introduction to the *Critique* argues that our knowledge of nature actually *requires* certain judgments which are "synthetic" rather than "analytic" (that is, not known to be true solely by virtue of the contents of the concepts involved in them, and thus independent of the principle of contradiction) and yet also knowable *a priori*, since no experience could ever be sufficient to establish them. Kant entitles the question how synthetic *a priori* judgments are possible the "general problem of pure reason" (B, 19), and proposes an entirely new science in order to answer it (A, 10–16; B, 24–30).

Transcendental philosophy

This new science, to which Kant applies the term "transcendental" (A, 11; B, 25), does not deal directly with objects of empirical cognition, but investigates the possibility of such objects and our experience of them by examining the mental capacities which are required for there to be any cognition of objects at all. Kant agrees with Locke that we have no *innate* knowledge, that is, no knowledge implanted in us (by God or nature) prior to experience. But experience is the product *both* of external objects affecting us and of the operation of our faculties in response to this effect (A, 1; B, 1). And Kant calls cognition "pure" or *a priori* when its source is the operation of these faculties themselves, rather than the effect on us of external objects through experience. Kant divides our cognitive capacities into the *receptivity* for sensations of objects, through which these objects are *given* to us in *intuition*, and the *active* faculty for relating intuitive data by thinking them under *concepts*, which is called *understanding* (A, 19; B, 33). This division is the basis of Kant's organization of the main part of the *Critique*, the "Transcendental Doctrine of Elements," into the "Transcendental Aesthetic" (which deals with sensibility, the source of intuitive data for cognition) and

"Transcendental Logic" (which deals with the operations of the understanding, and, as we shall presently see, also with the activities of *reason*).

Space and time

First Kant attempts to distinguish the contribution to cognition made by our faculty of receptivity from that made by the objects that affect us (A, 21–2; B, 36). Despite its brevity, the "Transcendental Aesthetic" is crucially important, since it argues for the paradoxical thesis of transcendental idealism that determines the course of the whole *Critique*. First, Kant proposes a new resolution to the debate about space and time between the Newtonians, who held space and time to be self-subsisting existences independent of the things that occupy them (perhaps even to be attributes of God), and the Leibnizians, who held space and time to be systems of relations, conceptual constructs based on the properties inhering in the things we think of as spatio-temporally related. Kant's revolutionary proposal is that space and time are only forms of our sensibility, hence *a priori* conditions under which objects of experience can be given at all and the fundamental principle of their individuation. Only in this way can we account adequately for certain features of our very *concepts* of space and time – their fundamental status in regard to nature, their necessary givenness throughout all experience as infinite magnitudes, and only in this way can we explain the *a priori* yet *synthetic* character of the mathematical propositions which give us cognition of the physical properties of quantities and shapes given in space and time (A, 22–5, 30–2; B, 37–41, 46–9).

Kant draws a paradoxical conclusion from his doctrine of space and time: that although space and time are *empirically real*, they are *transcendentally ideal*, and so are the objects given in them (A, 26–30, 32–48; B, 42–5, 49–73). This *transcendental idealism* is employed throughout the *Critique* in a variety of ways, both positively, to help account for the possibility of synthetic *a priori* cognition, and negatively, to limit the scope of our cognition to the appearances given to our sensibility. We will return presently to what the doctrine means.

The metaphysical and transcendental deductions

The longest and most varied part of the *Critique*, the "Transcendental Logic," contains two main divisions: the "Transcendental Analytic," which considers the *understanding* as a source of synthetic *a priori* cognitions, and the "Transcendental Dialectic," which investigates the faculty of *reason*, but chiefly as a source of illusory arguments and metaphysical pseudo-sciences. The "Transcendental Analytic" is viewed most sympathetically if it is seen as presenting a single, though extremely complex, line of argument, whose different phases or parts are interdependent, each of them persuasive only if they are seen to rest not only on the phases that have gone before but also on those that will come after. The argument begins with an analysis of our use of concepts in judgments and ends with the conclusion that certain concepts, especially substance and causality, apply systematically and *a priori* to all objects that can be given to us in experience.

Kant regards the understanding as the source of certain concepts that are *a priori* conditions of the possibility of any cognition. Twelve basic concepts, which Kant calls the *categories*, are *fundamental concepts of an object in general* and the basis of all *a priori* cognition. In a section of the "Transcendental Analytic" (A, 66–81; B, 91–116) which students of the *Critique*, following Kant's own usage in the second edition, nickname the "metaphysical deduction" of the categories (B, 159), Kant derives the twelve concepts from a table of the twelve logical forms of judgments, comprising three forms each of subject term (quantity), predicate term (quality), copula (modality), and relations either of subject and predicate within a judgment or between judgments themselves (as in hypothetical and disjunctive judgments) (A, 70, 80; B, 95, 106).

Yet it is one thing to establish that we have certain concepts *a priori*, and a rather more ambitious thing to show that these concepts apply (even apply necessarily) to the objects that are given in our experience. This ambitious claim is defended in the most famous and difficult chapter of the *Critique*, "The Transcendental Deduction of the Categories," which in the first edition he said had "cost him the most labor" but which he then completely rewrote in the second edition (A, 84–130; B, 116–69). Kant's argument in this chapter centers on the idea that nothing could count for us as an "experience" unless it could be ascribed to a single identical subject (via the "transcendental unity of apperception"), and the claim that representations could not belong to such a unity unless the elements given in intuition were synthetically combined in such a way that it presents us with objects which are thought through the categories.

Probably the most revolutionary aspect of this phase of Kant's argument is the way he makes *judgment* the fundamental act of the mind, and treats the conditions for judgment as constituting the indispensable condition of experience. This enables him to defend the conditions of objectivity (universal validity for all judging subjects) as conditions of experience, and to use the forms of judgment in traditional logic as universally applicable conditions for objects of experience. It thereby transforms many traditional issues about what is real ("in itself") – issues concerning which skeptical questions often seem unanswerable – into questions about the very conditions under which those skeptical questions themselves make sense. Kant's transcendental approach is therefore the prototype for many subsequent ways of dismissing metaphysical issues or skeptical doubts as unintelligible or as resting on philosophical assumptions that are themselves confused or dubious (including the ways employed by pragmatists, positivists, phenomenologists, ordinary language philosophers).

Principles of pure understanding

The transcendental deduction does not specify *how* each of the categories applies necessarily to the objects given in experience. This is Kant's task in Book II of the "Transcendental Analytic," the "Analytic of Principles." First it must be determined how instances of the categories can be recognized in an experience whose sensory content is originally given independently of them. In the opening chapter of the "Analytic of Principles," Kant indicates how this is possible by supplying for each of the categories a "transcendental schema" which exhibits each category in its application to *time*, which is the form of every sensible intuition whatever. The schema of cause, for example, is related to temporal *succession*, as "the real upon which, whenever it is posited, something else always follows [or] the succession of the manifold in so far as it is subject to a rule" (A, 144; B, 183).

In the next chapter Kant then organizes the principles of pure understanding under four headings, corresponding to the four groups of categories. The "Axioms of Intuition" guarantee that the magnitudes dealt with *a priori* by pure mathematics apply to the *extensive* magnitudes given in experience (to extended stretches of time or region in space) (A, 162–6; B, 202–7), while the "Anticipations of Perception" establish that these same mathematical quantities apply to *intensive* magnitudes, the "real in space" (such as sensations of color or heat, or material forces, such as weight or impenetrability) (A, 166–76; B, 207–18).

By far the most important principles, however, are the "Analogies of Experience," which concern the necessary *relations* among what is given in space and time. Here Kant argues (in the first analogy) that all change must consist in the alteration of states in an underlying *substance*, whose existence and quantity must be unchangeable (A, 182–6; B, 224–32). The second analogy maintains that every alteration must follow a necessary rule or causal law (A, 186–211; B, 232–56), and the third analogy that at any given instant of time the states of substance in different parts of space must stand in the mutual causal relation to one another of community or reciprocity (A, 211–15; B, 256–62). The second analogy is generally supposed to constitute Kant's answer to Hume's skeptical doubts about causality.

In the first edition of the *Critique*, the final section of the "Principles," the "Postulates of Empirical Thought," provides little more than an account of what the modal categories, possibility, existence, and necessity, mean in relation to objects of experience (A, 218–26; B, 265–74). In the second edition, however, Kant added a new argument, the "Refutation of Idealism" (B, 274–9), attempting to show that the very possibility of our consciousness of ourselves presupposes the existence of an external world of empirical objects spatially outside us and distinct from our subjective representations.

The third and final chapter of the "Principles," however, on the distinction between "phenomena" and "noumena," emphasizes the Kantian doctrine that objects of experience are always experienced by us only as they appear within our sensibility (as "phenomena"), and that, although through pure understanding (Greek, *nous*) we may *think* these objects independently of their sensible givenness, we can never *cognize* of them as such non-sensible entities (or "noumena") (A, 235–60; B, 294–315). His main target in this chapter is the Leibnizian idea that reality is grasped most truly when grasped through the understanding alone, and that sensible awareness consists only in confused thought. Against this, Kant reiterates his fundamental claim that the function of sense is to provide an intuition (immediate givenness) of determinate objects, without which thought could not amount to cognition at all. Following up on this, Kant concludes the "Analytic of Principles" with an important appendix, entitled the "Amphiboly of Concepts of Reflection" (A, 260–92; B, 316–49). In it he presents an important criticism of Leibnizian ontological conceptions by arguing that, through a confusion (or "amphiboly"), Leibniz has taken mere features of the concepts through which we think things to be features of the objects themselves. He thereby reinforces his critique of the Leibnizian–Wolffian account of essence, identity and possibility, and his insistence that empirical individuation and real possibility require sensible conditions independent of logical discernibility and non-contradictoriness.

Transcendental idealism

The most revolutionary and perplexing aspect of Kant's position in the *Critique* is surely his doctrine of transcendental idealism. It is perplexing not only because it explicitly demands a change in our perspective (allegedly analogous to that involved in the Copernican revolution in astronomy), but also because Kant's various statements of transcendental idealism do not clearly amount to any single coherent doctrine. The problems have to do with the relation between what Kant calls an "appearance" and the so-called "thing in itself" that, according to the doctrine, corresponds to this appearance.

Sometimes Kant contrasts a "thing existing in itself" with "its appearance," stating or suggesting that the former thing is the "cause" or "ground" of the latter. On this reading, transcendental idealism says that real things (things in themselves) *cause* appearances. Appearances are entities distinct from real things; they have no existence in themselves, but are only representations in us. Let us call this the *causality interpretation* of transcendental idealism. At other times, however, Kant speaks of appearances as though they were the very same things that exist in themselves, in so far as they are *considered* or *referred to* "as they appear." On this *identity interpretation* of transcendental idealism, real things (the very same things that exist in themselves) are cognized by us under certain conditions of sense and understanding. These things affect us, causing representations, whose *objects* are these same things *as they appear*. We distinguish these things *as* cognizable by us (appearances) from the same things *as* they are in themselves (which, as such, cannot be cognized by us); but we are speaking of the same entities in both cases.

The two interpretations agree that:

1   Real things exist.
2   They cause representations in us.
3   Objects of our cognition are given to us through the senses and thought through the understanding.
4   Sensing and thinking are subject to certain conditions that make synthetic *a priori* cognition possible.

But they return conflicting answers to the following questions:

1   Is an appearance the very same entity as a thing in itself?
    Causality interpretation: No (it is its effect).
    Identity interpretation: Yes (they are the same thing referred to in different ways).
2   Are appearances *caused* by things in themselves?
    Causality interpretation: Yes (that is the basic relation between the two).
    Identity interpretation: No (since nothing can be its own cause, and a real thing cannot be the same as the representation it causes).
3   Do the bodies we cognize in experience have an existence in themselves?
    Causality interpretation: No (appearances *never* have an existence in themselves).
    Identity interpretation: Yes (appearances *always* have an existence in themselves).

These three questions appear to require some determinate and self-consistent answer if transcendental idealism is to constitute a determinate and self-consistent hypothesis at all. Because the two interpretations answer them in conflicting ways, a sympathetic interpreter of *The Critique of Pure Reason* seems forced to choose between them. But the decision cannot be based on Kant's explicit statements, because *both* interpretations are explicitly supported by the texts. The following passages, namely, require the causality interpretation and are inconsistent with the identity interpretation:

> Objects in themselves are not known to us at all, and what we call external objects are nothing other than mere representations of our sensibility, whose form is space, but whose true correlate, i.e. the thing in itself, is not and cannot be cognized through them. (A, 30; B, 45)

> What the objects may be in themselves would still never be known through the most enlightened cognition of their appearance, which alone is given to us. (A, 43; B, 60)

> Appearances do not exist in themselves, but only relative to the [subject] in so far as it has senses. (B, 164)

> But we should consider that bodies are not objects in themselves that are present to us, but rather a mere appearance of who knows what unknown object; that motion is not the effect of this unknown cause, but merely the appearance of its influence on our senses; that consequently neither of these is something outside us, but both are merely representations in us. (A, 387)

Yet passages like the ones below equally require the identity interpretation and can in no way be reconciled with the causality interpretation:

> We can have cognition of no object as a thing in itself, but only in so far as it is an object of sensible intuition, i.e. as an appearance . . . We assume the distinction between things as objects of appearance and the very same things as things in themselves, which our critique has made necessary . . . (B, xxvi–xxvii)

> If we add the limitation of a judgment to the concept of its subject, then the judgment is unconditionally valid. The proposition "All things are next to one other in space" is valid only under the limitation that these things be taken as objects of our sensible intuition. If here I add the condition to the concept and say: "All things, as outer appearances, are next to one another in space," then this rule is valid universally and without limitation. (A, 27; B, 43)

> The things we intuit are not in themselves what we intuit them to be, nor are their relations so constituted in themselves as they appear to us. (A, 42; B, 59)

> The concept of appearances . . . already . . . justifies the division of objects into *phenomena* and *noumena*, thus also the division of the world into a world of the senses and of the understanding . . . For if the senses merely represent something to us **as it appears**, then this something must also be in itself a thing, an object of a non-sensible intuition, i.e. of the understanding . . . through which, namely, objects are represented to us **as they are**, in contrast to the empirical use of our understanding, in which things are only cognized **as they appear**. (A, 249)

If we cannot choose between the two interpretations on textual grounds, then we need to consider the philosophical grounds for preferring one interpretation to the other. On the *causality interpretation*, transcendental idealism appears to be similar to Berkeley's idealism, since appearances then seem to be reduced merely to ideas in individual minds. It seems impossible to save the objectivity of appearances, and Kant seems to condemn us to utter ignorance regarding objects that are truly real (i.e., that have an existence in themselves). Once we have done this, however, the thing in itself looks like a metaphysical extravagance, whose only function is to posit a reality we can never know. On the causality interpretation, moreover, Kant seems (as F. H. Jacobi famously alleged) to be guilty of an inconsistency when he charges that metaphysicians may not apply the concept of causality to things existing in themselves (as in the cosmological argument for God's existence); for on the causality interpretation, transcendental idealism itself involves precisely such an application of the concept of cause. Further, on this interpretation, transcendental idealism seems committed to the claim that the empirical self is not really the same entity as the noumenal self, so that when I know myself through experience, it is not really myself that I know but only some effect in the world of sense caused by me.

The identity interpretation too faces philosophical difficulties. For if space and time are essential properties of appearances, then how can the very same things not be spatio-temporal? Or if space and time are nothing in themselves, how can spatio-temporal things have an existence in themselves? Then again, Kant's solution to the mathematical antinomies appears to depend on his saying that appearances have no existence in themselves, a proposition which is asserted by transcendental idealism only on the causality interpretation but denied by it on the identity interpretation.

There is no space here to defend my own view that there are cogent responses to these objections, whereas the objections to transcendental idealism on the causality interpretation are insuperable. Throughout most of its history, transcendental idealism has most often been given the causality interpretation, making it a serious stumbling block to the acceptance of Kant's doctrines in the *Critique*. On the identity interpretation, however, transcendental idealism is actually a form of metaphysical *realism*, which is distinguished from other forms of realism by the fact that it holds our cognitive capacities to be limited and holds that we have ways of precisely determining what sorts of features of objects we are capable of cognizing and of referring to objects determinately *as* things that fall under our cognitive capacities (hence *as* "*appearances*"or real things in so far as they can appear to us).

The Transcendental Dialectic

As we noted earlier, it is really only in the second division of the "Transcendental Logic" that Kant turns to what has been from the beginning the chief task of the *Critique*, namely discrediting dogmatism and clearly displaying the limits of metaphysics. The "Analytic" has already prepared the way by indicating that synthetic *a priori* principles can be defended only within the limited domain of experience, and the final chapter and appendix to the "Principles" laid special emphasis on the limits of pure understanding in cognizing objects. But Kant's aim in the "Dialectic" is not only to show the failure of a metaphysics which transcends the boundaries of possible experience, but it is equally to demonstrate the inevitability of the questions which preoccupy it and to show that its arguments, though deceptive, cannot be dismissed because they tempt us for good reasons, and when these reasons are understood, they can even be put to good use for the cause of human knowledge. The doctrines of dogmatic metaphysics are not mere blunders; they resemble optical illusions in that they are based on the normal and healthy use of reason.

Ideas of reason

The opening book of the "Transcendental Dialectic" is therefore a derivation, even a defense, of the *transcendental ideas*, such as God, the immortal soul, and the free will, with which dogmatic metaphysics is preoccupied (A, 293–338; B, 349–96). *Reason*, the highest of all our cognitive faculties, is simultaneously the faculty of drawing inferences from principles and of seeking ultimate grounding principles. The ideas are generated *a priori* by our faculty of reason when it seeks, through regressive syllogistic reasoning, for what is *unconditioned* in respect of the objects given in experience, according to the principles of understanding which govern these objects.

The Leibnizian–Wolffian system, as presented in Baumgarten's *Metaphysica* (which Kant used as the textbook for his lectures on metaphysics for virtually his entire career) was divided into four parts: ontology, psychology, cosmology, and theology. The "Transcendental Aesthetic" and "Transcendental Analytic" may be seen as covering the ground of ontology, though in a new and critical way. The "Transcendental Dialectic," however, is dedicated to arguing that the other three parts of the system are pseudo-sciences resting on inevitable illusions of human reason attempting to extend itself beyond its proper limits. The three rationalistic pseudo-sciences are organized according to the traditional threefold division of syllogistic forms: categorical, hypothetical, and disjunctive. Kant argues that each type of syllogism leads to a different kind of rational idea. Seeking the unconditioned subject to which all our thoughts relate as predicates, we generate the idea of the soul as a simple non-empirical substance; seeking the unconditioned in respect of any of several hypothetical series arising in the world leads to ideas such as that of a first event in time, a simple substance, and a first cause. Finally, Kant derives the idea of a most real being or God as the ideal ground of the real properties constituting all other things.

Rational psychology: the paralogisms

Rational psychology is the topic of the "Paralogisms" (or fallacious inferences) of pure reason, which argue invalidly from the formal subjecthood, simplicity, and identity of the thinking to the conclusion that the soul is a simple (hence indestructible) substance which is self-identical throughout all experience (A, 341–66). In the first edition, the paralogisms also included a fourth, which defends the reality of external appearance in space (A, 366–405). But in the second edition the entire paralogisms chapter (B, 406–32) was rewritten and simplified, omitting this fourth paralogism altogether (since its place was taken by the new refutation of idealism in the postulates of empirical thought).

The invalidity of the inferences of transcendental psychology depends on the fact that the self-awareness (or transcendental apperception) which is the fundamental condition for the possibility of all experience is the *a priori* awareness of an activity (of our own minds) but it provides us with no direct cognitive access to (or intuition of) the entity which acts – of "the 'I' or 'he' or 'it' (the thing) which thinks" (A, 346; B, 404). Philosophical controversy still surrounds the question whether and in what way a materialistic science of nature (such as the study of the brain and nervous system) "explains" (or can ever hope to explain) consciousness or self-awareness. Kant's discussion in the "Paralogisms" returns a deeply pessimistic answer to those who hope to resolve these controversies. Whatever theory we may propose regarding the "mind–body" problem (whether the "pneumatism" that takes the soul to be an immaterial thing or the "materialism" that identifies it with something material), and whatever account we may propose of the causal interaction between thoughts and the body (whether the theory of "physical influence," which attracted Kant's teacher Martin Knutzen, or the occasionalist theory of "supernatural assistance" invoked by Malebranche and the later Cartesians, or that of "pre-established harmony" espoused by Leibniz and his followers), none of these theories can ever be established or even made fully intelligible (A, 379–96). Our own nature in our most intimate activity as thinking and experiencing beings must forever remain a mystery to us. The proposition that we are immortal spirits can neither be confirmed nor refuted.

Rational cosmology: the antinomies

By far the longest and most painstaking part of the "Transcendental Dialectic" is the "Antinomies of Pure Reason," which deals with the topics of *rational cosmology* (A, 405–583; B, 432–611). Here Kant thinks that reason's natural illusions, if left uncorrected by criticism, will lead it into actual contradictions. Kant argues that unless we accept transcendental idealism's distinction between appearances and things in themselves, we will be committed to accept the soundness of arguments both that there must a first beginning of the world in time and that there could not be such a beginning, both that there must be a limit in space and that there can be no such limit (the two halves of the first antinomy), both that there must be a simple substance and that there cannot be (the second antinomy), that there must be a first or uncaused cause and that there cannot be (the third antinomy), that there must be a being whose existence is necessary and that there can be no necessary being (the fourth antinomy).

The only way of resolving these contradictions, Kant argues, is by accepting that the natural world is a realm of appearances, not of things in themselves. Regarding the first two antinomies (which Kant calls "mathematical antinomies"), it has to be acknowledged that as regards its limits in space, time, or divisibility, there is no fact of the matter about the size of the world as a whole, because the natural world is never present in experience as a whole, but is rather given to us through a regressive series regarding time, space, and divisibility. We can always proceed *indefinitely* far in the regress, but can never reach a beginning, nor can we encompass the series as *infinite* either. Both sides of the mathematical antinomies, therefore, turn out to be false, because both rest on the common (and false) assumption that the world, as regards its extent in space and time or its divisibility, has a determinate magnitude (either finite or infinite). As to the third and fourth antinomies (which Kant calls "dynamical"), Kant's solution is somewhat different. Both sides here may be true, if the denial of a free cause or necessary being is taken to refer to the natural or sensible world and their affirmation is taken to refer to what might exist in a noumenal or supersensible world of things in themselves. Just as his thinking about the antinomies generally seems to have shaped his thinking about the structure and outcome of the entire "Transcendental Dialectic," so Kant's resolution of the third antinomy plays an important part in his moral philosophy, and indeed in his philosophy as a whole.

Rational theology: the ideal of pure reason

The third and last supposed metaphysical science is taken up by Kant in the final chapter of the "Transcendental Dialectic," which deals with *rational theology* (A, 567–642; B, 595–670). If an "idea" is a pure concept generated by reason, then an "ideal" is the concept of an *individual thing*, which concept is produced by reason alone. In the "Ideal of Pure Reason," Kant argues for the cogency, even the inevitability, of the idea of God as an *ens realissimum* or supreme individual thing, a being possessing all realities or perfections.

Kant organizes all theistic proofs under three headings: the *ontological* proof, based solely on the concept of God, the *cosmological* proof, based on the existence of a world in general, and the *physicotheological* proof, based on the particular constitution of the actual world (especially its exhibition of purposive design). First Kant attacks the ontological argument, through his well-known thesis that since existence is not a property or a perfection, it cannot be among the contents of the idea of God, and hence cannot be inferred from that idea alone. Then he claims about the cosmological and physicotheological proofs that if they are to establish the existence of a supremely perfect deity, they cannot succeed unless the ontological proof also succeeds. But then since the ontological proof is unsound, the entire metaphysical enterprise of proving the existence of God must be given up as hopeless.

Regulative use of the ideas

The outcome of the "Transcendental Dialectic," therefore, seems to be almost entirely negative. In an important appendix, however, Kant qualifies this result by arguing that the cosmological ideas have an important function as regards natural science if they are understood *regulatively*, that is, if they are taken to represent not metaphysical beings whose reality is supposed to be demonstrable, but rather goals and directions of inquiry, marking out the ways in which our knowledge is to be sought for and organized. He is concerned to emphasize, therefore, that the outcome of the dialectic of reason is in the end not entirely negative or skeptical, if we know how to make wise use of the ideas of reason.

The Transcendental Doctrine of Method

The "Transcendental Aesthetic" and "Transcendental Logic" (both the "Analytic" and "Dialectic") make up the "Transcendental Doctrine of Elements." *The Critique of Pure Reason*, however, contains a second major division, which tends to be neglected by its readers (perhaps just because the book is so long and the parts already surveyed are so exhausting). But, as indicated earlier, the "Doctrine of Method" includes some surprisingly important discussions.

The discipline of pure reason

Human reason, in its theoretical use, has been shown to be confined within narrow limits. Its primary task, a difficult one, is to discipline itself in light of this self-knowledge. Kant divides this discipline into four sections: (a) the "dogmatic" use of reason; (b) the "polemical" use of reason; (c) reason's hypotheses; and (d) reason's proofs.

The first section includes Kant's most complete discussion anywhere of the science of mathematics (A, 712–38; B, 740–66). Its aim is to argue against the attempt (found in the philosophies of Descartes, Spinoza, and Leibniz) to imitate the method of mathematics in other branches of philosophy (especially in metaphysics). Mathematics, he argues, has certain distinctive advantages over other sciences, owing to its inherent limitation to what can be exhibited *a priori* in the pure intuitions of space and time. Properly speaking, it is only in mathematics that we can find genuine definitions, axioms, or demonstrations. When philosophers present their theories as if they could avail themselves of these features of mathematics, they only deceive themselves, presenting arbitrary concepts and (necessarily groundless) inventions as if they could have the same kind of necessary and non-empirical grounding appropriate to mathematical theorems. The third and fourth sections further develop this critique of the methods of metaphysics by prescribing limits on what reason should employ as hypotheses or offer as proofs in matters that transcend empirical inquiry.

In the second section, dealing with the "polemical" use of reason, Kant turns to an ardent defense of freedom of public communication, and of a spirit of open-mindedness in the discussion of metaphysical issues, arguing that the very existence of reason itself depends on the free give and take of controversy between rational beings, which requires the liberty to come to one's own conclusions honestly and express them openly to others (A, 738–69; B, 766–97). This discussion is distinctive in that it directly connects the concerns of theoretical reason or science with considerations that are moral or political in nature. Chief among Kant's concerns here are to protect the liberty of thought and its expression against political repression that is motivated by *religious* concerns, and regards all critical questioning of religious dogmas as morally or spiritually harmful either to the individual soul or to the political order. Kant was to return to these issues many times in his later writings, especially in the essays *An Answer to the Question: What is Enlightenment?* (1784, Ak, 8: 35–42), *What Does It Mean to Orient Oneself in Thinking?* (1786, Ak, 8: 133–46), and *Conflict of the Faculties* (1798, Ak, 7: 5–116). After the death of Frederick the Great in 1786, Kant was also to incur the wrath of Prussian officials who attempted to act on precisely the kinds of views he argues against in this section of the *Critique*.

The canon of pure reason

In the second chapter of the "Doctrine of Method" Kant argues that reason's pretensions must be limited, but they cannot be checked externally by censorship; instead, they must be checked internally, by reason itself, which therefore requires a "canon," or set of principles determining how it should form its beliefs. Kant's principal thesis here is that reason requires such a canon not from a theoretical standpoint but only from a practical or moral standpoint, so that in matters that transcend its theoretical capacities, the propositions it holds to be true may be consistent with the moral duties reason prescribes to itself. The "Canon of Pure Reason" includes not only Kant's first systematic statements of his argument for rational faith in God on moral grounds, but also his most systematic discussion of moral philosophy prior to the *Groundwork for the Metaphysics of Morals* (1785).

The architectonic and history of pure reason

In the concluding two sections of the "Doctrine of Method," the "Architectonic of Pure Reason" and the "History of Pure Reason," Kant attempts to outline the entire system of philosophical knowledge in light of the findings of the *Critique*. The "History of Pure Reason," for all its tantalizing brevity, is an attempt by Kant to conclude by orienting the critical philosophy clearly in relation to the positions (dogmatism, empiricism, skepticism, indifferentism) he discussed metaphorically in the preface to the first edition.

Conclusion

The basic theme of *The Critique of Pure Reason* is the limitedness of reason. No philosopher has laid more stress than Kant did on the importance for human beings of keeping in mind the limited capacity of their reason in all the affairs of life, especially in the conduct of inquiry and formation of beliefs. Yet no philosopher ever asserted more ardently the absolute title of reason to govern human thought and action, or gave us sterner warnings concerning the inherent badness and the disastrous consequences of permitting human passions, enthusiasms, or inspirations, or the supernatural deliverances of authority or tradition, to usurp the authority of reason. The *Critique* gives the lie to all those who, standing in the Romantic tradition, assert that Enlightenment rationalism errs in overestimating our rational capacities or being insufficiently attentive to their limitations. On the contrary, the truly dangerous error is to imagine that human beings have access to some faculty or source of wisdom higher than reason, exempt from rational criticism, to be followed in preference to it. The importance of subjecting reason itself to critique lies precisely in the fact that beyond it there can be no legitimate appeal. Although this is the fundamental message of the most influential classic of modern philosophy, humanity remains in great peril because that message is under attack from many quarters. It therefore stands in constant need of being re-learned and re-appropriated, and that is why the study of Kant's *Critique of Pure Reason* is as important now as it ever has been.

Bibliography

Editions and translations

Immanuel Kants Schriften (1902–) Ausgabe der königlich preussischen Akademie der Wissenschaften. Berlin: W. de Gruyter. (Abbreviated in the text as "Ak." *Die Kritik der reinen Vernunft* is included in volumes 3 and 4 of this edition, but it is cited by pagination in the first (A) and second (B) editions. All other works will be cited in Ak by volume: page number.)

Kant, Immanuel (1998) *The Critique of Pure Reason*, ed. and trans. Paul Guyer and Allen W. Wood. Cambridge Edition of the Works of Immanuel Kant. New York: Cambridge University Press.

Studies

Allison, Henry (1983) *Kant's Transcendental Idealism*. New Haven, CT: Yale University Press.

Ameriks, Karl (1998) *Kant's Theory of the Mind*, 2nd edn. Oxford: Clarendon Press.

Aquila, Richard (1983) *Representational Mind: A Study of Kant's Theory of Knowledge*. Bloomington, IN: Indiana University Press.

Beck, Lewis White (1978) *Essays on Kant and Hume*. New Haven, CT: Yale University Press.

Beiser, Frederick (1987) *The Fate of Reason*. Cambridge, MA: Harvard University Press.

Bennett, Jonathan (1966) *Kant's Analytic*. Cambridge: Cambridge University Press.

Bennett, Jonathan (1974) *Kant's Dialectic*. Cambridge: Cambridge University Press.

Bird, Graham (1962) *Kant's Theory of Knowledge*. London: Routledge and Kegan Paul.

Brook, Andrew (1994) *Kant and the Mind*. New York: Cambridge University Press.

Cassirer, Ernst (1981) *Kant's Life and Thought*, trans. James Haden. New Haven, CT: Yale University Press.

Friedman, Michael (1992) *Kant and the Exact Sciences*. Cambridge, MA: Harvard University Press.

Guyer, Paul (1987) *Kant and the Claims of Knowledge*. New York: Cambridge University Press.

Guyer, Paul (ed.) (1992) *The Cambridge Companion to Kant*. New York: Cambridge University Press.

Henrich, Dieter (1994) *The Unity of Reason*. Cambridge, MA: Harvard University Press.

Keller, Pierre (1998) *Kant and the Demands of Self-consciousness*. New York: Cambridge University Press.

Kemp Smith, Norman (1923) *A Commentary on Kant's Critique of Pure Reason*. London: Macmillan.

Kitcher, Patricia (1990) *Kant's Transcendental Psychology*. New York: Oxford University Press.

Kitcher, Patricia (ed.) (1998) *Kant's Critique of Pure Reason*. Lanham, NJ: Rowman and Littlefield.

Longuenesse, Beatrice (1998) *Kant and the Capacity to Judge*, trans. Charles T. Wolfe. Princeton, NJ: Princeton University Press.

Melnick, Arthur (1993) *Kant's Analogies of Experience*. Chicago: University of Chicago Press.

Neiman, Susan (1994) *The Unity of Reason*. New York: Oxford University Press.

Paton, H. J. (1936) *Kant's Metaphysic of Experience*, 2 vols. London: George Allen and Unwin.

Pippin, Robert B. (1982) *Kant's Theory of Form*. New Haven, CT: Yale University Press.

Strawson, Peter (1966) *The Bounds of Sense*. London: Methuen.

Walker, Ralph (1978) *Kant*. London: Routledge and Kegan Paul.

Walker, Ralph (ed.) (1992) *Kant on Pure Reason*. Oxford: Oxford University Press.

Waxman, Wayne (1991) *Kant's Model of the Mind*. New York: Oxford University Press.

Wolff, Robert Paul (1963) *Kant's Theory of Mental Activity*. Cambridge, MA: Harvard University Press.

Wolff, Robert Paul (ed.) (1967) *Kant: A Collection of Critical Essays*. Garden City, NY: Doubleday.

Wood, Allen W. (1978) *Kant's Rational Theology*. Ithaca, NY: Cornell University Press.

Wood, Allen W. (ed.) (1984) *Self and Nature in Kant's Philosophy*. Ithaca, NY: Cornell University Press.

34

Immanuel Kant, *Groundwork of the Metaphysics of Morals* (1785)

Duty and Autonomy

Andrews Reath

Immanuel Kant's *Groundwork of the Metaphysics of Morals* is a seminal work in the history of moral philosophy that remains highly influential in contemporary moral theory. Some readers think that Kant succeeds in giving a systematic articulation of the core of moral thought, while others vigorously reject this assessment. But almost everyone agrees that it is a text with which one must contend if one wants to think seriously about ethics. The *Groundwork* is a difficult but immensely rich work. Kant claims to be articulating the fundamental principles that underlie ordinary moral thought, and, despite the forbidding terminology, his account of morality is driven by a few simple and powerful ideas. The aim of this chapter will be to state these ideas in intuitive terms and to help the reader navigate the intricacies of the extended argument that runs through the work.

Kant (1724–1804) describes the *Groundwork* as "nothing more than the search for and establishment of the *supreme principle of morality*" (*Groundwork*, 392; all quotations are from the 1997 edition, translator Mary J. Gregor, with page references [given in the margins of standard English translations] to the text in volume 4 of the Royal Prussian Academy of Sciences edition of Kant's collected works). The "search" for this principle occupies Sections I and II. Here Kant simply states the fundamental principle that guides ordinary moral thought, which he terms the "Categorical Imperative." However, these sections only offer an analysis of the basic concepts and principles found in ordinary moral thought, and do not go so far as to show that they have rational authority for us. That is, while we may actually employ the Categorical Imperative and related concepts in moral reasoning, these sections stop short of showing that this principle has a rational basis that applies to us. Section III completes the task by "establishing" the authority of the Categorical Imperative: it develops an argument intended to show that it is fully reasonable for us to endorse this principle.

The *Groundwork* may be understood as an inquiry into what is presupposed by the assumption of the ordinary person of good will that we are subject to duties. By reflecting on the idea of a moral requirement, Kant arrives at various statements of the fundamental principle. One version says that an action is right only if it is rational to will the principle of the action as a universal law from which anyone may act. Another version is a principle of respect for the dignity of persons – that one should always treat persons as "ends-in-themselves," and never as a means only. Though these principles seem different, Kant argues that they are equivalent – that they are different "formulae of the very same law" (1997: 436). Somewhat surprisingly, Kant also argues that we must be free and autonomous agents if we are bound by morality. One remarkable feature of Kant's theory is the way in which he connects duty and autonomy. Kant takes duty to be central to morality. But he argues that moral requirements are autonomously imposed in that they are based on principles that we legislate for ourselves through our own reason, independently of desire and other subjective influences. Indeed, we can account for the inescapable character of moral requirements only if we understand them as autonomously self-legislated in this way. Kant draws on the connection between duty and autonomy to establish the rational authority of morality. As rational agents we think of ourselves as possessing free choice. Since we most fully realize our freedom by acting from moral principles, as free agents we are committed to morality. Otherwise put, our reason for endorsing moral principles is that by doing so we realize our standing as free and autonomous agents. Let us now go through the main ideas of each section.

Preface

The task of establishing the fundamental principle of morality requires what Kant calls a "metaphysics of morals." By this phrase Kant means an account of moral principles that is *a priori*. *A posteriori* or empirical knowledge is based on experience. By contrast, there is no particular experience that is relevant to the truth or falsity of an *a priori* claim. *A priori* principles can, in that sense, be known independently of experience through reason alone. A metaphysics of morals is thus an account of the fundamental principles of morality that shows that they represent requirements on action based in reason. Moral principles need such a grounding because we regard them as ideal normative principles telling us how we ought to act. We cannot decide what is right simply by observing what people want, how they tend to act, or what is socially approved, since all of these may be morally improper. If moral principles are used to critically assess conduct and social values, they must be based in reason *a priori*.

Our common-sense concept of duty also points to the need for a metaphysics of morals. Referring to the idea of a moral law, or moral requirement, Kant claims that "everyone must grant that a law, if it is to hold morally, that is, as a ground of obligation, must carry with it absolute necessity . . ." (1997: 389) and that it must apply to any rational agent. Moral obligations are universal in that they apply to anyone in the same circumstances, regardless of their desires. The "necessity" refers to the special weight attached to moral obligations. When one decides that an action is morally required, one believes that one ought to perform the act whether one wants to or not.

The fact that one would prefer to ignore the requirement, or that acting on it does not promote one's interests, does not exempt one from the obligation. Somewhat more formally, we take moral requirements to apply "unconditionally." This concept of obligation evidently presupposes that morality gives us reasons for action that do not depend on our desires, and, indeed, take priority over desire-based reasons. To see how moral requirements can carry this kind of necessity and universality, we must uncover their basis in reason.

Section I

As we can see, Kant begins with certain assumptions about the shape of ordinary morality. Section I develops a philosophical statement of the fundamental principle implicit in ordinary moral thought from a set of assumptions about the special value of a "good will." A person with a good will is the conscientious agent committed to fulfilling his or her duties and pursuing his or her ends within the limits of morality. Such a person is disposed to do what is right, simply because it is right. Section I aims to uncover the fundamental principle of a person with a good will from assumptions about the unconditional value of a good will.

Kant asserts that the good will is the only thing that is good absolutely and without qualification. The opening three paragraphs that spell out this assertion contain several claims. First, while many things in the world are good, nothing is truly good unless its use is directed by a good will, i.e., by moral principles. For example, sound understanding and courage are desirable qualities, but we do not judge them good when used for bad purposes. We all value our own happiness, but do not think that it should be achieved by ignoring the rights of others. Second, a person with a good will is committed to maintaining her good will. She does not think that any other good (such as wealth or success) is worth having if it is achieved at the cost of violating a moral principle. She thus values her good will above all else. Third, the value of a good will does not depend on success in achieving one's aims. Someone who acts from morally good principles but fails to achieve his end still evokes our admiration. Thus what we value about that person must be his underlying principle of action. As Kant says, "a good will is not good because of what it effects or accomplishes . . . but only because of its willing – i.e., it is good in itself" (1997: 394).

One point to draw from these paragraphs is the special role of moral principles in setting limits on how we may pursue other desirable ends. The mark of the person with a good will, and the source of our esteem for this person, is his or her readiness to respect the demands of morality. This person has the general commitment to conform to moral principle, whatever that requires. Subsequently, Kant develops a more complete statement of the fundamental principle of a good will through a series of examples that focus on our esteem for actions that most clearly display a good will (1997: 397–403). Kant holds that actions display a good will, or, as he says, have "moral worth," only when they are done "from duty." Examining the underlying principle of actions done from duty then leads to the fundamental principle of a good will.

Kant begins by distinguishing between actions "in conformity with duty" and actions done "from duty." Actions in conformity with duty are perfectly permissible, but are performed from non-moral motives (such as self-interest, love of life, etc.). But in actions done from duty, one is motivated by the rightness of one's action. To see why Kant thinks that only actions done from duty have moral worth, we should look at the "maxims" of the agents in these examples. Kant thinks that rational agents always act from reasons which they can cite to explain their actions to others, and a "maxim" is the principle on which an agent acts in some situation that gives his or her reasons for the action. Typically, a maxim will state the action, its purpose, and the circumstances – all the information needed to explain why the agent thought the action worth doing.

Let us now consider some of Kant's examples. The "prudent merchant" has the maxim of charging everyone a fair price because it is good for business. He conforms with duty, but since he is moved by self-interest, his action has no particular moral worth. A second example depicts a "friend of humanity" who takes immediate pleasure in helping and helps another out of natural sympathy, for no ulterior purpose. In this instance, the agent acts on a maxim of helping another because he enjoys helping. Kant says that this action "deserves praise and encouragement but not esteem" (1997: 398). As amiable as the action is, it does not display the moral worth we accord to a good will. In a third example, Kant imagines that this same friend of humanity is burdened with personal sorrows that extinguish his natural sympathy, but performs a helping action all the same. In this case, he acts from duty and his maxim would be to help another because the other was in need, or perhaps to help because helping is morally required.

What sets the third example apart from the first two is that only the third maxim has "moral content." Only in this case do moral considerations figure in the agent's reasons for action – here the fact that the needs of others make moral demands. This is why Kant claims that only actions done from duty have moral worth. Here we might agree that an action does not have specifically *moral* worth, and does not display the characteristic feature of a good will, unless moral considerations figure in one's reasons for action.

These examples also support Kant's "second proposition": that "an action from duty has its moral worth not in the purpose to be attained by it, but in the maxim according to which it is decided upon" (1997: 399–400). In the second and third cases above, the friend of humanity has the same purpose – to help another person. What gives moral worth to the action in the third example is that the agent adopts this purpose for moral reasons. Thus what confers moral worth on an action is not its purpose, but the fact that the agent acts on a maxim with moral content.

Kant's third proposition – that "duty is the necessity of action from respect for the law" – points to a general feature of actions done from duty that leads to the basic principle of a good will. An agent who acts from duty recognizes the necessity of doing what is morally required and has the general principle of conforming to moral principle – as Kant says, of respect for moral law. Since moral principles are universal principles that hold for any rational agent, Kant thinks this equivalent to the principle of acting only from maxims that one can will as universal laws (1997: 402). Here we encounter Kant's first statement of the Categorical Imperative.

Section II

In Section I, Kant derives a statement of the Categorical Imperative from assumptions about the value of a good will. In order to connect this principle with reason, Section II provides several different formulations of the Categorical Imperative by undertaking an analysis of our capacity for rational choice. We will first look at Kant's distinction between "categorical" and "hypothetical" imperatives, then take up the three main formulations of the Categorical Imperative.

Rational choice and imperatives

Kant ascribes to rational agents "the capacity to act in accordance with the representation of laws, that is, according to principles . . ." (1997: 412). Rational agents are moved to act by their own judgments of what they have reason to do. As we have noted, an agent's reasons for action can be expressed in a maxim, and maxims are formed by the application of various principles of rationality to one's desires, ends, values, circumstances, etc. Since human beings are imperfect rational agents who are moved both by reason and by non-rational influences, our maxims do not always agree with reason and we experience the principles of rationality as constraints. Rational principles thus take the form of "imperatives," and judgments of what one has reason to do are expressed as judgments about what one ought to do.

Judgments about what we ought to do appear to fall into two general categories, corresponding to what Kant calls "hypothetical" and "categorical" imperatives. I might judge that I ought to train harder in order to place well in a race. Or I might judge that I ought to focus more on my family and less on my career because doing so will lead to a happier life. In these cases, my reasons for these actions are that they are means to a desired goal, and these reasons are conditional on my having certain desires and aims. If I did not care about placing well in the race, I would have no reason to train harder. If my career gives me more satisfaction than my family, my interest in happiness would give me reason to focus on my career. These judgments are both hypothetical imperatives: they represent an action as good as a means to an end, and apply only to someone who cares about the end in question. Both are instances of a formal principle of means–end rationality called the "Hypothetical Imperative," which Kant expresses as follows: "Whoever wills the end also wills (insofar as reason has decisive influence on his actions) the indispensably necessary means to it that are within his power" (1997: 417). In other words, take effective means to one's ends, or abandon the end.

We also make judgments about how we ought to act that do not simply prescribe the means to the satisfaction of our desires or previously adopted ends. I might judge that I ought to be honest in some situation, without considering whether that will advance my aims. Here an action is represented as good unconditionally – as one which I have reason to perform regardless of my desires and ends. Such imperatives are categorical, and they are the kind of imperatives needed to express moral requirements. The balance of the *Groundwork* tries to show how there can be principles of action whose rational authority does not depend on our desires and aims, or our interest in happiness.

The formula of universal law

Kant's first formulation of the Categorical Imperative comes from analyzing the concept of a categorical imperative. The passage leading to this principle is rather difficult:

> For since the imperative contains, beyond the law, only the necessity that the maxim be in conformity with this law, nothing is left with which the maxim of action is to conform but the universality of a law as such; and this conformity alone is what the imperative properly represents as necessary. (1997: 420–1)

Kant's analysis focuses on the formal features of categorical imperatives, or moral requirements – that they are requirements that apply with necessity to anyone. Kant appears to say that any categorical imperative will contain some law – a substantive requirement of acting in a certain way, such as telling the truth or helping others – that it represents as unconditional, as something that one ought to do regardless of one's desires and ends. The Categorical Imperative simply states a very general requirement implicit in any specific moral requirement: that one should conform one's maxims to universal law. Now how does one determine whether one's maxim conforms to universal law? Kant thinks that we can do so by asking whether it is rational to will the maxim as a universal principle on which anyone may act. The resulting principle is often referred to as the Formula of Universal Law (FUL): "Act only in accordance with that maxim through which you can at the same time will that it should become a universal law" (1997: 421).

We will note two of the four examples through which Kant illustrates the application of this principle. Kant considers a maxim of getting money by promising to repay a loan though one does not intend to keep the promise. This maxim cannot be willed as universal law because doing so would be self-defeating. If everyone was free to make deceptive promises, then either promises would no longer be believed or there would be no such thing as promising, and one could not achieve anything through this kind of deception. Since this maxim cannot rationally be willed as universal law, it is not a permissible way of advancing one's ends. Kant also considers someone whose policy is never to hinder anyone else in their pursuit of their aims, but never to come to another's aid. This maxim – call it the "maxim of indifference" – cannot rationally be universalized because doing so would produce a "contradiction in one's will." Any rational agent is committed to achieving his or her ends, and thus wants access to the means needed to achieve one's ends. But given the facts of human vulnerability, no one can guarantee that they will not at some point need assistance from another in order to achieve their ends and to continue functioning as a rational agent. Thus any rational agent wills that people be willing to help others whose ability to function as agents is threatened. Universalizing the maxim of indifference is inconsistent with this commitment. Since the maxim of indifference is thus impermissible, one ought to have the principle of helping others in need.

Maxims that cannot be universalized represent impermissible ways of pursuing one's ends. The second example above shows how the impermissibility of a maxim may also lead to a positive duty – in this case, a duty of mutual aid. Many questions need to be resolved about the success of the FUL in explaining ordinary duties, but it is equally important to ask why universalizability is morally significant. Here two brief comments are in order. First, one point of morality is to develop generally acceptable principles through which we can justify our actions to each other. An action is justifiable if it conforms to principles that anyone can accept. The FUL expresses the basic moral requirement of conforming to universally valid principles. You determine whether this requirement is satisfied by asking whether it is rational to will that anyone act in the way that you propose. Second, consider someone who acts on a non-universalizable principle – so that, for example, what makes it possible to act on the maxim is that most people do not. This agent appears to be granting himself a special privilege, as though he should count for more than others, and his action shows a failure to respect others as moral equals. Thus the FUL, in addition to expressing a requirement of conforming to universally valid principles, embodies a principle of respecting others as moral equals. As we shall see, this links the FUL to Kant's second major formulation of the Categorical Imperative, the Formula of Humanity.

The formula of humanity

Kant's first formulation of the Categorical Imperative focuses on the fact that we take moral requirements to apply unconditionally. He argues next that any such requirements must have as their "ground" some end with absolute value. That is, requirements that apply to anyone and that take priority over our desires and personal ends presuppose the existence of something that any rational agent cares about and regards as worthy of special respect. Something with this kind of value is an "end-in-itself" whose value puts inviolable limits on how it may be treated. Kant argues that "humanity" or "rational nature" is an end-in-itself.

By "humanity" Kant means the capacity for rational choice, understood broadly to include, among other things, the capacity to set ends for ourselves and to act from moral principles. Kant's argument turns on the idea that a commitment to valuing the capacity for rational choice is built into the perspective of rational agency. As a rational agent, I adopt ends that I regard as worth pursuing. I think that it matters whether I achieve my ends. But if I value my ends, I must also value myself – specifically, my capacity to set ends. So far this is a "subjective principle of human actions" – an attitude that any agent has toward him or herself. But it leads to an objective principle that is valid for any agent. What I value in myself is that I am a person with the capacity for rational choice. Thus, I value my ends and myself in a way that commits me to valuing rational nature generally, whether in myself or in others. Since this is true of any rational agent, rational nature is an end-in-itself.

This argument leads to the second main version of the Categorical Imperative, often called the Formula of Humanity: "So act that you treat humanity, whether in your own person or in the person of another, always at the same time as an end, never merely as a means" (1997: 429). The intuitive and very powerful idea behind this principle is that human beings, as rational agents, have a special value that renders them worthy of respect and gives rise to inviolable limits on how they may be treated. Kant thinks that the dignity of human beings as rational agents is the source of much of the content of morality, and that what explains our judgments about the wrongness of an action is its failure to respect rational nature, either in oneself or in others. Kant cites the same examples to illustrate this principle. If I make a deceptive promise to another, I manipulate him for my own purposes and he "cannot agree with my way of acting toward him, and so cannot himself contain the end of this action" (1997: 430). I treat the other "merely as a means" because he cannot rationally consent to my action. This line of reasoning leads to duties to refrain from deception, coercion, and the violation of others' rights. But full respect for rational nature also requires positive support for the development and exercise of rational capacities in oneself and others. It thus leads to a duty to perfect one's own capacities and to a duty of mutual aid.

Kant's discussion of these examples helps show why he thinks that these two versions of the Categorical Imperative are equivalent. One respects the rational nature of others when one acts in ways that one can justify to them. But an action is justifiable to others when it conforms to principles that anyone can accept, including those affected by one's actions. Briefly, one respects humanity as an end-in-itself by acting from universalizable principles.

Autonomy

Following the Formula of Humanity, an important shift occurs in Kant's argument. Up to this point, Kant emphasizes that moral agents are subject to duty and he presents the value of rational nature as a source of duties. Kant now argues that moral agents are not just subject to moral requirements, but are in some sense their "legislators." Moral principles originate in our own reason and are principles that we impose on ourselves through reason. At this point Kant introduces a third version of the Categorical Imperative, which he states simply as "the idea of the will of every rational being as a will giving universal law" (1997: 431). This is the idea of autonomy, and its purpose is to give us a new understanding of moral principles implicit in what has gone before: they are principles that we legislate for ourselves through reason to govern our interactions with each other as members of a community of rational agents.

One route to the idea of autonomy is to consider how moral requirements, understood as categorical imperatives, could have authority. If moral requirements apply unconditionally, the reasons for conforming to them cannot be based in desire or our interest in happiness. The alternative is that their authority comes from the fact that one accepts them as general principles of conduct stating how anyone ought to act. For a principle to apply unconditionally, we must impose it on ourselves through our own reason. Here consider someone with a duty to be truthful in some situation and ask what reasons she has for doing her duty. Truthfulness may serve her interests in various ways – for example by winning friends or establishing a good reputation, or by avoiding punishment or social disapproval. But if these are her reasons, she treats truthfulness as a hypothetical imperative telling her how to act on the condition that she values these other things. If truthfulness is treated as a categorical imperative, the reason to act truthfully must be that it is rational to accept truthfulness as a general principle for anyone in her situation.

There are many dimensions to Kant's notion of autonomy, but the basic idea is that moral principles do not get their authority from anything external to human reason. If we were to base the authority of morality in, for example, the will of God, social convention, or our interest in happiness, we would be treating moral principles as hypothetical imperatives that apply on the condition that one values these ends. The reason to act morally would be that doing so is pleasing to God, is socially approved, or serves one's long-term interests. If moral principles are categorical imperatives, as ordinary thought assumes, their authority must come from the fact that they are principles that we are committed to willing in so far as we are rational. That means that human reason is autonomous because it is not subject to any external authority. And individuals act autonomously when they act from moral principles because in doing so they follow the authority of their own reason.

Section III

Sections I and II state the basic principle of morality by analyzing the concept of duty that Kant thinks is central to ordinary moral thought. Somewhat oversimplifying, these sections argue that if we are subject to moral requirements, such requirements must be expressed as universal laws, they are grounded in the value of humanity as an end-in-itself, and they are principles that we legislate for ourselves as rational agents. But they do not yet show that we are subject to moral requirements. While they may articulate our moral beliefs, they leave open the possibility that these beliefs involve a kind of high-minded illusion. Perhaps there isn't any reason for us to give priority to morality when it conflicts with self-interest, as well-intentioned as that appears. Or perhaps we do not have the motivational capacities to act independently of desire that are presupposed by this conception of morality – so that the supposition that we can act from duty alone has no basis in reality. Section III attempts to close this gap. The details of the argument are notoriously difficult. But the basic idea is that we have reason to view ourselves as free and autonomous agents and that we realize our nature as free and autonomous agents when we act from moral principles.

Section III begins with a preliminary argument that draws analytic connections between freedom and morality and between rationality and freedom. First Kant argues that "a freewill and a will under moral laws are one and the same" (1997: 447). A freewill is not determined to act by anything external. But it must act on some reason or principle. Kant concludes that its freedom is autonomy – the power to act from laws that one gives to oneself, independently of any outside influence. Section II argued that the FUL is a principle of autonomy, since in acting from moral principles one acts from laws that one gives to oneself through reason, independently of desire and other subjective influences. Thus Kant claims that a freewill realizes its autonomy by acting morally. Second, Kant claims that a rational agent "acts under the idea of freedom" (1997: 448). Rational agents regard themselves as the "authors" of their actions because their actions result from their own judgment of what they have reason to do. That means that rational agents are never caused to act by their desires, and moreover can set their desires aside if they see reason to. Even the strongest desire leads to action only when the agent judges that it is a good reason for action. A rational agent "acts under the idea of freedom" because in order to act one must judge what one has reason to do and because it is up to the agent to decide what is and is not a reason for action.

The preliminary argument holds that rational agents with the capacity to set aside desire and act from reason alone "act under the idea of freedom," and that any such agent is subject to the moral law. But are we such agents? Our moral consciousness suggests grounds for ascribing this kind of freedom to ourselves because the belief that we are subject to duty supposes a capacity to act from reasons that make no reference to our desires. But since the task of the *Groundwork* is to validate ordinary moral consciousness, we need non-moral grounds for ascribing this kind of freedom to ourselves; otherwise, we would argue in a circle. At this point Kant draws on *The Critique of Pure Reason* and argues that our capacities for theoretical reason show that we are free in the sense required by his preliminary argument. Theoretical reason can form ideas that go beyond the information given by the senses and can use these ideas to guide empirical inquiry about the world. It is therefore a capacity for free and spontaneous activity. Since we have this kind of theoretical intelligence, it is reasonable to presume that our abilities to reason about action share the same spontaneity – that we are indeed rational agents who act under the idea of freedom.

If Kant has shown that we are agents who must act under the idea of freedom, he will have identified reasons for recognizing the authority of morality, and the project of the *Groundwork* will be complete. In acting we view ourselves as rational agents with autonomy, and it is by making the Categorical Imperative our fundamental principle of action that we realize our autonomy and become agents in the most complete sense.

Bibliography

Editions and translations

Kant, Immanuel (1785) *Grundlegung zur Metaphysik der Sitten*. In *Immanuel Kants Schriften*. Ausgabe der königlich preussischen Akademie der Wissenschaften, vol. 4. Berlin: W. de Gruyter, 1902– .

Kant, Immanuel (1959) *Foundations of the Metaphysics of Morals*, trans. Lewis White Beck. Indianapolis, IN: Bobbs-Merrill.

Kant, Immanuel (1964) *Groundwork of the Metaphysics of Morals*, trans. H. J. Paton. New York: Harper & Row.

Kant, Immanuel (1981/1993) *Grounding for the Metaphysics of Morals*, trans. James W. Ellington. Indianapolis, IN: Hackett.

Kant, Immanuel (1997) *Groundwork of the Metaphysics of Morals*, trans. Mary J. Gregor. Cambridge: Cambridge University Press.

Studies

Guyer, Paul (ed.) (1998) *Kant's Groundwork of the Metaphysics of Morals: Critical Essays*. Lanham, MD: Rowman and Littlefield.

Herman, Barbara (1993) *The Practice of Moral Judgment*. Cambridge, MA: Harvard University Press.

Hill Jr, Thomas E. (1992) *Dignity and Practical Reason*. Ithaca, NY: Cornell University Press.

Korsgaard, Christine M. (1996) *Creating the Kingdom of Ends*. Cambridge: Cambridge University Press.

O'Neill, Onora (1989) *Constructions of Reason*. Cambridge: Cambridge University Press.

Paton, H. J. (1947) *The Categorical Imperative*. Philadelphia: University of Pennsylvania Press, 1971.

Rawls, John (2000) *Lectures on the History of Moral Philosophy*. Cambridge, MA: Harvard University Press.

Wood, Allen W. (1999) *Kant's Ethical Thought*. Cambridge: Cambridge University Press.

35

Friedrich Schiller,
The Aesthetic Education of Man in a Series of Letters (1795)

The Play of Beauty as Means and End

Daniel O. Dahlstrom

Before Friedrich Schiller (1759–1805), there were ample testimonies to the impact of art, for good and for ill, on moral and political sentiments, just as surely as there were other voices placing art at arm's length from morality and politics, in effect, liberating it from the pulpit and the marketplace. Schiller's singular achievement in his work *The Aesthetic Education of Man in a Series of Letters* (hereafter *Letters*) is his elaboration of a conception of art and aesthetics that reconciles these seemingly contradictory voices. According to the *Letters*, precisely because an aesthetic state is the historical apotheosis of the human condition, art is the only means of transforming human beings and transcending the limitations of contemporary science, morality, and politics.

Born in Stuttgart in 1759 and originally educated as an army doctor, Schiller became a professor of history at the University of Jena in 1789. But he is best known as one of Germany's most celebrated dramatists, from his stormy plays of the early 1780s, such as *The Robbers* and *Intrigue and Love*, to brooding and conflicted historical pieces, *Maria Stuart* and *Wallenstein*, composed in neo-classical style just after the *Letters*, culminating in the year before his death – 1805 – with a paean to a people's struggle for freedom (through political assassination!): the illustrious *Wilhelm Tell*.

There is more than an echo of the dramatic and historically idealized character of this rich theatrical legacy in Schiller's *Letters*. Yet they owe their literary form, at least in part, to the fact that they were originally drafted to Schiller's benefactor, the Prince of Schleswig-Holstein-Augustenburg, in gratitude for a stipendium that Schiller, battling with illness and poverty, had desperately needed. When these letters were destroyed in a fire at the prince's castle, Schiller promptly composed the present version, publishing them in three groups (*Letters* 1–9, 10–16, 17–27) in his monthly, *Die Horen*, in 1795. Yet the form of the *Letters* is well suited to their programmatic character. For while the *Letters* proceed from an historical state of affairs (defined by the failures of the French Revolution and the inadequacies of the Enlightenment), they deliberately invoke "feelings no less often than principles" in an effort to educate readers to unrealized human possibilities and the singular means to their realization.

An Outline of the *Letters*

The first group of *Letters* demonstrates the need for such an education by depicting the dire state of contemporary culture. "Utility," Schiller charges, "is the great idol of our age," in which the savagery and indigence of the lower classes are matched by the perversity and indolence of the upper, dooming any hope for change, as events in France demonstrated only too well. In light of this gloomy assessment, preoccupation with art appears frivolous and self-indulgent. Yet neither the state nor reason, Schiller argues, can provide the way out of the age's maladies. Political reform is chimerical as long as citizens have not achieved moral self-sufficiency, resolving "the conflict of blind urges" within and among themselves. If reason and philosophy in an "enlightened" age are supposed to be the answer, "how is it then," Schiller asks, "that we remain barbarians?" The way to the head must be opened, he insists, through the heart. Hence, the thesis of the *Letters*: "If man is ever to solve the problem of politics in practice he will have to approach it through the problem of the aesthetic, because it is only through beauty that man makes his way to freedom" (Letter 2).

In the first group of *Letters*, the former military physician reviews the symptoms, makes his diagnosis, and proposes a cure. But the proposed cure is not only untested; experience speaks volumes against it. The second installment of *Letters* accordingly pursues a "transcendental path," fashioning "a purely *rational concept* of beauty" that, while abstracting from any actual instance, coincides with unrealized possibilities of the human condition. The final group of *Letters* refines this conception with a view to the contingent limitations of actual experience, as Schiller elaborates the necessary role played by an "aesthetic condition" in liberating and perfecting the individual and the species.

Schiller and Kant

By Schiller's own admission, several contemporaries influenced his thinking in the *Letters*. The turn from empirical observation to a speculative account of humanity and beauty explicitly incorporates Fichte's conception of basic drives and their reciprocity. The telling motto of the *Letters* is taken from Rousseau's *Julie ou la nouvelle Héloise* ("If it is reason that makes a man, it is sentiment that guides him") and the first installment of the *Letters* iterates Rousseau's diagnoses of the age and culture (though it rejects the Genevan's conclusions). Winckelmann as well as Schiller's friends, Goethe and Wilhelm von Humboldt, helped inspire Letter 6's enthusiastic portrait of the Greeks as a reason for continued hope in the possibilities of humanity in a degenerate age. Yet, Schiller probably has Herder to thank for resisting the nostalgic urge to portray the proposed aesthetic transformation as a Hellenistic revival. While Schiller admits that the Greeks are "our models" and "put us to shame," an aesthetic education of mankind, as he understands it, is a question of historical possibilities quite unavailable to the Greeks.

Yet no contemporary of Schiller casts a longer shadow on the *Letters* than Kant does. Schiller's relationship to Kant is complicated by a persistent struggle to take his predecessor's insights beyond their initial horizon. In the opening letter, for example, Schiller asserts that his remarks are based upon certain "Kantian principles," notably, the dominant ideas of Kant's practical philosophy. This apparent endorsement need not be disingenuous or purely rhetorical, but it must be qualified. For he immediately contrasts the much-debated technical form of those principles with the unanimous acceptance of them, based on "moral instincts" in human nature. Schiller thus makes appeal to the very naturalism and moral sense rejected by Kant as a foundation for morality. (For Kant, development of moral sense is necessary but ancillary to the foundational questions of ethics.)

Throughout the *Letters* Schiller sketches a dualistic picture of humanity that starkly resembles Kant's contrasts of experience's claims with those of pure practical reason. Yet, in defiance of Kant, Schiller rejects the notion that one pole of the dualism – notably, reason – should gain the upper hand. In "On Grace and Dignity," published by Schiller three years before the *Letters*, he objects, not to Kant's account of the moral obligatoriness of acting from duty, but to his presentation of that obligatoriness in the absence of grace, the expression of the harmony of duty and inclination. Kant himself responded that Schiller's problem arises only if duty, the dignity of which is necessarily independent of grace, is confused with virtue, the dignity of which is not. Schiller does not explicitly return to this foundational issue in the *Letters* and, as a result, one of their persisting ambiguities is whether they should be taken as complementing or subverting Kantian ethics.

If the relation of Schiller's concept of an aesthetic education to Kantian ethics is unclear, the same cannot be said for its relation to Kant's aesthetics. To be sure, Schiller freely adopts Kantian terminology but in this respect he plainly does so with the unabashed aim of transforming it. In other words, the aesthetic character of the education proposed by Schiller may be based upon Kantian ethics in some sense but it is not "aesthetic" in Kant's sense of the term. For Schiller, beauty possesses a vitality that transcends human subjectivity and, for that very reason, holds an incomparable historical promise for human beings.

Schiller fully agrees with Kant that aesthetics is a means of transition from a natural to a moral condition. Yet this agreement is misleading inasmuch as Schiller regards the culmination of that transition as an aesthetic state which topples barriers, erected by Kant and others, separating nature, morality, and aesthetics into insular domains of self-contained faculties. Such barriers, Schiller submits, reflect and reinforce the specialization and alienation plaguing modern humanity. Without denying that the antagonisms resulting from these divisions may serve some "cosmic purpose," Schiller insists that such divisions, if not healed, lead to barbarism. Thus, the proposed aesthetic education is not restricted to matters of taste in isolation from questions of science and politics. While a barbarian impulse may survive in techno-science's efforts to master nature, "the cultivated human being makes of nature his friend" (Letter 4).

The Objective Promise of Beauty: "The Play's the Thing"

The human being whom Schiller proposes to educate is torn. On the one hand, human beings are in a passive condition of ever-changing sensations and feelings, joy and sadness. On the other hand, every human being is a person, capable of self-consciously thinking, reasoning, and initiating action. Though mutually irreducible, being a person and being in a condition are equally necessary to being human, giving rise to two basic laws: "to externalize all that is within, and give form to all that is outside" (Letter 11). Corresponding to these two laws are two basic drives: a sensuous drive toward the material content of individual, momentary sensations, and a formal drive toward the necessary form of universal, eternal laws. Each drive is compelling, even coercive; the sensuous drive acting as a physical, the formal drive as a moral constraint. Though nothing might seem more opposed than these two drives, the "task" of culture and reason is to give each its due, intensifying both to the point where they moderate one another. Coordination, not subordination of one drive to another, is the order of the day.

Schiller admits that such a task is never fully attainable, that completion of it amounts to "the perfect consummation" of humanity. Yet if human beings were able to think and to feel at once, they would intuit their humanity completely and the objects that yield such intuitions would serve as symbols of mankind's destiny. Such experiences would, he adds, awaken a new drive, the play drive, reconciling the other two basic drives, albeit by canceling their respective coerciveness. In Letter 27 Schiller sketches a genealogy of play, from the physical play of an overflowing nature to the free play of human fantasy and association, culminating in aesthetic play with the capacity to transform sexual desire.

As the object of the sensuous drive is life and that of the formal drive is form, so the play drive's object is a living form, i.e., beauty. To those who consider such talk of play demeaning to humanity and beauty Schiller responds famously: "man only plays when he is in the fullest sense of the word a human being, and he is only fully a human being when he plays" (Letter 15). Moreover, precisely as the object of the play drive, beauty is "our second creatress," the key to our potential to transcend ourselves. The promise of beauty is the promise of humanity (and Schiller's anthropological aesthetics is equally an aesthetic anthropology). As noted above, Schiller restores to the notion of beauty an objectivity missing in many treatments of it in the eighteenth century by Kant and others. Beauty is no longer centered in some form of imagination or correlate to taste or aesthetic satisfaction. At the same time, as a living form, beauty concretely embodies the self-determining, autonomous unity of form and matter (virtue and happiness) that is, even in Kant's moral terminology, "the highest good."

Beauty and the aesthetic condition are thus for Schiller the ineluctable means to a moral condition. "Man in his *physical* condition merely suffers the dominion of nature; he emancipates himself from this dominion in the *aesthetic* condition, and he acquires mastery over it in the *moral*" (Letter 24). The step from the aesthetic to the moral condition is, Schiller adds, "infinitely easier" than that from the physical to the aesthetic condition. Yet he also warns against imagining that one might be only in one condition or that all three are not at hand as necessary conditions "in every individual perception of an object." Thus, if the aesthetic condition is necessary for moral mastery, its necessity is not something that we outgrow, like adolescence, on the way to maturity. It is accordingly necessary to distinguish a tyrannical mastery of the ever-rebelling animal in us from a graceful self-mastery in which our dignity and our happiness, our practical reason and our feelings, are not at odds. This graceful self-mastery is the epitome of moral, i.e., human freedom. Beauty is the living proof that such freedom is possible, "that a human being need not flee matter in order to manifest herself as spirit" (Letter 25).

The Paradoxical Truth of Art

Schiller is well aware that, in addition to experience and history, logic itself seems to speak against the task set by the *Letters*. Political change for the better requires a change in attitudes but attitudes are formed by the political culture. The only way out of this vicious circle – a version of the old Platonic quandary regarding the teachability of virtue – is to find some means not afforded by the state and not infected, at least not inevitably, by political corruption. In a further, paradoxical gloss on Plato, Schiller finds the way out in art, precisely as the semblance of truth. ("Semblance" itself is composed of, among other things, what contemporary philosophers call "qualia.") When nature has lost its nobility, "truth lives on in the illusion," as he puts it, and where attitudes are venal, he advises: "surround them with symbols of the noble until the semblance overturns the reality and art nature" – presumably the nature no longer noble (Letter 9).

Basic needs must be met, Schiller notes, before aesthetic semblance can be indulged, though such indulgence is also a natural development of seeing and hearing. These two senses do not simply receive but help produce their objects. In the process, the play drive develops, as people find enjoyment in mere semblance, followed by the mimetic drive to shape and form semblances as something relatively self-sufficient ("relatively" since it remains a human product and subject to human dictates). As these drives develop, the realm of beauty expands but also gives further definition to the boundaries between semblance and reality. Only in this world of semblance, more over, does the artist enjoy sovereign rights. What makes the artist an artist, and renders semblance aesthetic, is a certain honesty (no pretense of being real) and autonomy (dispensing with all support from reality).

In the end, the aesthetic semblance is self-reflexive and self-redeeming. In an important respect, art is the semblance of semblance, the illusion of illusion. The aesthetic education overturns a deficient, actual stage of human nature because art is capable of articulating ever higher human possibilities. These are possibilities, moreover, at the crossroads of the individual and the species. In contrast to the strictly private and needy undergoing of a sensual pleasure, the enjoyment of semblance is a pleasurable activity that is inherently shareable, yet not by virtue of some dictate of a *volonté générale*. Herein lies yet another side to the promise of beauty. Only in an aesthetic state (*Staat*) can we confront each other, not as enforcers of our respective rights ("the fearful kingdom of forces") or as executors of our wills ("the sacred kingdom of laws"), but as free and equal citizens: "the third joyous kingdom of play and of semblance" (Letter 27).

Schiller's claims for the mediating role of the aesthetic condition, on the one hand, and for the consummatory character of the aesthetic state, on the other, have been a source of continual debate among scholars. Slippage from one use of a term to another (e.g., "moral" and "ethical"), conflation of synchronic and diachronic perspectives, and the enormity of the task that he poses for himself in the *Letters* have clearly contributed to the confusion. Nor should the distance between a work of art and a work of character be minimized any more than that between funding the arts and feeding the hungry. Yet there is also good reason not to separate means from end in the never-ending quest for a holy human will. After all, for great artistry and nobility of character, practice is the means that must be constantly renewed and no stage is incapable of improvement. For Schiller, even the most elementary sort of aesthetic condition does not merely set the stage for human perfection; it already is the realization *in nuce* of that perfection. As he himself puts it, in a romantic flourish worthy of Novalis: "In the eyes of a reason that knows no limits, the direction is at once the destination, and the way is completed from the moment it is trodden" (Letter 9).

The Influence of the *Letters*

The *Letters'* theme of art's liberating possibilities exercised a lasting influence on the remarkable trio of young thinkers at Tübingen who would reshape German philosophy for the next two centuries: Hölderlin, Schelling, and Hegel. German idealists found a model of dialectic in the ways in which an aesthetic education reconciles opposites as a demand of reason. In Schiller's own words: "Nature (sense and intuition) always unites, intellect always divides; but reason unites once more" (Letter 18). Though Hegel would argue for the priority of philosophy over art, his praise of Schiller is unambiguous: "Schiller must be paid the great tribute of having broken through Kantian subjectivity . . . and of having dared to move beyond it, grasping unity and reconciliation as the ultimate truth" (Hegel, 1970: 89).

Bibliography

Editions and translations

Schiller, F. (1962) *Schillers Werke*. Nationalausgabe [*Schiller's Works*. National Edition], vol. 21; ed. B. von Wiese and H. Koopmann. Weimar: Böhlaus.
Schiller, F. (1967) *On the Aesthetic Education of Man*, ed. and trans. E. M. Wilkinson and L. A. Willoughby. Oxford: Oxford University Press.
Schiller F. (1993) *Essays*, ed. D. Dahlstrom and W. Hinderer. New York: Continuum.

Studies and references

Hegel, G. W. F. (1970) *Vorlesungen über die Ästhetik* [*Lectures on Aesthetics*]. Frankfurt am Main: Suhrkamp.
Martinson, Steven D. (1996) *Harmonious Tensions: The Writings of Friedrich Schiller*. Newark, DE: University of Delaware Press.

Miller, R. D. (1986) *A Study of Schiller's "Letters on the Aesthetic Education of Man."* Harrogate: The Duchy Press.

Pugh, D. (1996) *Dialectic of Love: Platonism in Schiller's Aesthetics.* Montreal: McGill-Queen's University Press.

Sharpe, Lesley (1995) *Schiller's Aesthetic Essays: Two Centuries of Criticism.* Columbia, SC: Camden House.

36

G. W. F. Hegel,
Phenomenology of Spirit (1807)

Thinking Philosophically without Begging the Question

Stephen Houlgate

For many, Hegel's *Phenomenology of Spirit* is one of the most original and profound works of Western philosophy. Yet others find the *Phenomenology* unintelligible and not worth the trouble to study. As Horst Althaus has put it, "the general impression which the *Phenomenology* leaves behind in the mind of the reader is almost invariably one of baffling obscurity" (Althaus, 2000: 99). In this chapter I hope to dispel some of that obscurity by explaining precisely what Hegelian phenomenology entails. In so doing I hope that some of the reasons why many see such originality and profundity in the *Phenomenology* – and regard it as still relevant to philosophy – will become apparent.

Logic and Metaphysics

Hegel (1770–1831) began writing the *Phenomenology* in 1805 when he was an unsalaried lecturer at the University of Jena. Printing started in February 1806, and Hegel was able to use the available pages in his summer course on "speculative philosophy or logic." According to his own account, he did not finish writing the main text until the night before the battle of Jena, which took place on October 14, 1806. (Earlier in the day on October 13, he had seen Napoleon – "this world-soul" – riding out of the city on reconnaissance.) The preface was completed in January 1807, and the book was finally published in the following April.

From the start the *Phenomenology* was conceived as an introduction to speculative logic, which was set out in several versions by Hegel over the coming years and given its most detailed articulation in the *Science of Logic* (1812–16, 2nd edn 1832). Prior to writing the *Phenomenology*, Hegel had separated logic from metaphysics. As he developed the new discipline of phenomenology, however, he fused logic and metaphysics into a single science. His position in the *Logic* is unequivocal: its subject matter, he writes, is "the science of logic which constitutes metaphysics proper or purely speculative philosophy" (Hegel, 1999 [henceforth *SL*]: 27). The same point is made in the 1830 *Encyclopedia Logic* : "*logic* coincides with *metaphysics*, with the science of *things* grasped in *thoughts*" (Hegel, 1991 [henceforth *EL*]: 56, para. 24). Hegel points out, however, that his metaphysics differs subtly from that of earlier philosophers, such as Leibniz and Wolff.

Previous metaphysicians, Hegel explains, assumed that there is a world "out there" (comprising, say, a single substance or an infinity of monads), and that our task is to formulate correct judgments about that world. Metaphysics did not, therefore, merely seek to understand the structure of our own understanding; it sought to know what the world itself is like. Hegel, by contrast, rejects the idea that metaphysics is directed out toward the world, and argues that it involves an examination of our own thought and fundamental categories. For Hegel, metaphysics thus coincides with logic or the study of what it is to think. In Hegel's metaphysical logic, "what we are dealing with . . . is not a thinking *about* something which exists independently as a base for our thinking and apart from it . . . on the contrary, the necessary forms and self-determinations of thought are the content and the ultimate truth itself" (*SL*, 50).

Yet does not Hegel's logic thereby forfeit any claim to being a genuine metaphysics? Does it not reduce itself to mere logic, to the simple study of thought in abstraction from the world? Hegel believes not, because he thinks that within the structure of thought (properly conceived) we discover the true structure of being itself. For Hegel, being has a logical or conceptual structure, and we discern that structure within that of thought and its categories. Logic is thus one and the same as metaphysics.

Now it can be argued that rationalist metaphysics prior to Hegel also coincides – at least, implicitly – with logic. After all, Spinoza tries to determine what substance is by examining the concept of substance. The explicit focus of Spinoza's attention is not, however, our concept of substance as such, but substance itself (together with its attributes and modes). In Hegel's logic, by contrast, the explicit object of study is our thought and its categories, within which the structure of being is to be discerned. Thought reveals the nature of being by unfolding its own logical structure. Consequently, "as science, truth is pure self-consciousness in its self-development and has the shape of the self, so that the absolute truth of being is the known Concept [*Begriff*] and the Concept as such is the absolute truth of being" (*SL*, 49).

The philosopher who directs Hegel's attention toward the categories of thought is Kant. According to Hegel, indeed, it was Kant's "critical philosophy" that first "turned metaphysics into logic" (*SL*, 51). Kant did so by demonstrating in his *Critique of Pure Reason* that the fundamental categories of thought contain the form of any object of experience.

Commentators disagree about how careful and reliable a reader of Kant Hegel is. What is clear, however, is that Hegel himself acknowledges a significant debt to Kant. In particular, he endorses Kant's conclusion that the categories impart objectivity to the things we perceive. Kant argued that things are not regarded as truly objective when they are merely perceived to be spatio-temporal or to have certain sensory qualities, such as color or smell. They are regarded as objective only when they are understood in terms of certain categories – categories which contain the form of any possible objectivity. For Kant, therefore, to be objective is to be a spatio-temporal object in certain intelligible (for example, causal) relations to other such objects.

Hegel accepts this Kantian association of objectivity with intelligibility: "Kant called what measures up to thought [*das Gedankenmässige*] (the universal and the necessary) 'objective'; and he was certainly quite right to do this" (*EL*, 83, para. 41, addition 2). Yet Hegel maintains that the categories contain the objective structure not just of the objects of human experience, but of being itself. This, of course, is a belief that Kant does not share. For Kant the categories allow us to understand as objective what we perceive, and so constitute the conditions of objective experience. They do not, however, disclose the intrinsic character of things themselves. Hegel goes beyond Kant, therefore, by retaining the metaphysical idea – embraced by Spinoza and Leibniz – "that thinking grasps what things are *in-themselves*" (*EL*, 66, para. 28, addition).

Nevertheless Hegel understands his metaphysics to build on, and not simply to reverse, Kant's philosophical achievement. For this reason, he insists that we seek the true nature of being by examining the logical structure of the *thought* or *category* of being. This pursuit of metaphysical truth by means of pure logic makes Hegel (in his own eyes at least) a post-Kantian metaphysician.

There is another feature of Hegel's metaphysics that makes it post-Kantian rather than pre-Kantian: the fact that it endeavors to be thoroughly self-critical and to assume as little as possible in advance about being or thought. Prior to Kant, metaphysicians began with definite assumptions about what there is. Spinoza begins the *Ethics* by assuming that whatever is, is either a substance or a mode thereof, and Leibniz opens his *Monadology* with the equally unequivocal assertion that monads are simple substances. Hegel believes that in the wake of Kant's critical turn one may no longer begin philosophy with such assumptions. Indeed, as he states in the *Logic*, "the beginning . . . may not presuppose anything" (*SL*, 70).

So what are we to start from? Hegel's answer is that we must start from the least that being can be understood to be; and that is not "substance" or "nature" or "God," but sheer indeterminate immediacy or pure being. Such indeterminate immediacy is not only the least that we can understand being to be, it is also the least that thought can be aware of at all. At its most minimal, Hegel claims, thought is the thought not of possibility (in opposition to actuality) but of utterly unspecified being – being that is not yet conceived as "existence," "actuality," or even the copulative "is" in a judgment. Such being is quite indeterminate, but it is nevertheless ineliminable. Indeed, it is found in the thought of sheer and utter nothingness: for even pure nothingness must be thought to *be* just that.

After Kant, Hegel believes, philosophy must be radically self-critical, presuppose as little as possible, and so begin from the least that thought and being can be. It must thus begin from the idea that thought is minimally the thought of indeterminate being. Furthermore, at the outset being cannot be taken to be anything more than the indeterminate immediacy of which thought is minimally aware. Consequently, Hegel's *Logic* opens with a simple sentence fragment: "*Being, pure being*, without any further determination" (*SL*, 82).

Note that Hegel understands thought to be a faculty of intellectual intuition: it is by its very nature the awareness of *being*. For Kant, on the other hand, thought and its concepts "deal with the mere possibility of an object" (Kant, 1987: 284, para. 76). Thought understands, through its categories, the form that anything would have to exhibit in order to count as an object, but it cannot itself bring to mind the immediacy of things. For Kant, it is through sensuous intuition or perception that we are conscious of something's being immediately before our eyes. Thought's role is simply to judge, by means of its categories, that what we intuit is an object of a certain kind.

According to Kant, therefore, thought is fundamentally discursive: it understands and categorizes what is given to it in sensuous intuition (Kant, 1997: 172, B33). Thought can thus claim with justification that it can determine the character of objects of human experience, but it may do no more than that. It may not claim to be able to determine directly what things are like in themselves, apart from the way they are perceived by us.

Kant's position appears to be a modest one that respects the "limits" of human knowledge. It restricts the objective validity of our categories to human experience and – sensibly, it would seem – denies that we can gain metaphysical knowledge of being itself through pure *a priori* reason. Yet, from Hegel's perspective, Kant's "modesty" rests on a significant and unwarranted assumption about thought: namely, that by itself it can entertain only the *possibility* of an object. This (alleged) characteristic is what requires thought to cooperate with sensuous intuition, if it is to yield knowledge of actual objects (of experience). For Hegel, however, the claim that thought by itself can conceive only of what is possible takes a great deal for granted: it assumes, for example, that we know what possibility is and how it differs from actuality. Accordingly, it is a claim that a fully self-critical philosopher should not make. Such a philosopher, in Hegel's view, must set aside all determinate assumptions about thought. He must suspend the idea that thought is necessarily the thought of substance, actuality, God, or possibility (in contrast to actuality), and he must begin from the least that thought can be. That, according to Hegel, is the thought of sheer indeterminate immediacy or pure being. Hegel takes issue with Kant, therefore, not because he has grandiose metaphysical ambitions, but because he believes that less is taken for granted in the thought of simple being or immediacy than in the thought of "mere" possibility.

This is not the place to discuss the relative merits of the Kantian and Hegelian positions. All I wish to note is that Hegel claims that thought is the thought of being because, in his view, that is the least one can say about thought. It thus constitutes the only appropriate starting-point for a fully self-critical philosopher. After Kant, therefore, the task of the philosopher is not to set out the conditions and (alleged) limits of human experience, but to analyze what is entailed by the bare thought of being, and so to do metaphysics by doing logic. Strange though it may seem, Hegel is led to his new, reformed Spinozism by what he understands to be the modern, Kantian spirit of radical self-criticism.

To begin the science of logic, therefore, nothing is needed except a willingness to set aside one's inherited assumptions about thought and being and to consider what thought minimally must be. At the outset, Hegel writes, "all that is present is simply the resolve [*Entschluss*] . . . that we propose to consider thought as such . . . To enter into philosophy . . . calls for no other preparations, no further reflections or points of connection" (*SL*, 70, 72). The thinking that sets aside its presuppositions in this way transforms itself into "pure" or "absolute" knowing. This is the knowing that knows it can discover the structure of being within thought because thought by its very nature is ontological and cannot but understand what it is to be.

Note that absolute knowing is not knowledge of some presupposed super-entity called the "Absolute." It is simply knowing that knows absolutely – that is to say, knows through pure thought alone that the structure of thought and being is identical. By recognizing this identity, absolute knowing understands being – which, on the one hand, is irreducible to our thought of it – to be logical and rational in itself. It thus not only finds the truth of being within thought, but also discovers the structure of thought within being and so can be described as "*pure* self-recognition in absolute otherness" (*Phenomenology of Spirit* [henceforth *PS*], 1977: 14). Either way, absolute knowing understands the structure of the object (or the "truth") and of our certainty (or thought) to be one and the same. "In absolute knowing," Hegel writes, "the separation of the *object* [*Gegenstand*] from the *certainty of oneself* [*Gewissheit seiner selbst*] is completely eliminated: truth is now equated with certainty and this certainty with truth" (*SL*, 49).

Thought becomes absolute knowing, therefore, when it sets aside a distinction that ordinary or "natural" consciousness takes for granted without question: namely, that between the object or truth that is known and our knowing or certainty of it. As Hegel puts it, "pure science presupposes liberation from the opposition of consciousness" (*SL*, 49). Such a suspension of our ordinary conception of knowledge and its object will not disturb the self-critical, "presuppositionless" philosopher; but it will clearly disturb ordinary consciousness itself, which is wedded to its everyday assumptions. Ordinary consciousness will find it bewildering to be told that the truth can be found within thought because, as far as it is concerned, the truth is out there in the world.

When ordinary consciousness encounters Hegel's "absolute" science of logic and tries to enter into its way of thinking, it finds itself, according to Hegel, "induced by it knows not what to walk on its head." Indeed, it experiences "the compulsion to assume this unwonted posture and to go about in it" as "a violence it is expected to do to itself, all unprepared and seemingly without necessity" (*PS*, 15). That is why Hegel wrote the *Phenomenology*. This text is designed to show that the perspective of absolute knowing is by no means as perverse as ordinary consciousness thinks because that perspective is in fact made necessary by the very certainties that ordinary consciousness itself holds dear.

Phenomenology and Logic

Philosophers who are willing to set aside their presuppositions and "consider thought as such" do not need to read the *Phenomenology*; but Hegel's text does need to be studied by any ordinary consciousness – including any philosophical mind steeped in the certainties of ordinary life – that wants to learn more about Hegel's speculative philosophy. This is because the standpoint of absolute knowing violates the fundamental principle on which ordinary consciousness rests. As consciousness sees things, the world is over there; so how can I possibly discover the true nature of being within my own thought?

Clearly, ordinary consciousness will not be able to engage in speculative philosophy unless it gives up its customary conception of knowledge and the world. Yet Hegel recognizes that consciousness is entitled to be shown by the philosopher why it should give up its favored view of things and adopt the "absolute" perspective. As Hegel writes, "the individual has the right to demand that Science should at least provide him with the ladder to this standpoint, should show him this standpoint within himself" (*PS*, 14). The purpose of the *Phenomenology* is precisely to meet this demand by demonstrating that absolute knowing is logically entailed by the certainties of consciousness itself. In this way Hegel aims to prove to ordinary consciousness that the perspective of absolute knowing is indeed justified.

> In the *Phenomenology of Spirit* I have exhibited consciousness in its movement onwards from the first immediate opposition of itself and the object to absolute knowing. The path of this movement goes through every form of the *relation of consciousness to the object* and has the Concept [*Begriff*] of science for its result. This Concept . . . needs no justification here [in the *Logic*] because it has received it in that work [the *Phenomenology*]; and it cannot be justified in any other way than by this emergence in consciousness, all the forms of which are resolved into this Concept as into their truth. (*SL*, 48)

Through this process of justification, Hegel believes, consciousness will be weaned off its everyday certainties and shown that true certainty and knowledge are to be found only in philosophy or "science." Consciousness will thus be educated by phenomenology and raised into the "ether" of absolute knowing. It will be taught to let go of its ordinary view of things and to become absolute knowing itself.

It is ironic, therefore, that the *Phenomenology* should be regarded by so many as obscure, since its *raison d'être* is to explain in terms that ordinary consciousness will understand why the seemingly perverse position of absolute knowing is necessary and rational. Like Plato, Hegel is interested not only in presenting the truth, but also in educating – indeed, converting – others (especially, non-philosophers) so that they may be able to comprehend that truth. Hegel undertakes this process of education, however, not through memorable images, such as the allegory of the cave, but through the discipline of phenomenology.

Although it is Hegel's most famous work, the *Phenomenology* does not set out his philosophical system. Its role is to lead consciousness to the standpoint of philosophy, which is then articulated in the disciplines of speculative logic, philosophy of nature, and philosophy of spirit. Hegel reminds us of the essential difference between phenomenology and philosophy (or science) at the end of the *Phenomenology*:

> Whereas in the phenomenology of Spirit each moment is the difference of knowledge and Truth, and is the movement in which that difference is cancelled, Science on the other hand does not contain this difference and the cancelling of it. On the contrary, since the moment has the form of the Concept [*Begriff*], it unites the objective form of Truth and of the knowing Self in an immediate unity. (*PS*, 491)

Philosophy starts out from the conviction that thought and being are identical in structure. Phenomenology, by contrast, examines the various ways in which consciousness distinguishes itself from its object. Phenomenology leads to philosophy, however, by showing that the structural identity of thought and being is implicit in the very distinctions that consciousness itself makes. In this way, phenomenology teaches consciousness to see in philosophy the unfolding of truth, rather than mere perversity.

Hegel undertakes this project of education, partly because he wants to overcome the traditional alienation of ordinary consciousness from pure, *a priori* philosophy. More importantly, however, he is acutely aware that philosophy may not simply insist against ordinary consciousness – as, for example, Fichte and Schelling do – that the ordinary point of view must give way to that of philosophy. He recognizes that "philosophy has no *prima facie* right to claim that natural certainty is unjustified or misplaced or, on the other hand, that the claims of philosophy are justified and validated against those of the natural attitude" (Flay, 1984: 8). Hegel is sometimes accused of presupposing the validity of absolute knowing in his phenomenology, but that is the last thing he wishes to do. He wants to avoid begging the question against ordinary consciousness, and to prove to consciousness – starting from assumptions made by consciousness itself – that the position of absolute knowing is justified. Indeed, Kenneth Westphal claims that "more than any other philosopher Hegel was sensitive to issues of begging the question against opponents and dissenters" (Westphal, 1998: 562).

We can certainly resolve to set aside all our presuppositions about thought and being, and start philosophizing in the "absolute" conviction that the true nature of being can be discovered within thought. Not everyone, however, will be prepared to carry out such a voluntary act of abstraction. Many will insist that the ordinary understanding of knowledge – which considers it to be distinct from the object known – is correct and should not be given up lightly. Hegel acknowledges that ordinary consciousness is perfectly entitled to take this stand and to demand that the philosopher prove to it that the absolute point of view is legitimate. The *Phenomenology* is intended to supply that proof. It is written not to explain Hegel's own philosophical position, but to convince ordinary consciousness that philosophy respects its point of view.

The Purpose of the *Phenomenology*

Hegel's wariness of simply taking things for granted is evident in the introduction to the *Phenomenology*. There he maintains that modern epistemologists (such as Locke and Kant) take it for granted that we should examine the capacities and limits of our faculty of knowledge before we set about actually knowing the world. They think this is possible because they assume that knowledge is an "instrument" or a "medium" through which we are put in touch with the truth (or, as Hegel calls it here, the "Absolute") and that it can be examined in isolation from that truth. Hegel points out, however, in a manner reminiscent of Berkeley, that such assumptions lead to skepticism because we can never be sure whether our knowledge takes hold of the truth or merely what can be known through our representations. Moreover, by making us doubt whether we can ever know the truth as such, they (artificially) "create the incapacity of Science" (*PS*, 48).

Such assumptions, Hegel tells us, are "natural" ones for philosophers to make, but they are made by epistemological *philosophers*, not by ordinary consciousness itself. Ordinary consciousness assumes that it is directly aware of the world out there and does not think of itself as walled up behind its own representations. As we have seen, Hegelian "science" does not share the assumptions of either the epistemologists or ordinary consciousness. It is closer in spirit to ordinary consciousness, since it claims to be in direct contact with being itself; but it considers the truth of being to be immanent within thought, rather than something that is just "out there."

Hegel may not, however, insist against the epistemologists and ordinary consciousness that his "absolute," logical-ontological standpoint just is the right one. Were he to do this, his "Science would be declaring its power to lie simply in its *being*"; but, of course, the "untrue knowledge" – representationalism and ordinary consciousness – "likewise appeals to the fact that *it is*, and *assures* us that for it Science is of no account." Hegel's insistence would thus get him nowhere in the eyes of his opponents: for, as Sextus Empiricus and Fichte have both reminded us, "*one* bare assurance is worth just as much as another" (*PS*, 49).

So how is Hegel's logical science to prove to its opponents that it is superior? There is only one option available: the philosopher must set his own standpoint to one side, enter into the perspective of his opponents, and show that that perspective itself makes the "absolute" point of view necessary. In other words, he must demonstrate the superiority of the "absolute" standpoint through an immanent critique of alternative points of view. In the later *Encyclopedia* Hegel undertakes an abbreviated immanent critique of classical empiricism and Kantian critical philosophy. In the *Phenomenology* he addresses ordinary consciousness.

The project of the *Phenomenology* is thus clear: it does not provide a logical-metaphysical account of the nature of being, but shows how the assumptions and certainties of consciousness lead by themselves to the standpoint of absolute knowing. Note that phenomenology, as Hegel conceives it, is not epistemology: it does not try to justify the claims of ordinary consciousness itself (and so is not interested in determining, for example, whether or not the colors we see are really there). Nor is phenomenology to be confused with transcendental philosophy (as practiced by Kant and Fichte): it does not aim to uncover the epistemic conditions of ordinary consciousness. Phenomenology is a new discipline that seeks to understand the perspective of consciousness on its own terms, whatever its conditions may be and whether or not its claims are justified.

Why is this discipline called "phenomenology?" The name is borrowed by Hegel from previous writers: J. H. Lambert, Kant and Reinhold (Harris, 1997: I, 16). It is particularly suited to Hegel's discipline, however, because the latter sets out the "logic of appearing" (Lauer, 1976: 3). It examines not what being is absolutely, but the way being is understood by, and so appears to, consciousness. Similarly, phenomenology does not try to establish definitively what knowledge or the mind is (and so is not philosophy of mind), but studies the way knowledge is understood by, and so appears to, consciousness. This is part of what Hegel means when he states that the *Phenomenology* presents "knowledge as it appears" or "phenomenal knowledge" (*das erscheinende Wissen*) (*PS*, 49).

There is, however, another, more positive nuance to Hegel's phrase. The *Phenomenology* also shows how absolute knowing is gradually caused to emerge or "appear" by the certainties of consciousness itself. Hegel's book thus examines both how knowledge appears to consciousness and how that very appearance leads logically and immanently to the appearance on the scene of absolute knowing. It is important to keep both aspects of Hegel's project in view. Hegel must examine the way knowledge appears to consciousness because he avoids begging the question against consciousness only by considering the latter on its own terms. At the same time, he undertakes this immanent, "presuppositionless" study of consciousness in the hope that he can demonstrate the necessity and validity of absolute knowing. What Hegel will seek to understand, therefore, is the specific way in which consciousness's own assumptions lead to the absolute standpoint. Or, to be more precise, he will seek to determine *whether* these assumptions lead to that standpoint: for, at the start of the *Phenomenology*, he may not simply assume in advance that they do so.

It should be emphasized, by the way, that the *Phenomenology* – if it succeeds – will do no more than show that an immanent, purely logical ontology is possible. The *Phenomenology* will not establish dialectic as the proper method of philosophy, or indeed establish any other rules of procedure for the science of logic. Nor will it demonstrate the existence of some mystical entity called the "Absolute." All the *Phenomenology* will demonstrate – if it succeeds – is that "the opposition in consciousness between a self-determined entity, a subject, and a second such entity, an object, is known to be overcome," and that thought and being prove within conscious experience itself to be identical in structure (*SL*, 60). Consciousness will come to recognize in this process that thought can, after all, determine from within itself what pure being entails. Yet that will leave the work of determining the true nature of being still to be carried out. The *Phenomenology* does not stipulate how it should be carried out, nor can it be used to anticipate what the *Logic* (and the rest of philosophy) will discover. In that sense it is a ladder that must be jettisoned, once one has climbed to the top.

The Method of Phenomenology

In the *Phenomenology* Hegel will not argue that every human being will be moved by his or her contingent historical experiences to see wisdom in speculative philosophy. Hegel's claim is, rather, that a sequence of experiences is generated *logically* by the formal structure of consciousness itself, and that this sequence culminates in absolute knowing. His point of departure in the *Phenomenology* is thus not (as it often is for Aristotle) the variety of things that people actually say about the world, but the minimal formal or logical structure that any consciousness must exhibit if it is to count as consciousness at all. This structure is very simple: all consciousness, for Hegel, is consciousness of that which it takes to be distinct from itself.

> Consciousness simultaneously *distinguishes* itself from something, and at the same time *relates* itself to it, or, as it is said, this something exists *for* consciousness; and the determinate aspect of this *relating*, or of the *being* of something for a consciousness, is *knowing*. But we distinguish this being-for-another from *being-in-itself* [*Ansichsein*]; whatever is related to knowledge or knowing is also distinguished from it, and posited as existing outside of this relationship; this *being-in-itself* is called *truth*. (*PS*, 52–3)

Now it is unlikely that many non-philosophers will describe what they encounter as "being-in-itself." They are more likely to say "There's the bus at last" or "The tea's gone cold." In saying such things, however, they assume that what they relate to is actually there and is whatever it is in itself. They may not formulate this assumption in the way Hegel does, but they make it none the less.

Although Hegel does not analyze what people actually say in everyday situations, his account of consciousness is immanent because he refrains from challenging the fundamental formal assumption that consciousness makes and "assum[es] nothing except what such knowledge itself assumes" (Loewenberg, 1965: 13). Hegel does not protest that consciousness is "really" aware only of its own representations, but accepts consciousness's claim that it relates to what is. He must do this because, as a phenomenologist, he is prohibited from entertaining any conception of being other than the one consciousness itself entertains. He must proceed, therefore, on the assumption that being is simply what consciousness is aware of and nothing beyond that. For Hegel, the phenomenologist, being just is that which consciousness knows.

I stated earlier that the *Phenomenology* examines the way being appears to consciousness. We now see that this does not mean that consciousness is caught up in the play of its own perceptions and cut off from what is real. It means that consciousness is directly aware of what is, but knows only those aspects of being that are apparent to it. It knows only those features of being that it is able to discern: being's immediacy, its unity and multiplicity, and the fact of its being "over there." Logical-ontological thought alone will discover the full truth of being.

At the end of the *Phenomenology* it is the very being of which consciousness is aware that will prove to be identical in structure to thought. For this reason, Hegel claims, "nothing is *known* that is not in *experience*" (*PS*, 487). When we pass from the *Phenomenology* to the *Logic*, we do not, therefore, move out of some putative realm of mere representation into the light of truth; we pass from the *consciousness* of being to the absolute *thought* of being. As far as Hegel is concerned (and *pace* Robert Pippin), consciousness is directly aware of being all along – the only realm of being we may assume there to be. At the end of the *Phenomenology*, however, we recognize that the true nature of what, for consciousness, is simply "over there" can be found within thought itself (see Pippin, 1989: 98–9, 114–15).

It is important to remember that Hegel makes no ontological claims of his own in the *Phenomenology*. He accepts the ontological claims made by consciousness and analyzes them phenomenologically. In the process, he discovers that consciousness itself mutates logically into the "absolute" standpoint from which he develops his own ontology. In this way, Hegel believes, his own ontology is shown to grow out of the ordinary view of things and so not to be as perverse as consciousness suspects.

At the outset of the *Phenomenology*, however, we may not assume in advance that consciousness will necessarily lead to absolute knowing. Nor may we presuppose the validity of the standpoint of absolute knowing and refer to that standpoint in order to judge that ordinary consciousness is deficient. Indeed, we may not measure ordinary consciousness against any other conception of knowledge at all, whether it be scientific, aesthetic, or religious. We must set aside all such external criteria of judgment, content ourselves with considering the internal coherence of the ordinary point of view, and wait to see whether or not that point of view issues in absolute knowing. What we must determine, therefore, is not whether consciousness knows being as well as absolute knowing does, but whether it lives up to its own standards and understands those aspects of being that are apparent to it quite as it thinks it does. If it does not do so, that might begin to explain why it leads eventually to absolute knowing.

Yet how could consciousness fail to know what it knows? Consciousness – in its own eyes and those of the phenomenologist – is nothing but the *consciousness* and *knowledge* of its objects. How, then, is it possible for it not to know those objects? Hegel's answer contains the key to the whole method of phenomenology.

Hegel points out that, although consciousness knows only what it knows, it draws a distinction between what it knows and its knowing of it. Indeed, this distinction is built into the very fact that consciousness knows something distinct from itself at all. This is not to say that there are two separate objects for consciousness. There is only one object, namely whatever it is that consciousness knows; but consciousness regards that object in two different ways – once as being what it is in itself, and once as being known or being for consciousness.

The fact that consciousness makes this distinction opens up the possibility that its knowledge of its object might not match the object itself. The problem is not that our knowledge might fall short of something (allegedly) lying beyond the reach of consciousness. The problem is that our knowledge might fall short of the object of which we are conscious: we might not know properly the very object we know. Ordinary consciousness may insist that it "knows what it knows," but Hegel's phenomenology shows that this is not necessarily the case. Furthermore, this difficulty is not imported into consciousness by the phenomenologist. It is inherent in consciousness itself, and is generated by the simple fact that consciousness knows something at all.

Yet consciousness need not despair, for it contains within itself the criterion by which to judge whether or not it knows its own object properly. That criterion is provided by whatever consciousness identifies as the object in itself. Consciousness does not, therefore, need to get outside its own perspective to compare its knowledge with what there is: for "in what consciousness affirms from within itself as *being-in-itself* or the *True* we have the standard which consciousness itself sets up by which to measure what it knows" (*PS*, 53). Consciousness says to itself "that is the object I know" and "this is how I know it to be," and in what it takes to be its object it has the criterion by which to judge the adequacy of its knowledge. Indeed, not only can consciousness compare its knowledge with its object, it cannot but undertake such a comparison.

> Consciousness is, on the one hand, consciousness of the object, and on the other, consciousness of itself; consciousness of what for it is the True, and consciousness of its knowledge of the truth. Since both are *for* the same consciousness, this consciousness is itself their comparison; it is for this same consciousness to know whether its knowledge of the object corresponds to the object or not. (*PS*, 54)

It is not we, therefore, who put consciousness to the test. Consciousness puts itself to the test, and "all that is left for us to do is simply to look on [*zusehen*]" (*PS*, 54).

The *Phenomenology* does not analyze the various ways in which we scrutinize and correct our understanding of things in our everyday lives. It analyzes the process of self-examination that follows *logically* from the very structure of consciousness as such. In the course of the book Hegel analyzes a sequence of "shapes" of consciousness, beginning with the simplest – sensuous certainty – and progressing through perception, understanding, self-consciousness, reason, and social, aesthetic, and religious spirit (or *Geist*) to absolute knowing. In each case (except the last), Hegel argues, consciousness learns that its knowledge does not actually correspond to the object as it holds it to be in itself. Consciousness starts out by identifying its object as *X*, but comes to know its object as *Y*. It thus discovers that it does not in fact know its object in the way it initially thought it did. Sensuous certainty, for example, takes its object to be a simple immediacy – *this*, *here*, *now* – but eventually comes to view its object as "an absolute plurality of Nows" and "a simple complex of many Heres" (*PS*, 64).

When knowledge turns out to diverge from the initial understanding of an object, "it would seem," Hegel writes, "that consciousness must alter its knowledge to make it conform to the object." That is to say, one would think that consciousness should correct its new view of the object in order to make it better correspond to the object as it first understands it to be. Yet such a move would be inappropriate here because the knowledge consciousness has acquired is nothing but knowledge *of the object*. Through the changes in our knowledge that have already occurred, we have gained a better understanding of what the object itself actually is. In the process the object has shown itself to be not just what it is first taken to be, but something different: "in the alteration of the knowledge, the object itself alters for it too, for the knowledge that was present was essentially a knowledge of the object: as the knowledge changes, so too does the object, for it essentially belonged to this knowledge" (*PS*, 54). We cannot, therefore, abandon what we have learned about the object and revert to our initial conception of it. On the contrary, we must give up that initial conception and accept what the object has now revealed itself to be. Consciousness must thus accept that its object is not a simple sensuous immediacy, but is indeed a complex unity of different spatio-temporal moments.

In this process, Hegel writes, consciousness learns "that what it previously took to be the *in-itself* is not an *in-itself*, or that it was only an in-itself *for consciousness*" (*PS*, 54). That is to say, it realizes that what it initially declared to be the object in itself was merely what it *declared* to be the object in itself, and that the object has now proved to be something different. In this way, Hegel maintains, there arises a new consciousness of what the object is in itself and a new criterion by which to judge our knowledge. The test is now to determine whether consciousness knows this newly conceived object properly, or whether it, too, will prove to be different from what it is first taken to be.

This process whereby a new understanding of the object – indeed, a new object – constantly emerges in consciousness is named by Hegel "experience" (*Erfahrung*). The *Phenomenology* is thus "the Science of the *experience of consciousness*" (*PS*, 56). (As consciousness later mutates logically into self-consciousness and, further, into social consciousness or spirit, Hegel's new science will turn into a phenomenology of spirit.) The experience Hegel describes does not involve an increase or change in our empirical knowledge of the world. It does not teach us, for example, that the object we believed to be a human being is really a tailor's dummy. The experience consciousness undergoes in the *Phenomenology* brings with it a change in the fundamental logical form of what it knows.

Consciousness initially takes its object in a certain way, but the experience that consciousness must logically make of that very object reveals it to have a more complex form and structure than is first thought. The very thing consciousness knows proves to be quite different from what it is first assumed to be. Experience does not completely invalidate the initial conception of the object: consciousness is not wrong to regard its object in that initial way. It becomes apparent, however, that its object is not merely what it is first taken to be, but harbors within it levels of complexity that are not immediately apparent. Indeed, what is implicitly disclosed in experience is the form of a new kind of object altogether.

Sensuous certainty, for example, initially takes its object to be nothing but *this, here, now*, but this object is actually experienced to be a complex unity of spatio-temporal moments. When consciousness accepts the lesson of its own experience, it mutates logically into perception. The object of perception is then experienced to have an inner unity underlying its evident multiplicity. When consciousness accepts this insight, it turns into understanding (*Verstand*). This inner unity itself proves to be law-governed and rational, like consciousness itself, and in this experience consciousness shows itself to be implicitly self-conscious. The object to which explicit self-consciousness relates then turns out to be not just a unified, law-governed entity standing over against consciousness, but an object of desire and labor. Later in the *Phenomenology* the object proves to be nature and, subsequently, the realm of being or "substance" that itself becomes self-conscious in human society, history, art, religion, and philosophy. At this point the form of the object is disclosed to be *spiritual* (*geistig*), and consciousness begins to experience aspects of its own spiritual world. When the object proves to be spiritual in this way, it does not cease altogether to be what it is earlier experienced to be. The realm of being or "substance" that becomes self-conscious in humanity still incorporates objects that can be desired, understood, and perceived and that have an immediacy. What is immediately there for consciousness has, however, proved – in consciousness's own experience – to be much more than mere perceivable, comprehensible, and desirable immediacy.

In the *Logic* Hegel will analyze the logical form that being or "substance" has in itself – the form that logical-ontological thought knows it absolutely to possess. In the *Phenomenology*, by contrast, Hegel analyzes the different forms of objectivity that become apparent in conscious experience. He examines – in what I believe is a unique style of philosophizing – the changing, dynamic structure of conscious experience itself. It is important to see that in each case the new object of consciousness – or the new form of the object – emerges out of the experience consciousness has just made of its current object. The new object is not introduced by the phenomenologist to resolve "contradictions" in a given shape of consciousness. As Werner Marx notes, "the new object is really the old one, albeit with the difference that the new contains the 'experience' gained of the old" (Marx, 1975: 80).

Hegel's own way of putting this is to say that "our knowledge of the first object, or the being-*for*-consciousness of the first in-itself, itself becomes the second object" (*PS*, 55). Hegel is aware, however, that this manner of expression could be misleading: for it might look as if the new object consists in nothing but the conscious realization or "reflection" that the initial object is not the object as it is in truth. On this reading, it would be hard to talk of the emergence of a new object of consciousness; all that would arise would be the awareness that the initial object has, as it were, been dethroned. Hegel reminds us, however, that this realization is itself produced by discovering what the initial object actually is. It is the experience of the true character of the object that causes consciousness to revise its initial assumption that the object as first conceived is the object as it is in itself.

This needs to be borne in mind when we read Hegel's claim that the new object consists in the "being-*for*-consciousness of the first in-itself." Hegel certainly points out that, in the experience of consciousness, the initial object "ceases to be the in-itself, and becomes something that is the *in-itself* only *for* consciousness" (*PS*, 55). The simple realization that this is the case does not, however, constitute the new object. The new object comprises what the first object is actually experienced and known to be – what that first "in-itself" actually proves to be for consciousness. In other words, the new object is what the initial object shows itself to be in the experience that brings about the realization to which we have referred.

The motor that drives phenomenology forward is thus the experience made by consciousness itself. This experience is "dialectical" because in it the object negates itself into a new kind of object. The culmination of this process is absolute knowing – the recognition by consciousness that what it is aware of is not just something distinct from itself, but that which is identical in form to itself. This idea that there is an identity of form between consciousness and its object in fact begins to emerge fairly early in the *Phenomenology*. It first surfaces when consciousness proves to be self-consciousness, or consciousness that finds itself in the other; accordingly, Hegel maintains, "with self-consciousness . . . we have . . . entered the native realm of truth" (*PS*, 104). Self-consciousness, however, is merely the beginning of absolute knowing. As such, it coexists with the idea that consciousness relates to something fundamentally distinct from the self, and, indeed, with the idea that the self is itself something alien to itself. This is why it soon proves to be an unhappy consciousness. Even spiritual consciousness, or *Geist*, regards its own social and historical context as an objective world "over there" to which it relates. That world is not understood to be "something alien" to consciousness, but is seen by consciousness as the space in which it is at home. Nevertheless, it is that which consciousness "opposes to itself as an objective, actual *world*," and so remains other than consciousness in its very homeliness (*PS*, 263–4). Genuine happiness or satisfaction is achieved only at the end of the *Phenomenology*, when consciousness becomes absolute knowing in the fullest sense. At that point consciousness finally overcomes the opposition between itself and its object by realizing that the true nature of the world over there is immanent within thought.

The Role of the "We"

The role of the phenomenologist is not to intervene in the experience of consciousness, but to let consciousness "move spontaneously of its own nature" (*PS*, 36). Only in this way, will we guarantee that the phenomenological analysis of consciousness is immanent.

Yet, toward the end of the introduction, Hegel notes that we are not to be purely passive observers of consciousness because it is our role to render explicit the fact that the experience of one shape of consciousness leads to a new object and a new shape of consciousness. With this remark Hegel refines, but does not retract, the account he has given so far. It remains the case that each shape of consciousness learns through experience that its object is not what it initially took it to be. It also remains the case that through the experience of one object a wholly new kind of object arises for consciousness. Hegel now points out, however, that, strictly speaking, a given shape of consciousness (such as perception) only ever understands itself to be learning more about one and the same object, and does not realize that the form of a new object altogether is implicit in its experience of the object it knows. We are the ones who recognize this and render it explicit. We are thus the ones who make the transition from the consciousness of one object to that of another and so from one shape of consciousness to another. As Hegel remarks, it is only thanks to "us" that "the new object shows itself to have come about through a *reversal* [*Umkehrung*] *of consciousness itself* " (*PS*, 55). It is through our activity, therefore, that the shapes of consciousness form a continuous development from sensuous certainty to absolute knowing.

Yet we do not force consciousness to follow a preordained route of our own devising. All we do is render explicit what is implicit in the experience of consciousness itself. Consciousness learns by itself that its own object is more complex than it first thought; but we make the move to the new shape of consciousness that accepts that there is now a new object. According to Hegel, therefore, no individual shape of consciousness sees the new object actually emerge from its experience of the old object, or catches itself in the act of mutating into a new shape; only the phenomenologist sees this. The new object is, of course, there for the new shape of consciousness. For consciousness, however, "what has thus arisen exists only as an object; *for us*, it appears at the same time as movement and as a process of becoming" (*PS*, 56). As Jean Hyppolite points out, "only the philosopher sees in force (the object of understanding) the result of the movement of perceiving consciousness" (Hyppolite, 1974: 25).

This explains why certain transitions in the *Phenomenology* appear at first sight to be somewhat obscure. It is not immediately obvious, for example, why the slave's consciousness (in the master/slave dialectic) should pass over into Stoicism. After all, the slave labors on material things, whereas the Stoic is content to grasp things in pure thought alone. Hegel claims, however, that the Stoic's understanding of the object is implicit in the slave's labor. This is not to say that the slave himself ends up transformed from a manual laborer into an intellectual. Hegel's point is more subtle than that.

The slave's relation to the object remains a practical one: he works on the thing and gives it a new shape. Yet in that new shape the slave sees the expression of his own freedom. He thus recognizes an aspect of himself in the object. In this respect, the slave does essentially what thought does: for thought is precisely that form of consciousness that knows its object to be just like itself (namely, rational). When something is "grasped *in thought*," Hegel writes, "consciousness remains *immediately* aware of its unity with this determinate and distinct being" (*PS*, 120).

The slave's practical activity is different from the Stoic's activity of thinking and understanding; Hegel does not attempt to conceal this difference. Nevertheless, in Hegel's view, the latter is implicit in the former. It is, however, we – not the slave – who render explicit the element of thought in the slave's labor and so make the transition to Stoicism. (By the way, although the Stoic position prefigures that of absolute knowing, it falls short of the latter because it still contrasts thought with those aspects of being it regards as inessential [*PS*, 121–2].)

It is clear from this brief discussion that the transitions between shapes of consciousness in the *Phenomenology* are logical, not historical. One shape of consciousness is made necessary logically by the one that precedes it because it is implicit in that preceding shape. It need not, however, follow that shape in time, though in later sections of the text there is some overlap between the logical sequence and modern European history. Nor (as some have argued) is every succeeding shape to be understood as the precondition of the one that precedes it. Hegel does claim that social and historical spirit is the "presupposition" of abstract shapes of consciousness, such as sensuous certainty and perception (*PS*, 264); but it is not the case that Stoicism is the precondition of the master/slave dialectic, or that absolute knowing is the precondition of aesthetic and religious experience.

The principal point, for Hegel, is that – whatever their historical relation to one another may be – each shape of consciousness (except the first, sensuous certainty) renders explicit the *truth* that is implicitly disclosed in the experience of the preceding shape. This includes the final shape of consciousness, absolute knowing, which Hegel describes as "the *truth* of every mode of consciousness" (*SL*, 49). Absolute knowing, for Hegel, is not the historical (or logical) presupposition of the other shapes of consciousness. It simply renders explicit what is implicit in, but also largely hidden from, every other shape of consciousness: namely, the truth that thought and being are actually identical in form.

Our role in the *Phenomenology* is not only to make the logical transition from one shape of consciousness to another; it is also to articulate the logical development of each individual shape of consciousness. We unfold the logic inherent in each shape's own experience, and must do so because we are the ones who present – or tell the story of – consciousness's self-examination. For some, however, the fact that we play this role prevents our account from being genuinely immanent. We approach consciousness (so it is argued) expecting it to conform to a predetermined logical pattern, and so inevitably fail to bring to light the internal dynamic proper to consciousness itself.

For Hegel, by contrast, the opposite is true. The fact that we approach consciousness as thinking beings, alert to the logic inherent within consciousness, is precisely what ensures that our account is immanent. For it is thought alone – not imagination, sensuous perception, or aesthetic intuition – that can set aside its own assumptions and attend to the unique "specificity" (*Eigentümlichkeit*) of each shape of consciousness (*PS*, 17, translation modified). In Hegel's view, only thought can "surrender [itself] to the life of the object" (*PS*, 32). A wholly immanent account of consciousness and its experience must, therefore, be a *logical* one.

This does not mean, as Stanley Rosen claims, "that the *Phenomenology* is not genuinely intelligible without a knowledge of the *Logic*" (Rosen, 1974: 129). If this were the case, the *Phenomenology* could not fulfill its specific task of leading to absolute knowing without taking the latter for granted. *Pace* Rosen, the thought that undertakes the phenomenological analysis of consciousness does not presuppose any particular conception of logic – dialectical or otherwise – but seeks to understand the internal structure of conscious experience, starting from nothing but consciousness's own assumptions.

In the course of the *Phenomenology* it becomes apparent that logical categories are, indeed, at work in conscious experience. Hegel points out, for example, that the "empty abstractions of a 'singleness' [*Einzelheit*] and a 'universality' [*Allgemeinheit*] opposed to it" are the "powers whose interplay is the perceptual understanding" (*PS*, 35, 77). Such categories also prove – in the course of the *Logic* – to be immanent in pure being itself. In this sense, "the development of [consciousness] . . . rests solely on the nature of the pure essentialities which constitute the content of logic" (*SL*, 28). The phenomenologist does not, however, presuppose those categories or their treatment in the *Logic*; rather, he *discovers* in consciousness categories that will also be discovered later by the speculative logician in the thought of pure being.

It is important to remember that phenomenology and speculative philosophy (or ontological logic) are separate disciplines for Hegel. Philosophy is the work of absolute knowing that knows that the truth of being can be found within thought itself. *Phenomenology* is also the work of thought or absolute knowing, in so far as it is a systematic, "scientific" study of consciousness. The phenomenologist, however, suspends his absolute, ontological certainty that thought can know being from within itself, and examines only what is immanent in conscious experience. The philosopher-as-phenomenologist hopes to show that such experience leads eventually to absolute knowing (in its full, ontological sense), but, as Lauer remarks, "he is willing to wait to see whether the path he has chosen really gets him there" (Lauer, 1976: 28).

The readers of the *Phenomenology* are ordinary individuals – modes of natural consciousness – who are also interested in finding out whether or not the certainties of ordinary consciousness lead logically to absolute knowing. Like the phenomenologist, they must adopt part of the standpoint of absolute knowing by thinking their way into the logic inherent in conscious experience, yet maintaining a skeptical distance from any ontological claims made by absolute knowing. The readers of the *Phenomenology* maintain this distance, however, not because they have suspended, but because they have yet to attain, the absolute certainty that being can be understood from within thought.

The phenomenologist and the readers of Hegel's text together constitute the "we" who think through the experience of consciousness and make the transition from one shape to another. They form the community of those who refuse to allow philosophy to beg the question against ordinary consciousness, but who are open to whatever proves to be logically implicit in conscious experience.

The "we" must be distinguished from the shapes of consciousness whose experience is analyzed in the *Phenomenology* itself (such as perception, the unhappy consciousness, and so on). The *Phenomenology* demonstrates that these shapes give rise to one another in a continuous logical sequence, culminating in absolute knowing. In the process, we, the readers, learn – and the phenomenologist proves – that absolute knowing is not a perverse standpoint after all, but one that is made necessary by the certainties of natural consciousness itself. There are, therefore, three things going on in the *Phenomenology*: as the shapes of consciousness mutate logically into one another, we readers are given a ladder to the standpoint of absolute knowing, and the phenomenologist demonstrates the validity of absolute knowing without begging the question against us.

At the end of the *Phenomenology*, the perspectives of the readers, the phenomenologist, and the consciousness being examined all coincide with that of speculative philosophy, or absolute knowing in its full, ontological (rather than merely phenomenological) sense. At that point, phenomenology has completed its task and the work of philosophy can begin.

Conclusion

The *Phenomenology* has exercised considerable influence on subsequent philosophers, including Marx, Heidegger, Kojève, Adorno, and Derrida. The most influential sections of the text have probably been those on sensuous certainty, the master/slave dialectic, and the unhappy consciousness; and the most significant insight bequeathed to us by Hegel may well be the idea that experience is not purely individual but mediated by our common social, historical, aesthetic, and religious heritage.

It does not appear, however, that many – if any – philosophers have adopted Hegel's phenomenological method. Neither Husserlian phenomenology, Heideggerian fundamental ontology, nor Derridean deconstruction examines the twists and turns of conscious experience in a Hegelian way. Yet, Hegel's phenomenological method continues to deserve serious attention, for it offers a unique solution to an enduring philosophical problem: how to prove to ordinary consciousness that philosophy (in particular, metaphysics) is a legitimate enterprise, without begging the question against such consciousness. From a Hegelian perspective, if one does not wish simply to assert that ordinary consciousness is wrong to be suspicious of philosophy, or to argue in a quasi-transcendental manner (like Nietzsche and Heidegger) that ordinary consciousness itself presupposes the very processes that philosophy discloses, then there is no alternative to a phenomenology that examines conscious experience on its own terms. Seen in this light, Hegel's *Phenomenology* does not set out an arcane and outdated philosophical system, but presents a mode of philosophizing that can still be defended, and is still needed, today.

Besides Hegel, many philosophers – from the empiricists to Wittgenstein and Austin – have explored the intricacies of ordinary experience. Yet none has sought as eagerly as Hegel to avoid interpreting such experience in terms of pre-established philosophical categories, and none has been as sensitive as Hegel to the subtle changes in perspective that conscious experience necessarily entails. For these reasons, Hegel's *Phenomenology* remains a text that modern philosophers should study closely.

Bibliography

Editions and translations

Hegel, G. W. F. (1970) *Phänomenologie des Geistes*, ed. E. Moldenhauer and K. M. Michel. Frankfurt am Main: Suhrkamp Verlag.

Hegel, G. W. F. (1977) *Phenomenology of Spirit*, trans. A. V. Miller. Oxford: Oxford University Press.

Hegel, G. W. F. (1980) *Phänomenologie des Geistes*, ed. W. Bonsiepen and R. Heede. Hamburg: Felix Meiner Verlag.

Hegel, G. W. F. (1991) *The Encyclopaedia Logic*, trans. T. F. Geraets, W. A. Suchting and H. S. Harris. Indianapolis, IN: Hackett.

Hegel, G. W. F. (1999) *Science of Logic*, trans. A. V. Miller. Amherst: Humanity Books.

Studies and references

Althaus, H. (2000) *Hegel: An Intellectual Biography*, trans. M. Tarsh. Cambridge: Polity Press (orig. pub. 1992).

Flay, J. (1984) *Hegel's Quest for Certainty*. Albany, NY: State University of New York Press.

Forster, M. (1998) *Hegel's Idea of a Phenomenology of Spirit*. Chicago: University of Chicago Press.

Harris, H. S. (1997) *Hegel's Ladder*, 2 vols. Indianapolis, IN: Hackett.

Houlgate, S. (1998) Absolute knowing revisited. *The Owl of Minerva*, 30(1): 51–67.

Houlgate, S. (2001) G. W. F. Hegel. In S. M. Emmanuel (ed.), *The Blackwell Guide to the Modern Philosophers from Descartes to Nietzsche*, pp. 278–305. Oxford: Blackwell.

Hyppolite, J. (1974) *Genesis and Structure of Hegel's Phenomenology of Spirit*, trans. S. Cherniak and J. Heckman. Evanston, IL: Northwestern University Press (orig. pub. 1946).

Kant, I. (1987) *Critique of Judgment*, trans. W. S. Pluhar. Indianapolis, IN: Hackett.

Kant, I. (1997) *Critique of Pure Reason*, ed. and trans. P. Guyer and A. W. Wood. Cambridge: Cambridge University Press.

Lauer, Q. (1976) *A Reading of Hegel's Phenomenology of Spirit*. New York: Fordham University Press.

Loewenberg, J. (1965) *Hegel's Phenomenology*. LaSalle, IL: Open Court.

Marx, W. (1975) *Hegel's Phenomenology of Spirit*, trans. P. Heath. New York: Harper and Row (orig. pub. 1971).

Pinkard, T. (1994) *Hegel's Phenomenology*. Cambridge: Cambridge University Press.

Pippin, R. (1989) *Hegel's Idealism*. Cambridge: Cambridge University Press.

Rosen, S. (1974) *G. W. F. Hegel: An Introduction to the Science of Wisdom*. New Haven, CT: Yale University Press.

Stewart, J. (ed.) (1998) *The Phenomenology of Spirit Reader*. Albany, NY: State University of New York Press.

Westphal, K. (1989) *Hegel's Epistemological Realism*. Dordrecht: Kluwer.

Westphal, K. (1998) Hegel, Harris, and the Spirit of the Phenomenology. *Clio*, 27(4): 551–72.

37

Karl Marx, *The Economic and Philosophical Manuscripts of 1844*

Radical Criticism and a Humanistic Vision

William McBride

The principal impact on Western philosophy of this relatively brief text, often referred to simply as *The 1844 Manuscripts* or (designating the place where they were written) *The Paris Manuscripts*, occurred, ironically, a century after their composition. Elsewhere, Marx (1818–1883) makes allusion to them as having been his effort to come to grips with, and to go beyond, the Hegelian philosophical tradition in which he had been immersed during his student years and immediately thereafter. Having achieved this goal to his satisfaction, he seemed content, as he wrote with reference to certain writings of the following year, to consign them to the gnawing criticism of the mice. It was from this incomplete and literally somewhat chewed-up state that, the original copies having been deposited in archives in Amsterdam, they were resurrected by Soviet researchers in the late 1920s and first published in their complete German version in Berlin in 1932.

Strong ideological constraints, however, prevented them from being widely disseminated until after World War II. Not only were the Nazi authorities in Germany committed to banning all Marxist works, especially works by Marx himself, but, for philosophical reasons which we shall be exploring, these *Manuscripts* were held in strong disfavor by Stalin's regime in the Soviet Union, as well. Hence, their "discovery" by larger numbers of philosophers and political theorists and their elevation to the status of a "classic" that is now rightly attributed to them was a phenomenon especially of the 1950s and 1960s, when they became a foundational text, so to speak, in the movement known as "Western Marxism."

The *Manuscripts*, essentially three in number with several sub-sections in the first and the third, present no evident structural coherence. What gives them their importance and allure is their assertion of a number of bold new conceptual claims, drawing primarily on the traditions of recent German philosophy and of British–French political economy, while inverting the seemingly conservative implications of both, in the service of a very radical critique of existing society and an equally radical but open-ended vision of future society. In contrast to the bulk of Marx's much later work, *Capital*, which consists largely of descriptive economic analyses based on a set of assumptions concerning the nature of material production under capitalism, the *Manuscripts*, in articulating many of those assumptions for the first time, do so in a rhetorical and dialectical way that reveals their ethical and even ontological roots. The best approach to summarizing the content of the *Manuscripts* may be to begin by focusing, in turn, on several of their themes that have attracted the most attention among readers and commentators before returning, at the end, to questions concerning their impact. The themes to which I propose to devote particular attention are the following: alienated labor, private property and communism, humanism/naturalism, and the critical rejection of the Hegelian legacy.

Alienated Labor

"Estranged labor" is in fact a better translation of Marx's German expression, *entfremdete Arbeit*, since the term that is more literally translated as "alienation," *Entaüsserung*, refers to a highly general characteristic of the movement of dialectics as Hegel understood it (wherein any entity, in the course of its development, necessarily becomes internally split and hence "goes outside itself"). But "alienation" has become the canonical term in English for the phenomenon which Marx explores in the best-known of the *Manuscripts*. It captures the situation of the ordinary worker in the present state of affairs, which according to Marx is one of antagonistic separation (1) from the object that he or she produces, (2) from his or her own life-activity, (3) from the human species as ideally conceived, and (4) from his or her fellow human beings. Under the coercive conditions of wage labor, whereby the typical worker's supposedly free choice is reducible to that of either undertaking whatever work is available or else starving, the product of that work takes on the role of a hostile ("alien") object. Producing things, which Marx's analysis identifies as the quintessentially human life-activity, has become, in the capitalist context, merely a painful means to the end of staying alive, so that the worker "feels himself to be freely active only in his animal functions – eating, drinking and procreating . . . – while in his human functions he is reduced to an animal" (*Economic and Philosophical Manuscripts* [hereafter cited as *MSS*], 1964: 125). Indeed – since Marx, as he goes on to say, has nothing against "animal functions" when they form part of an integrated, truly human life – the status of the worker is considerably lower even than that: he or she has become, within the work context, a *commodity*. This insight was to play an absolutely key role in the theory of *Capital*: the short section of the latter that is considered most reminiscent of this early manuscript on alienated labor is entitled "The Fetishism of Commodities and the Secret thereof."

The third aspect of alienation discussed by Marx here, alienation from the human species, depends for much of its force on a neologism, "species-being" (*Gattungswesen*) that was first devised by Ludwig Feuerbach, to whose critique of Hegel's theologically imbued system Marx pays special tribute in the preface to the *Manuscripts*. The idea of "species-being" is, roughly, that human beings, unlike other animals, are able to see themselves as a collective social and historical entity, capable of realizing by itself the positive attributes that traditional monotheistic religions have assigned, mistakenly, to an imagined "alien" Being, God. Marx self-consciously shifts the focus away from theology and toward the political and socioeconomic spheres, implying that a future overcoming of workers' present alienation from their common "species-being" is conceivable. Finally, the fourth aspect of alienation, identified as alienation from one's fellow human beings, manifested in enviousness and invidious competition, is said to follow logically from the third.

Private Property and Communism

In his very brief second manuscript, Marx elaborates on the theme that property relationships are historically relative, and that the current era of modern industry is witnessing the triumph of capital, or "movable property," over landed property, with the resulting change in status of the worker (who is by definition propertyless) into a "wage slave." In this and the succeeding sub-sections of the third manuscript, he makes frequent references to Adam Smith and other earlier economic theorists to buttress his case. At the same time, he begins to project a vision of what he denominates "communism," "the necessary form and the dynamic principle of the immediate future, but . . . not itself the goal of human development – the form of human society" (*MSS*, 1964: 167). The precise meaning of these words is in dispute, but at least part of their reference is to his depiction, several pages earlier, of various "stages" of communism (whether intended by him as mere conceptual possibilities or projected future historical probabilities is another disputed question), the first of which, "crude, egalitarian communism," is described in extremely negative terms. The problem with such a crude form of communism, as Marx explains in good dialectical fashion, is that it constitutes a "negation" or "overcoming" of private property which is still imbued with the latter's inherent tendencies toward domination and reliance on force, and simply universalizes these tendencies over the whole of society; hence it results in a leveling-down of talent and personality and, instead of abolishing the traditional role of the worker under capitalism, extends this role to *everyone*. In this same part of his text, while drawing the inference that such a barbaric society would also be characterized by universal prostitution, Marx remarks that the relationship between men and women is the key to judging the level of development of any given society – a claim that has often been cited with approval in feminist contexts.

The conclusion of the sub-section of the third manuscript to which editors usually give the title, "Private Property and Communism" (few sub-titles are to be found in the original *Manuscripts*), further elucidates Marx's point in rejecting communism as a long-term future goal. He regards the latter, "the form of human society," as an ever-evolving state of affairs in which private property would no longer be an issue in dispute at all, and a more positive form of social life, transcending the deformations occasioned by the present struggle against capitalist private property, could come about. He writes, in this context, of "socialist man" as the future ideal – confusing terminology for those who, as students of so-called "orthodox" Marxism–Leninism in the days of the Soviet Bloc, were taught that "socialism" designated their own societies and "communism" was the long-term goal.

Humanism/Naturalism

It is, however, the often rhapsodic quality of portions of this same sub-section of the *Manuscripts* that most conflicts with the tone and doctrine of later Marxist–Leninist ideology and explains the early hostility (sometimes replaced in later years by a be- mused distancing) of that ideology's proponents toward these *Manuscripts*. Marxism– Leninism stressed its allegedly "scientific" nature and the deterministic predictions that it was supposed to entail. Here in the *Manuscripts*, Marx engages in enthusiastic musings about the "emancipation of the human senses" that will come about in the society of the future, as well as a new appreciation of music, of love, and in short of all value-laden aspects of human life. He insists, it is true, that this emancipation will restore human beings to a lost harmony with nature, thus justifying his identification of his vision with both "humanism" and "naturalism," and that it will usher in a new and more correct understanding of the meaning of natural science. As he says: "Natu- ral science will then abandon its abstract materialist, or rather idealist, orientation, and will become the basis of a *human* science, just as it has already become – though in an alienated form – the basis of actual human life" (*MSS*, 1964: 163–4).

But this entire conception of a humanistic, or "anthropological," natural science of the future is in conflict at a deep level with the more positivistic, deterministic ap- proach to natural science that Marxism–Leninism inherited especially from the man who was later to become Marx's lifetime collaborator, Friedrich Engels. It suggests, rather, an aesthetically oriented and free society, unpredictable in detail and hence necessarily open-ended and vague, of the sort with which the work of various later "Western Marxists," such as Ernst Bloch and Herbert Marcuse, had much greater affinity than did that of typical Communist Party ideologists in the bygone era.

The Critical Rejection of the Hegelian Legacy

The final sub-section of the *1844 Manuscripts* consists of a full-scale assault on Hegel's philosophy, which had been the intellectually dominant force in Germany during Marx's recently completed student days. While rather technical in some of its details – for Marx had studied Hegel's philosophy closely – his critique may be summarized by saying that he finds Hegel's entire approach to be one of preserving the world as it is, after having identified the profound dialectical contradictions with which every aspect of human existence is rent, by resolving these contradictions strictly in the domain of philosophical thought. As Marx expresses it, for Hegel, "the true existence of religion, of the state, of nature, and of art, is the *philosophy* of religion, of the state, of nature, and of art" (*MSS*, 1964: 211). This leaves the real conditions of human alienation intact. Marx depicts Hegel as the quintessentially abstract, alienated thinker, for whom, at the end of the *Phenomenology of Spirit*, absolute knowledge is seen to be identical with full self-consciousness. To this approach Marx opposes both his naturalism, with its emphasis on the material, objective side of human existence, and his still-nascent sense of social activism. But he retains great respect for the dialectical method itself, with its capacity to identify contradictions within phenomena and to show how the dynamics inherent in their opposition inevitably lead to their overcoming and "supersession" by new phenomena with new contradictions. This respect was to endure throughout Marx's career, so that in *Capital* he would proudly claim adherence to the dialectical method of Hegel, widely regarded by that time as a "dead dog" in intellectual circles – but only to a totally inverted, materially based version of that method.

There is, to Marx's way of thinking, a close linkage between his critique of Hegel and his references to economic questions, such as the separation of capital from ground rent and the division of labor, which constitute the less frequently noted portions of the *Manuscripts*: "Hegel's standpoint," he says, "is that of modern political economy" (*MSS*, 1964: 203). He explains this by saying that Hegel, too, regards *labor* as the essence of the human, but he complains that Hegel only sees the positive side of labor, not the negative. In fact, one of the great charms of the Marx of these *Manuscripts* is his skill at juxtaposing ultimate value issues – questions about the meaning of human life itself, of the sort with which Hegel dealt – to problems of *economic* value, as he does most directly in a short sub-section concerning money. Here, he cites Goethe and quotes at length from Shakespeare's *Timon of Athens*, with its depiction of the character of a miser, by way of showing how the dominance of economic concerns distorts and subverts virtues, talents, and the human social bond itself. Marx thus appears as a committed humanist, angry at the many structural deformations (not all of them, clearly enough from this example, rooted strictly in the system of modern capitalism) that prevent the flourishing of a truly human existence, but also convinced that such a flourishing is a real future possibility.

Impact of the *Manuscripts*

A very hotly debated topic during the years, roughly the 1960s and 1970s, of the most extensive Marx scholarship among Western philosophers was that of the relationship between the "early" and the "later" Marx, the former being epitomized above all in the *Economic and Philosophical Manuscripts*. There is no doubt that there is a sharp difference of tone between these writings and *Capital*, and some of the *Manuscripts*' most central terms, such as, precisely, "alienation" and "species-being," appear rarely or never in the later work. The French philosopher, Louis Althusser, went so far as to assert that there had been an "epistemological break" in Marx's thinking, and in fact passages in Marx's own middle-period work, most notably a few autobiographical pages in the preface to *A Contribution to the Critique of Political Economy* from which my opening allusion to the "gnawing criticism of the mice" was taken, strongly imply that this, or something close to this, was Marx's own view of his intellectual evolution: from philosophy to economics, as it were. But I trust that I have already given sufficient indication of my belief that this view is greatly oversimplified, and that the impact of the "vision of a possible future," as I like to call it (as contrasted with a "prediction of a *certain* future"), that suffuses these writings underlay and in a sense motivated the more mathematically precise and – with occasional dramatic exceptions – generally more dispassionate Marxian texts of later years. To put the matter simply but, I think, accurately, the post-capitalist world of which Marx dreamed was one in which economic values would no longer predominate, and so he spent most of the rest of his life reading and writing economic theory with a view to demonstrating, through an internal (dialectical) critique of the premises of the great economic theorists as well as of the exploitative practices of the British industry of his day, that this dream was not idle.

But the more *direct* impact of these *Manuscripts* on Western philosophy and philosophers did not occur, as I indicated at the outset, until mid-twentieth century (although a few, notably Georg Lukács, had read them some years earlier, and among some Chinese philosophers they have only recently achieved a certain vogue). One of their effects at that earlier time, no doubt, was the perhaps important but not intellectually impressive one of making Marx more palatable to professional philosophers and even to the general public in Western countries in which a strong disciplinary and ideological animus against him had prevailed. Their more positive impact, I think, lay in their providing valuable new intellectual tools to help articulate the then-widespread liberation movements against colonialism in Asian and African countries still under European political control, to workers' movements especially in Europe, to peasant movements in Latin America, and even to dissidents within the Soviet Bloc, whom they enabled to cite Marx himself against oppressive practices that were being carried out in his name. I should also mention the small but significant *Praxis* group of Yugoslav philosophers who relied heavily on these writings to develop a social theory equally critical of capitalism and of the centralized Soviet economy.

Many of the conditions of those decades have since been greatly modified or ceased to exist entirely, and the premises of the worldview to which Marx's critique in the *Manuscripts* was directed – wage labor for capitalist profit as the optimal way of life – have become, if anything, more universally accepted than ever before. The sunny, rather romantic optimism of Marx's future vision that constituted the other side of this critique does not now seem particularly in vogue, to put it mildly. Nevertheless, these *Manuscripts* still constitute both a brilliant – highly general, philosophically sophisticated, uncompromising – articulation of some of our deepest discontents as the *homines oeconomici* (economic men) that modern capitalist society requires us, like it or not, to be, and a sort of regulative ideal of a society that would be at once far freer and more communal than our own.

Bibliography

Editions and translations

Marx, K. (1964) *Karl Marx: Early Writings*, ed. and trans. T. B. Bottomore. New York: McGraw-Hill.

Marx, K. (1982) *Ökonomisch-philosophische Manuskripte*. In *Marx–Engels Gesamtausgabe*, vol. I, Book 2. Berlin: Dietz Verlag.

Studies

Dupré, L. (1966) *The Philosophical Foundations of Marxism*. New York: Harcourt, Brace and World.

Maguire, J. (1973) *Marx's Paris Writings*. New York: Barnes and Noble.

Mészáros, I. (1970) *Marx's Theory of Alienation*. London: Merlin Press.

38

Søren Kierkegaard, *Concluding Unscientific Postscript to Philosophical Fragments* (1846)

Making Things Difficult for the System and for Christendom

Merold Westphal

The wickedly satirical title serves as a splendid preface. Hegel's philosophy of religion consists of two overarching claims. First, philosophy is (in Hegel's system) truly scientific knowledge, fully adequate to its object, the perfect, all-encompassing mirror of the real. Second, religion can be elevated from the faith of the many to the knowledge of the elite few by the systematic reinterpretation of scripture and creed to bring them into conformity with the categories of the speculative system. In 1846, with Hegelian thought dominating discussion in Denmark, to publish a philosophy of religion whose title declares it to be unscientific, a mere postscript at that, and, to make matters still worse, not a postscript to the system but to certain philosophical fragments or tidbits, is to make unambiguous its polemical intent. What is not immediately clear is that it is a dual polemic, against Hegelian philosophy (the distinction between Hegel and his followers not being important) and against a Christendom which Kierkegaard (1813–1855) sees throughout his authorship as the non-academic twin of the system: university and church as co-conspirators in smuggling Christianity out of Christendom (*nota bene* not by denying it but by domesticating it so that Christianity becomes the spiritual security blanket of those who have lapsed, in Nietzsche's words, into "wretched contentment"). Thus, in the first appendix, Johannes Climacus, the pseudonymous author, "does not make out that he is a Christian" but insists "that it must be the most difficult of all to become a Christian" (Kierkegaard, 1992: 617, 619; all citations are to this edition).

In the second appendix, we learn in what sense this "unscientific" contribution to philosophical discourse is a conclusion. For Hegel, since the truth is the whole, the conclusion is the *denouement*, the moment when all the pieces of the puzzle fall into place and the whole picture emerges with clarity and finality. But long since Climacus has argued that, while God may very well embody such totalizing thought, it is not available for us (1992: 118; cf. 141, 158); for humans, only those have style who are never finished (1992: 86). *Postscript* is the conclusion, not of the system, but (as Kierkegaard thought at the time) of his pseudonymous authorship, a series of eight works put forth by seven different authors or editors.

This means that *Postscript* is not by Kierkegaard but by Johannes Climacus, also the author of the *Philosophical Fragments* alluded to in the title. In the second appendix, Kierkegaard acknowledges that the pseudonyms are his creations, but insists that the works remain pseudonymous, that "in the pseudonymous books there is not a single word by me." To any who quote from these books, "it is my wish, my prayer, that he will do me the kindness of citing the respective pseudonymous author's name, not mine" (1992: 626–7). In other words, we are to treat the pseudonyms like characters created by a novelist, without attributing the views of any one character, much less all of them, to the novelist.

The point of post-publication pseudonymity, then, is not to hide Kierkegaard's identity; it is rather to distance himself from the reader. He does not wish to have his personality or notoriety influence the reader, either for or against. He wants to leave the reader alone with the content. He regularly insists that he writes "without authority" (being neither professor nor pastor), so there is no need to attach his name to the ideas presented.

In the context of the entire authorship, this move belongs to a deeper purpose, to leave the reader alone – before God, where human life at its deepest levels is lived. Kierkegaard's view of the self is every bit as relational as Hegel's, or Buber's, or Sartre's, or Levinas's; the difference is his emphatic insistence that the God relation is prior to all other relations. The radical individualism for which he is widely praised or blamed, often as the "father of existentialism," is badly misunderstood if it is seen as the affirmation of an isolated, atomic selfhood rather than as the attempt to keep society (the crowd, the present age, the herd) from coming between the individual and God, claiming in effect to be the "one mediator between God and humankind" (1 Tim. 2: 5).

Climacus, as we have seen, wants to make it difficult to become a Christian. With everyone else conspiring to make it "so very easy to be a Christian, it is certainly in order that a single individual . . . seeks to make it difficult, provided, however, that he does not make it more difficult than it is" (1992: 383). Like his predecessor, Johannes de Silentio, author of *Fear and Trembling*, he believes that faith is the task of a lifetime, one we never complete. The powerful elective affinities between Hegelianism and Christendom stem from the fact that "faith" has been turned into an achievement word (like winning) rather than a task word (like running) and, in the process, diluted beyond recognition. This process of personal becoming is what the system, which claims to be all encompassing, has left out, a fatal omission if, as Hegel claims, the truth is the whole.

Climacus' name for what Hegel and Christendom have overlooked is subjectivity. He stresses two features of objective knowledge, whether historical or metaphysical: (1) for human knowers it is always approximation, never final and complete; and (2) even if, *per impossibile*, it could be final and complete, it would not be faith. While "subjectivity" presupposes this analysis of human understanding, it is an existential rather than an epistemic category. It is about appropriation rather than approximation and concerns not the "what" but the "how" of belief. The question it poses is not "How certain is my knowledge?" but "How deep is my commitment?" to what I fallibly and always penultimately take to be true.

But Climacus links subjectivity to truth in the (in)famous slogan, "truth is subjectivity" (1992: 189–251). After complaining that for Hegel the highest human task is cognitive rather than ethical (1992: 129–88), he focuses attention on "essential knowing," the "ethical" and "ethical-religious" (1992: 198) knowing that concerns the deepest meaning of our existence. Here objective knowledge is not enough, even if we somehow get it right. In a parable he contrasts a pagan who prays to an idol "with all the passion of infinity" with a Christian who has "the true idea of God" but prays "in untruth" (1992: 201). With a rhetorical question he suggests that there is more truth in the former case (subjectivity), but not, *nota bene*, that the pagan has the true idea of God (objectivity).

Climacus assumes with his readers that the Christian's idea of God is a better approximation to reality than the pagan's; his point, however, is that the Christian's error is more serious than the pagan's relative to the following definition: "*An objective uncertainty, held fast through appropriation with the most passionate inwardness, is the truth*, the highest truth there is for an *existing* person," adding that this definition of truth "is a paraphrasing of faith" (1992: 203–4). Faith involves risk not because it is a lower form of cognition that, as Plato and Hegel will assure us, the philosophical elite can transcend, but rather because existential decision is called for in a context where objective certainty is not available to anyone, even to the intellectual elite.

Socrates is the paradigm of this subjectivity, not the Platonic Socrates who gives us the divided line, the ascent out of the cave, and proofs for the immortality of the soul, but the "historical" Socrates of the *Apology* who stakes his life and death on an immortality of which he cannot be certain. Socratic ignorance is an appropriate appropriation of the paradox of human existence, to be at once in time yet essentially related to the eternal.

This is not the specifically Christian paradox of the God-man that especially concerns Climacus; it only intensifies the already paradoxical nature of human existence which cognition can never neutralize. Accordingly, Climacus gives a long analysis of existential pathos (passion), the ethical-religious subjectivity which is (1) universally available to human existence and (2) the only legitimate context, as distinct from theory and speculation, for seeking to understand the specific claims of Christianity. Accordingly, we cannot stop with the objective question (approximation), "What is Christianity?" but will have to proceed to the subjective question (appropriation), "What does it mean to be, or rather, to become, a Christian?"

The initial expression of existential pathos is resignation. The task for human existence is not to understand the system but "*to Relate Oneself Absolutely to One's Absolute τέλος [goal, end] and Relatively to Relative Ends*" (1992: 387). One does not choose between the Absolute Good (God, the Eternal) and finite goods. Rather, like Abraham in *Fear and Trembling*, one holds to the finite goods in a state of resignation, deeply loving them but ready at any moment to give them up for the sake of the Absolute Good should they come into conflict with it. Learning resignation is a radical transformation that leads us to the second, essential expression of existential pathos, suffering.

This is not the contingent suffering of misfortune but the morally necessary suffering of dying to immediacy. In this context, "immediacy" signifies the natural condition in which we find ourselves to be absolutely committed to relative ends, a situation at once comic and tragic. Dying to immediacy is a task both painful and essentially incompletable. What distinguishes properly religious discourse from the complacent discourses of Hegelianism and Christendom is a constant awareness of this fact.

The third and decisive expression of existential pathos is guilt. By calling this guilt essential, total, and qualitative, Climacus indicates that it does not arise from occasional actions but rather characterizes our fundamental project, our original posture in the world. To be, as we immediately find ourselves to be, absolutely committed to anything other than the Absolute is to violate the Absolute by who we are and only subsequently by what we do. Since it does not arise from particular actions, we have awareness of this guilt not through memory but through recollection. In a dramatic turning of the tables on Plato and all the footnotes thereto, Climacus claims that the only thing recollection can give us is an awareness of our essential estrangement from the Good. This is the ultimate barrier to mediation, the Hegelian strategy for resolving the paradox of the finite in relation to the Infinite, the temporal in relation to the Eternal, the relative in relation to the Absolute in terms of the part in relation to the Whole. Guilt signifies a breach which destroys wholeness, which can only be restored through personal transformation, not speculative insight or bourgeois respectability.

Climacus calls the piety that understands itself in terms of the categories of resignation, suffering, and guilt Religiousness A. It is, he holds, a universal possibility for human existence, not dependent on special divine revelation or particular cultural tradition. Its relation to Christianity, which Climacus labels Religiousness B, is not that of another religion, like Buddhism or Islam, but more like that of the generic to the specific, where the genus–species relation has normative import. Just as a "dachshund" who lacked the generic characteristics of dogs would not be a dachshund at all but a fraud and a hoax, so a "religious" discourse that ignores or dilutes the strenuous categories of resignation, suffering, and guilt might be an aesthetic, or speculative, or even ethical discourse, but it is not authentically religious, however profound (Hegelianism) or pious (Christendom) it may appear.

Christianity, properly understood, or Religiousness B, intensifies the paradox already found in Socratic existence, not by introducing the notion of an eternal happiness but by linking it to something in time, namely the God-man, the God in time, in a word, Jesus as God incarnate. This is the point at which *Postscript* becomes a postscript to *Philosophical Fragments*, whose issue Climacus now restates as follows:

> The individual's eternal happiness is decided in time through a relation to something historical that furthermore is historical in such a way that its composition includes that which according to its nature cannot become historical and consequently must become that by virtue of the absurd. (1992: 385)

There is double paradox or, perhaps better, double scandal here. First, that anything historically particular should as such be of eternal significance goes against the notion that knowledge is recollection and that reason can be autonomous, for knowledge cannot recollect the historically particular and autonomous reason can only see it as an illustration for some general ideas it has already discovered on its own. There is a deep tension between the *logos* tradition inherited from Plato and the claim that Jesus is the *Logos* and not merely, like all the rest of creation, an expression and sign thereof.

This signifies the second paradox or scandal. It is not merely the historically particular as such that is central to Christianity but an historical being that combines two mutually exclusive natures, humanity and divinity. This absurdity is the Absolute Paradox, which goes not merely beyond but against reason. It is a contradiction.

It is easy to misunderstand Climacus here. He uses contradiction in its Hegelian sense in which it signifies not self-contradiction, the simultaneous affirmation of *p* and not-*p*, but rather the opposition between two conflicting elements, such as, for example, a mechanistic and a teleological interpretation of nature. Kierkegaard and his pseudonyms regularly contrast both (*A*) human understanding *vis-à-vis* (*B*) divine understanding and (*A*) secular human understanding, in which God is not an agent to be taken into account, and (*B*) a religious, sometimes specifically Christian understanding in which the biblical God is such an agent. In both cases there is an opposition between standpoint *A* and standpoint *B*: they contradict each other. Relative to the one, the other is paradoxical or absurd. Kierkegaard and his pseudonyms, including Climacus, think that Christian claims about Jesus as God incarnate are in contradiction to reason. But by "reason" they do not mean clear and coherent thinking but a specific interpretation of human understanding as an autonomous source of knowledge needing no divine teacher, a power of recollection that already has the truth within itself. If "faith" is the name for the understanding of human understanding as devoid of the truth within itself and needing a divine teacher, and if that is the actual situation in which we find ourselves, then faith and not reason will be the locus of our highest knowledge. It is to keep open the door to this possibility that Climacus introduces Religiousness B, Christianity as the Absolute Paradox (relative to merely human understanding).

Climacus' discussion of faith is a dual critique of Hegel, signifying two ways in which becoming a Christian is more difficult than the present age takes it to be. On the cognitive side, reason, understood as the self-sufficiency of philosophical speculation, is denied its hermeneutical authority in relation to scripture and creed. Religion within the limits of reason alone is a project of peace by colonial hegemony, and Christianity's Jerusalem remains an offense to philosophy's Athens. But beyond this, "faith" signifies not only a certain cognitive stance but also the subjective appropriation of what is believed, which involves a radical transformation of one's life. The categories of Religiousness A, blunted if not wholly ignored by speculation, are crucial here, but they have nothing specifically Christian about them – a fact which signifies a crucial incompleteness of *Postscript*. In relation to Religiousness A, Christianity must (1) be more than doctrinal belief and (2) must have its own distinctive form of existential pathos.

As a philosophy of religion, *Postscript* belongs to the analysis of the three spheres or stages of existence, aesthetic, ethical, and religious which Kierkegaard distinguishes. It is often taken to be his definitive statement, through Climacus, on the religious stage in general and on Christianity in particular. It is not! *Postscript* occurs about midway through Kierkegaard's entire authorship. In several of the works that make up his "second authorship" (see especially *Works of Love*, *Practice in Christianity*, *For Self-examination*, and *Judge for Yourself*) we encounter a Christianity that goes beyond (while presupposing) Religiousness B. We can call it Religiousness C. In it Christ is not merely the paradox to be believed but the paradigm or prototype to be imitated. As the metaphysics of the incarnation is completed in its ethics, the individual who has encountered God in Christ undiluted by the system or by Christendom is now sent back into the world of social relations with a more strenuous task to become not merely the faith that believes but the faith that works through love (Gal. 5: 6).

This is the greatest difficulty. Belief may be difficult for an intellectual elite indoctrinated in the self-sufficiency of human understanding. But for many, brought up in Christendom, it is easy to believe that Jesus is God incarnate. But once the hurdle of believing is crossed, whether with ease or with difficulty, there still lies an even greater hurdle, the task of imitating Christ in ways neither the system nor Christendom would dare to demand.

Bibliography

Editions and translations

Kierkegaard, Søren (1901–6) *Søren Kierkegaards samlede Værker*, vol. 7: *Afsluttende uvidenskabelig Efterskrift*, ed. A. B. Drachmann, J. L. Heiberg, and H. O. Lange. Copenhagen: Gyldendal.
Kierkegaard, Søren (1941) *Concluding Unscientific Postscript*, trans. D. F. Swenson and W. Lowrie. Princeton, NJ: Princeton University Press.
Kierkegaard, Søren (1992) *Concluding Unscientific Postscript to Philosophical Fragments*, 2 vols, trans. H. V. Hong and E. H. Hong. Princeton, NJ: Princeton University Press (orig. pub. 1846). Citations are to vol. 1 of this edition, which has marginal references to Kierkegaard (1901–6).

Studies

Evans, C. S. (1983) *Kierkegaard's Fragments and Postscript: The Religious Philosophy of Johannes Climacus*. Atlantic Highlands, NJ: Humanities Press.
Ferreira, M. J. (1991) *Transforming Vision: Imagination and Will in Kierkegaardian Faith*. Oxford: Clarendon Press.
Kirmmse, B. H. (1990) *Kierkegaard in Golden Age Denmark*. Bloomington, IN: Indiana University Press.
Perkins, R. L. (ed.) (1997) *International Kierkegaard Commentary: Concluding Unscientific Postscript to "Philosophical Fragments."* Macon, GA: Mercer University Press.
Westphal, M. (1996) *Becoming a Self: A Reading of Kierkegaard's Concluding Unscientific Postscript*. West Lafayette, IN: Purdue University Press.

39

John Stuart Mill, *On Liberty* (1859)

The Rational Foundations of Individual Freedom

G. W. Smith

The object of this Essay is to assert one very simple principle, as entitled to govern absolutely the dealings of society with the individual in the way of compulsion and control, whether the means used be physical force in the form of legal penalties, or the moral coercion of public opinion. That principle is, that the sole end for which mankind are warranted, individually or collectively, in interfering with the liberty of action of any of their number, is self-protection. That the only purpose for which power can be rightfully exercised over any member of a civilized community, against his will, is to prevent harm to others. His own good, either physical or moral, is not sufficient warrant. He cannot rightfully be compelled to do or forbear because it will be better for him to do so, because it will make him happier, because, in the opinion of others, to do so would be wise, or even right. (*On Liberty* [henceforth *OL*], Mill, 1991: 13–14)

The argument of John Stuart Mill's (1806–1873) celebrated essay revolves around the above "one very simple principle" (the so-called "Principle of Liberty") in two main ways. First, it is in terms of "harm to others" that Mill divides society into two exclusive spheres of conduct – the private (or, as he calls it, "self-regarding") sphere – in which actions cause no harm to non-consenting (adult) others, and the public (or "social," or "other-regarding") sphere – in which they do (or might). Second, it is upon this division that he grounds his claim that a free society is one in which it is recognized that there can be no morally justifiable reason for coercing individuals (whether by the law or through the pressure of public opinion) in the private sphere. Having established this framework, Mill pursues its implications, addressing a range of customary attitudes and practices where coercion is in his view misapplied, either being enforced where it should not be, or not being enforced where it should be – his major (though by no means exclusive) concern being with the former, that is, with violations of liberty, understood as interferences with private behavior so defined (Hamburger, 1999). Ever since its publication in 1859 *On Liberty* has inspired opponents of the intrusive state and of intolerant public opinion, and its principles and arguments continue to be invoked in a broad swathe of contemporary liberal causes, including freedom of speech, abortion, sado-masochistic behavior, recreational drug use, and general lifestyle permissiveness. Upon any understanding of the liberal canon, *On Liberty* is undoubtedly a classic of liberal philosophy.

However, liberalism comes in a variety of forms and in this regard the essay needs to be approached with care. The conviction that Mill is a liberal of a radically individual-istic stripe reflects a persistent opinion according to which *On Liberty* represents the culmination of the British tradition of liberal individualism. On this view, in the seven-teenth century John Locke establishes the case for individual political liberty, in the eighteenth Adam Smith does the same for economic freedom, and then Mill comes along to cap the tradition with his eloquent defense of what he calls "individuality," according to which the good society is the free society, understood as one whose *raison d'être* is to guarantee individuals the opportunity to live their own lives in their own way maximally free from interference by others. However, problems of whiggish historiography aside, Mill's thought does not in fact fit easily into this deceptively simple liberty-privileging story, for elsewhere in his extensive writings on economics, ethics, and culture he is at pains to reject unfettered individualism as a principle upon which any society could long endure. Some commentators see this as evidence of a failure of consistency on Mill's part and claim to detect the philosophically unsettling influence upon the argument of the essay of his politically radical wife, Harriet Taylor Mill. But this appears plausible only if we make the mistake of reading *On Liberty* as though Mill intended it in the spirit of his final statement of the necessary and suffi-cient conditions of the good society. On the contrary, as Mill plainly tells us in his *Autobiography*, his purpose in writing the essay was decidedly practical and very much a response to a specific socio-political problem: namely, the dangerous tendency in modern democracies for social authority to invade individual liberty – a tendency which, in the stifling social orthodoxy of mid-Victorian Britain was, in his view, particularly marked. Hence Mill's aim in the essay is basically a strategic one: to help redress this perceived imbalance by using all the eloquence at his command to remind his readers of the value of individual liberty, and by furnishing a principle in terms of which the proper sphere of freedom can be unambiguously identified and defended. It is in these "balance-redressing" terms that the accentuated individualism of the essay is best understood.

That Mill does not regard individualism as his "all-things-considered" view of the good life and the good society is evident enough from the very title of the most enthu-siastically individualistic chapter in the volume, chapter 3, where "individuality" is introduced as merely "*one* of the leading elements of well-being" in life (emphasis mine). Moreover, we need only turn to his other, almost equally famous, but much less immediately politically engaged book, *Utilitarianism*, to see him expanding upon the other "elements of well-being" tactically ignored in the essay, especially the essen-tially un-individualistic character virtues of "fellow feeling" and "social sympathy" (*OL*, 1991: 163–7). Although the essay invites misreading, Mill's ideal of human living, rather than privileging individuality *per se*, requires the integration of individuality with other desirable traits into what he calls a "developed character": a unique psycho-logical amalgam in each developed individual combining moral virtue (the same ideally in all) with aesthetic originality and grace (ideally different in each). Indeed, to grasp the full measure of Mill's very distinctive liberalism, *On Liberty* has to be placed in the context of his economic ideal of a system of worker-owned industrial and agricultural cooperatives, and the reader needs to bear in mind both his principled rejection of the central principle of liberty as it is commonly understood by liberal orthodoxy, namely the fundamental individual right to the private ownership of capital, and his low view of the associated conception of society as a system of external constraints designed merely to contain the activities of jostling individualists pursuing their own personal interests. With these *caveats* concerning the implicit parameters of Mill's argument in mind, let us now turn to the essay.

The Argument

The essentials of Mill's case for freedom are made in the first three chapters of *On Liberty*; in the final two chapters he applies his principles and considers borderline and other "hard" cases. The main structure of his argument is developed in chapter 1, although we need to draw on later chapters too in order to grasp the full implications, and difficulties, of his position. The argument opens with a brief characterization of the history of liberty. Freedom, Mill argues, is currently being threatened in a new and a dangerous way. Whereas historically the struggle for liberty has been a matter of the people resisting kingly and aristocratic misgovernment by establishing limited government and the rule of law, the recent growth of democracy in Europe and North America has encouraged the mistaken view that self-government is of itself a sufficient protection of liberty and that, consequently, collective power, as long as it is popular, represents no threat. On the contrary, however, it is precisely because "self-government . . . is not the government of each by himself, but of each by all the rest" that the establishment of clear limits to coercion is even more important now than in the past (*OL*, 1991: 8). Moreover, the emerging threat is not simply the political one of sheer numbers – the "majority tyranny" famously identified by the French liberal Tocqueville. It has a vital philosophical dimension too. For, on the important question of "where to place the limit . . . between individual independence and social control," the people have been brought erroneously to believe "that their feelings . . . are better than reasons, and render reasons unnecessary" (*OL*, 1991: 9–10). It is specifically in response to this novel moral epistemology, whereby the mere "feelings" of the people are democratically elevated to the utimate political authority, that Mill advances the "one very simple principle" as the rationally defensible alternative to having the crucial "limit" drawn according to the mere "likings and dislikings" of the multitude (*OL*, 1991: 11). Much of the strictly philosophical interest of *On Liberty* concerns the adequacy of Mill's handling of this question.

As a committed Utilitarian Mill insists that the basis of any rational ethics must be utility. "I forgo," he says, "any advantage which could be derived to my argument from the idea of abstract right . . . I regard utility as the ultimate appeal on all ethical questions" (*OL*, 1991: 15). His "one very simple principle" is, he claims, rational in two respects: it is a *principle* of decision – it substitutes an objective criterion, namely actual or potential "harm done," for mere arbitrary and subjective feelings; and it is a *morally justifiable* principle of decision – it conforms to the ultimate ethical require-ment that the general happiness must be maximized. However, Mill's position is com-plicated by the fact that he actually deploys two quite distinct principles. One is the aforementioned "one very simple principle," the so-called "Principle of Liberty." Strictly speaking, this is a "No non-consensual Harm to Others Principle" (NHP). As we have seen, it is in terms of the NHP that Mill defines and defends his key distinction be-tween the "self-regarding" (or private) and the "social" (or public) spheres of con-duct. The NHP is designed to secure the liberty of "all mentally competent adults," by stipulating as the necessary condition for *justifiable* coercion the occurrence of non-consensual harm to others. However, in addition to the NHP, he also identifies a class of strictly social, other-regarding, acts that are liberty-protected too; namely, those actions that do non-consensually harm (or threaten to harm) others, but where that harm is outweighed by general benefits. They come in two kinds. First, compensated harms, strictly understood; for example, examinations for public offices, the activity of trade and commerce, and the like. In cases such as these, although losers are undoubt-edly often harmed, in the broader interests of efficiency, and hence of the general happiness, such competitive practices may be permitted (*OL*, 1991: 104–5). Second, where the harm occurs with no compensating benefit to others, as in straightforwardly invasive or predatory behavior, although coercive punishment is *justifiable*, utility re-quires that a cost-benefit calculation must always be made about the effects on the general happiness of punishing in terms of the overall happiness produced before an actually *justified* case for coercion can be made (*OL*, 1991: 15–16, 104). For conven-ience we may embrace both kinds of case as instances of Mill's "Compensated Harm Principle" (CHP).

The effect, of course, is not only to broaden but also to complicate Mill's defense of liberty, since the relevant utility calculations under the CHP will often be difficult and debatable. In addition, the distinction serves to highlight the apparently anomalous standing of the NHP. Whereas the CHP is, in line with Mill's professed utilitarianism, manifestly grounded in general utility, the point of the anti-paternalistic NHP is pre-cisely to discount happiness-maximization as a reason justifying coercion in the strictly self-regarding activities of adult persons. This apparently glaring inconsistency has gen-erated much debate amongst Mill scholars and we shall return to it.

In chapter 2 Mill turns to the question of freedom of thought and discussion. Al-though speech and communication may well harmfully affect non-consenting third parties and are therefore other-regarding, since they are "practically inseparable" from the "inward domain of consciousness," which is manifestly private, Mill claims we can treat them anyway as falling under the protection of the NHP (*OL*, 1991: 16). In the event, he actually defends free speech in other-regarding CHP terms, arguing that free speech is vital to general utility because knowledge is an important means to utility, and freedom of speech is in turn instrumental to the discovery of truth. It is a matter, then, of utilitarianly balancing the short-term harms of free speech against the substan-tial long-term benefits of the growth of knowledge.

However, the utilitarian defense here is tricky since, apart from obviously malicious cases such as libel, blackmail, and intimidation – which Mill is of course happy to ban on fairly obvious cost-benefit grounds – speech can sometimes cause serious harm, and Mill is anyway the last person to underestimate the power of ideas. Moreover, can't harms of free speech be long term too? Particularly so, since Mill clearly wishes a free-speech policy to encourage individuals to think independently and to criticize the received ideas and values of society. Will not the result be an undermining of authority and a consequent erosion of social stability – serious long-term harms? A conventional liberal individualist would probably reply that it is individuals who matter, not social practices or institutions. But Mill, significantly, does not take this line. On the contrary, he recognizes that individuals can be harmed by the effects of debased or defective social practices – for example, the interests of women and children are harmed by "misapplied notions of [male and/or parental] liberty" in connection with the family (*OL*, 1991: 116–17). Instead he offers his "infallibility" argument. Censorship, he maintains, is indefensible because it implies a totally unjustifiable claim of infallibility on the part of the censors. But surely we can claim certainty about some things, and anyway might we not properly censor for other reasons, such as social peace? Mill has a powerful answer to the first part of this objection, although we need to go beyond the essay to connect the argument with elements of his broader philosophy. On the question of certainty, Mill is an empiricist and a fallibilist. Human knowledge is limited and contingent, consequently free intellectual competition is the only way to reduce our ignorance by protecting us against highly unfelicific illusions of false certainty. This is why censoring in the name of preserving the truth is tantamount to claiming infallibility. Nevertheless, we may ask why we should not censor in the name of social peace, especially if we are utilitarians. Moreover, the argument from truth apparently ignores the question of how to treat normative opinions, since they are not (or not obviously) matters of truth or falsity. In his epistemological writings Mill acknowledges that moral judgment is imperative rather than "fact-stating" in form. And it is precisely ethical and political disagreements that raise the issue of censorship in the most acute way. Mill offers other arguments in favor of free speech, but his CHP strategy represents his basic line. What is perhaps notable is the vulnerability of a utility-based defense, particularly in comparision with the typical liberal individualist line of defense in terms of freedom of speech as a basic "human right."

Chapter 3, "On Individuality as One of the Leading Elements of Well-being," reveals the spring of Mill's highly distinctive kind of liberalism and goes to the root of his justification of the crucial "one very simple principle" – the NHP. Mill paints a depressing picture of contemporary society. Commerce and manufactures may have spread wealth but they have also ironed out variety. Democracy has made things worse with "the ascendancy of public opinion in the State" and with politicians pandering to the prejudices of the multitude. Even the extension of education, something of which Mill of course otherwise highly approves, has increasingly brought everyone under "common influences." Indeed, pretty well everything in modern society encourages uniformity. Individual differences are submerged and suppressed and the social landscape flattened by an ethos of conformity and subjection to the "despotism of custom" (*OL*, 1991: 78). Allied to all this is the baneful "Calvinistic" ethos of Victorian social orthodoxy, which teaches that human nature is corrupt, that self-will is the greatest offense and self-abnegation the greatest virtue – attitudes that penetrate to the core of personality and bend the mind itself to the yoke of submission and social conformity.

Against this "pinched" and "hidebound" picture of human life Mill presents the animating ideal of *On Liberty*, namely "individuality." The ideal of individuality combines ancient Greek and modern German romantic ideals of living: it values above all energy, self-assertion, spontaneity, and originality, and it conceives human "well-being" in terms of the bold and independent exercise of individuals' powers of judgment and choice, and the confident self-development of their distinctive aptitudes, talents, and powers. For Mill, then, a necessary (though not a sufficient) test of whether a society is a good society is whether its practices and institutions are such as to guarantee liberty in this specific sense of facilitating and encouraging individuality. Hence the grounding claim of the essay: privacy is vital if individuality is to flourish, and the NHP – the "one very simple principle" – guarantees privacy.

Two points may be made about Mill's grounds for the NHP. First, the fact that he justifies the principle as protecting aspiring "individualists," that is, persons who actively desire to make something different of themselves, but who might well be inhibited from engaging in their own self-regarding "experiments in living" by the meddlesome interference of the passive and conforming majority, indicates that Millian liberalism is grounded in, and is intended to promote, a specific, and indeed controversial, ideal of human flourishing. Now liberalism is sometimes associated with a commitment to the ideal of state "neutrality" in relation to its citizens' conceptions of the good. Whether Mill's conception of individuality is a "neutralist" or a "perfectionist" one is a much-debated question, the answer to which largely depends upon the empirical status of his claim that people will in fact opt for individuality rather than conformity when given the chance. Second (and this is another aspect of the above-mentioned fundamental problem to which we must return), how can Mill possibly think that individuality grounds the NHP as an *unconditional liberty-preserving* principle? After all, his professed Utilitarianism commits him to the position that *all* values, including individuality, are *conditional* upon their *happiness-maximizing* effects. Must not the conditionality of the ideal inevitably transmit through to the NHP? In the absence of convincing answers to these questions, Mill's strategy of presenting his principles of liberty as the rational alternative to settling the limits of freedom and coercion by mere "likings and dislikings" is clearly much at risk.

Applying the Principles

In chapters 4 and 5 Mill turns to issues concerning the application of the NHP and CHP. In chapter 4, "The Limits of Authority of Society over the Individual," he raises two main questions. First, given that any free society must recognize and respect a private sphere, where then should we draw the line between the public and the private (this is the question of what counts as "harming" others)? Second, given that coercion of self-regarding actions is indeed illegitimate, are there other forms of intervention that are not (the question of what counts as "coercion")?

In respect of what triggers justifiable coercion, Mill is vague. Sometimes he talks in terms of conduct that "affects" or "concerns" others (which would of course reduce the private sphere to a nullity by excluding next-to-nothing); more frequently discussion is in terms of "harm to others," or "harm to the interests of others" (*OL*, 1991: 14, 16, 104). John Rees has claimed that a sympathetic reading of the essay can produce a good case for Mill in terms of harming the interests of others, and most commentators follow him (Rees, 1985). Mill's response to the temperance enthusiast is a good example. According to anti-drink reformers, intemperance is other-regarding and therefore should be controlled because in harming himself the drunk weakens and demoralizes the rest of us. In Mill's opinion, however, the abolitionists' position is tantamount to the manifestly oppressive claim that all mankind has a "vested interest in each other's moral, intellectual and even physical perfection, to be defined by each claimant according to his own standard" (*OL*, 1991: 98–100). Interference is justifiable only when other-regarding interests are directly violated – as, for example, with a policeman drunk on duty. But though Mill shows himself to be robustly committed to the thoroughly liberal proposition that sane adults may be assumed to know their own interests best, his handling of the line-drawing issue raises two important questions.

First, we might ask whether the interests in question are assumed to be simply matters of current recognition (e.g., the interests arising from property rights which exist *de facto* as the result of existing legal and customary arrangements), respect for which is, of course, highly unlikely to maximize the general happiness. Or whether what we should have in mind are "ideal" interests, that is, those interests whose actual recognition would conform to Mill's principle of maximizing general utility. If the latter, however, there can be no assurance that the resulting reformed system of political and economic rights and interests would resemble those characterizing what is commonly understood as a "liberal" society, except in the purely formal sense that some line or other between the private and the public would be drawn which would appropriately track those ideally defined rights and interests. (And, as has been pointed out, Mill's ideal economic structure would in any event generate a pattern of interests quite different from our current private property system.) On the second, "forms of intervention," question Mill, unlike modern "non-judgmental" liberals, insists that we not only have a right but a moral obligation to concern ourselves with whether other persons' lives are going well or badly. Hence, self-regarding defects of character, such as selfishness, "depravation of taste," rashness, conceit, obstinacy, and the like (intemperance is obviously another) are of legitimate concern and we may do what we can to persuade, exhort, and condemn – forms of intervention in Mill's view not inconsistent with freedom, as long as they are intended as advice rather than as coercion (*OL*, 1991: 85–6). Conventional liberal individualists will of course regard this view of interference as being indefensibly lax. But, again, we need to bear in mind Mill's distinctive ideal of the good society and his clear understanding that it requires social education in its widest sense if individuality is to be successfully integrated with the legitimate requirements of fellow feeling and sociability. The implications are the very reverse of a policy of individualistic lifestyle *laissez-faire*. Indeed, in the eyes of some critics they are decidedly elitist.

Mill concludes *On Liberty* with a chapter considering a range of "difficult" cases, where coercive interference in strictly self-regarding acts might appear to be justified. Should we prevent someone from crossing a manifestly unsafe bridge for their own good, or prevent a person from voluntary self-enslavement? To the first case Mill says no – we may inform but not impede; but yes to the second, on the grounds that "it is not freedom to be allowed to alienate [one's] freedom," although we may ask why not, since on the face of it it seems to be a fairly arbitrary exception to the professed anti-paternalism of the NHP (*OL*, 1991: 113–14).

Another category of problematic cases involves acts which are self-regarding, and may not even represent "defects of character," but which are none the less offensive if done in public. He has in mind natural bodily functions and the like. Since they can be as well, or better, done in private, Mill thinks they may be prohibited. However, again, it is not clear why, since on his own principles, harmless offensiveness is a matter of mere "likings and dislikings" rather than of harm done. Then there are "moral anomalies." For example, should third parties be permitted to instigate what is commonly, and properly, regarded as degrading or imprudent behavior? If individuals are permitted to do what concerns only themselves, they surely must also be free to consult with others about it. However, the advice might well not be disinterested since personal benefits are involved. Thus, should the pimp and gambling house be tolerated? On the one hand, they cause a moral hazard for the choosing individual; on the other, banning them involves the anomaly of punishing the accessory whilst allowing the principal to go free.

Mill's honest indecision here reminds us that he offers his principles, not as a replacement for moral judgment, but as a guide thereto. The book ends with consideration of a class of cases not strictly to do with liberty at all – cases in which the state might intervene to provide services so as to help rather than to restrain individuals. Mill's position on these is very much the conventional liberal one: the presumption must be against it; it is far better for people to do things for themselves rather than relying on government, and we should avoid wherever possible the "great evil" of adding unnecessarily to the power of government.

Assessment

On Liberty is a passionate and an eloquent book, rich in illustrative and telling examples, and an undoubted triumph of advocacy. However, its most enthusiastic admirers would be hard put to deny that Mill's logic is in many places puzzling. Looseness of expression is one problem – as with the rather casual way in which "harm to others" is characterized – although some difficulties here can be significantly eased by close reading and sympathetic interpretation along the lines mentioned earlier. More serious is the problem of Mill's philosophically important contrast between the "democratic" and "rational" methods of settling the limits of legitimate coercion, and the place of his professed utilitarianism therein. Critics have found Mill's fundamental strategy of argument somewhat odd for a self-professed liberal. For although his notion of a utility-maximizing mix of liberty and authority might be sufficient to rule out any Rousseauesque notion of the supreme democratic authority of the "will of the people," it still leaves him highly vulnerable to the charge that the "rational" Utilitarian requirement that the *general happiness* must always be pursued is manifestly at odds with the *priority* Mill accords to *individual freedom*. The apparent inconsistency surfaces most exigently in respect of the "one very simple principle" itself. After all, the whole point of the NHP is to stipulate that individuals must not be coerced merely "for their own good" but must be left free to harm themselves even if coercive intervention would (either in the short or the long run) make them happier. The apparently stark illogic of Mill's position has led some commentators to conclude that *On Liberty* reveals a mind irremediably riven between irreconcilable values (Berlin, 1969;

Himmelfarb, 1974). And, indeed, if his position turns out essentially to be a pluralist one, that is, one according to which the issue between liberty and utility must be settled by arbitrary decision, then the essay – understood in the way Mill clearly intends it to be understood, that is to say, as a foundational enterprise in the classically Western rationalistic sense – would have to be declared fatally damaged.

However, in recent decades influential "revisionist" scholars have advanced a defense of Millian liberalism, the basic strategy of which has been to argue that the charge of incoherence rests upon a serious misreading of the essay (Ryan, 1970; Gray, 1996). The mistake, the revisionists argue, has been to take *On Liberty* in isolation from the rest of Mill's social philosophy, with the result that his argument has been misconstrued, and the real strength of his position misrepresented. By gathering loose ends and making explicit the implicit connections with principles and positions developed and defended elsewhere in his writings on ethics, logic, and other related issues, the revisionists have attempted in various ways to buttress and reconstruct the philosophical basis of Millian liberalism. Mill's handling of the vexed question of the connection between his central value of individuality, the NHP, and utility is a good case in point.

Unfriendly critics charge that since the principle is manifestly happiness-indifferent its justificatory grounds, namely individuality, must be happiness-indifferent also. Consequently, Millian individuality must be construed deontologically, that is to say, as a strictly liberty-preserving quasi-Kantian conception of individual rational self-direction or "autonomy"; but then the incoherence re-emerges in the fact that Mill's two principles rest upon manifestly incompatible grounds, the CHP on general utility, and the NHP on individual autonomy. The revisionist response is to concede that the NHP is undeniably a liberty-preserving principle and it must indeed be grounded in individuality. However, there is no necessary inconsistency if we are prepared to read *On Liberty* in the context of positions and principles Mill develops elsewhere. Thus, in the first place, although he is explicit that the appeal must be to utility, he insists that "it must be utility in the largest sense, grounded on the permanent interests of man as a progressive being" (*OL*, 1991: 15). Second, man's "permanent interests . . . as a progressive being" are clearly seen as involving self-development, and hence choice, and hence individuality (*OL*, 1991: 71). Put together they show, it is argued, that individuality remains for Mill a utilitarian rather than a quasi-Kantian value. Third – and at this point the argument of the essay is buttressed by elements drawn from *Utilitarianism* – individuality is essentially a matter of a distinctively human kind of activity: choice-making is capable of yielding satisfactions of a qualitatively "higher" hedonic value than indulgence in the mere "passive" pleasures associated with the lower "animal" functions (*OL*, 1991: 139–43). Read inter-textually, then, consistency is preserved and utility-grounded individuality shown to support the NHP unconditionally because, even if it is possible to force individuals to be happy, it doesn't matter as coerced happiness is necessarily of the wrong, i.e., a humanly inferior, hedonic quality. As Mill famously says, "better to be Socrates dissatisfied than a fool satisfied" (*OL*, 1991: 140). This method of sympathetic prosthesis has been fruitfully applied to a broad range of issues bearing upon the argument of the essay, including the question of the connection between Mill's idea of justice, rights, and liberty, as well as his distinctions, vital to his conception of liberty, between morality, personal prudence, and aesthetics.

Although the debate continues, it cannot be denied that the revisionists have shown that the logic of Mill's distinctive version of liberal utilitarianism is both subtle and resilient (Gray and Smith, 1991: 1–20; Riley, 1998). Even so, it is perhaps unfortunate that the success of *On Liberty* as a classic of individualistic liberalism has tended to submerge the "other side" of Mill's thought. For, the doctrines of the essay represent but a facet (and perhaps, for the practical political reasons stated earlier, a somewhat exaggerated one at that) of a broader and deeper social ideal embodying a conception of human social relationships which recognizes that our need to connect with others in a shared community is as genuine as our need to free ourselves as independent individuals. It is his pursuit of this elusive synthesis that represents Mill's most challenging contribution to the liberal tradition.

Bibliography

Editions

Mill, J. S. (1991) *On Liberty and Other Essays*, ed. J. Gray, Oxford: Oxford University Press.

Studies

Berlin, I. (1969) John Stuart Mill and the ends of life. In Berlin, *Four Essays on Liberty*. Oxford: Oxford University Press.

Gray, J. (1996) *Mill on Liberty: A Defence*, 2nd edn. London: Routledge.

Gray, J. and Smith, G. W. (eds) (1991) *J. S. Mill's On Liberty in Focus*. London: Routledge.

Hamburger, J. (1999) *John Stuart Mill on Liberty and Control*. Princeton, NJ: Princeton University Press.

Himmelfarb, G. (1974) Introduction. *J. S. Mill On Liberty*, pp. 28–33, ed. G. Himmelfarb. Harmondsworth: Penguin.

Rees, J. C. (1985) *John Stuart Mill's On Liberty*, ed. G. L. Williams. Oxford: Clarendon Press.

Riley, J. (1998) *Mill on Liberty*. London: Routledge.

Ryan, A. (1970) *John Stuart Mill*. New York: Pantheon.

Skorupski, J. (1989) *John Stuart Mill*. London: Routledge.

Ten, C. L. (1980) *Mill on Liberty*. Oxford: Clarendon Press.

40

Friedrich Nietzsche, *Beyond Good and Evil* (1886)

Prelude to a Philosophy of the Future

Richard Schacht

Friedrich Nietzsche (1844–1900) today is one of the best-known figures in the history of philosophy; and *Beyond Good and Evil* (*Jenseits von Gut und Böse: Vorspiel einer Philosophie der Zukunft*, 1886, henceforth *BGE*) is one of his most celebrated works. At the time of its publication, however, he was virtually unknown to his contemporaries; and so he remained when his productive life ended abruptly in his forty-fifth year, just two and a half years later (in January 1889), owing to a complete physical and mental collapse from which he never recovered. The academic philosophical community was completely unaware of him; and he was only a fading memory among his erstwhile colleagues in classical philology, in which he had held his only academic position for a mere ten years at the Swiss university of Basle. After debilitating chronic health problems precipitated his resignation when he was but thirty-four, he never again held a position or had a permanent residence, living the ten active years remaining to him in obscurity in boarding houses in Switzerland, northern Italy, and southern France.

Nietzsche's first book, *The Birth of Tragedy* (1872), found little favor among his fellow philologists, but attracted some attention. His subsequent books sold poorly, however; and from *BGE* onward he was obliged to become his own publisher, financing their publication out of his small pension from Basle and his rapidly dwindling private funds. The first six hundred copies of *BGE* were printed at the press of C. G. Naumann in Leipzig in August of 1886. After ten months, a mere 114 had been sold. A second printing was not needed until 1891, two years after Nietzsche's collapse, when a second run of a thousand copies was made.

The status of a classic that *BGE* now enjoys thus was slow in coming, as was Nietzsche's own attainment of prominence. It was only some years later that his star began to rise – with *Thus Spoke Zarathustra* (rather than *BGE*) leading the way. And that owed as much to the efforts of his politically reprehensible sister, who controlled his literary estate until her death in 1935 and promoted the caricature of him as the philosopher of the radical right, as to the dawning recognition of the interest and importance of his philosophical thought, first in Europe, and more recently in the English-speaking world.

Nietzsche gave *BGE* the subtitle *Vorspiel einer Philosophie der Zukunft*, "Prelude to [or, more literally, "of"] a Philosophy of the Future"; and it is above all for his pro-vocatively revisionist conception of the future of philosophy that he is deserving of a place of major importance in the recent history of philosophy. The issues of just what that conception is, however, and of what is to be made of it, remain matters of intense controversy. He can be and has been interpreted as an early existentialist, positivist, naturalist, pragmatist, philosophical anthropologist, analytical philosopher, post-structuralist, and more – in each case, with a mix of justice and injustice. In this sense his thought has already proved to be a prelude to philosophy's future, during the century following his collapse, and quite remarkably so. And it may well be that we have not yet taken his full measure, and have yet to realize the promise of the kind of philosophizing he sought to begin.

I

BGE was written at what turns out to have been the high point of Nietzsche's all-too-brief philosophical life. It stands out among his writings as the book in which he most clearly conveys his hard-won understanding of the character and tasks of the kind of philosophy that will be most urgently needed in the human future that is now dawning – and the kind of philosophy that will itself be most deserving of a future. It admittedly offers only a "prelude" rather than extended treatment of any of the many matters on which it touches; but it is quite emphatic in its insistence that *interpretation* and *evaluation* must henceforth be recognized to be the main tasks of philosophy. And it is sufficiently suggestive of both the manner and the direction of Nietzsche's thinking to provide a clear indication of the course he was setting for himself, and was seeking to set for philosophy's future.

BGE is a most unusual book – particularly among philosophical classics – in both form and content. Like most of Nietzsche's other books from his "free spirit" series onward, it is neither a monograph nor even a set of essays. It consists of nearly three hundred consecutively numbered sections, ranging in length from a half-dozen to around eight hundred words, divided into nine parts, and framed by a short preface and a poetic postlude. The first part, "On the Prejudices of Philosophers," sets the stage for his kind of philosophical thinking, which is characterized in a preliminary way in the second, on "The Free Spirit," and elaborated in the sixth and seventh parts, "We Scholars" and "Our Virtues." The fourth part is a collection of aphorisms, "Epigrams and Interludes," providing a sort of light intermission between the heavy-going third and fifth parts, which deal both analytically and subversively with "religiousness" and with the "natural history" of morals. In the final two parts Nietzsche turns his atten-tion first to matters relating to the "peoples and countries" of his Europe and then beyond them, in a concluding part on the genesis and character of "noble" exceptions to the human rule and the conditions of their further possibility.

Nietzsche's style in *BGE*, as for the most part elsewhere, is highly unconventional in the philosophical literature. (Wittgenstein's may be its closest counterpart.) He rarely offers anything like a straightforward and decisive argument; and the arguments that he does offer are generally partial, provisional, and tentative. On the attack, he typically goes for what he takes to be the Achilles' heels of his targets, not lingering to finish the job once he thinks he has effectively put them out of play. And when advancing some line of thought of his own, he often is content simply to propose, suppose, conjecture, and sometimes flatly assert. Yet he is a powerful case-maker; and the ways in which he makes his cases, as he attempts to reposition philosophy for the new tasks he has in mind for it, are interesting and provocative even when they are less than compelling.

In *The Gay Science* (hereafter *GS*), four years earlier, Nietzsche had followed his observation that "God is dead" with the comment that "we – we still have to vanquish his shadow, too" (*GS*, 1974: 108), and with a call to "complete our de-deification of nature" and reinterpret ourselves in an accordingly "naturalistic" manner (*GS*, 1974: 109). By the time of *BGE* he had come to recognize that we must (as it were) *de-moralize* as well as "de-deify" our thinking, reinterpreting and revaluing virtually everything that matters in a post-moral as well as post-religious and post-metaphysical manner – "beyond" the moralism that centers upon the opposite categories of "good and evil" as well as beyond the other-worldly absolutisms related to it. Hence his choice of the phrase "Beyond Good and Evil" as the main title of the book. But he also had come to recognize the importance of guarding against the nihilistic rebound that was all too likely to attend the abandonment of any and all absolutes, moral as well as religious and metaphysical. He therefore now sought to supply his new "Yes-saying," life-affirming stance – to which he had given literary expression in *Zarathustra* – with a suitable philosophical repositioning and articulation.

The agenda of Nietzsche's "philosophy of the future," as he presents it in *BGE*, is a rich one. It begins with a reassessment of philosophy past and present, from which it will be departing. Another of its preliminaries is disentanglement from both religious and moralizing ways of thinking that might otherwise subvert it, by means of a mode of analysis serving to subvert *them*. It then calls for a reconsideration of how to go on to think about truth and knowledge; about science and philosophy itself; about our human reality and the world of which we are a part; and about a host of social, cultural, and intellectual phenomena that bear in various ways upon the character and quality of human life. But all of this will only serve to set the stage for a serious reckoning with the issues of *the future of humanity* in the aftermath of the "death of God"; of what matters and makes a difference in human life thus reconceived; and of what might be done about it. That is fundamentally what he has in mind in speaking of "great politics" in the last part of the book.

II

High on the reconstructionist part of Nietzsche's agenda is thus a consideration of how we – as both "the type 'human'" and the human types we are – have come to be as we are, what we have to work with, what our constraints and vulnerabilities are, and what we might yet make of ourselves. This might be conceived as the project of a thoroughgoingly naturalistic *philosophical anthropology*. It is vividly announced in one

of the more striking passages in *BGE*, which is full of them. "To translate man back
into nature," he writes; "to see to it that man henceforth stands before man as even
today, hardened in the discipline of science, he stands before the *rest* of nature . . . that
may be a strange and crazy task, but it is a *task* – who would deny that?" (*BGE*, 1966:
230). And Nietzsche further makes it clear in the course of the book that he considers
a number of kinds of inquiry and their differing perspectives to be indispensable to his
kind of philosophical anthropology: historical, physiological, sociological, linguistic,
cultural, and, perhaps most importantly, psychological. (This is one important sense in
which his talk of "perspectives" is to be understood.) Thus he calls psychology "the
path to the fundamental problems" (*BGE*, 1966: 23)

Nietzsche clearly takes various forms of morality and religion that have arisen in the
course of human events to admit of better-than-ordinary comprehension if approached
in this manner and spirit. And the same applies to a broad range of other such phenomena that are to be encountered within the compass of human life, history, and
experience. So he undertakes to reconsider a variety of phenomena that have long
been put on pedestals, in the perspective of a naturalistic philosophical anthropology –
and also to draw upon the analysis of these phenomena to enrich and develop that
anthropology itself. Among those he examines in *BGE* are phenomena of a moral,
religious, social, political, and cultural as well as of an intellectual, scientific, and otherwise cognitive nature.

"Translating man back into nature" thus is only the first part of Nietzsche's project
of reinterpreting our humanity naturalistically. A subsequent and ultimately more important part of it is to go on to translate it *out of* (mere) nature again – only this time
to get it right: to grasp the respects in which human life is no longer a *merely* biological
phenomenon, to understand how this could have come about in the course of entirely
naturalistic human events, and to comprehend the consequences. And this too is a part
of what Nietzsche is proposing and trying to do in *BGE*. It is at least a part of the
reason for the strong interest he evinces in social and cultural phenomena, and for that
matter in moral and religious phenomena as well. For he is convinced that they have
had a great deal to do with *the genealogy of our humanity* – and, further, that they
continue to have a profound influence upon the different ways human beings turn out,
individually as well as collectively.

Nietzsche's inquiries and reflections along these lines extend far afield, by conventional philosophical standards, even venturing into the treacherous terrain of sexuality
and gender. He is often pilloried for some of the things he says, in *BGE* (1966: 232–
9) and elsewhere, about gender, and more specifically about women. And it is undeniable that he invites and deserves at least some of this criticism; for some of his remarks
verge upon the ludicrous, even if they may have a certain cultural-historical and biographical comprehensibility, and even if he does aver them to be "very much only – *my*
truths" (*BGE*, 1966: 231). But he also deserves some credit in this connection. One of
the important questions he believes we must take seriously, philosophically as well as
humanly, is what to make of human differences – what they amount to, their historical
as well as biological genealogies, how much and in what ways they matter, how fixed
they are, and what might be done with as well as about them.

Even if many of Nietzsche's generalizations cannot be sustained, they are not simply
much ado about nothing. He certainly was fallible and all too human in his forays into

matters of sexuality and gender (and others of a like nature, such as what he loosely calls "race" or ethnicity). But he was not culpable for raising them, attempting to come to grips with them, or even venturing to make claims about them that we now have good reasons to reject. On the contrary, it was commendable of him to do so; and it is in the spirit of his own enterprise to make whatever adjustments in it turn out to be warranted by advances in human-scientific, historical, or other such understanding.

It is also (and relatedly) Nietzsche's intent, in *BGE* and elsewhere, to take serious account of new developments in the life sciences. The hazards of doing so are well illustrated by his Lamarckianism – "One cannot erase from the soul of a human being what his ancestors liked most to do and did most constantly" (*BGE*, 1966: 264) – which subsequently was discredited and generally abandoned. Nietzsche took more than a few such wrong turns in his wanderings in these mine fields. But what is more important than any of them is his insistence that these are matters to be grappled with philosophically in our efforts to understand ourselves – and, further, that philosophers must be readier than they long have been to back off from prior convictions and conjectures, when inquiry in these various disciplines discredits ideas that had previously seemed sound. He would be the first to insist that this readiness must begin at home, his equal readiness to take interpretive risks notwithstanding – and indeed precisely in consequence of it.

III

"Naturalizing" our understanding of ourselves, for Nietzsche, entails a recognition that our consciousness and thought are *human* phenomena. And this in turn requires a reconsideration of them – and consequently of humanly conceivable truth and humanly possible knowledge – in the context of our human constitution, resources, and circumstances. So he begins his preface to *BGE* by provocatively posing the question: "Supposing truth is a woman – what then?" This striking language has attracted so much attention for its problematic invocation and use of the figure of "woman" that it has tended to obscure the very point it was intended to make vivid, by capitalizing upon the feminine gender of the word for "truth" in German (*die Wahrheit*), and by drawing upon the familiar stereotype of the folly of pursuing a woman as though one were dealing with a man. And this point is not that there is no such thing as truth, but rather that philosophers have long misunderstood the sort of thing it is, and therefore have pursued it very ineptly. The preface is a polemic against dogmatism in philosophical thinking; against conceiving of truth in a manner attuned to it, as an all-or-nothing affair that must be fixed, final, and absolute if it is to obtain at all; and against conceiving of its pursuit in a manner that would only be appropriate *if it were* that sort of thing.

Nietzsche's insistence upon the *interpretive* character of thought in general and of philosophical and scientific thought in particular, and on the affective origins and motivation of all interpretation, is often supposed to entail his abandonment of the very ideas of "truth" and "knowledge." The fact that he readily avails himself of both notions throughout *BGE*, however, runs counter to this understanding of him. He does insist that no interpretation is immaculately conceived; but it is also one of his most important (but under-appreciated) points that, their origins notwithstanding, some interpretations *can turn out* to be better than others with respect to the comprehension they afford of the specific matters with which they deal. And for the Nietzsche of *BGE* (and of *GS* and *On the Genealogy of Morals* [hereafter *GM*]) this means: in terms of the *justice* they do their topics, conceived in terms of such things as the depth, subtlety, astuteness, explanatory power, and comprehensive sense-making of the accounts of these matters they enable one to provide. If such interpretations can be refined by a sufficiently rigorous, precise, and sophisticated intelligence; if a substantial evidential, circumstantial, and methodological case can be made for them; and if they prove capable of withstanding critical scrutiny, that is quite enough. For that, on his view, is what cognitive significance amounts to.

Nietzsche also makes much of the notion of "perspective" in *BGE*; and his emphasis upon it is also commonly thought to require the severe qualification or outright abandonment of any claim to knowledge that he might be thought to be making, either in this instance or in any other. But it does not follow, from anything he says about multiple and differing "perspectives" in *BGE*, that he takes them all to be on a cognitive par with each other. And that he does *not* do so is quite evident. So, for example, he suggests that "popular valuations" may well be "merely foreground estimates, only provisional perspectives . . . perhaps from below, *frog perspectives*, as it were, to borrow an expression painters use" (*BGE*, 1966: 2), clearly believing himself to be capable of doing better. And (not surprisingly, in view of the painterly origin of his use of the notion) he frequently contrasts such perspectives with others that may not only be different but also broader, more far-sighted, better situated, and less problematic than the former – even if no one of them is *the* right or definitive one where many matters (human affairs of any complexity in particular) are concerned, and even though there may often be something to be said (practically speaking) for "frog perspectives."

Nietzsche first sounds this theme in *BGE*'s preface, accusing Plato of "standing truth on her head and denying *perspective*, the basic condition of all life." The context of this remark is crucial to its understanding. Nietzsche is talking about "Plato's invention of the pure spirit and the good as such"; and his point is that there are no such things, but rather only particular forms of life, with particular constitutions and conditions of preservation, flourishing, and growth – and that it is only in some such "perspective" that "good" acquires specific and significant content. Thus he goes on to speak of "the perspective optics of life" (*BGE*, 1966: 11), and to assert: "There would be no life at all if not on the basis of perspective estimates and appearances" (*BGE*, 1966: 34). For he takes it to be the case that "the *narrowing of our perspective*" is "a condition of life and growth" for creatures like ourselves in a complicated world, as a way of getting us to focus on "the nearest tasks" (*BGE*, 1966: 188).

Nietzsche's "perspectival" theme in *BGE* is thus an interesting thesis; but it has to do with practical imperatives and the basic relation of value to them rather than our general cognitive predicament. And when he does subsequently extend it to our various commonplace and humanly possible kinds of knowing, his sense of its epistemic upshot would seem to be far from dire for the possibility of comprehension and its enhancement. So, for example, in his most explicit reflection on this matter in *GM* (which is cognitively ambitious with respect to the genealogy not only of "morals" but also of ourselves as knowers and as human), he couples the contention that "there is *only* a perspective seeing, *only* a perspective 'knowing'" with the idea that the crucial thing for us as philosophers, "precisely because we seek knowledge," is to develop "the ability *to control* one's Pro and Con and to dispose of them, so that one knows how to employ a *variety* of perspectives and affective interpretations in the service of knowledge" (*GM*, 1967: II, 12).

IV

The converse side of Nietzsche's philosophical-anthropological project is to give at least some consideration to the "nature" back into which (and then out of which again) our humanity is to be "translated." He frames his proposed interpretation of that larger reality, of which human life is a part, in terms of a general disposition he calls "will to power." "Life itself is *will to power*," he writes; "self-preservation is only one of the indirect and most frequent results" (*BGE*, 1966: 13). Or at any rate, he suggests, this conclusion would be warranted if it were to turn out to be possible to "explain our entire instinctive life" and "all organic functions," and even to "understand the so-called mechanistic (or 'material') world," in terms of "the will to power, as *my* proposition has it" (*BGE*, 1966: 36).

At the time he wrote *BGE*, it evidently was Nietzsche's intention to devote a future book to the elaboration of this interpretation; for on its back cover he announced a forthcoming book that was to be entitled "*The Will to Power: Attempt at a New Interpretation of All Events.*" He never carried out such a project – possibly because he abandoned it, or perhaps simply because his collapse precluded it. (The volume published under that title and in his name is only a posthumous collection, made by others, of notes from his notebooks of 1883–8.) But the "will to power" hypothesis does loom large in *BGE*; and his conviction of its soundness, at least with respect to "life," is clear: "If this should be an innovation as a theory – as a reality it is the *primordial fact* of all history" (*BGE*, 1966: 259). His surmise is that "all events" require to be understood not only dynamically but also in dispositional terms; and that if one supposes the disposition to the formation of power relationships to be the most basic of all dispositions, of which all others are "ramifications and developments," nothing more is needed to make sense of the kinds of change, development, organization, and dissolution that are to be observed at all levels of transaction we encounter within, among, and beyond ourselves (*BGE*, 1966: 36).

Nietzsche's chief concerns in *BGE*, however, lie elsewhere. Contending that conventional moralities are fundamentally "herd" phenomena reflecting social-group needs and dynamics (*BGE*, 1966: 199–201), he observes that "herd animal morality" is "merely *one* type of human morality beside which, before which, and after which many other types, above all *higher* moralities, are, or ought to be, possible" (*BGE*, 1966: 202). And what compels his interest in this matter is, on the one hand, his concern "for the over-all danger that 'man' himself *degenerates*" into "the perfect herd animal," and, on the other hand, his sense of "what, given a favorable accumulation and increase of forces and tasks, might yet *be made of man*." The stage is thus set for him to ask, "Where, then, must *we* reach with our hopes?" and to answer: "Toward *new philosophers*; there is no choice; toward spirits strong and original enough to provide the stimuli for opposite valuations and to revalue and invert 'eternal values,'" and to set "the will of millennia upon new tracks" (*BGE*, 1966: 203). It is to the consideration of what this will require – "the probable ways and tests that would enable a soul to grow to such a height and force that it would feel the *compulsion* for such tasks" – that Nietzsche devotes the concluding parts of the book.

Nietzsche's philosophical project thus encompasses matters of value, and extends even to considerations relating to value-determination and the politics of value-realization. So he accords an imporant place in *BGE* (and subsequent writings) to the necessary complement of his reinterpretation of our humanity: a new *theory of value*, also de-deified and naturalistic in character, but with a far greater reach and scope than one might have thought possible after "the death of God." And, for starters, it is to make possible a "revaluation of values" going well beyond a mere nihilistic devaluation of all prevailing values. This revaluation is exemplified by Nietzsche's intended dethronement of the morality of "good and evil," and by its proposed replacement with a quite different approach to morals and values. Its basis is the fundamental sort of *life-affirmation* to the possibility of which he had given powerful expression in *Zarathustra*; and its guiding ideas are those of "value for life" and "life-enhancement."

The "Yes or No . . . about life and the value of life" on which all ultimately depends for Nietzsche's kind of philosopher (*BGE*, 1966: 205) presupposes and yet also surpasses the disillusioned comprehension of the basic character of life and the world that is humanly possible. Nietzsche conceives of this "Yes or No" in terms of the possibility of a form of fundamental *affirmation*, beyond all illusion and disillusionment, that is no mere assent to a proposition, but also is neither a piece of knowledge nor a conclusion that can be validated or even warranted cognitively. It rather has the character of a kind of fundamental *expression* reflecting how one is or has come to be constituted (perhaps as thinker as well as human being). And making it, for Nietzsche, far from betraying a readiness to compromise in one's intellectual integrity, instead is associated with having sought and found "one's way" to a "right" and "even a duty" to such an expression (*BGE*, 1966: 205). It signals no abandonment of commitment to truthfulness, but rather the ascent to a further, highest humanly possible form of it. His formula for it is *amor fati* ("love of fate," echoing but replacing religion's fundamental affirmation, *amor dei*, "love of God"); his name for it is "Dionysian"; and his metaphor for it, in the language of *Zarathustra*, is "remaining faithful to the earth."

V

It is in this context that Nietzsche goes on to envision a role for philosophers of this sort in what he calls the coming "fight for the dominion of the earth – the compulsion to great politics," as the culture wars of the future unfold (*BGE*, 1966: 208). That role is neither the fantasy of somehow managing to seize the reins of government and to rule as philosopher-kings, nor the daydream of becoming the power behind the throne, but rather to affect the battles for minds and hearts on which much more ultimately depends. And Nietzsche conceives of this role as extending to what he calls the "creation" and even "legislation" of "new values," altering and enriching the landscape of different regions of human life. The idea that philosophers of any sort might actually "lead" or even "dominate" in such matters (as he sometimes suggests) may be difficult to take seriously. Not so, however, the idea of the genuine philosopher as one who can and does find ways of making a difference that matters in the direction, character, and quality of cultural life. Nietzsche himself was one such philosopher.

It is also with reference to considerations relating to life-enhancement that Nietzsche suggests a reassessment of certain sorts of phenomena that undeniably have had (and could again have) dismaying historical and real-world manifestations. They include things he is prepared to call by the harsh names commonly associated with their rudest forms, such as domination, exploitation, and even "slavery." So, for example, he observes that "Every enhancement of the type 'man' has so far been the work of an aristocratic society . . . a society that believes in the long ladder of an order of rank and differences in value between man and man, and needs slavery in some sense or other." And he takes the eventual attainment of forms of higher-human spirituality to require some such social modeling: "Without that pathos of distance which grows out of the ingrained difference between strata . . . that other, more mysterious pathos could not have grown up either . . . in brief, simply the enhancement of the type 'man' . . ." (*BGE*, 1966: 257).

One may well wonder whether Nietzsche even conceivably could be on to something worth taking seriously in passages of this sort. It is precisely here, however, where his language is at its most provocative and is most likely to give offense, that one must take the greatest care in reading him. Much of what he says along these lines is actually presented in the form of observations he makes of a genealogical nature, and conjectures he bases upon them. He at least purports to be attempting to learn from human history and from the kind of "psychology" he celebrates and commends at the end of the first part of *BGE*, and to be proceeding in the spirit of the "investigators and microscopists of the soul" he praises at the outset of *GM*, who "have trained themselves to sacrifice all desirability to truth, *every* truth, even plain, harsh, ugly, repellent, unchristian, immoral truth. – For such truths do exist" (*GM*, 1967: I, 1). He does at times go further; but as his denunciation of dogmatism in *BGE*'s preface makes clear, he knows that his claims are open to dispute, and are no stronger than the soundness and superiority of the case that can be made for them, in case-making competition with alternatives.

The fundamental question with which Nietzsche is concerned here is that of the *conditions of the possibility* of the attainment of "higher" forms of culture and humanity. At one level of his discourse, he is attempting to make comprehensible that and how forms of life of all sorts contrive, by whatever strategies are available and conceivable to them, to preserve and assert themselves in relation to whatever the competition may happen to be. At another level, however, he is very clearly taking sides, exhibiting a kind of partisanship on behalf of the flourishing and development of human life in ways enhancing its worth, and in opposition to others detrimental to them.

As has been observed, the question of how worth or value is to be conceived and articulated in this larger context, in the aftermath of "the death of God" and "beyond good and evil," is a major issue for Nietzsche. But from *Zarathustra* onward, he was convinced that profoundly important sense could be made of it. And much of what he has to say on both levels in *BGE* derives from his conclusion and conviction that, realistically speaking, when it comes to enhancements of life, there is no substitute in human life for *compulsion* in one form or another. So, for example, he writes: "What is essential and inestimable in every morality is that it constitutes a long compulsion." For "given that, something always develops, and has developed, for whose sake it is worth while to live on earth; for example, virtue, art, music, dance, reason, spirituality – something transfiguring, subtle, mad, and divine" (*BGE*, 1966: 188). And while it need not invariably be externally imposed, that is how he supposes it first came into human life, and is what it often continues to require.

Nietzsche's observations and conjectures along these lines may well be questioned. But he does have a point – or at any rate, a concern – that at least warrants serious consideration. *Can* highly complex and demanding forms of cultural life be sustained, flourish, and develop in the absence of a variety of forms of compulsion (internal if not external) sufficing for the continuing infusion of human resources and dedication of human effort they require over the long haul? That is indeed a question on which the jury is still out. Nietzsche is acutely aware of how much rides on it. He is right to insist that we face it squarely, not permitting ourselves the dodge of wishful thinking. And he is also right to maintain that this requires a willingness to take into account what can be learned both from human psychology and from human history.

BGE thus culminates in a determination to take seriously the relations between types of social arrangements and the ways human beings, human cultures, and so human life turn out, and the possibility of considerable differences along these lines. That is an important dimension of Nietzsche's conception of his and philosophy's responsibility to humanity. And if he goes astray and draws unwarranted or misguided conclusions, that is not the end of the enterprise, but rather is a matter for its self-correction. The penchant for interpretive and evaluative experiments and risk-taking that he commends and so paradigmatically exemplifies is essential and fundamental to his kind of philosophy. But so is the willingness and determination to subject *one's own* proffered observations and accounts to scrutiny, qualifying and amending or even abandoning various of them as may turn out to be warranted.

VI

Nietzsche's own version of his kind of philosophy, as it is displayed in *BGE*, leaves much to be desired, and much to be done. But there also is much to be admired in it, and much to be gained from a serious engagement with it. It offers a searching, critical examination and stock-taking of both our intellectual resources and ourselves, as they and we have been and have come to be; of the typically human and the all-too-human and of the human possibilities evinced by exceptions to the human rule; of the interpretations and evaluations we have lived by; and of the resources and abilities available to us by means of which we may be able to go beyond them.

Nietzsche's entire philosophical thought is what the subtitle of *BGE* proclaims the book to be: a "prelude" sounding the beginning of what at least could be philosophy's future. Complete agreement with it is as difficult to imagine as is indifference to it, on the part of anyone who shares something like his sense of philosophy's problems and tasks and his commitment to intellectual integrity. He does not hesitate to rush in where the angels among us may fear to tread; but that is no mere folly on his part. Nietzsche's kind of philosopher need not be as much of a risk-taker in new ventures of reinterpretation and revaluation as he was; but one who is no such adventurer is no such philosopher, and no true one either. Philosophers of the future neither are likely to be nor should be Nietzscheans, in the sense of staunch adherents to the full letter of *BGE*. (In that sense, even Nietzsche himself was no Nietzschean.) They could be kindred spirits, however, proceeding in a similar spirit with various of *BGE*'s tasks. One might well wish for nothing less.

Bibliography

Editions and translations

Nietzsche, Friedrich (1966) *Beyond Good and Evil*, trans. Walter Kaufmann. New York: Vintage Books.

Nietzsche, Friedrich (1967) *On the Genealogy of Morals*, trans. Walter Kaufmann and R. J. Hollingdale. New York: Vintage Books (original work, *Zur Genealogie der Moral*, pub. 1887).

Nietzsche, Friedrich (1968) *Nietzsche Werke: Kritische Gesamtausgabe*, ed. Giorgio Colli and Mazzino Montinari, vol. VI: 2, *Jenseits von Gut und Böse, Zur Genealogie der Moral*. Berlin: Walter de Gruyter. (*Jenseits* first pub. 1886).

Nietzsche, Friedrich (1974) *The Gay Science*, trans. Walter Kaufmann. New York: Vintage Books (original work, *Die fröhliche Wissenschaft*, pub. 1882; second expanded edn 1887).

Studies

Clark, Maudemarie (1990) *Nietzsche on Truth and Philosophy*. New York: Cambridge University Press.

Danto, Arthur (1965) *Nietzsche as Philosopher*. New York: Macmillan.

Hayman, Ronald (1980) *Nietzsche: A Critical Life*. New York: Oxford University Press.

Kaufmann, Walter (1974) *Nietzsche: Philosopher, Psychologist, Antichrist*, 4th edn. Princeton, NJ: Princeton University Press.

Magnus, Bernd and Higgins, Kathleen M. (eds) (1996) *The Cambridge Companion to Nietzsche*. New York: Cambridge University Press.

Nehamas, Alexander (1985) *Nietzsche: Life as Literature*. Cambridge, MA: Harvard University Press.

Schaberg, William H. (1995) *The Nietzsche Canon: A Publication History and Biography*. Chicago: University of Chicago Press.

Schacht, Richard (1983) *Nietzsche*. London: Routledge and Kegan Paul.

Schacht, Richard (1995) *Making Sense of Nietzsche*. Urbana, IL: University of Illinois Press.

Solomon, Robert and Higgins, Kathleen M. (eds) (1988) *Reading Nietzsche*. New York: Oxford University Press (includes chapters on *BGE* by Nehamas, on *GM* by Danto, and on *GS* by Schacht).

Warren, Mark (1988) *Nietzsche and Political Thought*. Cambridge, MA: MIT Press.

41

Gottlob Frege, "Über Sinn und Bedeutung" (1892)

A Fundamental Distinction

Michael Dummett

Among philosophers, this essay, first published in 1892 and here throughout referred to as "SuB," is the best known of Frege's (1848–1925) works, the most read, and the most frequently translated. It is also the least typical, going in detail into linguistic questions of little relevance to the philosophy of arithmetic, which was Frege's central concern until, in 1906, he came to realize that his project of constructing a definitive foundation for number theory and analysis had miscarried.

SuB expounds Frege's famous distinction between *Sinn* and *Bedeutung*. The word *Sinn* translates readily as "sense." The word *Bedeutung*, meaning in ordinary German "significance" or "meaning," was used by Frege eccentrically, as a technical term in his philosophy of language and symbolism. Neither of the English words, "meaning" and "reference," that have been used to translate it, as used in his writings, is satisfactory. It will here be left in its native form "*Bedeutung*."

SuB did not contain Frege's first announcement of the distinction: that occurred in his lecture *Funktion und Begriff* of 1891, complete with the most famous example, that of "the Morning Star" and "the Evening Star." Having in 1884 published his short masterpiece, *Die Grundlagen der Arithmetik*, in which he had expounded his philosophy of number theory and sketched his foundation for it, and having, in 1885, delivered a lecture arguing some main points of it, Frege entered a period of silence: five years, from 1886 to 1891, during which he published nothing. He was using the time to rethink his system and philosophy of logic. In the lecture of 1891, he gave a concise sketch of the new ideas attained during this silent period. Of these, the most important was the sense/*Bedeutung* distinction.

Most readers of *Grundlagen* would acknowledge that Frege's philosophy was crying out for such a distinction. For in Frege's writing before 1891 no distinction was drawn between the significance of an expression and what it signifies. The thesis that if an expression behaves indistinguishably from a singular term, and if a sense has been provided for every sentence in which it can occur, there must be something to which that expression refers cannot be ascribed to the author of *Grundlagen*, since he lacked the conceptual apparatus to frame it. Rather, the apparatus he employed takes such a thesis for granted. His term "content" is so used that it covers both a term's contribution to the content or sense of every sentence containing it and the object we use that term to talk about. By drawing the distinction between sense and *Bedeutung*, Frege belatedly filled this large lacuna in his philosophical apparatus. The need to distinguish the significance of an expression from what it signifies was not, and still is not, apparent to all philosophers.

Frege's concern, in SuB, was to persuade philosophers to accept his new distinction; that is why it is devoid of mathematical examples. It begins by drawing the distinction for singular terms; and it is often said that this was Frege's prime objective in drawing the distinction. This view is probably wrong: he was more concerned with whole sentences such as arithmetical equations. In any case, it was essential for Frege that the distinction applied to expressions of *every* type, though that is not made fully apparent in SuB, which, famously, starts with the question "What is identity a relation between?" Frege's tactics were impeccable: a puzzle is presented which must arouse the interest of all philosophers, however little they are concerned with questions of logic or of language.

"Is identity a relation between objects?," Frege asks. If so, it is a highly exceptional one, holding between every object and itself but between no object and any other object. But this raises a problem about the cognitive value of statements of identity – the information conveyed by them. The information conveyed by an ordinary relational statement, say "George VI was the brother of Edward VIII," is that the relation in question obtains or obtained between the objects or individuals named. But if identity is a relation between objects, then, to anyone who understands what relation it is, it can be no information that some given object stands in that relation to itself, since *every* object stands in that relation to itself. But valuable information *is* often conveyed by means of statements of identity, for instance, long ago, by the statement that the sun that rose on one day was the same as the sun that rose the next day. So is identity not after all a relation between objects?

Frege remarks that in his *Begriffsschrift* of 1879 he took identity to be a relation between names of objects. He objects to this theory that we should then not express any proper knowledge by statements of identity, since our choice of names to use for objects is arbitrary. By "proper knowledge" Frege means knowledge that is not about how the names are used: a statement of identity may be informative to one who already knows how both names are used.

If one designation "*a*" differs from another one "*b*" only in respect of its appearance, then, if "*a* = *b*" is true, it can convey no more ("proper") information than "*a* = *a*," Frege argues. (For him, only true statements have cognitive value. If sense is to be correlated with cognitive value, it would be better to take information to include misinformation, since false statements have sense: the cognitive value of a false statement is the information that a subject takes him- or herself to be acquiring when he or she holds the statement to be true.) Since a true statement of the form "*a* = *b*" can convey more information than "*a* = *a*," Frege argues that it follows that, whenever it does so, there must correspond to the difference in the signs "*a*" and "*b*" some other difference: what Frege calls "*die Art des Gegebenseins des Bezeichneten*." This phrase is generally translated as "the mode of presentation of the thing designated": we come closer to Frege's way of thinking if we say "the way that the designated object is given." Kant said that every object is given to us in a particular way, and Frege was of the same mind. The way that an object is given to us is the way in which we conceive of it as identified.

One might think that different objects could be given in the same way to different subjects. But this would conflict with a fundamental principle of Frege's, that the sense of an expression determines what it refers to (its *Bedeutung*): hence if the object referred to differs, so must the sense. This principle is not enunciated in SuB; it is indeed remarkable how many essential features of Frege's doctrine of sense and *Bedeutung* are left unmentioned in it.

Frege never explained definite descriptions or other complex singular designations along the lines of Russell's theory of descriptions. In a semantic analysis of a sentence containing a definite description, the description would remain as a semantic unit, whose function was to denote a particular object. In SuB he goes on to explain his use of the term "proper name" as applying to any term, whether simple or complex, used to denote some one specific object. It is more convenient to reserve the title for semantically *simple* singular terms.

Frege now states his thesis: to every designation is connected, not only the object it designates, but its *sense*, which conveys the way in which that object is given. The object denoted he calls its *Bedeutung*; besides its *Bedeutung* it has a sense. It is obvious enough that the meaning of a complex singular term such as a definite description cannot consist solely in the object which it denotes, or in its denoting that object: the meanings of the component words must be ingredients in the meaning of the whole. It is therefore uncontroversial that we must ascribe a sense to such a complex singular term in addition to its denotation or *Bedeutung*. But Frege wishes to draw the distinction for proper names in the narrow sense. He proceeds to give his most famous example. The *Bedeutungen* of "the Morning Star" and of "the Evening Star" are the same; but they have different senses. Several pages later, Frege offers a proof that the two proper names have different senses: someone who understood both of them might still believe the sentence "The Morning Star is illuminated by the Sun" to be true without believing the sentence "The Evening Star is illuminated by the Sun" to be true. This argument he had already used in *Funktion und Begriff*. As he explains in a footnote, he uses the term "thought" to mean, not an act of thinking, but its content, which may be shared with many other subjects – what other philosophers call a "proposition." Frege was to use the same test on several other occasions. For him, the thought expressed by a sentence is composed of the senses of its component words – another ingredient of his theory of sense not stated in SuB, though implicit in the connection made between the cognitive value of statements and the senses of the words. Hence, if two sentences express the same thought, then anyone who understands both must regard either as true if he or she regards the other as true. When two sentences fail this test, the thoughts they express must differ; so if two such sentences differ only in that one contains a given expression where the other contains a different one, the senses of those two expressions must differ. Frege treated the condition only as a necessary one for the coincidence of the thoughts expressed, never as a sufficient one.

This principle clearly indicates, as does the correlation between sense and cognitive value, that Fregean sense is a cognitive notion: it has to do with what a subject who understands an expression can and cannot believe, and with what he takes himself to know when he recognizes a statement as true. Frege's argument fails to prove that the sense of an expression must be the same for every competent speaker of the language. He asserts that the sense of a proper name is grasped by everyone familiar with the language but immediately adds a footnote allowing that the sense of the name "Aristotle" may vary from one speaker to another. The footnote is unfortunate in giving the impression that Frege believed in a description theory of (ordinary) proper names, equating them to definite descriptions. He had no such theory; but his epistemology was undeniably hazy, and he had no very clear account of the senses of either proper names in the narrow sense or of demonstrative and indexical terms. There are two requirements on a notion of sense if it is to agree with Frege's. First, the sense of any expression must be something that can be known, and which any speaker who understands the expression does know. Second, the sense of a singular term must serve to identify an object as the *Bedeutung* of that term; further, since two terms may have the same sense, this identification must not involve reference to that term. Clearly, a name, distinguished solely by its pronunciation and spelling, may have different uses and hence different senses: "Georgia" is the name of a country in the Caucasus once part of the Soviet Union and also of a southern state of the USA.

A child may take a message on the telephone that Mr Redmayne will be at home after six, and pass it on. In doing so, the child may genuinely refer to Mr Redmayne; but, having never heard of Mr Redmayne before, the child cannot be said to believe that Mr Redmayne will be at home after six. The most the child can be said to believe is that someone called "Mr Redmayne" will be at home after six. The child will know the sense of the name, as Frege conceives of it, only if he or she can be said to believe (or disbelieve) the thought expressed by a sentence containing it. Frege never went into the question in any depth; that does not invalidate his contention that to grasp the thought expressed by a statement containing a proper name, a speaker must attach to the name a sense which identifies the bearer.

That someone knows, of an object, that a certain name stands for it can never be a complete account of the knowledge that he or she has: the object must be given to him or her in a particular way. It does not follow that it must be given to every speaker in the same way. This is necessary because any two speakers must be able to be sure that they are speaking of the same object. If one speaker attached one sense to a name and the other attached a different sense to it, then, for all they knew, one might rightly judge the statement to be true while the other rightly judged it to be false. Frege says that to each expression of a language there ought to correspond a definite sense, but that, in natural languages, we must be content if the same word has the same sense in the same context. That everyone should then attach the same sense to it is an ideal of which in practice we fall short; but communication depends upon its being possible to ensure that a word is being used in the same sense by different speakers.

Frege distinguishes sharply between the sense of an expression and the mental image, which he calls the "idea" (*Vorstellung*), which it may arouse in someone's mind. The latter is subjective; one person cannot have another's idea. Sense is objective, and is therefore not a constituent of the mind: the very same sense, and the very same thought, may be grasped by many. In this denial that thoughts and their constituent senses are mental contents in the same respect as sensations and mental images, Frege was following in the tradition inaugurated by Bolzano. It was an immensely important step: it liberated the philosophy of meaning from appeals to psychological processes, turning it toward what makes our statements true. Frege distinguishes between the sense of an expression and its coloring, which concerns the ideas it evokes; this is important in poetry, but does not affect the thought expressed. From later writings we learn that the sense comprises only what may affect the truth-value of a sentence; "I'm an honest man" and "I'm an honest guy" differ in coloring, but express the same thought.

Frege allows that a singular term may have a sense but lack a *Bedeutung*, giving examples of definite descriptions to which no object answers. But when we use a term in making a serious assertion, we presuppose that it has a *Bedeutung*. Since its lacking one is a possibility, how can we be sure that any of our words have *Bedeutungen* at all? Frege brushes this skeptical question aside by remarking that we certainly intend to speak about the *Bedeutung* of any term we use. Later, he remarks that in a logically complete language stipulations must be made that guarantee a *Bedeutung* to every well-formed term.

Frege observes that words do not always have their ordinary *Bedeutungen*, for instance when they are in direct or indirect speech. In the first case they are used to speak about themselves; enclosure in quotation marks indicates this special use. Frege then states his famous theory that the *Bedeutung* of a word in indirect speech is its ordinary sense: that of a sentence following ". . . said that" or the like is the thought it would ordinarily express. In such cases an expression has its *indirect Bedeutung*; Frege infers that it will also have an indirect sense. To say that it retains its ordinary sense, but has a special *Bedeutung* in virtue of the special context, would violate the principle that the *Bedeutung* of an expression is determined by its sense; it would also violate the characterization of sense as the way the *Bedeutung* is given. The indirect *Bedeutung* of an expression is given to us as the (ordinary) sense of that very expression.

Frege now turns to ask after the *Bedeutungen* of whole assertoric sentences. This is a surprise to the reader, since so far the notion of *Bedeutung* has been presented only as the relation between a name and its bearer, a singular term and what it is used to refer to. It seems extremely doubtful that a whole sentence stands to anything in this relation: but Frege does not argue that it does, but, rather, assumes that it does, and asks to what it so stands. A full knowledge of his theory of *Bedeutung*, as developed in other writings, reveals that it plays for him the same role as that of semantic value in later theories. Frege implicitly assumes in SuB that the *Bedeutung* of any complex expression is determined by the *Bedeutungen* of its components; since, as he argues, the *Bedeutung* of a sentence is its truth-value, the theory of *Bedeutung* is a theory of how the truth-value of a sentence is determined in accordance with its composition: the *Bedeutung* of an expression is what goes to determine the truth-value of any sentence containing it. Furthermore, as is argued in SuB, a complex phrase containing a component which lacks a *Bedeutung* must itself lack *Bedeutung*: if there is no such country as Ruritania, there is no such city as the capital of Ruritania. Hence, if a sentence contains a component which lacks a *Bedeutung*, it must lack a truth-value. It follows that any expression that can affect whether a sentence is true or false must have a *Bedeutung*. Since a sentence may be a component of a more complex sentence, it must have a *Bedeutung*, which goes to determine the truth-value of the whole.

Frege argues that the *Bedeutung* of the sentence cannot be the thought it expresses, since, by replacing a part of the sentence by an expression with a different sense but the same *Bedeutung*, we cannot change the *Bedeutung* of the whole, but will change the thought it expresses: that thought must therefore be, rather, the sense of the sentence. A sentence may have a sense even though part of it, say the name "Odysseus," lacks a *Bedeutung*; but the sentence will not then have a truth-value: the name will be taken to have a *Bedeutung* by anyone who regards the sentence as either true or false. If we are unconcerned with its truth-value, as when we enjoy the *Odyssey* as poetry, we are likewise unconcerned with whether the name has a *Bedeutung*; this becomes a concern when we are interested in whether the sentence is true. We are thus driven to take the *Bedeutung* of the sentence to be its truth-value; there is nothing else that is guaranteed to remain unchanged throughout a series of replacements of constituent expressions by others with the same *Bedeutungen*.

The argument shows that it is the *Bedeutungen* of the components of a sentence that determine its truth-value; it does not follow that the truth-value of a sentence is its *Bedeutung*. That depends on showing that a sub-sentence contributes to the truth-value of the whole only through its own truth-value. The discussion of the last nineteen pages – by far the greater part of SuB – is devoted to this question.

Apparent exceptions arise in three ways: when a sentence has its indirect *Bedeutung*; when it is not truly a complete sentence, but involves an indefinite indicator (a variable bound by a quantifier with wider scope); and when, although there are two clauses, three thoughts are expressed. The latter happens with such a sentence as "Because Karl was asleep, he did not hear the burglar." We deny the thought expressed by the whole sentence without thereby denying that expressed by either clause when we say "It was not because Karl was asleep that he did not hear the burglar." Frege does not apply the same analysis to sentences with concessive clauses, since negating the whole does not have a similar effect: rather, he holds that "although" merely affects the "coloring" of the sentence, not its sense. The apparent exceptions to the identification of the *Bedeutung* of a sentence with its truth-value are all thus explained away.

The two truth-values are objects known, at least implicitly, to everyone who makes a judgment. Here, then, are objects whose existence cannot be doubted even by the skeptic (and can thus serve in stipulations guaranteeing a *Bedeutung* to every well-formed singular term). Truth does not stand to thoughts as predicate to subject: when we try to predicate truth to a thought, we do not make that advance from the thought to a truth-value which a judgment effects, but merely express the very same thought. The judgment distinguishes parts within the truth-value. This formulation Frege was later to reject: he opened one of the lectures attended by Carnap in 1913 by saying, "The *Bedeutungen* of the parts of a sentence are not parts of the *Bedeutung* of the sentence, but the sense of a part of the sentence is a part of the sense of the sentence."

Bibliography

Editions and translations

Frege, G. (1892) Über Sinn und Bedeutung. *Zeitschrift für Philosophie und philosophische Kritik*, 100: 25–50.

Frege, G. (1980) *Translations from the Philosophical Writings of Gottlob Frege*, 3rd edn, ed P. Geach and M. Black. Oxford: Blackwell.

Frege, G. (1984) *Collected Papers on Mathematics, Logic and Philosophy*. Oxford: Blackwell.

Studies

Dummett, M. (2000) On Frege's term *"Bedeutung."* In D. P. Chattopadhyaya, S. Basu, M. N. Mitra, and R. Mukhopadhyay (eds), *Realism: Responses and Reactions, Essays in Honour of Pranab Kumar Sen.* New Delhi: Indian Council of Philosophical Research.

Kenny, A. (1995) *Frege*, ch. 7. London: Penguin.

42

Edmund Husserl, *Logical Investigations* (1900–1901)

From Logic through Ontology to Phenomenology

David Woodruff Smith

The Significance of Husserl's *Logical Investigations*

How logic led through ontology into phenomenology and epistemology: that is the story of Edmund Husserl's *Logical Investigations*. This work launched the discipline of phenomenology: the study of forms of conscious experience, especially their content or meaning. Moreover, it integrated the four disciplines above in closer detail (arguably) than anywhere else in the history of philosophy.

Husserl (1859–1938) was 41 years old when this 1,000-page work appeared in 1900–1. With the *Logical Investigations*, Husserl matured into a fully fledged philosopher. In the 1880s he worked as a mathematician. This period of his development culminated in his early philosophy of mathematics, specifically of number, in *Philosophy of Arithmetic*, published in 1891. There, following Franz Brentano's empirical psychology, Husserl developed an analysis of the mental operations involved in dealing with numbers. The analysis has often been glossed as an immature exercise in psychologism, seeking to reduce mathematical truth to patterns of mental activity. Yet this was never Husserl's goal. In the *Investigations* he would analyze, much more clearly, forms of meaning in mental acts that represent or are directed toward typically independent objects, be they numbers or physical objects. Husserl's works following the *Investigations*, from *Ideas* I (1913) to the late works on "transcendental logic" and the "life-world," would develop phenomenology in great detail, but all his later results are circumscribed by the wide philosophical system outlined in the *Investigations*.

Husserl's *Logical Investigations* synthesize two long philosophical traditions, which we may call logical theory and psychological theory. The tradition of logical theory stretched from Aristotle's theory of syllogism to the modern propositional and quantifier logic emerging in Husserl's day. The tradition of psychological theory stretched from Aristotle's theory of form "in" mind (in *De anima*) to Franz Brentano's and William James's detailed empirical psychologies of Husserl's day. The result was Husserl's theory of "intentionality": an act of consciousness is directed through an ideal meaning toward that object which the meaning represents. For Husserl, the structure of intentionality is fundamental to mental activity, while the structure of meaning is fundamental to logical deduction, and these structures come together in Husserl's analysis.

Kant had sought to define the mind's role in our knowledge of objects, seeking a middle way between rationalism and empiricism in *The Critique of Pure Reason* (1781). While post-Kantians from Fichte to Hegel ramified nineteenth-century idealism, anti-idealists from Bolzano to Lotze promoted an ontology of objective "ideas" in logic. Then, in the *Logical Investigations*, Husserl urged a robust ontology of "ideal" entities including numbers, logical forms and meanings, intentional contents, and universals – each playing appropriate roles in mind, language, and the world.

The phenomenon of mind-*cum*-language (if you will) was the great philosophical theme – one could almost say discovery – of twentieth-century philosophy. Phenomena of mind and language were explored in very different ways by both the analytic and Continental traditions. Husserl's deep and detailed studies in the *Logical Investigations* laid much groundwork for subsequent theorizing. The themes of this work were explicitly followed, extended, and also opposed, as the Continental tradition spread from phenomenology into existentialism, structuralism, post-structuralism, and so on. In the analytic tradition, though Husserl was not widely read by logic-minded philosophers or science-minded philosophers of mind, retrospection shows that Husserl's *Investigations* none the less charted the flow of theory throughout the century in analytic philosophy of logic, language, and mind – from philosophical logic to philosophy of mind allied with cognitive science.

Husserl's most original contribution in the *Logical Investigations*, arguably, lies in his analysis of intentionality and meaning, relating mind and language to the rest of the world. Beyond the structures of consciousness and language, however, lie basic ontological structures which Husserl analyzed with often novel insight in the *Investigations*. The theory of universals began in the West with Plato and Aristotle, and dominated much of medieval philosophy. Husserl sought a renewed theory of universals, or "ideal species," and at the same time tied "ideal meanings" into the logical structure of language and thought. Moreover, at work in all his results were his conception and application of part–whole theory, or mereology (as distinct from set theory).

What, then, makes Husserl's *Logical Investigations* a classic of Western philosophy? First, in the *Investigations* Husserl initiated the discipline of phenomenology – merely implicit in earlier thinkers such as Descartes, Hume, and Kant. Second, in the *Investigations* Husserl developed the theory of intentionality, marking distinctions that advance philosophy beyond the theories found in Descartes, Kant, et al. Third, Husserl's analysis, in the *Investigations*, of the role of ideal form in logic, mathematics, language, and intentional experience was novel and pathbreaking, charting salient issues in today's theory of mind and language (in ways not yet widely recognized). Fourth, Husserl's *Investigations* was the seminal influence on the Continental European tradition of the twentieth century, which developed rich interpretations of cultural forms in experience, language or discourse, the arts, and ultimately politics. Fifth, the *Investigations* unfolds a systematic, often novel ontology, grounding his detailed analyses of language, consciousness, and knowledge. The full significance of the *Logical Investiga-*

tions cannot be fully appreciated, however, I maintain, until we see the remarkable unity of the *Investigations* – a main theme to follow.

The Text of the *Logical Investigations*

The *Logical Investigations* (*Logische Untersuchungen*) occupy some 1,000 pages in three volumes in the German edition: including the Prolegomena and six Investigations numbered I–VI. The first edition was published in 1900 and 1901. The second edition, with revisions through Investigation V, was published in 1913; the second edition of Investigation VI, with revisions, was published in 1922. There was no English translation of the whole work until that by J. N. Findlay (1970): 877 pages in two volumes, translating the full second edition. We shall cite the Findlay translation, with reference to the German terms (and occasional modification of the translation).

Many scholars think that Husserl held a form of metaphysical realism in 1900 but moved to a form of idealism by 1913 in *Ideas* I, a neo-Kantian transcendental idealism asserting that external objects are "constituted" in consciousness and so dependent on consciousness. These scholars claim that Husserl's revisions of the *Investigations* in the second edition incorporate his new-found idealism and thereby modify his original realist position. A different view finds Husserl's "transcendental idealism" joined with a realist ontology, so that his philosophy did not change metaphysics over this period, but rather came to give greater emphasis to intentionality in both methodology and ontology.

The present interpretation follows the second paradigm. We pursue a unifying interpretation of the whole of the second edition of the *Logical Investigations*, viewing this work not only in the context of Husserl's own development, but also in the context of the broad Western tradition.

Overview of the Content of the *Logical Investigations*

Husserl unfolds a complex philosophical system, we shall see, over the long course of the Prolegomena (P) and six Investigations (I–VI). In highlight:

P   Logic is the theory of theories. A theory (*Theorie*) is a unified system of propositions. A proposition (*Satz*) is an objective ideal meaning (*Sinn*) (expressible by a declarative sentence).

I   Language consists in expressive acts of speech (or writing). A speech act intimates an underlying act of thought or judgment and expresses the objective ideal content or sense (*Sinn*) of that act. That sense serves as the meaning (*Bedeutung*) of the expression uttered.

II Concrete spatio-temporal objects (particulars) share ideal species (universals). Ideal species are not spatio-temporal but are objective. Meanings are a type of ideal species.

III An object that is a whole or unity has parts. An independent part or "piece" can exist apart from the whole, but a dependent part or "moment" cannot. An instance of an ideal species is a moment in an object that is a member of that species.

IV   Part–whole relations apply to meanings. Propositions contain concepts as parts, some as dependent parts.

V   An act of consciousness has a subject or ego ("I"), a content or sense, and an object. An act is "intentional" in so far as it is directed toward its object (if such object exists). It is directed through its content or sense, a meaning, which represents the object.

VI   Objective knowledge begins with "intuition" (*Anschauung*), an intentional experience whose meaning is fulfilled by evidence. Sensory perception is the paradigm, but in "categorial" intuition we grasp logical and ontological forms.

These seven courses of investigation look quite independent, exploring different domains altogether, from logic to ontology to phenomenology to epistemology. Yet there are strong ties that bind these pieces of theory together, as I shall try to show. Let us turn to these seven studies one by one.

Prolegomena: Philosophy of (Mathematical) Logic – a Neo-platonic Idealism of (Mathematical) Logical Form

The *Logical Investigations* opens with a book-length study: "Prolegomena to Pure Logic," the entire first volume of the German edition. Through most of the Prolegomena Husserl is exercised to refute psychologism, the dominant position in nineteenth-century philosophy of logic. On that view, logic is about how we happen to reason, a matter of human psychology. Husserl argues at length that logic is not about contingent psychological processes of inference, nor about historical social conventions of inference, nor about normative principles of how people ought to reason. Instead, Husserl argues that logic is about objective forms of propositions and objective deductive relations among them. What makes a form of inference valid, then, is not something about the human mind, or human convention, but something in the essence of propositions themselves: objectively existing ideal meanings.

Husserl's own, positive view of logic emerges in the final chapter of the Prolegomena (11), titled "The Idea of Pure Logic." Husserl's guiding light is Bernard Bolzano's *Theory of Science* (*Wissenschaftslehre*) of 1837. Following Bolzano, Husserl conceives pure logic as "the theory of theories" (§66). A particular *theory* (*Theorie*) has a systematic unity defined by deduction of theorems from "basic laws" or axioms (§63). This ideal is basically the same as that of later logicians, including Gödel, Tarski, and Quine, though Gödel's results on completeness and incompleteness were thirty years down the road. But Husserl's focus is on meanings: meanings are ideal entities, like Platonic forms; to be more precise, they are like Bolzano's conception of objective versus subjective ideas (*Vorstellungen*), especially the notion of a proposition in itself (*Satz an sich*), which is grasped in thought and expressed in language but exists in its own right. We need not think of objective ideas as occupying a Platonic heaven; rather, we should simply think of them as having their own kind of objective being.

Husserl divides logic into three parts: the theory of logical categories or forms, the theory of inference, and the theory of possible forms of theories (§§67–9). These three ranges of logical theory resemble what today's logicians call syntax, proof theory, and model theory. Yet Husserl's conception of these areas was unusually rich, both in the ontology of propositions and in their relation to intentionality. What we call semantics was an integral part of Husserl's conception of pure logic as addressing correlations among three levels of logically relevant entities: expressions, meanings, and objects.

Logic begins, for Husserl, by fixing *categories of meaning, categories of objects* (represented by meanings), and the lawful correlations of meanings and the objects they represent (§67). The categories of meaning are determined by "the concepts: Concept, Proposition, Truth, etc." together with "[t]he concepts of the elementary connective forms . . . of propositions, e.g. the conjunctive, disjunctive, hypothetical linkage of propositions" (§67, p. 237). Every meaning is thus a certain form of concept or combination of concepts in a proposition. Corresponding to these formal meaning categories are "formal objective categories" determined by "concepts such as Object, State of Affairs, Unity, Plurality, Number, Relation, Connection, etc." (§67, p. 237). For instance, corresponding to a proposition of the form "S is p" is a state of affairs of the form that S is p. Of course, meanings are expressed by expressions of certain categories or forms, but Husserl leaves the nature of expressions for Investigation I. Where today's logicians begin with categories of expression, Husserl takes that for granted and focuses on corresponding categories of meanings expressed and objects represented.

The basic forms or categories of object are defined in the discipline Husserl called *formal ontology* (in *Ideas* I, §10). So pure or formal logic includes or presupposes formal ontology in that meanings of certain forms are said to represent objects of certain forms. Notably, propositions represent states of affairs, where a state of affairs "formally" combines objects with relations, qualities, or species.

Given categories of meaning and object, logic proceeds to state formal *laws* that govern both meanings and objects (§68, pp. 238–9): this is the second part of logic. The formal laws of meanings include theories of inference, concerning which propositions entail which by virtue of their form: Frege's logic was well known to Husserl. Formal laws of correlative *objects* include, for Husserl, the "pure theory of pluralities" and the "pure theory of numbers": early set theory and early number theory were well known to Husserl. Thus, Husserl's conception of logic was of a piece with the emerging discipline of mathematical logic allied with set theory, number theory, and so on.

The third part of logic, for Husserl, is to develop "the theory of the possible forms of theories or the pure theory of manifolds" (§69, pp. 239ff). Husserl's story here is less clear: he is projecting an ideal not yet developed. A *theory* is a system of propositions, concerning certain kinds of objects and their properties and relations. The theory of possible *forms of theories* concerns, then, what unifies a group of propositions into a proper *theory*: a theory includes axiomatic propositions and all propositions deducible from them. This much is familiar today. Now, the *objective structure* corresponding to a particular theory is a structure of objects bearing properties and relations: a very complex state of affairs. And its form is, I propose, what Husserl obscurely calls a "manifold" (*Mannigfaltigkeit*, a term also used earlier by Cantor for sets). Here Husserl envisioned a future mathematical theory of "manifolds" that would realize Leibniz's dream of a "*mathesis universalis*" (§60, p. 219) understood as a universal formal theory of objects of any kind. The third part of logic, in Husserl's vision, is thus a rich type of formal semantics.

Investigation I: Philosophy of Language – a Theory of Meaning, Reference, Speech Acts, and Expression of Thought

Investigation I, titled "Expression and Meaning," expands Husserl's philosophy of logic into a philosophy of language. Husserl's analysis addresses meaning, reference, truth, expressions (spoken and written), speech acts (asserting, etc.), acts of thought or judgment given voice, and the complex relations among these things. Language encompasses all these things, on Husserl's analysis. Over the course of the twentieth century, analytic philosophers (Russell, Carnap, Austin, Quine, Kaplan, et al.) have studied these phenomena of language, its form and its use, in considerable detail. None the less, the field of analytic philosophy of language today still lacks a unified theory that puts these things in their place, especially in relation to intentionality. The outlines of such a theory can be drawn from Husserl's first Investigation.

The overriding meta-theory of the Prolegomena is Husserl's Neoplatonic idealism of meaning and logical form. As we look back today on the development of modern logic, we focus on forms of linguistic expressions, featuring a syntax with rules of formation of well-formed formulas: sentences formed from terms, predicates, connectives, and quantifiers. For Husserl, however, the primary entities that logic deals with are not linguistic expressions, but rather the ideal meanings they express, including propositions and their constituents and combinations. What then are ideal meanings (propositions, concepts)? And how are they related to linguistic expressions (sentences, terms)? These are the concerns of Investigation I.

Husserl's theory of language and meaning is a detailed formulation of the traditional view that language expresses thought and serves to communicate contents of thought. This basic model is familiar, almost common sense, with a long history including versions in Aristotle, Ockham, Aquinas, Locke, and so on. However, Husserl offers much closer detail than his predecessors, thanks to his careful analysis of intentionality. The new logic of Frege et al. was familiar to Husserl, and he sought to ground this logic in an ontology of ideal meanings (as did Frege). However, in the 1890s Husserl was laying the groundwork for his theory of intentionality, whence he tied his ontology of meanings together with an ontology and a phenomenology of intentional acts including both speech and thought. From today's perspective, the main thing lacking in Husserl's philosophy of logic-*cum*-language was an explicit semantics of truth-conditions. That style of semantics, which has proved so useful, was developed by Tarski in the 1930s, extended toward everyday language in the 1940s, and rendered a nearly canonical form of philosophical semantics by the 1970s. None the less, what Husserl did not yet envision on the formal side of semantics, he made up for on the wider philosophical front, with his account of the role of intentionality and intentional content in language. Let us outline Husserl's account of meaning, then, bringing in his special terminology.

Some objects *indicate* or are *signs* of others, Husserl notes (§1). Fossils are signs of ancient animal life, while a flag is the sign of a nation (§2). A thing is a sign or indication if and only if "it serves to indicate something to some thinking being" (p. 270). Language in particular is an indication to others of a speaker's intentional activity (§2). Specifically, an *expression* – a sentence – uttered by a *speaker* serves as a sign that indicates to the *hearer* the *speaker's thoughts* (§7). As Husserl puts it, the expression *intimates* the speaker's *inner experience* of thinking such-and-such. Intimation of thoughts is thus a special type of indication. Expressions function in this way to *communicate* the speaker's thoughts to his or her hearers. Husserl outlines here a theory of speech acts central to the social use of language; what later speech-act theory (Austin, Searle, Grice) would add is the social effect of language on the hearer. (This model is designed for the case of a declarative sentence: the paradigm of Husserl's model. It needs to be expanded to cover interrogative and imperative sentences.)

The speaker's underlying thought *lends* its content or sense to the expression uttered and thus *gives meaning* to the expression. Accordingly, Husserl calls the intimated thought a *sense-giving* act (§9). On Husserl's ontology, language involves two types of ideal entities (§11): species or types of expression, and species or types of mental act. The type of sound produced in speaking is the ideal form of expression; the type of thought intimated is the ideal form of thinking, its shareable intentional content. With this latter entity, the structure of language reaches into phenomenology (§§9–11), into intentional structure that is analyzed further in Investigation V.

An expression gains objective reference (§12), Husserl holds, in a type of intentional relation (§13). For example, "Two names can differ in meaning but can name the same object, e.g., 'the victor at Jena' – 'the vanquished at Waterloo'" (§12, p. 287). But "an expression only refers to an objective correlate *because* it means something, it can be rightly said to signify or name the object *through* its meaning" (§13). These words formulate a well-known model of reference (shared with Frege's famous doctrine): reference is mediated by meaning or sense. However, in a prescient analysis of pronouns like "this" or "I" (studied decades later by Kaplan and others), Husserl holds that such "essentially occasional" expressions have two levels of meaning (§26): one type of ("semantic") meaning that remains constant in different uses, and a second type of ("indicated") meaning that varies with the occasion, specifically with the speaker's perception of the object referred to. Thus, the semantic meaning of "this" is constant, but its "indicated" meaning varies with the occasion of use and depends on the speaker's perception of the object being referred to in saying "this." The peculiarly occasional content of perception, or "intuition," is pursued further in Investigation VI.

While language is thus an expression of contents of thought to be communicated from speaker to hearer, these contents themselves are drawn from the realm of ideal meanings, to which the science of logic is devoted.

> Pure logic, wherever it deals with concepts, judgments [propositions], and syllogisms, is exclusively concerned with the ideal unities that we here call "meaning" [*Sinn*]. (§29, p. 322)

> As numbers – in the ideal sense that arithmetic presupposes – neither spring forth nor vanish with the act of enumeration . . . so it is with the ideal unities of pure logic, with its concepts, propositions, truths, or in other words, with its meanings. They are an ideally closed set of general objects, to which being thought or being expressed are alike contingent. (§35, p. 333; last page of Investigation I)

What then are ideal unities?

Investigation II: Metaphysics – a neo-Aristotelian Ontology of Universals

Investigation II, "The Ideal Unity of Species and Modern Theories of Abstraction," is a study in pure ontology, a study of the ancient problem of universals and particulars. On Husserl's ontology, species (*Spezies*) are ideal entities, like Plato's forms; yet species are realized in concrete instances, like Aristotle's qualities or accidents, which exist only in particulars, such as this redness in this flower. Husserl calls such instances of species "moments" (*Momente*), borrowing an older term in German philosophy. Most of the Investigation is a critique of the British empiricists' theories of abstraction, with Husserl charging Locke, Berkeley, Hume, and Mill with collapsing or confusing distinctions and missing the nature of both universals and our knowledge of them.

Husserl begins Investigation II (Introduction) by marking the distinction among: a red object, the instance or "moment" of red in the object, and the species red (red *in specie*). Husserl's positive theory consists largely in stressing this distinction and the "ideal" status of species. When we look at a red object in perception and think or speak of "red," we can mean either its particular redness (its red-moment) or the ideal species red. The red object is a "real" individual, in space and time; the species red is an "ideal" object, not in space or time; the red-moment is a part of the real individual and an instance of the ideal species. "To talk of 'idealism' is . . . not to talk of a metaphysical doctrine [reducing physical things to ideas], but of a theory of knowledge which recognizes the 'ideal' [species] as a condition for the possibility of objective knowledge . . ." (p. 338).

Against nominalists and conceptualists, Husserl insists on the objective existence of "universal objects," or species (*Spezies*), and our "consciousness of universality" (§§1–2). Then he denies "the reduction of ideal unity [*Einheit*] to dispersed multiplicity [or manifold: *Mannigfaltigkeit*]" (§4): so a species, an ideal unity, is to be distinguished from its extension, a set or "manifold" (in Cantor's sense). Ending his long critique of the empiricists, Husserl concludes Investigation II with a series of distinctions about "abstraction" and "abstract" concepts and objects. In abstraction, he writes,

> we directly grasp the specific unity Red "itself" on the ground of a singular intuition [*Anschauung*] of something red. We look at its red-moment, but we perform a peculiar act whose intention is directed to the "Idea," the "universal". Abstraction in the sense of this act is wholly different from the mere attention to, or emphasis on, the red-moment . . . (§42, p. 432; translation altered)

This act of abstraction Husserl would later call "intuition of essence" (*Wesenschau*), in *Ideas* I.

Notice that intuition of meaning is a special case of this type of abstraction, since a meaning is the ideal species of an intentional act (Introduction to II, p. 337). Phenomenology, more fully elaborated in *Ideas* I, centers on intuition and analysis of intentional contents, or meanings. (More on Husserl's evolving ontology of meanings below.)

To understand Husserl's conception of "moments," which tie universals to particulars, we must turn to Husserl's ontology of part and whole.

Investigation III: Mereology – a Novel Ontology of Part–Whole and Dependence

Investigation III, "On the Theory of Wholes and Parts," extends Husserl's ontology of universals: ideal species with concrete instances. He analyzes *instances* of species as proper *parts* of concrete objects: *essentially dependent* parts. He incorporates this notion into a proper ontology of part–whole and dependence.

Following Stumpf's psychology (following Brentano following Aristotle), Husserl focuses primarily (and I think misleadingly) on parts of mental acts and their sensory contents, especially seeing a colored expanse (§2). In the wake of the British empiricists, he addresses our abstraction of color from an object of perception. And, in a partly Aristotelian vein, he treats this white of this object as a concrete instance of the pure species white. Aristotle called these instances "accidents" or simply "qualities" understood as particulars; Husserl calls them "moments."

Making explicit this notion of part, Husserl writes:

> *Dependent* [*unselbstständig*: non-independent] *objects are objects belonging to such pure species as are governed by a law of essence to the effect that they only exist (if at all) as parts of more inclusive wholes of a certain appropriate species* . . . [T]hey are parts that only exist as parts, that cannot be thought of as existing by themselves. The color of this paper is a dependent "moment" of the paper. It is not merely an actual part, but its essence, its pure species, predestines it to partial being: a color *in general and purely as such* can exist only as a "moment" in a colored thing. (§7, p. 447, translation slightly altered)

Here we see Husserl's synthesis of Plato and Aristotle on the ontology of universals: there are ideal species, but they gain actual existence only in their instances in particulars, instances called moments. But moments are cast as *bona fide* parts of concrete objects.

Husserl proceeds to elaborate this notion of dependent objects as dependent parts of a whole, in a partly axiomatized theory of part–whole. First he defines the formal relation of foundation (*Fundierung*) (§14). Suppose there is a "law of essence" that an *A* cannot exist except in relation with an *M* within a whole, and suppose A_0 and M_0 are respectively "determinate instances of the pure kinds *A* [and] *M*, actualized in a single whole," in the required relations to each other in the whole. Then we say A_0 is *founded* on M_0 – and so A_0 is dependent, or non-independent.

Given this notion of dependence or foundation, Husserl then distinguishes two kinds of part: independent parts, or *pieces*, and dependent parts, or *moments*. This page of this book is a piece of the book, a part that could exist separately from the book. But this instance of white in this piece of paper is a "moment" of the paper, a part that could not exist separately from the paper. Stated more formally: "*Each part [Teil] that is independent relative to a whole W we call a piece [Stück], each part that is dependent relative to W we call a moment [Moment] (an abstract part) of this same whole W*" (§17, p. 467, translation slightly altered). Husserl uses the term "abstract" differently from many philosophers today: something is "abstract" if it can exist only in thought by virtue of "abstraction."

Husserl does not separate the notion of dependence from that of dependent part, assuming that dependent objects exist only in wholes of which they are dependent parts. This is arguably a mistake or a limitation. But consider next Husserl's further application of the notion of dependent part: to ideal meanings.

Investigation IV: Grammar – a Part–Whole Ontology for Propositions

Investigation IV, "The Distinction between Independent and Dependent [Non-independent] Meanings and the Idea of Pure Grammar," pursues the ontology of meaning. Here Husserl applies the ontology of dependent parts, surprisingly, to ideal meanings. The distinctions Husserl develops for complex forms of propositions lead to an account of logical analytic truths and nonsensical combinations of meanings. Finally, these reflections lead Husserl toward the ideal of a "pure grammar," an ontology of forms of meanings and their permissible combinations.

Husserl holds that complex expressions express complex meanings (§§1–3). Just as language includes simple and complex expressions, physical signs spoken or written, so the realm of ideal meaning includes simple and complex meanings. A proper name like "Schultze" expresses a simple meaning, according to Husserl: "The proper name *P* names the object, or its 'proper meaning' means the object, in a single 'ray'" (§3, pp. 497–8). By contrast, Husserl implies, the proposition "Schultze is German" is a complex meaning, which represents the state of affairs that Schultze is German: a complex meaning representing in a complex way a complex object. Remember that a meaning is an ideal intentional content, taken as the ideal species of an act of consciousness, here thinking that Schultze is German. So the complexity of a meaning mirrors the complexity of the intentional force of an act with that meaning as content.

It is traditional to distinguish "categorematic" from "syncategorematic" expressions, Husserl notes (§4): categorematic expressions, such as "the founder of ethics," have meaning by themselves, or are "complete"; syncategorematic expressions, such as the connective "and," do not, or are "incomplete." Remarkably, Husserl holds that the same distinction applies to meanings (§§5–7): we must distinguish also categorematic and syncategorematic *meanings*. To elaborate on some of Husserl's (cryptic) examples, the proposition "the founder of ethics was Greek" is categorematic, while the connective-meaning "and" is not. In a novel move, Husserl explicates this distinction in terms of his ontology of dependence: these types of meaning are respectively *independent* and *dependent* meanings. Thus, the proposition "the founder of ethics is Greek" is an independent meaning: it could exist by itself. I take it that that entails it has the force of autonomously representing something, namely, the state of affairs that the founder of ethics is Greek. By contrast, the meaning "and" is a dependent meaning: it cannot exist by itself, but only in complex propositions of the form "*P* and *Q*." And I take it that Husserl holds "and" does not play a role in representing except as a dependent part of such a complex proposition.

So simpler meanings can be combined into more complex meanings, and propositions can be combined by connective meanings such as "and": Husserl's model is clearly the new logic of his day (Boole, Frege, et al.), extended from expressions to ideal meanings. Now, "*meanings are subject to a priori laws regulating their combination into new meanings*" (§10, p. 510). Thus, Husserl writes, "We can construct verbal strings such as 'if the or is green', 'A tree is and', etc., but such strings have no graspable single meanings. It is an analytic truth that the forms in a whole cannot function as its materials, nor vice versa, and this obviously carries over into the sphere of meanings" (p. 512). Another kind of nonsense occurs, Husserl holds (§12), with names such as "wooden iron" and "round square" or sentences such as "All squares have five angles": "An object (e.g. a thing, state of affairs) which unites all that the unified meaning conceives as pertaining to it by way of its 'incompatible' meanings, neither exists nor can exist, though the meaning itself exists" (p. 517).

The "formal laws of meaning" that Husserl envisions, systematically developed, would define "the Idea of a grammar of pure logic" (§14). At the level of meanings, traditional logical laws of "Contradiction, Double Negation, or the Modus Ponens" are "*laws of the avoidance of formal absurdity*" (p. 523). Here we see Husserl's conception of logic as a theory of ideal meanings extended through his account of speech and expression while using his ontology of species and dependent parts – all in the service still of logical theory. But meanings are ideal intentional contents: that is the theme of the next Investigation.

Investigation V: Phenomenology – the Theory of Intentionality Coming of Age

Investigation V, "On Intentional Experiences and their 'Contents,'" develops Husserl's theory of intentionality: the foundation of his conception of phenomenology – the science of the essence of consciousness (as he puts it later in *Ideas* I). Husserl mapped out for the first time an adequate analysis of intentionality. The core of Husserl's analysis was a series of careful distinctions among an act of consciousness, its content, and its object. These distinctions parallel distinctions in logical theory among an act of expression, its meaning, and its object of reference. But since Husserl has argued that language is founded on mind, in that an act of expression is founded on an underlying act of thought, Husserl grounds intentionality, or objective reference, in thought.

Husserl begins with Brentano's view of "inner" consciousness in "experience": I am conscious of being conscious of this or that object (§§3ff). What defines consciousness, Husserl finds, is its *intentional* character, as Brentano held (extending Aristotle and Aquinas) (§§9–10). But Husserl painstakingly draws a variety of distinctions that were never carefully drawn by his great predecessors, from Descartes to Kant and Bolzano. In the structure of an intentional experience Husserl distinguishes four types of entity: ego, act, content, and object.

The "pure I" (*Ich*, translated often by the Latin "ego") is the "I" that thinks or experiences, the being from which intentional relations proceed (§8). In the first edition of the *Investigations* Husserl joined Hume, saying "I must frankly confess . . . that I am quite unable to find this I, this primitive, necessary center of relations" (p. 549, translation altered). In the second edition Husserl famously recanted, adding in a footnote (p. 549), "I have since managed to find it . . . ," learning not to be "led astray . . . through corrupt sorts of I-metaphysic." Thus, the "I" is simply that being which has the intentional experience.

The "act" of consciousness is the concrete "inner experience" in which I am conscious of something, say, in seeing or thinking-about or wanting such-and-such. In an act I am "presented" or see or judge-about something: a consciousness *of* something (§12). The fundamental structure of consciousness is thus a *relation* of an act or I to an object. This consciousness of an object Husserl calls an *intentional* relation, and he comes to call this relation *intentionality*.

The "object" of the act is whatever object I am seeing, judging-about, etc. But we must distinguish between the object and the "content" of the act (though the latter term has been used for the former) (§§16–21). The act's content is not the object, but the way the object is "intended" in the act. Husserl divides the content into the "quality" and "matter" of the act (§20). The quality of an act is its "general act-character" as being "merely presentative, judgmental, desiderative, etc." (p. 586). The matter of an act defines what is presented, judged, desired, etc., for instance, that "there are intelligent beings on Mars." Quality and matter together define the act's character of being, say, an act of judging that there is life on Mars.

But we must distinguish "real" and "ideal" content. The "real" content of an act is a *part* of the act: a moment. This moment is an instance of an ideal species, which is the "ideal" content of the act: the *intentional essence* of the act (§22). So the intentional content of an act is, fundamentally, a type of ideal essence: it is this ideal content that determines the act's intentionality, the way it is directed toward an object.

The structure of intentionality, or "objective reference," is unique. First, an act of consciousness can be directed toward, or "intend," something that does not actually exist. In that case, we say the act has no existing object, though it has a content. Second, the same object can be intended in different ways in different acts. Thus, to recall the semantic example, Napoleon may be thought of as "the victor at Jena" or "the vanquished at Waterloo": same object, different contents – different ideal meanings. So the intentional relation between an act or I and an object is mediated by a content or meaning. There is no other type of "relation" like that!

For Husserl, we saw, language is founded on thought. Husserl's philosophy of logic-cum-language, we can now see, is grounded in his theory of intentionality. Specifically, his analysis of linguistic meaning and reference in Investigation I presupposes his analysis of intentionality in Investigation V. For the ideal contents of thought are the same entities that serve as ideal meanings expressed in language. Logic studies ideal meanings drawn from this class of entities. In that way, for Husserl, logic is founded on phenomenology. Alternatively, phenomenological analyses are discernible in logical analyses of different forms of meaning, reference, and truth. In the language of Investigation IV, indeed, we might say that phenomenology begins in the "grammar" of intentional contents, the meanings of different forms of experience.

In his subsequent work *Ideas* I (1913) Husserl introduced a new terminology for intentional content or meaning, drawn from the Greek: the real content of an act he there calls a "noesis," a pure "thinking"; the ideal content of the act he calls a "*noema*," what is thought, an ideal meaning, be it a concept (representing an object or a property or relation) or a proposition (representing a state of affairs).

Investigation VI: Epistemology – Perception, Intuition, and a Novel Theory of Knowledge

Investigation VI, "Elements of a Phenomenological Eludication of Knowledge," is a 200-page treatise in epistemology. Briefly, Husserl offers a phenomenological theory of knowledge that is a genuine alternative and successor to rationalism, empiricism, and Kantianism. For Husserl, knowledge begins in "intuition" (*Anschauung*), "intuitive" or "self-evident" experience. Intuition includes sensory perception of physical objects (compare Kant's account of intuition formed from sensations and concepts). But intuition also includes intuitive abstraction of ideal species (with "insight") and intuitive reflection on the structure of consciousness. Phenomenology proceeds by intuitive analysis of the sense of an intentional experience, a form of abstraction. And pure logic proceeds by intuitive analysis of propositions and their logical forms. Both logic and phenomenology assume thus the "grammar" of ideal meanings, and our intuitive grasp thereof.

According to Husserl's phenomenology of "intuitive" experience, an act of intuition divides into an "interpretive" meaning-bearing intention and a "fulfilling" evidence-bearing intention (chs 1–3). Where the interpretive intention has the character of pointing to an object as presented in a certain way, the fulfilling intention has the character of "evidence," through which the object is intended as actually there. Accordingly, the intentional content of the act divides into an "interpretive" sense (*Auffassungssinn*) and an "intuitive" sense (*Anschauungssinn*), where the former prescribes the object of the act and the latter fulfills the former.

An important example clarifies Husserl's theory of intuition. When I see a blackbird and say "this blackbird flies up," the meaning of my uttering "this" is supported by my perception of "this blackbird," which has a unique form of intuitive intention (§5). Of this form of intention, Husserl writes:

> When I say "this," I do not merely perceive, but a *new act of pointing (of this-meaning) builds itself on my perception, an act directed upon the latter and dependent on it, despite its difference. In this pointing reference, and in it alone, our meaning resides.* (p. 683)

What Husserl seems to have in mind here is that the perceptual intention presents "this" object before me, and the meaning of my saying "this" depends on that perceptual intention on that occasion. To fill in Husserl's story here, the perceptual intention includes an intuitive intention that points to this particular object before me, and the act of referring by "this" draws only on that part of the perception, and not on any further conceptualization of the object intended, say, its presenting it as a "blackbird." In the use of the demonstrative pronoun "this," then, we see a model of purely "intuitive" intention, with its unique type of content or sense.

Near the end of Investigation VI Husserl distinguishes "categorial" from "sensory" intuition. *Categorial* intuition, Husserl holds, is the intuitive grasp of "categorial forms" corresponding to formal (logical) words such as "is," "not," "the," "some," "and," "or," etc., and their meanings (formal parts of propositions) (§40). These forms – "objective correlates" of the formal words and meanings – are not "real" (*reale*) features of "real" objects (§44). As we know from the Prolegomena, these forms are ideal entities: the objective categories set out in pure logic along with categories of meaning and expression. Suppose I see this bird and judge that this is a raven. Then the bird is intuitively given (with various properties) in sensory intuition, or perception. But the *form* of the state of affairs judged – corresponding to the predicative form "this *is* a raven" – is intuitively given in categorial intuition. Husserl explores in detail the way in which the intention of categorial form, here "being [thus-and-so]", can be fulfilled in a categorial intuition *founded* on a sensory intuition. Suffice it to say that such categorial – if you will, "logical" – intuition is a type of abstraction carried out by considering examples and coming to "see" the relevant form at work (§§45–9). So the phenomenology of intuition finally makes good on the method of pure logic, in Husserl's system. Or alternatively, the method of pure logic finally is at work in the phenomenology of certain forms of experience.

Husserl thus brings his final Investigation full circle to meet his Prolegomena. Epistemology, phenomenology, ontology, and logic are joined in a philosophical circle arcing over 1,000 pages of philosophical investigations.

Categories and Ideal Entities

Husserl's discussion, over the long course of the *Logical Investigations*, raises the problem of how many types of ideal entities are posited in his overall ontology. "Ideal" (*ideale*) entities contrast with "real" entities. Material things (*Dinge*) and events are "real" (*reale*), or located in space–time, and mental acts or experiences are "real" (*reelle*), or located in time (within the stream of consciousness), whereas ideal entities are non-spatial and non-temporal. However, it is best to think of ideal entities as defined ontologically not by the negative feature of not being located in space and/or time, but rather by the positive features adduced in Husserl's accounts of these kinds of entities. But which kinds of entities are ideal?

The Prolegomena posits meanings, including concepts and propositions, along with their logical forms: all are ideal entities that play their roles in logical formation and deduction. Investigation I again assumes meanings as ideal entities, which now play their roles in language, in communication of what is thought. As Investigation I closes (p. 333), Husserl calls meanings ideal unities, or species: not species of objects like trees, but species of intentional acts of thinking intimated in language use. The ontology of species *per se* is then the theme of Investigation II.

So it seems that Husserl categorizes meanings under species. We need to address the problem of universals – species – in our overall ontology. So if we assume that meanings are a kind of species, then we simplify our ontology of ideal entities.

Still, Husserl began his *Logical Investigations* with the assumption that numbers are ideal unities not captured by psychologistic analyses of number (as a pattern of enumeration in thinking "one, two, three, . . ."). And by the end of the Prolegomena, Husserl is found positing, with passion, at least two apparently distinct kinds of ideal entities: numbers (and indeed other mathematical entities like sets) and meanings (including propositions). But are either numbers or meanings properly categorized as *species*?

It might be suggested that the number 2 is the species comprising pairs of objects. (On one influential analysis, the number 2 is the set of sets of two objects. Here we consider a richer ontology, since a species is not a set, an extensional collection, but rather an Aristotelian universal, as we find in Investigation II.) Then numbers would be a kind of species. Again, it might be suggested that the proposition "snow is white" is the species comprising mental acts of thinking that snow is white. Then propositions, like numbers, would be a kind of species. The differentiating character defines what falls under the relevant species.

This reduction of all ideal entities to species seems to fit much of Husserl's discussion. But it conflicts with his refined approach to ontological categories. Thus, in the Prolegomena (§67) Husserl gives an explicit but open-ended list of formal meaning categories: "Concept, Proposition, Truth [True Proposition], etc.," and an explicit, open-ended list of formal objective categories: "Object, State of Affairs, Unity, Plurality, Number, Relation, Connection, etc." Notice that numbers are given their own category here, alongside categories for unities, relations, etc. Thus, when Husserl gets serious about the categorial status of numbers, he does not categorize numbers as a kind of species, since the entities traditionally called universals – pluralities ("many-nesses"), relations, etc. – are divided here among distinct formal objective categories. Where are species on this list? They could appear under a separate formal objective category Species, since (notably) biological species are a very special kind of grouping of individual living things. But since Husserl takes species to be "ideal unities," the formal category of Unity subsumes different kinds of species, all being ideal unities. Either Unity is identical with Species, or Species is subsumed under Unity. Numbers follow unities and pluralities in this scheme, under Unity, Plurality, Number: a unity gathers many things, their plurality distributes them, and their number quantifies them. Here we see formal distinctions not always carefully observed.

And what of meanings? If they are a kind of species, they fall under Species, under Unity. However, by the time of *Ideas* I (1913) and the second edition of the *Logical Investigations* (1913/1922), Husserl concluded that meanings are not a kind of ideal species, but a unique kind of ideal individual object: *noema*. In *Ideas* I Husserl gives meanings (still ideal intentional contents) the Greek name "*noema*," and often he calls species "essences" (*Wesen*: from what-something-is). The more mature position of Husserl on the categorial status of meanings, then, is that they fall under the formal category Object, rather than under Species. And they are ideal objects with their own special role in consciousness: a role detailed in Investigation V.

It may be, however, that Husserl allows the term "species" to range rather widely over all ideal entities: not only classical universals (kinds, qualities, the one over the many), but also numbers (and sets and other mathematical entities), and meanings. After all, in the second edition of the *Logical Investigations*, he does not alter the claim that meanings are ideal unities, ideal species: why not?

The Unity (and Power) of the *Logical Investigations*

For a hundred years Husserl's *Logical Investigations* has been read mostly as a patchwork of disjoint studies of unrelated issues, a meandering prelude to the "mature" transcendental phenomenology Husserl developed in *Ideas* I. A very different perspective emerges when we come to appreciate the unity of the *Logical Investigations*. Husserl's phenomenology takes its place in his larger system, and so potentially do other lines of philosophical theory.

The patchwork reading misses the ties of presupposition or dependence that bind together the diverse theories mapped out in the Prolegomena and the six Investigations: ties I have tried to underscore along the way above. Ironically, these dependencies are themselves covered by the theory of dependent part laid out in Investigation III, and these ties bind the seven studies into a unified theory, with a unity that is itself an instance of the unity of theory set out as the ideal of "pure logic" in the Prolegomena. The *Logical Investigations* thus includes its own meta-theory uniting logic, ontology, phenomenology, and epistemology – as never before.

In this classic work, then, Husserl has laid out a philosophical *system*. The system covers a remarkable range of traditional philosophy, while launching phenomenology, with ties throughout to Husserl's salient ideals: meaning, abstraction, and intentionality.

Bibliography

Editions and translations

Husserl, E. (1900) *Logische Untersuchungen*, vol. 1: *Prolegomena zur reinen Logik*. Halle an der Salle: Max Niemeyer (2nd edn, 1913). Republished as *Husserliana* vol. XVIII: *Logische Untersuchungen*, vol. 1: *Prolegomena zur reinen Logik*, ed. E. Holenstein. The Hague: Martinus Nijhoff, 1975.

Husserl, E. (1901) *Logische Untersuchungen*, vol. 2: *Untersuchungen zur Phänomenologie und Theorie der Erkenntnis*. Halle an der Salle: Max Niemeyer (2nd edn in two parts, 1913/ 1922). Republished as *Husserliana* vol. XIX: *Logische Untersuchungen*, vol. 2: *Untersuchungen zur Phänomenologie und Theorie der Erkenntnis*, 2 vols, ed. U. Panzer. The Hague: Martinus Nijhoff, 1984.

Husserl, E. (1913) Ideen zu einer reinen Phänomenologie und phänomenologischen Philosophie. *Jahrbuch für Philosophie und phänomenologischen Forschung*, I: 1–323. Republished as *Husserliana* vol. III, ed. W. Biemel. The Hague: Martinus Nijhoff, 1950.

Husserl, E. (1969) *Ideas [pertaining to a pure phenomenology and a phenomenological philosophy, first book]: General Introduction to Pure Phenomenology*, trans. W. R. Boyce Gibson. London: George Allen and Unwin (first English edn, 1931; German original, first pub. 1913. Called *Ideas* I).

Husserl, E. (1970) *Logical Investigations*, 2 vols, trans. J. N. Findlay. London and New York: Routledge and Kegan Paul.

Husserl, E. (1994) *Early Writings in the Philosophy of Logic and Mathematics*, trans. Dallas Willard. Dordrecht: Kluwer (original German texts, from 1890 to 1901).

Studies

Hill, C. O. and Rosado Haddock, G. E. (2000) *Husserl or Frege?* LaSalle, IL: Open Court.

Mohanty, J. N. (ed.) (1977) *Readings on Edmund Husserl's Logical Investigations.* The Hague: Martinus Nijhoff.

Smith, B. (ed.) (1982) *Parts and Moments.* Munich: Philosophia Verlag.

Smith, B. and Smith, D. W. (eds) (1995) *The Cambridge Companion to Husserl.* Cambridge: Cambridge University Press.

Smith, D. W. and McIntyre, R. (1982) *Husserl and Intentionality: A Study of Mind, Meaning, and Language.* Dordrecht: Reidel.

Willard, D. (1984) *Logic and the Objectivity of Knowledge: A Study of Husserl's Early Philosophy.* Athens, OH: Ohio University Press.

Zahavi, D. and Stjernfelt, F. (eds) (2002) *100 Years of Phenomenology: Husserl's Logical Investigations Revisited.* Dordrecht and Boston: Kluwer Academic.

43

William James, *Varieties of Religious Experience* (1902)

Dimensions of Concrete Experience

Sandra B. Rosenthal

William James's *Varieties of Religious Experience* (hereafter *VRE*) is a towering work in the corpus of religious literature. The first edition was published on June 9, 1902, and in a letter to Frank Abauzit the following April, James wrote that "they have just printed and bound 1500 more making in all 11,500 copies in the first year" (*VRE*, 1985: 554). Over the next fifty years, the original publisher made forty impressions of the book, in addition to which there have been numerous reprints and foreign-language translations. It is presently available as the fifteenth volume in *The Works of William James*, which was sponsored by the American Council of Learned Societies, and is the only edition prepared and annotated in keeping with modern standards of textual scholarship.

The *Varieties* consists of the twenty Gifford Lectures James (1842–1910) delivered at the University of Edinburgh in 1901–2. This was one of the highest honors a philosopher could receive, and came to him when he had attained international reputation as one of America's most original and important thinkers. Initially James intended that the first ten lectures should portray the features of religious experience and the second ten provide a philosophical interpretation of the previous account. However, descriptive considerations occupied most of the lectures, with his philosophical conclusions condensed into just one lecture. This is a bit misleading, however, as his general philosophical stance pervades many of them.

The work is at once religious, philosophical, and psychological, the intertwining of which themes is anticipated in the generally ignored subtitle of the work: "A Study in Human Nature." It incorporates vivid, penetrating descriptions of the various dimensions of religious experience that transcend the confines of particular religions or particular worldviews within which to locate these experiences. For those interested in viewing the work in the context of James's general philosophical position, it provides an excellent example of the application of his pragmatism, pluralism, and radical empiricism to a specific area, at the same time offering insights into these interrelated facets of his philosophy. Thus, it is not only a work of unique stature in the area of religion but also a vital part of any in-depth study of his philosophy in general, and all the facets of it are intimately intertwined and mutually illuminating. As one scholar (Myers, 1986: 464) has encapsulated this diversity of dimensions, "in *Varieties* he took religious experience to academics and philosophical interpretations of that experience to the people."

Religion meant for James not particular dogmas of institutionalized theology, which he considered "second hand" religion, but a common experiential content. James's empiricist approach focused on religion as manifest in the fullness of the concrete lives and experiences of individuals rather than on religion as institutional or theological. Thus his working definition of "religion" in the *Varieties* is: "the feelings, acts, and experiences of individual men in their solitude, so far as they apprehend themselves to stand in relation to whatever they may consider the divine" (*VRE*, 1985: 34).

He finds the distinctiveness of the religious attitude, as opposed to the moral attitude, in the fact that in the religious state the assertive, strenuous attitude of the moral life has been displaced by a willingness to "close one's mouth," to let go and "be as nothing in the floods and waterspouts of God" (*VRE*, 1985: 46). In the religious attitude the individual is moved to respond "solemnly and gravely," as well as "tenderly" (*VRE*, 1985: 39).

While with morality fear is held in abeyance, in the religious state it is positively washed away, completely expunged. The religious feeling, which is not wholly volitional, but rather is attained by a surrender, is not, however, just an escape, for it carries with it the strong conviction that worldly evil has been permanently overcome; "tragedy is only provisional and partial, and shipwreck and dissolution are not the absolutely final things" (*VRE*, 1985: 407).

In the *Varieties* James first set out to provide a descriptive survey of religion which encompasses numerous and varied examples of sorts of religious experience, in the process grouping, comparing, and analyzing them. He examined reports of regeneration, religious conversion, saintliness, prayer, revelation, and mystical communion. In accounting for religious experience, he made use of scientific findings when relevant. However, his scientific psychological accounts in no way reduce religious experience to physiological or neurological "causes" but rather focus on the natural religious dimension of human nature in its fullness and the resultant beliefs to which it gives rise. In keeping with his radical empiricism, which is far richer than the then dominant classical British empiricism, James always respected the holistic concreteness of experience. Indeed, Seigfried (1990: 14) finds that his "best formulation" of his "knowing-things-together" is to be found in the *Varieties*. As James here expresses his holistic understanding of experience: "A conscious field *plus* its object as felt or, thought of *plus* an attitude towards the object *plus* the sense of self to whom the attitude belongs . . . is a *full* fact, even though it be an insignificant fact; it is of the kind to which all realities whatsoever must belong . . ." (*VRE*, 1985: 393). Thus for James, dealing with the cosmic or the general can give us only "symbols of reality," while in dealing with private, personal phenomena "we deal with realities in the completest sense of the terms" (*VRE*, 1985: 393). For this reason James was determined to reaffirm the aspect of feeling in religion and subordinate its intellectual dimension, for "individuality is founded in feeling." This focus on religious feeling is a manifestation of his concern throughout his philosophy to call attention to the irreducible dimension of feeling as a vital force in shaping the ways in which we organize experience and hence the ways in which we actively engage reality.

James focused heavily on exaggerated cases of first-hand reports of religious experience which he saw as offering the best illustrations of the features of religion, but which led to criticisms that he gave too much emphasis to extreme instances that often bordered on the abnormal. Skeptical critics viewed these as pathological cases that could be scientifically explained away. Anticipating this type of objection, he worked hard in his first lecture to prevent prejudice against such cases.

James devoted two full lectures to conversion experience, which he understood as a regeneration or transformation of the self from divided and imperfect to a higher unified self. The psychological theory of the subliminal self allowed him to give a natural account of this in terms of a subliminal or transmarginal consciousness from which a transforming power emanates. For James, however, the divided self could not achieve unification if it were the ultimate source of the power, and this issue of the "more" of religious experience becomes dominant in the final pages of the work. There is no conflict between the psychological and supernatural interpretations, but rather for James the subliminal consciousness can allow for an openness on to further realities.

James's categories of the once-born and the twice-born, borrowed from Francis W. Newman, as well as the sick soul, have become well entrenched in discussions of religion. He describes the once-born as being cheerful, viewing the world as kindly, and thinking all obstacles can be overcome by maintaining an optimistic attitude, while the twice-born are well aware of the evil of the world that cannot be overcome by humans and come to terms with the anguish and fear in their lives. The former view evil as a "mal-adjustment with things" and correctable, while the latter view evil as "more radical and general, a wrongness or vice" in one's essential nature which requires a supernatural force to correct.

Although "the religion of healthy-mindedness" of the once-born has a value in meeting psychological needs, James considers it inadequate as a philosophical doctrine because it fails to acknowledge evil as a dimension of reality; hence the most complete religions "are those in which the pessimistic elements are best developed" (*VRE*, 1985: 138). The kind of religiousness one achieves out of "quivering fear" and anxiety houses a richer mixture of attitudes than does the religion of the once-born. Both the sick soul and the divided self belong to the twice-born. However, John Smith (*VRE*, 1985: xxxii) has well noted that in discussing the sick soul James was more attentive to the variety of psychological states and moods involved, while in his discussion of the divided self the focus is on the fundamental nature of the discordance within the self and the ways in which the self can become unified in conversion. Though James seems to make a sharp dichotomy between the once-born and the twice-born, he offers a brief clarification which mitigates it. He observes that the consciousness of union with the divine that each type ultimately reaches has for the individual the same practical significance, and different temperaments "may well be allowed to get at it" through the different channels. Moreover, in numerous instances whether one is classed as once-born or twice-born is quite arbitrary (*VRE*, 1985: 385n).

The discussions of saintliness that James provides are more than descriptions, for they contain a sustained attempt to evaluate it on the basis of its fruits, both for individuals and for the entire sweep of culture. Here James, in keeping with his rejection of theological criteria, tests religion by turning to "practical common sense" and the method of empiricism. The mixture of qualities of saintliness which James elicits through his concrete descriptions are seen as a genuinely creative social force which tends toward making real a level of virtue which only the saintly assume to be possible. But he was not admiring of religious extravagances which bore no useful fruits, and his descriptions of such cases contained appropriate criticisms. Moreover, James did not consider saintly virtues to be superior in some absolute sense. Nor did he characterize the saint as some "ideal type," holding instead that any attempt to do so would be as impossible as trying to define an "ideal horse."

In the lectures on mysticism James approaches the question of the truth of religion and of mystical claims to see truth in a special way, pursuing the question as to whether such experiences furnish any warrant for the truth of supernaturalism, pantheism, or twice-bornness, all of which it favors. He concludes that while well-developed mystical states have a right to be, and usually are, authoritative for individuals who have them, they offer no authority for those standing outside them. They do, however, break down the authority of practical or rational consciousness based only on the understanding and the senses; they open up the possibility that there may be other orders of truth.

James's focus on concrete cases and the fullness of experience that can never be adequately conceptualized does not lead him to dismiss the philosophical enterprise or intellectual rationality in general. In the lecture devoted to philosophy he concludes that, though it cannot demonstrate by rational means alone the truth of religion, yet if philosophy will abandon the deductive method of arguing and turn to criticism and induction from concrete experience, thereby transforming itself from theology into a science of religion, it can be enormously useful (*VRE*, 1985: 359). What James sought was a science of religion which provided a hypothesis that was too much in keeping with the facts to be readily dismissed and which was broad enough to transcend the diversity of various religious beliefs.

James holds that there is a certain uniform deliverance to be found in all religions, which is more fundamental than the various discrepancies among their respective religious creeds and which consists of two parts: an uneasiness that there is something wrong about us as we naturally exist and a solution to this in the sense that we are saved from this through proper connection with higher powers. One becomes conscious that the higher part of one's self is continuous with a "more" of the same quality, which operates in the universe outside one's self, and with which one can keep in working contact and in this way "save himself when all his lower being has gone to pieces in the wreck." The question then arises as to the truth of this common content.

The *Varieties* manifests a complexity to James's pragmatic theory of truth which is too often ignored by his critics. Although James held that the various sorts of religious experiences provided spiritual strength and possess "enormous biological worth," he observed that these were "only psychological phenomena" and might be no more than a "subjective way of feeling things." In light of this, he found it important to deal with the question as to "What is the objective 'truth' of their content?" (*VRE*, 1985: 401). As James clarifies, "The word 'truth' is here taken to mean something additional to bare value for life, although the natural propensity of man is to believe that whatever has great value for life is thereby certified as true" (*VRE*, 1985: 401n).

The development of James's "pragmatic theory of religion" at its fullest takes place in the last chapter and the postscript to the *Varieties*, where he is concerned not with "mere utility" but with the intellectual content itself. The question of truth arises in relation to the "more of the same quality" with which the individual's higher self seems to enter into harmonious relation. What comes into play in the diverse interpretations of the objects of the religious attitude is what James calls "over-belief," belief in the nature of the more or beyond which is not within the experience itself but is rather an over-belief as to the nature of that with which in religious experience we feel ourselves connected. The various theologies as well as James's own theistic belief, which comes to light here, all agree that the "more" does really exist, though they differ in the various specifics attached to this real existence. Religion houses the belief that there is an unseen order and that our supreme good lies in harmoniously adjusting ourselves to it; the natural world is not exhaustive of reality.

His approach to the truth of religious belief was in keeping both with the experimental method embraced by his pragmatism and with his radical empiricism. Religion cannot be justified by some privileged origin, nor can it be reduced to some bodily state. Rather, it must be evaluated in the way everything must be evaluated, by the way its consequences make a difference in some future. The over-belief is an experimental hypothesis, with features similar to those "a good hypothesis in science must have" (*VRE*, 1985: 407). As in the experimental method used by science, the over-belief or hypothesis is the creative, interpretive stance from which one views so-called objective evidence or facts. This hypothesis directs our continuing activity. Finally, the test of its truth is via consequences: does the hypothesis work in positing and accounting for facts beyond those predicted by natural science? And, as James has made quite clear, these consequences are not merely the production of social utility or types of subjective states.

The world interpreted religiously is richer, more intricately built, than the reality that science recognizes. Reality has a constitution different in some ways than the materialistic world recognized by science, such that different events can be expected in it and different conduct is required. New facts are postulated, which are verifiable or falsifiable in the future, thus withstanding the pragmatic test of truth. This is James's "thoroughly 'pragmatic' view of religion" (*VRE*, 1985: 408). For James, however, no reality stands over against the individual as an objective truth to be apprehended in its pristine purity. Rather, facts exist for us within an interpretive interactive context of our ways of engaging the world. "We count and name whatever lies along the special lines we trace, whilst the other things and the untraced lines are neither named nor counted" (*VRE*, 1985: 346n). We get interested in certain kinds of arrangements, and whenever we find them within experience they hold our attention. There is selectivity in the way in which we organize and view the world.

The world viewed from the religious perspective is not merely the ordinary world seen from a different perspective, the whole of nature cast in a different light. In contrast to this "universalistic supernaturalism," which leaves the "laws of life" just as science finds them, with no hope of remedying bad results, James calls his position "piecemeal super-naturalism" (*VRE*, 1985: 409): it admits miracles and providential leanings, accepts the causal force of the ideal realm as determining details of the world. It is this piecemeal supernaturalism which, he holds, maintains the essence of practical religion.

In keeping with his pragmatic understanding of a pluralistic, unfinished, "restless" universe, James thought any final philosophy of religion must seriously consider a pluralistic hypothesis. His radical empiricism, which embraces continuity and the direct experience of "felt relations" rather than merely the traditional discrete data of British empiricism, led him to accept a wide range of experienced and continuous relations. Far from leading him to some monistic position, however, it was part and parcel of his commitment to pluralism. For James, novelty and pluralism are built into the very nature of the world. All that the facts require is that the power be other than and larger then our conscious selves. It need be neither infinite nor solitary. As John McDermott (James, 1977: xlix) observes, James sees a pluralistic, unfinished universe as "liberating with regard to the human situation."

Ralph Barton Perry (in Seigfried, 1990: 260–1), commenting on James's letter to a friend concerning the *Varieties* (to Pauline Goldmark, August 1, 1902), observes that, although James wrote that "both God's friends and his enemies apparently find in it ample justification for their differing views," yet the impression that is left on the reader "is that God's friends get much the best of it." While this impression does seem to be accurate, James in this work captures dimensions of concrete human existence in its full richness which must resonate, in some sense, with both "God's friends and his enemies."

Bibliography

Editions

James, William (1977) *The Writings of William James*, ed. John J. McDermott. Chicago: University of Chicago Press (orig. pub. 1967).
James, William (1985) *The Varieties of Religious Experience*. In *The Works of William James*, vol. 15, ed. Frederick H. Burkhardt. Cambridge, MA: Harvard University Press.

Studies

Myers, Gerald E. (1986) *William James: His Life and Thought*. New Haven, CT: Yale University Press.
Perry, Ralph B. (1996) *The Thought and Character of William James*. Nashville, TN: Vanderbilt University Press (orig. pub. 1948).
Seigfried, Charlene H. (ed.) (1990) *William James's Radical Reconstruction of Philosophy*. Albany, NY: State University of New York Press.

44

G. E. Moore, *Principia Ethica* (1903)

Ethical Analysis and Aesthetic Ideals

Thomas Baldwin

Principia Ethica was published in 1903 when G. E. Moore (1873–1958) was aged thirty. It remains his most famous book (it is the only one currently in print). Moore was then acquiring a reputation as a leader of the new Cambridge school of analytical realism which, at the start of the twentieth century, successfully challenged the hegemony of absolute idealism within British philosophy.

Moore begins *Principia Ethica* by maintaining that the difficulties and disagreements which are characteristic of ethics have one "very simple cause," namely a failure to undertake the work of "analysis and distinction" which is necessary to differentiate the questions to which inquiries in ethics should provide an answer. In particular, Moore argues, almost all moral philosophers have been guilty of mistaking questions concerning actions which are "right" for questions concerning the kinds of thing that have "intrinsic value." This is a mistake, Moore holds, because there can be no justification for beliefs of the latter type since truths concerning intrinsic value are self-evident, whereas beliefs concerning what it is right to do always stand in need of a justification which shows how an action which is right brings into existence things that have intrinsic value.

Three points stand out from this opening discussion. First, Moore's criticism of others for their lack of preliminary analysis indicates the importance that he attaches to the work of analysis and his faith that, once this work has been completed successfully, ethics should give rise to no significant disagreements and difficulties. Second, Moore's emphasis on intrinsic value shows that he takes this to be the fundamental concept of ethics. Third, Moore's contrast between questions concerning what it is right to do and questions of intrinsic value shows that right and wrong are not, for him, intrinsic values.

These three points suggest much of the substance of the book. The first point is characteristic of Moore's Cartesian philosophical method, in which he relies on analysis to clarify the questions at issue in such a way that he can present his main ethical thesis as "so obvious, that it runs the risk of seeming to be a platitude" (¶113). In truth the thesis is far from platitudinous, for it is the claim that "by far the most valuable things, which we can know or imagine, are certain states of consciousness, which may be roughly described as the pleasures of human intercourse and the enjoyment of beautiful objects" (¶113). I return below to this thesis, but the point to grasp here is that Moore's method precludes him from offering any argument for it. The result is that, in so far as Moore does present interesting arguments, these belong to the preliminary analysis of ethical questions; the substantive ethical theory itself is supposed to be too obvious to admit of any argument or justification.

The second point, concerning the fundamental status of the concept of intrinsic value, is indeed the main point of interest in Moore's preliminary analysis. The main conclusion Moore seeks to establish here is that intrinsic value is unanalyzable. Thus the analytic method is used to identify that which is unanalyzable, so that questions involving these concepts can be used as a basis for answering further questions whose concepts are analyzable. The final point, concerning the distinction between questions about right action and questions about intrinsic value, is one application of the previous point: what it is right to do depends upon the kinds of thing with intrinsic value and the connections (causal and constitutive) between the actions available to one and the existence of things with intrinsic value.

Goodness

Moore holds that goodness is the only intrinsic value. In discussing this point he contrasts things that are "intrinsically good" with things that are only "good as means" or "good as a part" in a way which suggests at first that he holds that there are three kinds of goodness. But the point of these contrasts is that things which are only good as means or good as parts are not, as he puts it, good *in themselves*. Things which are only "good as means," such as money, are things whose goodness resides only in their intrinsically good consequences; and things that are merely "good as a part" contribute to the intrinsic goodness of some complex situation of which they are a part without being themselves intrinsically good. Moore holds that knowledge is in this sense often good as a part of intrinsically good complex states of mind (for example, emotions such as love) despite not being good in itself. In both cases, therefore, only the one fundamental form of goodness is in play, and within *Principia Ethica* this is the only intrinsic value.

These two contrasts imply that a thing's intrinsic goodness is independent of its causal and constitutive relationships; indeed, it is for Moore independent of all the thing's relations: in this sense "intrinsic" implies "non-relational." But, in another sense, intrinsic value is inherently relational. For it comes in degrees and the basic structure of value is one of the relative intrinsic value of things, positive (i.e., goodness) or negative (i.e., badness). Although a thing's degree of intrinsic value is independent of its relationships, it is not, for Moore, an altogether independent quality of the thing, like its color or shape. As Moore puts it, a thing's intrinsic value is not a "part" of it and does not contribute to its "substance" in the way in which its natural qualities do (¶26). Instead, Moore implies, a thing's intrinsic value depends upon the kind of thing it is. In the preface to the second edition of *Principia Ethica* he maintains that a thing's intrinsic value depends upon its "intrinsic nature" without itself contributing to it. So the fundamental truths concerning intrinsic value are truths concerning the relative intrinsic value of different kinds of thing. These truths, Moore holds, are abstract necessary truths, comparable to the truths of arithmetic, independent of all questions concerning what actually exists (¶73–4).

The Naturalistic Fallacy

Moore says that the denial of this doctrine, i.e., the affirmation that the fundamental truths concerning intrinsic value concern the nature of what actually exists, is "the root of the naturalistic fallacy" (¶73). This introduces us to the most famous claim of *Principia Ethica*, the thesis that almost all previous ethical theories have been guilty of a fallacy (he exempts from this charge just Plato and his teacher, Henry Sidgwick), which he calls the "naturalistic fallacy." Thus he represents his own position as a new start, one which, by identifying and avoiding this fallacy, puts ethics on a "scientific" foundation for the first time; hence the title of the book, with its obvious attempt to remind the reader of Newton's *Principia*. This emphasis on science implies, however, no substantive dependence of ethics upon the natural sciences; that would involve precisely the naturalistic fallacy. Instead, Moore has in mind the Cartesian conception of science, which leads him to claim that his position provides, for the first time, "a clear discussion of the fundamental principles of Ethics, and a statement of the ultimate reasons why one way of acting should be considered better than another" (¶33).

What, then, is the fallacy which subverts almost all previous ethical theories? It is the misrepresentation of the fundamental truths concerning the intrinsic value of different kinds of things as an analysis or definition of intrinsic value. One implication of such a definition is that all other truths concerning intrinsic value are regarded as reducible to truths of the type specified in the definition. Because the standard examples of such theories define intrinsic value by reference to "natural" properties (for example, by defining goodness as that which we desire to desire, so that truths concerning intrinsic value are reduced to truths concerning our psychology), Moore calls this fallacy the "naturalistic fallacy." But, as he makes clear, someone who defines goodness in theological terms, for example, as that which is willed by God, commits essentially the same fallacy although this definition is "metaphysical" and not "naturalistic." In both cases, because it is denied that there are any fundamental truths concerning the intrinsic value of different kinds of things, all questions concerning intrinsic value are reduced to questions concerning the nature of what "actually exists" – be it human psychology or the will of God.

Because the thesis that it is a "fallacy" to define intrinsic value raises a question concerning the analysis of ethical questions, arguments in its favor are, for Moore, legitimate. The main argument Moore advances in support of his thesis has become known as the "open question" argument, to the effect that once we consider any alleged definition of intrinsic value, we can readily recognize that the truth of the underlying hypothesis remains an "open question" in a way which is incompatible with its being simply a matter of definition (¶ 14). Thus Moore argues that the hypothesis that one can define what it is for something to be intrinsically good by saying that it is something which we desire to desire cannot be correct since we can see that, whereas it is not an open question whether something which we desire to desire is something which we desire to desire, it is inescapably a significant question whether something which we desire to desire is really good (¶ 13).

Sometimes Moore suggests that we can tell that an alleged definition is spurious just because we can sensibly doubt it; but this sets the standard for definitions too high, and his more considered claim is that what undermines the possibility of a definition of intrinsic value is the fact that we persist in finding the truth of any alleged definition a significant question (¶ 24). Some later philosophers have claimed that even this argument sets the standard for definitions too high, since "synthetic" definitions of the kind established in the natural sciences (e.g., water = H_2O) show us that there can be definitions which are also significant truths; but whether these provide a model for the positions Moore opposed remains disputed.

Ethical Non-naturalism

Moore connects the thesis that intrinsic value is indefinable with the further claim that it is not itself a "natural" or a "metaphysical" property. In truth these points are distinct: the first is an anti-reductive thesis, the second a further thesis about the kind of property intrinsic value is. One can endorse Moore's anti-reductionism while still holding that intrinsic value is a natural or metaphysical property. Indeed, contrary to Moore's characterization of other ethical theories, positions of this kind are common: Aristotle's ethical theory is a case of the former and most theologies exemplify the latter. Moore, however, takes the further step of maintaining that intrinsic value is not a natural property. Indeed, it is only because he takes this further step that he can conclude that the fundamental truths concerning intrinsic value are altogether independent of questions concerning what actually exists.

Principia Ethica does not contain any straightforward arguments for this further claim which Moore tends to confuse with his anti-reductive thesis. But his thesis that goodness is not a natural property because it does not contribute to the "substance," i.e., the intrinsic nature, of good things (¶ 26) suggests a line of thought here – that if goodness were a natural property it would play an explanatory role in the understanding of good things, whereas in truth their goodness is only an inherently "consequential" property, and not an explanatory one at all. Whether this is altogether persuasive is a question that must be left open here; it will certainly be disputed by those "virtue theorists" who take the virtues and vices to be fundamental, since these are supposed to be both explanatory and ethical.

Intuitionism

Moore's ethical non-naturalism is a metaphysical doctrine concerning value. It is closely connected to the epistemological doctrine known as intuitionism. Moore calls his fundamental truths concerning intrinsic value "intuitions" because our knowledge of them cannot be justified by reference to knowledge of other truths; these truths are to be self-evident if evident at all. Moore stresses, however, that his talk of "intuition" is not intended to imply a special cognitive faculty. Instead, he holds that the way to gain knowledge of intrinsic value is to practice a method of "reflective isolation," by which we "consider what things are such that, if they existed *by themselves*, in absolute isolation, we should yet judge their existence to be good" (¶112).

It is not obvious that this method is a reliable way of gaining ethical knowledge. But it does show well the distinctiveness of Moore's position: on the one hand, he does not aspire to the type of "rational intuition" Sidgwick sought. Moore denies that ethical truths are truths of reason in this sense. On the other hand, Moore equally rejects any appeal to common-sense "intuitions" concerning right and wrong. For, he holds, because judgments of this type are not judgments of intrinsic value they cannot be self-evident. So Moore aims to provide an intuitionist position which is intermediate between these two.

Ideal Utilitarianism

As we have seen, Moore holds in *Principia Ethica* that judgments concerning right and wrong are not judgments of intrinsic value; instead, he defines them by reference to judgments concerning goodness: "'I am morally bound to perform this action,'" he writes, "is identical with the assertion 'This action will produce the greatest amount of good in the Universe'" (¶89). As Russell immediately pointed out to him, this claim is vulnerable to his own "open question" argument: the truth of this account of moral obligation is not a matter of definition alone. As a result, Moore switched thereafter to the more familiar thesis that we ought to act in whatever way has the best consequences, where this is not a matter of definition, but a substantive moral theory. One implication of this revision is that Moore had to accept that there is another type of intrinsic value: moral obligation.

Moore's argument for his "ideal" utilitarian position is just that it is absurd to hold that one might be doing what one ought to do even though the action involved did not have the best available consequences. Moore's critics have argued otherwise, on the grounds that our responsibilities are restricted and do not include a requirement to maximize "the . . . amount of good in the Universe." But the distinctive feature of Moore's position, as compared with classical utilitarianism, is that it allows for a variety of intrinsically good ends; thus as well as the causal-consequentialist reasoning characteristic of utilitarian moral theories, determining what one ought to do requires a comparative assessment of the relative value of the various intrinsic goods which might be affected by one's choice of action. Hence, although the position avoids the narrow emphasis on the maximization of happiness characteristic of classical utilitarianism, it no longer makes it at all straightforward to decide what one ought to do. Indeed, Moore complicates matters further by introducing a "principle of organic unities" according to which the value of a complex situation is not determined by the value of its constituent elements; there is also, according to Moore, an ever-present possibility of a further holistic aspect, the extra intrinsic value "as a whole" of the situation. While this principle enables him to accommodate some moral judgments that are characteristically troublesome for utilitarians, it makes it all the clearer that his position does not offer any method for calculating what one ought to do.

Moore himself draws this conclusion in an exaggerated form: "we can never have any reason to suppose that an action is our duty" (¶91). Thus Moore is a moral skeptic: we lack knowledge of what we ought to do. But, Moore affirms, we can arrive at some reasonable beliefs, in particular that, by and large, we ought to act in accordance with the rules of conventional morality. This is because, he thinks, adherence to these rules is necessary for the existence of "civilised society," which is in turn a necessary condition of the existence of any significant intrinsic goods (¶95). This defense of conventional morality is not, however, argued for in any detail, and was the aspect of Moore's theory which his friends within the Bloomsbury Group, such as Maynard Keynes and Lytton Strachey, did not accept.

The Ideal

One of the odd features of *Principia Ethica* is that Moore's endorsement of conventional morality precedes his account of "the ideal," his account of the things which are good and evil. Given his ideal utilitarianism, one would have expected an account of morality to be dependent upon the identification of intrinsic value, in the way he had suggested in his preface. It is, however, his moral skepticism which explains this reversal in the order of exposition; and this point equally helps to explain the way in which his account of the ideal is so detached from the concerns of ordinary morality.

Moore holds that there are indefinitely many kinds of things that are intrinsically good and evil; this is indeed one implication of the principle of organic unities. But he singles out three for special emphasis: pain (¶127), which is in itself a great evil; the enjoyment of beautiful objects (¶113); and "the love of love," which is "far the most valuable good we know, and far more valuable than mere love of beauty" (¶122). All these three involve either pleasure or pain; so although Moore is not a hedonist in the tradition of classical utilitarianism, his favored goods and evils belong within the hedonist tradition. What is chiefly unsatisfactory about the resulting position, however, is that Moore cannot allow himself to provide any argument for this ideal, since it is supposed to be self-evident. Hence, although it suggests a certain conception of human life and aesthetic community, which which was indeed subsequently practiced within the Bloomsbury Group, these considerations do not enter into his discussion.

As a result, Moore's aesthetic ideal remains undeveloped in *Principia Ethica*. None the less, *Principia Ethica* remains a seminal reference point for twentieth-century ethics. It established a distinctively analytical approach to the metaphysics of value and gave a strong impetus to the priority assigned to "meta-ethical" questions which was characteristic of much twentieth-century British moral philosophy. In particular, the thesis that there is a "naturalistic fallacy" at the heart of traditional ethics has influenced much subsequent discussion and debate.

Bibliography

Editions

Moore, G. E. (1903) *Principia Ethica*. Cambridge: Cambridge University Press.

Moore, G. E. (1912) *Ethics*. London: Williams and Norgate.

Moore, G. E. (1942) A reply to my critics. In P. A. Schilpp (ed.), *The Philosophy of G. E. Moore*, pp. 535–627. LaSalle, IL: Open Court.

Moore, G. E. (1993a) *Principia Ethica*, rev. edn. Cambridge: Cambridge University Press.

Moore, G. E. (1993b) The conception of intrinsic value. In G. E. Moore, *Principia Ethica*, rev. edn, pp. 280–98. Cambridge: Cambridge University Press.

Studies and references

Baldwin, T. R. (1990) *G. E. Moore*. London: Routledge.

Keynes, J. M. (1949) My early beliefs. In *Two Memoirs*. London: Hart-Davis.

Sylvester, R. P. (1990) *The Moral Philosophy of G. E. Moore*. Philadelphia: Temple University Press.

45

Charles Sanders Peirce, *1903 Harvard Lectures on Pragmatism*

The Practice of Inquiry

Vincent Colapietro

Three years after C. S. Peirce (1839–1914) delivered his *Lectures on Pragmatism*, William James famously described them as "flashes of brilliant light relieved against Cimmerian darkness!" (James, 1981: 10). This seems, however, too slighting. For Peirce's series of lectures is one of the most indispensable documents for understanding his mature philosophy; moreover, it represents a pivotal moment in the history of pragmatism, the upshot of which only becomes clearer when two years later Peirce publicly distanced himself from James and F. C. S. Schiller by announcing the birth of "pragmaticism" (a word "ugly enough to be safe from kidnappers" [Peirce, 1934: 5.414]).

Peirce, who in 1903 was living a somewhat reclusive life, clearly wanted to take full advantage of the rare opportunity of presenting his most central ideas to a learned audience. He could not confine himself to a narrowly circumscribed topic, but outlined the entire philosophical system. Though his substantive metaphysical and cosmological ideas are largely in the background, tychism, synechism, and evolutionism are at times unmistakably visible. In contrast, some of his main methodological preoccupations occupy center stage.

The introductory lecture begins by recalling Peirce's own formulation of the pragmatic maxim and proceeds by stressing the need to go beyond uncritical reliance upon this logical directive to a defense of its truth. It concludes by invoking the name of Hegel. Peirce reminds his listeners that "we do not come to this inquiry [into the truth of pragmatism] any more than anybody comes to any inquiry in that blank state that lawyers pretend to insist upon as desirable" (in *The Essential Peirce* [henceforth *EP*], 2: 142). We come to this inquiry, in general, as implicated inquirers and, in particular, as ones inclined toward the presumption that there is enough truth in pragmatism to render worthwhile a painstaking examination of its own pragmatic meaning. We are, willy-nilly, implicated in practices of searching for answers to questions, for means of appeasing the uneasiness of often pressing, persistent doubts; and we are, as a result, molded into agents committed (however unconsciously) to a set of norms and ideals. To conceive inquiry in this way points to ethics, since investigation is a manner of comporting ourselves that demands of investigators conscientious and deliberative decisions of how to carry on the tasks taken up by them. In turn, ethics points to aesthetics in the sense of a sustained, systematic reflection on what is inherently admirable (or, as Peirce occasionally puts it, adorable, i.e., worthy of adoration).

The three normative sciences of *logic* (the investigation of self-controlled inquiry), *ethics* (the investigation of self-controlled conduct generally), and *aesthetics* (the determination of that which is intrinsically worth while) are, however, dependent on a logically prior investigation. Their work would be utterly blind and groping were it not for a set of clues by which to relate these disciplines to one another but also to suggest possible courses of inquiry, systems of relationship, and ways of guessing. In Peirce's judgment, phenomenology provides nothing less than such a set of clues.

The movement of Peirce's thought in these lectures is, beginning with Lecture II, from phenomenology to normative science. Lectures II, III, and IV make up the phenomenological prolegomena for Peirce's defense of pragmatism, whereas Lectures V, VI, and VII make up the normative prolegomena. Interspersed in the earlier lectures we catch glimpses of both the system of sciences in which philosophy in its totality (including cosmology and metaphysics) is to be located *and* the system of philosophy in which the doctrine of pragmatism, in its varied senses, is itself to be situated.

Accordingly, these lectures are best interpreted as prolegomena for a defense (or "proof") of pragmatism, rather than as an attempt to defend fully this doctrine. They aim to make plausible the need for a revision of what constitutes "proof" and, closely allied to this, what constitutes a sufficiently comprehensive framework for describing, analyzing, and assessing the three modes of inference (deduction, induction, and abduction) and, more inclusively, the various forms of successful inquiry. The incomparable successes of such experimental sciences as physics and chemistry reveal that knowing is, at bottom, a game of guessing; thus, the theory of inquiry ought to make intelligible the efficacy of these practices. It can only do so by according the framing of hypotheses a more central place than logicians have yet granted this process. In addition, a sufficiently comprehensive framework for the description, analysis, and evaluation of the modes of argumentation or inference needs to be nothing less than a truly general theory of signs. In sum, formulating a *logic of abduction* becomes the most urgent task for any logic able to account for what have emerged as the most authoritative modes of human knowing. But developing *a theory of signs* becomes an equally pressing matter for anyone committed to illuminating how the continuous renovation and critical monitoring of diverse signs makes possible the advance of science, the growth of knowledge.

In "What Pragmatism Is," "Issues of Pragmaticism," and numerous unpublished manuscripts, though not so much in these 1903 lectures, the link between pragmatism and semiotic is highlighted. In his lectures on pragmatism, the emphasis falls on the logic of hypothesis, not the theory of signs. The heuristic function of Peirce's three categories resides in their capacity to goad and guide inquiry; and this means their power to widen the field of imaginable hypotheses, by recursively generating an expanding array of formal possibilities. Simply put, the categories provide invaluable clues for what guesses to make. So understood, it is explicable why they occupy such an important place in what are after all methodological explorations.

Pragmatism is a guess made by an inquirer for how he or she and others ought to conduct inquiry. Its validation can only be circular, for it involves a guess concerning the logic of guessing; but its circularity must not be too narrow, for otherwise the "proof" of pragmatism will be utterly vacuous or viciously circular (or both!). It is no surprise, then, that Peirce found it so difficult to present in a persuasive or even intelligible form his apologia for pragmatism. In so far as the lectures make little formal use of his semiotic, they are potentially quite misleading (for Peirce's general theory of signs is vital to his radical revision of logic and any compelling defense of pragmatism). But, in so far as they give a central role to his categories, they help us see the systematic character of not only Peirce's substantive metaphysics but also his methodological investigations, at the center of which is, in one or more senses, his pragmatism. It is just this aspect of his methodology that Peirce brings forth in his 1903 lectures.

Thus, these lectures are not what they initially announce themselves to be. Nor are they what they superficially appear to be. They *are* a significant contribution to Peirce's quest of quests, his inquiry into the conditions for the success of quite diverse forms of inquiries. They imply a virtue theory of inquiry: the success of our investigations depends significantly upon the cultivation of a mutually supportive set of dispositions (truly quite plain or ordinary – though far from commonplace! – virtues, such as humility, courage, hope, tolerance, veracity, and a sense of fallibility). They encompass a normative theory of inference and, herein, a pragmatic account of abduction. Finally, they underwrite an emphatically communal approach to knowing: "one man's experience is nothing, if it stands alone. If he sees what others cannot, we call it hallucination. It is not 'my' experience, but 'our' experience that has to be thought of; and this 'us' has indefinite possibilities" (Peirce, 1934: 5.402, n3).

In the opening paragraphs Peirce creates the impression that he is interested in assessing the logical warrants for adopting the pragmatic maxim. But the focus shifts away from assessing these warrants. The very meaning of pragmatism also appears to be altered in the course of these presentations: what is introduced as simply a maxim pertaining to the meaning of terms playing key roles in objective investigations becomes in the final lecture nothing less than the "logic of abduction." The scope of this doctrine thus expands to include a previously unrecognized mode of inference. The framing of fruitful hypotheses takes its rightful place alongside the drawing of necessary inferences (deduction) and the weighting of relative likelihood (induction). There is certainly a connection between the narrower and wider conceptions of pragmatism: the pragmatic clarification of meaning is a crucial part of the fallible conduct of inquiry and, in turn, the explicitly pragmatic formulation of our hypotheses is the innermost center of our potentially instructive guesses.

Yet even this fails to convey the scope of Peirce's pragmatism as enlarged in these lectures. The penultimate paragraph of the last lecture alludes to the most appropriate context in which to situate Peircean pragmatism, the context of purposive action and by implication human agency ("The elements of every concept enter into *logical* thought at the gate of perception and make their exit at the gate of purposive action; whatever cannot show its passports at both those gates is to be arrested as unauthorized by reason"; *EP*, 2: 241, emphasis added). The ideal of a life shaped in accord with the *summum bonum* – the continuous growth of concrete reasonableness – finds one of its most arresting expressions in the irreducibly communal forms of experimental inquiry, in the actual life of some recognizable scientific community. We discern, at the heart of such communities, the self-critical participation of fallible agents in the continuing work of an historical community animated by a distinctive form of *eros*. Peirce's lectures on pragmatism express the sensibility of one whose life has been shaped by his devotion to this ideal.

Peirce initially steps to the podium of these lectures in the roles of logician and mathematician. Two years later he kisses his child goodbye and christens his doctrine "pragmaticism." The logician is trying to wrest his own doctrine from the clutches of *littérateurs* and humanists who have very little patience for subtle distinctions and formal argumentation (*EP*, 2: 334). In a letter to James (March 7, 1904), he concedes that the "humanistic element of pragmatism is very true and important and impressive" but insists that the doctrine cannot be *proved* in that way; and though the "present generation likes to skip proofs" the logically inclined Peirce could not help but judge harshly this tendency. So he approaches his topic by stressing at the outset that his goal is to submit to his auditors' judgment "in half a dozen [following] lectures an examination of the *pros* and *cons* of pragmatism by means of which I hope to show you the result of allowing to both *pro* and *con* their full legitimate values" (*EP*, 2: 133–4). In brief, his principal concern is to examine the *logical* case to be made for the pragmatic approach.

Peirce was animated by purposes other than that of proving the validity of pragmatism. It is, indeed, likely that he was principally concerned to seize this opportunity to sketch a comprehensive account of his philosophical system, at the heart of which is his categoreal scheme. He appears to take the lectures as an occasion to win a hearing for his categories but also for the system of sciences structured by the recursive use of these categories. Thus, his system of sciences is an exemplification of the power of his categories, for these categories allow him to organize the bewildering array of scientific pursuits into a systematic whole. This organization itself serves the purpose of inquiry: it helps inquirers understand the deeper nature of their own endeavors and also helps them to identify the investigations with which their own is most closely allied, hence the ones from which they might fruitfully borrow. Peirce's categories are tools of inquiry useful for countless purposes, including mapping the terrain of not only historically developed disciplines but also potentially fruitful ones, perhaps even simply imaginable ones (for example, Peirce's own projected science of signs).

Somewhat surprisingly, then (especially given his early emphasis on weighing the *pros* and *cons* of the case), Peirce's lectures on pragmatism offer not so much a proof of this doctrine as an articulation and application of his categories. This would obviously explain the detailed attention paid in Lecture II to phenomenology, understood as a doctrine of categories. It would also make clear the amount of attention paid in Lecture III to defining each of his three categories and, then in Lecture IV, using them to classify various systems of metaphysics. But this appears to leave unexplained the last three chapters. If the heuristic function of Peirce's categoreal scheme, however, is taken seriously (if we interpret his categories mainly as tools of inquiry), then these chapters too become explicable. In having a heuristic function, Peirce's categories have a normative status: they *ought* to goad and guide inquiry. Accordingly, the most basic questions concerning normative discourse are unavoidable. (What are the most basic forms of such discourse? What, in anything, is the relationship among these forms? What are the defining foci of these normative discourses or, in Peirce's lexicon, sciences?) So, after explaining and illustrating his categories phenomenologically and then metaphysically, Peirce turns in Lecture V to a detailed discussion of the normative sciences. The relationship among the normative sciences of logic, ethics, and aesthetics is itself established by means of the categories.

At the outset of these lectures, then, Peirce recalls the seemingly simple maxim he proposed in 1878 for helping us to become clearer about what we mean when we use such terms as *hardness, weight, force,* or *reality.* He however moves very quickly into a dense discussion, packed with mathematical equations, of the pragmatic meaning of probability. Part of his purpose is to show that the only appropriate way of dealing with probability is in explicitly mathematical terms. Another part seems to be to suggest that the pragmatic clarification of this term cannot be attained through the translation of one mode of symbols into another mode ("Pragmatism is completely volatilized if you admit that sort of practicality"; *EP,* 2: 141). One gets the sense that Peirce is, to some extent, showing off: it is almost as if he wants to lose his audience in the technicalities of his treatment of probability. But he is not simply showing off; he is making what for him is a crucial point – the severe discipline of mathematics is indispensable for the successful execution of philosophy. Only such discipline instills the requisite sense of exactitude and rigor as well as the ability to handle utterly abstract conceptions, exceedingly complex relationships of a purely formal character, and recursive operations. A mind disciplined in mathematics is one suited to take up the task of phenomenology, at least in Peirce's sense. Though necessary, this discipline is not sufficient. In Lecture II, then, Peirce notes that a finely attuned *aesthetic* receptivity or attentiveness is even more valuable. Phenomenologists need first and foremost the faculty of seeing what stares them in the face, "unreplaced by any interpretation" (*EP,* 2: 147). Peirce immediately adds that: "This is the faculty of the artist who sees for example the apparent colors of nature [just] *as they appear*" (emphasis added).

So, precisely what was left implicit in his inaugural presentation of pragmatism is made more explicit in this mature articulation, for the doctrine of categories pervades and structures Peirce's lectures on pragmatism. While the deletion of his categories makes for an economy of presentation and hence ease of understanding, their inclusion contributes to the fullness of exposition and thus adequacy of understanding.

Peirce's lectures embody one of the most compelling formulations of his mature thought. In them, readers glimpse Peirce's architectonic conception of philosophical inquiry, embedded in the broader context of an elaborate classification of the various sciences. This itself reflects the influence of Kant and expresses Peirce's identification with scientists and, by implication, his antipathy to *littérateurs.* Peirce's growing appreciation of the normative sciences, especially in their intimate relationship to one other, is also discernible in these lectures. As a maxim of logic, pragmatism calls for an understanding of the discipline of logic precisely as a normative science. In turn, an understanding of this specific normative science calls for a general understanding of the formally normative disciplines of logic, ethics, and aesthetics as well as a precise account of the connections among these disciplines. In his scheme, philosophy is located between mathematics and those disciplines most readily identified as sciences in the narrow modern sense (for example, physics, chemistry, biology, and psychology).

All of the main branches of philosophical inquiry (phenomenology, the normative sciences of logic, ethics, and aesthetics, and metaphysics) are positive sciences, distinguished at one end from mathematics (the most abstract of all the sciences) by making categorical (not simply hypothetical) assertions about the actual world and at the other end from the special (or *idioscopic*) sciences. Moreover, Peirce ranks, among the distinctively philosophical disciplines, three normative sciences (logic, ethics, and aesthetics). Since pragmatism is, in its most exact meaning, a maxim of logic designed to assist us in clarifying abstract conceptions and otherwise insufficiently clear notions, an understanding of normative science in general and logical analysis is helpful. Peirce is offering a normative account of a specific form of human conduct, thought in its strictly logical sense: conduct in general is self-controlled action, whereas inquiry is self-controlled thought. The insistence that, at root, thinking is a mode of conduct is central to Peirce's pragmatism; so, too, is his anti-psychologistic approach to logical operations.

Peirce's lectures on pragmatism are invaluable in aiding us to see how he saw his own undertakings. In reference to his intellectual predecessors, he stresses his affinity with Aristotle, Kant, and Reid; exhibits his ambivalence toward Hegel; and reveals his indebtedness to medieval authors. In reference to the distinct theoretical endeavors aiming at truth in its (broadly) scientific sense, he presents pragmatism as a logical doctrine but also logic as a normative science and, thus, a communal practice devoted to identifying, (when appropriate) formalizing, and refining the norms and ideals constitutive of human inquiry in its myriad forms. Peirce the logician looked to phenomenology for a set of categories to be used recursively in guiding and goading his inquiry into inquiry. Moreover, he traced the trajectory from logic to metaphysics and, within normative science itself, from logic through ethics to aesthetics. He did so from the perspective of one who felt compelled to acknowledge his indebtedness and own up to his inheritance.

Bibliography

Editions

Peirce, C. S. (1934) *The Collected Papers of Charles Sanders Peirce*, vol. 5: *Pragmatism and Pragmaticism*, ed. Paul Weiss and Charles Hartshorne. Cambridge, MA: Harvard University Press.

Peirce, C. S. (1997) *Pragmatism as a Principle and Method of Right Thinking: The 1903 Harvard Lectures on Pragmatism*, ed. Patricia Ann Turrisi. Albany, NY: State University of New York Press.

Peirce, C. S. (1998) *The Essential Peirce Selected Philosophical Writings*, vol. 2: *1893–1913*, ed. the Peirce Edition Project. Bloomington, IN: Indiana University Press.

Peirce, C. S. (1999) *The Essential Peirce: Selected Philosophical Writings*, vol. 1: *1867–1893*, ed. Nathan Houser and Christian Kloesel. Bloomington, IN: Indiana University Press.

Studies and references

Anderson, Douglas R. (1995) *Strands of System: The Philosophy of Charles Peirce.* West Lafayette, IN: Purdue University Press.

Apel, Karl-Otto (1981) *Charles S. Peirce: From Pragmatism to Pragmaticism,* trans. John Michael Krois. Amherst, MA: University of Massachusetts Press.

Brent, Joseph (1998) *Charles Sanders Peirce: A Life.* Bloomington, IN: Indiana University Press.

Colapietro, Vincent M. (1989) *Peirce's Approach to the Self.* Albany, NY: State University of New York Press.

Fisch, Max H. (1986) *Peirce, Semeiotic, and Pragmatism: Essays by Max H. Fisch,* ed. Kenneth Laine Ketner and Christian J. W. Kloesel. Bloomington, IN: Indiana University Press.

Hausman, Carl R. (1993) *Charles S. Peirce's Evolutionary Philosophy.* New York: Cambridge University Press.

Hookway, Christopher (2000) *Truth, Rationality, and Pragmatism: Themes from Peirce.* Oxford: Clarendon Press.

James, William (1981) *Pragmatism.* Cambridge, MA: Harvard University Press.

Kent, Beverley (1987) *Charles S. Peirce: Logic and the Classification of the Sciences.* Kingston and Montreal: McGill-Queen's University Press.

Ketner, Kenneth Laine (ed.) (1995) *Peirce and Contemporary Thought: Philosophical Inquiries.* New York: Fordham University Press.

Murphey, Murray (1993) *The Development of Peirce's Philosophy.* Indianapolis, IN: Hackett.

Potter, Vincent G. (1997) *Charles S. Peirce: On Norms and Ideals.* New York: Fordham University Press.

Rosenthal, Sandra B. (1994) *Charles Peirce's Pragmatic Pluralism.* Albany, NY: State University of New York Press.

46

Bertrand Russell, "On Denoting" (1905) and "Mathematical Logic as Based on the Theory of Types" (1908)

Metaphysics to Logic and Back

Stewart Shapiro

According to Alberto Coffa's *The Semantic Tradition from Kant to Carnap* (1991), a major item on the agenda of Western philosophy throughout the nineteenth century was to account for the (apparent) necessity of mathematics and logic without invoking Kantian intuition. Coffa suggested that the most fruitful development in this task was the "semantic tradition," running through the work of Bolzano, Wittgenstein, and Frege, and culminating with the Vienna Circle. Its aim was to locate the source of necessity in the use of *language*: necessary truth is truth by definition. The semantic tradition developed and honed many of the tools we use today. It is now common to look to language, and to logical form, for metaphysical or epistemological insights. Much of Russell's work was pivotal in these developments.

"On Denoting" (1905)

The topic of this essay is what Russell (1872–1970) calls "denoting phrases." Instead of a definition, he gives a list of examples, which includes: "a man, some man, any man, . . . the present King of England, the present King of France . . ." (Russell, 1905: 479). A denoting phrase seems to be what linguists call a "noun phrase," the sort of thing that can go in subject position in a simple declarative sentence.

For Russell, well-formed declarative sentences express propositions, and two sentences express the same proposition if they have the same meaning. Simple propositions are made up of objects, properties, and relations. For example, the constituents of the proposition expressed by "Bill loves Hilary" include the persons Bill and Hilary and the relation of love. Complex propositions are structured much like formulas in formal logic, containing connectives, quantifiers, and variables. In some cases, however, the grammatical form of a sentence may not correspond to the make-up of the expressed proposition.

Russell begins with denoting phrases like "a man," "some man," and "every man." Suppose that I utter the sentence, "I met a man," and the man I met was Socrates. Then I met Socrates. But clearly the sentences "I met a man" and "I met Socrates" do not have the same meaning and so they do not express the same proposition. A philosopher might be duped into thinking that the proposition expressed by "I met a man" contains a strange entity called "a man." Presumably this thing, "a man," is indeed a man, but he (or it) is not any particular man.

Russell suggests instead that the proposition expressed by "I met a man" is " 'I met x and x is human' is not always false" (1905: 481). This much is now common practice. In contemporary notation, the proposition expressed by C (a man) has the form:

$$\exists x(C\,x\ \&\ Hx)$$

which is a reasonable gloss on Russell's analysis. Note the essential use of quantifiers and bound variables.

As Russell points out, his account leaves the expression "a man" "by itself, wholly destitute of meaning, but gives a meaning to every proposition in whose verbal expression 'a man' occurs" (1905: 481). This is the central feature of his account of denoting phrases.

The bulk of the essay concerns definite descriptions, or, as Russell put it, denoting "phrases containing *the*" (1905: 481). To focus on an example, consider "the Prime Minister of the UK at the start of the year 2000." This denotes Tony Blair. One might think that the components of the proposition expressed by "the Prime Minister of the UK at the start of the year 2000 is frugal" consist of the man Blair and the property of frugality. If so, the proposition is the same as that expressed by "Blair is frugal."

Russell pointed out several problems with this suggestion. First, what are we to make of definite descriptions that fail to denote? For example, what would be the components of the proposition expressed by "the Prime Minister of the USA at the start of the year 2000 is frugal"? Second, and more important, "the Prime Minister of the UK at the start of the year 2000 is frugal" does not have the same meaning as "Blair is frugal." Someone who does not know that Blair was Prime Minister might sincerely believe that Blair is frugal but doubt that the Prime Minister is frugal.

Russell follows the lead of his analysis of quantified expressions, and attempts to provide a meaning for every legitimate sentence containing the denoting phrase:

> Take as an instance "the father of Charles II was executed." This asserts that there was an
> x who was the father of Charles II and was executed. Now *the*, when it is strictly used,
> involves uniqueness . . . Thus when we say "x was *the* father of Charles II" we not only
> assert that x had a certain relation to Charles II, but also that nothing else had this relation

. . . Thus, "the father of Charles II was executed" becomes:
> "It is not always false of *x* that *x* begat Charles II and that *x* was executed and that 'if *y* begat Charles II, *y* is identical to *x*' is always true of *y*." (1905: 482)

It is straightforward to render Russell's analysis into contemporary notation. Let *Bxy* stand for "*x* begat *y*"; let *Ex* stand for "*x* was executed"; and let *c* stand for Charles II. Then "the father of Charles II was executed" becomes:

$$\exists x(Bxc\ \&\ Ex\ \&\ \forall y(Byc \to y = x)).$$

Russell's account of denoting phrases plays an important role in his overall epistemology. In order to assert or even grasp a proposition, one must be directly "acquainted" with the constituents of the proposition (see Russell, 1912). If Blair were a constituent of "the Prime Minister of the UK at the start of the year 2000 is frugal," then I could not assert this proposition unless I were acquainted with Mr Blair. But I have never met the man.

Presumably, then, I am acquainted with the constituents of the final analysis of any proposition I contemplate. In the case at hand, these constituents include the properties of Prime-Ministerhood and frugality, and the relation of identity. What of "the UK"? If this is a (logically) proper name, then I would have to be acquainted with the entity it stands for, the nation. Since the expression "the UK" contains the word "the," perhaps it is a definite description, in which case we would apply Russell's analysis a second time. But what is the description? Presumably something like "the largest sovereign nation on the British Isles." If so, then I cannot contemplate the proposition about the Prime Minister's frugality unless I am acquainted with the British Isles. How am I acquainted with the geographic entity? What if I have never been there? So we should replace "the British Isles" with a definite description, and apply the analysis once more. What of "the year 2000"? If I am not acquainted with this temporal entity, then it, too, should be replaced with a definite description. On Russell's view, the proposition expressed by this ordinary English sentence is rich and complex indeed.

"Mathematical Logic as Based on the Theory of Types" (1908)

Although it is widely held today that logic has no distinctive subject matter, Russell was part of a tradition in which logic is taken to deal with items like propositions, properties, relations, and classes. Presumably, this is because one must invoke such items in order to reason at all.

The essay considered here appears to conflate sentences (and formulas) with propositions (and properties), and it falls into use–mention confusions. Some (but not all) of these problems can be attenuated if we follow the above suggestion and think of propositions and properties as structured much like the formulas of formal systems.

Russell had a fascination with paradoxes, especially those concerning logic and mathematics. He begins the essay with a list of them. The first is the Liar: consider a person "who says 'I am lying'; if he is lying, he is speaking the truth, and vice versa" (1908: I, 222). The second is now known as "Russell's paradox": let "*w* be the class of all those classes which are not members of themselves" (1908: I, 222). That is, w is $\{x \mid x \notin x\}$. Then we have that $w \in w$ if and only if $w \notin w$. Russell's list includes the paradoxes attributed to Richard, Cantor, and Burali-Forti, and two more.

On Russell's diagnosis, these antinomies arise because of self-reference. For example, the definition of the class w in Russell's paradox includes a quantifier ranging over "all classes." The trouble results when we try to apply this definition to w itself (to see if $w \in w$).

As a remedy, Russell lays down the *vicious circle principle*: "Whatever involves *all* of a collection must not be one of the collection" (1908: I, 225). This deals with the Liar, since the subject makes a statement about all of his assertions, and then applies that statement to the asserted generalization.

With Russell's paradox, things are not quite as straightforward. The definition of the class w has a variable ranging over classes. So this *definition* should not be in the range of that variable. But what of the class itself? Perhaps Russell thought that a class somehow "involves" whatever is involved in its definition. But this cannot be correct, since some classes have many definitions. The underlying idea is that some of the items of logic and mathematics – classes, propositions, etc. – *presuppose* other items. The vicious circle precludes items that presuppose themselves, and presumably the class w runs foul of that dictum.

In the essay under study, Russell sketched a formal system that does not violate the vicious circle principle. Following Frege, he defined a *propositional function* to be the result of replacing a constituent of a proposition with a variable (or several constituents with several variables). The value of the function expressed by "x is a dog" for the argument Lassie is the proposition expressed by "Lassie is a dog."

The result of binding the variable of a propositional function with a universal quantifier results in a proposition, which is true if and only if every instance of the propositional function is true. The proposition expressed by "all dogs go to heaven" is analyzed as "for every x, if x is a dog then x goes to heaven." Russell calls the x here an *apparent variable*. In contemporary terms, it is a *bound* variable. In these terms, the vicious circle principle becomes: "Whatever contains an apparent variable must not be a possible value of that variable" (1908: IV, 237). A propositional function thus *presupposes* whatever lies in the range of the bound variables it contains.

In contemporary treatments of type theory, the universe is first divided into levels. We begin with a ground type of "individuals," which does not include propositions, propositional functions, or the like. Propositional functions of individuals constitute another level, which we call "level 1 propositional functions." Level 2 propositional functions are propositional functions of level 1 propositional functions. Propositional functions of individuals and level 1 propositional functions constitute another level; propositional functions of those things constitute yet another level, etc. The level structure results in the so-called *simple type theory*. The system avoids (but perhaps does not resolve) the paradoxes that concern mathematical notions like class and cardinality, but does not touch semantic paradoxes like the Liar. It runs against Russell's belief that the paradoxes all have a common solution.

Russell's theory of propositions and propositional functions, called *ramified type theory*, is more complex than this simple type theory. Each level is further divided into ranks. A level 1 propositional function is of rank 0, if it can be defined without referring to (or does not presuppose) propositional functions at all. A level 1 propositional function is of rank 1 if it is not of rank 0, but can be defined with reference to rank 0 level 1 propositional functions only. A level 1 propositional function is of rank 2 if it is not of rank 1 but can be defined with reference to rank 1 level 1 and rank 0 level 1 propositional functions only. And on it goes. There is a similar rank structure for every level. See Hazen (1983) for a readable and sympathetic development of ramified type theory, and Jung (1999) for a careful analysis of Russell's theory (or theories).

There is a discrepancy between Russell's and contemporary terminology. Russell uses the words "type" and "order" for what I call here a "rank," whereas today the words "type" and "order" are used for what I call a "level." We adopt Russell's terminology here, so that a "type" is a rank, not a level. I shall continue to use the word "level" for what is today called a "type."

For Russell, the vicious circle principle demands that the legitimate range of a bound variable is always a type (rank), or part of a type. The essay under study here is hard to follow because Russell does not explicitly invoke the "level" structure. To be consistent, he cannot invoke that structure: the vicious circle principle precludes reference to, say, "level 1 propositional functions," because there is no type (rank) that contains all of them.

Russell notes that the vicious circle principle seems to prevent statements of the basic laws of logic, in so far as those very laws are generalizations on propositions and propositional functions. Consider, for example, the law of non-contradiction:

for any proposition Φ, it is not the case that both Φ and not-Φ.

Note the initial quantifier over propositions. The vicious circle principle requires that any legitimate statement of the law must be restricted to a single type. For example, we can state that for any level 1, rank 0 proposition Φ, it is not the case that both Φ and not-Φ. But, clearly, the law of non-contradiction is not so restricted; it applies to *any* proposition whatsoever.

Russell's solution is to think of the law as systematically ambiguous; it does not express a proposition by itself, but it becomes a legitimate proposition once we specify a type for the quantifier. In laying down the ambiguous law, we commit ourselves to each of its instances. Russell makes a distinction between the word "any" (or "each") and the word "all." For Russell, it is appropriate to assert that *any* instance of the law is valid, but we cannot assert that *all* of the instances are valid. The former is an acceptable systematic ambiguity, whereas the latter invokes an illegitimate apparent variable whose range is the totality of propositions.

Russell calls a symbol like Φ a "real variable." It corresponds to what is now called a "free variable." Russell's framework seems consonant with the contemporary practice of construing axioms and rules of inference as schematic. But Russell does not distinguish the meta-language from the object language, and so does not distinguish schematic letters from free variables.

Russell was aware that his type restrictions make the development of standard mathematics impossible: "it is absolutely necessary, if mathematics is to be possible, that we should have some method of making statements which will usually be equivalent to what we have in mind when we (inaccurately) speak of 'all properties of *x*'" (1908: V, 241).

Consider, for example, the induction principle: n is a natural number if and only if for every propositional function Φ, if Φ holds of 0, and if Φ is closed under successor (i.e., $\forall x(\Phi x \rightarrow \Phi sx)$), then Φ holds of n. This contains a quantifier ranging over all propositional functions – in direct violation of the vicious circle principle. A restriction to a single type might render the induction principle false.

Russell defines a propositional function to be *predicative* if it has no apparent variables of higher type than the objects that go for its free variable. For example, a propositional function of natural numbers is predicative if it has no apparent variables of type higher than that of the natural numbers. In contemporary treatments, a propositional function Φx is predicative if it is of rank 0 for its level. Note that both of these definitions of predicativity violate the vicious circle principle, in so far as they invoke a bound variable ranging over types (or ranks or levels).

Russell uses the notation $\Phi!x$ to indicate that Φ is predicative. The *principle of reducibility* is that any "propositional function is equivalent, for all its values, to some predicative function" (1908: V, 242–3). It can be expressed as follows:

$$\exists \Phi!(\forall x(\Psi x \equiv \Phi!x)).$$

Like the law of non-contradiction, this "axiom" is systematically ambiguous, summarizing infinitely many instances. The symbol "Ψ" is a real (free) variable, and has no type restriction, while "$\Phi!$" is an apparent variable (of the same level as Ψ), ranging over a single (predicative) type.

We can, then, formulate a legitimate version of the principle of mathematical induction: n is a natural number if and only if for every *predicative* propositional function $\Phi!$, if $\Phi!$ holds of 0, and if $\Phi!$ is closed under successor, then $\Phi!$ holds of n. If we come across a propositional function Ψ of natural numbers, reducibility entails that there is a predicative propositional function $\Phi!$ extensionally equivalent to Ψ. We can apply the induction principle to $\Phi!$

Let $\chi(\Phi)$ be a propositional function whose argument Φ is itself a propositional function. Say that χ is *extensional* if whenever $\forall x(\Phi x \equiv \Psi x)$ then $\chi(\Phi) \equiv \chi(\Psi)$. The propositional functions studied in mathematics are extensional.

In extensional contexts, a variable ranging over a type of predicative propositional functions thus serves as a variable ranging over the corresponding *level*. Thus, the effect of the axiom of reducibility is to wipe out the rank structure and introduce the level structure. As with simple type theory, the paradoxes concerning mathematical notions like classes are still avoided. Moreover, the axiom of reducibility does not reintroduce semantic paradoxes like the Liar, since the relevant propositional functions are not extensional. I leave it as an exercise for the reader to check this.

Russell expressed ambivalence over the axiom of reducibility throughout his career. In the essay under study, he offers no justification for it, other than its role in developing standard mathematics. He proposed two additional axioms (and expressed similar ambivalence toward them). One is a principle stating that there are infinitely many individuals (i.e., level 0 items), and the other is a version of the axiom of choice. With these in place, he sketched the resulting theories of arithmetic, real analysis, classes (and relations), cardinal numbers, and ordinal numbers. He also provided a rigorous formulation of the account of definite descriptions (see above).

Whitehead and Russell (1910–13) is a (much) more complete development of ramified type theory. Russell (1919) remains a readable, less technical account.

The specific topics of the two essays discussed are quite different. In the earlier essay, Russell shows how to accommodate certain types of seemingly "denoting" phrases without presupposing some strange entities denoted by them. The second essay is a start on a systematic treatment of logic in order to avoid the paradoxes and place mathematics on a secure foundation. His account of indefinite descriptions is now orthodoxy, and the account of definite descriptions has some advocates today. However, both essays are tied to Russell's overall atomistic metaphysics and his theory of propositional functions, neither of which is widely held today. Moreover, not many logicians accept the strictures of ramified type theory, and the issue of the axiom of reducibility was never resolved. Independent of the specific accounts and theories, however, these two essays were influential in setting the tone for philosophy throughout the twentieth century, and beyond. Russell shows how to use the rigorous techniques of mathematical logic to shed light on philosophical problems, a major plank of the semantic tradition. By all accounts, this brings the discussion of problems to a higher, more refined level.

Bibliography

Editions

Russell, B. (1905) On denoting. *Mind*, n.s. 14: 479–93; repr. in B. Russell, *Logic and Knowledge: Essays 1901–1950*, pp. 41–56, ed. R. C. Marsh (London: Allen and Unwin, 1956); and in *Readings in Philosophical Analysis*, pp. 103–15, ed. H. Feigel and W. Sellars (New York: Appleton-Century-Crofts, 1949).

Russell, B. (1908) Mathematical logic as based on the theory of types. *American Journal of Mathematics*, 30: 222–62; repr. in B. Russell, *Logic and Knowledge: Essays 1901–1950*, pp. 150–82, ed. R. C. Marsh (London: Allen and Unwin, 1956); and in *From Frege to Gödel*, pp. 152–82, ed. J. van Heijenoort (Cambridge, MA: Harvard University Press, 1967).

Russell, B. (1912) Knowledge by acquaintance and knowledge by description. In B. Russell, *Problems of Philosophy*, pp. 46–59. Oxford: Oxford University Press.

Russell, B. (1919) *Introduction to Mathematical Philosophy*. London: Allen and Unwin/New York: Macmillian (repr. New York: Dover, 1993).

Whitehead, A. N. and Russell, B. (1910–13) *Principia mathematica*, 3 vols. Cambridge: Cambridge University Press.

Studies

Coffa, A. (1991) *The Semantic Tradition from Kant to Carnap*. Cambridge: Cambridge University Press.

Hazen, A. (1983) Predicative logics. In D. Gabbay and F. Guenthner (eds), *Handbook of Philosophical Logic*, vol. 1, pp. 331–407. Dordrecht: D. Reidel.

Jung, D. (1999) Russell, presupposition, and the vicious-circle principle. *Notre Dame Journal of Formal Logic*, 40: 55–80.

47

Henri Bergson, *Creative Evolution* (1907)

Analysis and Life

F. C. T. Moore

On June 13, 1907, William James sent a copy of his newly published *Pragmatism* to Bergson, with a letter praising *L'Évolution créatrice*, which was published in the same year. The letter began "O my Bergson, you are a magician," and included the remark "To me at present the vital achievement of the book is that it inflicts an irrecoverable death wound upon Intellectualism" (Henry James, 1920: 291). Five years later, Bertrand Russell gave a talk at the University of Cambridge in which he expressed a reaction somewhat similar in content, but with a very different verdict: "Instinct is fundamental in his philosophy . . . with instinct as the good boy and intellect as the bad boy." Or again: "Intellect is the misfortune of man, while instinct is seen at its best in ants, bees and Bergson" (Russell, 1912: 321; see also Russell, 1914).

Creative Evolution remains Bergson's (1859–1941) most well-known work. Here we shall explore Bergson's views about evolution, and his views of the scientific enterprise in general, including the biological sciences, as well as considering to what extent the initial reactions of William James or of Bertrand Russell were sound. We shall begin by providing an outline of Bergson's views about reason, durance, and intuition.

The Role of Reason

The role which Bergson gives to "intuition" has led many to describe him as an irrationalist. Though such a description can be defended in certain respects, what we find in Bergson is not so much a devaluation as a revaluation of reason. He wrote:

> human intelligence is in no way the kind of intelligence depicted by Plato in the allegory of the Cave. It does not have the function of watching vain shadows pass by any more than of turning round and contemplating the blazing sun. It has other things to do. Yoked, like plough-oxen, to a heavy task, we feel the play of our muscles and joints, the weight of the plough and the resistance of the soil: the function of human intelligence is

to act and to know that it is acting, to enter into contact with reality and even to live it, but only in so far as it is concerned with the job being done and the furrow being ploughed. (Bergson, 1907: 192 [201–2])

In other words, the intellect arose in evolution as an aspect of and adjunct to our need and capacity for action, and bears the marks of this origin. (Note that the translations from Bergson's writings are mine; references to the published English translations are given in square brackets.)

Bergson also compared and contrasted intellect and instinct. They were divergent solutions to the same problem for life: creating local stores of energy within us from what surrounds us, and using them (Bergson, 1907: 144). Each had its advantages and disadvantages and importantly different characteristics, though we should avoid erecting from these differences a systematic philosophical doctrine in which instinct would become pure or automatic mechanism, and reason pure contemplative detachment. This kind of system-making is to be avoided. It is the occupational hazard of the intellect, the counterpart to its pragmatic strengths.

The Nature of *Durée*

In his early work, Bergson elaborated a view of "durance" (for the translation, see Moore, 1996: 58–9) or duration. Movement or change can be decomposed into component parts (e.g., successive states or events), and for many purposes it is essential for us to do this. But having decomposed a movement in this way we are then tempted to regard the movement as nothing other than the arrangement of these components in time. Bergson often explains why he considers this an error by using the example of melody. A melody can be analyzed as a succession of notes: indeed, musical notation and musical instruments are commonly designed in just this way. However, remember the dictum: "The worst crime is to play notes instead of making music" (Griffin, 1993, attributing the saying to Isaac Stern). The intellectual mistake corresponding to this musicianly crime would be to think that a melody is nothing other than a sequence of notes *played in a certain way*. Of course, the activities which involve attending to individual notes and their relations do have a place: we may need as performers to practice a difficult sequence of notes, attending, say, to evenness of timbre, rhythm, or dynamics, or we may wish to make an effort in the case of earlier music to retrain ears, voices, or fingers that have become more or less accustomed to even temperament. And so forth. But such note-oriented activities are secondary to the melody, which is prior to the sequence of notes. The existence of the melody (actually or potentially) and our awareness of it are, in Bergson's view, preconditions of analyzing it into certain components. In another musical comparison, Bergson suggested that our experience of change is the experience of a complexity of "rhythms," with no general procedure enabling us to determine their beginnings or endings.

At first, Bergson treated durance psychologically. The realities of movement not captured by analysis were those grasped in the sphere of consciousness. Later, however, he held that a similar approach could be applied more generally. Indeed, we can view *Creative Evolution* as an application of his account of durance to the phenomenon of life.

Intuition and the Absolute

In 1903, Bergson introduced his notion of "intuition" (Bergson, 1903). This has been widely regarded as irrationalist or mystical. However, it is in the first place more down to earth. Bergson often gave the common example of a simple action, like raising one's arm. Consider, for instance, the following passage:

> If I raise my hand from A to B, this movement presents itself to me under two aspects at the same time. Felt from within, it is a simple, indivisible act. Seen from outside, it is the traversal of a certain curve AB. In this line, I shall distinguish as many positions as I wish, and it will be possible to define the line itself as a certain coordination of these positions. . . . Mechanism would consist here in seeing only the positions. Finalism would take account of their order. But mechanism and finalism, each of them, would sidestep the movement, which is the true reality. In a certain sense, movement is more than the positions and their order . . . [having] in addition something which is neither order nor position, but which is of the essence: mobility. In another sense, the movement is *less* than the series of positions with the order which connects them, since, to put points in a certain order, it is necessary to start by representing the order to oneself, and then instantiate it using points: we need assembly work and we need intelligence, where the simple movement of the hand contains none of all that. (Bergson, 1907: 91–2 [96])

Such movements, he thought, are known as simple "from the inside," though they can be decomposed by the intellect into appropriate components. Similarly, a movement can be decomposed analytically into cinematographic frames, which can, depending on the technology, simulate real movement. In fact, it was as a result of reading Bergson that Russell paid his first visit to the cinema. He wrote: "At last we went out to a cinematograph to see if it bore out Bergson's philosophy, which it did" (Russell, 1912: 318). No doubt this was just a joke in Russell's letter, alluding to jerky images. But for Bergson, the example illustrates an epistemological contrast between what is achieved by analysis, and what is achieved by intuition. Analysis is indispensable to us as active beings, and thus is "relative," while intuition is in the first place our awareness of ourselves as agents, and is "absolute." The new step in 1903 is the claim that, since we are ourselves part of the world, intuition can also provide an instrument for understanding features of the world at large. It was this step that made it possible for Bergson to move from his earlier exploration of topics in the philosophy of mind to new explorations of other issues raised by the sciences, in particular evolutionary theory (Bergson, 1907), and relativity theory (Bergson, 1922).

Radical Mechanism and Radical Finalism

Bergson's propositions about the *élan vital* have led many to view him as a "vitalist" (i.e., one who postulates a force present in animate but not inanimate matter, and appeals to it to explain living phenomena). However, it is important to note his extensively stated position, that radical mechanism and radical finalism are two sides of the same coin, and that both are unacceptable. Radical mechanism is a general position illustrated most notably in Laplace's global determinism (Bergson, 1907: 38 [40]). When applied more specifically to the theory of life it can take a Darwinian form (though at the cost of introducing "chance" events, i.e., mutations, in the biological realm). Radical finalism is also a general position illustrated, for instance, in the Aristotelian teleological view of reality. When applied to life, it can yield varieties of vitalism.

Mapping Movement

How could it be that radical mechanism and radical finalism should be viewed as two sides of the same coin? Because, according to Bergson, they share a geometric or spatialized view of time. On this view, the actual evolution of events and states could be mapped in a diagram or directed graph. The nodes of such a diagram would be specific states or events (actual, hypothesized, or anticipated) which can be isolated from the continuing rhythms of change (this is part of the work for which intellect evolved). The lines between the nodes would represent causal connections between states or events, able to be verified through mechanistic hypotheses or at least statistical data (further work of the intellect). Bergson repeatedly expressed respect for the importance of this work, both in everyday life and in scientific endeavor. But such work was, in its evolutionary origin, pragmatic. We should avoid erecting it into a metaphysics such as that of Einstein, who passionately denied the reality of time as experienced. Indeed, on the death of a friend of fifty years' standing, he wrote: "Now Besso has preceded me a little by parting from this strange world. This means nothing. To us believing physicists the distinction between past, present and future has only the significance of a stubborn illusion" (Speziali, 1972: 538). We may imagine that this was not on Einstein's part heartless adherence to a scientific orthodoxy, but an attempt to turn it into a sort of consolation. For Bergson, by contrast, such a view would be a self-imposed blindness.

The *Élan Vital*

I now present a difficulty for the interpretation of Bergson's position which I suggest. He writes of the "original surge of life" (*l'élan originel de la vie*), and says "This surge, conserving itself in the evolutionary lines between which it is divided, is the deep cause of variations, at least of those which are regularly transmitted, which agglomerate, and create new species" (Bergson, 1907: 88 [92]). Surely, an appeal in these terms to the "surge of life" as a "deep cause" can be construed only as a form of vitalism. Those who do construe Bergson's position in this way can readily recruit this and other similar texts to their banner. However, his reference to a "cause" here should be treated with caution, especially since this blithe phrase is in some respects inconsistent with Bergson's clear and argued rejection of radical finalism elsewhere. The question is whether Bergson really intended to hypothesize a hidden force to explain the phenomena of life: the answer, I think, is that he wanted rather to turn our attention toward having a good sense of these rhythms in their variety and originality, undistorted either by a mechanistic or by a finalist ideology.

Nevertheless, life can be viewed as an organization of matter, and this gives reason for a mechanistic approach. But though, in a mechanism, simpler parts are assembled into a more complex working whole, it is a key claim of Bergson that this is not, or is not always, how life works. Consider the case of an embryo. Here "*life does not proceed by association and addition of elements, but by dissociation and splitting*" (Bergson, 1907: 90, original emphasis).

The dissociative processes characteristic of the *élan vital* operate in diverse and sometimes conflicting ways. The coming into being from species A of two new species B and C is a form of dissociation. The way in which an organism maintains its identity (to the extent that in its own particular way it does so) creates a particular dissociation between it and its environment which should not be viewed in mechanistic terms. Nor consequently should adaptation be viewed in mechanistic terms either (as fitness to a relatively fixed environment, with the properties of the organism and those of the environment playing, as it were, predetermined roles). If we include two organisms in our model, assuming that each makes a different dissociation of itself from an environment, then we have the following instability. In this model life has already dissociated itself globally from brute matter. But the view that we might now have two life forms in competition in the *same* environment is misleading, first because it is not the same environment (for reasons already indicated), and secondly because the environment for each of them includes the other. A mechanistic model of this situation would, in principle, rapidly run up against an analog in the biological realm of the three-body problem in mechanics. Recent work in coevolution, for instance, attempts to face up to at least part of this difficulty (see Mullarkey, 1999: esp. 62ff).

Natural Philosophy

To what extent is Bergson an adversary of "natural philosophy" (or, as we now say, "natural science")? Answer: not at all. In fact, he engaged in extended and serious study of scientific work related to topics which interested him. His frequent detailed comments on empirical work in the psychology, biology, and physics of his day can sometimes create the impression that he thinks philosophy to have the critique of scientific work as one of its tasks (this would not be a new opinion). Nevertheless, when he confronted this issue directly, this is what he said:

> Here is someone who has followed a certain scientific method over a long period and laboriously achieved his results, and who tells us: "Experience, helped by reasoning, leads to this point; scientific knowledge starts here and ends there; these are my conclusions"; and the philosopher is supposed to have the right to reply: "Fine, leave that with me! Just look what I can do with it! I shall complete the knowledge which you brought to me incomplete. What you brought in a disjointed form I shall unify . . ." Really, what a strange pretension! How can the profession of philosophy entitle a practitioner to go further than science? . . . Such a conception of the role of the philosopher would be injurious for science. But how much more injurious for philosophy! (Bergson, 1911: 135–6 [122–3])

Conclusion

This summary account of Bergson's *Creative Evolution* should be enough to make us wary of Russell's reaction to it. It is not adequate to describe Bergson as an irrationalist (in the sense of thinking that human reason should not be trusted), as a vitalist (in the sense of appealing to a hidden force supposed to be responsible for life), or as an opponent of science (in any sense). He could perhaps better be seen rather as William James wanted to see him: as a kind of pragmatist. The work of science should be done on the ground, and is, as may be expected, very useful – indeed, indispensable; but we should be cautious of grander and more radical philosophical claims which scientific work may sometimes tempt us to make. The main mistake is the one which leads us, in effect, to side-step or dismiss the realities of change. Philosophical reflection should not pretend to correct or improve upon the work of science, but it should guard us against the dogmas and factitious problems to which we are liable because of our evolutionary history, and it may open or re-open our eyes to those realities in the world in general, and the living world in particular, which are not fully captured by analysis.

When scientists or others make some of the grander claims, they are philosophizing, and the hazard of philosophizing is its tendency to create "systems" of thought. Some may view the position put forward in *Creative Evolution* as just such a system. But we should beware. These are Bergson's own remarks in his last published work on the dangers of system-making:

> Philosophical systems are not made to the measure of the reality in which we live. They are too big. Take any suitably chosen example, and you will find that it would apply equally well to a world without plants or animals, in which there was nothing but people, in which people did not eat and drink, in which they did not sleep, dream or wander off the point; in which they were born decrepit and died as nurselings; in which energy went up the slope of dispersal; in which everything went backwards and everything was topsy-turvy. This is because a real system is a set of conceptions which are so abstract, and therefore so vast, that it would fit not only what is real, but also what is possible, and even some things that are impossible. It is the explanation which sticks to its object that we must judge satisfactory. (Bergson, 1938: 1 [11])

We may suppose that this sober advice had a purpose. *Creative Evolution* had a massive impact in its day and later. Bergson hopes to discourage us from entering the heady arena of "sheer disputation," and from enrolling his work in causes foreign to his philosophical practice.

Bibliography

Editions and translations

Bergson, Henri (1903) Introduction à la métaphysique. In *La Pensée et le mouvant: essais et conférences*. Paris: Presses Universitaires de France, 1938. Translated by M. L. Andison as "Introduction to Metaphysics" in *The Creative Mind*. New York: Philosophical Library, 1946.

Bergson, Henri (1907) *L'Évolution créatrice*. Paris: Presses Universitaires de France.

Bergson, Henri (1911) L'Intuition philosophique. In *La Pensée et le mouvant: essais et conférences*. Paris: Presses Universitaires de France, 1938. Translated by M. L. Andison as "Philosophical Intuition" in *The Creative Mind*. New York: Philosophical Library, 1946.

Bergson, Henri (1920) *Creative Evolution*, trans. Arthur Mitchell. London: Macmillan.

Bergson, Henri (1922) *Durée et simultanéité : à propos de la théorie d'Einstein*. In *Mélanges*, ed. A. Robinet. Paris: Presses Universitaires de France, 1972.

Bergson, Henri (1938) *La Pensée et le mouvant: essais et conférences*. Paris: Presses Universitaires de France. Translated by M. L. Andison as *The Creative Mind*. New York: Philosophical Library, 1946.

Bergson, Henri (1959) *Oeuvres*, ed. A. Robinet. Paris: Presses Universitaires de France.

Bergson, Henri (1965) *Duration and Simultaneity*, trans. L. Jacobson. Indianapolis, IN: Bobbs-Merrill.

Studies and references

Griffin, Jasper (1993) Citation of Isaac Stern. *The University of Oxford Gazette*, 124, no. 4309 (2 December).

James, Henry (ed.) (1920) *The Letters of William James*. London: Longmans, Green and Co.

James, William (1907) *Pragmatism*. New York: Longmans, Green and Co.

Moore, F. C. T. (1996) *Bergson: Thinking Backwards*. Cambridge: Cambridge University Press.

Mullarkey, John (1999) *Bergson and Philosophy*. Notre Dame, IN: University of Notre Dame Press.

Russell, Bertrand (1912) The philosophy of Bergson. In John G. Slater (ed.), *Bertrand Russell: Logical and Philosophical Papers 1909–1913*, London and New York: Routledge, 1992.

Russell, Bertrand (1914) *The Philosophy of Bergson*. Cambridge: Bowes and Bowes.

Speziali, Pierre (1972) *Albert Einstein – Michele Besso: Correspondance 1903–1955*. Paris: Hermann.

48

Ludwig Wittgenstein, *Tractatus Logico-philosophicus* (1921)

The Essence of Representation

Hans-Johann Glock

The dominant tradition in European philosophy after Descartes evolved around epistemological problems. Do we have knowledge of reality? How can we arrive at beliefs that are true and justified? Wittgenstein's *Tractatus* brought about a radical reorientation. It is devoted to the relation between thought and language on the one hand, and reality on the other. Yet the focus is on logical or semantic questions that are in some respects prior to those of epistemology. The issue is not how we can represent reality accurately, but rather: how can we represent reality at all, whether truly or falsely? What gives content to our beliefs and meaning to our sentences? What enables them to be about something?

The *Tractatus* is devoted to two major themes: the essence of representation or intentionality, on the one hand, and the nature of logic and philosophy on the other. The two are interconnected, since for Wittgenstein logic comprises the most general preconditions for the possibility of representation. We represent reality through thought. But the *Tractatus* breaks with the traditional view that language is merely a medium for transmitting a prelinguistic process of thought. Thoughts are intrinsically linked to their linguistic expression. Wittgenstein's first masterpiece evolves around a striking account of the essence of symbolic or linguistic representation – the famous picture theory of the proposition – which at the same time furnishes a novel understanding of logic, a metaphysical account of the basic constituents of reality, pregnant remarks about the mystical, and a revolutionary if controversial conception of the proper task and method of philosophy itself.

Background

Ludwig Wittgenstein (1889–1951) was born into a wealthy and cultured Viennese family of Jewish descent. An interest in the foundations of mathematics led him to the writings of Frege and Russell. In 1911 he went to Cambridge to work with Russell. The *Tractatus* is the result of the ensuing labor. It was finished in 1918, while Wittgenstein served in the Austrian army, and it remained the only philosophical book he published during his lifetime. He always referred to it as *Logisch-Philosophische Abhandlung*. Nevertheless, the title Moore suggested for the English edition, *Tractatus Logico-philosophicus*, has carried the day and is now an academic household name. Unfortunately, the work itself has remained obscure.

Part of the difficulty, and of the appeal of the book, lies in the fact that it combines the formal with the Romantic. "The work is strictly philosophical and at the same time literary, but there is no babbling in it," as he wrote in a letter to von Ficker. Another obstacle is that the marmoreal remarks are extremely condensed. They are not aphorisms, since they are rigidly fitted into a tight structure. But in his attempt to avoid babbling Wittgenstein adopted a laconic tone and compressed his remarks into what Broad called "syncopated pipings." The famous system of decimal numbers (used in my subsequent references) is supposed to indicate the importance and place of individual remarks, yet the *Tractatus* does not apply it consistently. Still, the main propositions 1–7 can be seen as chapter headings.

Wittgenstein had great difficulties finding a publisher for the *Tractatus*. It was eventually published in 1921 in Oswald's *Annalen der Naturphilosophie*, and a year later in an English–German parallel edition. To ensure publication, Russell wrote an introduction, which Wittgenstein condemned as superficial and misleading, with partial justification.

Frege and Russell pioneered logicism, the reduction of mathematics to purely logical concepts and principles. To this end, they replaced the old syllogistic logic by a more powerful one. They analyzed propositions not into subject and predicate, but into *function* and *argument*, and they introduced the device of variable-binding quantification. Thus, "Caesar conquered Gaul" is analysed not into the subject "Caesar" and the predicate "conquered Gaul" but into the name of a function "x conquered y" and the names of its two arguments, "Caesar" and "Gaul." Similarly, "All Greeks are bald" is analysed not into a subject "All Greeks" and a predicate "are bald," but into the name of a complex function "if x is Greek then x is bald" and a quantifier "For all x."

According to Frege, the value of such a function is either one or other of two "logical objects," "the True" and "the False." For example, the value of the function named by "x conquered y" is the True for the arguments Caesar and Gaul, the False for Alexander and Russia. In an ideal language, all sentences are proper names of the True or the False, and these objects are both arguments and values of the truth-functions denoted by the logical constants. Negation, for instance, maps a truth-value onto the converse truth-value (if "p" is true, "$\sim p$" is false).

Frege distinguished between two aspects of the content of signs: their meaning, which is the object they refer to, and their sense, the "mode of presentation" of that referent. The meaning of a sentence is its truth-value; the sense of a sentence is the thought it expresses (what is asserted). The meaning of a proper name is what it stands for; its sense the descriptions through which we identify that bearer. For instance, for some the sense of "Aristotle" is given by the description "the pupil of Plato," for others by "the teacher of Alexander."

Frege's logical system is the first complete axiomatization of first-order logic, and it is capable of formalizing inferences involving multiple generality, which are essential to mathematical reasoning. Frege defined numbers (the basic concept of arithmetic) as sets of sets with the same number of members. The number two is the set of all pairs, the number three the set of all trios, and so on. Alas, this ingenious procedure made unrestricted use of the notion of a set, and therefore led to the paradox of the set of all sets which are not members of themselves. Russell, who had devised the paradox, developed a logical system closely resembling Frege's. He endeavored to protect logicism from the paradox by means of a theory of types which prohibits as nonsensical formulae that predicate of sets properties which can only significantly be predicated of their members (as in "The class of lions is a lion").

Russell's system differed from Frege's in other notable respects. The value of a function like *x conquered y* is not a truth-value, but a proposition; for example, its value for the arguments Caesar and Gaul is the proposition that Caesar conquered Gaul. As a consequence, Russell denied that sentences name truth-values, and he repudiated Frege's sense/meaning distinction. For Frege, in natural languages a sentence of the form "The *F* is *G*," e.g., "The king of France is bald," expresses a thought but lacks a truth-value if nothing which is *F* exists. Russell's Theory of Descriptions analyzed such sentences into a quantified conjunction, viz. "There is one and only one thing that is *F*, and that thing is *G*." If nothing which is *F* exists, this proposition is not truth-valueless, but false.

Like Frege, Russell thought of his formal system as an ideal language that avoids the logical defects (indeterminacy, referential failure, type confusions, etc.) of natural languages. Unlike Frege, he used this language to advance a logical atomism. Complex propositions from diverse areas of discourse are analyzed into truth-functions of simple "atomic propositions." These in turn are further analyzed into "logically proper names," that is, names which, unlike ordinary proper names and definite descriptions, are proof against referential failure. According to Russell, the only expressions that satisfy this requirement are demonstratives that refer to sense data. By the same token, atomic propositions are statements like "This is red"; they refer to a sense datum with which the speaker is presently acquainted, and the existence of which is therefore immune to skeptical doubt.

Logic, Thought, and Language

Wittgenstein took over and transformed important elements of Frege's and Russell's logical systems, notably the idea that a proposition is a function of its constituents and that it is composed of function and argument. Moreover, he followed Russell in identifying philosophy with the logical analysis of propositions. But his "philosophy of logic" departed radically from his predecessors. With considerable chutzpah, he includes their work under the label "the old logic," and castigates them for having failed to clarify the nature of logic (4.003f, 4.1121, 4.126).

At the turn of the century, there were three accounts of the nature of logic. According to psychologism, logical truths or "laws of thought" describe how human beings (by and large) think, their basic mental operations, and are determined by the nature of the human mind. Against this, Platonists like Frege protested that logical truths are objective, and that this objectivity can only be secured by assuming that their subject matter – logical objects and thoughts – are not private ideas in the minds of individuals, but abstract entities inhabiting a "third realm" beyond space and time. Finally, Russell held that the propositions of logic are supremely general truths about the most pervasive traits of reality.

Wittgenstein eschews all three accounts, by exploiting a Kantian idea that he may have picked up from Schopenhauer or Hertz. Necessary propositions are not statements about the way people actually think, or about a Platonist *hinterworld*, or about the most pervasive features of reality. Philosophy cum logic is a second-order discipline. Unlike science, it does not itself represent any kind of reality. Instead, it reflects on the (quasi-transcendental) preconditions of representing reality. Philosophy is the "logical clarification of thought." It investigates the nature and limits of thought, because it is in thought that we represent reality. Echoing Kant's critical philosophy, the *Tractatus* aims to draw the bounds between legitimate discourse, which represents reality, and illegitimate speculation – notably metaphysics (4.11ff). At the same time, it gives a linguistic twist to the Kantian tale.

> Thus the aim of the book is to draw a limit to thought, or rather – not to thought but to the expression of thoughts: for in order to be able to draw the limits of thought, we should have to find both sides of the limit thinkable (i.e. we should have to be able to think what cannot be thought). It will therefore only be in language that the limit can be drawn, and what lies on the other side of the limit will simply be nonsense. (preface)

Language is not just a secondary manifestation of something non-linguistic. For thoughts are neither mental processes nor abstract entities, but themselves propositions, sentences which have been projected on to reality (3.5f). Thoughts can be completely expressed in language, and philosophy can establish the limits and preconditions of *thought* by establishing the limits and preconditions of the *linguistic expression of thought*.

Indeed, these limits *must* be drawn in language. They cannot be drawn by propositions talking about both sides of the limit. By definition, such propositions would transcend the bounds of meaningful thought. The limits of thought can only be drawn *from the inside*, namely by delineating the "rules of logical grammar" or "logical syntax" (3.32–3.325). These rules determine whether a combination of signs is meaningful; that is, capable of representing reality either truly or falsely. What lies beyond these limits are not unknowable things in themselves, as in Kant, but only nonsensical combinations of signs, e.g. "The concert-tone A is red." The special status of necessary propositions is due not to the fact that they describe a peculiar reality, but to the fact that they reflect "rules of symbolism" (6.12ff). These rules *antecede* questions of truth and falsity. They cannot be overturned by empirical propositions, since nothing contravening them counts as a meaningful proposition.

Wittgenstein's "logic of representation" (4.015) comprises the most general preconditions for the possibility of symbolic representation. Consequently, there is no such thing as a logically defective language. Any language, any sign-system capable of representing reality, must conform to the rules of logical syntax. The systems of Frege and Russell are not ideal languages that avoid the logical shortcomings of natural languages, they are attempts at providing an "ideal notation," a symbolism that displays the logical structure that natural languages possessed all along (see 4.002ff, 3.325). Russell's introduction and numerous subsequent commentators have gone wrong, therefore, in treating the *Tractatus* as a contribution to ideal language philosophy.

The focus on the preconditions of representation also resolves another exegetical problem. According to "ontological" interpretations (Pears, Hacker, Malcolm), the *Tractatus* is the climax of a metaphysical tradition for which the structure of thought and language has to mirror the essence of a mind-independent reality. According to "linguistic" interpretations (Anscombe, McGuinness, Ishiguro), the *Tractatus* anticipates Wittgenstein's later work in regarding language as autonomous, and the so-called essence of reality as a mere projection of the structure of language. In fact, however, the emphasis is neither on language nor on reality, but on *the relation of representation between them*. Wittgenstein's central idea is that there must be an *isomorphism* – a structural identity – between language and reality, if the former is to be capable of representing the latter. The essential logical form of language is identical with the essential metaphysical form of reality because it comprises those structural features which language and reality must share if the former is to be capable of depicting the latter. "To state the essence of the proposition is to state the essence of all description, and thus the essence of the world" (5.4711).

The linguistic interpretation is correct in that Wittgenstein's ontology is a fall-out of his account of language. At the same time, the ontological interpretation is right in that language is prior only with respect to the *ordo cognescendi*, not the *ordo essendi*; language provides a guideline to ontology precisely because it has to mirror reality. The rules of logical syntax are not linguistic conventions (as the logical positivists later held). Logic is a "mirror image of the world" and describes its "scaffolding" (6.13, 6.124, see 5.511).

The Picture Theory and the Metaphysics of Logical Atomism

The *Tractatus* starts out with an ontological discussion according to which the world is the totality of facts (1–2.063), and then proceeds to investigate a subset of that totality, namely pictures, in particular propositions, i.e., facts which are capable of representing other facts (2.1–3.5). That the world is the totality of facts rather than things (1f) means that in order to *represent* the world we have to represent facts, how things are. In that sense the actual world cannot consist of, i.e., be identified with, its ultimate constituents, the "objects" (*Gegenstände*), since the latter are common to all *possible* worlds. These objects are essentially *simple*, while *complexes*, e.g., ordinary material objects, are combinations of simples. They form the fixed "substance of the world": all change is the combination or separation of objects, consequently the objects themselves are *unchanging* and *indestructible*; what can vary is only the way they are combined (2.02–2.027).

Objects have both "internal properties" (or "form") and "external properties" (2.01ff). The internal properties of an object A determine what other objects it *can* combine with; by contrast, it is an external property of A to be *actually* being combined with certain other objects. It is an internal property of a visual object *not* to have a pitch but to have *some* color (and vice versa for a note), an external property to have, for example, the color red. A possible combination of objects is a "state of affairs" (*Sachverhalt*); the obtaining of such a combination is a "fact." The representation of a state of affairs is a model or picture. It must be isomorphic with what it represents; that is, it must have the same "logical form" – logical multiplicity and structure. Propositions are "logical pictures," maximally abstract pictures that do not rely on a particular medium, by contrast to speech, writing, painting or sculpture, for instance (2.18ff, 3, 4.032ff, 5.474f).

The logical analysis of propositions yields "elementary propositions" which are logically independent of each other because their truth depends solely on the obtaining or non-obtaining of the state of affairs they depict. The ultimate constituents of elementary propositions are unanalyzable "names" or "simple signs" which stand for the indecomposable objects that are their meaning (3.144–3.26). Their logico-syntactical form (combinatorial possibilities) mirrors the metaphysical essence of the objects they stand for (2.012–2.0272).

Like Frege, Wittgenstein distinguished between sense (*Sinn*) and meaning (*Bedeutung*). Unlike Frege, he recognized that there is a crucial difference between names, on the one hand, and propositions on the other. Propositions are not names; they do not stand for either a truth-value (Frege) or a fact (Moore, Russell). Conversely, simple names go proxy for objects directly, without the mediation of a sense (description). As a result, the *Tractatus* maintains that names have a meaning but no sense, while propositions have a sense but no meaning (3.142, 3.203, 3.3). The sense of an elementary proposition is the state of affairs it depicts, and it is a function of the meanings of its constituent names.

The picture theory is an attempt to solve complex puzzles concerning the nature of intentionality. How can a thought or proposition depict the world? More specifically, how can it "reach right up to reality" (2.151f). If the proposition "*p*" is true, it depicts a fact, i.e. what it says *must be* what is the case, namely that *p*. But if the proposition "*p*" is false, it does not depict a fact, i.e., what it says *cannot* be what is the case. Yet the content of the proposition, what it says, must be the *same* in both cases, irrespective of whether it is true or false.

These puzzles defy both Russell's dual-relation theory of judgment, according to which the content of a proposition is a fact (a complex of things) and Frege's account of sense, according to which it is a thought, an abstract entity that stands between the proposition and the fact which verifies it if it is true. By contrast, the picture theory explains how a proposition can reach right up to reality by holding that its sense is a potentiality. Whether or not my thought is true, its content is one and the same *possibility*, which is actualized in the first case but not in the second. *What I think* is the "sense of the proposition," the state of affairs depicted, a possible combination of objects (*Tractatus* 3.11, 4.021). The possibility of that combination is guaranteed by the proposition making sense (2.203, 3.02). The world – how things are – only decides whether or not the place in logical space determined by the proposition is filled. Propositions are not just bivalent, as Russell had it, i.e. either true or false, but *bipolar*. That is to say that they are capable of being true but also capable of being false. In this they reflect what they represent. A state of affairs (combination of objects) either does or does not obtain; but, being a potentiality, it cannot obtain necessarily.

For a proposition to depict, no fact need correspond to it as a whole. But two things are required. First, something must correspond to its *elements*. There must be a one-to-one correlation between these elements – its constituent names – and the elements of the situation it depicts – the objects. Second, it must be determined what relationships between the names depict what relationships between things. If both "pictorial relation" and "structure" are in place, the *fact* that the elements of the picture are related to each other in a determinate way represents that the corresponding things are related to each other in the same way, whether or not they actually are. To depict falsely is to depict a *non-existing combination of existing elements*. "In a proposition a situation is, as it were, assembled by way of experiment" (4.031f). A proposition is true if the objects for which its names stand are combined in a way that matches the combination of those names (2.1–2.15, 4.01–4.1, 4.5).

In the *Notebooks* leading up to the *Tractatus*, Wittgenstein wavered between assigning the role of objects to physical atoms, on the one hand, and minimal objects of perception like points in the visual field and unanalyzable perceptual qualities on the other. But in the *Tractatus* he is reticent on the issue of what the objects, names, and elementary propositions postulated by his logical atomism look like. His main concern there is to insist that there *must be* such elements of reality, on the one hand, and of language, on the other, if the latter is to represent the former (*Tractatus* 5.55ff, 4.221; *Notebooks* 14–17.6.15). According to the picture theory, an elementary proposition can only depict a possible state of affairs because each of its ultimate constituents – each simple name – stands for an object. If these objects could fail to exist, however, the capacity of the elementary proposition to depict a possible state of affairs would be contingent on the truth of another proposition, namely one which asserts the existence of the objects to which the names of the first proposition refer. This would run counter to Wittgenstein's conviction that the sense of a proposition must antecede all matters of fact. Consequently, the objects for which names stand must be indestructible.

The Nature of Logic

The picture theory of elementary propositions is only one part of Wittgenstein's account of representation. The other part is his explanation of how elementary propositions combine to form molecular propositions. This explanation is shaped by what he calls his "fundamental thought" (4.0312). The logical constants (propositional connectives and quantifiers) are not *names* of logical objects or functions, as Frege and Russell had it, but express the truth-functional *operations* through which complex propositions are constructed out of simple ones. The truth-value and the sense of the result of such an operation *are* a function of the truth-values and senses of their bases. But the operations do not name relations between propositions, they express *what has to be done* to one proposition to turn it into another, e.g. that "$p \vee q$" has to be negated to obtain "$\sim p . \sim q$" (5.21–5, 5.3). In contrast to genuine function-signs such as "x is red," *nothing in reality* corresponds, for example, to "$\sim$." Although "p" and "$\sim p$" have opposite senses, both are about the same configuration of the same objects (4.0621). "$\sim$," "$\supset$," "$.$," "(x)," "$(\exists x)$," etc. are interdefinable; hence they are neither "primitive signs," as Frege and Russell assumed, nor do they denote different entities (5.42, 5.441).

All possible forms of truth-functional combination can be generated out of a single operation (joint negation). Furthermore, all meaningful propositions are the result of truth-functional operations on the set of elementary propositions (the so-called thesis of extensionality). As a result, *all* meaningful propositions share with elementary propositions the feature of saying how things are, of depicting situations that may or may not obtain. The *essence of all propositions* – "the general propositional form" – is to say "Things are thus-and-so" (4.5–5.01, 5.54). All logical relations (entailment, incompatibility) between propositions are due to the fact that they are the result of such truth-functional combination. The sense of a molecular proposition is given by its "truth-conditions," i.e., the possible combinations of truth-values among its constituents – under which it comes out as true in a truth-table: "$p . q$" is true if and only if both "p" and "q" are true (4.431).

There are two limiting cases of truth-functional combination, namely "tautologies," which are unconditionally true, and "contradictions," which are unconditionally false. They constitute the propositions of logic. Just as the *signs* of logic (the logical constants) do not name logical objects, the *propositions* of logic do not describe such objects. The necessity of tautologies simply reflects the fact that they combine bipolar propositions in such a way that all information cancels out. They exclude and hence *say nothing*, which means that they are senseless, i.e., have zero sense. "Either it is raining or it is not raining" says nothing about the weather. The hallmark of logical propositions is not their supreme generality, as traditionally assumed. For this statement is strictly necessary, while general principles like the law of induction are merely contingent (4.46ff, 6.123ff). At the same time, the fact that a certain combination of bipolar propositions says nothing about the world *shows* something. Thus, that "$\sim(p . \sim p)$" and "$((p \supset q) . p) \supset q$" are tautologies shows, respectively, that "p" and "$\sim p$" contradict each other and that "q" follows from "$p \supset q$" and "p".

Logic is a fall-out from the essence of representation in general, and of elementary propositions in particular. Both logical propositions and logical inferences arise out of the truth-functional complexity of propositions, which in turn is the result of applying truth-operations to bipolar elementary propositions (4.31–4.461, 5.47ff, 6.1–6.13). Contrary to the axiomatic systems of Frege and Russell, all logical truths are on the same level, and there is no need to appeal to rules of inference. That one proposition entails another will be evident, once the two are properly analyzed.

Saying and Showing

By contrast to logical propositions, which are limiting cases of propositions with a sense, the pronouncements of metaphysics are nonsensical "pseudo-propositions." They try to say what could not be otherwise, e.g., that red is a color, or 1 is a number. What they seem to exclude – e.g., red being a sound – contravenes logic, and is hence nonsensical. But the attempt to refer to something nonsensical, if only to exclude it (as in Russell's theory of types), is itself nonsensical. For we cannot refer to something illogical like the class of lions being a lion by means of a meaningful expression. What such

philosophical pseudo-propositions try to *say* is *shown* by the structure of genuine propositions (e.g., that "red" can combine only with names of points in the visual field, not
with names of musical tones). The only necessary propositions which can be expressed
are tautologies and hence analytic.

The *Tractatus* combines reflections on the nature of representation with mystical
themes, which were inspired by Wittgenstein's experiences during the war and influenced by Schopenhauer. Indeed, Wittgenstein seems to have adopted a linguistic version of transcendental idealism: what projects sentences on to reality are acts of meaning
or thinking something, acts which, by the lights of the *Tractatus*, could only be performed by a metaphysical self (see 3.11; *Notebooks* 26.11.14, 22.6.15). Like the eye of
the visual field, this subject of representation is not itself part of experience, it cannot
be represented through meaningful propositions (5.6ff). The metaphysical self is ineffable, and so is what Wittgenstein calls "the higher," the realm of ethical, aesthetic,
and religious value (6.42, 6.432).

The distinction between what can be said by meaningful propositions and what can
only be shown pervades the *Tractatus* from the preface to the famous final admonition
"Whereof one cannot speak, thereof one must remain silent." In a letter to Russell,
Wittgenstein referred to it as "the main point of the book." Part of its importance lies
in the fact that it holds together the two parts of the book, the logico-semantic reflections on the essence of symbolic representation and the mystical pronouncements about
ethics, aesthetics, the self, and death. What unites them is the contrast with the bipolar
propositions of science. While the latter make factual statements, depict combinations
of objects that may or may not obtain, the former attempt to say things that could not
be otherwise. The pronouncements of the *Tractatus* itself are in the end condemned
as nonsensical because they concern the essence of representation rather than contingent facts.

> My propositions serve as elucidations in the following way: anyone who understands me
> eventually recognizes them as nonsensical, when he has used them – as steps – to climb up
> beyond them. (He must, so to speak, throw away the ladder after he has climbed up it.)
> He must transcend these propositions, and then he will see the world aright. (6.54)

This paradoxical conclusion provoked Russell into observing that "after all, Mr
Wittgenstein manages to say a good deal about what cannot be said." Similarly, it
invites Ramsey's complaint that if you can't say it you can't say it, but then you can't
whistle it either. If philosophy is nonsense, we should simply refrain from it. Recent
commentators like Diamond (1991) have repudiated such criticism. According to them,
Wittgenstein was not trying to whistle it. His confession that the sentences of the book
are nonsense must be taken literally – they are plain nonsense rather than attempts to
say something that can only be shown. The *Tractatus* does not hold that there are
ineffable metaphysical truths that can be shown yet cannot be said. On the contrary, it
is a pedagogic performance designed to condemn the idea of metaphysical truths and
to reveal the pointless nature of all philosophy.

The "plain nonsense" interpretation promises to rescue the *Tractatus* from the charge
of being self-defeating. Alas, it has several fatal drawbacks. First, it is at odds with the
external evidence, numerous writings and conversations before and after the *Tractatus*

in which Wittgenstein professed his allegiance to the idea of ineffable truths. Secondly, it employs hermeneutical double standards. On the one hand, it must reject as deliberate nonsense remarks which insist that philosophical pseudo-propositions are attempts to say something that can only be shown, and that the proper method of philosophy is to "signify what cannot be said by clearly delineating what can be said" (4.115, see 4.122, 5.535, 6.522). On the other hand, it must accept as genuine those remarks that provide the rationale for declaring philosophical pronouncements to be illegitimate (notably the claim that any well-formed sentence with a sense must be bipolar and that "formal concepts" like "proposition," "object," "fact," etc. cannot be employed in meaningful propositions). Yet these two types of remarks are inextricably interwoven. The only consistent interpretation of the text is therefore that it condones the idea of truths that language, by its very nature, cannot express.

Finally, if the pronouncements of the *Tractatus* were meant to be mere nonsense, Wittgenstein would have to be neutral between, for example, Frege's and Russell's idea that propositions are names of objects and the idea that they differ from names in saying something, or between the claim that the propositions of logic describe abstract objects and the claim that they are tautologies. This is obviously not the case; indeed, Wittgenstein continued to defend the latter ideas even after abandoning much of the *Tractatus*. The "plain nonsense" interpretation demeans the book, by sweeping aside its hard-won insights and assimilating it to an existentialist gesture or a protracted nonsense poem with a numbering system.

At the same time, we need not rest content with lumbering the text with the idea of ineffable truths. It is crucial to take seriously the *propadeutic* nature of the *Tractatus* explicit in 6.53. The book *is* self-defeating because, in delineating the essential preconditions of representation, it violates its own restrictions on what it makes sense to say. But it does so only to attain a "correct logical point of view" (4.1213), an insight into the essence and structure of language which allows one to engage in critical logical analysis, *without* committing any further violations. Once we have achieved an ideal notation that displays the logical structure of meaningful propositions, we can throw away the ladder on which we have climbed up, namely the pronouncements on the essence of meaningful propositions that we needed to construct the ideal notation.

Russell's aspiration to introduce scientific method into philosophy is misguided. Proper philosophy cannot be a doctrine, since there are no philosophical propositions. It is an *activity*, not of deliberately uttering nonsense with the aim of debunking it, however, but of *logical analysis*. Without propounding any propositions of its own, it clarifies the logical form of the meaningful propositions of science, but also demonstrates that the propositions of metaphysics violate the rules of logical syntax (6.53).

The Impact of the *Tractatus*

Wittgenstein later realized that such critical analysis cannot and need not push away the ladder. It cannot assume a *once-and-for-all vision* of the essence of language. Rather, it is a dialectic process, namely of showing that metaphysicians create conceptual confusions by using words according to conflicting rules. This process must involve continuous observations of how philosophically relevant words are actually used. The attempt to capture the essence of representation is misguided, since "formal concepts" like "thought," "proposition," "language" are family-resemblance concepts that cover diverse cases. Thus "proposition" applies not just to the bipolar propositions of science, but also to "grammatical propositions" that express rules for the use of words. In criticizing philosophical mistakes we can and must rely on grammatical propositions concerning terms like "meaning," "nonsense," "proposition," etc.

In this respect, as in many others, the *Philosophical Investigations* builds on the *Tractatus* both by way of continuation and by way of self-criticism. It further develops what Wittgenatein called "the transition from the question of truth to the question of meaning." Philosophy is not a cognitive discipline, but an activity which aims at clarity. But the ineffable metaphysics is dropped, and the mere promise of critical analysis is replaced by a therapeutic practice: philosophy dissolves the conceptual confusions to which philosophical problems are alleged to owe their existence.

Wittgenstein also retains the idea that philosophy and logic are rooted in language, while abandoning the picture of language as a calculus of hidden rules that must be unearthed by logical analysis. Ironically, it is precisely this picture through which Wittgenstein has exerted his strongest influence on contemporary philosophy of language, in particular on the project of constructing a theory of meaning for natural language.

The *Tractatus* was the major inspiration behind logical positivism, which in turn became the most influential philosophical movement of the twentieth century. Through its linguistic conception of thought, its explanation of logic by reference to rules for the combination of signs, and its conception of philosophy as the critical analysis of language, the *Tractatus* initiated the *linguistic turn* of analytical philosophy. Even those analytic philosophers who are going back on this turn are in its debt, however, because it placed the nature of representation or intentionality at the center of the subject, and thereby set the agenda for current theories of meaning and content. Furthermore, its enigmatic yet beautiful style and its sibylline pronouncements have inspired continental philosophers and artists alike. Last but not least, the *Tractatus* was the starting-point for Wittgenstein's later work, which has had an equally profound impact on contemporary thought.

Bibliography

Editions and translations

Wittgenstein, Ludwig (1961) *Tractatus Logico-philosophicus*, trans. D. F. Pears and B. F. McGuinness. London: Routledge and Kegan Paul.

Wittgenstein, Ludwig (1979) *Notebooks 1914–16* (German–English parallel text), rev. edn, ed. G. E. M. Anscombe and G. H. von Wright, trans. G. E. M. Anscombe. Oxford: Blackwell. (These contain not just the notebooks on which Wittgenstein worked during the war, but also two pre-war dictations, *Notes on Logic* and *Notes dictated to Moore in Norway*, as well as some letters to Russell.)

Wittgenstein, Ludwig (1989) *Logisch-Philosophische Abhandlung*, Kritische Edition, ed. B. McGuinness and J. Schulte. Frankfurt: Suhrkamp (orig. pub. 1921; also contains a preliminary version from 1917, the "Prototractatus").

Studies

Anscombe, G. E. M. (1959) *An Introduction to Wittgenstein's Tractatus.* London: Hutchinson.

Black, M. (1964) *A Companion to Wittgenstein's "Tractatus."* Cambridge: Cambridge University Press.

Copi, I. M. and Beard, R. W. (eds) (1966) *Essays on Wittgenstein's Tractatus.* London: Routledge.

Crary, A. and Read, R. (eds) (2000) *The New Wittgenstein.* London: Routledge.

Diamond, C. (1991) *The Realistic Spirit.* Cambridge, MA.: MIT Press.

Fogelin, R. F. (1987) *Wittgenstein.* London: Routledge.

Glock, H-J. (1996) *A Wittgenstein Dictionary.* Oxford: Blackwell.

Glock, H-J. (ed.) (2001) *Wittgenstein: A Critical Reader.* Oxford: Blackwell.

Hacker, P. M. S. (1986) *Insight and Illusion.* Oxford: Clarendon Press.

Hacker, P. M. S. (1996) *Wittgenstein's Place in Twentieth Century Analytical Philosophy.* Oxford: Blackwell.

Kenny, A. J. P. (1973) *Wittgenstein.* Harmondsworth: Penguin.

McGuinness, B. (1988) *Wittgenstein, a Life: Young Ludwig 1889–1921.* London: Penguin.

Malcolm, N. (1986) *Nothing is Hidden: Wittgenstein's Criticism of his Early Thought.* Oxford: Blackwell.

Monk, R. (1990) *Wittgenstein: The Duty of Genius.* London: Cape.

Mounce, H. O. (1981) *Wittgenstein's Tractatus: An Introduction.* Oxford: Blackwell.

Pears, D. (1987) *The False Prison*, vol. 1. Oxford: Clarendon Press.

Schulte, J. (1992) *Wittgenstein: An Introduction.* Albany, NY: State University of New York Press.

49

John Dewey, *Experience and Nature* (1925)

What You See is what You Get

John McDermott

Unless one suffers from the lamentable and self-defeating trait of doing philosophy as ideology or holds to the current staple that features the benign neglect of the history of philosophy, it can be said that John Dewey's (1859–1952) work, *Experience and Nature*, is a "philosophical classic." I take "classic" to mean a work that is deeply rooted in its immediate philosophical landscape and yet is profoundly originating such that it becomes a landmark, ever bequeathing new insights, approaches, versions, and contentions, which remain as "funded" throughout the subsequent history of philosophy. One thinks here, among others, of Plato's *Theaetetus*, Aristotle's *Metaphysics*, Aquinas's *On Being and Essence*, Descartes's *Meditations*, Spinoza's *Ethics*, and Kant's *Critique of Pure Reason*. Philosophical inquiry subsequent to these works was different and, in some instances, Kant, for example, radically different. No matter how conflicted these classics become as interpretations mount, their presence is perennial. They cannot be dismissed or gainsaid.

Of all the philosophical classics, *Experience and Nature* has the deepest, albeit querulous, kinship with Aristotle's *Metaphysics*. Actually, legend has it that the *Metaphysics* was the goad for Dewey's writing *Experience and Nature*. Constantly complaining about Aristotle's positions, Dewey received advice from his colleague at Columbia University, F. J. E. Woodbridge. Quite simply, Woodbridge suggested to Dewey that he stop complaining and write his own version of Aristotle's *Metaphysics*. Consequently, we have *Experience and Nature*.

Another comparison could view *Experience and Nature* as a proletarian equivalent to A. N. Whitehead's *Process and Reality*. Appearing four years after Dewey's work, *Process and Reality* shares with *Experience and Nature* the systemic inspiration and influence of the thought of William James. And both works hold to the decisive move from the traditional use of "substance" to that of "process" as the major interpretive metaphor for understanding "anything."

Some others among us note a distinctive affinity between *Experience and Nature* and Heidegger's *Being and Time*, published in 1927. Both works have as irreducible contexting for philosophical inquiry, temporality and finitude. Yet, *Being and Time*, as with *Process and Reality*, differs from *Experience and Nature* in that Dewey avoids any language that is arcane, covert, private, neologistic, or egregiously technical. Dewey's language is thick, freighted, and layered, but it is never used for its own sake. To the contrary, he always writes into and out of the experiences we share and understand. To use a contemporary byword, *Experience and Nature* is accessible.

If the reader has a penchant for a philosophical labeling of this work, Dewey, himself, offers three appellations: (a) empirical naturalism; (b) naturalistic empiricism; and (c) humanistic naturalism (*Experience and Nature* [henceforth *EN*; all references are to *The Later Works of John Dewey*, vol. 1 , 1981, ed. Boydston], 10). Whichever nomination presides, Dewey rejects the assumption that experience is a "veil," which blocks us from nature and, in turn, denies that we need any "transcendent" source if we are to understand the meaning of nature. Clearly, this project is characterized by the attitude of an unvarnished philosophical naturalism and by the use of the empirical method.

It is of signal note that the term "pragmatism" does not occur in these entitlements. In fact, "pragmatism" is not indexed in *Experience and Nature* and occurs in the text but a few times, in passing, as it were. Obviously, this is not a book about pragmatism, a philosophical label that Dewey eschewed, firmly and consistently, in his later philosophical works. Still, it is of equal significance that in *Experience and Nature* we find constant reminders of the importance of "consequences' for all assumptions, contentions, and decisions. Pragmatism as a descriptive term for the philosophy of *Experience and Nature* – NO. Pragmatic sensibility as a necessary accompaniment to matters of judgment and evaluation – YES.

I would describe this work as one on philosophical anthropology, namely, an attempt to diagnostically describe *how* we have, lose, connect, disconnect, celebrate, loathe, revere, and lament our ineluctable place, binding, and resolution in, of, and about nature. As anthropology, the approach is anthropocentric in version, but *not* in power. As a way of doing philosophy, we can know it as a metaphysical ecology, thoroughly enhanced by Dewey's familiarity with the life sciences, especially physiology, biology, and botany.

Given John Dewey's life-long concern with education, both in its institutional form, the schools, and in its pedagogical form, teaching, it should not come as a surprise that *Experience and Nature* has, riding beneath its surface, a philosophical pedagogy. In synoptic terms, this pedagogy can be expressed as Dewey's fidelity to philosophical inquiry as "how" to do it rather than as a series of scraps over competing conceptual schema. The former is a persistent and needful activity, whereas the latter is always up for contentious grabs, whereby names of experiences speak to each other in a form of conceptual incest, quickly losing their original grounding in how nature actually "goes on." With Dewey, here following William James, we have an empiricism which affirms that concepts trail percepts and vision proceeds, equivalently, from our hands and feet as well as from our eyes.

Present throughout *Experience and Nature* are two interpretive prongs. One could refer to them as philosophical assumptions but Dewey had long held them and they became "warranted assertions" in his fundamental philosophical stance, having passed, for him, the inquiring test of a submission to the crucible of experience.

The first prong is Dewey's relentless opposition to all forms of dualism. Following William James, once again, "separation" is the *bête noire* of metaphysics, for the intervening space is filled, inevitably, with a concept, replicating itself until the philosophical description has strayed far from the original experience. Among his many lamentations over the persistence of dualism as a philosophical method of explanation and, ironically, clarity, Dewey points to the long-standing "split in Being itself, its division into some things which are inherently defective, changing, relational, and other things which are inherently permanent, perfect, self-possessed" (*EN*, 102). Seeing this division as a veritable Pandora's Box, Dewey then lists the dualistic fall-out "between sensuous appetite and rational thought, between the particular and the universal, between the mechanical and the telic, between experience and science, between matter and mind" as substantiations of the dualism which sliced Being itself (*EN*, 102).

The most noxious form of dualism in Dewey's purview is the separation of the human organism from nature. He takes at face value that "a living organism and its life processes involve a world or nature temporally and spatially 'external' to itself but 'internal' to its functions" (*EN*, 212). When "consciousness is gratuitously divided from nature and when nature is denied temporal and historical quality" it is at that point we ascribe, without an experiential legitimacy, "mystery," the mysterious, "eulogistic predicates" to events, happenings, and otherwise palpable manifestations of the natural.

The second interpretive prong in *Experience and Nature* is Dewey's insistence on the presence of evocative messages precisely as a characteristic, better, a generic trait, of the transacting relationship of the human organism and nature. Dewey holds that:

> When events have communicable meaning, they have marks, notations and are capable of con-notation and de-notation. They are more than mere occurrences; they have implications. Hence inference and reasoning are possible; these operations are reading the message of things, which things utter because they are involved in human associations. (*EN*, 138)

We anticipate here Dewey's text, cited below, that experience reaches down into nature, has elasticity, and can stretch. "That stretch constitutes inference" (*EN*, 12). That stretch catches messages, utterances, the speaking of nature in a way, in ways, directly continuous with our human organic presence in, of, and about nature. Note also that Dewey believes "Of all affairs, communication is the most wonderful" (*EN*, 132) and that "nature is an affair of affairs" (*EN*, 83).

The *project* of *Experience and Nature*, its overarching intention, can be described as probing philosophical analysis of "how things go on." The phrase is colloquial, a commonplace, but the purpose is to explode the ordinary texture of our reflective lives such that we are able to grasp, capture, and elucidate the organic webbing of nature in its affairings, its happenings, and its rhythms. So, too, does Dewey intend to sort out the "generic traits" of all existences, ineluctably present in all human doings, havings, and undergoings.

The matricial text, which acts as a lodestone for this work, is found early in chapter 1, "Experience and Philosophic Method." Having written "that experience as an existent is something that occurs only under highly specialized conditions" (*EN*, 12), Dewey then tells us that when experience does occur "it enters into the possession of some portion of nature and in such a manner as to render its precincts accessible" (*EN*,

12). In short, we are not alien to nature or to naturals. On this behalf, Dewey cites a series of taxonomic judgments by which we render nature as accessible. The upshot of this version of experience as an existent leads to the central contention of *Experience and Nature*.

> These commonplaces prove that experience is *of* as well as *in* nature. It is not experience which is experienced, but nature – stones, plants, animals, diseases, health, temperature, electricity, and so on. Things interacting in certain ways *are* experience; they are what is experienced. Linked in certain other ways with another natural object – the human organism – they are *how* things are experienced as well. Experience thus reaches down into nature; it has depth. It also has breadth and to an indefinitely elastic extent. It stretches. That stretch constitutes inference. (*EN*, 12)

Nature, for Dewey, has a life of its own, undergoing its own relatings, its own "affairings," which, in turn, become what we experience. Our own transactions with the affairs of nature cut across the givenness of nature and our ways of relating. This is *how* we experience *what* we experience. Dewey was a realist in the sense that the world exists independent of our thought of it. Yet, he maintained an idealist strand in holding that the meaning *of* the world is inseparable from our *meaning* the world. Experience, therefore, is not headless, for it teems with relational leads, inferences, implications, comparisons, retrospections, directions, warnings, and with the gift of mapping the scape of experiences had, having, and able to have. All of these activities are related as in an organic mosaic rather than in an atomistic or contiguous string of singles. Crucial to the philosophy of John Dewey is his insistence that the "rhythm" of *how* we experience is constitutive of who we are as persons, as reflective naturals. This rhythm, this "howing" shows us as living aesthetically, or anaesthetically, and is found especially in the relationship between anticipation and consummation. Our accessibility to the precincts of nature is neither opaque nor dull, being rather characterized by mishap, loss, boredom, or listlessness as well as by celebration, nesting and building.

The philosophic method invoked here by Dewey is distinctively empirical, alternating its focus from the way things are to the *how* things are had, that is, undergone by us. Undergone in such a way that we are brought back to the messages of nature. Thereby, our experience is both the starting-point or, speaking philosophically as with Descartes and Husserl, the point of departure and, equally so, the method by which we enable nature to disclose itself for what it is, for those precincts of nature made accessible to us.

The remaining nine chapters of *Experience and Nature* can be described as a series of reflective landings on the tissue and texture of nature, each with a perspective in hand, for instance, mind, history, art, and values. I offer a gloss on these chapters seriatim.

Chapter 2, "Existence as Precarious and as Stable," takes as its task the explication of the starting-point, "namely, that the things of ordinary experience contain within themselves a mixture of the perilous and uncertain with the settled and the uniform" (*EN*, 5). Designated by Dewey as a generic trait of existence, he refers frequently to this mixture elsewhere as the rhythm between the stable and the precarious. Although these traits alternate as both moods and events in our lives, they never exist wholly separate from each other. As one or the other trait predominates our situation, the other remains poised to appear, sometimes for a reason but often, tychastically, by some happy or unhappy chance. On this matter, namely, the freighted living of life on its own terms, John Dewey is crystal clear. "We confine ourselves to one outstanding fact: the evidence that the world of empirical things includes the uncertain, unpredictable, uncontrollable, and hazardous" (*EN*, 43).

Chapter 3, "Nature, Ends and Histories," finds Dewey stressing his approach that "when nature is viewed as consisting of events rather than substances, it is characterized by histories, that is, by continuity of change proceeding from beginnings to endings" (*EN*, 5–6). This contention enables Dewey to adumbrate the flow of nature as experienced in terms of setbacks and consummations, of accrued versions known to us as histories or, more telling, as "stories" (*EN*, 69, 70). Immediate experiences, for Dewey, are ineffable but when contexted by the inevitable "memorandum of conditions" they can become a knowledge (*EN*, 74).

Chapter 4, "Nature, Means and Knowledge," develops further the "memorandum of conditions" by which immediate experience becomes a knowledge. "By its nature technology is concerned with things and acts in their instrumentalities, not in their immediacies" (*EN*, 101). Given his firm commitment to the inexorable temporal quality of reality, Dewey offers that our relationship to and with nature is best understood by "tooling," that is by an "instrument" which "denotes a perception and acknowledgment of sequential bonds in nature" (*EN*, 101). In this chapter we find the seedbed for a philosophy of technology that bypasses the regnant dualisms between applied and pure, or between the everyday and the ethereal.

Chapter 5, "Nature, Communication and Meaning," considers discourse and communication as both "instrumental and consummatory" (*EN*, 144). Instrumental in that it bridges naturally the "factitious and gratuitous" gulf between essence and existence. Consummatory in that communication yields "an immediate enhancement of life, enjoyed for its own sake" (*EN*, 144). The everyday activity of making sense defies the long-standing opprobrious philosophical habit of hypostatizing essences, thereby cutting them off from the discourse which, in fact, constitutes most of our active life. "When the instrumental and final functions of communications live together in experience, there exists an intelligence which is the method and reward of the common life, and a society worthy to command affection, admiration and loyalty" (*EN*, 160).

Chapter 6, "Nature, Mind and the Subject," and chapter 7, "Nature, Life and Body–Mind," both address the emergence of personality, selfhood, and subjectivity as "complexly organized interactions, organic and social" (*EN*, 162). Dewey denies the approbation of "mystery" to the presence or activities of mind. "In ultimate analysis the mystery that mind should use a body, or that a body should have a mind is like the mystery that a man cultivating plants should use the soil" (*EN*, 211). Throughout these chapters, in a wide variety of exampling sustenance, Dewey reaffirms the inseparable continuity of nature and experience.

Chapter 8, "Existence, Ideas and Consciousness," focuses on the traits of living creatures and the twin functions of consciousness, the first pertaining to our response to "qualities of things of sentiency" and the second pertaining to the denotation of "meanings actually perceived, *awareness* of objects" (*EN*, 226). Systemically reminiscent of the work of William James on consciousness, Dewey moves to get beyond the lexicographical tangles of the word "consciousness" and seeks rather to provide an analysis of its behavioral activities. Of note here is Dewey's remarkable grasp of the "inchoate" in our experiencing landscape, our consciousness as fringed, as inferential.

Chapter 9, "Experience, Nature and Art," continues Dewey's opposition to any form of dualism, in this case, the separation of the consummatory from the instrumental, which renders "art" esoteric, negatively understood. It is in this chapter that Dewey sets out the parameters for his very influential work, *Art as Experience*, published ten years later, in 1935. The message in both settings is the need to recover an aesthetic of the everyday, of the ordinary, and the rejection of setting art in "a niche apart." Philosophers of whatever persuasion should be cheered by Dewey's assessment of their major activity. "Thinking is preeminently an art; knowledge and propositions which are the products of thinking, are works of art, as much so as statuary and symphonies" (*EN*, 283).

The tenth and final chapter in *Experience and Nature* is entitled "Existence, Value and Criticism." Dewey takes values to be naturalistically interpreted as "intrinsic qualities of events in their consummatory reference" (*EN*, 9). More than a search for these "intrinsic qualities," philosophy takes as its responsibility a forging of a "criticism," an evaluation of these qualities in the light of human needs. "Criticism is discriminating judgment, careful appraisal, and judgment is appropriately termed criticism wherever the subject-matter of discrimination concerns goods or values" (*EN*, 298). To that end, philosophy is a generalized "criticism of criticisms" (*EN*, 298).

For most philosophical classics, it can be said that the sum is greater, more important, than the parts. It is often the take, the message, the philosophical point of departure that is remembered, historically enshrined. Not gainsaying that Dewey's overarching position is also remembered, I suggest that, of this work, we can say that the sum is not as important as its parts. The intellectual and philosophical power of this work is the dogged, penetrating articulation of virtually every way in which we have our experiences. Acknowledging Dewey's long-standing aversion to philosophical labels, I offer that *Experience and Nature* can be read as a phenomenological diagnosis, broadly considered, of the entire, natural situation in which we find ourselves, behaviorally and reflectively undergone. The phenomenological appellation has to do with a "return to the things," not so much to the ineffability of "themselves," as to their activity, their processes, their "affairings" as Dewey would have it.

His opponents are clear: the tradition for which experience blocks us from the alleged secrets of nature; those who hold experiencing to be headless, in need of conceptual assistance if we are to obtain its fundamental messages; those who hypostatize concepts as if they were nature itself rather than "eulogistic predicates," rhetorically fancy but without hands and feet; and those for whom divisions, separations, disconnections, and dualisms come ready-made and can only be closed by the imposition of philosophical systems.

John Dewey urges us to trust our "common sense" because "it is innocent of any rigid demarcation between knowledge on one side and belief, conduct, and aesthetic appreciation on the other. It is guiltless of the division between objective reality and subjective event" (*EN*, 318). To be sure, there is nothing fluffy nor banal, nor naïve about Dewey's use of common sense.

I urge the reader of this chapter not to be satisfied with knowing that *Experience and Nature* is a classic by reputation and by this or some other evaluation. This is a work that has to be read line by line in order to catch what Dewey is providing for us; namely, a way to conduct our own diagnosis of just how we have our experiences and just how it is with us as a reflective natural. For me, trees, bugs, stars, strife and song, tragedy and escapes, the opaque, the shrill, the subtle and the explosive all take on a thickness and yet a luminosity if I follow Dewey and forgo conceptual preconditioning as my philosophic method. If I have Dewey right, his message is for us to employ the empirical method, one which requires that we have every experience at dead reckoning. I take that literally, for as a natural, my death is an inescapable shroud for all I do, for all I am. Avoid then masquerading versions which claim to protect us from this naturing, from this hard-scrabble of ordinary, everyday life. As unsettling as this may be, I see no other authentic way to assess events, happenings, assertions, promises, or disappointments.

On more than one occasion, inquiring persons will ask me what they should read to know how philosophers go about their version of living in the world. I respond, try *Experience and Nature* by John Dewey. Read it slowly and deliberately, matching his thoughts with yours on how you have the world, see, hear, and feel the world, and what you think about someday your inevitable losing of the world. There is no cure for being a human organism; mortality is its final upshot. Still, Dewey's philosophical approach cast in accessible language can be ameliorating if given a respectful hearing. And we should recall that, in the first edition of *Experience and Nature*, Dewey encouraged us to have "Intellectual piety toward experience" which will generate tolerance, cooperation, and free us from "patronage, domination and the will to impose" – a Deweyan experiment well worth undertaking!

Bibliography

Editions

Dewey, John (1969–72) *John Dewey: The Early Works, 1882–1898*, 5 vols, ed. Jo Ann Boydston. Carbondale, IL: Southern Illinois University Press.

Dewey, John (1976–83) *John Dewey: The Middle Works, 1899–1924*, 15 vols, ed. Jo Ann Boydston. Carbondale, IL: Southern Illinois University Press.

Dewey, John (1981–90) *John Dewey: The Later Works, 1925–1953*, 17 vols, ed. Jo Ann Boydston. Carbondale, IL: Southern Illinois University Press.

Dewey, John (1981) *The Philosophy of John Dewey*, 2 vols, ed. John J. McDermott. Chicago: University of Chicago Press.

Dewey, John (1998) *The Essential Dewey*, 2 vols, ed. Larry A. Hickman and Thomas M. Alexander. Bloomington, IN: Indiana University Press.

Studies

Alexander, Thomas M. (1987) *John Dewey's Theories of Art, Experience and Nature: The Horizons of Feeling*. Albany, NY: State University of New York Press.

Bernstein, Richard J. (1966) *John Dewey*. New York: Washington Square Press.

Campbell, James (1995) *Understanding John Dewey*. LaSalle, IL: Open Court.

Eldridge, Michael (1998) *Transforming Experience: John Dewey's Cultural Instrumentalism.* Nashville, TN: Vanderbilt University Press.

Hahn, Lewis E. and Schilpp, Paul A. (eds) (1989) *The Philosophy of John Dewey* (The Library of Living Philosophers). LaSalle, IL: Open Court.

Hickman, Larry A. (1990) *John Dewey's Pragmatic Technology.* Bloomington, IN: Indiana University Press.

Hook, Sidney (1981) Introduction. In Jo Ann Boydston (ed.), *John Dewey: The Later Works, 1925–1953*, vol. 1: *Experience and Nature*, pp. vii–xxiii. Carbondale, IL: Southern Illinois University Press.

Pasch, Alan (1958) *Experience and the Analytic: A Reconsideration of Empiricism.* Chicago: University of Chicago Press.

Randall, Jr, John Herman (1958) Substance as a cooperation of processes: a metaphysical analysis. In *Nature and Historical Experience*, pp. 143–94. New York: Columbia University Press.

Sleeper, R. W. (1986) *The Necessity of Pragmatism: John Dewey's Conception of Philosophy.* Chicago: University of Chicago Press.

50

Martin Heidegger, *Being and Time* (1927)

Authentic Temporal Existence

Bernard N. Schumacher

Martin Heidegger (1889–1976) wrote his principal work, *Being and Time* (*Sein und Zeit*), while holding a junior position at the University of Marburg, the cradle of neo-Kantianism and one of Germany's most reputed universities. Pressured by the time constraints posed by his candidacy for a post as full professor, the young philosopher completed the work on April 8, 1926. It appeared for the first time in February 1927 in the journal edited by Husserl, *Jahrbuch für Philosophie und phänomenologische Forschung*, and was published in the spring of the same year by Max Niemeyer. *Being and Time* fell like a bombshell on the German philosophical world, moving neo-Kantianism out of the central place it then occupied. Soon thereafter, Heidegger would succeed Husserl in his prestigious chair at the University of Freiburg in Breisgau.

Whereas neo-Kantianism conceived of philosophy as devoted chiefly to questions relative to the principles and methods of science as well as to a critique of knowledge, Heidegger, by contrast, maintained that philosophy should seek above all to reflect upon Being and its meaning. He was fascinated by the possibility of engaging in a radical interrogation about the meaning of Being, particularly Being as it comes to be apprehended under the guise of temporality. By questioning the very meaning of Being – a stance which Heidegger claims had been forgotten since Aristotle – *Being and Time* was (and in many ways still is) a revolutionary work. Its explicit goal was "to raise anew *the question of the meaning of Being*" (*Being and Time* [henceforth *SZ*; quotations are taken from the translation of Macquarrie and Robinson, 1962, with occasional modifications; the pagination refers to the German edition of 1927, which is reproduced in the margin of the English translation], p. 1), by concentrating upon the Being (*Sein*) of a being (*Seienden*), rather than simply upon particular beings. Heidegger's aim was thereby to explain (in a manner even more radical than the ancients) that which makes every being a being, that is, that by which each being exists.

None the less, Heidegger acknowledges that we find before us a multitude of different kinds of beings. Of these beings, the one most appropriate to consider in fundamental ontology is the being that Heidegger terms *Dasein*. Literally "being-there," *Dasein* denotes the everyday human existent, namely, the very being who is daily confronted with Being, and who raises the question of its meaning. In so far as *Dasein* takes part in this questioning, it contains a mode of being proper to itself that differentiates it from all other beings. These others Heidegger characterizes as being simply "there" (*da*); they are in repose, as it were. *Dasein*, by contrast, is incessantly engaged in active questioning. Nevertheless, *Dasein* should not be understood as the conscious subject, as some have interpreted Heidegger. *Dasein*, rather, is a being that exists, a being that is concerned with Being, a being that has a relation of being to its very own Being, and that understands Being in time.

The project of fundamental ontology will, Heidegger argues, return philosophy to its status as the theoretical "arch-science." By retrieving the authentic meaning of Being, philosophy will likewise recover its lost primacy. For these reasons, Heidegger insists that philosophers should not concern themselves chiefly with our knowledge of being, for then they would achieve only an understanding of the knowledge of being, and not of Being itself. Such a restricted point of view would take them no further than the neo-Kantians, for whom philosophy is made subject to the claims of progress, and is forced to imitate the procedures of the natural sciences. By comparison, philosophy, as Heidegger conceives of it, in fact occupies an autonomous domain of research: its investigation is directed to the Being of a being that, by nature, is inaccessible to the sciences. The method proper to this search for the meaning of Being is borrowed from hermeneutic phenomenology. Heidegger presupposes that there are no uninterpreted facts. Phenomena are always given to us in the context of our interpretation and understanding.

Although Heidegger tells us that his primary aim in this work is "to work out the question of the meaning of Being" (*SZ*, 1), *Being and Time* actually proposes an analysis of Being under the aspect of temporality. The work thus consists only of a third of what its author had originally planned. The original plan contained two parts and only the first two sections of the first part were ever written. Heidegger developed certain ideas for the third section of the first part and for the second part in various later studies. These constitute what is commonly referred to as "Heidegger's turn": from 1930 on, the pursuit of Being and its meaning gives way to a reflection upon the truth of Being.

Despite the fact that it remains unfinished, *Being and Time* is still the object of many lively discussions. Heidegger's election on April 21, 1933 as rector of the University of Freiburg in Breisgau and his Nazi involvement have recently aroused – particularly with the publication of Victor Farias's (1989) book – a lively and passionate debate. Some think of Heidegger as the most important thinker of the twentieth century, whereas others consider him a poet and a mystic, rather than a philosopher. One fact is certain, however: notwithstanding the numerous attacks against its author, *Being and Time* has survived beyond the initial enthusiasm which met its publication and has considerably influenced several currents of contemporary philosophy. One might mention, for example, the existentialism of Jean-Paul Sartre, the ethical thought of Emmanuel Levinas, the deconstructionism of Jacques Derrida, the hermeneutics of Hans-Georg Gadamer or Paul Ricoeur and, to a certain extent, the work of Michel Foucault and Richard Rorty. It cannot be denied that, without Heidegger, continental philosophy in the twentieth century would not be what it is. Contemporary theology has also been influenced by this work, whether we think of Paul Tillich or of

Rudolf Bultmann, both of whom have employed the existential hermeneutical perspective proposed by Heidegger, or of Karl Rahner, who has developed a transcendental approach to dogmatic theology.

Existential Analytic of *Dasein*

Heidegger describes his preliminary focus on *Dasein* as an *existential analytic*. This analytic is not conducted on the ontic level, as some have mistakenly thought, but rather with an eye to the fundamental structure of existence. The object of an ontic analysis is a particular being formed within a determinate region; for this reason, the object of such an analysis is, in a sense, already revealed before a particular science seeks to reveal it. A particular science adopts an already existing pre-scientific attitude toward the beings that it studies. An ontological analysis, on the other hand, is characterized by its universality and its neutrality toward every conception of the world. It transcends the "regionality" of the ontic sciences, being devoid of presuppositions. Its object is the Being that is the foundation of beings and the *a priori* condition of their possibility without, however, being identified with the essence of Being. Being, as such, does not appear in the world. Rather, it is the foundation of the phenomena of the world and determines what appears in it. Independent of all "regions," the ontological science aims at making explicit the conceptual pre-understandings which characterize ontic sciences. The question of the meaning of Being is thus anterior and foundational with respect to any particular being. Thus *Being and Time* seeks to analyze the existential attitude of *Dasein* – the Being of that being which questions – in order to arrive at a better understanding of *Dasein*'s existential dimension.

Focusing his reflection on *Dasein* and, more particularly, on its manner of being, Heidegger maintains that the essence of *Dasein* is its *existence*. This does not mean that *Dasein* is a Being-present-at-hand indifferent toward its Being – as is the case of other beings – but rather that it is concerned with Being and related to its Being, that is, to its potentiality-for-Being as its most proper possibility, and engaged in a relation of self to self. *Dasein* does not subsist; it exists. Its essential characteristic does not reside in the *ego sum*, but in the *mineness* (*Jemeinigkeit*) which is to-be (*Zu-sein*), a having (so as) to appropriate. *Dasein* has the possibility of finding itself, or of never finding itself. Having to be existentially neutral, the existential analytic of the ontological structures of *Dasein*'s existing begins with a description of its *everydayness* which is a mode of being in which *Dasein* is indifferent to itself. Such an analysis facilitates the distinction among *Dasein*'s modes of being and the constitutive determinations of human existing. These modes Heidegger terms *existentialia* (*Existenzialien*); he takes care to contrast them to the classical ontological categories.

Dasein as Being-in-the-world

The first section of the book discusses *Being-in-the-world* (*In-der-Welt-sein*) of *Dasein*. Although other beings are found "in the world," they do not "have" a world, whereas *Dasein* does. Contrary to the Cartesian ego which exists separately before becoming related with the beings of the world, the Heideggerian *Being-in-the-world* expresses *Dasein*'s "original" relation to the world from which it is in a position to relate to other beings. This relation does not, however, exist in a neutral and disinterested manner. *Dasein*'s everyday *Being-in-the-world* is characterized by concern, i.e., by its absorption in the hustle and bustle of daily life. *Dasein* as *Being-in-the-world* is equally a *Being-alongside-the-world* (*bei der Welt*), which is to say that it is affected by its environment (*Umwelt*). The beings that *Dasein* encounters with concern in its everyday environment are not perceived primarily under the aspect of their substantiality but of their instrumentality. A tool appears to *Dasein* under the guise of its serviceability as determined by numerous references in a given framework. A hammer, for example, refers to something else which in turn refers to still another thing within a workshop. *Dasein* makes use of the tool for a particular purpose. The world of beings is thus constituted by a system of references and of meaning in which the daily existence (everydayness) of *Dasein* is conducted.

Being-with and the "They"

It is not only utensils that *Dasein* encounters with concern in its everydayness, but also other *Dasein*. The Other is always present. *Dasein* is thus defined as fundamentally a *Being-with* and *Dasein-with* (*Mit-sein und Mit-Dasein*). This essential relation between *Dasein* is expressed in everydayness under the aspect of *Being-with-one-another* (*Miteinandersein*) in which the other has a hold on my "mineness" (*Jemeinigkeit*) that is in some sense dispossessed of its Being. *Dasein* is in the first instance a public-being before it is a singular thinking ego. It succumbs to the dictatorship of the "they" (*Man*) which is, in fact, no one: it is determined by what "they" say, think, and do, and it flees itself through babbling and curiosity. This dictatorship of the "they," called *falling* (*Verfallen*), strips *Dasein* in a certain sense of its Being and acquits it of authentic living with respect to itself and its possibility-for-Being. The "they" dispossesses it of Being. If *Dasein* desires to be and to live in authenticity, to be itself, it must break away from the "they."

  Dasein discovers the world with the help of three existential attitudes: *state-of-mind* (*Befindlichkeit*) reveals to *Dasein* its thrownness in the world (*Geworfenheit*), its facticity, which is to say that it is continually thrown in a world already present to it; *understanding* (*Verstehen*) is not a theoretical attitude of *Dasein* but expresses, as the structure of *Dasein*'s Being, its openness with respect to plans and possibilities, its projection toward the future, its proper potentiality-for-Being; *discourse* (*Rede*) is the attitude that expresses what *Dasein* understands before this understanding is articulated in language.

Anxiety and Care

By contrast to fear, whose object is a concrete being of the world, *anxiety* reveals a fundamental experience of nothing which is none the less not nothing, but rather the experience of *Being-in-the-world* as such, in its nakedness. In this existential attitude of anxiety which reveals the insignificance of the world, *Dasein* is individualized, finding itself alone in the world. This experience of "solipsism" expresses a free choice of being by leading *Dasein* back to the possibility of being itself and of living in authenticity. "Anxiety makes manifest in *Dasein* its *Being towards* its ownmost potentiality-for-Being – that is, its *Being-free for* the freedom of choosing itself and taking hold of itself" (*SZ*, 188). Anxiety projects *Dasein* in an attitude of uncanniness (*Unheimlichkeit*) which breaks with the habitual and the familiar of the world and with the reassuring effect of the "they" in order to lead *Dasein* back to its Being-in-the-world and, more specifically, to its fundamental potentiality-for-Being, that is, to the very possibility to-be-itself.

The fundamental structure of *Dasein* as Being-in-the-world is characterized by existentiality (*Dasein* as projected toward its possibility-for-Being), facticity (the being in the world), and Being-fallen. These three existential determinations constitute the entirety of what Heidegger refers to as *care* (*Sorge*), a term which indicates the fundamental structure of *Dasein* as Being-in-the-world. Care is, first of all, the expression of *Being-ahead-of-itself* (*Sich-vorweg-im-sein*), that is to say, of *Dasein* as projected toward the possible, as a being toward its potentiality-for-Being, in search of itself. It is, second, *in-already-being-in-a-world* (*im-schon-sein-in-einer-Welt*) such that this projection toward the possible is realized in a world: *Dasein* is factual. Third, care is *Being-alongside* (*Sein-bei*) which is expressed in the tension between the authenticity and inauthenticity of the "they."

Dasein's Possibility of Being-a-whole and Being-toward-death

After having analyzed, in the first section of *Being and Time*, the fundamental constitution of *Dasein* from the perspective of its everydayness, Heidegger examines in the second and final section, entitled "*Dasein* and Temporality," the meaning of *Dasein*'s Being from the perspective of its authentic existence under the aspect of temporality.

The fundamental problem, as Heidegger sees it, consists in reconciling the totality of *Dasein* (its Being-a-whole) and its constant state of being unsettled (its *ständige Unabgeshlossenheit*): (a) *Dasein* ceases to be when it no longer has something before it (*nichts mehr aussteht*), but (b) as long as it is, it is fundamentally open and unfulfilled, never having attained or being able to experience its totality, its Being-a-whole. In order to resolve this conflict between openness (unfulfilled existence) and totality, Heidegger appeals to the notions of *not-yet-being* and *end*.

As already mentioned, *Dasein* is not, from an ontological point of view, a reality *present-at-hand* (*Vorhandenheit*), a given fact, but rather it exists to the extent that it refers to its possibility, remaining outside of what is "present-at-hand." Heidegger presents the category of possibility as ontologically constitutive of *Dasein*, which is to say that *Dasein* is "primarily Being-possible" (*SZ*, 143), open to an infinite variety of possibilities. As long as *Dasein* exists, there is always something for which it waits, namely that which it can be and that which it will be. As long as *Dasein* exists, it is related to its end as potentiality-for-Being, which expresses its anticipative character: it tends toward its possibilities, toward the authentic wanting-to-be, the potentiality-for-Being itself. This "projective" character of *Dasein* is directed toward the future: it is "possible only as something in the future" (*SZ*, 325). Whenever it finds itself, radically speaking, without a future, it ceases to be. The future does not however signify a "now" that is not yet real and that will only be realized in a more or less distant coming, but rather "the coming [*Kunft*] in which *Dasein*, in its ownmost potentiality-for-Being, comes towards itself" (*SZ*, 325).

In maintaining the priority of the future over the present and the past (which is to say that the temporal is realized from the perspective of the future, that "place" in which possibilities are possibly realized), Heidegger distances himself from both the "vulgar" (Husserlian) conception of time (with its retention–protention dynamic) and the Augustinian conception according to which the present is primary: the present of the past (memory), the present of the present (vision), and the present of the future (waiting). The primary sense of Heideggerian existentiality, by contrast, consists in the future, from which originate all the *existentialia* (*Existenzialien*).

> But ontologically, being toward one's ownmost potentiality-for-Being means that in each case *Dasein* is already *ahead* of itself [*ihm selbst . . . vorweg*] in its Being. *Dasein* is always "beyond itself" [*über sich hinaus*], not as a way of behaving towards other entities which it is *not*, but as Being towards the potentiality-for-Being which it is itself. (*SZ*, 191–2)

Being primordially a projection toward its own potentiality-for-Being, ever tending toward the future, *Dasein* is fundamentally a *Being-ahead-of-itself* (*Sich-vorweg-sein*). It is characterized by a state of perpetual unfulfillment: its ability-to-be itself is never quite "realized."

The extreme of that which is yet to come, of that which *Dasein* can be, is identified with *Dasein*'s end. To clarify the point, Heidegger distinguishes two different meanings of "end" as applied to *Dasein*. On the one hand, the word signifies a real arrival at an end, a *Being-at-an-end* (*Zu-Ende-Sein*), an achievement, that is the actualization of *Dasein*'s potentialities. One might infer from such a conception of the end, which is bound up with the category of (ontic) possibility, that death constitutes the fulfillment of *Dasein*. This inference, however, does not adequately explain death, for death often comes as a surprise to human beings, stripping them of their future possibilities and anticipations. *Dasein*'s end does not necessarily coincide with its achievement. This is why the end might also signify a state of being in relation to the end understood in the first sense: a *Being-toward-the-end* (*Sein-zum-Ende*). Here the not-yet-being of the end does not express the anticipation of a fullness, which is to be realized in the future. It is not extrinsic to Being but already formally belongs to the present both by way of anticipation and as being "something constitutive" of *Dasein* which is *"already its 'not-yet'"* (*SZ*, 244). If the essence of *Dasein* is its potentiality-for-Being, then it must, as long as it exists, *"not yet be* something" (*SZ*, 233). As long as it is, it is already its "not-yet" which is "its death": it is a Being-toward-the-end but not yet a Being-at-an-end.

Death appears in the context of *Dasein*'s direction toward its end, for the end proper to *Dasein* is not extrinsic (as if coming from a distant future), but rather intrinsic. *Dasein* "is already its end," that is to say, "its death." It is orientated toward its totality which it does not reach at the moment of its death, but, rather, in a moving relation toward the extreme possibility of death. *Dasein* cannot be outstripped of its intimate potentiality-for-Being which is death; it "exists as Being thrown *toward* its end" (*SZ*, 251). Death expresses *Dasein*'s relation toward its own certain end which impregnates it from the moment of its projection in the "worldhood" (*Weltlichkeit*). Death belongs to *Dasein* in a distinctive sense, being ontologically immanent to it as a constant possibility.

> Death is a possibility-of-Being which *Dasein* itself has to take over in every case. With Death, *Dasein* stands before itself in its ownmost potentiality-for-Being. This is a possibility in which the issue is nothing less than *Dasein*'s Being-in-the-world. Its death is the possibility of no-longer being-able-to-be-there . . . This ownmost non-relational possibility is at the same time the uttermost one. As potentiality-for-Being, *Dasein* cannot outstrip the possibility of death. Death is the possibility of the absolute impossibility of *Dasein*. Thus death reveals itself as that *possibility which is one's ownmost, which is non-relational, and which is not to be outstripped* [*unüberholbare*]. As such, death is something *distinctively* impending. (*SZ*, 250)

Death consists in the intrinsic end of the Being-ahead-of-itself of *Dasein* and is derived from *Dasein*'s very finitude, for death is the radical impossibility which denies all possibilities. "Death, as possibility, gives *Dasein* nothing to be "actualized," nothing which *Dasein*, as actual, could itself *be*. It is the possibility of the impossibility of every way of comporting oneself toward anything, of every way of existing" (*SZ*, 262). But death remains a certain possibility for *Dasein* since *Dasein* is, in its essence, a Being-toward-death. The indetermination of the factual "when" of death allows us also to speak of a possible possibility.

Reversing the Cartesian *cogito sum*, Heidegger founds the existential solipsism, the principle of *Dasein*'s individuation, in the *sum moribundum* (the "I am dying") or the *moribundus* (the "destined to die") (as distinct from ontic death, i.e. the moment of death). Ontological death is the absolute certitude founding all other certitudes. It precedes the *sum*, giving it meaning, for it is death that allows *Dasein* to affirm the *ergo sum*, its "ipseity." The possibility of the impossibility of being constitutes the proper structure of *Dasein*, the foundation of its Being. *Dasein*'s Being is the Being-possible with regard to the extreme of possibility of death. *Dasein* cannot be other than a Being-toward-death.

The absolute certitude of death, which is attained independently of ontic experiences is none the less accompanied by an uncertainty regarding the "when," for the moment of death escapes all determination. This uncertain certitude is expressed by Heidegger as follows: "*death, as the end of Dasein, is Dasein's ownmost possibility – non-relational, certain and as such indefinite, not to be outstripped*. Death is, as *Dasein*'s end, in the Being of this entity *toward* its end" (*SZ*, 258–9).

The attitudes of *expecting* death and of *brooding* over it (*SZ*, 261) strip death, in a certain sense, of its possibility by actualizing it. The meditation upon the instant of ontic death and the manner in which it is realized expresses a weakening of death's power through a calculating will to dispose of it. Waiting anticipates the realization of the possible and no longer considers the possible as possible. Only the attitude of *anticipation* (*Vorlaufen*) of (the possibility of) death leaves intact the comprehension of death as an existential possibility of *Dasein*: Being-toward-the-end of existence. This *anticipation* makes it possible to live the anguish of nothingness, hence does not objectivize death, contrary to the unauthentic life which de-subjectivizes death (thereby rejecting the expression of anguish by a flight from death). Moreover the anticipation of death allows *Dasein* to seize, as a pure possibility, the extreme and intimate possibility of its being which is the impossibility of existence, the return to nothing, even if the moment of the (ontic) possibility of the impossibility is undetermined. Ensuring the certitude of the "must die," that is, Dasein's anticipation of death, reveals to *Dasein* the authenticity of the Being-toward-death. The projection of this possibility is not accomplished within the framework of a temporality marked by the tension between the present and the future. Nor does it refer here to an intellectual transposition to the future moment of death with the help of the imagination, as occurs in waiting and in suicide. Rather, this anticipation is a movement of *Dasein* toward its most intimate possibility, attaining a proximity to death outside of time and permitting the retention of its possibility. The anticipation in the Being-toward-death makes it possible to accept death as possibility, and therefore of *Dasein*'s attainment of authenticity and liberty.

   Dasein authentically exists as the Being-toward-death which is its most proper possibility and liberates it of the influence of the "they," permitting it to find its most proper potentiality-for-Being and to assume its most proper Being, to choose itself as itself. *Dasein*'s pressing call to be delivered from its loss in the "they" – so as to develop its most proper potentiality-for-Being – is exteriorized with the help of the strange and undetermined voice ("'it' calls") (*SZ*, 276) of conscience which breaks from the voices of the everyday. *Dasein* lives authentically by responding to this call to extricate itself from the influence of the "they" – that which constitutes a non-choice of itself – so as to understand itself and to discover itself in relation to itself in an attitude of silence and truth.

Time: Expression of the Authentic Coming to Itself

Heidegger concludes his reflection on the relation between *Dasein* and temporality by emphasizing the idea that original time is limited by its very essence. *Dasein*'s time is inextricably rooted in death because death is at its origin. "The *moribundus* first gives the *sum* its sense" (Heidegger, 1979: 437–8).

> As a way of being for *Dasein*, history has its roots so essentially in the future that death, as that possibility of *Dasein* which we have already characterized, throws anticipatory existence back upon its *factical* thrownness, and so for the first time imparts to *having-been* its peculiarly privileged position in the historical. *Authentic Being-toward-death – that is to say, the finitude of temporality – is the hidden basis of Dasein's historicality.* (*SZ*, 386)

Dasein can only be temporal by reference to the three "ekstases" of past, present, and future. In defining the Being of *Dasein* the future necessarily has priority over the past and the present. Temporality permits *Dasein* to find itself in authenticity and to escape the non-authenticity which marks the tyranny of the "they" within the public sphere. In its anticipation of death, *Dasein* returns to itself and accepts its possibilities as effectively its own. *Dasein* thereby finds itself as fundamentally limited with deep historical roots, a heritage, and a fate. Time expresses the possibility of an authentic coming to itself, of a true "ipseity," and allows *Dasein* to embrace its historicity.

Although Heidegger was unable to bring the original project of *Being and Time* to completion (which would have resulted in a much fuller discussion of the meaning of Being), he nevertheless made great strides in developing an ontology of *Dasein* in its everydayness. The elaboration of this existential analytic allowed him to spotlight *Dasein*'s Being-in-the-world and its Being-with-one-another. With a pathos that would move many a subsequent reader (especially existentialists such as Jean-Paul Sartre), Heidegger spoke eloquently of *Dasein*'s irrepressible liberation from the dictatorship of the "they," and its aspiration to authentic freedom. For *Dasein* this amounts to assuming the innermost, most proper Being which it carries within itself. Moved to the very center of philosophical investigation (where it belongs), Being thereby stands as a constant call to authentic existence.

Bibliography

Editions and translations

Heidegger, M. (1927) Sein und Zeit, *Jahrbuch für Philosophie und phänomenologische Forschung.* 8: 1–438.

Heidegger, M. (1927) *Sein und Zeit.* Halle an der Salle: Max Niemeyer.

Heidegger, M. (1962) *Being and Time,* trans. J. Macquarrie and E. Robinson. New York: Harper and Row.

Heidegger, M. (1979) *Prolegomena zur Geschichte des Zeitbegriffs.* In *Gesamtausgabe,* vol. 20. Frankfurt am Main: Klostermann.

Heidegger, M. (1996) *Being and Time,* trans. J. Stambaugh. Albany, NY: State University of New York Press.

Studies

Courtine, J-F. (1990) *Heidegger et la phénoménologie.* Paris: Vrin.

Dahlstrom, D. O. (2001) *Heidegger's Concept of Truth.* New York: Cambridge University Press.

Dreyfus, H. L. (1991) *Being-in-the-world: A Commentary on Heidegger's "Being and Time."* Cambridge, MA: MIT Press.

Farias, V. (1989) *Heidegger and Nazism,* trans. P. Burell. Philadelphia: Temple University Press.

Figal, G. (1988) *Martin Heidegger Phänomenologie der Freiheit.* Frankfurt am Main: Athenäum.

Gelven, M. (1989) *A Commentary on Heidegger's Being and Time.* DeKalb, IL: Northern Illinois University Press.

Greisch, J. (1994) *Ontologie et temporalité: esquisse d'une interprétation intégrale de Sein und Zeit.* Paris: Presses Universitaires de France.

Guignon, C. B. (1993) *The Cambridge Companion to Heidegger.* Cambridge: Cambridge University Press.

Hermann, F-W. von (1985) *Subjekt und Dasein: Interpretation zu "Sein und Zeit."* Frankfurt am Main: V. Klostermann.

Kaelin, E. F. (1987) *Heidegger's Being and Time: A Reading for Readers.* Tallahassee, FL: University Presses of Florida.

Kisiel, T. (1993) *The Genesis of Heidegger's Being and Time*. Berkeley, CA: University of California Press.

Macann, C. (1992) *Martin Heidegger: Critical Assessments*, 4 vols. London: Routledge.

Marion, J-L. (1989) *Réduction et donation: recherches sur Husserl, Heidegger et la phénoménologie*. Paris: Presses Universitaires de France.

Philipse, H. (1998) *Heidegger's Philosophy of Being: A Critical Interpretation*. Princeton, NJ: Princeton University Press.

Pöggeler, O. (1987) *Martin Heidegger's Path of Thinking*. Atlantic Highlands, NJ: Humanities Press.

Richardson, W. J. (1963) *Heidegger: Through Phenomenology to Thought*. The Hague: Martinus Nijhoff.

Sallis, J. (1986) *Delimitations: Phenomenology and the End of Metaphysics*. Bloomington, IN: Indiana University Press.

Schumacher, B. N. (2003) *Auseinandersetzung mit dem Tod*. Darmstadt: Wissenschaftliche Buchgesellschaft.

Taminiaux, J. (1991) *Heidegger and the Project of Fundamental Ontology*. Albany, NY: State University of New York Press.

Van Buren, J. (1994) *The Young Heidegger: Rumor of the Hidden King*. Bloomington, IN: Indiana University Press.

51

Alfred North Whitehead, *Process and Reality* (1929)

Scientific Revolutions and the Search for Covariant Metaphysical Principles

George R. Lucas, Jr

Process and Reality, subtitled "An Essay in Cosmology," was the title given by Harvard philosopher Alfred North Whitehead (1861–1947) to his Gifford Lectures, which were delivered at the University of Edinburgh during the 1927–8 academic term. The text of this unusually technical and complex lecture series was subsequently revised and considerably expanded for publication by Cambridge University Press in England, while a slightly different edition was published in the United States by Macmillan in 1929. Both editions suffered from a host of typographical errors and other textual anomalies which were resolved, in so far as was possible, in a "corrected edition" of the text published in the United States in 1978, which serves as the standard reference edition of this classic work.

Whitehead was a prolific and highly popular lecturer and author, especially during his later years. *Process and Reality* is his most famous, and arguably his most difficult, work of philosophy. It is rivaled only by the magisterial but ultimately failed attempt to provide an exact grounding for mathematics in logic in the *Principia mathematica* (three volumes, co-authored with his pupil and colleague, Bertrand Russell), and by the author's attempt to develop an alternative to Albert Einstein's theory of general relativity in *The Principle of Relativity* (1922), a work in which Whitehead sought to avoid some of the more problematic ontological features of Einstein's theory, such as the radical discontinuity of space, the paradox of simultaneity, and the reversibility of time.

Process and Reality was written at about the same time as Martin Heidegger's *Being and Time*, and relatively soon after Ludwig Wittgenstein's *Tractatus Logico-philosophicus*. *Process and Reality*, however, is utterly unlike either of these other two classic works of early twentieth-century philosophy. It is most often characterized as a work of systematic and speculative metaphysics in the grand tradition of Hegel, Spinoza, and

Aristotle, and its author is considered the last in a long line of speculative thinkers in the Western philosophical tradition. Whitehead thus appears to exemplify habits of philosophy which both Heidegger and Wittgenstein decry. Whether this book, and Whitehead himself, represent a relic of philosophy's past or a harbinger of its future remains a matter of spirited debate.

This characterization of his major work is surprising in light of Whitehead's reputation and career. For much of that career, Whitehead stood in the mainstream of what has since come to be called Anglo-American analytic philosophy; indeed, he, Russell, Wittgenstein, and their mutual friend and colleague, G. E. Moore, were among its principal architects at Cambridge University at the beginning of the twentieth century. Whitehead's earlier writings from the late 1890s well into the mid-1920s are primarily works on the philosophy of mathematics, logic, epistemology, and the philosophy of science. It is standard convention to attribute his later "metaphysical" turn to his migration to Harvard upon retiring from the Imperial College of Science and Technology at the University of London in 1924. Much is made of his relatively advanced age, 63, and of the new opportunities and relative intellectual freedom afforded by this "second career" in America.

In *The Concept of Nature* (1920), however, written while Whitehead was still allegedly in the grip of anti-metaphysical and largely logical and empirical approaches to philosophy, he discusses for the first time the concept of an "event" – a well-defined temporal activity or episode of finite duration, a "quantum" of experience – as an alternative fundamental notion to that of matter or substance at a single location in space and time. He likewise introduced the notion of a non-temporal "form of definiteness" or "enduring object" (examples include geometrical shapes or the color blue) as among the components or constituents of events, the particular combination or "togetherness" of which in a concrete episode of experience defines its novelty or uniqueness. The twin themes of permanence and change that dominate Whitehead's later philosophical works – including attention to the "flux of becoming," the radical temporality and transitory nature of discrete events, as set against the enduring, eternal backdrop of timeless, Platonic forms, everlastingly available as potential ingredients in finite, temporal experience – are thus quite evident in rudimentary form in this and other earlier works from Whitehead's "analytic" period. The deeper challenge is to understand why all four of the Cambridge philosophers associated with the heyday of analysis and logical empiricism in Britain each, in their own way, came to repudiate this early emphasis on logical precision, exactness, and rigor in favor either of broad and speculative metaphysical views (Whitehead, followed much later by Russell) or of the incorrigible ambiguities and indefiniteness of ordinary language and common life (Moore, followed by Wittgenstein).

Process and Reality is unquestionably Whitehead's crowning achievement, but it can be viewed either as the culmination of an extraordinary burst of intellectual energy channeled into unconventional paths between 1925 and 1929, or else as the culmination of a much more sustained and long-standing attempt to develop a descriptive metaphysical system commensurate with early twentieth-century relativistic cosmology and quantum mechanics. In either case, Whitehead's thoroughgoing efforts to invert the traditional metaphysical priorities that historically (from Plato and Aristotle, to Locke, Spinoza, and Newton) seem to give priority and pride of place to substance over process, being over becoming, permanence over change, and inert matter at a specific location over the pervasive interactivity of force and energy fields are what led to the choice of title for this work, and to the subsequent tendency of scholars to identify Whitehead's thought with the label, "process philosophy."

Process and Reality is a work which is virtually impossible to summarize in a simple and coherent fashion. It is replete with technical (some would say "arcane") terminology that Whitehead held it necessary to invent for the sake of precision and clarity. In this he unfortunately follows Aristotle's lead in transforming ordinary, familiar but vague terminology into precise but less transparent technical terminology, thereby unintentionally driving a wedge between the philosopher as steward of highly specialized and technical mysteries and the ordinary individual who cannot possibly be privy to them. It was likewise this elite "guild" mentality that the later Wittgenstein joined Moore in eschewing. Following his exploration of the intricacies of process metaphysics in this work, Whitehead forever after abandoned the overly technical and formidable approach to philosophy that characterizes this work, and spent the remainder of his life and career expounding his views in clear and often elegant prose.

Process and Reality consists of five parts. The first provides an introductory overview or glossary of terminology and fundamental propositions informing the work, outlining what Whitehead terms his "speculative scheme." Part II, entitled "Discussions and Applications," is thought by some scholars (e.g., Ford, 1984, 2000) to contain the bulk of the material originally presented in the Gifford Lecture series. It consists of an historical conversation in which Whitehead sets forth his so-called "philosophy of organism" as an alternative to a metaphysical synthesis that he identifies with classical modern thinkers from Descartes, Locke, and Newton to Leibniz, Spinoza, Hume, and Kant. This discussion is considered by many scholars largely as a further refinement and exemplification of views first set forth by the author in his 1925 Lowell Lectures, *Science and the Modern World*. There are, however, important differences that are introduced in this later material. Whitehead coined terms like "organic mechanism" and "philosophy of organism" in the mid-1920s to signal his challenge to the Newtonian metaphysical synthesis variously termed mechanism or "scientific materialism." By the time of the Gifford Lectures, however, his initial conception of a process or ceaseless creative activity as a single, underlying, Spinoza-like substance whose "modes" are the discrete objects of ordinary experience is replaced in *Process and Reality* by an atomistic, Leibnizian doctrine in which ordinary experience is held to be composed of discrete episodes or quanta of process, termed "actual occasions" or "actual entities."

Part III of *Process and Reality*, entitled "The Theory of Prehensions," seems intended to revise and reformulate many of the discussions and conclusions developed in Part II. Readers today in fact take the discussion there of positive "prehensions" as "feelings," together with the detailed distinction between what are termed physical, conceptual, and hybrid feelings, as evidence of Whitehead's conversion to idealism and a kind of mystical panpsychism. This tendency has been encouraged by a legion of process disciples, led by the late Charles Hartshorne and his students. In fact, Whitehead is in this section of his work dramatically re-contextualizing a once well-known discussion of feelings by the British idealist, F. H. Bradley (McHenry, 1992). He argues in effect, against Bradley, that the origin of consciousness and the so-called "higher phases" of experience in more complex organisms can be shown to be a continuous and natural outgrowth of more rudimentary processes, rather than proof of a radically distinct order of being, or of the unreality of concrete, everyday experience. It is an unfortunate irony that Whitehead, as a result of this treatment and of his profound respect (even in disagreement) with Bradley, is thus mistakenly thought to espouse mystical positions that he instead sought to explain and discard as vestiges of the metaphysical dualism he sought to overcome.

The two most pervasive terms employed in these first three portions of the book are "actual entities" (or "actual occasions") and "eternal objects." The first pair of terms represent a translation into English of Descartes's terminology in the *Meditations*, where the question is considered: "what are the *res verae*" (that is, what are the *actual things* or *actual entities* that truly exist or that are real)? Whitehead invokes this Cartesian terminology to indicate that his inquiry, too, is aimed at discovering the true nature of being. The shift toward the term "occasion" and away from "entity" in turn suggests that those actualities are not entitative, substantive, or material in the traditional sense, but are episodes or occasions of pure activity or "process." "Actual occasions" are the fundamental quanta, units, or building blocks ("monads") of which (according to Whitehead's so-called "Ontological Principle") all entities of whatever sort are composed. The Ontological Principle establishes the claim that, at the core, change and becoming are the primary characteristics of "true things," while being conceived as unchanging substance (Aristotle, Locke) or inert matter (Newton, Descartes) is either the product or the appearance of episodes or "occasions" of creative, generative activity.

The discrete properties that occasions of experience possess, however, stem from two quite different sources. Each occasion or episode "prehends" (that is, grasps or actively appropriates, either to incorporate as "feelings" or eliminate) elements or features achieved in past occasions of experience. This fundamental act of prehension distinguishes the present from the past; past occasions are themselves no longer active as prehending subjects, while the concrete results or outcomes of their brief episodic experience are available as determinate objects to be "prehended" by subsequent subjective occasions of experience. Whitehead describes this as his Reformed Subjectivist Principle, also addressed in his Principle of Relativity: "subject" and "object," in contrast to Descartes, do not designate distinct categories of being. Nature is not divided into two quite distinct ontological categories: rather, these terms are temporally relative. Every actual occasion is at first an active subject, grasping and incorporating elements of its environment (its past) and synthesizing these elements into a new and unique occasion of experience, after which this occasion, too, "perishes" (loses its subjective immediacy) and persists thereafter indefinitely as an "object" or datum for future experiences to take account of ("feel") or ignore.

There is, however, a second source of determinateness that contributes to the novelty and uniqueness of each experience. In *The Concept of Nature*, Whitehead had recognized that there are properties (like geometrical shapes and the color blue) that not only are ingredients of specific occasions of experience, but seem to appear and reappear, or to be replicated, in precisely the same fashion in myriad different objects and states of affairs over time. Whitehead called these "enduring objects" or "forms of definiteness." In *Process and Reality* he coins the term "eternal objects" for these Platonic universals, to distinguish them from the characteristics of earlier, objectified occasions prehended as data in each new occasion of experience, or "concrescence." These "eternal objects" bear close comparison to the sense data, sensibilia, universals, or (as the psychologists prefer) qualia that permeated the epistemological theories of early twentieth-century analysis. Again, according to the Ontological Principle, such "objects" are not "actual," as they are not events or processes themselves, but are components or ingredients in actual occasions.

The problem with which Whitehead is wrestling, somewhat in contrast to British and American sense-data theorists, is the origin of novelty (and the explanation, without resort to dualism, of differing degrees of novelty) in the process of becoming. He also must address the question of how a "process" ever issues in anything determinate. How is "being" produced by "becoming?" Whitehead's metaphysical project subsumes their epistemological concern, since he must explain not only how a conscious subject (or even a sentient being) perceives and develops reliable knowledge of its surroundings, but how any entity of whatever sort interacts with its world, weaving elements of that world into its own self-constitution. The epistemological problem of perception and knowledge simply turns out to be a highly specialized variant of a much more generalized and pervasive activity, characteristic of all entities. In this manner, the problem of Cartesian dualism is avoided. Likewise, what for Kant are categories of understanding and limitations or "categoreal obligations" on reason become, for Whitehead, categories of experience generally, and categoreal obligations to which all experience, of whatever sort, must conform. Kant's twelve epistemological "Categories of Understanding" and the resulting categoreal limitations they impose on pure reason are replaced in Whitehead's architectonic by eight metaphysical "Categories of Existence" which collectively impose twenty-seven limitations or "categorial obligations" on experience generally. Such views illustrate Whitehead's gradual migration away from the epistemological concerns of his British analytic colleagues and toward the uniquely American focus on a "metaphysics of experience" as discerned in the thought of C. S. Peirce, William James, and John Dewey.

As noted earlier, the transition from past to present is achieved when a new occasion synthesizes the objective data from its past. This process is termed "perception in the mode of causal efficacy." It characterizes every experience of whatever grade of complexity. Much hangs on whether the replication is indeed precise or approximate. If approximate, then previous finite instantiations of particular qualities and properties might simply be inherited or transmitted from one occasion to the next, without recourse to the notion of "eternal objects" at all. If *the same* color or shape, however, is instantiated identically in occasions separated by substantial distance and time, then causal transmission and repetition do not fully account for the origins and multiple "ingressions" (Whitehead's terminology) of these forms in concrete but discrete episodes of experience. Once again, this is a common problem in sense-data theory, and Russell, Moore, Broad, Ralph Barton Perry, and many others likewise struggled mightily with it. Whitehead finds in favor of a modified Platonism, holding that the definiteness and timelessness of these forms as repeated in experience demonstrates that they "exist independently" in some sense as objects.

This generates a puzzle. Such objects are not themselves *res verae*, and if they "exist" in some sense outside of the flux of ordinary occasions, they can only be characteristics of (or subsumed as properties within) some other kind of actual occasion. Whitehead postulates an everlasting actual occasion, "God" or the "Principle of Concretion," whose principal function seems to be a "primordial envisagement" of the totality of eternal objects in an abstract hierarchy which defines the most perfect possible arrangement of the possibilities collectively available for actualization within each concrete episode of experience in the world. This proposal bears close comparison to Leibniz's pre-established harmony, except that the harmony here is relative, changing, and never fully established. Instead, an initial prehension of the prospects for actualization represented in this divine primordial envisagement repeatedly constitutes the starting-point for each new finite occasion of experience, with each occasion weaving "feelings" of its past of various intensities more or less according to the pattern of possibilities offered by this "initial subjective aim."

It is possible to do without this elaborate account, however, if one abandons the notion of "eternal objects" and, along with them, the view that forms are precisely and repeatedly instantiated in concrete occasions of experience. Causal efficacy, the power of the past, is sufficient to account for the repetition of form, while novelty is an outgrowth both of the inexactness of that replication and the uniqueness of the "weaving" of physical and conceptual feelings or prehensions of the past by present occasions of experience. There is no reliance of process upon a prior conceptual ordering or abstract hierarchy of possibilities, and thus no need to postulate God either as the locus of eternal objects, or as the means by which their ideal ordering is mediated in concrete experience. The price to be paid for this is not only loss of the unusual theological dimensions of Whitehead's thought, but also the notions of "ideal order" and "harmony" themselves – the sort of things that Bertrand Russell uncharitably dismissed as "qualities which only governesses love." Instead, such order and organization, or achievements of value (or of disvalue), as are attained in the world are solely a function of the achievements and accidents of the finite and concrete occasions of experience that constitute the world as we find it.

Whitehead's discussion of "prehension," perception, and causality led to a surprisingly far-sighted evolutionary epistemology that anticipated much of the current discussion of this topic. Causal efficacy is the underlying feature of connectedness between past and present, characteristic (as we have noted) of all entities. As a result of the comparatively sophisticated sentient experience possible for complex, conscious, and self-conscious organisms, however, such organisms are able to isolate and abstract certain precise features from the underlying flux of "blooming, buzzing confusion" (William James) or "firstness" (C. S. Peirce), and attend to these features in detail. This, according to Whitehead, occurs in perception in the mode of "presentational immediacy." Early analytic philosophers had mistaken this kind of perception as the starting-point for analysis, but on Whitehead's account, this "primitive experience" is in fact a very complex mode of perception supervening upon the more fundamental experience of causal efficacy. Moore and his students (if Whitehead is correct) would have eventually discovered that the "brown color patch" and the oblong spheroid that they analyzed as among the primitive sense data constituting their conference table were in fact the end result of a long process of selective abstraction from the concrete experience of transition, conceptual reversion, and isolation in presentational immediacy of the "eternal objects" ingredient in the events that actually constitute the *appearance* of a solid, circular, brown-colored table out of the ceaseless interaction of energy fields.

The remaining two parts of *Process and Reality* are, by comparison, quite brief, and have had a decidedly different historical impact. Part IV, "The Extensive Continuum," continues Whitehead's decades-long study of relativistic geometry, setting forth his views on the nature of the space–time manifold, on measurement, and on the derivation of geometrical points and temporal "point-instants" (which are abstractions) as a limit of overlapping finite volumes (which are concrete events). This material is seldom cited or studied in detail, and its important continuity with Whitehead's earlier work in general relativity theory accordingly is seldom acknowledged (Stolz, 1995).

The obscure fate of Part IV stands in marked contrast to the impact of the equally brief concluding Part V, Whitehead's "final interpretation" devoted to the theme, "God and the World." The poetic remarks here were likely coined in compliance with the terms of the Gifford Lecture series, which require that the lecturer reflect on the implications of his work for natural theology. These twenty pages of modest and touching theological reflection have generated perhaps more commentary than all parts of the rest of the work combined, and have given rise to an entire, distinct field known as "process theology," which has had enormous influence throughout the world since Whitehead's death. Here God is not only conceived as an actual occasion, but as unique in that this episode has as yet no determinate outcome.

According to Whitehead, the "subjective immediacy" of divine experience never "perishes," but is everlasting; hence, God's nature is not fully determinate or complete. God not only provides abstract conceptual aims (hierarchical orderings of eternal objects) for the world that guide or "lure" creativity toward its most optimal outcome (the "Primordial Nature" of God), but also "feels" the resultant experience of the world. The determinate outcome and achievements of the activity of discrete and finite actual occasions are thus ceaselessly "causally objectified" in God's own being, in what Whitehead terms "the Consequent Nature" of God. God is thus somewhat like Hegel's conception of "absolute knowing" in the *Phenomenology of Spirit* (1807): a state of perfect recollection, in which all that is and has been is preserved and held together in an everlasting and perfect harmony as one. Hegel was, of course, no mathematician, and was therefore perhaps less entitled to this elegant restatement of Pythagorianism than the mathematical and logical genius, Whitehead. But it is significant that for both, as for Plato and Pythagoras before them, recollection is the key to immortality.

Bibliography

Editions

Whitehead, Alfred North (1929) *Process and Reality*. New York: Macmillan.
Whitehead, Alfred North (1929) *Process and Reality*. London: Cambridge University Press.
Whitehead, Alfred North (1969) *Process and Reality*. New York: The Free Press.
Whitehead, Alfred North (1978) *Process and Reality: Corrected Edition*, ed. David Ray Griffin and Donald W. Sherburne. New York: The Free Press.

Studies

Ford, Lewis S. (1984) *The Emergence of Whitehead's Metaphysics: 1925–1929.* Albany, NY: State University of New York Press.

Ford, Lewis S. (2000) *Transforming Process Theism.* Albany, NY: State University of New York Press.

Kline, George L. (ed.) *Alfred North Whitehead: Essays on his Philosophy.* New York: Prentice-Hall.

Lowe, Victor (1985/1990) *Alfred North Whitehead: The Man and his Work*, 2 vols. Baltimore, MD: The Johns Hopkins University Press.

Lucas, Jr, George R. (1979) *Two Views of Freedom in Process Thought: A Study of Hegel and Whitehead.* Atlanta, GA: Scholars' Press.

Lucas, Jr, George R. (1983) *The Genesis of Modern Process Thought.* London and Metuchen, NJ: The Scarecrow Press.

Lucas, Jr, George R. (1989) *The Rehabilitation of Whitehead: An Analytic and Historical Analysis of Process Philosophy.* Albany, NY: State University of New York Press.

Lucas, Jr, George R. (1995) Whitehead and Wittgenstein: the critique of Enlightenment and the question concerning metaphysics. In Jaako Hintikka and Klaus Puhl (eds), *Wittgenstein and the British Tradition in Twentieth Century Philosophy*, pp. 122–37. Proceedings of the Seventeenth International Wittgenstein Symposium. Vienna: Verlag Holder-Pichler-Tempsky.

McHenry, Leemon B. (1992) *Whitehead and Bradley: A Comparative Analysis.* Albany, NY: State University of New York Press.

Rescher, Nicholas (1996) *Process Metaphysics: An Introduction to Process Philosophy.* Albany, NY: State University of New York Press.

Schilpp, Paul Arthur (ed.) (1941) *The Philosophy of Alfred North Whitehead* (The Library of Living Philosophers, vol. 20). LaSalle, IL: Open Court.

Sherburne, Donald W. (1963) *A Key to Whitehead's Process and Reality.* Chicago: University of Chicago Press.

Shields, George W. (ed.) (2002) *Process and Analysis.* Albany, NY: State University of New York Press.

Stolz, Joachim (1995) *Whitehead und Einstein.* Frankfurt am Main: Peter Lang.

52

Karl Popper, *The Logic of Scientific Discovery* (1934)

Not Logic but Decision Procedure

Mariam Thalos

In his *magnum opus, The Logic of Scientific Discovery* (first published in German in 1934, English translation, 1959), Karl Popper (1902–1994) makes two fundamental philosophical moves. First, he relocates the center of gravity of the philosophical treatment of science around what he calls the *problem of demarcation*. This is the problem of distinguishing between science, on the one hand, and everything else on the other. (By contrast, his contemporaries of the Vienna Circle, whose positivism would prove the most influential brand of empiricism of the day, located the center of gravity around the problem of linguistic meaning, and used a criterion according to which a statement is meaningful to the extent that one can identify verification conditions for it.) Popper excludes from science such things as logic, metaphysics, Freudian psychoanalysis, and Marx's theory of history.

Second, Popper propounds the doctrine of falsificationism, which handles the problem of demarcation, as well as answers David Hume's shattering attack on science as the premier form of knowledge centuries before. The arguments he mounts for falsificationism would function also as an attack on any account of the scientific enterprise that, like positivism, adheres to the idea that science progresses logically from instances (given in observation or experience) to the high-order generalizations characteristic of mature scientific theory.

In this small space I shall undertake neither to illuminate the nuances of Popper's position, nor to trace the (numerous) lines of criticism that have accumulated against it some seventy years later. I shall busy myself instead with tracing a trajectory of thought on the subject of scientific *reasoning* and its relation to individual *decision-making*, reflecting on Popper's contribution and on how his legacy might be further enlarged.

Reasoning

Hume, like many of his contemporaries and predecessors, divided reasoning into two kinds: theoretical reasoning and practical reasoning. Practical reasoning has the function of controlling action or decision: its point is to figure out what to do. This is contrasted with theoretical reasoning, whose work is to figure out how things stand in the world, rather than what to do about them. Hume and his contemporaries held, moreover, that theoretical and practical reasoning operate independently of one another. This (if true) preserves the impartiality of theoretical reasoning, by way of ensuring that the opinions we hold as to how things stand in the world are not influenced by how we might wish things stood. And this, in turn, guarantees that science is never compromised by wishful thinking.

There is agreement between Hume's empiricist camp and Immanuel Kant's counter-empiricist camp on the subject of having to divide, and subsequently to separate in their operations, the functions of theoretical and practical reasoning. But there is disagreement between them about how each form of reasoning proceeds. For instance, Kant and his followers believed that practical reasoning itself has to be subdivided further, into moral reasoning (which has the office of figuring out what matters – what is *worth* wanting) and the instrumental reasoning that figures out how to achieve it, whilst Hume's followers held that practical reasoning is means–ends reasoning through and through. To this day Humeans maintain that there is no place in practical reasoning for figuring out what is worth wanting, and no point anyway, since one is in no position to *decide* to want; one either does or doesn't, and deciding simply can't swing things one way rather than another.

Humeans and Kantians disagree too about how theoretical reasoning proceeds. Hume's camp believed that theoretical reasoning *vis-à-vis* contingent matters of fact (like, for example, whether the sun shall rise tomorrow, or whether bread nourishes) must proceed from the instances (of the sun having risen in the past, or of bread having nourished in the past) to the sort of universal generalizations that would license inference to future such events. Thus they sought a *logic of induction* for the purposes of science. But Hume, for one, despaired of devising a logic, and resigned himself to skepticism. His followers amongst the positivists (such as Moritz Schlick and Rudolf Carnap) were more optimistic, at least at first, but no more successful.

The Kantians, and Henri Poincaré in particular, sharing Hume's pessimism about a logic of induction, advanced various forms of conventionalism. They held that certain matters could not be left up to observation. One famous example is the choice between Euclidean and non-Euclidean geometry, which they held could not be made by appeal to observation. Conventionalism holds that this choice cannot be made by appeal to how things stand in the world at all. This choice, and others like it, are purely matters of convention – matters of discretion, and of utter indifference for the purposes of science.

The conventionalist's position introduces the idea of *decision* as something narrower than – but none the less performed in the course of – reasoning. Decision-making, according to the conventionalists, is conducted in *both* practical *and* theoretical reasoning. Popper would introduce an even more perplexing twist into this tangle of ideas.

Science and Decision

In no era of Western philosophy before the twentieth century have empiricists tolerated in scientific reasoning (or any academic subject) a garden-variety decision process, such as is occasioned when someone or some group is deciding where to go for lunch. Positivists are no exception: they sought a logic for the advancement of knowledge, not a decision procedure. Their thought was that science – as the premier form of knowledge – would grow exactly in proportion to the growth in the number, variety, and precision of empirical observations. Popper was to be the antidote to their brand of optimism.

First, Popper argued that the positivists' division between meaningful statements (among which are the scientific ones) and everything else (which of course would then deserve being called nonsense) is just arbitrary, resting as it does on an arbitrary – and thus itself unscientific – decision about what to regard as meaningful, namely their verificationist criterion. Popper then argued that observation *alone* could not advance a true scientific hypothesis ahead of its competitors, since any given body of observations will be consistent with numerous and mutually incompatible bodies of theory. What is needed is an account of how an idea, however initially outrageous, can *grow into* something that takes a rightful place amongst the ranks of dignified scientific theories, to the point of overthrowing older and initially better-regarded theories. Such a thing can occur only if there exists a (unique) *scientific method for testing one theory against another*. That method, says Popper, is the method of falsification, which also marks the difference between science and other things. A theory is scientific to the extent that it *excludes* or *prohibits* certain possibilities that are in principle observable (and is *ipso facto* falsifiable). And it is corroborated to the extent that it survives tests aimed at falsifying it.

This position would appear to commit Popper to a certain doctrine, also espoused by the positivists: to wit, the doctrine that observation is in some sense primary or fundamental – at least that it is independently distinguishable from scientific theory as such. But Popper does not seem happy with such a commitment. Like those in Kant's camp (for example N. R. Hanson and the later Ludwig Wittgenstein), Popper repudiates the view that observation is either infallible or foundational. He argues that they are not mere reports of sensations passively registered, but are instead descriptions of what is observed *as interpreted in the light of a theoretical framework*. And this is what he means when he says that perception is an active process, in which the mind assimilates data against a backdrop of theory – that observation is therefore theory-laden. Accordingly, he asserts that statements of observation are open-ended hypotheses: they are not a function of experience alone, nor can they be verified by experience as such. But if this is true, then how can a scientific theory be falsified? How can it even be testable, as it must be if it is even to qualify as scientific? For if it is a matter of judgment, and not of simple fact, whether an observation sentence is true, where is the objectivity in the test? Here now is Popper's twist.

Popper states that acceptance of observation statements is "prompted" by experience, but not determined by it. Therefore observation statements "are accepted as the result of a decision or agreement, and to that extent they are conventions. The decisions are reached in accordance with a procedure governed by rules" (Popper, 1959: 106). All the same, they are free decisions; we have a genuine choice:

> From a logical point of view, the testing of a theory depends upon basic statements whose acceptance or rejection, in its turn, depends upon our *decisions*. Thus it is *decisions* which

settle the fate of theories. To this extent my answer to the question, "how do we select a theory?" resembles that given by the conventionalist; and like him I say that this choice is in part determined by considerations of utility. But in spite of this, there is a vast difference between my views and his. For I hold that what characterizes the empirical method is just this: that the convention or decision does not immediately determine our acceptance of *universal* statements but that, on the contrary, it enters into our acceptance of the *singular* statements – that is, the basic statements. (1959: 108–9)

Popper is very aware of the move he is making: he is saying that scientific reasoning is decision-making *all the way down*. Even the method of testing, while distinguishing science from non-science, still involves a form of decision-making. Now does this view obliterate the distinction between practical and theoretical decision-making? And where, in the end, is there room for the sort of open-ended criticism, and the decisive, or at least genuine, testing of hypotheses against evidence, that Popper so venerates? To the end of his life Popper had no satisfactory answer.

Some of Popper's successors hold that once the potential for genuine, bona fide falsifiability is gone, there is no longer any room for justification of any scientific methodology, in the strict objective sense insisted upon by Popper. For example, Thomas Kuhn and his followers too speak of maintaining and overthrowing scientific theories (Kuhn, 1962). But Kuhnians hold that, when it comes to the question of deciding between competing scientific hypotheses, the affair is social, subject to sociological laws, and not the simple and dignified matter of checking (albeit piecemeal) against the gold standard of evidence. So evidence, in and of itself, can never play the role of absolute and final arbiter, as Popper would have liked. The scientific enterprise, on this view, becomes indistinguishable from the putatively pseudo- or non-scientific. The only standards there can be are the inconstant, shifting standards of (as they might put it) "professional practice." There are no now-and-forever methodologies by means of which science can expect to grow by simple accretion.

This is the doctrine of naturalized epistemology – that there are no now-and-forever, sure-fire methodologies for increasing or refining knowledge of the world. It is nowadays pervasive, and Popper, much as he should have fought it, seemed incapable even of resisting it. Indeed he called himself a naturalist, and was content to acquiesce in some of the naturalist's favorite axioms. For example, he acquiesced in the idea that we should learn about scientific methodology from the history of science. He was fond of using episodes in the history of science himself to reinforce his falsificationist proposal, and in that way blurred the distinction between the context of discovery and the context of justification.

Epistemology: the Individual and the Citizenry

Sometimes a certain contrast is drawn between Popper and Kuhn. Popper, some people have said, is a staunch defender of scientific Reason with a capital R, whilst Kuhn is not. This assessment is too simplistic, as Kuhn himself points out (in Lakatos and Musgrave, 1970: 1–23). After all, it is not at all clear how precisely Popper shall sustain a place for the critical objectivity he holds in such high regard, once one appreciates his position on the nature of evidence and observation. Both Kuhn and Popper acknowledge the role of decision throughout scientific practice, and both ascribe a methodology, or at least a pattern, to scientific activity. To be sure they do not see entirely eye to eye on what the pattern of scientific change looks like in the real-life history of science, or on whether there is genuine advancement in science. (The rather minor differences here are two: (1) Popper does not acknowledge a difference between what Kuhn terms "normal science" and "scientific revolution," whereas Kuhn himself makes much of that difference; and (2) Popper is more on the side of genuine advancement than Kuhn.) Even so, there is a substantive difference between Popper's position and Kuhn's.

That difference lies in their starting positions on the subject of the relation between the history of science and the status of proper scientific methodology. Popper's position is more enduring, and it holds the possibility for a host of developments that Popper himself was not in a position to envision. He can (though he did not himself, possibly for political reasons that I shall not go into here) defend rather well against criticism alleging that he has no logical space for open-ended criticism and objective testing of theory by evidence.

Kuhn begins by examining various episodes in the history of science, and concludes that science does not progress by accretion. Theories, he tells us, are overthrown rather than built upon. He makes no antecedent separation between the subject matters of discovery and justification, and is content, when he fails to find a pattern of growth in the transmitted body of theory, or a pattern to the succession of superseded bodies of theory, to dismiss the idea of now-and-forever methodology entirely. It is not at all clear what sorts of conclusions about matters of methodology he is entitled to draw from the historical and sociological data he amasses. Popper, by contrast, begins (like his positivistic predecessors) with a crisp distinction between the question of methodology and the question of discovery. And there is a path that leads from here to a defense against criticism that alleges no room in his system for objectivity.

Let us call the view that a decision as to what theory to accept (or recommend, or place in high regard, or what have you) is just another practical matter, *pragmatism*. It is the view that the imperatives of science fall under the imperatives of practical life, as a special category. Pragmatism does not distinguish between the decisions of a collective and the decisions of individuals. Now Popper, by acquiescing in the idea that experimentation and observation in science are just more decision-making, adheres to or at least leans in the direction of pragmatism as we have just defined it. And thus he becomes vulnerable to criticism that his methodology is not objective.

But it need not have gone this way. Popper could have acquiesced in the idea that observation *by individuals* is an ordinary matter of individual decision, and thus subject to theoretical bias. But he could have remained firm in the idea that decisions *vis-à-vis* a body of evidence, assembled and preserved by citizens acting, not with personal aims for personal gain, but rather as faithful public officers, are not like everyday personal matters of decision. He could have insisted that decisions of that sort are not similarly subject to such bias because they are subject instead to canons of collective decision, whose standards transcend those of personal decision. Thus Popper could have made effective use of a distinction between individual and collective reasoning, in a way that would have set him apart from all his predecessors. And this move could have rehabilitated and indeed sharpened, rather than blurred, the difference between justifying one theory in preference to another, in relation to a body of evidence, and merely overthrowing the latter in favor of the former.

Now, of course, such a move, if someone were to make it, would require giving a normative account of collective decision, and decision *vis-à-vis* theory acceptance in particular. No such account, or anything remotely like it, exists at this time. But surely the time is now ripe. Perhaps someone will insist that this move is *ad hoc*. And why in particular should the falsificationist be entitled to it? For surely it is available even to the inductivist. There are very good reasons for viewing this move as especially suited to the Popperian position, and far from being *ad hoc*. These reasons are rooted in what we can anticipate a normative account of collective reasoning to look like. In particular we have very good reasons for thinking that an account of collective reasoning *vis-à-vis* theory acceptance (or anything else) could not take the form of a logic, but instead must take the shape of a decision procedure. Hence such an account would fit quite naturally into a Popperian system consisting of decision-making all the way down. Moreover, that decision procedure will by necessity look very much like the criticism-friendly one suggested by Popper. Among many-membered decision-making bodies, the most functional, and certainly the most democratic (in a broad sense), govern themselves by something like Robert's Rules of Order. These rules come quite close to the procedure of critical evaluation Popper esteems. And nothing even remotely like a logic (in the inference-drawing sense) exists for governing the proceedings of any group. This would suggest, though of course it does not prove decisively, that any decision procedure worthy of the name of science shall incorporate just the sort of critical examination of hypotheses *and* evidence that Popper might have sought.

Bringing it up to Date

There is a revival in the inductivist church that has come with the rise of naturalized epistemology. Bayesianism – made possible by certain advances in the application of probability theory – is a marriage between contemporary decision theory, and Bishop Butler's much-admired dictum (endorsed by nearly everybody) that probability is the very guide of life. Very roughly, Bayesians acknowledge that the question for a scientific methodology to address is not "which theory shall we accept (or attach high probabilities to)?" but instead "how must we proceed – in as mechanical a way as possible – from one set of (given) opinions to another, with each new observation, as responsible empiricists ought to do?" And they leave the arrival at a theory for the initial application of their principles as a matter of personal taste. The algorithms they propose for massaging probabilities are perhaps as much in the way of a *logic* as one can hope for. Still, their view accommodates quite well Popper's original idea that everything rests on a bedrock of decision.

The neo-Popperian, who embraces the distinction between the individual and the citizenry that I have sketched, will of necessity tangle with the Bayesian. Their struggle (in the twenty-first century) will be over the role of evidence in the *formation* of scientific theory – with the Popperians having the cloud of history's weightiest opinions on their side.

Bibliography

Editions and translations

Popper, K. (1935) *Logik der Forschung: Zur Erkenntnistheorie der Modernen Naturwissenschaft.* Vienna: J. Springer (orig. pub. 1934).

Popper, K. (1959) *The Logic of Scientific Discovery.* London: Hutchinson.

Popper, K. (1963) *Conjectures and Refutations.* London: Routledge.

Studies and references

Kuhn, T. (1962) *The Structure of Scientific Revolutions.* Chicago: University of Chicago Press.

Lakatos, I. and Musgrave, A. (eds) (1970) *Criticism and the Growth of Knowledge.* New York: Cambridge University Press.

Radnitzky, G. and Andersson, G. (eds) (1978) *Progress and Rationality in Science.* Boston: Reidel.

Thornton, S. (2002) *Popper, Karl.* In Edward N. Zalta (ed.), *The Stanford Encyclopedia of Philosophy* (http://plato.stanford.edu/entries/popper/).

53

Jean-Paul Sartre, *Being and Nothingness* (1943)

The Prodigious Power of the Negative

Thomas R. Flynn

Jean-Paul Sartre (1905–1980) was the quintessential not just French or even urban but Parisian philosopher. Born in Paris, his life and examples seemed to revolve around the capital, in fact the Left Bank, to be exact. Though he loved to travel abroad, he considered his brief boyhood residence in La Rochelle a kind of exile. And yet his conceptual rigor and his powers of psychological description and analysis gave his works, both literary and philosophical, a universal appeal. They earned him a nomination for the Nobel Prize in Literature (1964), which he characteristically refused. Sartre is arguably the most famous philosopher of the twentieth century. And though, like Darwin's *Origin of Species*, it is more mentioned than read, *Being and Nothingness* is his most famous philosophical work.

Published during the Nazi occupation of Paris in 1943, *Being and Nothingness* became the emblem of French existentialism in the immediate post-war years. Its message of individual responsibility ("We are condemned to be free") coupled with the promise that we can always transcend but never discount our situation ("We are free only in situation") gave theoretical impetus to a flood of artistic works that set the cultural style in the West for the next decade.

Part of the book's success came from riding on the wave of an increased interest in "concrete" philosophy epitomized by Jean Wahl's *Vers le concret* (1932). Edmund Husserl's phenomenological method answered this need by its close description of the "givens" of our situation "in their respective modes of givenness." By suspending our ontological commitments to the existence of the objects of our consciousness "in themselves" and limiting ourselves to the rigorous description of what appear (phenomena) in their characteristic ways of appearing, the phenomenologist opened a vast field of investigation that extended from perceptual objects and recollections to aesthetic objects and emotions. It was this possibility of descriptive "argument" that attracted Sartre. It resonated with his considerable gifts for psychological observation and imaginative construction. Not the least of the attractions of *Being and Nothingness* is its series of insightful phenomenological descriptions of shame consciousness, anguish, bad faith, and the like that constitute concrete, experiential "proofs" of Sartre's case at important junctures of his work.

The subtitle of the book is "An Essay on Phenomenological Ontology." Mention of "ontology" suggests the second major presence after Husserl in this opus, namely, Martin Heidegger. Its very title echoes the latter's famous *Being and Time* and the link between time and nothingness is not accidental. But the anthropological and the ethical dimensions of Sartre's work are much more in evidence than in Heidegger's volume, and the detailed discussions of our "situation" that make the Sartrean study so concrete and attractive to a large public are readily dismissed by Heidegger as merely "ontic" in nature. Still, Sartre's concerns were as ontological as were Heidegger's. In an interview toward the end of his life, Sartre argued that this ontological interest was what distinguished him from the Marxists in the final analysis.

The work begins with an introduction that Sartre claims was written last and should be so read. Though assuredly among the most difficult portions of the book, the introduction initiates Sartre's careful progress from a high degree of abstraction to increasingly more concrete determinations of its subject matter in succeeding chapters. Critical of Kant's distinction between phenomenal and noumenal domains, Sartre insists that at least some of the phenomena or appearances that he is describing give us a kind of immediate access to being, what he calls the "being of the phenomenon." Such experiences as boredom and nausea (the title of his philosophical novel that imaginatively anticipates key concepts of the present work) constitute this awareness of the being of the phenomenon. They simply articulate non-conceptually the appearance of that being. What saves Sartre from a phenomenalism that would reduce being to its appearances is his insistence on this experience as an immediate awareness, though not a conceptual grasp, of the being of phenomena. Such phenomena as nausea and boredom are thus "ontological" because they reveal the *trans*phenomenal character of being. But, unlike the Kantian noumenon, the being of the phenomenon is coextensive with every phenomenon and not an entity hidden behind it. Yet this being cannot be subject to the phenomenal condition, namely, that it exist only in so far as it reveals itself. Such is Sartre's core objection to idealism. Unlike Berkeley's famous adage, the "to be" of the being of the phenomenon is not "to be perceived." In other words, the being of the phenomenon surpasses the knowledge we have of it and provides the basis for such knowledge.

What is this being and how may we characterize it? Sartre calls it "being-in-itself" and his phenomenology reveals features that contrast markedly with its counterconcept, the as yet only briefly described being of consciousness (being-for-itself). Being is "in-itself," that is, it is self-identical. The principle of identity applies to it as it does to all being according to Aristotle. Being-in-itself is solid (*massif*), beyond becoming, fully positive, knows no otherness, is not subject to temporality, and can never be derived from another existent by causal necessity. Since possibility belongs to consciousness, being-in-itself or the non-conscious is neither possible nor impossible; it simply is. It is contingent. In the well-known phrase from *Nausea*, it is superfluous (*de trop*). In sum, being is; it is in-itself; and it is what it is. Each of these features distinguishes it from the second basic form of being, being-for-itself or consciousness.

Though Sartre claims being-in-itself and being-for-itself are of equal importance, he devotes a much larger portion of his book to the latter. After reminding us that the concrete reality which he is describing is what Heidegger calls "being-in-the-world," Sartre betrays his anthropological concerns by translating this expression as "man-in-the-world" and raising two questions: "What is the synthetic relation which we call being-in-the-world?" and "What must man and the world be in order for a relation between them to be possible?" In effect, Sartre is posing descriptive and analytical questions, while insisting that our grasp of concrete reality demands a synthesis of the responses to each. His descriptive account of being-for-itself or, roughly, consciousness focuses first on our questioning relation to the world. Our very questioning is questioned. Like Heidegger, Sartre takes this interrogative relation to be basic and yet to presume a pre-interrogative familiarity with being. Again like Heidegger, he examines the negative dimension of our questioning, namely, its assumption that a negative answer is possible; indeed, that the very raising of a question indicates a "pre-judicative comprehension of non-being." Other philosophers have admitted that negation is a quality of our judgments, but Sartre and Heidegger insist that there is a transphenomenal negativity that we disclose when we make such judgments and which is enunciated by such phenomena as fragility and absence just as boredom and nausea reveal the being of phenomena. In this case, the transphenomenality of non-being or nothingness places us in touch with the fundamental relation between man and world that Sartre calls "nihilation" and which is a defining characteristic of consciousness as being-for-itself. In other words, human reality (man) simply "is" that nihilating relationship between consciousness and things. Man is the being by which nothingness enters the world. We must employ scare quotes to say that human reality "is" this relationship because, by its very nature, consciousness or what we may now call "no-thingness" is the internal negation of whatever being ("thingness") one might wish to ascribe to it. Being-for-itself is an exception to the principle of identity. In Sartre's paradoxical formula: human reality is what it is not, and is not what it is; whatever it is, it is in the manner of not-being (nihilating) it.

The remainder of the book elaborates this claim in many ways. Each trades on the ambiguity of this internal negation and offers a more concrete determination of the still abstract concept of being-in-the-world. But one must keep in mind that the ontological root of the freedom that Sartre claims is the definition of "man" is this very lack of self-coincidence which consciousness brings into the very world it constitutes. Human reality, Sartre insists, is free because it is not a self (a thing, being-in-itself) but a presence-to-self (a no-thing, an internal negation of any identity one might fix on it).

Perhaps the best-known example of such elaborations of this ontological paradox which is human reality is Sartre's account of bad faith. A form of self-deception, what makes bad faith possible is the fundamental dividedness of human reality. But since the for-itself excludes appeal to an unconscious awareness (Sartre denies the existence of an unconscious and supplants much psychoanalytic discourse with appeals to bad faith), the source of this lie to oneself must rest in the consciously lying subject. The possibility of self-deception rests in a twofold duality of the subject. Consciousness may comprehend at a pre-reflective level more than it knows reflectively. But this "duality" obtains even at the pre-reflective level, for we are aware of our ontological state of non-self-coincidence and hence can undertake the bad-faith project of denying this situated freedom by acting as if it were not so. This duality within our conscious life makes it possible for us to enter into a project of self-deception that is pre-reflectively sustained and carried out while reflectively ignored or denied. Toward the end of the book, Sartre will introduce the hermeneutic of what he calls "existential psychoanalysis" as the method of bringing such pre-reflective comprehension to reflective awareness. But he admits that this process has yet to find its Freud.

The ontological paradox comes to full focus in his account of "situation." Every human reality is being-in-situation, which is a more concrete form of being-in-the-world. Humans are not free except in-situation. Situation is a synthesis of the givens of our lives such as our past, our geographical place, our physical characteristics, our death, on the one hand, and our manner of living these features by surpassing (not-being) them, on the other. Sartre calls the former aspect of any situation "facticity" and the latter "transcendence." But situation is an ambiguous phenomenon. It is impossible to determine the precise contribution of "facticity" and "transcendence" to any given situation. Bad faith consists in lying to ourselves about this ontological duality either by trying to collapse our transcendence into our facticity as the determinists do or by volatilizing our facticity into transcendence through wishful thinking. The former claims "that's just the way I am," whereas the latter, ignoring the facts of the case, pretends by sheer velleity to become whatever it wishes. Bad faith is the practical denial of our situated freedom and its attendant responsibility.

But the ontological paradox that human reality engenders extends to the temporal domain as well. Human reality "is" not; it "temporalizes" itself according to three fundamental ekstases. In fact, one could say that the perennial paradoxes of time are given ontological status in the Sartrean notion of being-in-situation. For Sartre, "objective" clock-time is derived from an original, ekstatic temporality. From the temporal viewpoint, facticity is the past, transcendence is the future as possibility, and the present is "presence-to." But these distinctions are aspects of our fundamental intuition of temporality as a moving whole. They are not juxtaposed slices in search of some atemporal binding. Rather, they are aspects of a revolving, internal relation that Sartre calls "myness" and which he will later analyze as the "circle of selfness." That revolving cycle of reflection-reflecting is Sartre's alternative to the Cartesian "thinking thing." If Hume found only a bundle of impressions and ideas when he reflected in search of a substantial self, Sartre discovers an interminable circle of reflection that by virtue of its non-self-identity "temporalizes" itself in three dimensions. He captures this paradoxical nature of being-for-itself by saying it "is" not but rather "is/was," a neologism that catches ephemeral temporalization on the wing.

Presence-to is the for-itself in its core non-self-identity. Whenever we try to reduce human reality to its temporal "moment" we encounter the indissoluble dyad, being and nothingness. There is always a temporal "spread" into the immediate past and future that prevents human reality from collapsing into an atemporal instant. In fact, the instant is the locus of our possible conversion to another life-directing "choice." As such, the instant haunts our present direction with the pre-reflective awareness that we are radically free to "choose" otherwise, indeed, that we are free to be other than we are. This awareness is the famous existential *Angst*. To be is to choose and to cease to choose is to cease to be. But the fundamental "choice" that gives our lives unity and direction is the sustaining force for all the secondary choices that characterize our daily lives. Such fundamental "choice" is not the selection from a list of motives or reasons.

Rather, it is what renders our reasons reasonable and makes our motives motivate. We discover our defining "choice" by interpreting its indications in the secondary choices we make every day. "Choice" in this original sense simply is the sustaining direction of our secondary choices. The latter are the symbolic expression of the former. We accept or flee our radical responsibility for this value-constituting "choice" in good faith or bad, but we cannot escape the anguished awareness of its presence or its utter contingency.

The third basic ontological dimension is being-for-others. If nausea reveals the brute existence of being-in-itself and anguish the responsibility of our radical freedom, shame consciousness is the index of our awareness of the Other (Sartre's term for the other as subject). In his phenomenological description of a person's being caught in a voyeuristic act, Sartre parses our experience of embarrassment as a complex awareness of both our embodiedness and another's consciousness. His point is that this awareness of both dimensions is immediate and intuitive. It carries a certitude which exceeds the probability of arguments from analogy to the existence of other minds. This new dimension of being, with its distinctive characteristics, is the result of our encounter with the Other. One cannot deduce this aspect from either the in-itself or the for-itself. It would seem to follow that human reality is only accidentally social in character; that the interpersonal dimension of its being is an accident of the "spontaneous upsurge" of other subjects. And yet, this merely means that the existence of the Other is no less contingent (*de trop*) than my own. There are features of my facticity that depend essentially on my being-for-others. To ignore them is to wander in abstraction.

Given the ocular basis of our awareness of other subjects (the looking/looked-at model of interpersonal relations), it is not surprising that our concrete relations with others are described in terms resembling a game of mutual stare-down: we either transcend the other's transcendence or are transcended by it. In *Being and Nothingness*, Sartre equates alienation with this objectification and considers our relations with each other to be originally conflictive, a view that he will modify in his later work. So the love relationship in this text is interpreted as one instance of this project of recovery of my freedom, objectified and possessed by the Other's gaze. But like all attempts at synthesizing transcendence and facticity, such would-be fusion of consciousnesses is bound to fail. In a problematic footnote, Sartre admits that "an ethics of deliverance and salvation" is not thereby excluded but this would require a "radical conversion which we can not discuss here" (Sartre, 1956: 412, n14). He offers reflections for such an ethics in his posthumously published *Notebooks for an Ethics*. There he speaks of authentic love and non-objectifying interpersonal relations, implying that the alienating relations described in *Being and Nothingness* are historically conditioned and not insuperable.

The concept of situation renders Sartre's account still more concrete. Of its many features, he selects five for detailed consideration: my place, my past, my environment, my fellow man (where he discusses language), and my death. The ambiguity of the given and the taken (facticity and transcendence) pervades each of these categories as it does situation generally.

Each turn of the spiral of Sartre's argument toward greater concreteness seems guided by one overriding concern: to underscore our freedom and responsibility for every dimension of our existence. If there is no freedom without situation nor situation without freedom, human reality finds its responsibility qualified but not reduced by the various facets of its being-in-situation. Yet human reality itself is abstract in comparison with the individual person, which Sartre equates with our fundamental project uncovered by existential psychoanalysis. *Being and Nothingness* provides the fundamental ontology that prepares the ground for such an analysis by offering us a theory of human reality at its more abstract levels of being. But he reserves for the hermeneutics of individual actions to reveal the process of personalization that is the concrete living individual. His subsequent "biographies" commence this undertaking.

Sartre will elaborate the concept of situation as he builds a social ontology in his *Critique of Dialectical Reason*. But by then he will have supplemented, if not replaced, the looking/looked-at model of interpersonal relations with one of *praxis* (human action in its historical context). Correspondingly, the dichotomies of in-itself and for-itself are moderated in a practical dialectic that issues in group activity and mediated reciprocity rather than conflict. Still, despite a practical unity that sustains social predicates, the Other remains "out of reach" because of the internal negation that continues to constitute the subject-agent even in Sartre's later works, testifying once again to the prodigious power of the negative.

Bibliography

Editions and translations

Sartre, J-P. (1943) *L'Être et le néant*. Paris: Gallimard.

Sartre, J-P. (1956) *Being and Nothingness*, trans. H. E. Barnes. New York: Philosophical Library.

Sartre, J-P. (1976) *Critique of Dialectical Reason*, vol. 1, trans. A. Sheridan-Smith. London: New Left Books (orig. pub. 1960).

Sartre, J-P. (1991) *Critique of Dialectical Reason*, vol. 2, trans. Q. Hoare. London: Verso (orig. pub. 1985).

Sartre, J-P. (1992) *Notebooks for an Ethics.*, trans. D. Pellauer. Chicago: University of Chicago Press (orig. pub. 1983).

Studies

Catalano, J. S. (1974) *A Commentary on Jean-Paul Sartre's Being and Nothingness.* New York: Harper and Row.

Detmer, D. (1986) *Freedom as a Value: A Critique of the Ethical Theory of Jean-Paul Sartre.* LaSalle, IL: Open Court.

Flynn, T. R. (1984) *Sartre and Marxist Existentialism: The Test Case of Collective Responsibility.* Chicago: University of Chicago Press.

Howells, C. (ed.) (1992) *The Cambridge Companion to Sartre.* Cambridge: Cambridge University Press.

Santoni, R. (1995) *Bad Faith, Good Faith, and Authenticity in Sartre's Early Philosophy.* Philadelphia: Temple University Press.

Schilpp, P. A. (ed.) (1981) *The Philosophy of Jean-Paul Sartre.* LaSalle, IL: Open Court.

54

Maurice Merleau-Ponty, *Phenomenology of Perception* (1945)

How is the Third-person Perspective Possible?

Stephen Priest

If the 1945 work of the French existential phenomenologist Maurice Merleau-Ponty (1908–1961) *Phenomenology of Perception* deserves the status of a classic it is for its thesis that the existence of one's own body (*le corps propre*) is prior to the problems of philosophy, science, and common sense. The concepts needed to think about mind and matter, space and time, self and other, things and the world depend on a primordial, practical, and pre-reflective embodiment in the world. The truth of the descriptions of Merleau-Ponty's existential phenomenology is putatively prior to any scientific claim because it is necessary for its formulation, necessary for its truth or falsity, and, *a fortiori*, necessary for any knowledge of its truth or falsity. Here I describe the purported primordiality of *le corps propre* and identify some of the limits it usefully exposes in scientific explanations of the distinctively human.

In a partial repudiation of Husserl's 1913 *epoché* but a partial endorsement of the Moravian's mid-1930s doctrine of the *lifeworld* (*Lebenswelt*), Merleau-Ponty says that the world is not what I think but what I live through. The subject is his body and *le corps propre* is a living agent. The Heideggerian existential category *being-in-the-world* (*in-der-Welt-sein*) is substituted for Husserl's methodologically solipsistic reduction of the world to its givenness to a pure ego (*reine Ich*) within the field of transcendental subjectivity. Over-cognitive philosophical and scientific conceptions rely on *pre-reflective experience* or *the pre-predicative life of consciousness* (*la vie antéprédicative de la conscience*) which is always embedded in a finite situation in a way that ultimately depends upon the irreducible and inextricable *being-in-the-world* of *le corps propre*, the terms of which may be separated in abstract thought but not in existence. Merleau-Ponty hopes to disclose and describe the ambiguous but primordial levels of being that make any theorizing possible, but in a way that eschews sensationalist foundationalism. The sensation is not "the unit of perception." There are no uninterpreted sensations so no "sense-data." By describing the pre-objective domain (*domaine préobjectif*), a number of dualisms which constitute metaphysical problems will be exposed as not existentially fundamental, but as constituted by consciousness.

Le Corps Propre

Merleau-Ponty thinks *le corps propre* has characteristics incompatible with its being only an *object* (*objet*). Although my body is physical, and from the point of view of the other it appears as an object, my body *qua* mine is a *body subject*.

For something to be an object is for it to be at some distance from me, paradigmatically standing in front of me. Even if most objects are not present before me, if I think of a physical object I think of it as if it were present to me. This is its paradigmatic mode of phenomenological presentation and is suggested by the Latin etymology of *objet* (in *objectus*: *a lying before* or *opposite*). A physical object is in principle observable with the objectivity or detachment that observation entails. If a physical object is in practice unobservable, its being an object is partly its being thinkable as something observable and thereby remote (*éloigné*). We can think of objects in the abstract because some of them are directly present within our tactile or visual fields.

I can manipulate a physical object, tour it, or pick it up. A physical object gains and loses properties but nevertheless remains the object it is through such transitions. A physical object presents *sides* (*côtés*), or *profiles* (*profils, Abschattungen*) and would be presented as an idea (*idée*) and not as a thing (*chose*) if it were not presented in that way. Something can be an object only to the degree to which it can be moved away from me (*éloigné*), and ultimately disappear from my visual field. Merleau-Ponty says that in the case of a physical object its presence entails its possible absence. His phenomenology also entails that its absence entails a possible presence.

The way in which the existence of my own body is phenomenologically presented to me is radically different from these. My body is constantly kinaesthetically or subliminally perceived by me, even though the practical articulation of my body renders "kinaesthetic sensation" a naïveté. Physical objects are intermittently and non-kinaesthetically perceived by me. I do not leave my body and my body does not leave me. My body is not at the extremity of some indefinite exploration. It defies clinical, objective, third-person observation or exploration by me. My body exhibits a peculiar phenomenological subjectivity because it always presents itself visually to me from the same angle. Its continuing existence is not a continuing existence in front of me in the world. It is not an objective particular that I could encounter, tour, or pick up. Its existence is continuous from my subjective point of view. I am my body but phenomenologically not quite it. My body is always intimately "near" me. My body is always "there" for me in the sense of never absent from me. My body is never wholly and objectively before me. I cannot single it out as one particular amongst others in my visual field. My body is perpetually *marginal* in every perception that is mine. My body is *with* me in a sense that is more intimate than accompaniment or mere objective juxtaposition.

Although physical objects also never expose one of their sides to me without thereby concealing the others, in their case I can choose which side they present by moving my body or by moving them. My body in contrast only ever presents part of the front of my torso and my legs within my visual field and if I move then I do not thereby cause a very different aspect of my body to appear.

My habitual actions are part of the original structure of my own body, rather than contingent appendages to it, because *le corps propre* is essentially an agent. My dispositions are instrumental complexes integral to my body and my body itself may be correctly described as my *basic* habit. It makes possible and explains all my other behavioral habits.

My body is as permanent as I am. It is where I am. It is when I am. Its unvarying perspective is a necessity in the quasi-transcendental sense of being a necessary condition for my experiences and for their being mine. It follows that nothing in the course of my experience could refute the claim that my body exists. To that extent, my existence *qua* body-subject is *a priori* and, in that weak Kantian sense of "necessary" which means "not refutable by experience," necessary.

I use my body to observe physical objects, manipulate them, examine them, walk round them, so *le corps propre* is not another thing which I manipulate, observe, or tour. For this to be possible I would need a meta-body which itself would be unobservable without a meta-meta-body and so on. The absence of my body is inconceivable by me whereas the absence of any object is readily conceivable. I cannot see my own head, except perhaps parts of my nose end and the rims of my eye sockets. I have never seen my own face. I can see my eyes in mirrors but they are the eyes of another seen from the outside not my living eyes as I see through them. Although startled to see myself in a mirror in a shop window, I cannot easily catch myself seeing myself. The nearer the aspects of *le corps propre* considered are to the eyes, the less plausibly it can be construed as an object. My body is a phenomenological quasi-space.

To the extent that my body sees or touches the world it cannot be seen or touched by me. I move objects by using my body but I move my body by moving. I do not find my body in one region of objective space and then move it to another. I have no need to search for my body, it is already with me. I am located in a certain place from which I see objects and which I cannot see. My body is a *subject–object*, not just an object.

Subjective Points of View

The theory of the body is already a theory of perception. We can perceive physical objects only because we are body-subjects. When I walk round my apartment, the various aspects it presents to me could not appear as views of one and the same thing if I did not know that each presents the apartment seen from one spot or another. I have to be a persisting body-subject adopting a sequence of subjective points of view in order for the apartment to be presented as the same apartment to me. Merleau-Ponty also thinks I have to be at least implicitly aware of the continuity of my own body during this process in order for anything to be presented as the same thing to me through my fluctuating perceptions of it.

There are two kinds of objectivity. On the one hand, something might be presented to me from the front, as detached, or "over-there." On the other hand, something might be presented from above or in plan. The plan view is typically more complete than the front view, not more true or accurate. It is the apartment seen from above. I have a subjective point of view on the neighboring house which thereby presents some sides but not others. If I change my viewpoint or use an aeroplane the house presents other aspects. Merleau-Ponty judges it meaningless to speak of the house *seen from nowhere* (*vue de nulle part*) because seeing is always seeing from somewhere. An object *seen from nowhere* would be invisible. From the subjective point of view of my body I never see the six sides of the cube as equal in length (even if the cube is transparent). Nevertheless, I have a concept of the whole cube and "cube" has a meaning. The cube as it is in itself, beyond its phenomenological *Abschattungen*, has six sides of equal length. This concept of objectivity depends upon a series of phenomenological presentations which depend in turn on *le corps propre*.

Making Space

Space is neither a "container" nor an "ether" because these concepts apply only to objects, not to the space objects occupy. According to Merleau-Ponty, a direction can only exist for a subject who adopts it and the orientation of what is presented within the visual field is inexplicable by the existence of my body construed only as an object in objective space. It is explicable by my body as *le corps propre*; a pattern of possible actions in a phenomenological quasi-space defined by tasks and practical situations. Things are presented to my body in a pattern of possibilities and impossibilities depending on my practical projects, depending on what is to be done. Space as we think of it, in the abstract, or in geometry, physics, or geography depends upon the primitive and practical orientations of *le corps propre* in the world. Hiking over the landscape makes geography possible.

The pre-reflective space of *le corps propre* is prior to rationalism and empiricism about space. Space as an object of thought or space as a sensory presentation would not be possible without lived spatial routes taken through the world. Merleau-Ponty thinks there is an *absolute here* (*un ici absolu*) which common-sensical spatio-temporal location depends upon phenomenologically. Something can only be presented as here, or in another place, if it is presented to a body-subject who is "here," in phenomenological quasi-space. Nevertheless the *absolute here* is an absolute "within the relative" (or relational) because no subject can adopt a *view from nowhere* (*spectacle de nulle part*).

The Thing

Merleau-Ponty analyzes the thing as an *intersensory entity* (*chose intersensorielle*). The problem is how an object can be presented as numerically identical through a sequence of experiences each of which presents a qualitatively distinct content given that no single *quale* need endure through any sequence of perceptions of the same object, nor does endure through the exercise of different sensory modalities. Merleau-Ponty's solution is to say that the object is presented as a whole even in a partial perception of it. Indeed, being presented with a part is only intelligible if it is or could be being presented with part of a whole. The properties of a thing which appear are properties of one another and thereby constitute one and the same thing. Merleau-Ponty postulates no quasi-Lockean substance or *substratum* that the properties of the object are properties of. That would be phenomenologically illegitimate and arguably neither necessary nor sufficient for the endurance of numerically the same object over time.

Other Subjects

Merleau-Ponty raises the question of how the word "I" can be put into the plural. He rejects the conjunctive Cartesian assumption that first-person singular psychological ascriptions are certain and indubitable but third-person psychological ascriptions are uncertain and dubitable. The existence of what he calls *the human world* (*le monde humain*) makes possible a degree of certainty and uncertainty about both one's own reality and the reality of others. The human world would be unintelligible without the subjectivity of others. The human world is intelligible, so there is the subjectivity of others. For example, someone uses the pipe for smoking, the spoon for eating, the bell for summoning. The artifacts of the human world have a *human atmosphere* (*une atmosphère de l'humanité*) and carry the stamp (*la marque*) of human purposes and acts and so presuppose the embodied subjectivity of the other.

Merleau-Ponty also rejects the Cartesian assumption that the body of another is inhabited (*habité*). It is a mistake to think of the person as divided into two parts, one wholly mental and the other wholly physical. Already in *The Structure of Behaviour* he had introduced the distinction between "human predicates" and "mental predicates" and argued that our having the concept of the whole human being is a necessary condition of our ascribing mental or physical properties to that human being. A person is not a combination of a mental soul and a physical body so nothing psychologically inner or private dwells in the body. The body of the other is a body-subject. Indeed, it is not a phenomenological or a sincere psychological option for me to assume that the other is not a whole living *corps propre*. The other's body is not given only as an object for me. The trace (*la trace*) of the other is the other as not fully present and not fully absent. The trace resists any clean assimilation to mind or body, interior or exterior, subject or object. *Any* lived body is a *subject–object* (*sujet–objet*).

Self and other are mutually dependent. There is no such being as myself without others who I am not, and no such being as the other without some self whom he or she is not. That we have a concept of ourselves living together in one public human world as anonymous subjects of perception entails that there exists the primordial phenomenon of *the body-for-us*.

Nevertheless, because I have a body which presents a physical exteriority to the other, I may be reduced to the status of an object beneath the other's gaze in a quasi-Hegelian or Sartrean antagonistic power struggle. Then I no longer count as a person for him/her. In a parallel fashion I may master the other through turning my look (*regard*) on him/her. Because the other has a hold over me, a hold over what I am, I cannot ultimately and authentically doubt his/her existence, the reality of his/her physical subjectivity. We constitute each other as mutually constituting one another.

Soulless Cartesianism

Because I am most fundamentally a body-subject I am not a pure subject such as a Husserlian transcendental ego (*transzendentale Ich*) or a Platonic or Cartesian soul. Nor, on the other hand, am I a pure object like a physical object. Merleau-Ponty rejects mind–body dualism because he rejects the view that I am or have a mind that could exist independently of my embodiment. He rejects materialism because any purely physicalist explanation of my lived subjectivity is inadequate to its phenomenology. He rejects idealism as inconsistent with yet presupposing my embodiment in the physical world. Merleau-Ponty also repudiates Husserl's endorsement of Augustine's dictum that truth inhabits the inner man. Not only does truth not inhabit the inner man, there is no inner man. The human being is inextricably in the world, and only in the world does he/she know him/herself.

Nevertheless, there are strong residual Cartesian elements in *Phenomenology of Perception*. Merleau-Ponty thinks it impossible to doubt one's own existence, even though Descartes was wrong to think that being in a mental state entails knowing that one is in that state. Merleau-Ponty thinks that each person has to think the Cartesian *cogito* in application to their own case to perceive its truth. It cannot be appreciated in the abstract or if couched in covert or overt third-person grammatical form.

Despite his repudiation of incorrigibility, Merleau-Ponty endorses the Cartesian thesis that consciousness entails self-consciousness in the strong, not merely dispositional, form that all occurrent consciousness entails occurrent consciousness of that consciousness by that consciousness. He thinks this is a necessary condition for consciousness having an object. He holds that Cartesians are right to insist that how significance and intentionality could consist in only molecular structures or masses of cells can never be understood. If we do not view ourselves only as objects but as body-subjects this problem need not arise. Because the subject is a body-subject, on the one hand the subject cannot be a series of psychic events and on the other cannot be eternal.

In and Out of Time

Time presupposes a *supplément* of time (*un supplément de temps*); a standpoint which is outside time in allowing a view of time, but inside time because itself temporal. Any cognitive grasp of time is grounded in the unreflected lived experience of time. In any science, phenomenology, or philosophy of time *le corps propre* is presupposed. *Le corps propre* is temporal, *le corps propre* constitutes time so, Merleau-Ponty concludes, time constitutes itself (*il se constitue*). In thinking of time one tacitly assumes a witness in a particular spatial location viewing successive events. Time is not like a river, not a flowing substance but events are cut out (*découpés*) by a finite observer from the spatio-temporal totality of the objective world. If we abstract from the perspectives of the real or ideal observer then we can make no phenomenological sense of the idea of an event. The Parmenidean consequence is that the event has no place in the objective world and the world itself is simply one indivisible and unchanging being (*un seul être indivisible et qui ne change pas*). Merleau-Ponty concludes that time is not a real or subject-independent process.

Unblocking the Roads to Freedom

Following Sartre, Merleau-Ponty thinks that putative obstacles to freedom are really devices deployed by freedom. For example, a rock face counts as "unclimbable" only for some (actual or possible) person intending to climb it. The projects of *le corps propre* carve out meanings from the uniform mass of the *in-itself* and cause a disambiguated world to arise, a world of significant things. Nothing can limit freedom, except those limits that freedom has set itself. *Le corps propre* fashions the world that limits me, so the body-subject constitutes the world and the world constitutes the body-subject. However, neither the world nor the living subject is ever fully constituted. We are always free in the sense of retaining the capacity to choose; the disposition or power of doing or thinking one thing rather than another but only within a constituted situation. *That* we may choose is a fact. *What* we may choose is circumscribed by our situation. The world is the totality of situations, not as their mere aggregate, but as the situation of all situations.

How Scientific is Science?

Science rests upon assumptions that cannot be justified scientifically. The scientist is a body-subject in the human world but bodily subjectivity and the human world sharply resist reductivist scientific explanation. Reductivist science is inauthentic because it denies the reality of that which makes it possible. Merleau-Ponty says that he cannot conceive of himself as only a part of the world, as only an object of biological, psychological, or sociological inquiry. I cannot reduce myself to just what science says I am. It is not just that it is psychologically impossible to do this, or requires immense self-deception, although it is partly that. The scientific reductivist view is self-refuting.

The failure of science to explain human reality originates in its obsession with objective thought: the treating of any subject matter as *only other* or as *only abstract*. Of course, Merleau-Ponty does not mean that scientific claims should be reconstrued as mere matters of opinion. He means that objective thought cannot explain subjective subject matter. Merleau-Ponty recovers and describes a primitive and practical bodily experience of the world which is scientifically inexplicable. Psychologists, especially those of a behaviorist or materialist persuasion, adopt the standpoint of objective thought and thereby reduce persons to objects. This is self-refuting because the psychologist is himself a body-subject phenomenologically similar to the persons he studies.

Merleau-Ponty thinks that everything that I know about the world, including any science, is gained from my own particular point of view. Without the *being-in-the-world* of *le corps propre* and the point of view of *le corps propre* the symbols of science would be meaningless. He argues that all science is built upon the world as directly experienced or "lived" (*le monde vécu*). People are worthy of moral respect because they are subjects not just objects. If we allow the scientific view of the world to destroy subjectivity, individuality, and freedom in theory, we allow a spurious legitimacy to their destruction in practice.

Bibliography

Editions and translations

Merleau-Ponty, Maurice (1942) *La Structure du comportement*. Paris: Presses Universitaires de France.
Merleau-Ponty, Maurice (1945) *Phénoménologie de la perception*. Paris: Gallimard.
Merleau-Ponty, Maurice (1962) *Phenomenology of Perception*, trans. Colin Smith. London: Routledge.
Merleau-Ponty, Maurice (1965) *The Structure of Behaviour*, trans. A. L. Fisher. London: Methuen.

Studies and references

Husserl, Edmund (1950) Pariser Vorträger. In *Husserliana – Edmund Husserl, Gesammelte Werke. Auf Grund des Nachlasses veröffentlicht vom Husserl-Archiv (Louvain) unter Leitung von H. L. Van Breda*, vol. I, pp. 3–39. The Hague: Martinus Nijhoff.
Husserl, Edmund (1975) *The Paris Lectures*, trans. P. Koestenbaum. The Hague: Martinus Nijhoff.
Moran, Dermot (2000) New books on Merleau-Ponty. *International Journal of Philosophical Studies*, 7 (3): 393–402.
Priest, Stephen (1991) *Theories of the Mind*. London: Penguin.
Priest, Stephen (1998) *Merleau-Ponty*. London and New York: Routledge.
Priest, Stephen (2000a) Merleau-Ponty's concept of the body-subject. *Nursing Philosophy*, 1: 1–2.
Priest, Stephen (2000b) Taking Merleau-Ponty literally: reply to Dermot Moran. *International Journal of Philosophical Studies*, 8 (2): 247–51.

55

R. G. Collingwood, *The Idea of History* (1946)

History as the Science of Mind

Jonathan Rée

In his touching but astringent *Autobiography*, published in 1939, R. G. Collingwood (1889–1943) said that the main aim of his intellectual endeavors had always been "to bring about a *rapprochement* between philosophy and history." He recalled a chance encounter at the age of nine with an antique textbook on meteorology, geology, and the movements of the planets. He was already an enthusiast for modern physics, and his astonishment on seeing how science had changed in the past two hundred years gave him his first glimpse of the "secret" that was to fascinate him for the rest of his life: that historicity pervades our lives, and even our most absolute truths "have a history of their own" (Collingwood, 1939: 77, 1–2).

With the help of his father, a painter and archeologist, the young Collingwood became an expert on Roman Britain, and as an adult he maintained a leading position amongst professional historians (see, for example, Collingwood, 1923, 1930, 1936). But when he became a student and then teacher of philosophy at Oxford University before World War I, he was confronted by a fashion for "realism" – an echo of the self-styled anti-Hegelianism of G. E. Moore and Bertrand Russell – and conceived a life-long antipathy to it. (The British philosophical establishment responded by ignoring him.) Collingwood had many criticisms of realism, but his principal complaint was simply that it "erred through neglecting history" (Collingwood, 1939: 28; it should be noted that Collingwood took care to be etymologically correct, always using the word "history" to designate discourses about the past rather than the past itself).

Collingwood's double life as philosopher and historian convinced him that history had undergone a scientific revolution in the nineteenth century, comparable to the one that had transformed physics in the seventeenth. And just as philosophy since Descartes had busied itself with the implications of scientific physics, so, he argued, it should now attend to those of scientific history (Collingwood, 1939: 78–9). According to Collingwood, history had become a science in fundamentally the same way as physics: historians had realized that science is not so much a repository of true propositions as a workshop in which problems are formulated and investigated, and that it progresses not by stockpiling masses of "truths" but by asking a few "good questions" and insisting on "right answers." They had, in other words, implicitly repudiated the "logic of propositions" and replaced it with a "logic of question and answer" (see Collingwood, 1939: 36–7). History became a science when it gave up "scissors and paste" – Collingwood's characteristically homely phrase for the chronicler's practice of making compilations of all available memories, opinions and anecdotes – just as physics became one when it realized that nature was not so much a Sphinx asking us riddles as a prisoner under interrogation. In science, it was always ourselves "that did the asking" (Collingwood, 1939: 78–9).

When Collingwood said that history had become scientific, he did not mean that it had adopted the methods of natural science, but, on the contrary, that it had forged a quite distinctive scientific method of its own. This method, as Collingwood expounded it in *An Autobiography*, boils down to six fundamental points, all of them somewhat surprising if not counter-intuitive:

1   The subject matter of history has a continuing life, rather like a habit of smoking which lingers even in someone who has given it up; hence "the past which an historian studies is not a dead past, but a past which in some sense is still living in the present" (Collingwood, 1939: 141, 97).
2   The raw materials of history, such as documents, inscriptions, or artifacts, must be treated not as testimony but as evidence; in other words they must be cajoled or tortured into yielding solutions to our own problems – answering statistical or economic questions which might never have occurred to their makers, or revealing facts which they were consciously or unconsciously trying to conceal (Collingwood, 1939: 96, 133).
3   Historical understanding is concerned not with "the past" as a whole but only with humans and their "actions" (human responses to the eruption of Vesuvius in AD 79 are of historical interest, for example, but the eruption itself is not); and since actions are performed in the light of the "situations" people take themselves to occupy – their self-interpretations as we might say – they must be seen as expressions of "thought"; hence "all history is the history of thought" (Collingwood, 1939: 102, 128 n1, 110).
4   The main task of history is to identify the problems that people have set themselves in the past; an account of political theory, for example, should not be "the history of different answers given to one and the same question, but the history of a problem more or less constantly changing" (Collingwood, 1939: 62–3).
5   The identification of past problems requires that ideas and knowledge from the past be rethought and relearned in the present (historians cannot understand ancient mathematics historically, for instance, unless they grasp it mathematically as well); so in general "historical knowledge is the re-enactment in the historian's mind of the thought whose history he is studying" (Collingwood, 1939: 111, 112).
6   Hence – strangest of all – the historian must become a "microcosm" in which past thoughts are repeated, and history is nothing less than "the self-knowledge of mind" (Collingwood, 1939: 114–15).

Collingwood knew that the conception of history as self-knowledge would be mocked by his "realist" colleagues with their philistine axiom that "knowing makes no difference to what is known" (Collingwood, 1939: 44). They would accuse him of rampant idealism: of postulating an occult "life" linking the historian to the events of the past, of neglecting economics and production in favour of "thought," and of relativizing history to the solipsistic subjectivity of the present. Collingwood was sure he could fend off such attacks, but confessed that his arguments were buried in a mass of notes and not yet ready for publication. It was "only a question of time and health," he said optimistically; but although he was only forty-nine when he wrote *An Autobiography*, he had already suffered a stroke and knew he was not likely to live long (Collingwood, 1939: 117). He drove himself courageously for four more years, but when he died in 1943 his work on history was unfinished.

The Idea of History (henceforth *IH*) is a selection from Collingwood's manuscripts and papers put together by T. M. Knox, who based himself mainly on a text of thirty-two lectures delivered in 1936. The series had opened with some general remarks about the nature of history, but soon opened into a critical history of history which surveyed the stages through which history had passed on its way to becoming scientific. First there was the Greco-Roman discovery of the mutability of human fate, which unfortunately exempted certain principles (such as justice, humanity, or Rome) which were treated as perennial and incorruptible. The classical sense of history was radicalized by Christian doctrines of the folly and fragility of earthly existence, which ensured that "the process of historical change was no longer conceived as flowing, so to speak, over the surface of things, and affecting their accidents only, but as involving their very substance" (*IH*, 49). The third phase, romantic history, ultimately led to the realization that the character of a society is not fixed by nature but "made what it is by that people's historical experience" (*IH*, 91). Fourth and last, history had recently become an autonomous science, confidently pursuing its own problems in the knowledge that "reality consists neither of isolated particulars nor of abstract universals but of individual facts whose being is historical" (*IH*, 190, 141).

After this survey, which apparently follows the (now lost) text of the 1936 lectures quite closely, Knox placed a substantial set of metaphysical essays ("Epilegomena") based partly on the lectures but also on various published articles and selections from a late manuscript entitled *The Principles of History*, which Knox considered unworthy of publication in full. It is, of course, ironic that Knox resorted to "scissors and paste" in reconstructing Collingwood's view of history, and his editorial procedure led to various inconsistencies and repetitions. Nevertheless, *The Idea of History* became one of the classics of British philosophy – though appreciated more by historians than by philosophers – and it went a long way toward dispelling the aroma of crazy idealism that clung to Collingwood's treatment of history in *An Autobiography*.

(1) The idea that "the past which an historian studies . . . is a past which in some sense is still living in the present" might suggest that the present is haunted by ghosts from the past, intent on propelling it toward some preordained future; and the impression would not be immediately removed by passages in *The Idea of History* which assert that particular "monographic" histories are bound to converge eventually on a single "universal history" or "history of the world" (see *IH*, 37, 51; cf. 88, 104, 127, 246, 264). But the difficulty disappears in the light of Collingwood's insistence that history is "autonomous," in the sense that it is made by historians rather than the past, just as paintings are made by artists rather than their subjects (*IH*, 236; cf. 256). The "living

past" and the unity of world history were not mysterious metaphysical compulsions, but simply the practical goal of the creative labors of historians.

(2) The rule that the raw materials of history should be treated as present evidence rather than past testimony also flows from the doctrine of the autonomy of the historian. "Scissors-and-paste" chroniclers trust their sources implicitly, but scientific historians will realize that documents can be expressions of ignorance, bias, delusion, or deceit, and that "truth is to be had, not by swallowing what our authorities tell us, but by criticizing it" (*IH*, 243; cf. 259). Indeed, Collingwood suggested that history had much to learn from detective fiction: Sherlock Holmes and Hercule Poirot proceed "exactly like an historian," he said (*IH*, 253, 280–2; cf. 266–78, 320), except that their forensic deductions are always absolutely confirmed by a confession, whereas "in history, as in all serious matters, no achievement is final" (*IH*, 248).

(3) Just as Holmes and Poirot proceed by trying to penetrate the "mind" of the criminal – the calculations and "motives" behind the outward facts of a crime – so, according to *The Idea of History*, historians must attempt to enter into the ideas and interpretations which produced the facts which constitute their evidence. Scientific history, in Collingwood's sense, is concerned not with "external events" but with "the thought out of which these events grew," and that is why "all history is the history of thought" (*IH*, 132; cf. 115). Even a history of material production must focus on "inwardness": neolithic implements, for example, will not yield genuine historical knowledge unless we can work out the "purpose" with which they were made (*IH*, 199). Moreover (though *The Idea of History* is frustratingly inexplicit about the point), historians cannot claim to have identified a thought or purpose if they themselves cannot make sense of it. The past may contain a fair share of folly and unreasonableness, but it is up to historians to make its irrationalities intelligible, at least in terms of the situations in which they occurred. History may not be absolutely rational (unless perhaps we follow Hegel and treat irrationality as "essential to reason itself"), but it cannot be properly understood except as a "logical process" (*IH*, 117–19).

(4) *The Idea of History* draws the boundaries of the history of thought wide enough to take in most kinds of human practice, including the favorite topics of old-fashioned historians: politics, warfare, trade, production, and morality. But Collingwood located the heartland of history in art, science, religion, and philosophy. These fields had hitherto been neglected, but Collingwood was sure that they would yield rich returns provided historians took care to identify the problems which preoccupied the artists, scientists, believers, and thinkers of the past, rather than being content simply to catalogue their results (*IH*, 309–15). Sometimes Collingwood suggests that fundamental problems change so radically from one period to another that there can be no comparison between them – a view which could well lead to the disheartening conclusion that past intellectual worlds are utterly inaccessible and that no thinking has any validity beyond its own epoch (see *IH*, 229). But at other points (see e.g. *IH*, 63) he notices that – as his own practice as a historian of history testifies – revolutionary transformations need not rupture the underlying continuity of a tradition. If he had lived a little longer, he would no doubt have sought to resolve the inconsistency. Perhaps he would have built on his very suggestive idea that intellectual progress always depends on history, in that a new theory cannot claim acceptance merely because it accounts for some facts; it also has to demonstrate its superiority to the theory it

hopes to replace – its ability "to explain all that the first theory explained, and also to explain types or classes of events or 'phenomena' which the first ought to have explained but could not" (*IH*, 332).

(5) When Collingwood stated in *An Autobiography* that "historical knowledge is the re-enactment in the historian's mind of the thought whose history he is studying" (Collingwood, 1939: 112) his readers may have thought he was calling for some kind of sentimental identification with the actions and personalities of the past. But in *The Idea of History* he makes it clear that historical understanding has nothing to do with emotional sympathy: the discovery that the Greeks tried to control their population by exposing newborn babies, for example, was "no less true for being unlike anything that happens in the experience of contributors to the Cambridge Ancient History" (*IH*, 240). And whilst Collingwood's notion of the "history of thought" was broad enough to cover politics, warfare, economics, and morality, it was also strict enough to place certain aspects of the human past beyond the bounds of historical knowledge (*IH*, 309). In particular, there could never be "a history of memory or perception," of "how the flowers smelt in the garden of Epicurus," for example, or "how Nietzsche felt the wind in his hair as he walked on the mountains" (*IH*, 307, 296). Emotions and sensations do, of course, leave traces in the documentary record, and they can be reconstructed more or less plausibly by historical novelists. But they do not form logical or dialectical patterns, so however vigorous our sympathetic imagination, we cannot genuinely think our own way through them and thus subject them to the kind of verification – the test of logical intelligibility – that scientific history requires. I can never be sure how Plato felt about his philosophical companions, for example; but when I read one of his arguments, and "follow it in my mind by re-arguing it with and for myself," then I am, to some reliable degree, exactly reproducing his thoughts (*IH*, 301). Such intellectual repetition or re-enactment "is not a passive surrender to the spell of another's mind," Collingwood says, but "a labour of active and therefore critical thinking" (*IH*, 215; cf. 300, 202).

(6) The greatest implausibility of *An Autobiography* was the doctrine that the historian is a "microcosm" of the past and that history is "the self-knowledge of mind." At first sight the extravagance is magnified by the explanation of intellectual re-enactment in *The Idea of History*: the insistence that historians must rely on their "present" judgments of "present" evidence sounds like a license for present-centeredness if not self-glorification and reckless subjectivism. But in fact it is little more than a reminder of the principle that historical judgments are made not by the past but by historians; and it is connected to the fact that "the historian himself" will understand that the present is itself historical and that "together with the here-and-now which forms the total body of evidence available to him, [he] is a part of the process he is studying." He will recognize that he "has his own place in that process, and can see it only from the point of view which at this present moment he occupies within it" (*IH*, 248). Hence, the attempt to re-enact past thinking in the present is not an acceptance of epistemological defeat but a bid for historical rationality and objectivity; and when it is successful we enter into the minds of others and thus expand our own as well. History thus becomes a science of mind in a way psychology can never be; for psychology, according to Collingwood, is concerned with the natural processes of the soul (or "psyche") rather than the rational and normative aspirations of thinking or spirit which alone are prop-

erly called "mind"; and in the absence of other claimants it follows that history is "the only knowledge that the human mind can have of itself" (*IH*, 231, 220). From this point of view, he might have added, the tasks of history more or less coincide with those of philosophy.

For all its imperfections, *The Idea of History* successfully performs the explanatory task which Collingwood himself did not live to complete. No doubt most historians would like to rehabilitate various kinds of history that fall short of its exacting standards of scientificity, and most philosophers would reject the claim that history should avoid contingencies because "contingency means unintelligibility" (*IH*, 151). Collingwood scholars will also want to put *The Idea of History* in context, especially following the discovery, in 1995, of the long-lost manuscript of *The Principles of History* (Collingwood, 1999). But this new text contains few surprises, apart from its failure to pursue the theme of re-enactment; and in any case the contingencies of the past have conspired to make Knox's *Idea of History* into the classic statement of Collingwood's conception of history. And this conception has proved not only penetrating but enduring. It anticipates a range of philosophical developments which did not gather momentum till the 1960s: Thomas Kuhn's discovery of a "role for history" in the philosophy of science and elsewhere (Kuhn, 1962); Jean-Paul Sartre's exploration of "praxis" and the intelligibility of history (Sartre, 1976); and Hans-Georg Gadamer's recognition (with acknowledgment to Collingwood) of the interaction between past meanings and present interpretations (Gadamer, 1975).

But even if many of its themes have been absorbed into later philosophy, *The Idea of History* can still pack a punch. Collingwood's fundamental criticism of "realist" theories of knowledge – that they "not only ignore historical thinking but are actually inconsistent with there being such a thing" (*IH*, 233) – has not lost its pertinence. And his suggestion that "the right way of investigating mind is by the methods of history" (*IH*, 209, cf. 174, 219) would transform the field known as "philosophy of mind" if it were treated with the seriousness it deserves. Perhaps Collingwood will never get proper credit for his attempts to bond philosophy with history, but as he said in *An Autobiography* (Collingwood, 1939: 119): "If there are any who think my work good, let them show their approval of it by attention to their own."

Bibliography

Editions

Collingwood, R. G. (1923) *Roman Britain*. Oxford: Oxford University Press (rev. edn, 1932).

Collingwood, R. G. (1930) *The Archaeology of Roman Britain*. London: Methuen (rev. edn, 1969).

Collingwood, R. G. (with Myres, J. N. L.) (1936) *Roman Britain and the English Settlements*. Oxford: Oxford University Press.

Collingwood, R. G. (1939) *An Autobiography*. London: Oxford University Press.

Collingwood, R. G. (1940) *An Essay on Metaphysics*. Oxford: Oxford University Press.

Collingwood, R. G. (1942) *The New Leviathan*. Oxford: Oxford University Press.

Collingwood, R. G. (1946) *The Idea of History*, ed. T. M. Knox. Oxford: Oxford University Press.

Collingwood, R. G. (1993) *The Idea of History*, rev. edn, ed. Jan van der Dussen. Oxford: Oxford University Press.

Collingwood, R. G. (1999) *The Principles of History and Other Writings in the Philosophy of History*, ed. W. H. Dray and W. J. van der Dussen. Oxford: Oxford University Press.

Studies and references

Boucher, David (1989) *The Social and Political Thought of R. G. Collingwood*. Cambridge: Cambridge University Press.

Boucher, David, Connelly, James and Modood, Tariq (eds) (1995) *Philosophy, History and Civilization: Interdisciplinary Perspectives on R. G. Collingwood*. Cardiff: University of Wales Press.

Donagan, Alan (1962) *The Later Philosophy of R. G. Collingwood*. Oxford: Clarendon Press.

Dray, William H. (1995) *History as Re-enactment: R. G. Collingwood's Idea of History*. Oxford: Oxford University Press.

Gadamer, Hans-Georg (1989) *Truth and Method*, 2nd rev. edn, trans. Joel Weinsheimer and Donald G. Marshall. London: Sheed and Ward.

Johnson, Peter (1988) *R. G. Collingwood: An Introduction*. Bristol: Thoemmes Press.

Krausz, Michael (ed.) (1972) *Critical Essays on the Philosophy of R. G. Collingwood*. Oxford: Clarendon Press.

Kuhn, Thomas S. (1962) *The Structure of Scientific Revolutions*. Chicago: University of Chicago Press.

Mink, Louis O. (1969) *Mind, History, and Dialectic: The Philosophy of R. G. Collingwood*. Bloomington, IN: Indiana University Press.

Russell, Anthony F. (1984) *Logic, Philosophy, and History: A Study in the Philosophy of History based on the work of R. G. Collingwood*. Lanham, MD: University Press of America.

Sartre, Jean-Paul (1976) *Critique of Dialectical Reason I: Theory of Practical Ensembles*, trans. Alan Sheridan-Smith, ed. Jonathan Rée. London: New Left Books (orig. pub. 1960).

Taylor, Donald S. (1988) *R. G. Collingwood: A Bibliography. The Complete Manuscripts and Publications, Selected Secondary Writings, with Selective Annotation*. New York: Garland.

56

Gilbert Ryle, *The Concept of Mind* (1949)

A Method and a Theory

Laird Addis

Gilbert Ryle (1900–1976), writing more than two decades after publication of *The Concept of Mind* (hereafter *CM*), reported that his primary purpose had been "meta-philosophical," that is, designed to illustrate a philosophical method rather than to illuminate a subject matter, and that the title came to him only at the last moment (Wood and Pitcher, 1970: 12). Yet the book's name captures perfectly the ambitious content of what is – after its ancient predecessor in both spirit and content, Aristotle's *De anima* – almost certainly the most famous essay on the nature of mind in Western philosophy.

Although he didn't like either label, Ryle's theory in *CM* is almost universally regarded as a *materialist* one of the *behaviorist* sort. Behaviorism has its purely methodological form but, as applied to Ryle, it refers to the ontological thesis that the mind is only behaviors and dispositions to behaviors. Ryle's target, in any case, was *dualism*, an ontology of mind that asserts the distinct being and natures of body and mind. As persistently pressed by Ryle, the two major problems of dualism are its inability to explain how mind and body interact causally and how anyone could ever know the contents of another person's mind. If, as Ryle taught, the mind instead is something "about" the body itself and therefore something publicly observable, these problems will not even seriously arise. His task, then, was to excise what he called the "ghost in the machine"; and, although his attack on dualism may sometimes fail to distinguish the several forms of dualism, one can regard it as an attempt to undermine both the mainly "continental" tradition of the mind as mental acts and mental substance and the largely "analytic" tradition of the mind as "ideas" or "percepts" or "sense data" and the like.

Portraying Ryle as a modern Aristotelian fits well, at a personal and institutional level, with Ryle's life-long association with Oxford University. At the level of general ontology, it reflects Ryle's early rejection of "abstract" objects, whether resident in a Platonic world of forms or in this world as universals or as publicly unobservable things. In the ontology of human being, it recalls the one-substance theory of Aristotle in which the mind is conceived as the "form" of a fundamentally biological being. If, at yet another level, Ryle seems more at home with the humanistic atmosphere of Plato than the scientific one of Aristotle, one need only remember that arguably the most important event of Western civilization was the rejection of Aristotelian "common sense" by the emerging modern science. Ryle's love of Plato, despite his vehement anti-Platonism, is evident in many of his publications.

Ryle was not the first materialist nor the first of the behaviorist variety in the Western philosophical tradition. Indeed, in the two decades preceding the publication of *CM*, some of the logical positivists had, from what they took to be required by a commitment to scientific respectability, explicitly argued for a behaviorist theory of mind. But *CM*, in its detailed treatment of the numerous and sundry ways in which we talk about mental phenomena, seemed to many philosophers to achieve a hitherto unattained plausibility to this conception of the mind. If, by the nature of the topic, one could not demonstrate in all cases, perhaps not even in all *categories* of cases, that statements about the mind can be recast as statements about behaviors and dispositions to behaviors, Ryle was thought to have succeeded in enough cases to make the comprehensive claim worthy, if not of unconditional assent, at least of serious consideration. For Ryle, however, it was not so much a matter of the nature of mental phenomena as the *meanings* of statements about mental phenomena, such meanings to be disclosed by the philosophical technique of *linguistic analysis*.

Ryle had arrived at his idea of proper philosophical method during his more than two decades of philosophical reflection prior to *CM*. Although in sympathy with philosophers of the preceding decades who had sought to free philosophy from the errors of psychologism (the thesis that certain apparently "objective" truths, especially those of mathematics and logic, are really about how people think), Ryle rejected what he called the Platonism of Meinong, Russell, and others who had maintained that those truths are about "abstract" objects. Sharing also the importance many of his recent predecessors attached to the distinction between the logical and the merely grammatical forms of propositions and, accordingly, their concern with the distinction between the meaningful and the meaningless, Ryle took his own distinctive route – not that of Austin nor Wittgenstein nor anyone else – in coming to regard philosophy as about language itself. More precisely, the position of the mature Ryle was that philosophical propositions are about the *categories* of (usually non-philosophical) propositions. Thus, *CM* is a book that intends to categorize everyday propositions about mental phenomena. But, of course, this thesis about the nature of philosophy is itself a proposition that would identify the category of a certain set of propositions; namely, philosophical propositions. While in *CM* Ryle is almost exclusively interested in *illustrating* this conception of philosophy, he explicates and defends it in the earlier "Systematically Misleading Expressions" and "Categories" and the later *Dilemmas*.

Appearing in 1949, *CM* is a book of ten chapters and about 325 pages. After a brief introduction, Ryle, in his first chapter, states and attacks what he calls "Descartes' Myth," that is, dualism. The next three chapters are devoted, respectively, to what have often been regarded as the three supreme "faculties" or "activities" of the mind – knowing, willing, and feeling. The crucial fifth chapter, "Dispositions and Occurrences," sets out the basic idea of the nature of dispositions and of the mind as certain kinds of dispositions to behavior. In the next four chapters, Ryle applies the basic idea to self-knowledge, sensations, imagination, and the intellect. In a short final chapter, he discusses the idea of scientific psychology and its relation to his theory of the mind.

In that first chapter, Ryle argues that dualism is a "category mistake" in treating minds and bodies as two sets of entities existing side by side, so to speak. This mistake is said to have originated in the misguided search for special *causes* of intelligent behavior, on the assumption that if those causes were of the usual sort, the distinction between intelligent and mechanical behavior could not be explained. Instead, one should proceed, Ryle insists, by asking by what publicly observable *criteria* we actually do make the distinction. That dualism is absurd Ryle takes to be shown by its inability to provide coherent accounts of how a mind, conceived as a non-physical, "private" entity, could cause a physical event such as behavior and how its contents could ever be known to anyone except its possessor.

In what is probably the best-known chapter of *CM*, "Knowing How and Knowing That," Ryle begins with a statement of his general thesis that mental episodes are physical processes considered as the exercises of certain dispositions. But the main theses of the chapter are, first, that much of intelligent behavior is only knowing *how* to do something and, second and more important, that the "intellectualist legend" that knowing how to do something presupposes knowing that something is the case is false. In his argument, Ryle uses one of his favorite techniques: attempting to show that the opposing thesis entails a vicious infinite regress. Ryle observes that, as the consideration of propositions, knowing *that* is itself something that can be done better or less well and so, on the theory, would require a prior knowing *that*. The general intent is to show that a sizable class of behaviors, the consideration of which as intelligent might be thought to support dualism, can instead be understood as behaviors that are the expressions of certain dispositions. Thus one is indeed going "beyond" the behavior in describing it as intelligent, referring not to an "occult" (non-physical) *cause* but instead to a (physical) *disposition*. What makes the behavior intelligent is that the disposition will include the tendency to look for and correct errors, to observe and learn from how others do it, and so on. The dispositions involved are thus complex and multi-track dispositions, ones that can be manifested in numerous ways and circumstances.

In his third chapter, "The Will," Ryle rejects what he calls the "myth of volitions," the widely held theory that voluntary behavior is that caused by a (non-physical) event of willing. His general objection is, of course, that this is dualism; but his specific arguments against it are that nobody ever describes behavior that way in daily life, that no one could ever know whether or not another person's behavior was voluntary, that no intelligible account can be given of the required causal transaction between the non-physical and the physical, and that either answer to the question of whether or not an act of willing is voluntary leads to absurdities. Much of the chapter forwards his account of the everyday distinction between the voluntary and the involuntary, attempting to show that it in no way requires volitions. Nor, Ryle emphatically insists, is the distinction grounded in whether or not the behavior is fully caused. Ryle decries what he calls the "bogy of mechanism," not because he believes that some events fall, even in part, outside the causal realm but because, while all events are fully subsumable under mechanical laws, some of those events admit of other kinds of descriptions and explanations, ones that involve purpose and voluntariness.

The chapter called "Emotion" deals with several aspects of mind that Ryle says are not usually distinguished, including inclinations, moods, feelings, and motives. Motive explanations are said to be dispositional, not causal, and so provide no grounds for non-physical causes. Inclinations and moods (a species of what Ryle calls "frames of mind") are propensities to behavior. Feelings are, to be sure, occurrences – "agitations" or signs thereof – but, Ryle claims, they play no essential role in the explanation of behavior.

Although he adumbrates it earlier in the book, it is only with "Dispositions and Occurrences," *CM*'s fifth chapter, that Ryle states his theory of dispositions in detail. The fundamental idea is that while disposition statements such as "John knows French" have truth-values, they do not state facts or ascribe properties. Instead, they are, like law statements as Ryle conceives them, what he calls "inference-tickets," which enable us to explain and predict particular occurrences as in "John is speaking French." Thus disposition statements are mainly propositions about what someone or something *would* do or *could* do, not about what is happening or being done. Many pages are devoted to a discussion of differences among kinds of dispositions: inclinations, tendencies, capacities, competences, habits, liabilities, and so on. But there is also a sizable section on mental *occurrences*. Ryle wrestles somewhat uncomfortably with such things, which, for many, give the most support to dualism. His tentative solution is that a mental occurrence is a usually overt behavior done in a certain "frame of mind." But a "frame of mind" is not itself an unobservable occurrence: it is a short-term disposition. Thus does Ryle attempt to preserve his theory that the mind is only behaviors and dispositions to behaviors.

In "Self-knowledge" Ryle attacks some central theses of traditional dualism and also what is now known as foundationalism in epistemology: states of consciousness as necessarily self-knowable, introspection as privileged access to private things and events, and a rigid distinction between the directly and the indirectly knowable. Distinguishing several senses of "consciousness," he uses an infinite regress argument to show that consciousness cannot be that of which a person always is or can be aware. The main argument against introspection as traditionally conceived is that self-knowledge has a better explanation and that we learn about our own minds in much the same way as those of others – by induction from observable behavior. The chapter concludes with two sections on the self, culminating in an account of the "systematic elusiveness of 'I' " by way of the phenomenon of self-awareness.

"Sensations and Observation" opens with a concise statement of the general theory:

> To talk of a person's mind is not to talk of a repository which is permitted to house objects that something called "the physical world" is forbidden to house; it is to talk of the person's abilities, liabilities and inclinations to do and undergo certain sorts of things, and of the doing and undergoing of these things in the ordinary world. (*CM*, 199)

Ryle argues that it is a mistake to suppose that we can *observe* our sensations; sensations are neither observed nor observings (although, he says, they can be noticed). Hence there is no *given*, according to Ryle, and thus no basis for sense-data and phenomenalist theories or any other that would support dualism. At the beginning and the end of this longest chapter, Ryle wonders if it is really true that perception does require sensations.

CM's eighth chapter, "Imagination," is mainly concerned with demolishing the theory that imagining consists, even in part, in observing images. Thus another candidate for non-physical entities is rejected. Of course, there are imaginative behaviors, but no special faculty or objects of imagination. Ryle uses this chapter also to consider pretending and memory, the former involving the problematic notion of "frames of mind," the latter, like imagination, *not* involving the observation of images.

In his penultimate chapter, "The Intellect," Ryle is eager to show that while the intellect does have a kind of primacy, it is not that of being the hidden causal source of certain activities. The intellect is, instead, certain "powers, propensities and performances," that is, certain dispositions and behaviors. Just what powers and propensities Ryle attempts to indicate by way of extended elucidation of such notions as judgment, inference, abstraction, pondering, thinking, and many more. In particular, the notions of schooling and didactic point to the correct conception of the intellect's primacy – as "cultural" in so far as it identifies the task of those who have had and who give formal education, that is, education by "didactic discourse." Because such labor often involves the construction, understanding, and application of theories, Ryle devotes several pages to such matters, hoping once more to show that they require no hidden, non-physical acts or entities. Finally, proper understanding of the intellect leaves no room for traditional epistemology; all that remain for the theory of knowledge, Ryle asserts, are the study of the structures of theories and the psychology of learning.

A short but important chapter, "Psychology," closes the book by attempting to describe what scientific psychology, characterized as the study of behavior and not of private, non-physical entities, can hope to achieve. Behaviorism in psychology has been of "revolutionary importance" in discrediting dualism, as Ryle sees it. The advocates of behaviorism, however, would not accept Ryle's claim – in the spirit of his Aristotelianism and its distinction of "natural" and "unnatural" behavior – that ordinarily we know full well what explains our own behavior and it is only when we are "deceived" that the special knowledge and techniques of the scientist are relevantly invoked. Possibly this is why Ryle characterizes Sigmund Freud as "psychology's one man of genius." Behaviorism in psychology also tends to "mechanism" and thus the identification of thinking with saying. But human behaviors, in the most important sense, are not to be understood by their causes, whether the existent physical ones of the scientists or the non-existent non-physical ones of the dualists, but by the dispositions of which they are the exercises.

No general characterization of *CM* should fail to mention its flowing and effortless style nor its sly but effective pokes at the solemnity of much academic philosophy. Sympathetic critics have questioned this or that particular description of language use about minds. Less sympathetic critics have wondered whether or not what Ryle calls "frames of mind" and what he calls "silent soliloquy" may not be just what some dualists were talking about and also have suggested that Ryle has overestimated the importance of the motive of explaining behavior for the defenders of dualism. Yet more radical critics (for example, Addis, 1965) have maintained that Ryle's analyses largely ignore what those critics say constitute the essence of mind – namely, mental acts or acts of awareness – and concentrate instead on what may always have been more dubious candidates for existence or non-physicality such as, in one category, sense data, images, and sensations and, in another category, mental substance. And some philosophers (for example, Lyons, 1980: ch. 2) have challenged Ryle's method.

Ryle rarely responded directly to criticisms in subsequent publications, although some of them extend or modify some theses of *CM*.

For many years, *CM* was a book read by all English-language graduate students in philosophy and often used as a text for seminars and conferences. Few of today's students encounter the book except, possibly, as excerpted in anthologies. While there was an abundance of reviews and articles about the book in the two decades following publication, interest and conviction in behaviorism have severely waned since, and the literature on Ryle's book had, accordingly, diminished to a trickle by the century's end. But no more can be said of any book of the first half of the century, and *The Concept of Mind* remains the *locus classicus* for an extended and detailed exposition and defense of a major philosophical theory of the mind.

Bibliography

Editions

Ryle, Gilbert (1949) *The Concept of Mind*. London: Hutchinson.

Studies

Addis, Laird (1965) Ryle's ontology of mind. In L. Addis and D. Lewis (eds), *Moore and Ryle: Two Ontologists*. The Hague: Martinus Nijhoff.

Lyons, William (1980) *Gilbert Ryle: An Introduction to his Philosophy*. Brighton: Harvester.

Wood, Oscar P. and Pitcher, George (eds) (1970) *Ryle: A Collection of Critical Essays*. New York: Anchor.

57

Ludwig Wittgenstein, *Philosophical Investigations* (1953)

Clarity versus Pretension

Newton Garver

Ludwig Wittgenstein's (1889–1951) work from beginning to end was dominated by an austere conception of the role of philosophy. Metaphysical theories and explanations are nonsense, often because of a pretentious usurpation of the task of science. The goal of philosophy is clarity, and one main theme is to describe the dynamics of nonsense through describing the patterns for making sense. His early work developed this theme through a brilliant and profound elaboration of the logic of Frege and Russell. In his later work he saw flaws in the early work and reworked the theme with no reliance at all on the technicalities of logic or any other scholarly discipline. It is an astonishing achievement, which throws light not only on what philosophy ought to be but also on what it always has been, when not obscured by scientistic or moralistic pretensions.

Philosophical Investigations (hereafter *PI*), never approved for publication by its author, was published posthumously in 1953, two years after Wittgenstein's death. The text has been lost, so there can never be a critical edition. In spite of these scholarly problems, it presents an accurate and stunning picture – a "perspicuous representation," to use one of its important expressions – of Wittgenstein's philosophical thought in the last two decades of his life. It consolidates his powerful attack on the Cartesian paradigm that had dominated philosophy for three centuries, a paradigm that conceives philosophy as a kind of *knowledge* (in the scientific sense) and hence as requiring a *theory* that depends epistemologically on *basic truths* whose truth it is *impossible* to doubt, and that depends metaphysically on *simple substance* or *absolute non-empirical* reality. Wittgenstein had attacked this paradigm in his earlier work, *Tractatus Logico-philosophicus* (*TLP*), but the attack itself was in the form of a theory, which (at the very end of *TLP*) he compares to a ladder which has to be thrown away after it is used. In *PI* he shows (as the ladder simile already suggests) that the theoretical structure of *TLP* was part of the problem. *PI* is, from this perspective, a vast improvement on *TLP*, dispensing with theory as well as with both epistemological and metaphysical foundations, and thereby giving his attack on Cartesian philosophy increased cogency.

PI is a revision and refinement of central themes of *TLP*, that philosophy is like logic and is utterly different from science, and that its task is clarification rather than finding new truth. Wittgenstein was fierce in self-criticism, and his vehemence about his own "errors" has led some scholars to suggest that in *PI* he completely abandoned his earlier ideas. Certainly there are new themes and a different tone. But there are striking continuities: (1) the basic problem of philosophy is how statements and other utterances make sense; (2) philosophy is therefore akin to logic, conceived as a framework of basic principles of meaning and inference; (3) statements differ from stones and trees in that they have two indispensable and perhaps complementary aspects; (4) one aspect is that they are events in the world and therefore presuppose a world; (5) the other aspect is that what we say makes sense because of our human intentional activity; (6) therefore what makes sense in one context might be nonsense in another context; (7) a principle to work with is that a sentence makes sense if and only if its negation makes sense; (8) language and linguistic expression have limits; (9) transgressing such limits leads to nonsense and to both moral and intellectual confusion; (10) these problems about meaning and language are philosophical problems, not scientific problems; (11) the main object of philosophy is clarity, and clarity for its own sake; (12) philosophical problems are utterly different from scientific problems, and philosophical clarity is utterly different from scientific clarity; (13) there are very important things that lie beyond the limits of both language and knowledge; (14) which things can become clear through seeing them in the right way or through actions. No one can understand *PI* without appreciating the differences from his earlier work, but the continuities provide context for understanding the changes.

The Practice of Philosophy

Wittgenstein left Cambridge in 1914 and joined the Austrian army. While serving at the front, he recorded philosophical thoughts in notebooks, and during periods of leave he sifted, polished, and organized these thoughts into *TLP*, which was complete by the time he was taken prisoner by the Italians. This prodigious intellectual effort ended in 1918, followed by a decade of philosophical inactivity. Wittgenstein was jarred back into philosophical work partly by a lecture on mathematics by Brouwer, partly by questions from Ramsey, partly by conversations with Schlick, and decisively by his return to Cambridge in 1929.

Soon after returning to Cambridge, Wittgenstein began giving lectures, an important part of his philosophical work. The lectures were well prepared but they were never read, and those who heard them had the impression that they were hearing philosophy in the making. What they did not then know is that Wittgenstein continued to work as before, filling notebooks with thoughts which he later sifted, refined, and reorganized. Such work persisted throughout the remainder of his life, the great bulk of it surviving. Georg von Wright has catalogued it, scholars are familiar with its general shape and content, and bits and pieces (beginning with *Investigations*) have been published over the five decades since Wittgenstein's death.

The preface to *PI* (written in 1945) allows us to see distinctive features of Wittgenstein's work:

- The same point might look different from different approaches.
- It is therefore difficult, perhaps impossible, to find a definitive expression for any one of these points.
- While truth may well be important, the expression of any point needs to be tailored to fit the context, and the critical criterion for presenting a good picture of the landscape is more aesthetic than scientific.
- Presenting a good picture, or "perspicuous representation" (*bersichtliche Darstellung*), resists the analytic clarity that Frege rightly demanded for scientific statements.
- For a good picture of the landscape, the organization and trimming of the points is as important as their truth.
- The picture must be comprehensive, for otherwise it will not be perspicuous.
- Between 1929 and 1945, Wittgenstein revised not only the expression of the individual points but also the overall organization.
- Since these revisions are "connected with the very nature of the enterprise," philosophy is utterly different from science.

We can see a definite strategy in Wittgenstein's later philosophy, although he never spelled it out. First, what is basic must be what is right in front of our eyes, facts of a certain sort. This starting-point in natural history is a revision of the opening words of *TLP*, that the world is all that is the case. Second, we ought to investigate the range and variety of distinctively human activities, our language-games. Wittgenstein referred to this great variety to avoid the sort of hierarchical system favored by traditional metaphysics, where the foundation justifies or explains the superstructure. His alternative metaphor is that "these foundation-walls are carried by the whole house" (*On Certainty*, 1969: 248). Third, certain human experiences are common to other animals as well; fear, for example, belongs to the natural history of dogs and birds as well as humans. Fourth, we can perspicuously represent the variety of human activities only by clearly describing all of them and all their differences – "the whole hurly-burly of human actions" (*Zettel*, 1967: 567). The framework for perspicuity continues to be comprehensive and all-inclusive, as in *TLP*. Fifth, it is especially characteristic of humans that our activities are bound up with the use of language: "Our talk gets its meaning from the rest of our proceedings" (*On Certainty*, 1969: 229). It is therefore a distinctive feature of "this complicated form of life" (*PI*, 174) that we humans master the use of a language.

The Beginning: Language-games

It is worth noting how Wittgenstein begins *PI* because it is different from the beginning of prior efforts in the early 1930s. The work begins with a quotation from Augustine in which Augustine recounts how, as it seems to him, he learned language by noting what object adults meant when they used individual words. His account seems deliberately to avoid the *context* and *use* of words. Wittgenstein then proceeds with a concrete example that applies Augustine's "picture of language" to words used in the context of shopping. On a shopping list an expression has meaning in the context of an *activity*. This utterly natural reliance on context to fill out the meaning of the words introduces, without fanfare, a vastly broadened version of the context principle he adopted from Frege in *TLP*, that a name has meaning only in the context of a proposition. In *PI* it is never explicitly stated, but it holds in practice for all expressions, for sentences as well as for names. Wittgenstein, near the beginning of *Investigations*, insists that we take note of actions rather than just words when he explains what he means by "language-games": "Here the word 'language-*game*' is meant to bring into prominence the fact that the *speaking* of language is part of an activity, or of a form of life" (*PI*, 23). We do not understand sentences entirely, or perhaps not even principally, through understanding their elements (as in *TLP*), but rather through understanding how they work together with our actions, what role they play in our lives. "Commanding, questioning, recounting, chatting, are as much a part of our natural history as walking, eating, drinking, playing" (*PI*, 25). It is therefore activities rather than sentences that now provide context.

In contrast to *TLP*, where the *only* language-game is stating facts, Wittgenstein avoids discussing statements (truth-claims) in the early sections of *PI*. He begins with the shopping list, and then in *PI*, 2 he introduces his famous builders – the builder and his assistant – who have only four expressions in their language, and who use language only in connection with their construction activity. This is, as he says, a primitive language-game: we can conceive its being learned without anyone having to have learned anything else. Wittgenstein is not saying that this is how and where language began, but (1) that it could be and (2) that it aptly illustrates the intertwining of language and activity. When he presents his list of twenty-odd language-games in *PI*, 23 there are half a dozen for which truth would be a standard, but these involve other standards as well, and they are outnumbered by language-games (such as "asking, thanking, cursing, greeting, praying") in which truth is not primarily at issue, or not at issue at all.

Wittgenstein's language-games have an affinity to Aristotle's *categories* (but not to Kant's). Aristotle defines categories as kinds of "things that are said." Both Aristotle's categories and Wittgenstein's language-games are differentiated contextually rather than analytically. Just as for Aristotle a statement makes sense only if it belongs to some category or other, so too for Wittgenstein an expression makes sense only if it is a move in some language-game.

In *PI*, 23 Wittgenstein says that there are *countless* language-games. The reason is not that we could never complete the counting, but that we have no idea how to begin. We cannot begin because language-games lack the individuating identity conditions necessary for counting. They are individuated neither spatio-temporally (as are apples and oranges) nor analytically (as are chemical elements and biological species). Language-games are identified and explained ostensively and contrastively, by examples and differences. Teaching differences in order to explain concepts is a form of definition in a broad sense. Like ostensive definitions, but unlike analytic or Aristotelian definitions, explanations by contrasts are inherently and unavoidably vague, even when they are perfectly clear. Here is a powerful example:

> Compare *knowing* and *saying*:
>   how many feet high Mont Blanc is –
>   how the word "game" is used –
>   how a clarinet sounds.
> If you are surprised that one can know something and not be able to say it, you are perhaps thinking of a case like the first. Certainly not of one like the third. (*PI*, 78)

Wittgenstein here gives no definitions and no analysis but the example makes a clear and convincing point. Nothing further is needed.

Consider some paragraphs where Wittgenstein sets forth differences that belong to psychology:

> Emotions. Common to them: genuine duration, a course. (Rage flares up, abates, vanishes, and likewise joy, depression, fear.)
>   Distinction from sensations: they are not localized (nor yet diffuse!) (*Zettel*, 1967: 488)

> Love is not a feeling. Love is put to the test, pain not. One does not say: "That was not true pain, or it would not have gone off so quickly." (*Zettel*, 1967: 504)

Several emotions are mentioned in these passages, but the important distinction is between emotions on the one side and feelings or sensations on the other. Nothing is exact or well defined. We could no doubt ask more questions and take further considerations into account. The principal distinction is none the less undeniable, and is clearly set forth.

To recognize differences, and for clarity about the basic ideas involved, we have no need for exactness, any more than we have need for it in cases of ostensive definition. Recognizing differences, like recognizing context, is a prior, more primitive, more animal activity. In order to *count* things, on the other hand, they must be defined. Counting, like more advanced forms of measurement, is indispensable for scientific clarity, but it is based on a more primitive clarity achieved through contrasts and examples. The contrast between these two forms of clarity is one of the most distinctive and controversial features of Wittgenstein's later work, expressed dramatically in *On Certainty*, 308: "'Knowledge' and 'certainty' belong to different *categories*."

Clarity without Analysis

Clarity is related to understanding, so we can get more perspective on Wittgenstein's conception of clarity without analysis by considering what understanding is. "What really swims before us when we understand a word? – Isn't it something like a picture? Can't it be a picture?" (*PI*, 139). This question of Wittgenstein's seems to presuppose that understanding might be private or subjective, as it is in the passage in which Augustine recounts how he first learned language. Wittgenstein makes the alternatives clearer by distinguishing three cases:

> Let us remember that there are certain criteria in my behavior for the fact I do not under-

stand a word: that it means nothing to me, that I can do nothing with it. And criteria for my 'thinking I understand', attaching some meaning to the word but not the right one. And lastly criteria for my understanding the word right. In the second case one might speak of a subjective understanding. And sounds which no one else understands but which I '*appear to understand*' might be called a "private language". (*PI*, 269)

For Kant and for scientists, understanding something consists in bringing it under a law or concept. Intuitions and perceptions must fall under concepts, and concepts under categories. Data (phenomena) are explained scientifically through empirical laws. Wittgenstein regards philosophic understanding differently, as a matter of perspective rather than knowledge, seeing how something fits into a picture that consists of ever broader and vaguer facts, customs, and institutions, the broadest and vaguest of which is our form of life:

> It is not possible that there should have been only one occasion on which someone obeyed a rule. It is not possible that there should have been only one occasion on which a report was made, an order given or understood; and so on. – To obey a rule, to make a report, to give an order, to play a game of chess, are *customs* (uses, institutions).
>
> To understand a sentence means to understand a language. To understand a language means to be master of a technique. (*PI*, 199)

Such contextual explanation makes use of *grammar* (in the sense of practices rather than rules and regulations) and *perspicuous representation*. It also presupposes that we can recognize the contexts in question straight off, without needing definitions. About the widest and vaguest of the contexts, forms of life, Wittgenstein suggests that it is "what has to be accepted, the given" (*PI*, 226).

"What has to be accepted, the given" seems powerful, provocative, and puzzling because it combines facts (reality) and possibilities (modality). Mastering speech is a *fact* of human natural history, but the mastery means *being able* to understand many possible sentences that have never been expressed. One cannot explain or describe mastery of a language without referring to such possibilities. There none the less remains an uneasy puzzle about how the factual or empirical can include the modal in this way, partly due to the trickiness of "*use*." We learn the "use" (*Gebrauch*, pattern of employment, usage) of a word through its "use" (*Anwendung*, employment) on a number of occasions. Most commentators have noticed that *use* is central in explanations of meaning in Wittgenstein's later work, but fewer have noticed the varieties of *use*, or that such explanations are always contextual.

PI retains traces of the Tractarian distinction between names (which have reference but not sense) and sentences (which have sense but not reference) in the difference between "use in the language" (*PI*, 43) and employment in the course of an activity. The first sections of *PI* emphasize the latter, and it makes little difference (see *PI*, 19) whether the verbal expressions are words or sentences. In *PI*, 20 the individual words become important because they differentiate between possible sentences that would indicate different actions. The immediate context of individual words is therefore not activities but the possibilities of our language, which get prominence when Wittgenstein discusses names: "For a *large* class of cases – though not for all – in which we employ the word 'meaning' it can be defined thus: the meaning of a word is its use in the language" (*PI*, 43). Wittgenstein speaks here of words rather than sentences, of "*Bedeutung*" rather than "*Sinn*," and of "*Gebrauch in der Sprache*" rather than "*Anwendung*" or "*Verwendung*" or "*Benützung*." The dualism of the symbolism of *TLP* is therefore not completely erased. It is, however, no longer clearly defined, and the underlying niceties that are involved at this point are deep and rich.

Interesting and important concepts in philosophy are unavoidably vague. For Wittgenstein this is intimately connected with giving up analytic philosophy, no longer recognizing an essential distinction between words and sentences, understanding both "*Sinn*" and "*Bedeutung*" in terms of varieties of context (employment in a game or practice, use in the language), and his ingenious use of both contrast and context in formulating "perspicuous" representations. The opposition between analytic and contextual explanations makes clear that the foundations and principles of Wittgenstein's philosophy after his return to Cambridge in 1929 were not analytic at all. But the demand for clarity remains.

Philosophy as Grammar

We need to take a closer look at what replaces analysis and analytic clarity. For the last twenty years of his life, the years of his greatest productivity and his profoundest work, Wittgenstein identified what he was doing, and what other philosophers really do, with *grammar*. This perspective is as carefully considered as it is puzzling. It emerged out of earnest and continuing work, it has roots in *TLP*, and its implications are felt throughout his later philosophical investigations. Although he settled into this general conception of philosophy soon after his return to Cambridge, he never gave a clear and orderly account of what he meant.

Wittgenstein began by identifying philosophy with logic. In his "Notes on Logic" of 1913 (*Notebooks*, 1979: 106) Wittgenstein says: "Philosophy consists of logic and metaphysics: logic is its basis." In *PI* this thought gets transformed into, "*Essence* is expressed by grammar . . . Grammar tells what kind of object anything is" (*PI*, 371–3). Wittgenstein maintained a deflationary posture toward foundationalist metaphysics, but clearly also remained interested in what kinds of things there are. His descriptions of feelings and emotions cited above, and also his comments about knowing and saying, are examples of the realities he investigated. Since their essence, and any other "essence," is expressed by grammar, philosophy is a branch of grammar (in a broad sense).

PI uses "grammar" in a broad sense, as he had used "logic" in a broad sense in his *Notebooks*. Just as it is impossible to conceive logic as the basis of philosophy if logic were nothing but the "peculiar crotchets and contrivances" of *Principia mathematica*, it would be impossible to grasp Wittgenstein's later conception if one identified grammar with morphology and syntax. The broader view is that grammar consists of *all* the rules and practices that govern our use of language. He once said that he was using "grammar" in its usual sense but applying it beyond its usual range – for example, to the clues and circumstances that make something a threat rather than a prediction, a feeling rather than an emotion, a demand rather than a wish, or a stipulation rather than a theory. Such distinctions are vital to the realities of life, and their basis resides in that part of "grammar" where language-games are differentiated from one another.

Wittgenstein's view of philosophy as an extension of grammar is a generalization of his earlier view of philosophy as "logic and metaphysics: logic is its basis." Logic is still inherent in truth-claims, but truth-claims are only one of countless uses of language. Wittgenstein's grammar differs from logic in being descriptive, and differs from linguistics by focusing on uses of language (language-games), by not being systematic, and by being self-referential. Wittgenstein's view therefore implicitly incorporates elements of naturalism, Kant, and linguistic methodology; but it forces us to rethink what these traditions mean if we are to see clearly Wittgenstein's relation to them and the use that he makes of their ideas.

Simples

Simples (elements) are essential to analysis, and whether one leans toward analytic or contextual explanation in philosophy will be inextricable from one's attitude toward simples. Something is simple if it cannot be defined or analyzed. It could then, one would think, be learned only ostensively, by pointing to it and naming it. Wittgenstein sees this idea not only underlying the picture suggested by Augustine but also as central to both *TLP* and Plato's *Theaetetus*, and as crucial to philosophical analysis. Without absolute simples, philosophical analysis can never come to an end. Nor could concepts have definite boundaries, as Frege required. Since this picture is one that held Wittgenstein captive at the time he wrote *TLP*, he attacks it methodically in *PI*, 27–67. In *PI*, 67 he introduces the metaphor of "family resemblances." With this metaphor Wittgenstein abandons analysis and embraces vagueness – the principal feature of his critique of *TLP*. He continues discussing the hollowness of the demand for "exactness" through *PI*, 81, a discussion which must have cost anguish and effort, for it involves sharp explicit rejection not only of the analysis of *TLP* but also of central ideas of Frege, whom he continued to admire.

Rules and Practices

At *PI*, 82 Wittgenstein begins talking about rules – a perfectly reasonable topic, since rules are central to both logic and grammar. After an interlude in which he discusses what philosophy is (*PI*, 89–133), *PI*, 143 begins a long examination of proceeding by following rules. This discussion completes the attack on philosophical analysis, for analysis requires rules by which to proceed as well as simples at which to stop. Rules are not rejected any more than simples are. The point is rather that, just as nothing can be *absolutely* simple and so must emerge from analysis instead of providing the basis for it, so also rules require stage-setting in order to determine action. Rules emerge from practices rather than providing the basis for them. So what we must learn is mastery of a technique (*PI*, 199, quoted above). Mastering a technique means knowing how to use the relevant tools and instruments – in this case words and sentences. For communication to work, the persons involved must follow the same rules in the same way.

That is they must share the practice, or have it in common. Wittgenstein here argues further that following any rule presupposes a custom or institution and therefore is inherently social.

The Impossibility of Private Language

One main conclusion of the discussion of rule-following comes at *PI*, 202: "And hence also 'obeying a rule' is a practice. And to *think* one is obeying a rule is not to obey a rule. Hence it is not possible to obey a rule 'privately': otherwise thinking one was obeying a rule would be the same thing as obeying it." This conclusion is stated clearly and forcefully, but the discussion of rule-following continues for another forty-one sections before the question of private language is taken up for extended discussion in *PI*, 243–315. These sections, especially 243–70, constitute Wittgenstein's famous "Private Language Argument." Why, one may ask, take the matter up again and at such length, when it has already been presented as a consequence of his consideration of rule-following? A good question, since no new conclusions seem to be reached.

One part of the answer is given in Wittgenstein's preface to the work, in which he warns us that he will approach the same point from different directions. Another part might derive from Wittgenstein's admiration of Kant's *Critique of Pure Reason*. In the "Transcendental Analytic" Kant lays out his conception of judgment and knowledge, and in the "Dialectic" he applies this conception to key philosophical problems of his day, diagnosing "dialectical illusions." For Wittgenstein the illusions to be identified are "grammatical" rather than "dialectical." In 243–315 (as in Kant's "Dialectic") no new principles of meaning are introduced, but there are powerful arguments against a popular picture of language and meaning, one that had held Wittgenstein himself captive.

The conclusion is not that there are no private languages, but that no private language is possible. This is a logical or grammatical point, rather than a metaphysical or empirical one, because it follows from the very nature of language and meaning: it is not that we understand what "private language" is and see that there aren't any or that our theory prohibits it, but rather that when we look more closely we realize that we cannot understand what a "private language" (in the philosophical sense) would be. The various ways in which Wittgenstein demonstrates the incoherence of the idea are ingenious and fascinating but will not be reviewed here.

Seeing Aspects of Things

Language may involve "practices, customs, institutions," but *we* learn it. So *we* must be able to "see" the point of the contrasts and examples upon which learning a language depends. Wittgenstein had referred to the Neckar cube in *TLP* 5.5423, so the interest he shows in "aspect-seeing" and "aspect-blindness" in section xi of Part II has deep roots. It is in this section that he refers to the "duck–rabbit" and that he says, "If a lion could talk, we could not understand it" (*PI*, 223). One sees affinities with the descriptive side of *Gestalt* psychology. More important, however, is Wittgenstein's probing of the "aesthetic" dimension of language-learning: that each of us (if we use the same language) learns to see the same squiggles as the same letters and to hear the same sound patterns as the same words and phonemes. The very description of this phenomenon involves us in two senses of *seeing*, for the very same figure that we "see" on the page we sometimes "see" as a rabbit and sometimes as a duck. Wittgenstein has no interest in explaining the two senses and their interrelation, but only in describing their subtleties. One passage (*PI*, 222) contains a dramatic echo of the Private Language Argument:

> I can know what someone else is thinking, not what I am thinking.
> It is correct to say "I know what you are thinking", and wrong to say "I know what I am thinking."
> (A whole cloud of philosophy condensed into a drop of grammar.)

While the lack of further editing results in diminished perspicuity compared with Part I, an appreciation of the material in this section reveals something Wittgenstein saw to be needed – in addition to rules, customs, and training – in order to master the use of language. Aspect-blindness would stifle language-learning, and hence becoming human.

Nonsense and Silence

It remains astonishing to think of *philosophy* as *grammar*. Philosophy seems something grand, grammar anything but grand. Wittgenstein's philosophical conscience (unlike his personality) would allow no domineering pretensions. Philosophy is possible only because of its limits. Philosophers become confused and fraudulent when they deliberately or even inadvertently cross over those limits. In this way philosophical and moral clarity go hand in hand; conversely, for those who slip, there is no easy separation of intellectual from moral confusion. That is one reason why Wittgenstein saw philosophy as "treatment of an illness" (*PI*, 133, 255), not only as conceptual clarity and argument.

In his renunciation of the pretensions of dogmatic metaphysics and moral or political pronouncements, there is a moral message, as there was in *TLP*. The message is one of humility. As "grammarians," philosophers have no special knowledge of truth or goodness, for grammar is at best a servant of the sciences rather than another epistemic discipline undergirding or overseeing them. Wittgenstein's philosophy does not help us to improve the world (as medicine and engineering may do) or to act well in the world (as moral rules may do) but only to think in a certain way about life and the world – to see things as they really are and in proper perspective. This is not easy, and Wittgenstein's life was an awesome struggle to keep trying. The various limits are features of reality, but observing them (or not) is a matter of will as well as intellect, and therefore a matter in which Wittgenstein saw righteousness as well as wisdom.

Epilogue

PI articulates with perspicuity and convincing argument a radically different conception of philosophy from one that dominated the field for three centuries and that continued to grip his tutors and colleagues. None the less its place in the history of philosophy remains uncertain. Its greatness is acknowledged, but most philosophers continue to spin out theories, as if his work were either non-existent or mistaken, and there is little recognition of how his work relates to that of other great philosophers. His naturalism restates a central thrust of Aristotle's while avoiding the trap of scientism, and his language-games implicitly generalize Aristotle's categories in a brilliant way that few Aristotelian scholars acknowledge. There is little recognition among Kantian scholars that *PI* provides a genuinely self-referential critical philosophy, such as Kant demanded, without such reliance on specific scientific doctrines as proved the Achilles' heel of Kant's effort. His remarks on ethics echo existentialist themes, with little recognition from existentialists. Since Wittgenstein worked without footnotes, his extensive indebtedness to Plato, Augustine, Spinoza, Hume, Kant, and even Frege and Schopenhauer often remains shrouded or invisible. Furthermore the fact that he did not break his work down into the conventional domains, and his thoughts about mathematics do not lead to theorems nor does his thought on morals lead to rules of conduct, tempts many professional philosophers and philosophy teachers to regard his work as irrelevant. These uncertainties about his historical impact are compounded by his own successful determination not to found a school: no one has or can have the one right reading of *PI*.

Because it is not scholarly (not *wissenschaftlich*), *PI* is sometimes dismissed (or even praised) as being more literary than philosophical, and because Wittgenstein rejects and ridicules theoretical generalizations he is sometimes thought a relativist or historicist or particularist. Rorty (1989), for example, stresses the irony in Wittgenstein's writing and associates him with such literary figures as Derrida and the German Romantics, and Winch (1958) suggests a cultural relativism. Affinities there certainly are. Wittgenstein is a consummate stylist, and he uses irony when he suggests that maybe dogs are too honest to lie, or that if a lion could talk we could not understand it. He was influenced by the ironic aphorisms of Lichtenberg and Schopenhauer as well as by the satire of Karl Kraus. But in *PI* irony and satire are never ends in themselves, nor merely literary devices. They remain firmly in the service of Wittgenstein's unrelenting quest for clarity. Irony is used to mark distinctions necessary for seeing the whole picture clearly. And the distinctions and differences he insists on are not between particulars (whether cultures or persons) but between *types* of action or experience common to all. Without such distinctions obscurity results from confusing things that are different, as feelings are often confused with emotions and as Cartesians generally confuse knowledge with certainty. Clarity, not irony, is the master motive for Wittgenstein in *PI* – clarity for its own sake rather than as a preliminary to something else.

PI is therefore not an historical or scholarly achievement, and not just a literary achievement, but a philosophical achievement. Descartes separated mind from matter, leaving mind and the soul to faith (religion) and matter to reason (science), with philosophy naturally being assimilated more to science and reason than to religion and faith. The problem of how to overcome doubts became the central problem for philosophy. *PI* points out that our thinking and our language begin with certainties, not with either doubts or knowledge, and in Aristotelian fashion *PI* takes this to be just a matter of human natural history. From this starting-point, *PI* presents a description of how language works and how words and sentences have meaning, shattering one theory after another along the way. The resultant philosophy cannot tell us what to believe, cannot explain why things are as they are, and cannot tell us how to conduct our lives – limitations which make it possible for philosophy to be what it is. Only illusion can result from ignoring these limits, just as only illusion can result from supposing that *Principia mathematica* can be both complete and consistent or that light can travel instantaneously. Recognition of limits characterizes the twentieth century. *PI* transposes this spirit into philosophy, reshaping the discipline into one aiming at understanding through clarity rather than knowledge, with clarity and understanding always requiring an overview of the whole scene as well as attention to details. Such clarity is an exceedingly tough taskmaster. But, as Spinoza famously remarked, all things excellent are as difficult as they are rare.

Bibliography

Editions and translations

Wittgenstein, Ludwig (1958) *Philosophical Investigations*, 3rd edn, ed. and trans. G. E. M. Anscombe. Oxford: Blackwell (this edition continues to be available with German and English on facing pages).

Wittgenstein, Ludwig (1961) *Tractatus Logico-philosophicus*, trans. David F. Pears and Brian McGuinness. London: Routledge and Kegan Paul.

Wittgenstein, Ludwig (1967) *Zettel*, ed. G. H. von Wright and G. E. M. Anscombe, trans. G. E. M. Anscombe. Oxford: Blackwell.

Wittgenstein, Ludwig (1969) *On Certainty*, ed. G. H. von Wright and G. E. M. Anscombe, trans. Denis Paul and G. E. M. Anscombe. New York: Harper and Row.

Wittgenstein, Ludwig (1979) *Notebooks 1914–1916*, 2nd edn, ed. G. H. von Wright and G. E. M. Anscombe, trans. G. E. M. Anscombe. Oxford: Blackwell.

Wittgenstein, Ludwig (2001) *Philosophische Untersuchungen*. Kritisch-genetische Edition, ed. Joachim Schulte in collaboration with Heikki Nyman, Eike von Savigny and George Henrik von Wright. Frankfurt am Main: Suhrkamp Verlag.

Studies

Finch, Henry LeRoy (1977) *Wittgenstein – The Later Philosophy: An Exposition of the Philosophical Investigations*. New York: Humanities Press.

Garver, Newton (1994) *This Complicated Form of Life*. LaSalle, IL: Open Court.

McGinn, Marie (1997) *Wittgenstein and the Philosophical Investigations*. London: Routledge.

Pears, David F. (1987, 1988) *The False Prison*, 2 vols. Oxford: Clarendon Press.

Rorty, Richard (1989) *Contingency, Irony, and Solidarity*. New York and London: Cambridge University Press.

Savigny, Eike von (1988–94) *Wittgenstein's "Philosophische Untersuchungen": Ein Kommentar für Leser*, 2 vols. Frankfurt am Main: Klostermann.

Schulte, Joachim (1992) *Wittgenstein: An Introduction.* Albany, NY: State University of New York Press.

Stern, David G. (1995) *Wittgenstein on Mind and Language.* Oxford: Oxford University Press.

Winch, Peter (1958) *The Idea of Social Science and its Relation to Philosophy.* London: Routledge and Kegan Paul.

58

P. F. Strawson, *Individuals: An Essay in Descriptive Metaphysics* (1959)

The Rehabilitation of Metaphysics

David Bell

In Britain in the 1950s a number of factors converged, the overall effect of which was to encourage the belief that there was something deeply problematic and even disreputable about anything that had the temerity to call itself "metaphysics." These factors included, for example, the rejection of metaphysics as unverifiable nonsense on the part of those, like Carnap and Ayer, influenced by Viennese positivism; a distaste for the pretensions, the obscurities, and (many felt) the intellectual dishonesty not only of earlier speculative thinkers like Hegel and Bradley, but, even more, of contemporary thinkers like Sartre and Heidegger; the dominance in Britain during the 1940s and 1950s of the piecemeal, non-speculative, non-systematic, and metaphysically timid thought of the so-called "Oxford philosophy" or "ordinary language philosophy" practiced at that time by Austin, Ryle, Grice, and Strawson (b. 1919) himself; the increasing influence of Quine's naturalistic rejection of all ineluctably *philosophical* modes of explanation; and, perhaps most influentially of all, the contagious hypersensitivity Wittgenstein communicated concerning what genuinely philosophical activity should comprise, and whether there could, indeed, be any such thing.

Within this climate, therefore, it is significant that Strawson's *Individuals* proclaims itself, in its very title no less, to be an essay in metaphysics. In 1959 this was a provocative and unfashionable claim – a claim, moreover, whose boldness was only slightly diminished by the author's insistence that the metaphysics to be essayed would be of a rather modest kind, to which he gave the name "descriptive metaphysics." The major historical significance of *Individuals* in Britain, then, was not merely that it signaled, but that it was influential in securing, the rehabilitation of metaphysics as a respectable enterprise.

Strawson's book was also influential, more specifically, for arguing that concrete spatio-temporal material objects are basic particulars; that one needs to refer to other people and their psychological states if one is to be able to refer to oneself and one's own; that the concept *person* is a primitive concept and one, moreover, to which both physical and psychological predicates must equally be capable of attaching. In addition, the book contains novel and illuminating treatments of a variety of further topics including, amongst others, identification and re-identification, demonstrative and descriptive thought, reference and predication, the ownership of mental states, solipsism, and skepticism.

Descriptive Metaphysics

The aim of descriptive metaphysics, we are told, is to "describe the actual structure of our thought about the world." As such, it is intended to contrast, on the one side, with speculative or revisionary metaphysics which "is concerned to produce a better structure," and, on the other side, with mere piecemeal or *ad hoc* conceptual analysis. Revisionary metaphysics, Strawson suggests, is over-ambitious; mere conceptual analysis, however, is not ambitious enough, for its results "are not general enough and not far-reaching enough to meet the full metaphysical demand for understanding." That demand is to be satisfied, according to Strawson, by an investigation of a broadly Kantian kind which takes as given certain very general features of our thought about the world, and then attempts to demonstrate what must be the case if it is to be possible for those general features to obtain at all. Strawson later explained that in *Individuals*:

> I found myself using the technique of arguing from the conditions of the possibility of making certain distinctions or achieving certain results. For example the conditions of the possibility of distinguishing between oneself and one's states of consciousness on the one hand, and what wasn't oneself or a state of consciousness of oneself on the other; or again the conditions of the possibility of identifying certain items. Now these are Kantian types of argument. (Magee, 1971: 123)

Strawson resurrected the Kantian term "transcendental argument" to characterize such attempts to demonstrate that a certain structural feature is a necessary condition of the very possibility of any conceptual scheme we can make intelligible to ourselves.

A particular, and hugely influential, use to which, more or less in passing, Strawson applies the technique of transcendental argument is in connection with the refutation of skepticism. If it can be established, say, that a commitment to the existence of material objects, or other minds, or causal relations is indeed a necessary condition of the very possibility of our conceptual scheme, then, Strawson argues, a skeptic who attempts to deny or doubt such commitments can be charged with a particular form of incoherence:

> He pretends to accept a conceptual scheme, but at the same time quietly rejects one of the conditions of its employment. Thus his doubts are unreal, not simply because they are logically irresoluble doubts, but because they amount to the rejection of the whole conceptual scheme within which alone such doubts make sense. (Strawson, 1959: 35)

(The ensuing debates about the nature and viability of transcendental arguments, and about their efficacy in the refutation of skepticism, have been extensive. For an overview, see Stern, 1999.)

In so far as descriptive metaphysics aims to explore, from within, the *actual* structure of *our* thought about the world, it may seem that its results will be inevitably and objectionably parochial: are there not other possible – perhaps even actual – ways of thinking about the world? Is it not at the very least an open, empirical question whether the thought-structure of an Oxford philosopher in the middle of the twentieth century is the same as that of an Egyptian pharaoh, a Phoenician sailor, or a Hopi indian? And is it not the case that our own conceptual scheme has changed and developed over time? (These issues are discussed, for example, in Mei, 1961; Hacking, 1968; Davidson, 1974; and Haack, 1979.) Strawson is largely unmoved by such questions as these, and simply asserts that he intends to explore the "massive central core of human thinking which has no history" and which is shared by all thinking human beings. He does, however, somewhat indirectly address the possibility of coherent, intelligible, yet different conceptual structures in *Individuals*. He considers, for example, the alternative conceptual schemes that would be appropriate in a purely auditory world which lacks a spatial dimension (chapter 2), in a Leibnizian world of conscious but non-spatial monads (chapter 4), and with respect to a feature-placing language which lacks subject-predicate articulation and is thus unable to secure reference to particular objects (chapter 7). In all cases the diagnosis is the same: either the structure of the alternative conceptual scheme coincides sufficiently with our own for it to be judged viable, or there is insufficient coincidence, in which case it is judged incoherent.

Basic Particulars

One notion which dominates the philosophical investigations conducted by Strawson is that of *ontological priority*. Broadly speaking, a given category of entity, of type-α, say, would be ontologically prior to some other category, of type-β, if it were the case that

> the ability to talk about β-particulars at all was dependent on the ability to talk about α-particulars, but not vice versa. This fact could reasonably be expressed by saying that in our scheme α-particulars were ontologically prior to β-particulars, or were more fundamental or basic than they. (1959: 17)

Now throughout the work Strawson advances and defends a variety of claims concerning *relative* ontological priority – that persons, for instance, are prior to such "private particulars" as mental states, sensations and sense data; that everyday medium-sized objects like tables and trees are ontologically more basic than theoretical entities of physics like quarks and neutrinos; and that objects are, as such, more ontologically basic than such things as events, processes, states, and conditions.

There can be no doubt, however, that the dominant goal of Strawson's investigation is to establish a claim about *absolute* ontological priority – namely, that there are two types of entity which are, in the sense defined above, ontologically prior *tout court*, that is, ontologically prior to all other types of entity whatsoever. Strawson calls them *basic particulars*. Our ability to talk about basic particulars, he argues, is a necessary condition of the possibility of our talking about anything at all.

There are two major strands to Strawson's strategy here. The one aims to specify precisely which things are to be counted as basic particulars. The other aims to analyze what is involved in "our ability to talk about anything." The former strand culminates in the claim that *material bodies*, and *persons*, are "in our conceptual scheme as it is, . . . the basic or fundamental particulars," and that "the concepts of [all] other types of particular must be seen as secondary in relation to the concepts of these" (1959: 11). The other strand results in an analysis of such notions as *reference, identification, re-identification, existence, predication, proposition*, and the like, in so far as they are involved in an account of how we are able to pick out objects, and say something about them.

Talking about Material Bodies

Strawson's analysis of the most fundamental skills we must possess if we are to be able to talk about something – about anything at all – conforms to a number of plausible, common-sense assumptions. Talking, for instance, is not something we usually do by ourselves. It is an activity which typically involves at least a speaker and a hearer; and for there to be a successful act of communication, both partners must of course understand each other. In particular, the hearer must know what it is that the speaker is talking about. In Strawson's terminology, if the speaker makes an identifying reference to a particular, the hearer too must correctly identify that very particular as the one being currently referred to.

This hearer-identification can take many forms. Linguistically, for example, we employ proper names, descriptive phrases, personal pronouns, demonstratives, and other devices to enable a hearer to identify what is being talked about. Non-linguistically, we may point, draw pictures, mime, show photographs, and so on. Now clearly some forms of hearer-identification, though entirely successful and unobjectionable, are nevertheless parasitic on other successful identifications. Thus a hearer's correct identification of a particular person (Mr Brown) to whom a speaker refers by using the phrase "Mrs Smith's accountant" requires the hearer correctly to identify *another* particular person (Mrs Smith).

At this point Strawson makes three strong demands on any form of hearer-identification that is to be non-parasitic. He requires (1) that to identify a particular the hearer must know "an individuating fact" about that particular, that is the hearer must "know that such-and-such a thing is true of that particular and of no other particular whatever." We can call this the requirement of *uniqueness*. He requires (2) that "the known individuating fact must not be such that its statement essentially involves identifying any other particular by reference to which it is identified." We can call this the demand for *independence*. And (3) he requires that a non-parasitically identified particular must be in principle capable of being identified more than once, and by more than one person. (This follows trivially from the claim that, while they are talking, both a speaker and a hearer must be correctly identifying the same particulars.) Such things must, that is, be capable of *re-identification*. Knowledge meeting these three conditions will identify a basic particular.

With these three demands in place, Strawson argues negatively that there are many types of thing about which we talk – including mental states, sense data, properties, classes, universals, physical events, economic conditions, numbers, times and places, works of music or literature, sub-atomic particles, and the like – which fail to fit the bill. Hearer-identification of such "secondary" things requires, and is necessarily made on the basis of, the identification of other particulars. More positively, and more influentially, Strawson argues that non-parasitic hearer-identification can only be accomplished when the particulars in question "are, or possess, bodies." Bodies, in Strawson's terminology, are concrete particulars which are located in a single space, which persist through time, which possess empirical properties (like shape, color, sound, smell, texture, taste, and the like) perceivable by both a speaker and a hearer, and which can be demonstratively identified. For, Strawson argues, only things conforming to these specifications can simultaneously satisfy the demands (noted above) for uniqueness, independence, and re-identifiability, and are thus fit to "secure to us one single common and continuously extendable framework of reference, any constituent of which can be identifyingly referred to without reference to any particular of any other type."

In a conclusion that owes much to Bertrand Russell's treatment of descriptions and logically proper names, and that has in turn influenced thinkers like Gareth Evans and John McDowell, Strawson denies that any purely descriptive or exclusively general identification is ever sufficient to secure *uniqueness* of reference. Individuation of a particular on the basis merely of its possession of certain properties (as, for example, "whichever particular is *F*, and *G*, and *H*, etc."), although perfectly legitimate, is inevitably parasitic on a specification of precisely *which particular it is* that uniquely possesses these properties. That specification, Strawson argues, can only be provided demonstratively, via a direct indication of a perceptible particular that is present in the immediate environment of both the speaker and the hearer, and by the use in that context of phrases such as "*that* person," "*this* pen," "*your* nose," and the like. However, as Strawson observes: "To accept this solution [is] to accept the general theoretical position that the identification of particulars rests ultimately on the use of expressions with some demonstrative, or egocentric, or token-reflexive, force" (1959: 117).

Talking about Oneself and Others

The third chapter of *Individuals* is devoted to an exploration of the place occupied within the conceptual scheme we in fact possess by the concept *person*. "What I mean by the concept of a person," Strawson writes, "is the concept of a type of entity such that *both* predicates ascribing states of consciousness *and* predicates ascribing corporeal characteristics, a physical location &c. are equally applicable to a single individual of that type" (1959: 102). Predicates of the former kind – those that ascribe or presuppose the applicability of states of consciousness, such as "is thinking," "is in pain," or "is writing a letter" – Strawson dubs *P-predicates*. Those of the second kind – those that "also apply to material bodies to which we would not dream of applying predicates ascribing states of consciousness," for example "weighs ten stone," "is six feet tall," "is in the kitchen," and the like – he calls *M-predicates*.

The central claim defended in this chapter is that there is a single, univocal concept of a person, as a particular to which both *P*-predicates and *M*-predicates can equally be applied, which is a logically primitive concept. The very primitiveness of the concept is claimed to have a number of philosophically significant consequences. For example, Strawson suggests, if the concept of a person is primitive, then certain forms of skepticism about the self, and certain traditional versions of the mind–body problem, cannot even be coherently formulated. The fact that the notion of a person is a single, univocal notion, on the other hand, is taken to mean that it applies in the same way to *all persons*. In other words it applies to me, my actions, experiences and conscious states in precisely the same sense in which it applies to those of anybody else. This symmetry between first-person and third-person talk about people and their mental states makes Strawson's notion strongly and intentionally anti-solipsistic. It also allows him to ignore the many asymmetries between first-person and third-person ascriptions of *P*-predicates upon which Wittgenstein had recently insisted (see Wittgenstein, 1953).

Strawson proceeds by identifying two forms of objectionably "revisionary" metaphysics in this context, and devotes some effort to discrediting them. On the one hand, that is, there is any broadly Cartesian account according to which a person is essentially an ego, a conscious subject of experiences, and only contingently if at all a corporeal being. And, on the other hand, there is any theory which attempts to dispense entirely with the notion of a conscious subject and deny that experiences and conscious states are owned or "had" by a subject at all. In the last analysis, Strawson's verdict is this: "both the Cartesian and the no-ownership theorists are profoundly wrong in holding, as each must, that there are two uses of 'I.'"

Commitment to the primitiveness and, especially, the unambiguousness of the concept of a person is only sustainable, as Strawson himself clearly recognizes, if *P*-predicates themselves have the same sense whenever and however they are ascribed to a person. In particular, the sense of a *P*-predicate must be the same irrespective of whether it is self-ascribed ("I am feeling sad") or other-ascribed ("he is feeling sad"). In the last analysis, Strawson's highly contentious verdict is this: in order to understand *P*-predicates:

> one must acknowledge that there is a kind of predicate which is unambiguously and adequately ascribable *both* on the basis of observation of the subject [in other-ascription] *and* not on this basis [in the case of self-ascription]. If there were no [such] concepts . . . we should not have our concept of a person. . . . To refuse to accept this is to refuse to accept the *structure* of the language in which we talk about [states of consciousness]. (1959: 108)

Now the two verdicts mentioned in the previous paragraphs are both vital to Strawson's case, and both are reached by a similar line of argument. That line of argument, however, depends crucially on an appeal to contingent facts about how we talk and use language. In effect, in both cases a philosophical proposal is defended on the grounds that it is "in harmony with our actual ways of talking," and does not "flout the conceptual scheme we actually employ" (1959: 134). Here, I think, we have "descriptive metaphysics" at its most conservative. Indeed, at this point it becomes virtually indistinguishable from precisely the naïve form of "ordinary language philosophy" which it was supposed to supplant, and in which substantial philosophical conclusions are read off from merely contingent facts about the way we talk.

An immediate influence of *Individuals* as a whole, and in particular of the treatment it contains of "persons," was to open up a space within which *metaphysical* debate could again respectably take place. Ironically, however, the very modesty and conservatism of Strawson's own practice may in the longer term have fueled an appetite for even more robust metaphysics. A contemporary reviewer of *Individuals* asked: "Are its conclusions possibly a little bit too reassuring, and its answers to skepticism and to the wilder kinds of speculation a little too comforting, like the political views of a class that feels secure in its privileges?" (Pears, 1961: 173). Perhaps Strawson himself came to feel attracted to an affirmative answer: certainly with his next major work, *The Bounds of Sense*, he became still more metaphysically adventurous, and still more committed to the move away from ordinary language philosophy and toward full-blooded transcendental arguments.

Bibliography

Editions

Strawson, P. F. (1959) *Individuals: An Essay in Descriptive Metaphysics.* London: Methuen.
Strawson, P. F. (1966) *The Bounds of Sense. An Essay on Kant's "Critique of Pure Reason."* London: Methuen.

Studies and references

Davidson, D. (1974) On the very idea of a conceptual scheme. In D. Davidson, *Inquiries into Truth and Interpretation*, pp. 183–98. Oxford: Oxford University Press.
Haack, S. (1979) Descriptive and revisionary metaphysics. *Philosophical Studies*, 35: 361–71.
Hacking, I. (1968) A language without particulars. *Mind*, 77: 168–85.
Magee, B. (1971) *Modern British Philosophy*. London: Secker and Warburg.
Mei, T-L. (1961) Subject and predicate, a grammatical preliminary. *Philosophical Review*, 70: 134–45.
Pears, D. F. (1961) Critical study: Strawson's "Individuals." *Philosophical Quarterly*, 11: 172–85.
Stern, R. (1999) *Transcendental Arguments: Problems and Prospects.* Oxford: Clarendon Press.
Van Straaten, Z. (ed.) (1980) *Philosophical Subjects: Essays Presented to P. F. Strawson.* Oxford: Clarendon Press.
Wittgenstein, L. (1953) *Philosophical Investigations.* Oxford: Blackwell.

59

W. V. O. Quine, *Word and Object* (1960)

The Metaphysics of Meaning

Randall Dipert

Word and Object is W. V. O. Quine's (1908–2001) most significant philosophical book, and his most extensive foray into the philosophy of language. It is not merely a collection of previously published essays, and was written as a long-term philosophical project that began in 1951 (Quine, 1985: 241), continued at Oxford in 1954 and especially at Princeton in 1956–7 (Quine, 1985: 248, 268), and was triumphantly completed at Stanford in 1958–9 (Quine, 1985: 281).

Word and Object was preceded in Quine's *oeuvre* by most of his work on logic, and by his famous attack on the analytic–synthetic distinction ten years earlier in "Two Dogmas of Empiricism" (Quine, 1950). In many ways, *Word and Object* is a work that goes to the heart of the matter concerning the analytic–synthetic distinction: it attempts to show that the very notion of analyticity – and the supposed contrast with what it is to be synthetic – is problematic because the notion of meaning is problematic. Quine himself described *Word and Object* as the "scaffold" on which to hang the many things he had wanted to say (Quine, 1985: 281).

Cast in terms of wider currents in the whole history of philosophy, the general tenor of *Word and Object* is empiricist and pragmatic. This is not always easy to discern and Quine resisted both the former and especially the latter term. In place of the usual foundational empiricist notions such as sensation, Quine rejects characterizing anything as a basic experience and instead casts "experience" simply as what the natural sciences study. His pragmatism is narrowed from what concepts and beliefs are helpful for a full human life or for conduct, as James or Peirce would have understood it, to what is demonstrably required for scientific understanding as we now conceive it.

In the opening pages of *Word and Object*, Quine self-consciously positions himself against empiricist attempts to construct reality solely from sense data. He mentions Berkeley, but it is clear his difference was with the then greatest living empiricist and his former mentor, Rudolf Carnap (to whom the book is in fact dedicated). It is perhaps not precisely with empiricism that he parts ways so much as with *foundationalist* empiricism.

His arguments here and elsewhere in the book have all of the succinct verbal charm that one associates with his writing style. Quine saw earlier attempts to craft an empiricist protocol language as to propose a "fancifully fancyless medium of unvarnished news" (1960: 2). Yet despite this effort, "entified" physical things are not banished because "they hold this language together" and connect the dots between various past and continuing sensations. It is not only the assumption of physical objects that troubles Quine, but also an over-reliance on the memory of sensations. These memories are neither indefeasible nor purely sensuous, being typically recalled in a conceptualized form. We remember not precisely a clear image of the hulking, blackened cathedral in Cologne, but *that* we saw it.

Our notions of physical objects are thus not constructed or justified from immediate sense data, as the logical positivists had claimed. Quine appears to show, here and elsewhere, an abiding distrust of atomistic foundations and the use of pure or ideal notions – such as sense data or analyticity.

Belief in physical objects is rational, but for other reasons, and such objects are merely "posits" – a favorite word of Quine and his followers, as important as "paradigm" was in the influence of Thomas Kuhn. Posits are fallible hypothetical constructions that derive their utility from the whole fabric of the explanatory enterprise of which they are a part. While successful, they need not be superior to alternative constructions.

Quine's Critique of Meaning

If there is a single leitmotiv to *Word and Object*, it is probably the contention that there does not exist anything that is the meaning of a word or sentence. Gilbert Harman (1999) calls this the "death of meaning." More precisely expressed in Quine's own vocabulary, "meaning" is not a notion that is necessary for a science of language. It is not even a useful posit. He describes this general view as "dispensing with intensional objects." Meanings are one major kind of intensional object. Words and phrases (at least some of them) retain an ability to refer to things, but do not require separately and secondarily to indicate abstract entities.

In a sense, Quine believes words and sentences *do* have meanings, but they are not anything like traditional notions of meaning, such as Frege's *Sinne*. Sentences have "stimulus meaning": this is the set of all circumstances that would result in a speaker's assent to the assertion of that sentence (1960: 32). In another sense, too, Quine does not reject the claim that sentences and words-in-context have meaning (are useful, sensible, etc., or not). Rather, he objects to the relational notion of meaning: while "Snow is white" has meaning, there exists no X such that we can helpfully claim that the meaning of "Snow is white" is X.

Quine locates the attraction to traditional notions of meaning in several arguments (1960: 206–7). Most importantly, he believes there has been a myth that when we correctly translate a sentence from one language into a sentence of another language, what makes it a correct translation is thought to be that something – the sentence's meaning – remains invariant. More generally, the notion of synonymy, sameness of meaning, within or between languages would require that sentences have meanings which can be compared. His famous reply is that there are no perfect, empirically derivable, criteria for correct translation (or correct paraphrase); instead, there is a "radical indeterminacy of translation." Hence there is no synonymy. This is one sense in which *Word and Object* is a more general scaffold for his earlier attack on the analytic–synthetic distinction.

Quine notes two other arguments that propositions, primarily identified as the meanings of sentences, exist or are necessary posits: philosophers have believed they are necessary as "truth vehicles" (what are now called, following D. M. Armstrong, truthmakers), and that they are necessary as the objects or content of propositional attitudes, such as believing. Quine does not fully address these arguments. It is a curious assumption in most analytic philosophy that meanings of sentences (as described in a science of natural language), what is true (what is a basic description of reality – roughly, the description of facts), and what we believe or want to be so are all taken to be the same basic *kind* of entity.

The Indeterminacy of Translation

Quine's doctrine of the Indeterminacy of Translation is widely cited, and has formed the basis for an extensive secondary literature. It is often confused with what we might call the "Impossibility of Translation." The Impossibility of Translation would claim that for some, many, or all sentences of one language there do not exist any sentences in the second language that are perfect translations. Even stating this claim requires that sense can be given to two sentences having exactly the same meaning. Since this is precisely what Quine denies, he cannot be taken to be saying that translation is impossible.

Quine's doctrine is rather that meanings are at best fuzzy and underdetermined. A mature science of language would not use them at all. His supposed demonstration of the phenomenon of indeterminancy of translation uses one of the most famous examples in analytic philosophy, the mock foreign expression, "Gavagai."

We are linguists who are thrust into a foreign culture of which we have no previous understanding. We point to a rabbit and look perplexed. A native says, "Gavagai." We see another rabbit and say emphatically, "Gavagai!" and the native nods. (This example seems to require previous knowledge of what it is to assert or assent in this culture; this lingering naïveté ultimately presents obstacles for Quine's goal of a pure, objective behavioral account of "stimulus" meaning.)

We go through many similar examples, which only tend to confirm our growing suspicion that "Gavagai" *means* the same thing as "rabbit." Quine's question is this. How many such experiments, or which other experiments, would establish that "Gavagai" means "(There's a) rabbit" and a quizzical "Gavagai?" means "Is this a rabbit?"

Quine responds to the example as follows. Although we may reasonably take "Gavagai" to refer to an animal kind, our verbal exchanges are compatible with the native in fact meaning (thinking) such things as "Over there is an exemplification of the property of rabbitness," "There is a temporal slice of a rabbit-in-action," "There are some animate, connected rabbit-parts," and so on. Saying "Rabbit!" might be co-extensive with – have the same truth conditions as – "That's my favorite animal,"

"There is rabbit meat before processing," "I am hereby referring to a rabbit," and so on.

Quine's point is that what constitutes a correct translation cannot be discovered through any empirical means, free of all theoretical frameworks. He does so by considerings phrases in English that are co-extensive (that is, refer to the same entities) but have different meanings: same extension (reference), but differing intension (sense, connotation, etc). Thus "rabbit" and "connected, animated rabbit parts" are different ways of thinking about the same entities in the world, but refer to the same entities. However, since every theoretical entity is, in isolation, similarly beyond confirmation, Quine must also show that meanings are eliminable: that they are not necessary or useful even as posits.

One peculiarity of the Gavagai example is that it requires us to use the idea of what we might call private mental activity of thinking about entities in a certain way – as regarding rabbits in a certain way. It is unlikely that such an argument would have much appeal to someone who, from the beginning, is suspicious of private or non-physically manifest mental activity, such as Gilbert Ryle, or much later and forcefully, Ludwig Wittgenstein. Another criticism is that it is only a linguistic facet of the more general ambiguity of confirmation explored by Quine's Harvard colleague Nelson Goodman in his Grue Paradox.

The bulk of the middle portion of *Word and Object* is devoted to showing how a successful, complete, and relatively simple theory of language can be developed that lacks this secondary aspect of words and phrases, namely, their meanings. In these sections, accounts are given of relative terms and phrases, abstract terms, proper names and descriptions, and so on.

A special problem that has to be solved is with so-called opaque contexts (1960: 141–56). These are contexts in which substitution of one phrase by another with the same reference or extension does not preserve the truth of the sentence. Frege, as well as important contemporaries of Quine such as Alonzo Church, had regarded the existence of such phenomena as conclusive proof that words and phrases have this secondary dimension of meaning, beyond bare reference. An example of opacity is this. The pre-Socratic philosopher Thales believed that water was everywhere, since he believed that everything was in some sense ultimately water. We now know water is H_2O. Therefore, Thales believed that hydrogen–oxygen molecules were everywhere. This conclusion seems false, even though the argument form, of substitution of identicals, is generally valid. It is virtually impossible that Thales had any thoughts whatsoever about oxygen (which was isolated millenniums later and not understood in the modern way until the late eighteenth century). The context of what one believes is said to be "opaque" because it does not allow substitution of co-referential expressions. Quine's solution is essentially to accept the conclusion after all – that Thales believed hydrogen–oxygen molecules were everywhere – but only after re-writing it so that the replaced phrase ("H_2O" for "water") is in a position where co-referential substitution does no harm to its truth: roughly, "It turns out that there is something, H_2O, identical to that (water) which Thales believed to be everywhere." This device of paraphrasing in order to bring a term to the subject position, where it can be logically manipulated, was in fact discovered by medieval logicians, and called the "oblique syllogism"; they used it to derive valid conclusions that were quantified and relational.

Quine, himself an immaculate and elegant writer, realizes full well that the resulting paraphrases are clumsy. He believes that the occasional added difficulty is more than made up for by the elimination of an entire ill-understood category of abstract objects, "meanings." All we require for a complete theory of language are concrete linguistic terms and the concrete entities to which they refer. However, Quine also believes that when expressed in an ideal language, and not the natural language of, for example, English, we have inherited, such paraphrases are not at all awkward or even very complex.

First-order Logic as a Canonical Language

In two respects, Quine departed from previous empiricist accounts, including his mentor Carnap's. First, there are no fixed basic elements – not sensations nor even the bare notion of physical object. Second, there is no philosophically useful notion of analyticity, nor even of "meaning." This shatters the distinction between merely linguistic truths and genuinely empirical ones. Left to ponder the undoubtedly rational but nevertheless unempirical claims of logic and mathematics, logical positivists had argued that these were surely analytical truths. Blanketing all of the territory of both of these positions is a view we might call Quine's "relativistic holism." The holism is most clearly developed in his later (with J. Ullian) *Web of Belief* (1970) and the relativism in his *Ontological Relativity and Other Essays* (1969). No single statement, or posit – not even one usually thought to be analytical – is indubitable or absolutely epistemologically secure. Instead, its epistemic merit is to be measured entirely in its success as part of a larger project to explain the world. Although he rejects the ordinary language approach (1960: 3–5), his own holism and theory of meaning come dangerously close to the doctrine of "meaning is use." Furthermore, there may be quite different worldviews that equally well explain the world, although, to be sure, most worldviews do not succeed as well as the one Quine defends, especially one that contains intensions or a surfeit of abstract entities. Quine's relativism could perhaps better be called conventionalism, and is likely derived from Pierre Duhem and Henri Poincaré, perhaps via Thomas Kuhn. However, other than the narrow case of geometric conventionalism that inspired Poincaré and others, no one seems to have built up whole metaphysical systems that minimally overlap with our usual metaphysics and yet can be demonstrated to be equally workable.

In another respect, however, Quine is indeed the heir to the tradition of Carnap and the other logical positivists. He believes that there is a single, ideal language for clearly expressing any worldview, and this language is an artificial one deriving from the extensive logical discoveries of the nineteenth and twentieth centuries. In particular, he believes that the first-order predicate calculus is both sufficient to express anything worth expressing, in a perfectly clear and unambiguous way, and that it is the minimum such language. While two-thirds of *Word and Object* are devoted to an attack on meanings, and to developing a full and elegant theory of language that does not appeal to them, the last third of the book is devoted to defending a certain conception of this ideal language – an ideal scientific language that was the goal of Leibniz, among many others. While he says that "temporary" and "opportunistic" deviation (1960: 157) from polished natural language had occasionally been useful in the first sections of the book, he argues that a full reform of language is necessary in order to achieve a "central motive of theory," simplification (1960: 158).

A first-order language quantifies over individual entities. A second-order language quantifies over properties (and relations) as well. He is concerned with what entities are quantified because of his view that the entities a formal language quantifies codify the kinds of things its user takes to exist (Quine, 1948). Although it is not trotted out on every occasion where it could be, Quine clearly believes there exists one principle above others when choosing a preferred ontology: namely, Ockham's razor, by which he understands that metaphysical categories of things should not be posited if a successful explanatory theory does not require them. We do not require properties and intensions. He more often disguises his frequent use of the maxim by instead employing value-laden words such as appealing to simplicity or "austerity" (1960: 228) when speaking of first-order predicate logic. The need to employ the razor arises because of the profligate tendency of natural languages toward nominalizing (such as the nouns "glint" or "sake" and in the -ness and -hood forms of English): nominalization begets illicit entification. Nevertheless, we may not jettison a type of entity unless we can demonstrate its dispensability (1960: 124) – as Quine believes he has done with intensions.

The theory of sets is the one domain of *abstracta* that causes Quine to blink. He himself refers to sets and classes, and wrote a book about sets (Quine, 1963); at the same time, he strongly criticized those who hypocritically use abstract entities in which they feign not to believe (1960: 241). He proposes that the reduction of the notion of order to sets is a paradigm of analysis. (His account has both historical and possible philosophical flaws; see Dipert, 1982.) He endorsed stimulus meaning as a *set* of circumstances. In a carefully written later chapter of *Word and Object*, "Whither Classes?" (pp. 266–70), he extols sets for their "versatility" and "power" (p. 267) and expresses difficulty in accepting a completely nominalist account without sets, especially for mathematics.

Except for this flirtation with sets, especially in the unusual system explored in *Set Theory and Its Logic* (1963) and first proposed in 1937, Quine endorses a physicalist nominalism (1960: 233–8; Quine and Goodman, 1947). The evidence for physical objects is admittedly not immediate, but is less "far fetched" (1960: 234) than evidence for other kinds of entities. Without explanation, this is argumentation by *bon mot*. Quine doesn't tell us whether his plausible physical objects are the mesoscopic objects of common sense or the strange microscopic apparitions of quantum mechanics; he is similarly untroubled by the precise metaphysical status of space and time – occurring in his reduction of tensed sentences to time-indexed "eternal sentences" (1960: 170–6, 190–5).

Conclusion

Although it is a bit early to assess the importance of *Word and Object* in the whole history of philosophy, or its impact on future analytic philosophy, one might hazard a few words. If there is an American analytic philosopher of the twentieth century who will emerge as a major thinker in the history of philosophy, it is probably Quine (Stroll, 2000: 251–4). While Quine did propose a system of philosophy that he single-mindedly pursued throughout his career, it nevertheless does not seem to be one that even touched some central areas of human concern, such as politics, ethics, or art. Seen from the perspective of the decades since 1960, *Word and Object* is a pivotal work of the period for the philosophy of language, logic, and their interface. It is unlikely, however, that the teacher of a graduate-level seminar in the philosophy of language would now feel compelled to place the complete *Word and Object* on its reading list (though some of Quine's articles have acquired a status that *is* nearly canonical).

For one thing, its dominant method, or meta-philosophy, namely of Ockhamite simplicity, is itself too simple of a value. Its reductionism – especially of intension, but also of mathematical entities – seemed refreshing at the time, but the tide in philosophy is now turning toward a robust view of philosophical issues and the metaphysics that might be needed to account for them. Its behaviorism (in its characterization of "stimulus meaning," for example) is something of an embarrassment, as even Quine later sometimes admitted, though he defended it in Quine (1995). Its relativism and holism seem either dated or are now taken for granted (we can see in hindsight from works of Kuhn, Wittgenstein, and others that it was part of a broad fashion). At the same time, in failing to consider the possibility of radically different alternatives to first-order logic or set theory as we happen to have come to them, his fallibilism seems tepid. Why don't formal languages, too, have a "disposition to keep on evolving" (1960: 3)? His pragmatism seems too unspecific, or too tied to the status quo in the natural sciences – what Stroll (2000: 188) calls his "scientism." What is it about science, for example, that gives it its privileged position in being the very measure of epistemic adequacy? What is it about layman's physics ca. 1950 that is privileged?

Word and Object thus occupies a paradoxical position in twentieth-century philosophy. It is the most important book of a very important philosopher. It undergirds and summarizes views expressed in essays that are undoubtedly of major importance and influence. Yet it is probably not itself a book of the importance of Wittgenstein's *Philosophical Investigations* (admittedly a non-book), or even Carnap's *Aufbau* that it was in some ways intended to supersede.

Bibliography

Editions

Quine, W. V. O. (1948) On what there is. Reprinted in W. V. O. Quine, *From a Logical Point of View*. Cambridge, MA: Harvard University Press, 1953.

Quine, W. V. O. (1950) Two dogmas of empiricism. Reprinted in W. V. O. Quine, *From a Logical Point of View*. Cambridge, MA: Harvard University Press, 1953.

Quine, W. V. O. (1960) *Word and Object*. Cambridge, MA: MIT Press.

Quine, W. V. O. (1963) *Set Theory and Its Logic*. Cambridge, MA: Harvard University Press.

Quine, W. V. O. (1969) *Ontological Relativity and Other Essays*. New York: Columbia University Press.

Quine, W. V. O. (1985) *The Time of my Life*. Cambridge, MA: MIT.

Quine, W. V. O. (1995) *From Stimulus to Science*. Cambridge, MA: Harvard University Press.

Quine, W. V. O. and Goodman, N. (1947) Steps toward a constructive nominalism. *Journal of Symbolic Logic*, 12: 97–122.

Quine, W. V. O. and Ullian, J. (1970) *The Web of Belief*. New York: Random House.

Studies

Arrington, Robert and Glock, Hans-Johann (eds) (1996) *Wittgenstein and Quine*. New York: Routledge.

Barrett, Robert and Gibson, Roger (eds) (1990) *Perspectives on Quine*. Cambridge, MA: Blackwell.

Dipert, Randall R. (1982) Set-theoretical representations of ordered pairs . . . *Canadian Journal of Philosophy*, 12: 353–74.

Hahn, Lewis and Schilpp, Paul (eds) (1986) *The Philosophy of W. V. Quine*. LaSalle, IL: Open Court.

Harman, Gilbert (1999) *Reasoning, Meaning and Mind*. New York: Oxford University Press.

Leonardi, Paolo and Santambrogio, Marco (1995) *On Quine: New Essays*. New York: Cambridge University Press.

Stroll, Avrum (2000) *Twentieth-century Analytic Philosophy*. New York: Columbia.

60

J. L. Austin, *How to Do Things with Words* (1962)

An Active View of Language

Nicholas Fotion

By all appearances, *How to Do Things with Words* (hereafter *HTD*) is not a classic work in philosophy. The title makes it sound as if it is a "how to fix it" manual of some sort. It is also seemingly too short, a mere 163 pages, to sustain much original thought. Further, Austin's breezy writing style makes it seem that he is not engaged in serious thought. But appearances can be, and in this case are, deceiving.

HTD was published after Austin (1911–1960) died. During his time at Oxford, he had given lectures which evolved over the years under the title of "Words and Deeds." In 1955, he took his notes on "Words and Deeds" to Harvard to deliver the William James lectures. It is these notes that J. O. Urmson edited and that subsequently emerged as *HTD*.

HTD is a classic work in the philosophy of *language*. Attending to language for its own sake, and as a way of doing philosophy, had come into vogue before World War II. At that time, the most aggressive thinkers engaged in language analysis were the logical positivists. Those in the group included R. Carnap, H. Feigl, H. Hahn, M. Schlick, F. Waismann from Vienna, and A. J. Ayer from Oxford. As a group, they were great admirers of the hard physical sciences and so were inclined to argue that language gains meaning in so far as it is used to report observations and insights having scientific import. A. J. Ayer expressed this line of thought most famously when he said that a sentence is meaningful if and only if it is assessable at least in principle as either true or false (Ayer, 1946: 35). He added that to assess a sentence in this way it had to be based on observation or fall into the class of "analytic" sentences (those devoid of observational content such as "All triangles are three sided" and "All red roses are red"). If a sentence fails to fit into one of these two categories, it was said to be meaningless (i.e., neither true nor false).

This line of thinking puzzled Austin. In *HTD* he asks: are not "I name this ship *Queen Elizabeth*" and "I bet you sixpence it will rain tomorrow" meaningful (*HTD*, 5)? We understand what is said, so they certainly seem meaningful. But, more importantly, such utterances satisfy certain standards of meaning that Austin calls felicity or happiness conditions. One such standard is that a certain accepted procedure exists;

another is that the right person(s) carry out the procedure; a third that the procedure is carried out correctly; and a fourth that it is carried out completely. In the *Queen Elizabeth* example we know the first condition is happy since a naming procedure for ships exists. In addition, if the Queen herself comes to "christen" the ship, then the right person is in place to do the job. Beyond that if she carries out every step of the procedure correctly and completely even to the point of smashing the champagne bottle smartly against the bow of the ship, then the ship is named. If, in contrast, someone not authorized to name the ship tries to do the job, the ship is not named. We then have, as Austin would say, a procedural misfire. But if the Queen does her job properly, the ship is indeed named. In that case Austin says that the Queen *did* something with language. She performed linguistically. In saying "I name this ship *Queen Elizabeth*" she has issued a performative utterance (*HTD*, 6). Similarly, the person making the sixpenny bet is performing linguistically because, first of all, there is a betting procedure in place in society, he is the right person to make the bet (if the money he is betting is his, he is an adult, etc.), he offered the bet properly, and he carried it out completely.

Having argued for the meaningfulness of performative utterances (e.g., "I promise . . .," "I order you to . . .," "I congratulate you . . ."), Austin contrasts them with sentences he calls constatives (*HTD*, 3). These are the sentences that the positivists claimed are the exclusive carriers of meaning. But Austin, without denying that constatives are meaningful, has gone on to show that meaning can be carried far beyond the borders of science and the "analytic" realm (of definitions, mathematics, and the like). Having done that much, Austin has already taken steps to shake the positivist tradition to its roots.

But his new dichotomy of constatives and performatives posed some problems for Austin. If *making* a promise is doing something with language, isn't *reporting* that someone made a promise a performative also? Puzzling about this and similar questions, Austin saw that it is not clear what *doing* with or in language means. He also saw that he had to explore the relationship between constatives and performatives since now it appears that our natural language is schizophrenic. There seem to be two separate realms to our language, and apparently they have nothing to do with one another.

In his rather wandering attempts to deal with these problems, Austin arrived at a cluster of important distinctions. In one such he distinguishes what he calls perlocutionary action. If a speaker says something that frightens the hearer, the speaker has performed a perlocutionary act. We can also speak here of the perlocutionary effect on the hearer. The effect, fright in this case, is causally brought about *by* what was said. Another example of a perlocutionary act and/or effect is when the speaker tells a story and thereby convinces the hearer that what was said is true. Still another is when what is said convinces the hearer to vote for a different candidate from the one he would have voted for.

Strictly speaking, the perlocutionary act is not an act performed within language. Rather, it is an act brought about after something has been said. This is not the case with what Austin calls the locutionary act. This act is performed within language and also within the total speech act. A locutionary act is like moving a foot while in the process of performing the larger act of moving the whole leg. However, although the locutionary act is part of a larger act, it too has parts. Within it are the smaller acts *of* referring and predicating. Thus, if one says "The rose is red" the locutionary part of the whole is that concerned with the words "the rose" and "red." The locutionary act, in effect, presents the subject matter of the total act.

Austin next tells us about the third and most important of the distinctions he needs to help in understanding what it means to *do* something with language. This is the illocutionary act. The illocutionary act is the full performative. It is performed *in* saying something. Force is added to the locutionary act (to referring and predicating) to create the full performative. The speaker says "I *order* you to move that table," or "I *promise* to help you," or "I *apologize* for running into you." The words "order," "promise," "apologize" each add force to the locution found in each of these utterances.

Having these distinctions in hand, Austin focuses on the notions of illocutionary act and force to help him decide what the relationship is between constatives and performatives. It is clear right off that there are all sorts of forces at play in our language and thus all sorts of illocutionary acts. In addition to ordering, promising, and apologizing, we can issue illocutionary acts where we are asking, pleading, congratulating, thanking, declaring (war), swearing (to tell the truth), advising, proclaiming, excommunicating, conceding, and on and on. Evidently we can play an indefinite number of language-games with our native language. But are there even more games here? Take hypothesizing. Is that a performative? What about estimating? What about affirming? They seem to have force and so they too seem to be performatives. But they are all thought of as falling in the constative camp. What about stating? The speaker says "I state that Smith was at the party where the murder took place." It's a constative, but it sounds like a performative. It has illocutionary force; and can be analyzed just like any other performative. We can ask if there is a convention for stating. There certainly is. Just as there is for promising. We can also ask if the speaker is the proper person to make the statement and receive the answer "Yes he is, since he has good eyesight, was himself at the party and stayed sober throughout the whole affair." Further, he made his claim about Smith correctly (he spoke in good English) and completely. In other words, the conventions that constatives satisfy are comparable to those of other performatives.

Further, what the speaker said satisfies other conditions that Austin says belong to performatives. When Austin discusses other performatives he says that they are supposed to satisfy what he calls the sincerity condition. With a promise the speaker satisfies this condition if he intends to carry out the promise. With an order the speaker's sincerity condition is satisfied if she wants what is ordered done. But notice that the constative "I state that Smith was at the party where the murder took place" also has a sincerity condition: viz., the speaker believes what he said.

So it is beginning to appear that language is not divided schizophrenically into constatives and performatives, but that all language is performative. The realm of constatives is not separate. Rather, it seems that constatives form one or more kinds of performative and that other performatives, such as promises and orders, play roles in forming other kinds. Obviously Austin's next task is to decide just how many kinds of performatives there are and what their properties are. This is a formidable task since, as already noted, a host of performatives grace our natural language.

Austin concludes, cautiously, that all performatives fall into five groups. The easiest group to understand he calls commissives. He says that their point "is to commit the speaker to a certain course of action" (*HTD*, 156–7). He analyzes performatives by listing (performative) verbs and verb expressions that he thinks belong in this group. Not surprisingly "promise" heads the list. But, among others, he also adds "give my word," "contract," "covenant," "undertake," "mean to," "plan," "propose to," "vow," "guarantee," "espouse," "bet," "swear," and "favour." When used in a complete performative, all these verbs commit the speaker, but some more strongly than others. "I vow to catch the criminal" is stronger than "I mean to . . . ." Still other commissives have different features. Contracting and betting, for example, require two speakers at least to get the performative properly done.

A second group of performatives Austin labels behabitives. Of these he says that they "include the notion of reaction to other people's behaviour and fortunes and of attitudes and expressions of attitudes to someone else's past conduct or imminent conduct" (*HTD*, 159). Up to a point this group is fairly easy to grasp as well. A congratulations is clearly a behabitive. When I say "I congratulate you for your victory" I am reacting to someone else's behavior and fortune. Some of the verbs he lists under this grouping are "thank," "commiserate," "condole," "compliment," and "apologize." Notice that with "apologize" the speaker's behavior is at issue, not the hearer's.

He broadens this group still further. It includes expressions of greetings such as "welcome" and "bid your farewell" and expressions of the speaker's wishes. So verbs such as "bless (you)," "curse," "toast," and "drink to" are included. He also includes verbs relating to challenging others. So "dare," "defy," and even "challenge" are in his list.

The last three groupings are not so easy to understand. One of these he calls verdictives. He characterizes it as consisting "in the delivering of a finding, official or unofficial, upon evidence or reasons as to value or fact" (*HTD*, 152). He adds that verdictives represent judicial as against legislative or executive acts. The verbs he associates with this group include: "find" (as in "We find the defendant guilty"), "rule" (as in "I rule that you were out"), "grade," "rate," "describe," "measure," "acquit," "convict," and "diagnose." One thing to note about this group is that it contains performatives that formerly were said to be constatives.

The next group he labels exercitives. With these, the speaker is exercising power or authority. As against verdictives, which are judicial, exercitives are legislative and executive in nature. The verb list here is wide ranging. It includes "appoint," "dismiss," "excommunicate," "name," "sentence" (as in "I sentence you to five years in jail"), "proclaim," "recommend," "annul," and "bequeath."

The final class Austin calls expositives. These he says are "used in acts of exposition involving the expounding of views, the conducting of argument, and the clarifying of usages and references" (*HTD*, 150). His long list of these verbs includes "affirm," "deny," "state," "describe," "inform," "accept," "concede," "apprise," "analyze," "define," "mean" (as in "I mean by the word 'God' . . ."), and "object to."

What Austin wants to do with this fivefold grouping is bring order to chaos. He supposes that our language is not composed of an indefinite number of unrelated language-games. But is his ordering system the best that can be found? Even Austin wonders about that. He notes repeatedly that his allocation of this or that verb can be disputed. He wonders, for example, whether "analyze" in the expositive camp really belongs in the verdictive. But there are other problems. "Describe" is classed both as an expositive and a verdictive. "Swear" is both an expositive and a commissive. There are more serious problems. Some former constatives are classed as verdictives, while others are classed as expositives. Further, it is not at all clear why some belong under one heading rather than another. Still another problem is that there is no consistent set of criteria for identifying the groups. The notion of an expositive, for example, seems to apply not to performatives but to discourse (i.e., a string of performatives). Although the other classes do indeed apply to performatives, it is not clear why, with the case of exercitives, they are not divided in two: one for legislative thinking and one for executive. In short, it is not clear why just those five groups emerged as the ones to best bring order to our language.

Sensing these and other problems with Austin's system, John Searle tried to rectify things in an article entitled "A Taxonomy of Illocutionary Acts" (Searle, 1979). Seizing on the idea that performatives can best be classed mainly in terms of their purpose, he developed the following system. Interestingly, his "taxonomy" also contains five types of performatives or, as he calls them, "speech acts" (Searle, 1979: 12–20).

1 *Assertives.* The purpose of these is to commit speakers to the truth of what they say. This is an improvement over Austin's system since all constatives fall under one heading. Scientific claims, ordinary observations, and even reports about definitions (i.e., analytic claims) belong under this heading.
2 *Commissives.* These are much like Austin's. No change here. The purpose of these speech acts is to commit the speaker one way or another.
3 *Directives.* The purpose of these speech acts is to try to get the hearer to do something. This category gathers in Austinian performatives mainly from the exercitive camp.
4 *Expressives.* The purpose of these speech acts is to express the psychological state of speakers with respect to what they are talking about. Mostly, these speech acts are found in Austin's behabitive category. Thus when one apologizes, congratulates, greets someone in the morning on the way to work, etc. the "sincerity" of what the speaker says is expressed in the speech act.
5 *Declarations.* The purpose of these speech acts is to bring about a state of affairs simply by issuing a speech act. Thus when the tyrannical employer says to the employee "You're fired" the employee is an ex-employee. Also, when the meeting organizer declares the meeting open, it is open. Saying it makes it so. In terms of Austin's system, declarations come mainly from the exercitive category.

So Searle completes some of the work Austin started in *HTD*. This is not surprising since *HTD* is best seen as an exploratory work. One would not expect Austin to get things right all the way through. What he got right was the discovery of performatives, the roles some of these performatives play in language, and the relationship between constatives and performatives. He also got right the relationship between the locutionary, perlocutionary, and illocutionary acts. And, finally, he got it right that order can be found in our language. Our language is not a jumble of disconnected performatives or speech acts. That he did not get the actual order right is only a minor consideration when seen against the revolution he started in giving us a far better understanding of how our natural language works and how it is structured.

Bibliography

Editions

Austin, J. L. (1962) *How to Do Things with Words*. New York: Oxford University Press.

Studies and references

Ayer, A. J. (1946) *Language, Truth and Logic*. New York: Dover (orig. pub. 1936).

Fann, K. T. (ed.) (1969) *Symposium on J. L. Austin*. New York: Humanities Press/Routledge and Kegan Paul (see especially Part IV containing articles on *HTD* by Walter Cerf, P. F. Strawson, Max Black, L. W. Forguson, L. Jonathan Cohen, and Mats Furgerg).

Searle, John R. (1969) *Speech Acts*. Cambridge: Cambridge University Press.

Searle, John R. (1979) A taxonomy of illocutionary acts. In *Expression and Meaning: Studies in the Theory of Speech Acts*. Cambridge: Cambridge University Press.

Searle, John R. and Vanderveken, Daniel (1985) *Foundations of Illocutionary Logic*. Cambridge: Cambridge University Press.

Tsohatzidis, Savas L. (ed.) (1994) *Foundations of Speech Act Theory: Philosophic and Linguistic Perspectives*. London and New York: Routledge.

61

Thomas S. Kuhn, *The Structure of Scientific Revolutions* (1962)

"Relativism" Hits the Headlines

Endre Begby

It is, perhaps, a bizarre twist of fate that one of the most hotly debated books in twentieth-century philosophy (and perhaps its only real best-seller – recent reports number sales at more than a million copies in English alone, not counting its twenty-five translations) was written by a self-avowed non-philosopher. The story of Thomas Kuhn (1922–96) is the story of a physicist, turned historian of science, turned (somewhat unwillingly) the philosopher of science who was blamed for almost single-handedly creating a crisis of rationality in contemporary philosophy.

Kuhn's primary concern when writing *The Structure of Scientific Revolutions* (1962) was with the nature of scientific discovery, and, by implication, with our view of scientific progress. Nowhere did he intend to challenge the *rationality* of science as such. To his contemporaries, however, this was just what his book seemed to do. For what could Kuhn's forceful and polemical attack on time-honored notions such as truth, progress, and objectivity amount to, if not an attack on science itself? In short, would not Kuhn's insistence on radical discontinuities and revolutionary upheavals in the history of science, together with his emphasis on the contingency inherent in every research situation, seem to project the specter of relativism on to that supposed bastion of rationality, natural science? And if natural science is not free from such factors, can any other sphere of human inquiry claim immunity?

Paradigms and Normal Science

To challenge the then dominant "development-by-accumulation" view of scientific progress, Kuhn characterizes mature science as having passed through a number of distinct stages. All candidates for the status of "scientific discipline" must first undergo a period of "immaturity" before becoming a science proper. This transition to mature science coincides with the discipline's reception of its first *paradigm*. This term, introduced by Kuhn in *The Structure of Scientific Revolutions* (henceforth *SSR*), has become common currency in academic discourse. The notion is notoriously difficult to delimit and has taken on a life of its own apart from his writings. In *SSR*, however, it was intended to capture something along the lines of an *exemplary achievement*: a work that serves "implicitly to define the legitimate problems and methods of a research field for succeeding generations of practitioners" (*SSR*, 10). Frequently cited examples of such works are Newton's *Principia* and Lavoisier's *Chemistry.*

Science practiced under a paradigm is what Kuhn refers to as *normal science*. The transition from immaturity to normal science is marked by a distinct narrowing of scope; for every paradigm rigidly defines both what is to count as a problem and the range of acceptable solutions. The transition to normal science can only happen when scientists have at their disposal clear-cut criteria of relevance. These are what enable them collectively to work on one set of problems while discarding others.

Kuhn describes the tasks of normal science as threefold: (1) the determination of significant facts; (2) the matching of facts with theory; and (3) theory-articulation. All three are, in Kuhn's distinctive parlance, "mop-up work," and nowhere do they constitute the kind of "testing" of the theory that was deemed so important on the traditional view. Normal science simply does not aim at producing major novelty: "Instead, its object is to solve a puzzle for whose very existence the validity of the paradigm must be assumed. Failure to achieve a solution discredits only the scientist and not the theory" (*SSR*, 80).

Anomaly and Crisis

Yet, although innovation is not the *aim* of normal scientific research, we can rest assured that novelty will not be suppressed forever. Over time, research will produce *anomalies*– facts that thwart theoretical expectations and cannot readily be assimilated into the paradigm. The existence of anomaly does not by itself constitute sufficient reason to discard a paradigm (after all, no scientific theory, no matter how successful, has ever explained all phenomena relevant to it). The accumulation of anomaly will, however, induce in scientists a greater willingness to articulate and investigate alternative ways of accounting for the recalcitrant phenomena. The continued resistance of anomaly to traditional modes of accommodation forces scientists to bend the paradigmatic applications in ways that under normal circumstances would seem arbitrary and *ad hoc. Extraordinary science* comes about when the discipline enters a period of *crisis*. In such a situation, "the rules of normal science become increasingly blurred. Though there is still a paradigm, few practitioners prove to be entirely agreed upon what it is" (*SSR*, 80).

This state of crisis will resolve in one of three ways: (1) normal scientific resources will ultimately prove able to account for the seeming anomaly; (2) the problem will be deemed insoluble for the present time and set aside for future research; or (3) a new candidate for paradigm will emerge, and with it the ensuing battle over its acceptance (*SSR*, 84). This last possibility is, needless to say, the one that is of most interest to

Kuhn. This, in his opinion, is what traditional philosophy of science has crucially over-looked. If a crisis ends with the acceptance of a new paradigm, a *scientific revolution* will have taken place.

Scientific Revolutions and Incommensurability

Nothing in the foregoing account is in principle incompatible with the story of scientific development as cumulative. The notion of a scientific revolution was in circulation long before Kuhn, and was used to designate particularly great scientific advances, for example, the Copernican revolution. Kuhn did, however, introduce a number of twists in the tale, ultimately provoking some critics to outrage. The revolutionary transition from paradigm to paradigm should not be called a cumulative process, he argues: "Rather, it is a reconstruction of the field from new fundamentals . . . When the transition is complete, the profession will have changed its view of the field, its methods, and its goals" (*SSR*, 94).

Kuhn is far from oblivious to the political connotations of his choice of terminology, and explores these to find interesting parallels to scientific development. Political and scientific revolutions alike start from a growing awareness within an estranged sub-community that existing institutions fail to deal satisfactorily with a certain set of problems. Seeking redress for their grievances, "revolutionaries" opt to change these political institutions in ways that the institutions themselves prohibit, or even to overthrow them altogether. In the interim between old and new, the community is inevitably split in two, and communication across the divide will be only partial. Since standards of adequacy and failure are exactly what are under dispute, and since neither party acknowledges any supra-institutional framework, standard forms of political recourse necessarily fail. Applying this political analogy to revolution in science, Kuhn observes that both involve a special kind of choice:

> Like the choice between competing political institutions, that between paradigms proves to be a choice between incompatible modes of community life. Because it has that character, the choice is not and cannot be determined merely by the evaluative procedures characteristic of normal science . . . Each group uses its own paradigm to argue in that paradigm's defense . . . The status of [this] circular argument is only that of persuasion. It cannot be made logically or even probabilistically compelling . . . As in political revolutions, so in paradigm choice – there is no standard higher than the assent of the relevant community. (*SSR*, 94)

As if this were not enough to infuriate his critics, Kuhn would then go on to introduce the notorious notion of *incommensurability*. Adopted from mathematics and meaning "no common measure," Kuhn used the term to pinpoint the predicament of paradigm choice in science. If we think of paradigms as languages expressing divergent cognitive commitments, two paradigms will then be incommensurable if there is no way of effecting a translation between them. Incommensurable paradigms may employ many of the same concepts (for example, space, motion, mass), but each paradigm will use them differently, since the meaning of these concepts is anchored in the theoretical structure of their respective paradigms. Kuhn thereby bids farewell to the time-honored idea that "nature" or "reality" (the supposed common measure) provides us with a neutral court of appeal, a court that would allow us unproblematically to decide between theories. "[P]aradigm changes do cause scientists to see the world of their research engagement differently. In so far as their only recourse to that world is through what they see and do, we may want to say that after a revolution scientists are responding to a different world" (*SSR*, 111).

Kuhn thus rejects the idea of a clear separation between fact and theory; between nature and the way we conceptualize it. We simply cannot analyze a paradigm to parcel out "empirical content" from "theoretical framework." A major scientific innovation does much more than simply alter the scientific community's interpretation of given data. Rather, the "proponents of competing paradigms practice their trades in different worlds" (*SSR*, 150). In other words, there exists no pre-established neutral ground by which cross-paradigmatic comparison may be effected. Nor will it be possible to decide between theories simply on the basis of their relative problem-solving ability. Different paradigms define differently what are the relevant problems that need to be solved.

Kuhn's views provoked much controversy among philosophers of science. His book was said to render theory choice in science *irrational*, or at least *arational*, and in Imre Lakatos's famous phrase, "*a matter for mob-psychology*" (Lakatos and Musgrave, 1970: 178). Kuhn's exploration of the political analogies to theory choice in science was not well received in the conservative halls of the American academy. Further chagrin was caused by the fact that Kuhn initially sought to explain incommensurability and scientific revolutions in terms of *gestalt switches* and *conversion experiences* (*SSR*, 111–14). While striking and even provocative, Kuhn himself later came to realize that drawing on concepts from individual psychology to explain what are ostensibly collective processes was clearly misguided. Moreover, *gestalt* switches and conversion experiences are typically described as non-composite events, instantaneous flashes with no rationally discernible internal structure. Small wonder, then, that Kuhn's critics were dumbfounded when he later came to describe scientific revolutions in terms of argumentation and negotiation, in order precisely to highlight their rational character.

Over the ensuing decades, Kuhn found in the philosophy of language a fruitful approach to the troublesome phenomenon of incommensurability, one better suited to the task than his earlier emphasis on individual psychology. This has done much to strengthen the general plausibility of his argument. Although the exact status of the incommensurability thesis remains a point of contention in the continuing debates over Kuhn's legacy, it is also one of the most influential aspects of his work, an idea that has reverberated through a number of academic disciplines.

Kuhn's View of Scientific Rationality

All in all, then, should we read Kuhn as asserting that paradigm changes in science have no rational basis whatsoever, as some of his critics have claimed? Of course not; scientists have numerous "good reasons" to appeal to in the period of transition between paradigms. Kuhn even cites five "characteristics of a good scientific theory"

(Kuhn, 1977: 321–2) – accuracy, consistency, broadness of scope, simplicity, and fruitfulness – as standard criteria in theory evaluation. The point remains, however, that these criteria, even in conjunction, cannot always dictate a unique conclusion. There will always be ample room for disputes about their application and relative merits. Additionally, one or several of these criteria may, and frequently will, conflict with the others. These criteria cannot, then, form anything like a neutral *algorithm* of theory choice; they can only function as *values* which inform, but not determine, our choices. The kind of unequivocal decision procedure that the received view took to be the essence of scientific rationality can only exist within the confines of a single scientific tradition, and cannot be used to legislate between competing traditions.

Is this a problem? Should we shudder at the thought that an understanding of theory choice in science must ultimately refer back to the group whose decision it is, in the sense of having to take into account values and commitments that are to some extent specific to this group? Does such an idea open the door to all kinds of subjective impulse and arbitrary fancy, thereby reducing scientific rationality to mob psychology? Kuhn, obviously, did not think so. As he aptly put it in a later text:

> [T]o describe [my] argument as a defence of irrationality in science seems to me not only absurd but vaguely obscene. I would describe it . . . as an attempt to show that existing theories of rationality are not quite right and that we must readjust them or change them to explain why science works as it does. To suppose, instead, that we possess criteria of rationality which are independent of our understanding of the essentials of the scientific process is to open the door to cloud-cuckoo land. (Kuhn, 2000: 159)

Science-as-praxis, on Kuhn's account, is not an imperfect, *ex post facto* approximation of "pure science," but is in fact an integral element in its development. To understand science, we must understand it as practiced, or not at all. Rationality and rational validation cannot be specified independently of this practice, and cannot automatically be applied across the board. Different practices at different times will have different notions of rational validation. Still, the incommensurability of highly technical languages of scientific inquiry does not leave us bereft of the means to communicate. Rather, incommensurability forces us to meditate on the fact that science – even science! – remains embedded in the larger context of community and history, where communication is never beyond our grasp.

The Popper–Kuhn Controversy

Karl Popper was perhaps the most influential philosopher of science at the time that *SSR* was published, and he and his followers were quick to take up the challenges that Kuhn's book posed. In 1965 a colloquium was arranged (documented in Lakatos and Musgrave, 1970) which saw a distinguished group of Popperians line up against what they perceived as the many dangerous shortcomings of Kuhn's work. In his contribution, Popper conceded that he had largely overlooked the phenomenon of normal science, having directed his attention almost exclusively to extraordinary science. That concession made, Popper goes on to claim that Kuhn's normal scientist cuts a sorry figure; he is a victim of indoctrination. Kuhn, Popper claims, has confused *is* and *ought*. Although Kuhn may have supplied a *descriptively* correct account of science, Popper, by comparison, meant his account to be *normative*. His "logic of discovery" attempts to lay out the proper procedure for scientific inquiry. The failure of normal science to conform to this norm only underscores the importance of a philosophy like his. The normalcy of normal science is, Popper writes, "a danger to science and indeed to our civilization" (Popper, 1970: 53).

Popper, apparently, wants science to develop through an unbroken string of revolutions. However, the danger of dogmatism that Popper sees as endemic to normal scientific research is, Kuhn claims by contrast, essential to science as we know it.

> Because they can ordinarily take current theory for granted, exploiting it rather than criticizing it, the practitioners of mature sciences are freed to explore nature to an esoteric depth and detail otherwise unimaginable. Because that exploitation will ultimately isolate severe trouble spots, they can be confident that the pursuit of normal science will inform them when and where they can most usefully become Popperian critics. (Kuhn, 2000: 141)

Popperian revolutions-in-permanence leave nothing to revolutionize. Only with the patience bred by confidence in the ultimate potential of the paradigm – a patience that cannot be instilled by proof or conclusive argument – can scientists afford to momentarily overlook the problems facing any new theory and thereby get to work on its broader articulation. Kuhn's positive and constructive point is that this gap between shared values and uniform decision is not a predicament but is in fact indispensable to scientific progress, however else we wish to define it.

Indeed, there are many ways in which Kuhn remained a firm believer in scientific progress. He believed, for one, that a successor paradigm was superior to its predecessor in terms of both theoretical sophistication and problem-solving ability. He refused to believe, however, that scientific progress can usefully be said to carry us ever closer to *the truth*. He makes this point by recalling Darwin's theory of evolution. The most controversial aspect of Darwin's work, Kuhn points out, was neither the notion of species change nor of man's descent from the apes. What bothered Darwin's contemporaries was the fact that his account had no teleology – *evolution ceased to be a goal-directed process*. Kuhn, then, invites us to see the progress of science as an evolution *from* primitive beginnings but *toward* no goal (*SSR*, 171).

Conclusion

Looking back over the forty years that have passed since *SSR* was first published, it seems clear that the work's most striking impact has been to ignite a number of fierce debates on relativism and rationality. These debates have surfaced in a number of disciplines, not just in philosophy, and they continue unabated to this day. Kuhn is commonly held to be one of the first thinkers of his generation to take an explicitly historical (or "hermeneutic") approach to the philosophical study of science, betraying a kinship to thinkers such as Collingwood and Gadamer. While that is true, we should not underestimate his affinities with philosophers pursuing a very nearly perpendicular axis, namely naturalists such as Wittgenstein, Quine, and Sellars. Indeed, the way in which *SSR* faces up to this tension between naturalistic and historical approaches to the philosophy of science may be a crucial key to explaining its originality and enduring appeal.

Bibliography

Editions

Kuhn, Thomas S. (1957) *The Copernican Revolution*. Cambridge, MA: Harvard University Press.

Kuhn, Thomas S. (1962) *The Structure of Scientific Revolutions*. Chicago: University of Chicago Press (2nd rev. edn, 1970; 3rd edn, 1996).

Kuhn, Thomas S. (1977) *The Essential Tension*. Chicago: University of Chicago Press.

Kuhn, Thomas S. (1978) *Black-body Theory and the Quantum Discontinuity 1894–1912*. Oxford: Oxford University Press.

Kuhn, Thomas S. (2000) *The Road Since Structure*, ed. James Conant and John Haugeland. Chicago: University of Chicago Press.

Studies and references

Feyerabend, Paul (1975) *Against Method*. London: Verso (3rd edn., 1996).

Hacking, Ian (1983) *Representing and Intervening*. Cambridge: Cambridge University Press.

Horwich, Paul (ed.) (1993) *World Changes: Thomas Kuhn and the Nature of Science*. Cambridge, MA: MIT Press.

Hoyningen-Huene, Paul (1993) *Reconstructing Scientific Revolutions: Thomas Kuhn's Philosophy of Science*. Chicago: University of Chicago Press.

Lakatos, Imre and Musgrave, Alan (eds) (1970) *Criticism and the Growth of Knowledge*. Cambridge: Cambridge University Press.

Popper, Karl (1959) *The Logic of Scientific Discovery*. London: Hutchinson.

Popper, Karl (1970) Normal science and its dangers. In I. Lakatos and A. Musgrave (eds), *Criticism and the Growth of Knowledge*. Cambridge: Cambridge University Press.

Name Index

Subject Index